**Varieties of Skepticism**

# Berlin Studies
# in Knowledge Research

Edited by
Günter Abel and James Conant

# Volume 5

# Varieties of Skepticism

---

Essays after Kant, Wittgenstein, and Cavell

Edited by
James Conant and Andrea Kern

**DE GRUYTER**

*Series Editors*
Prof. Dr. Günter Abel
Technische Universität Berlin
Institut für Philosophie
Straße des 17. Juni 135
10623 Berlin
Germany
e-mail: abel@tu-berlin.de

Prof. Dr. James Conant
The University of Chicago
Dept. of Philosophy
1115 E. 58th Street
Chicago IL 60637
USA
e-mail: jconant@uchicago.edu

ISBN 978-3-11-048179-2
e-ISBN 978-3-11-033679-5

**Library of Congress Cataloging-in-Publication Data**
A CIP catalog record for this book has been applied for at the Library of Congress.

**Bibliographic information published by the Deutsche Nationalbibliothek**
The Deutsche Nationalbibliothek lists this publication in the Deutsche Nationalbibliografie;
detailed bibliographic data are available in the Internet at http://dnb.dnb.de.

© 2014 Walter de Gruyter GmbH, Berlin/Boston
Printing: Hubert & Co. GmbH & Co. KG, Göttingen
♾ Printed on acid-free paper
Printed in Germany

www.degruyter.com

# Table of Contents

James Conant and Andrea Kern
# Introduction: From Kant to Cavell

This volume brings together work by a number of contemporary philosophers, all of whom share the conviction that there is much philosophical gain still to be had from reflection on the sources and nature of skepticism. One might wonder what distinguishes this collection from any number of other volumes on the same subject. After all, the topic of philosophical skepticism has constituted a central part of the professional fare of contemporary philosophers since at least the 1970s. Whole volumes, conferences, and journals continue to be devoted to it. Yet throughout these copious discussions, one rarely encounters a sense that there is anything deeply *disquieting* about the problem of skepticism. It is generally treated as just one philosophical puzzle among others, a puzzle upon which a professional philosopher might or might not sharpen her analytical teeth. One of several respects in which the contributions to this volume resemble one another more than they do a great deal of other contemporary work on skepticism is that they all share, as a fundamental aspect of their philosophical standpoint, the conviction that the problem of skepticism is *not* just any old philosophical puzzle. Their many disagreements notwithstanding, the philosophers brought together in this volume are united by the following two thoughts: first, that a proper appreciation of the depth of the skeptical challenge must reveal it to be deeply disquieting, in the sense that, although it is first and foremost an *intellectual* puzzle, skepticism threatens not just some set of theoretical commitments, but also—and fundamentally—our very sense of self, world, and other; and second, that skepticism is the proper starting point for any serious attempt (a) to make sense of what philosophy is, and (b) to gauge the prospects of philosophical progress.

Though "skepticism" means different things to different philosophers, it is no mere accident that these varieties of philosophical puzzlement have all come to be labeled "skepticism." The contributions to this volume are primarily concerned with exploring three such problems: (1) the possibility of knowledge of the external world, (2) the possibility of knowledge regarding the meanings of words and hence the possibility of mutual comprehension (and the related problem of our capacity to go on in the same way in attempting to follow a rule), and (3) the possibility of knowledge of other minds (and thus of our capacity to acknowledge the thoughts and feelings of others). The first of these problems takes center stage in Part One of this volume, the second in Part Two, and the third in Part Three. However, many of the articles contained here draw attention to all three problems, with those in the final part most consistently concerned to keep all in view at once.

There are three figures in the history of modern philosophy whose work represents the polestars by which our authors navigate their way through this philosophical terrain. Those figures are Kant, Wittgenstein, and Cavell. The essays contained in this volume have been sorted according to their relation to these figures: those concerned most with Kant can be found in Part One, those concerned most with Wittgenstein in Part Two, and those concerned most with Cavell in Part Three. This is not to say that the division is clear-cut. Over half of the contributions bear, prominently, the stamp of all three figures. Thus, judging into which part of the volume a given essay best fits generally came down to weighing the comparative degrees to which the essay manifests the imprint of our three guiding figures. Furthermore, this is not to say that sorting the contributions according to their relation to Kant, Wittgenstein, and Cavell presupposes some clear, overarching understanding of what it means to bear the stamp of one of these figures. On the contrary, a central point of contention in Part One is what it means to claim of a particular philosophical treatment of skepticism that it can properly be said to bear the stamp of Kant. Likewise, the essays in Part Two assume different stances on what it means to take Wittgenstein's teaching about skepticism to heart. Perhaps this kind of disagreement is most explicitly thematized in Part Three, where the central issue in several of the essays is just that of what fidelity to Cavell's response to skepticism requires of its philosophical audience.

These points of contention among our authors are related to another point on which they have differing views—namely, the question of what would constitute a satisfying response to skepticism. To what extent is the philosophical task here primarily a *therapeutic* as opposed to a *theoretical* one? Does philosophical skepticism so much as admit of a theoretical refutation, or does it require some other form of philosophical response? If so, is the response in question one that reveals it to be nonetheless in some way false or mistaken? Or, if skepticism is to be turned back, then is it on some other ground than that of its claim—or lack thereof—to truth? Should the philosophical skeptic's doubt be regarded even as making sense? If not, what does it mean to charge the skeptic with speaking nonsense? What sort of philosophical views does such a charge presuppose? With respect to one or more of these questions, each of our authors disagrees with at least several of the others. In some cases, these disagreements take the form of explicit engagements among or between our contributors. For the most part, however, such disagreements remain implicit, but no less pointed for that.

# Part I: After Kant

The first part of this volume investigates different ways to understand and articulate the lesson to be learned from a Kantian perspective on the problem of skepticism. A central concern of the papers in Part One is the problem of how to understand the very possibility of knowledge, especially knowledge regarding the so-called "external world." All of the authors in Part One agree on the following point: it was Kant's ambition to solve external-world skepticism by setting out to undermine its fundamental premise. Our authors disagree, however, not only on how to characterize the supposed premise in question (which, on each of these versions of Kantianism, is taken to constitute the root of epistemological skepticism), but also on the extent to which Kant himself achieved, or the extent to which some modified form of a Kantian position can hope to achieve, its goal, namely, to liberate us from such skeptical problems.

Our authors are at best only secondarily concerned with purely exegetical questions concerning how to interpret the writings of Kant and various post-Kantians. Their primary aim is, first, to develop an account of the skeptical problem that takes its cue from such authors and, second, to offer their own diagnosis of the root of skepticism. In each case, the result is a novel philosophical contribution to the literature, yet one of a form that can be seen to contain either an implicit interpretation of the central point of the Kantian philosophy or an attempt to bend the letter while preserving the spirit of that philosophy. A common thread running through these papers is the effort to develop a philosophical position that manages to avoid skepticism by adumbrating of a *third* (critical) position, one that shows the way beyond the central dilemma haunting this area of philosophy. Put in Kantian terms, the dilemma is that of empiricism and rationalism. Put in more contemporary terms, the dilemma is that of foundationalism and coherentism. For all of their differences, our authors appear, therefore, to be united in the following thought: In order to escape skepticism, one must first find a way to render non-obligatory the apparently inescapable problem of having to choose between the horns of the aforementioned dilemma. The individual philosophical differences between our authors first come strikingly into view at the moment in which each seeks to characterize what is involved in the possibility of maintaining such a "third" position, a position supposedly free of the problematic philosophical commitments that give rise to skepticism. The disagreements here go quite deep. They disagree regarding both how to characterize the details of any properly Kantian diagnosis of the skeptical problem and how to elaborate the details of a successful Kantian treatment. They also differ widely regarding the exegetical question of the extent to which Kant himself managed to furnish the philosophical materials required for such a diagnosis or treatment. Therefore, the question that lies at the heart of Part One, in the first instance, is not merely whether Kantianism can lay claim to having developed a philosophical route out of or beyond skepticism; rather—and above all—the central question is how we ought to characterize and understand any philosophical approach that is to merit the title of Kantianism.

In his article, "Skepticism After Kant," Paul Franks explores three forms of skepticism that emerged in the wake of the publication of Kant's *Critique of Pure Reason* in the late-eighteenth century. Franks argues that although Kant intended his transcendental idealism to abolish skepticism, certain central features of his philosophical project turned out to have the opposite effect: they directly contributed to the rise of even more radical forms of skeptical thought than those Kant had sought to answer. In addition, Franks argues that all three of these forms of skepticism remain of contemporary philosophical interest. That this is the case has often been missed because these early reactions to Kant tend to be underestimated in most contemporary narratives of the history of post-Kantian thought.

The first of the three forms of post-Kantian skepticism that Franks brings to our attention is the one thematized by one of Kant's earliest and most vocal critics, Friedrich Jacobi. Jacobi himself shared Kant's thought that it was a central task of philosophy to help us avoid skepticism. But he thought Kant had radically failed in this regard. According to Franks, Jacobi's central point tends to be misunderstood. Jacobi is often mistakenly read as accusing Kant of himself championing a position that amounts to a form of what Kant calls, in "The Refutation of Idealism," problematic idealism, i.e., the sort of philosophical position that Kant associates with Cartesianism. Against such a reading, Franks reconstructs an interpretation of Jacobi that emphasizes the central role played by the problem of rational justification in his critique of Kant. Jacobi, on this reading, accuses Kant of pushing the demand for justification too far. According to Jacobi, Kant overreaches when he attempts to extend the demand for rational justification to our everyday knowledge-claims. In doing so, Kant destroys our everyday faith in our immediate perceptions of ordinary things, reducing them to mere appearances, whilst bringing it about that the supposedly true "things in themselves" are caused to recede to a position forever beyond our cognitive grasp. Franks suggests that Jacobi's overall approach to the problem of skepticism is helpfully compared with that of Stanley Cavell. Both philosophers, on Franks's reading of them, seek to highlight a moment at which philosophical questioning—in attempting to press a demand for the justification of ordinary knowledge-claims beyond the point tolerated by our ordinary practices for entering and assessing such claims—comes upon a point where the demand becomes empty: the philosopher oversteps the moment where such a demand still makes sense. On this criticism of a certain approach to answering the skeptical challenge—a criticism Franks finds in both Jacobi and Cavell—a form of philosophical questioning that seeks to avoid skepticism by answering its demand for justification is unmasked as in fact, contrary to its own aim, contributing to the intensification of skeptical nihilism—making it seem as if skepticism is the only possible outcome of philosophical reflection.

The problem of rational justification is treated in all the papers that figure in this part of the volume, including Michael Williams's contribution, "Knowledge, Reasons, and Causes: Sellars and Skepticism." In contrast to Franks, who follows Jacobi and Cavell in holding that the problem of skepticism cannot be solved by rational means, Williams undertakes to show that it can be. His paper seeks to uncover an anti-skeptical line of argument inspired by the work of Wilfrid Sellars, whose philosophical approach in turn is explicitly rooted in Kant's theoretical philosophy. In following Sellars, Williams's ambition is to chart a course between the two horns of a fundamental dilemma in epistemology, that of a dogmatic foundationalism, on the one hand, and a coherence theory of knowledge on the other. Just as Kant sought to overcome the dilemma between empiricism and rationalism by developing a third, critical alternative, so Sellars wants to overcome the dilemma between dogmatic foundationalism and a coherence theory of knowledge by developing his own variant of a third way. According to Williams, however, the version of the dilemma Sellars confronts presents a specific kind of obstacle to any such approach. The official position that Williams finds in Sellars is one that concedes a great deal to the empiricist/foundationalist thought that observational knowledge is fundamental to all of our knowledge insofar as it provides a necessary external constraint on the formation of the worldview of the knower. The problem with which Sellars struggles is that a subject of an observational belief must know that her belief-forming mechanism is reliable. She must be able to draw a *reliability inference*. However, the only way she can justifiably do this is on the basis of the very sort of knowledge—i.e., perceptual knowledge—that, we are given to understand, becomes available to her only *through* her drawing such an inference. This difficulty would seem to indicate that Sellars has not actually managed to find a way between foundationalism and coherentism. His account of observational knowledge tilts in a coherentist direction insofar as it would appear to require the following justificatory circle: on the one hand, perceptual knowledge presupposes some prior form of explicit knowledge of the reliability of the subject's belief-forming mechanism, while, on the other hand, the latter sort of knowledge would appear to require perceptual knowledge as its source. Sellars's solution to this problem consists in proclaiming that reliability-knowledge is essential to thinking beings. But this still leaves the question open whether a thinking being must merely *believe* that she knows herself to be reliable or whether she must actually *know* herself to be reliable. Williams suggests that the proper way to resolve this difficulty is to appreciate the locally situated default-and-challenge character of epistemic justification. The resulting position, which Williams finds intimated in some of Sellars's remarks, is one according to which reliability-knowledge is seen to play a continuously essential role as a background condition on the possibility of perceptual knowledge without necessarily always being relevant as part of the explicit justification of particular instances of such knowledge. Its relevance depends on the context in which the claim to knowledge is made.

A variant of this general form of argumentative strategy, which we might call *epistemological contextualism*, is also adopted by Hilary Putnam in his essay, "Skepticism, Stroud, and the Contextuality of Knowledge." Putnam's primary concern in his paper is to respond to a particular form of objection which has been advanced against such contextualist accounts, most famously by Barry Stroud. The argumentative aim of Putnam's article is to demonstrate that if Stroud's attack on the very possibility of the contextual character of knowledge were to go through, it would entail a form of wholesale skepticism that we ought to find untenable. Putnam is happy to concede that under ordinary circumstances we take the claim, "I know that p," to imply the further commitment that the speaker is in a position to exclude possible doubts concerning the truth of p. The key to a sane contextualism, according to Putnam, is to appreciate that this commitment extends not to every possible doubt that might overturn p, but only to a certain class of contextually relevant doubts. Since every reasonable doubt presupposes a determinate question, each ground for doubt must rest on a reasonable basis; in this respect, grounds for doubt function just as claims to knowledge do. In objecting to this form of contextualism, Stroud argues that even if one has the most favorable grounds for the claim, "I know that p," it is still possible that p will be overturned by an unlikely and unforeseeable event E, in which case the corresponding knowledge claim will be rendered false. Hence, the mere conceivability of E suffices to defeat the knowledge-claim. We may say that the speaker's claim was perfectly reasonable when assessed by our everyday standards for entering such claims, but this does not gainsay the fact that it turned out to be false. Since we are never in a position to exclude every possibility of overturning p (e. g., the possibility that we may be dreaming, or that we are deceived by Descartes's evil demon), Stroud's point would seem to concede the game to the epistemological skeptic. (It should be noted that Stroud's own point is not that epistemological skepticism is true, but only that contextualist approaches underestimate the strength of the skeptic's position.) Putnam claims that the manner of deploying the expression "to know" that Stroud goes in for in his attempt to bring out the strength of the skeptic's position is in fact a case of language going on a holiday: The expression is here employed outside of any determinate context of use that could confer a definite meaning on it. Why would language ever contain an expression whose employment requires truth conditions of such a sort that they obviously can never be met? The skeptic's understanding of "to know" seems to rely on a conception of the meaning of the expression that transcends every actual employment of the term, while at the same time failing to specify how it is that we are so much as able to understand something determinate by the expression in question.

The papers by Andrea Kern and Sebastian Rödl are united in taking up an equally critical perspective towards both skepticism, on the one hand, and contextualist responses to the skeptic, on the other. They both take their cue from the Kantian thought that the deadlock between skeptical and anti-skeptical philosophical positions is to be traced to common philosophical assumptions shared by both parties in the dispute, making the truth in each apparently unreconcilable with the truth of the other. Thus, the fundamental task remains one of diagnosing the philosophical root of the dispute.

Andrea Kern's paper, "Why Do Our Reasons Come to an End?", critically examines the idea present in much contemporary philosophy (and exemplified in this volume by the positions advocated by Franks, Williams, and Putnam), namely, the idea that the crucial misstep that plunges the skeptic into doubt consists in his misconceiving the ideal of knowledge. The skeptic, according to this line of criticism, operates with an overly demanding conception of justification, one in which the ideals of certainty and indefeasibility are accorded a false privilege. For finite beings such as us, this cannot be an appropriate ideal of knowledge. Our ideal of knowledge is to be properly adumbrated in more modest terms—for example, in the sorts of terms that the contextualist allows for, when she proposes that something less than an indefeasible form of warrant may suffice to justify our knowledge-claims. Andrea Kern argues that one cannot overcome philosophical skepticism by correcting its conception of the ideal of knowledge in this way. Following a line of thought she traces back to Kant, Kern suggests that the skeptic does not entertain a false conception of our *ideal* of knowledge. Rather, she goes wrong in his manner of conceiving of our *finitude*. On Kern's reading, Kant wants to say that the skeptic is a skeptic not because she overestimates our ideal of knowledge, but because she underestimates our finitude. The skeptic considers our susceptibility to error to be the deepest characteristic of our finitude, and therefore thinks of our finitude as an epistemological matter, one which characterizes the nature of our grounds for knowledge. According to a proper Kantian perspective, Kern argues, we are finite not (merely) because we are capable of error, as the skeptic (as well as the contextualist) concedes, but rather because we depend on the world to provide us with sensory appearances in order to be so much as able to entertain beliefs about the world in the first place. That the human intellect has finite knowledge does not mean that he can only finitely justify his beliefs; rather, it means that his beliefs have the sort of content they do only in virtue of a justification that ends in a claim about the world, a claim whose standing depends upon the fact that the world itself has first sensuously impressed something upon him.

In a different but related vein, Sebastian Rödl argues against the contextualist answer to the problem of how to deal with the so-called regress of justification we seem to face whenever we try to justify our knowledge-claims. On a contextualist's view, as Rödl presents it, the skeptic falsely assumes that a subject cannot know anything if she cannot exclude all grounds for doubting that which she purports to know. Knowledge merely requires that she be capable of excluding those grounds that are relevant or justified. Rödl rescues the skeptic's assumption from the contextualist's attack by showing that grounds for knowledge cannot claim to be sufficient when they exclude some but not all grounds for doubt. If a putative ground of knowledge leaves some grounds for doubt untouched, as it sometimes must (e.g., regarding claims to know how the dice will roll), it cannot be considered a sufficient ground for knowledge. Rödl locates the skeptic's mistake elsewhere, namely, in the assumption that one's ground for knowledge may be the same in situations in which one has knowledge and in situations in which one fails to know. A sufficient ground for knowledge must be a ground for thinking that a general truth bears on a particular case (e.g., that in general, one's faculty of perception operates normally, and that this is an instance of its operation). When a particular situation is not as the general truth specifies, then one does not have a sufficient ground. Whether I have a sufficient ground thus depends on the situation in which I find myself. The finitude of human knowledge, Rödl suggests, consists not in any inability to exclude grounds for doubting whether one has knowledge, as both the skeptic and the contextualist assume, but in the situation-dependence of all (empirical) grounds for knowledge.

# Part II: After Wittgenstein

Part Two of this volume investigates Wittgenstein's contribution to our understanding of the problem of philosophical skepticism. The particular form of skepticism that lies at the heart of Cora Diamond's article is the same as that which concerned our authors in Part One, namely, epistemological skepticism. The other papers in this part of the volume—those by Wellmer, Stone, and Bridges

—focus instead on skepticism about meaning and rule-following. All four papers, however, are concerned to one extent or another with the general philosophical question of the nature of skeptical problems and what is involved in making progress with them, as well as with the more narrowly focused exegetical question of whether Wittgenstein himself managed to furnish us with the philosophical resources required to make such progress. Wellmer thinks that Wittgenstein's suggestion for how to make progress with such problems is in an important respect flawed. The other three authors are concerned to bring out how certain apparent flaws in Wittgenstein's treatment of skeptical problems arise from a misunderstanding of both what he thought those problems were and what would count as offering a satisfactory response to them. (Stone, in particular, is concerned to bring out how something Wellmer sees as a flaw in Wittgenstein's response to skepticism about rule-following is essential to its success.) Though none of our four authors in this part of the volume draw explicit connections between Kant and Wittgenstein, there are numerous parallels in philosophical concern and approach that unite the essays in Part Two with those in Part One, not least their common effort to provide a diagnosis of the true source of skeptical perplexity that is sufficiently deeply grounded to permit certain familiar forms of philosophical impasse to come to an end.

Cora Diamond's paper concerns Wittgenstein's ideas about skepticism at the time he was writing his early *Notebooks* and the *Tractatus*. According to Diamond, Wittgenstein means to respond in these texts to Russell's attitude towards skepticism, i. e., to his claim that universal skepticism is irrefutable. Wittgenstein links this skeptical claim with Russell's conception of philosophical method, both of which he seeks to reject. In particular, Russell thinks of skepticism on the model of a hypothesis considered within the sciences, which may or may not fit the data. The mistake here is not merely that Russell models philosophy on scientific method, but that he also misunderstands scientific method as working with 'ordinary generalizations.' According to Wittgenstein's early philosophy, the generality of scientific statements, like those to which philosophy aspires, is different in kind. Unlike ordinary generalizations, scientific generalizations are not complete specifications of truth-conditions, but rather serve a different sort of use. This shifts the question about skepticism away from a dispute about what entities there are to a dispute about the use served by talk about what entities there are. This yields quite a different account of Wittgenstein's response to skepticism than that which is commonly found in the secondary literature on his philosophy. Wittgenstein's response to skepticism does not involve first assuming that the skeptic is attempting to make an ordinary generalization about the non-existence of objects, and then going on to object to that generalization on the grounds that it violates some supposed principles about meaningfulness whose special standing Wittgenstein seeks to uphold. Rather, what Wittgenstein wants us to see is that the skeptic has not determined the use that his words are intended to have and has thus failed to say anything with them. Such a form of criticism of the skeptic does not require that we first ascribe to Wittgenstein an attachment to some general set of principles for when words mean something and when they do not.

In his essay "Skepticism in Interpretation," Albrecht Wellmer discusses the hermeneutic skepticism concerning the possibility of understanding the true meaning of the spoken and written word within a linguistic community. Wellmer's discussion takes its point of departure from Wittgenstein's arguments against a form of skepticism that makes it appear as if there is no such thing as genuinely sharing in a common understanding of what words mean and in what it would be to go on using them in the same way. Wittgenstein's approach to avoiding the skeptical impasse is to insist that there is a way of grasping a rule that is not an interpretation, and that in such cases we follow the rule blindly. Wellmer parts ways with Wittgenstein on this point, however, insisting that interpretation is indeed the key to understanding how it is that we are able to share a language. Recalling arguments by Kripke and Davidson, Wellmer argues that the concepts of meaning and understanding presuppose the priority of the second-person perspective, hence that meaning is always subject to contextual interpretation. As a skeptical consequence, the plurality of perspectives and ambiguous contexts lead to the possibility of infinite misunderstanding. Consequently, hermeneutic skepticism expresses the concern that we can never get a grip on the real meaning of words and thus that our interpretative understanding could always appear to be nothing more than arbitrary. Wellmer's rebuttal of this hermeneutic skepticism is twofold. First, he denies its core presupposition of objective meaning existing behind linguistic representation. If understanding always asks for an act of interpretation, why should we assume the existence of real meaning beyond interpretation? The presupposition of objective meaning needs justification before it can provide the ground for a skeptical doubt. Secondly, in order to meet the concern of arbitrariness, Wellmer discusses the possibility of a standard of correctness for interpretation. Our understanding follows the hermeneutic principle of intelligibility that only allows for content that is subject to debate within our social space of reason. This space limits interpretation in a threefold manner: through our use of words, through the particular communicative situation, and through a narrative context. Wellmer denies the existence of an Archimedean point with which to judge understanding outside of this very process of interpretation; rather, he relies on the internal normative standard of a linguistic community to disarm the hermeneutic skeptic.

Whereas Wellmer holds that no understanding is possible without interpretation, Martin Stone, in his paper, denies precisely this. He discusses the claim implicitly shared by many authors that an act of interpretation (of rules, texts, etc.) is a condition for every act of understanding. This is the position that Stone calls "interpretivism." While Wellmer is of the view that it must be possible to develop a form of interpretivism that is free of skeptical consequences, Stone is concerned to show, on the contrary, that merely conceding the opening assumption of interpretivism is already sufficient to give the skeptic what he most desires. Interpretivism, according to Stone, is based on the thought that rules are, in a fundamental sense, unable to determine the particular case that falls under them. Stone argues that interpretivism is based on a misunderstanding of the nature of rules. He argues that it is constitutive of rules that we consider them as immediately guiding, i. e., as applicable without interpretation. If there are no cases with respect to a rule for which it is immediately guiding, then we cannot think of there being any rule in play at all. Hence, the idea that rules are as such indeterminate with respect to particular cases mistakes a secondary phenomenon for the general case. Rules do sometimes require interpretation. This is a phenomenon that is made possible against the background of cases in which it would be possible for us to follow the rule in question without interpretation. The interpretivist misunderstands this basic concept of 'rule' because she regards uncertainty about the sense of a rule as generally operative in the understanding of rules. Stone suggests, following Wittgenstein, that one source of this misunderstanding is a "queer picture of rules," according to which the way in which they are to determine an action is not "normative," but "mechanical." Stone attempts to clear up this misunderstanding by suggesting that the correct manner in which to conceive of the clarity of rules has to do not with the way in which they determine each particular action, but in the sense in which they prescribe an "action type."

Jason Bridges is concerned to understand and lay bare the philosophical importance of the same stretch of sections in Wittgenstein's *Philosophical Investigations*, those on rule-following, that play a central role in Wellmer's and Stone's papers. His focus and interest, however, lie to some extent elsewhere. In his contribution, "Rule-Following, Properly So Called," Bridges takes on Saul Kripke's famous "rule-following paradox." On his view, the real source and nature of Kripke's skeptical paradox have been largely misunderstood. In contrast to previous commentators, he claims that the central target of the paradox is the idea of rational explanation, i. e., explanations that account for what people do by giving their reasons for doing so. More particularly, he argues that the paradox arises from what he calls "the guidance conception" of such explanations, according to which a person's grasp of her own reasons involves a mental item that guides her performance. According to Bridges, conceiving of the skeptical paradox in these terms not only yields a better understanding of Kripke's text, it also allows for an appreciation of the real scope and depth of the skeptical problem. Moreover, it allows us to understand Wittgenstein's appeal to practices and customs in his own discussions of rule-following as challenging the intuitions that fuel the guidance conception of rational explanation.

# Part III: After Cavell

Part Three of this volume investigates the understanding of skepticism at work in the writings of Stanley Cavell. The first two papers, by Stephen Mulhall and Steven Affeldt, are in direct conversation with each other (and, indeed, represent a continuation of an ongoing dialogue). Their topic is directly related to the papers by Wellmer, Stone, and Bridges in Part Two, namely, the place of rules in Wittgenstein's vision of language. This aspect of Wittgenstein's work takes on a remarkable and renewed significance in the light of Cavell's interpretation of Wittgenstein's account of how criteria allow us to share our lives in and through language. Yet, as the first two papers in this section clearly bring out, there is considerable space for disagreement about what the role of criteria are in this vision of language and how it relates to Cavell's overall response to skepticism. Whereas both Mulhall and Affeldt seek to defend Cavell's account of criteria (while disagreeing with one another over what Cavell's view of the matter actually is), the last paper in this part of the volume, by Simon Glendinning, takes issue with a fundamental aspect of that account. Christoph Menke, in his contribution, is also interested in Cavell's treatment of skepticism, but rather than concentrating on Cavell's interpretation of Wittgenstein (as our other authors in this part of the volume do), Menke shifts the focus to Cavell's reading of Shakespeare and the light it sheds on the nature of skeptical problems. The penultimate paper in this part of the volume, by Arata Hamawaki, nicely ties together themes that run not only through this section of the volume, but through the volume as a whole, revealing the degrees of alignment and misalignment between Cavell's treatment of skepticism and those of Kant and Wittgenstein.

In his paper "Inner Constancy, Outer Variation: Stanley Cavell on Grammar, Criteria, and Rules," Mulhall seeks to flesh out the vision of language in the work of Wittgenstein and Cavell by showing how this vision of language is at work in their responses to a particular form of skeptical perplexity, namely, that which arises from reflecting on how it could be that we are entitled to use words in one way rather than another. Mulhall argues that many critics of Wittgenstein's view of language as normative, i. e., as rule-governed, tend to misunderstand the form of normativity in question. Both defenders and critics of Wittgenstein alike tend to presuppose that Wittgenstein envisions our use of words as guided by the sort of rules that could be codified in a book. Mulhall follows Cavell in seeing this as a misunderstanding of the sort of normativity Wittgenstein has in mind. The misunderstanding makes it appear as if it were possible to adjudicate disagreements over the legitimacy of the use of a word by appealing to an external, impersonal authority. Mulhall claims that, on the contrary, what is needed—and what Wittgenstein and Cavell both seek to provide—is a way of looking at our lives with language that is able, on the one hand, to accord a proper place to the ways in which a speaker must herself assume responsibility for the particular uses of language she makes and accepts in others, while, on the other hand, remaining sensitive to the almost unimaginable range and systematicity that govern these exercises of responsibility. According to Mulhall, such a conception is found in Cavell's notion of the grammatical schematism of words. It entails that concepts essentially possess both 'inner' constancy and 'outer' variation. Concepts possess 'inner' constancy in that they implicitly possess criteria locating them in a system of concepts that informs and is informed by our human forms of life. They possess 'outer' variation in that judgments regarding the correct projections of concepts are highly context-specific and dependent upon the speaker's individual capacity to justify her uses of concepts in these contexts.

In his paper, "The Normativity of the Natural," Affeldt scrutinizes Mulhall's account of Wittgenstein's and Cavell's philosophies of language. Affeldt claims that Mulhall's focus on rules and rule-following misinterprets Wittgenstein and Cavell and also fails to provide an adequate representation of the normativity of language-use. Affeldt aims to reject Mulhall's theses on the basis of three objections. First, Affeldt denies Mulhall's claim that Wittgenstein's discussion of rule-following is meant to provide an account of linguistic meaning. According to Affeldt, it is no part of Wittgenstein's ambition to provide a substantive philosophical theory of such matters. Such a theory would try to solve problems and answer questions that are themselves based on an unjustified skepticism regarding our natural practices. Second, Affeldt questions Mulhall's claim that our uses of language are essentially cases of rule-following. Rather, Affeldt takes Wittgenstein and Cavell to argue that rule-based conceptions of language fundamentally distort our understanding of human language and of our life with and in language. There are many types of normative practices that can be retrospectively described by rules even though rules play no role in our partaking in these practices. Third, Affeldt argues that Mulhall's conception of rules is incoherent, since Mulhall oscillates between a strong characterization of rules as essential determinants of our uses of language and a weak characterization of rules as open, flexible, and without any final authority. Affeldt argues that this view leaves us with no resources for understanding how disagreements about how to use language are to be resolved. For Affeldt, any such approach to problems in the philosophy of language remains locked within a form of skepticism unable to come to terms with the way in which language simply is part of our natural history as human animals and is spoken essentially by embodied, desiring creatures—a form of skepticism against which Wittgenstein's work is recurrently directed.

In his essay "Tragedy and Skepticism: On *Hamlet*," Menke's engagement with Cavell's work is less explicit than is that of the other three authors in their contributions to Part Three, but it is no less indebted to it and no less sustained in its effort to reveal its significance. Menke not only shares Cavell's interest in the relation between skepticism and tragedy, and more particularly in the particular understanding of the sources and nature of skepticism that are in play in Shakespearean tragedy, but he also follows Cavell in thinking that Shakespearean tragedy itself constitutes nothing less than an investigation of the modern skeptical attitude. In this essay, Menke seeks to highlight the complex contours of the form of skepticism on display in Shakespeare's *Hamlet*. According to Menke, tragedy in general "replaces trust and confidence with doubt and uncertainty" and, in this sense, gives expression to and has consequences for a certain form of skepticism. In classical tragedies, skepticism takes on a particularly *practical* form, calling into question our ability to act successfully and to lead a self-directed life. Modern tragedies, on the other hand, seem to be concerned, not with our practical capacities, but with the failure of our epistemic capacity to know; they give expression to an *epistemic* skepticism. On the surface, what seems to corrode Hamlet's capacity for successful action is his epistemic uncertainty, his lack of secure knowledge. According to Menke, however, the relationship between practical and epistemic skepticism in *Hamlet* is far more complex. For, he argues, *Hamlet* presents a kind of genealogy of modern epistemological skepticism. In a first step, epistemic uncertainty is shown to be the consequence of what Menke calls Hamlet's "attitude of reflective spectatorship." Such a reflective attitude makes the search for certainty both necessary and, at the same time, unrealizable. It is thus the ground of epistemic skepticism. In a second step, however, this attitude is itself traced back to a form of *practical* uncertainty. For, on Menke's view, the question as to what role we should accord to the attitude of reflection is itself a practical question; and the essential tragic experience in *Hamlet* consists in the absence of any ground upon on which this question could be rationally decided.

In his paper "Cavell, Scepticism, and the Idea of Philosophical Criticism," Arata Hamawaki undertakes to draw a parallel between Kant's treatment of the problems of special metaphysics in the transcendental dialectic and Cavell's treatment of skepticism. Just as for Kant the idea of definite answers to meta-physical questions is based on a transcendental illusion that leads to unavoidable contradictions when trying to answer them, so for Cavell skepticism and traditional attempts at its refutation rest on the illusion that the skeptic can make himself intelligible by means of criteria that govern the use of his concepts. Hamawaki's aim in drawing this parallel is to lay bare the precise extent of Cavell's inheritance of the idea of Kantian critique. He makes perspicuous just where Cavell follows Kant's model and locates the exact moments at which Cavell is compelled to depart from it, and why. He thereby seeks to illuminate both the nature of Cavell's unique engagement with skepticism and the special conception of philosophy that arises from and informs this engagement.

In the final paper in Part Three, "Cavell and Other Animals," Simon Glendinning expounds his understanding of human finitude on the basis of an appreciative yet critical reading of Cavell's interpretation of Wittgenstein's conception of the role of "criteria" in our understanding of concepts. On the one hand, Glendinning follows Cavell in rejecting the standard, or epistemological, interpretation of Wittgensteinian criteria. According to this interpretation, the point of Wittgenstein's appeal to criteria is to provide for a novel form of refutation of skepticism concerning other minds, enabling us to attain *certainty* about inner states or events on the basis of outer states or events. As opposed to this, Cavell sees the role of Wittgensteinian criteria as one of determining the application of concepts employed in statements about the inner states of others rather than as one of establishing some form of certainty with regard to the existence of those states. Glendinning's dissatisfaction with Cavell's account of these matters sets in at the point in Cavell's account where he insists that the capacity to convene and master such criteria is something that is exclusively the concern of human animals. As Glendinning sees it, this is a sign of the extent to which Cavell continues to be captivated by a traditional classical humanist picture—one which introduces an overly sharp distinction between human and non-human animals—a picture which renders the nature of our own human animality incomprehensible. In contrast, Glendinning wants to get clear about a dimension of our lives that, while not being exclusive to human beings, is central to our animal finitude and which can neither be accounted for by reductive naturalism nor by classical humanism. This dimension can be seen in forms of interaction between humans and non-human animals that display an uncanny mutual understanding and thereby suggest that criteria have application beyond the human province.

The volume as a whole seeks to bring out the varieties of forms of philosophical skepticism that have continued to preoccupy philosophers for the past couple of centuries, as well as the specific varieties of philosophical response that these have engendered—above all, in the work of those who have sought to take their cue from Kant, Wittgenstein, or Cavell—and to illuminate how these various philosophical approaches are related to and bear upon one another.

**Part I:   After Kant**

Paul Franks
# Skepticism after Kant

Skepticism is regarded by some philosophers today as a problem that is, or ought to be, *superseded*—an issue of the past, to which we should not bother respond-ing.[1] Yet it would be no exaggeration to say that others regard skepticism as in some way *defining* philosophy's contemporary task.[2]

A similar division is found among interpreters of Kant. Some think that Kant is not concerned to argue against skepticism, since he believes that nobody could be a serious skeptic in the face of Newton's accomplishments. Yet others measure Kant's accomplishments by his success or failure in replying to the skepticism of Hume.[3]

In this paper, I want to ask: what is the effect upon skepticism of Kant's phil-osophical revolution? I will pursue the question in two ways. First, I will consider Kant's own attitude to skepticism, and whether, by his own lights, there should

---

1 Three ways of dismissing skepticism stand out as influential over the last few decades. What is striking is that views that are so very different should have conspired to produce a common effect. According to Quine, classical epistemology has been largely concerned with the ju-stification of knowledge against skepticism. But that project has failed. See Quine 1969, 72: "The Humean predicament is the human predicament." So classical epistemology should give way to a naturalized successor-discipline without justificatory pretensions. According to Rorty 1979, 140: "The Cartesian mind simultaneously made possible veil-of-ideas skepticism and a disci-pline devoted to circumventing it." Since, then, we can dispense with the Cartesian theory of the mind, we can also dispense both with (modern) skepticism and with the epistemological dis-cipline concerned to refute it. According to Chisholm, however, Quine and Rorty share a false presupposition: classical epistemology has never been solely or necessarily concerned to refute skepticism. Pure, theoretical analysis of the structure of justification is logically independent of any interest in skeptical doubt, which is in any event of doubtful coherence. So classical epi-stemology should continue, but without the interest in skepticism that has motivated some of its practitioners. See Chisholm 1966, 24–7.

2 See Williams 1996, xii–46, for discussion of what he calls the New Skepticism or New Hu-meanism of, e. g., Cavell, Nagel, and Stroud, who hold, in their different ways, that skepticism is deeply rooted in the very activity of philosophizing and so must be confronted in any self-reflective philosophy. Some who rhetorically dismiss skepticism may nevertheless, in effect, reinforce the sense of its standing importance. For example, Quine's remark about Hume, cited in the previous footnote, may be taken that way.

3 The prevailing view in recent—especially but not exclusively Anglophone—literature has been that Kant's achievements must be measured against his ability to refute skepticism. See, e. g., Wolff 1963, Chapter 1; Walker 1978, vii; Henrich 1989, 37; Stroud 1983. For an approach that focuses on Kant's relation to Newton, see Friedman 1992b, and for a careful examination of Kant's attitude to skepticism, see Engstrom 1994 and Hatfield 2001.

be any place for skepticism after Kant. Second, I will turn to Kant's effect on skepticism during the last two decades of the eighteenth century, asking whether there emerged at that time any skepticism that might be called genuinely post-Kantian, by which I mean a new skepticism, made possible by Kant's revolution.[4]

# I Kant and Skepticism

Turning first to Kant, I will argue that he holds *both* of the attitudes mentioned above. That is, Kant thinks *both* that skepticism defines the task of philosophy *and* that skepticism is, or ought to be, a problem of the past. To understand Kant's view of skepticism, we must see how he *could* hold these two—apparently opposed—attitudes.

Few passages are more frequently cited in accounts of Kant's motivation than the passage from the *Prolegomena* in which he says that his recollection of Hume first interrupted his dogmatic slumber.[5] However, it is important to note that Kant never says that he was provoked into attempting a *refutation* of Hume's *skepticism*. Rather, the description of their relationship suggested by the passage is that Hume helped Kant to *ask* the central *question* of transcendental philosophy. To inaugurate transcendental philosophy, Kant needed first to *generalize* Hume's skeptical question and then to ask that question in a different *tone* or *mood*. Whereas Hume may be said to have asked, "How *could* we *possibly* be justified in employing the concept of cause?", Kant found a way to ask, "Under what conditions *can* we employ the concept of cause?" or, more generally, "How are synthetic judgments *a priori* possible?"[6] Skepticism, Kant says

---

**4** The term "post-Kantian" is here meant philosophically, not chronologically. In fact, the varieties of post-Kantian skepticism that I will discuss here all arise chronologically after Kant's first *Critique*. But I would not be averse on principle to the claim that some chronologically pre-Kantian philosopher—say, Aristotle, Descartes, or Hume—could be interpreted as in some way addressing a skepticism that is, in my sense, post-Kantian. To make out such a claim, one would need to show that the philosopher in question was committed to some version or anticipation of Kant's revolution. Thanks to Rupert Read for raising this question in discussion.

**5** Kant 1900–, IV 260. (All Kant citations are by Academy volume and page, except for citations from the *Critique of Pure Reason*, which use the A/B format. All translations are from Kant 1999.)

**6** Compare Lear 1998, 285–6: "A transcendental argument for X . . . will answer the question 'How is X possible?' when that question is asked with a straight face rather than a skeptical sneer." For Lear, too, the mood in which the question is asked is crucial. But must a skeptical question be accompanied by a sneer rather than, say, a wild-eyed look of horror or a disillusioned shrug of the shoulder?

later in the *Prolegomena*, is "a way of thinking, in which reason moves against itself with such violence, that it could never have arisen except in complete despair [*in völliger Verzweiflung*] of achieving satisfaction with respect to reason's most important aspirations."[7] Hume's skeptical question is asked in a mood of *despair*, while Kant's transcendental question is asked in a mood of what Kant elsewhere calls *hope:* hope that reason can fulfill its aspiration to self-knowledge.[8]

This is how skepticism defines the task of philosophy for Kant. It is not that philosophy must seek, above all, to refute skepticism. Rather, philosophy must learn from skepticism which questions to ask, while transmuting the skeptic's mood of despair. Thus, transcendental philosophy may be described, not only as an account of the conditions of the possibility of synthetic judgments *a priori*, but also as an account of the conditions of the possibility of skepticism. For the list of synthetic judgments *a priori* is at the same time a list of judgments that are vulnerable to skeptical doubt. There is a genuine problem about these judgments, a problem articulated—at least, in part—by Hume. For we can easily grasp that the ground of synthetic judgments *a posteriori* is experience, and we can readily see that the ground of analytic judgments is the general logic of our concepts, but we cannot understand the ground of synthetic judgments *a priori* unless we alter the direction of our gaze. As Kant says in several passages, Hume gave up too hastily and was thus driven to skeptical despair.[9] He missed the possibility that some judgments might be neither enabled by experience nor independent of experience but, rather, conditions for the possibility of experience.

What sustains Kant in his hopefulness is precisely his generalization of Hume's problem. For once Kant has arrived at the general idea of synthetic judgments *a priori*, he sees that the problem arises as much for mathematics and for what he calls the general science of nature as it does for causal judgments. But mathematics and mathematical physics are, for Kant, beyond reasonable doubt, and he is confident that Hume would have said the same if he had realized that

---

7 Kant 1900–, IV 271.

8 See also A407/B433 – 4, where Kant refers to "skeptical hopelessness [*Hoffnungslosigkeit*]." The notion of rational hope plays a crucial role in Kant's doctrine of the highest good. On reason's aspiration to self-knowledge, see A745/B773, where Kant imagines Hume answering a question about the purpose of skepticism by saying that we have been made vulnerable to skepticism "[s]olely in order to advance reason in its self-knowledge, and because of a certain indignation at the violence that is done to reason by those who, while boasting of its powers, yet hinder it from candid admission of the weaknesses which have become obvious to it through its own self-examination."

9 IV 258; A762–3/B790 –1.

his problem extended to them. If Hume's problem is soluble in the cases of mathematics and mathematical physics, then we have reason to hope that it is soluble more generally. Any view that gives up the quest for a general solution, abandoning itself to despair, is—as Kant says of empiricism in the introduction to the transcendental deduction—"refuted" [*widerlegt*] through the *Faktum* of mathematical and natural science.[10]

So skepticism defines philosophy's task by teaching it to ask transcendental questions. But skepticism is *also* a problem of the past. Once the mood has changed from despair to hope, no further refutation of skepticism is called for, and Kant's central arguments do not seek to provide one. This attitude goes along with a certain picture of the skeptic's motivation. Skeptics like Hume, Kant thinks, are driven by reason's interest in self-knowledge. When they find reason's way to its objective apparently blocked, they prefer candid admission of their despair to disingenuous pretense that all is well. Consequently, skepticism is—at least, so far—an *academic* problem, a problem that affects those who want to fulfill reason's aspirations by setting metaphysics on the sure path of a science.[11] Moreover, there should be no room for skepticism proper—that is, for skeptical despair—after Kant's inauguration of transcendental philosophy. At most, there is room for the deployment of skeptical arguments against philosophy's recurring seduction into transcendent dogmatism by dialectical illusions.[12] For Kant recognizes no drive to skeptical doubt as such. There is only the drive to knowledge, which used to get diverted into skepticism, prior to Kant's critical restoration of hope.

---

10 B128. See also B4–5, where Kant claims that it is easy to show that there are pure *a priori* judgments in human knowledge, whether scientific or ordinary, and that, even without appealing to such examples, it is possible to show that pure *a priori* principles are indispensable for the possibility of experience, which could not derive its "certainty" from anywhere else. At any rate, Kant says, "we can content ourselves with having displayed the pure use of our cognition as a fact [*Tatsache*] together with its indication [*Kennzeichen*]." Evidently, no refutation of skepticism is required to establish this fact.

11 See Bxxxiv–xxxv: "Through criticism alone can we sever the very root of *materialism, fatalism, atheism,* of free-thinking *unbelief,* of *enthusiasm,* and *superstition,* which can become generally injurious, and finally also of *idealism* and *skepticism,* which are more dangerous to the schools and can hardly be transmitted to the public." Any attempt to restrain academic freedom in order to protect the public is therefore misguided, argues Kant.

12 See A297–8/B354–5.

# II Three Possibilities of Post-Kantian Skepticism

If Kant is successful, then, there ought to be no skepticism after Kant. But of course there is. And some varieties presuppose precisely that Kant's arguments have succeeded. One frequently mentioned possibility is that transcendental idealism, the conclusion that should be established by Kant's arguments if they are successful, simply amounts to skepticism. In the next section, I will say more about this possibility, which Kant would certainly want to resist.

In addition, there are at least two ways in which the argument of the *Critique of Pure Reason* itself leaves open the *logical* possibility of post-Kantian skepticism.[13]

First, recall Kant's description of his deductive method in "The Discipline of Pure Reason":

> through concepts of the understanding... [pure reason] certainly erects secure principles, but not directly from concepts, but rather always only indirectly through relation of these concepts to something entirely contingent, namely, *possible experience*; since if this (something as object of possible experiences) is presupposed, then they are of course apodictically certain, but in themselves they cannot even be cognized a priori (directly) at all. . . although [the proposition that everything that happens has its cause] must be *proved*, it is called a *principle*, not a *theorem* because it has the special property that it first makes possible its ground of proof, namely experience, and must always be presupposed in this.[14]

This is, I think, generally understood as follows: Kant undertakes to show that synthetic *a priori* principles—such as the principle of causality—are necessary conditions for the admittedly contingent possibility of experience; since, as a matter of fact, we actually have experience, it follows that the application of the principles is justified. If this interpretation is correct, then the assumption that we actually have experience plays a crucial role in transcendental argumentation.[15] Were there reason to *doubt* that we actually have experience, the prin-

---

**13** This is in no way intended as an exhaustive list. And I do not intend here to reconstruct the details of Kant's arguments. I will merely assume standard characterizations of those arguments and, for the sake of this investigation, I will assume the validity of the arguments, so characterized.

**14** A737/B765.

**15** In fact, although this is not the place to explore the point, I think it likely that when Kant refers to "something as object of possible experience," he has in mind the sum-total of the *materials* for possible experience, a finite spatiotemporal version of the *ens realissimum*. Kant's method could presuppose the actuality of this material sum-total without presupposing the actuality of experience itself. On the *ens realissimum*, see Longuenesse 1995. On the role of a

ciples in question would not have been demonstrated beyond reasonable doubt, *even if* Kant's argument that they are conditions for the possibility of experience were accepted as logically *valid*. Consequently, it is logically possible to accept the argumentation of the Analytic in Kant's first *Critique* and yet to doubt the actuality of experience which Kant assumes. In this way, it is possible to be a post-Kantian skeptic.

Now, it may well seem that Kant excludes this possibility in advance, when he adds the Refutation of Idealism to his B-edition of the *Critique*. For he describes that refutation as showing that we have, of outer things, *experience*, and not merely imagination.[16] In the first place, however, the Refutation of Idealism takes aim against a particular opponent: "the problematic idealism of Descartes" which, according to Kant, admits that I have immediate, inner experience of my own existence, but regards judgments about outer objects as involving problematic inferences.[17] Doubt about whether we have experience at all is not the Refutation's concern. Furthermore, it is important to see that, *by Kant's own methodological standards*, the Refutation of Idealism cannot, even if it is successful, establish straightforwardly *that we have experience of outer things*. At most, the Refutation can show that *problematic idealism* is absurd; that one cannot coherently hold that we have inner experience, but not outer experience. But Kant himself points out elsewhere that, in transcendental philosophy, apagogic proofs—that is, arguments by *reductio ad absurdum*—cannot *establish* the *opposite* of the opinion reduced to absurdity. Here is Kant, from the Discipline of Pure Reason:

> Apagogic proof... can be allowed only in those sciences where it is impossible to *substitute* that which is subjective in our representations for that which is objective, namely the cognition of what is in the object. Where the latter is the dominant concern, however, it must frequently transpire that the opposite of a certain proposition either simply contradicts the subjective conditions of thought but not the object, or else that both propositions contradict each other only under a subjective condition that is falsely held to be objective, and that since the condition is false, both of them can be false, without it being possible to infer the truth of one from the falsehood of the other. . . The transcendental attempts of pure reason... are all conducted within the real medium of dialectical illusion, i.e., the subjective, which offers itself to or even forces itself upon reason, as objective in its premisses.

---

finite analogue of the *ens realissimum* in Kant's transition project, see Friedman 1992b, 308 – 11; Förster 2000.

**16** B275.

**17** B274. Cf., A367– 9, where Cartesianism is called empirical idealism, divided into dogmatic and skeptical idealism at A377.

Now here it simply cannot be allowed that assertions of synthetic propositions be justified by the refutation of their opposites.[18]

Of course, this view of Kant's underlies what, in his treatment of the antinomies, he calls his "skeptical method."[19] Both opinions may be rejected. Or, if they are reformulated so that they do not conflict, both may be accepted. If we apply this line of thought to the Refutation of Idealism, then we see a second logical possibility for post-Kantian skepticism. That empirical idealism is absurd does not entail that empirical realism is coherent. There could be another antinomy, in which *not only* idealism *but also* realism is reduced to absurdity. But that would place us, once again, in a state of skeptical despair. For there would be no reason to affirm either realism or idealism. There would be reason only to abstain from judgment—that is, reason only for skepticism.

Remarkably, as I hope to show, all three possibilities for post-Kantian skepticism were actualized in the period of Kant's first reception, in the 1780s and '90s. At that time, it was not unusual for a philosopher who considered himself a Kantian to think that, far from superseding skepticism, Kant had shown how deep a problem it really was, or even that Kant had given rise to a more thoroughgoing skepticism than any hitherto encountered. In 1794, Karl Friedrich Stäudlin published a groundbreaking two-volume work on the history and spirit of skepticism. His opening words were:

Skepticism is beginning to become a sickness of the age, and—which is a rare phenomenon in history—is beginning to spread itself among more classes and to express its effects on a large scale. The most recent revolution in philosophy was supposed to overthrow it, but according to a new discovery it is supposed to have bent not a hair on its head or, rather, even to have strengthened it.[20]

How could Kant's revolution have so paradoxical an effect?

This is not only an historical question. For even today many of us continue to grapple with problems that may justifiably be called Kantian or post-Kantian. In order to indicate the contemporary relevance of my investigation, I will adduce a contemporary analogue for each of the post-Kantian skepticisms discussed below.

---

**18** A791–2/B819–20.
**19** A424/B451.
**20** Stäudlin 1794.

# III Transcendental Idealism as Nihilistic Skepticism

I want first to consider the thesis that transcendental idealism, even if success-fully established, amounts to some kind of skepticism. The problem with this thesis is that, as it is typically formulated, it seems to depend on an interpreta-tion of Kant as, in effect, a *pre*-Kantian.[21] I do not think that any such interpre-tation is correct. Indeed, my own thesis would be in trouble if it were, for if there were no Kantian revolution, then there would be no post-Kantian skepticism in any interesting sense. It is tempting to dismiss the claim that transcendental ide-alism amounts to skepticism as a pseudo-post-Kantian skepticism. However, I will argue that there are genuinely post-Kantian ways of reformulating the claim.

The *locus classicus* for the idea that Kant's revolution, if successful, leads to a new kind of skepticism is a supplement to Jacobi's 1787 book of dialogues in-spired by Hume.[22] This supplement, with its complaint of a presupposition with-out which one cannot enter the critical philosophy but with which one cannot remain within it, is as famous as any reaction to Kant. Yet it is all too often read in total isolation from Jacobi's other writings, in isolation even from the text to which it is a supplement. The result is widespread misunderstanding, not only of Jacobi's own position, but also, as I hope to show, of the ultimate im-port of his criticism of Kant.

In the supplement on transcendental idealism, Jacobi argues that Kant is torn between two incompatible commitments. On the one hand, Kant is commit-ted to the genuine receptivity of outer sense. Indeed, Kant's talk of sensibility would be meaningless unless he intended "a distinct real intermediary between one real thing and another, an actual means *from* something *to* something else," hence unless he presupposed "the objective validity of our perception of objects outside us as things in themselves."[23] Without that presupposition, Jacobi found for some time that he could not enter into the Kantian system. For without it he could make no sense of the distinction between sensibility and understanding.

On the other hand, Kant is committed to the transcendental idealist doctrine that we know only appearances. As Jacobi puts it, ". . . what we realists call ac-

---

**21** Certainly, the Garve–Feder review, which shared the interpretation in question, attributing to Kant the Cartesian view of the mind as an inner realm of mental objects or states, concluded that Kant had contributed nothing new. For a translation, see Sassen 2000.

**22** See Jacobi 1994, 331–8.

**23** Jacobi 1994, 336. For a later version of the point, made in 1815 when Jacobi had clarified his position and was able to refer to Kant's later works, see 546.

tual objects or things independent of our representations are for the transcendental idealist only internal beings *which exhibit nothing at all of a thing that may perhaps be there outside us, or to which the appearance may refer. Rather, these internal beings are merely subjective determinations of the mind, entirely void of anything truly objective.*"[24] So Jacobi cannot stay within the Kantian system as long as he continues to credit Kant's presupposition of a genuine faculty of *outer* sense.

It is simply impossible, Jacobi argues, for Kant to maintain both his realistic commitment to genuine sensibility and his idealism. So Kant faces a dilemma. He must give up one or the other if he is to be consistent. Now, Jacobi is himself a thoroughgoing realist, as he has stated clearly in the main body of the text.[25] So it goes without saying in the supplement that Jacobi himself would recommend realism to Kant. What Jacobi emphasizes in the supplement, for his own dialectical purposes, is the consequence of rejecting realism to become a consistent transcendental idealist. Someone who grasped that horn of the dilemma would have to profess what Jacobi calls "transcendental ignorance," a thoroughgoing repudiation of knowledge about so much as the probability of the existence of things outside us in a transcendental sense.[26] This "absolute and unqualified ignorance" would be accompanied by "the strongest idealism that was ever professed," since all that could ever be known would be merely subjective and internal. If one wants to be a consistent transcendental idealist, one "should not be afraid of the objection of speculative egoism."[27] Of course, Jacobi means to be presenting the Kantian with a *reductio ad absurdum.* Yet, presumably because his words have been taken out of the context of his realism and, indeed, out of the context of the book in which those words appear, he is often quoted as if he is *recommending* "speculative egoism."[28]

---

24 Jacobi 1994, 334. For a later version, see 552–3.

25 See, e.g., Jacobi 1994, 275–7, where it is argued that the realist must reject the assumption that representations, as determinations of the self, are epistemically prior to knowledge of outer objects, which requires inference.

26 Jacobi 1994, 338.

27 Jacobi 1994, 338.

28 For a recent example, see Collins 1999, 27: "Kant does not actually assert any idealist conclusion, which he would do only if he contended that there are no things-in-themselves but only ideas that seem to be ideas of such things, or if he argued that we cannot know for sure whether there any things-in-themselves in addition to our ideas of such things. These views would amount to a dogmatic or a problematic idealism concerning things-in-themselves. *Jacobi seems to adopt the latter position*, but Kant himself propounds neither. It is in the context of these understandings that German idealism turns away from Kant's commitment to things-in-themselves" (emphasis added). Collins does an excellent job of reinterpreting Kantian passages

Jacobi's criticism of the inconsistency of Kant's transcendental idealism, and his argument that a consistent Kantian idealism would amount not only to skeptical *doubt*, but to *denial of the very possibility of knowledge of external objects*, was immensely influential in his own day, and is still echoed today.[29] However, it is not hard to see that Jacobi is interpreting Kant against Kant's explicit protests, as an idealist akin to Berkeley. Of course, Jacobi is hardly alone in doing so. Kant is similarly interpreted, not only in the Garve–Feder review that so provoked Kant, but also in much twentieth-century Anglophone literature.[30] Admittedly, Jacobi wrote his supplement before Kant produced the *Prolegomena* and the B-edition of the first *Critique*. But those clarifications did not lead Jacobi, or many more recent Anglophone commentators, to retract the ascription to Kant of a Cartesian conception of the mind as veiled from the external world by its own representations.

That ascription has recently been challenged with great thoroughness and effectiveness, notably by Arthur Collins, who provides alternative ways of reading even the A-edition passages that have seemed Cartesian to Jacobi and to many others. Jacobi finds these passages so obviously Cartesian that it is sufficient merely to *quote* them in order to bring out the side of Kant that is incompatible with realism about external objects. For example, at A491/B519, Kant characterizes transcendental idealism as follows: "everything intuited in space or time, and hence all objects of an experience possible for us, are nothing but appearances, i.e., mere representations, which, as they are represented, as extended beings or series of alterations, have outside our thoughts no existence grounded in itself." And at A101, Kant says: ". . . appearances are not things in

---

that one can feel compelled to read as espousing a Cartesian conception of the mind, hence as espousing pre-Kantian empirical idealism. But he seems to have no reservations about attributing the pre-Kantian, Cartesian conception not only to Jacobi, who explicitly rejects it, but also to German idealists whose apparently pre-Kantian formulations may also be reinterpreted in the way Collins reinterprets Kant himself, and who may thus be seen as the post-Kantians they explicitly profess to be. See Collins 1999, 25, 161, 180.

**29** Jacobi may have influenced Schulze's widely read work of 1792, *Aenesidemus*, which echoes and develops some of Jacobi's criticisms of Kant and which throughout neglects the transcendental–empirical distinction and presupposes a Cartesian interpretation of Kant. Fichte seems to accept Jacobi's view of those he called Kantians, who read Kant literally, but not of Kant himself, as read spiritually. For recent echoes of Jacobi, see Stroud 1984; Williams 1996, 20.

**30** See Collins 1999, 153 – 82 for discussion of the persistence of the Cartesian interpretation, not only in Paton, Kemp Smith, and Strawson, who might acknowledge it, but also in Allison and Pippin, who mean to be offering non-Cartesian interpretations.

themselves, but rather the mere play of our representations, which in the end come down to determinations of inner sense."[31]

There is no doubt that these passages *sound* Cartesian. Indeed, as Collins notes, at A368 Kant uses almost identical language to describe the Cartesian or problematic idealist, for whom, "it always remains doubtful... whether... all the so-called outer perceptions are not a mere play of our inner sense, or whether they stand in relation to actual external objects as their cause." Yet Kant explicitly distinguishes his *transcendental* idealism from the *empirical* idealism of the Cartesian in that very context, in the Fourth Paralogism of the A-edition. Apparently, this distinction is insufficient to prevent Jacobi from drawing some of his most compelling proof-texts from the Fourth Paralogism itself. Indeed, although Kant protests vehemently against the suggestion that he is an empirical idealist, and although he drops some of the apparently damning language (e. g., A101), he does not drop all of it (e. g., A491/B519), and he even reuses some of it in the *Prolegomena* despite the fact that that text was meant to refute the charge of empirical idealism.[32] If there is no way to interpret these passages other than the obvious Cartesian way, then Kant is a very confused man.

But there *is* another way. First, one needs to take seriously Kant's own remark in the Fourth Paralogism that the expression "outside us" is "unavoidably ambiguous," having both an empirical and a transcendental sense.[33] Indeed, one needs to generalize this remark, so that a range of terms, including "inside us" and "representation," are also treated as having both empirical and transcendental senses. Kant does not say as much about this crucial distinction as he might have. He does not emphasize that "unavoidable ambiguity" must affect his entire enterprise. This is not the place to explore Kant's motivation for deploying precisely the language used by empirical idealists and skeptics while allowing the transcendental character of his inquiry to give that language a sense that must be unfamiliar to his readers, nor to investigate why he is so remarkably unguarded against the standing possibility of misinterpretation that must, on his

---

**31** Cited by Jacobi 1994, 334. Kemp Smith makes clear his Cartesian interpretation of the passage by translating *"auf Bestimmungen des inneren Sinnes auslaufen"* as "reduce to determinations of inner sense"." Jacobi also cites extracts from the Fourth Paralogism (A367–80), the Aesthetic (A36), and the A-deduction (A125–6).

**32** See, e. g., Kant 1900–, IV 337: "... the question of whether bodies (as appearances of outer sense) exist *outside my thought* as bodies in nature can without hesitation be answered negatively." For discussion, see Collins 1999, 33.

**33** A368.

own account, threaten his central arguments and claims.[34] It will suffice here to say something about the difference between the empirical and the transcendental senses of the claim that, say, all objects of experience are mere representations.

Empirically speaking, to say that all objects of experience are mere representations is to make an ontological claim. It is to say that all objects of experience are mental, whether they are mental objects or mental states. Whatever is mental cannot exist outside thought, because thought is the essence or medium of the mental. Indeed, according to some highly influential lines of thought, whatever is mental may exist independently of any non-mental thing and may be individuated solely in terms either of its own intrinsic properties or of the intrinsic properties of the mind of which it is a state.

If, however, one says that all objects of experience are representations in the *transcendental* sense, no such ontological claim is being made, either about the mental status of empirical objects or about their independence from the non-mental. Rather, the claim in its transcendental sense is like the claim that an object has a certain property when viewed from a certain perspective.[35] If I say that a bridge, viewed from my window, is obscured by an intervening building, I am not saying that the bridge *in itself* has the property of being obscured. Being obscured is not an intrinsic property of the bridge.[36] Of course, being obscured is

----

34 Collins provides invaluable help by providing transcendental readings of passages that one is sorely tempted to read empirically. But he does not seem interested in asking why Kant writes this way. Indeed, he leaves the impression that Kant just committed an inexplicable tactical error. Collins himself prefers to stick to the empirical sense of idealism and hence to insist that Kant was simply *not* an idealist. See, e.g., Collins 1999, 2: "Kant is not an idealist, and 'transcendental idealism' is a misleading title in so far as it seems to advertise a thesis that merely corrects the errors of the defective versions of idealism Kant expressly refutes." To my mind, this leaves unexplained the intimacy of the relationship between empirical and transcendental idealism, symbolized by the possibility of expressing them in the same language, which must be connected to their different ways of responding to the same skeptical doubt.

35 See Collins 1999, 37–45, from whom the bridge example that follows is drawn. The analogy between transcendental idealism and ordinary perspectival claims helps to explain Kant's famous invocation of Copernicus. For Copernicus's revolution depends upon the insight that observations may have unobserved conditions, hence that it may be harder than we realize to distinguish apparent from real motions, which is of course not to say that apparent motions are mental. See Ewing, *Kant's Critique of Pure Reason*, 16.

36 This formulation coheres with what Ameriks calls the essence theory of transcendental idealism, according to which "a thing's properties are merely phenomenal simply if and only if they are contingent, that is, do not belong to the real essence of the thing" (Ameriks 2000, 267). Thus a thing-in-itself is a thing considered with respect to its real essence or intrinsic properties,

not an intrinsic property of my mind either. It is, rather, a perspectival property, a relational property of a specific kind, which cannot exist without the perspective in question and which therefore could not exist if there were no minds capable of occupying that perspective. Now, the fact that a perspectival property cannot exist "outside my thoughts" in the sense just explained does not entail that the property is mental, let alone that it may exist or be individuated independently of any non-mental thing.

Of course, Kant's transcendental claim is not exactly like ordinary perspectival claims. A variety of ordinary perspectives is available to us. If I view the bridge from elsewhere, it is not obscured. But Kant's argument is that all human beings occupy the same *transcendental* perspective—that there are conditions of our experience to which *all* empirical properties are relative—and that no *alternative* perspective in that sense is available to us. *None* of the empirical properties we ascribe to things are intrinsic properties of those things, or properties of those things considered *in themselves*. Still, the analogy remains: Kant's transcendental claim does not entail that all empirical properties are mental, let alone that they are intrinsic properties of mind, independent of the non-mental. So the perspectival character of transcendental idealism is very different from the ontological character of empirical idealism.

Now, if Jacobi's influential claim—that consistent transcendental idealism entails "absolute and unqualified ignorance" of external things—depends on the mistaken ascription to Kant of *empirical* idealism, then the claim must surely be rejected. According to Kant's transcendental idealism, we *can* know external things, but we cannot know them as they are in themselves. A *specific kind* of knowledge is denied to us, but this denial seems very different from skeptical doubts or denials with respect to knowledge *as such*, especially since the kind of knowledge denied to us is not, Kant argues, a kind to which we ordinarily lay claim.[37] So it seems that Jacobi has not led us to a species of post-Kantian skepticism.

---

while an appearance is a thing considered with respect to its relational or extrinsic properties. For a development of this interpretation, see Langton 1998.

**37** My talk of a specific kind of knowledge could be misleading if taken to mean some kind of knowledge on a par with other kinds that are accessible. Discussion of Kant's account of reason would be required to clarify the point and to earn the following formulation: the idea of knowledge of things-in-themselves is of a way of fulfilling reason's demand for the unconditioned theoretically; although that mode of fulfillment is not even in principle possible for us, we may fulfill reason's demand by interpreting it practically, as a demand for determination of the will, not determination of the intellect. In a sense, then, nothing is denied to us. To conceive human finitude as a denial is part of the problem, not part of the solution.

However, if Jacobi's criticism of Kant is situated within the context of the criticism of philosophy developed in his work as a whole, then that criticism may, I believe, be reformulated in an adequately post-Kantian manner.

At the end of his life, Jacobi characterized his earlier response to Kant as follows:

> The Dialogue *On Idealism and Realism*, which was published a year earlier than Kant's *Critique of Practical Reason*, considers only the first, theoretical, part of his system. It is objected that that first part leads to nihilism, and that it does so with such an all-devastating power that no rearguard intervention could recoup what had been lost. It was lost once and for all.[38]

Jacobi's criticism of Kant must be understood within the context of his general argument that philosophy as such leads to *nihilism*—a term that Jacobi first popularized within philosophical discussion.[39]

Now, Jacobi is very far from being a systematic philosopher. In fact, he is the seminal critic of systematic philosophy, one who demands a return from philosophical attempts at rational justification and explanation to pre-philosophical, non-systematic, ordinary, rational *faith*. It is hard to find clear lines of argument in Jacobi although, according to his own views, the claim that philosophy leads necessarily to nihilism *ought* to be expressible in clear and compelling arguments, unlike his own way of escaping nihilism. Here I will present, in broad outline, a reconstructed line of argument that is rooted in Jacobi's texts, although it is never presented in just this way.[40]

In Jacobi's view, the long descent into nihilism begins with the Aristotelian demand for justification of what ordinarily requires no justification. Once the demand is accepted, the philosopher is confronted with some version of Agrippa's trilemma: any justification cited will be either a brute assertion that itself lacks justification, or a justification that has another justification, or a justification that presupposes some claim whose justification has already been demanded.[41]

---

**38** Jacobi 1994, 544.
**39** Jacobi does not use the term "nihilism" until 1799, but speaks of the threat of annihilation already in 1789. See Jacobi 1994, 362, 374–5 n., 519. On the history of the concept of nihilism, see Süss 1974; Pöggeler 1974; Gillespie 1996.
**40** See Franks 2000a.
**41** See Diogenes Laertius 1925, IX 88. For discussion, see Fogelin 1994; Williams 1996, 60–8. Jacobi does not explicitly address Agrippa's trilemma, but he seems to have been deeply concerned with the avoidance of both infinite regresses and arbitrary terminations or annihilations from childhood. See Jacobi 1994, 183, 362.

So any response to the demand will either terminate arbitrarily, or lead to an infinite regress, or move in a vicious circle.

What would count as escaping from the trilemma? It seems that one could escape only if one could cite something that is *intrinsically* justified, or justified *in itself*. Now it is important to see that the trilemma and the aspiration to intrinsic justification may be found in every part of philosophy. It is not only that epistemology hopes to find some intrinsically justified object of knowledge. Metaphysics hopes to find some intrinsically justified subject of predication, logic hopes to find some intrinsically justified premise, and ethics hopes to find some intrinsically justified principle of action.

The problem with all these escape attempts, in Jacobi's view—and of course he recognizes that the attempts have come in many varieties and that some are better than others—is that their effect is entirely destructive. Every brilliant appeal to some new kind of intrinsic justification succeeds only in raising the demand for justification about something else that was hitherto taken for granted. Thus, for example, Descartes' *cogito* leads, not to the security of an Archimedean point, but rather to Hume's disturbing discovery that the subject is no more substantial than its objects. The end of philosophy is not intrinsic justification but the total annihilation of justification, not an absolute something but an absolute nothing. Epistemic skepticism is only one aspect of the justificatory void that philosophy as such cannot avoid.

The only genuine escape from the Agrippan trilemma, according to Jacobi, would be to reject the demand for justification or, better yet, to stop raising it. To make our escape, we need to see that justification is not *mediation* by some ground, as the philosophical tradition would have it, but the *immediacy* of ordinary life and perception. Ordinary things and persons just *are*, immediately—except for their dependence on God, which is known with as much immediacy as is the existence of ourselves and others. Reason is not a faculty of inference, but a faculty of perception.[42] As soon as we raise the philosophical demand for justification, it is too late, because we have already lost our natural faith in reason, or else we would not have raised the demand. Once lost, the immediacy of the ordinary can never be replaced by any philosophical absolute. On the contrary, to seek a philosophical absolute—an intrinsic justification—is to continue to raise the demand for justification that is, at the same time, the loss of faith, the loss of the only justification there can be.[43]

---

42 Jacobi 1994, 541.

43 See Jacobi 1994, 583: "The moment a man sought to establish scientifically the veracity of our representations of a material world that exists beyond them, and independently of them, at

Nihilism, then, is the annihilation of the ordinary, where that annihilation is either a condition or an aspect of the activity of philosophizing. If Jacobi prefers to speak of nihilism rather than skepticism, it is, I think, because he takes himself to have uncovered a deeper diagnosis of philosophy's power of negation than the notions of doubt or ignorance would suggest.

Jacobi's criticism of Kant may easily be seen to instantiate the general pattern of his thought. In order to save what Kant *calls* the immediacy of sense, he argues that all objects of experience are merely internal representations, including the subject insofar as we experience it. But Kant has salvaged only a pseudo-immediacy. He has argued, perhaps even more cogently than Hume, that neither the subject nor its objects can be known in any intrinsically justified way. And he has missed Hume's naturalistic insight, from which Jacobi takes some of his inspiration, that the targets of philosophical questioning are ordinarily taken on what can only be called faith and that philosophy and ordinary faith can never be reconciled.

I have argued that, insofar as Jacobi's accusation of nihilism is based on the interpretation of Kant as an empirical idealist, it is to be rejected. However, now that the focus has been broadened, Jacobi's accusation can be reformulated, this time in a register that seems more metaphysical than epistemological.

In Jacobi's massively influential book on Spinoza—the first edition of which was published in 1785, after Kant's first *Critique* and before Jacobi's criticism of transcendental idealism—he confronts a philosopher who is not, in his opinion, an empirical idealist. Indeed, one reason for Jacobi's fascination with Spinoza is precisely that Spinoza sees clearly how to avoid epistemological nihilism, but nevertheless follows, with unprecedented rigor and clarity, the metaphysical road to what Jacobi later calls nihilism.[44] Inspired by the principle of sufficient reason—which Jacobi prefers to formulate as *"a nihilo nihil fit"*—Spinoza's uncompromising quest for genuine substance—for an intrinsically justified subject of predication—leads him to a remarkable formula: *"Determinatio est negatio, seu determinatio ad rem juxta suum esse non pertinet."* As Spinoza glosses the formula: "Individual things, therefore, so far as they only exist in a certain determinate mode, are *non-entia*, the indeterminate infinite being is the one single

---

that very moment the object that the demonstration wanted to ground disappeared before their eyes. They were left with mere subjectivity, with *sensation*. And thus they discovered idealism.

**44** Jacobi acknowledges Spinoza's influence in epistemological matters. Thus, Jacobi derives his conception of the natural faith of reason not only from Hume and Reid, but also from Spinoza, "who drew a clear distinction between being certain and not doubting." See Jacobi 1994, 193 n. 7. Jacobi also credits Spinoza for influencing his rejection of empirical idealism. See Jacobi 1994, 292–3.

true *ens real, hoc est, est omne esse, et praeter quod nullum datur esse.*"[45] That is, Spinoza's attempt to escape the Agrippan trilemma with respect to being annihilates the being of the individual things of everyday life.

In a remarkable footnote, Jacobi cites Kant's first *Critique* to illustrate his point about Spinoza.[46] The implication, although not developed explicitly, is that, just as Spinoza annihilates the positive being of everyday things by making them dependent on the substantial unity of God, so Kant annihilates the positive being of everyday things by making them dependent on the transcendental unity of apperception. What Kant calls a phenomenon is not a thing in itself, with its own positive character, but a *non-entity*, whose being is determinate only in relation to the whole of which it is a part and, ultimately, to the transcendental conditions that make up the human perspective.

Here is a metaphysical version of the charge that transcendental idealism amounts to a new kind of philosophical negation, to a nihilism that is even more destructive than empirical idealism and the skepticism with which it is associated. And this version is not so easily rejected. Kant himself argues that:

> ... everything in our cognition that belongs to intuition... contains nothing but mere relations; namely, of places in one intuition (extension), alteration of places (motion), and laws in accordance with which this alteration is determined (moving forces). But what is present in the location, or what it produces in the things themselves besides the alteration of place, is not given through these relations. Now through mere relations no thing in itself is cognized; it is therefore right to judge that since nothing is given to us through outer sense except mere representation of relation, outer sense can also contain in its representation only the relation of an object to the subject, and not that which is internal to the object in itself. It is exactly the same in the case of inner sense...[47]

As I have argued above, this passage must be read in an appropriately transcendental way, not as an expression of the empirical idealist view that the objects of sense are *mental* representations relative to a subject, but rather as an expression of the view that the objects of sense are accessible to us only via ineliminably perspectival properties. Nevertheless, the passage says that the objects of sense have determinate being, not in virtue of their own individual characters, but rather in relation to the spatiotemporal dynamic whole of which they are parts. And, as Kant goes on to argue in the Analytic, that spatiotemporal dynam-

---

**45** Jacobi 1994, 220. The last eleven words of the quotation are from Spinoza 1925, II 29 (I 34 in the English translation): "... the origin of Nature ... is a unique and infinite being, beyond which there is no being."
**46** Jacobi 1994, 223 n. 43, citing A107.
**47** B67.

ic whole itself has determinate being only in relation to the transcendental conditions that make up the human perspective. So if, as Jacobi insists, ordinary things have determinate being in virtue of their own individual characters, then Kant has annihilated ordinary things, substituting for them the phenomena of Newtonian physics, all of whose properties Kant has now shown to be ineliminably perspectival.

I can now reformulate Jacobi's nihilism accusation in a metaphysical register. On the one hand, transcendental idealism annihilates everyday things with their immediately determinate being. On the other hand, Kant himself acknowledges that genuine entities have individual characters. That is why he insists that we not only *can* but *must* think things-in-themselves as the grounds of appearances: "For otherwise there would follow the absurd proposition that there is an appearance without anything that appears."[48] Here, Jacobi might say, is a residue of Kant's pre-philosophical faith in ordinary individual things. But that residual realism is incompatible with transcendental idealism, and it is inevitable that a more thoroughgoing Kantian will eliminate the thing-in-itself. For the thing-in-itself cannot do what, on this view, it is intended to do. Kant's imperceptible things-in-themselves are not the perceptible individuals of ordinary life, and the insistence that they exist cannot restore the ontological immediacy that Kant's Copernican revolution has annihilated. If things-in-themselves cannot be perceptually known, then in what sense can they be the things that appear? Transcendental idealism *is*, in effect, the absurd conclusion that there can *only* be appearance without anything that appears. Kant's explicit recognition of the absurdity of this nihilistic conclusion cannot save him from it.

In my reformulated version, Jacobi may once again confront Kant with a dilemma. Either Kant may develop his philosophy consistently by embracing nihilism, meaning, in this case, the view that there can be no genuinely individual entities whatsoever. Or Kant may retain his residual faith in genuinely individual entities, but only by giving up his philosophy—indeed, only by rejecting the philosophical demand for justification altogether.

This reformulated version counts, I claim, as a kind of post-Kantian skepticism.[49] It amounts to a puzzle: after Kant's Copernican revolution, how is everyday knowledge of individual things and persons so much as possible? Or, how is

---

48 Bxxvi–xxvii.

49 I do not mean to imply that Jacobi, or any post-Kantian, advocates such a skepticism. Rather, the point is that some critics of Kant may criticize transcendental idealism because it amounts to skepticism in this way and that some post-Kantians may find that their acceptance of Kant's revolution makes this kind of skepticism a source of anxiety for them.

it so much as possible that there *are* any everyday individuals to know?[50] As these two formulations are supposed to suggest, the question may be put epistemologically, but it seems primarily metaphysical or, say, ontological. Any post-Kantian skepticism should, I think, have this characteristic, since it will inherit some version of the claim, central to Kant's revolution, that "[t]he *a priori* conditions of a possible experience in general are at the same time conditions of the possibility of the objects of experience."[51]

This species of post-Kantian skepticism has a contemporary analogue in some strands of Cavell's thinking about skepticism. First, Cavell speaks of "the skeptic as nihilist," of both skepticism and its attempted refutations as participating in an "annihilation" that has already occurred as soon as the philosophical question has been raised, if not before.[52] Second, what is annihilated in or before the philosophical demand for justification is precisely the everyday.[53] Hence no appeal to the everyday—say, to the criteria of our ordinary concepts—can refute skepticism, for once the skeptic's question has been raised, those everyday modes of justification are precisely what have already been lost or repudiated.[54] Third, what Cavell calls *acknowledgment*—like what Jacobi calls faith—is intended to articulate the ordinary's vulnerability to annihilation. However, Cavell guards against the charge that "in offering an alternative to the human

---

50 The question may also be ethically inflected: how is it possible that there are genuine persons with individual characters? The main character of Jacobi's novel, *Edward Allwill's Collection of Letters*, is, one might say, an ethical nihilist. For his will is entirely perspectival, flowing entirely into passions that are relative to given situations and lacking any genuine individual character. He is all will, and therefore nothing, just as Spinoza's God and Kant's transcendental subject are all being, and therefore nothing. This version of the problem of free will (how can a will give itself determinacy and not merely be determinate in response to the whole of which it is a part?) differs from the more familiar version (how can a will determine itself and not be determined by efficient causes?). But I find that the unfamiliar version plays a significant role in German Idealism, perhaps a more significant role than the familiar version.

51 A111. Cf., A158/B197: "The conditions of the possibility of experience in general are at the same time conditions of the possibility of the objects of experience."

52 For "the skeptic as nihilist," see Cavell 1988, 89. For an early formulation of skepticism as responding to a "loss of presentness," see Cavell 1976, 322–6; Cavell 1988, 172–4; Cavekk 1987, 5–6. Also crucial is the relationship between skepticism and "death-dealing passion." See Cavell 1979, 451–2; Cavell 1988, 55–56; Cavell 1987, 6–7.

53 See, e.g., Cavell 1988, 170–1.

54 Cavell sometimes describes this as "the major claim I make in *The Claim of Reason* about Wittgenstein's idea of a criterion, namely that while criteria provide conditions of (shared) speech they do not provide an answer to skeptical doubt. I express this by saying that criteria are disappointing, taking them to express, even to begin to account for, the human disappointment with human knowledge" (Cavell 1988, 87).

goal of knowing . . . [the idea of acknowledgment] gives up the claim of philosophy to reason"—just the charge to which Jacobi seems open—by insisting that the idea is proposed "not as an alternative to knowledge but rather as an interpretation of it."[55]

Finally, Cavell's criticism of Kant's settlement with skepticism bears comparison to Jacobi's. Cavell says that Kant's settlement fails to satisfy because he did not *deduce* the thing-in-itself,[56] or because he deprives appearances of "our sense of externality": "Our sense not of each object's externality to every other, making nature a whole, showing it to be spatial; but their externality to me, making nature a world, showing it to be habitable."[57] Thus Kant seems "to deny that you can experience the world as world, things as things; face to face, as it were, call this the life of things."[58] One might take Cavell to be charging Kant with empirical idealism. Certainly, he regards Kantian appearances as too internal, or as internal in the wrong way. But, as I hope the above quotations suggest, Cavell may more charitably be interpreted as charging Kant with participating in the nihilistic violence of skepticism against the ordinary—in something like the way I have reformulated Jacobi's famous criticism of Kant. With respect to the differences between Cavell and Jacobi, it may suffice here to note that for Cavell—unlike Jacobi—there can be no *salto mortale* from the threat of annihilation, both because the possibility of annihilation can never be decisively excluded from human life, but is definitive of it, and because there can be no return to the pre-philosophical everyday.

# IV Transcendental Rule-Following Skepticism

Some of Kant's first respondents, unlike Jacobi, explicitly rejected the Cartesian interpretation of Kant, yet still found Kant not to have extirpated, but rather to have deepened, skepticism. An important example is Salomon Maimon, the Lithuanian Talmudist-turned-philosopher, who appeared suddenly on the German philosophical scene in 1790, with his *Essay on Transcendental Philosophy*.[59]

---

**55** Cavell 1988, 8. On faith, see Cavell 1979, 242–3; Cavell 1988, 136. On the charge that Jacobi repudiates reason, see Jacobi 1994, 538–90, and Franks 2000a, "All or Nothing," 96, 111 n. 5.
**56** Cavell 1972, 106–7 n.
**57** Cavell 1979, 53.
**58** Cavell 1988, 53. For discussion of Kant, see also 30–1. For individuality—our ability to count one another, to count for one another—as at stake in skepticism, see 127.
**59** For Maimon's rejection of the Cartesian interpretation, see, e.g., Maimon 2000, V 358–9, where he criticizes Aenesidemus for arguing that transcendental idealism is skepticism because

The three post-Kantian skepticisms I want to discuss now all have roots in his work, although others—notably Fichte—played a role in developing them.[60]

The second possibility for post-Kantian skepticism mentioned above involves accepting as valid Kant's argument that synthetic *a priori*—or categorial —principles make experience possible, while at the same time finding reason to doubt that we actually have experience, hence reason to doubt that the categories may be justifiably applied to the objects of perception.

This must sound bizarre. For, in the Anglophone philosophical tradition, to have experience is roughly equivalent to having a life of the mind in the thinnest sense. This may be understood either in empiricist fashion—as the raw impressions given to the senses prior to conceptualization—or in Cartesian fashion— as the flow of mental events within the self-enclosed space of an individual mind. Indeed, Kant's transcendental deduction has frequently been construed as an attempt to show that categorial principles make experience *in one of these thin senses* possible—that they make possible a life of the mind. One reason why this view has attracted so many interpreters is that it allows them to view Kant as attempting a *refutation* of skepticism—as arguing, from a premise that not even a skeptic would deny, to a conclusion incompatible with skepticism.[61]

But Maimon does not in fact doubt the actuality of experience in the thinnest empiricist or Cartesian sense. His view seems less bizarre when situated within the context of a line of interpretation initiated by Johann Friedrich Schultz, Kant's friend and, later, designated spokesman. As Beiser has pointed out, Schultz is the first to draw attention to the difficulties attending Kant's conception of experience and its role in the Deduction.[62] Indeed, Schultz's discussion is

---

it does not enable assessment of the correspondence between our representations and things in themselves.

**60** For more detailed examination of Maimon's skepticism, see Franks 2003.

**61** See, e.g., Strawson 1966, 85: "If it would be a disappointment of our analytical hopes to find an argument resting on the assumption (or definition) that experience necessarily involves knowledge of *objects*, the topics of *objective* judgments, how much more would those hopes be disappointed by an argument which assumes that experience is necessarily of an objective and spatio-temporally unitary world." For Strawson, the Deduction's starting point is, rather, "The notion of a single consciousness to which different experiences belong," and those experiences need not, by assumption or definition, be of objects, let alone "of an objective and spatio-temporally unitary world" (Strawson 1966, 98). The task of the Deduction is to show that we could not have any experiences in the minimal sense unless we had some experiences of an objective and unitary world.

**62** Beiser 1987, 205–8. Beck argues that Kant used the term "experience" ambiguously in the opening sentences of the B edition (Beck 1978), and Guyer has argued that there is a related ambiguity in the method and goal of the Transcendental Deduction (Guyer 1987, 79–86). For a decisive refutation of the ambiguity charge, see Engstrom 1994, n. 6. See also Kant 1900–,

fateful, because it is determined, not directly by the Deduction, but by Kant's distinction in the *Prolegomena* between judgments of perception and judgments of experience, a distinction whose relationship to the A and B versions of the Deduction remains controversial and oblique.[63] Other contemporaneous discussions, including Maimon's, follow Schultz's path, whether under his influence or because of the direct impact of the *Prolegomena*. Thus, when Maimon argues that Kant has illicitly assumed the actuality of experience, he is construing Kantian experience as the employment of judgments of experience, in which pure concepts of the understanding are applied to objects given to the senses, expressing putatively necessary and universal connections among appearances.[64] As Maimon reads the Transcendental Deduction, Kant's argument depends on the assumption that we actually have experience *in this sense*, an assumption that is open to dispute not only by Cartesian skeptics but also—and, for Maimon, more significantly—by Humean empiricists.

Maimon has two grounds for doubting that we actually make judgments of experience. His first argument is that Kant has given an inaccurate description of our actual practices of judgment, and that the inadequacy of this account has led Kant to assume *without justification* that no Humean, psychological account of those practices can ever be given. Unlike Kant, Maimon distinguishes sharply between everyday and natural-scientific practices. In neither case, Maimon maintains, do we apply categories to objects of perception, forming judgments of experience. *Scientific* causal judgments do not apply the category of causality because their analysis shows that they make no claims whatsoever about universal and necessary connections.[65] *Ordinary* causal judgments do not apply the cat-

---

*Prolegomena*, IV 305 n., where he distinguishes between the perception in an experience, which can ground merely contingent judgments, and judgments of experience, which claim necessary and universal validity. This distinction is helpful in clarifying apparent ambiguities elsewhere.
**63** Judgments of perception express "only the logical connection of perceptions in a thinking subject," claiming to "hold only for us (i.e., for our subject)" and, indeed, "only in my present state of perception." In contrast, judgments of experience subsume perceptions under categories, and thus claim to be "valid at all times for us and for everybody else." See Kant 1900–, IV 297–301. Collins has no proposal for avoiding a Cartesian interpretation of Kant's claim in the *Prolegomena* that all our judgments are at first only of perception, although he does not exclude the possibility of avoidance (Collins 1999, 52). For a useful attempt at non-Cartesian interpretation, see Longuenesse 1998, 167–95.
**64** Maimon is aware that Kant's usage merits special scrutiny. See Maimon 2000a, II 192 for a reference to experience "in Kant's sense." Throughout the *Essay*, Maimon makes it clear that the "empirical propositions" discussed by Kant are judgments of experience claiming necessary connections among sensuously given objects. See, e.g., Maimon 2000a, II 4–5, 73, 127–8, 184–5.
**65** See Maimon 2000a, II 140: "For what does one understand in natural science (*Naturlehre*) by the word 'cause,' except the development and dissolution of a phenomenon; so that one finds

egory of causality because, although their analysis shows that they purport to make claims about universal and necessary connections, their use belies the claims they purport to make. Unlike scientific causal judgments, then, ordinary causal judgments are based upon an illusion or self-deception.[66]

This is not the place to evaluate Maimon's proposed accounts. Suffice it to say that one may reject those specific accounts and still find reason to question the assumption that we apply the categories in both scientific and ordinary explanation.[67] If one does question that assumption, then one may agree with Kant that judgments of experience would be impossible if categorial principles were invalid, while nevertheless regarding skepticism about the validity of categorial principles as unrefuted, because the possibility of judgments of experience itself remains unproven and open to doubt.

---

the sought after continuity between it and the antecedent phenomenon?" Maimon's idea is, in brief, that when continuity—maximal identity or minimal difference—is judged to occur between two phenomena, then the transition from the first to the second is judged to be an *alteration* of a single underlying determinable, not a transition between phenomena grounded in distinct determinables. But no claim is made about the *necessity* of the transition or about its exemplification of a *universal* law governing relations between phenomena of the relevant types. See also Maimon's commentary on Chapter 68 of Maimonides' *Guide for the Perplexed* in Maimon, in Maimon 2000b, 102.

**66** See Maimon 2000a, IV 74: "I deny, says my [skeptical] friend, that 'Fire decomposes wood,' this expression so very useful in practical employment, is a judgment of the understanding (having necessity and universality). With justification, one can assert only that one has found it to be so whenever one has perceived fire in the vicinity of wood, but not that it *must* be so. The fact that the common man gives this expression the form of a necessary and universal judgment rests upon a *lack of philosophical knowledge* and of insight into the difference between a putatively necessary and universal judgment made with justification, and this [judgment] which is taken for one by means of an illusion." See also Maimon 2000a, IV 301–2: "Skepticism doubts the fact and seeks to establish that the witness of common sense is not valid, since it rests on an illusion explainable psychologically." See also Maimon 2000a, VII 667: "The Kantian critical philosophy is indeed sufficiently grounded *formaliter*; it has the form of a complete system. But not *materialiter*. The facts, which are laid at the ground of this system, are not provable. The testimony of the common sense is indeed not valid, but rests rather on this self-deception." See Maimon 2000a, III 44 for the claim that the Kantian categories are transcendental fictions, not genuine concepts of the understanding. On common usage, see also Maimon 2000a, VII 58–9. For Maimon, genuine categories are mathematical. See Maimon 2000a, V 229–53.

**67** For example, Russell argues that "the law of causality" plays no role in mature science, which instead employs the mathematical idea of a function. See Russell 1917, 180–208. More recently, Anscombe has argued that the ordinary concept of causation does not involve universality and necessity (Anscombe 1971). For developments of Anscombe's arguments, see Harré/Madden 1975; Putnam 1999, 75–6, 141–2, 144–5.

Kant does indeed seem to assume that we actually make judgments of experience. For it is his view that a Humean approach to the categories may be legitimately excluded *in advance* of the detailed argument offered in the Transcendental Deduction, apparently for two reasons. First, any empirical derivation of, say, the concept of causality would be, not an *explanatory* account, but rather a *revision* of our practices of causal judgment:

> to the synthesis of cause and effect there belongs a dignity that can never be expressed empirically, namely, that the effect does not merely come along with the cause, but is posited *through* it and arises *from* it. The strict universality of the rule is therefore not any property of empirical rules, which cannot acquire anything more through induction than comparative universality, i.e., widespread usefulness. But now the use of the pure concepts of understanding would be entirely altered if one were to treat them only as empirical products.[68]

Second, the categories may be deduced either empirically or transcendentally, but not both. If they may be empirically deduced, then skepticism about their application to sensuously given objects is insuperable. But "the *empirical* derivation, however, to which both of them [Locke and Hume] resorted, cannot be reconciled with the reality of the scientific cognition *a priori* that we possess, that namely of *pure mathematics* and *general natural science*; and is therefore refuted by the fact."[69]

Now, Maimon agrees with Kant that Hume cannot account for the *a priori* knowledge attained in pure mathematics. So he agrees that the concepts of pure mathematics cannot be empirically derived. But what implications does this have for natural science? That categories are applied to objects of perception in Newtonian physics needs to be argued, not assumed as a "fact." Indeed, even if it is a fact, we are hardly mathematical physicists in everyday life. So even if the possibility of an empirical deduction of the categories—hence, the possibility of empirical skepticism—has been excluded by the fact of natural science, skepticism about ordinary causal judgments remains a threat.[70] Finally, Maimon does

---

**68** A91–2/B123–4.

**69** B128.

**70** See Maimon 2000a, VII 58, where Philalethes, Maimon's representative, responds as follows to the Kantian claim that the concept of causality in common usage involves the strict universality of a rule and that a Humean empirical derivation would amount to a loss of the concept: "One cannot build with certainty upon the commonest use of the understanding. The [commonest usage] distinguishes itself excellently from the scientific use of the understanding insofar as the latter seeks the *ground* and the *mode of origination* of some given *knowledge*; [while] the former satisfies itself with this *knowledge in itself* and its application in common life; thus the common human understanding can deceive itself and believe itself to be in possession of a cognition which has no *objective ground*. As an example, you bring forth the proposition that all

not accept Kant's argument that an empirical derivation of a putatively *a priori* concept amounts to a revision, not an explanation. This argument, in effect, rules out any explanation of a judgmental practice that entails skepticism about that practice. Rather than weighing the consequences of a putative explanation, we should consider whether the explanation is a good one, or whether it may be improved. As Maimon says, "It is a well-known proposition, which Newton lays at the foundation of his philosophy of nature, that one should assume no new principle for the explanation of a phenomenon, which may be explained from other, long since known principles."[71] If there is a good empirical explanation of the acquisition of the concept of cause—and Kant has not argued that there is not—then we should not throw away the explanation we have in order to seek a transcendental explanation. But that is exactly what Kant does, just before he begins his Transcendental Deduction. He simply excludes from consideration any account of our practices of judgment developed within empirical psychology. In contrast, Maimon finds empirical psychology to be a discipline worthy of development. If the explanations promised by the discipline entail skepticism about certain practices of judgment, then the proper response is to change those practices insofar as that is possible, not to throw out the explanations because their implications are unsettling.

Maimon's second reason for doubting that we actually have experience may be seen as a response to the following Kantian objection to what has just been said. To be sure—the Kantian may concede—Kant says, before beginning the Transcendental Deduction, that skepticism is refuted by the fact of pure mathematics and natural science. Nevertheless, the argument of the Deduction as a whole provides independent grounds for excluding a Humean empirical derivation of the categories. For it is *not* a premise of the Deduction that we actually make judgments of experience, subsuming the sensuously given under some category. The relevant premise is rather that we have "some empirical knowledge," that we actually make synthetic *a posteriori* judgments that do not apply any cat-

---

alterations must have a cause, and you say that the concept of cause would be wholly lost if one were to [explain] it as Hume did, etc., because it contains necessity and strict universality. But friend! Here you are doing the honourable Hume a great injustice. He derives from association of ideas and custom, not the *concept* of cause, but only its supposed *use*. Thus he doubts only its *objective reality*, since he shows that the common human understanding could have arrived at belief in the *use* of this concept through the confusion of the merely *subjective* and *comparatively universal* with the *objectively* and *absolutely universal*."

**71** Maimon 2000a, IV 239n.

egory and that make no claims to necessity and universality.[72] Kant argues, in brief, that such judgments presuppose the transcendental unity of apperception—strikingly absent from the discussions of both Schultz and Maimon—which in turn requires principles for the unification of the sensuously given manifold provided only by the categories. Such an argument does not purport to refute the Cartesian skeptic. But it does not obviously beg the question against the Humean skeptic by assuming any actual judgments of experience.

This is an important objection, because Maimon's reading of the Transcendental Deduction is obviously objectionable as it stands.[73] However, Maimon's second argument does not depend on the disputable claim that Kant assumes the actuality of judgments of experience as a premise. For even if Kant assumes only the actuality of some empirical knowledge, without any claims of universality and necessity, he surely wishes, in the argument of the Analytic as a whole, to show that the principles presupposed by that knowledge *render judgments of experience possible*. But Maimon's second argument, if correct, can be taken to entail that even if we actually have some empirical knowledge that presupposes categorical principles, the presupposed principles are nevertheless *indeterminate* and cannot be rendered determinately applicable to the sensuously given in particular judgments of experience. Thus, it is the Analytic of Principles, rather than the Analytic of Concepts containing the Transcendental Deduction, that is directly threatened by Maimon's second argument. Still, if the Analytic of Principles yields only indeterminate principles, then the Deduction seems to accomplish less than we hoped for—less than a demonstration of the objective reality of the categories, of their applicability to determinate, sensuously given objects.

---

**72** See Ameriks 1978, 273–87. "On this interpretation Kant's premise is not, as is often assumed, Newtonian and Euclidian, but is the relatively weak assumption of some empirical knowledge" (Ameriks 1978, 282). Such an interpretation is suggested by Kant's examples (the perception of a house and of the freezing of water) at B162. I am grateful to Ameriks for helpful discussion of this and related issues.

**73** However, a similar reading has been given considerable weight in the extensive discussions of the Deduction in Guyer 1987. See Guyer 1987, 85, where a classification of forms of the Deduction is given, and where form IA is said to be exhibited by arguments or interpretations maintaining that, "[j]udgments about empirical objects are possible, and these actually contain some synthetic *a priori* knowledge which implies the *further a priori* knowledge of the categories." Thus, Maimon's interpretation is an example of form IA, while the form of argument recommended in the Kantian objection considered here is Guyer's IB: "Judgments about empirical objects are possible, and although these do not themselves *assert* any claims to *a priori* knowledge, they do *presuppose a priori* knowledge." So it is noteworthy that Guyer,121–4, argues that some versions of IB collapse into IA.

In the Second Analogy, Kant argues that the possibility of judging that some successions of perceptions are not subjective but objective—that they express, not just events in the mental life of the subject, but events in the careers of objects—depends on the assumed principle that every event presupposes something from which it follows according to a rule. Thus the *a priori* assumption of the principle of causality plays a crucial role: it makes synthetic *a posteriori* judgments of objective succession possible. But Maimon argues that Kant has not shown that, in order to distinguish objective from subjective successions, we actually need to *apply*—or even to be *able* to apply—the concept of causality to given objects. Kant has shown only that we need to assume that every event has some indeterminate cause, but he has not shown that we need to *assign* any determinate cause to any event, nor has he shown *how* we *could* assign any determinate cause. Maimon is prepared to endorse some version of Kant's argument; he is even prepared to argue that the mere perception of *subjective* succession presupposes a version of the principle of causality.[74] But he does not think that Kant's argument shows either the necessity or the possibility of determinate applications of the principle in causal judgments.

Now Maimon's point is of great importance and has only recently attracted the attention of interpreters of Kant's Second Analogy, without Maimon receiving any credit.[75] But the extent to which it counts against Kant is unclear, because it is a point of which Kant himself—unlike some of his interpreters—is fully aware. Thus Kant says, "there is an order among our representations, in which the present one (insofar as it has come to be) points to some preceding state as a correlate, to be sure still undetermined, of this event that is given, which is, however, determinately related to the latter, as its consequence, and necessarily connected

---

74 This strengthening of the Second Analogy seems licensed by the Refutation of Idealism. For Kant argues there that consciousness of myself as determined in time, which presumably involves the ability to judge the temporal order of subjective states, requires perception of something permanent. As perception of something subject to objective alterations, perception of something permanent must be the kind of perception shown in the Second Analogy to presuppose the causal principle. However, Maimon's version of the Principle of Causality differs from Kant's, and depends on Maimon's claim that the natural-scientific conception of causality is a conception of continuity. See Bergmann 1967, 127–37.

75 See Buchdahl 1969, 649–50. One may accept the idea that the Second Analogy argues only for an indeterminate version of the causal principle without accepting Buchdahl's controversial claim that it is arguing only for the principle that every event has some cause, not for the principle that every event of the same type has a cause of the same type. For criticism of Buchdahl's claim, see Friedman 1992a. Allison, defending his version of the Buchdahl interpretation against Friedman, effectively concedes that the principle at stake is that every event of the same type has a cause of the same type; see Allison 1996.

with it in the temporal series."[76] And Kant is no less explicit in his statement that determinate causal judgments require determinate experiences, not the causal principle alone: "Now how in general anything can be altered, how it is possible that upon a state in one point of time an opposite one may follow in the next—of these we have *a priori* not the least concept. For this acquaintance with actual forces is required, which can only be given empirically, e. g., acquaintance with moving forces, or what comes to the same thing, with certain successive appearances (as motions) which indicate such forces."[77] But this is mysterious, since Kant insists on the impossibility of arriving at any genuinely causal judgment by induction from experiences. As Michael Friedman has emphasized, Kant's *full* story about how we arrive at determinate causal judgments requires, not only the Analytic of Principles, but also the account of the mathematization of appearances in Kant's *Metaphysical Foundations of Natural Science*.[78] In Kant's own words: "a separate metaphysics of corporeal nature does excellent and indispensable service to *general* metaphysics, insofar as the former furnishes examples (instances *in concreto*) in which to realize the concepts and propositions of the latter (properly transcendental philosophy), that is, to provide a mere form of thought with sense and meaning."[79] So Kant concedes Maimon's claim that, the result not only of the Transcendental Deduction, but also of the Analytic of Principles, is nothing more than categorial principles that are, to be sure, necessary conditions of possible experience, but only as "mere forms of thought," without determinate "realizations." But he also promises to make up for this merely formal result in his account of the metaphysical foundations of mathematical physics.[80]

Still, Maimon's point suggests the route to a post-Kantian skepticism. For even if Kant can show that Newtonian physics is genuine science, he must do so by showing the genuineness of the Newtonian *mathematization* of the sensuously given, since "in every special doctrine of nature only so much science proper can be found as there is mathematics in it."[81] If judgments of experience

---

76 A198–9/B244.
77 A207/B252.
78 Friedman 1992b, 136–64; Friedman 1992a. As Friedman emphasizes, the task of the Phenomenology chapter of Kant's *Metaphysical Foundations of Natural Science* is to transform "appearance," which Friedman identifies with the *Prolegomena*'s judgments of perception, into genuine "experience" (Friedman 1992b, 165–210). See Kant 1900–, IV 555; Friedman 1992b, 142, 144, 169, 184–5.
79 Kant 1900–, IV 478.
80 For Maimon's reaction to Kant's *Metaphysical Foundations of Natural Science*, see Freudenthal 2003.
81 Kant 1900–, IV 470.

are shown to be possible only through a proof of the possibility of *mathematization*—as Kant and Maimon agree—then *how are ordinary, non-mathematical judgments of experience possible?* How can the determinate causal explanations we give in everyday life count as actual judgments of experience or as grounded in the categorial principle of causality?

Maimon's position, then, is as follows. He agrees with Kant that philosophers should investigate the transcendental conditions for the possibility of experience. He also thinks that Kant has demonstrated decisively that experience would be impossible if not for principles or rules of necessary connection that constitute the objects of experience. However, Maimon differs from Kant in thinking that we can operate with categories or with rules of necessary connection only in the mathematical sciences. We do not employ such rules in everyday judgment, and the successes of mathematical physics give us no reason to hope that we could ever operate as mathematical physicists in our everyday lives. Consequently, Maimon thinks, we should be transcendental philosophers about the *hypothetical* conditions for the possibility of experience—that is, for the mathematization of the objects of our perceptions. But we should be Humean skeptics about *everyday* practices of judgment, which should be explained psychologically, as functions of custom or habit that cannot, as they stand, amount to knowledge.

Unlike Kant, then, Maimon does not think that the time for skeptical despair is past. Nor does he think that it ever will be. In Maimon's memorable image, the relationship between transcendental philosophy and skepticism resembles that of man and the serpent after the fall, as expressed in God's words to the serpent in Genesis 3:15: "He will strike at your head, but you will strike at his heel." The transcendental philosopher will strike at the skeptic's head, by articulating the necessary conditions for the possibility of knowledge, but the skeptic will strike at the transcendental philosopher's heel, by reminding her of the extent to which those conditions have actually been fulfilled.[82]

Of course, there is much more to say about Maimon's arguments, both as responses to Kant and in their own right. But I hope to have made it clear that this is a genuinely *post-Kantian* skepticism, one that would be impossible without some fundamentally Kantian notions. Instead of the pre-Kantian empirical idealist division between the inner and the outer, Maimon's skepticism focuses on the division between that which is mathematical and scientific, and that which is ordinary and merely psychological.

---

**82** Maimon 2000a, IV 80.

I should like to call this second kind of post-Kantian skepticism *transcendental rule-following skepticism*. For Maimon accepts the Kantian idea that empirical knowledge is possible only in virtue of transcendentally constitutive rules. However, because he thinks those rules would have to be something like the rules constitutive of mathematical objects, he finds reason to doubt that any ordinary practice of judgment could count as following those rules, hence could count as attaining empirical knowledge.

For a contemporary analogue, consider Kripke's interpretation of Wittgenstein. On that interpretation, Wittgenstein is responding to "a new form of skepticism"[83] about the ability of rules to determine the judgments in which we take ourselves to be following those rules. As in Maimon's case, mathematical rules are taken to be exemplary:

> Ordinarily, I suppose that, in computing '68 57' as I do, I do not simply make an unjustified leap in the dark. I follow directions I previously gave myself that uniquely determine that in this new instance I should say '125'. What are these directions? By hypothesis, I never explicitly told myself that I should say '125' in this very instance. Nor can I say that I should simply 'do the same thing I always did,' if this means 'compute according to the rule exhibited by my previous examples.' That rule could just as well have been the rule for quaddition (the quus function) as for addition.[84]

The problem is not merely, "How do I know which rule I mean, hence whether my computation is correct?"[85] but, "How is it possible to mean one rule rather than another, or how is computation possible at all?" Soon the indeterminacy is argued to also affect generalized non-mathematical rules that constitute the meanings of our words.[86] Consequently, the skeptical problem is, "How can we show *any language* at all (public, private, or what-have-you) to be *possible?*"[87] As Kripke himself notes, "So put, the problem has an obvious Kantian flavor."[88] An obvious difference is that on Kripke's interpretation, the indeterminacy of

---

83 Kripke 1982, 62.

84 Kripke 1982, 10 – 11.

85 See Kripke 1982, 39: "such merely epistemological skepticism is *not* in question."

86 Kripke 1982, 19: "Can I answer a sceptic who supposes that by 'table' in the past I meant *tabair*, where a 'tabair' is anything that is a table not found at the base of the Eiffel tower, or a chair found there?" On Kripke's assimilation of the ordinary to the mathematical, see Cavell 1990, 89 – 90.

87 Kripke 1982, 62.

88 I do not mean to suggest that transcendental rule-following skepticism *must* depend on conceiving the transcendental rules as mathematical or as quasi-mathematical. But it is noteworthy that some such conception figures centrally in the thinking of both Maimon and Kripke.

rules affects pure mathematics, whereas, for Maimon, the indeterminacy affects only the application of mathematical rules to empirical cases.[89]

# V Transcendental-Antinomy Skepticism

The third possibility mentioned above was the possibility for an antinomy of idealism and realism. In fact, Maimon also formulates his skepticism in just this way. In his article on truth, reprinted in the *Philosophische Wörterbuch* of 1791, he sketches what he calls:

> a general antinomy of thinking as such. For thinking as such consists in relating a form (rule of the understanding) to a matter (the given subsumed under it). Without matter one can never attain consciousness of the form, consequently the matter is a necessary condition of thinking—that is, for real thinking of a form or rule of the understanding, a matter to which it relates must necessarily be given; however, on the other hand, completeness in thinking of an object requires that nothing be given therein, rather that everything should be thought. (162)

Now, the skepticism expressed in this passage seems in one way stronger than that explored in the previous section. So far, Maimon has found reason to doubt that we actually make judgments of experience, judgments that render what we perceive intelligible in light of rational principles. If it is doubtful that we have experience in this sense, then Kant's deduction of categorial principles as necessary conditions of the possibility of experience, even if it is valid, fails to legitimate our present attempts to follow those principles. Maimon finds it questionable whether both scientific and everyday practices of judgment count as actual experience in Kant's sense. But everyday practices are especially doubtful because, given their non-mathematic status, it is hard to see how they could *ever* count either as actual experience or as the potential for scientific experience. In the passage just quoted, however, Maimon seems to be saying, not only that there is reason to doubt whether experience is *actual*, but that there is reason to doubt whether experience is so much as *possible*. For among the necessary conditions for the possibility of experience, two conditions cannot be simultaneously satisfied.

---

**89** I do not mean to suggest that transcendental rule-following skepticism *must* depend on conceiving the transcendental rules as mathematical or as quasi-mathematical. But it is noteworthy that some such conception figures centrally in the thinking of both Maimon and Kripke.

To be sure, in the passage Maimon speaks not of experience but of "thinking as such." But what he means is, I think, something very like what Kant means by "experience." For Maimon, thinking is not merely conjoining concepts, or even conjoining concepts and objects, in a grammatically permissible way and without contradiction. To think is to make things intelligible. An arbitrary thought, which predicates a concept of an object without exhibiting any reason for the predication, is not a genuine thought at all.[90] For a genuine thought would make some actual thing intelligible, would exhibit the conceptual structure of actuality by grounding what is actual in rational principles. A genuine thought would be what Kant calls synthetic *a priori*.[91] It would be a judgment of experience.

Why does genuine thought—"thinking as such"—seem impossible? On the one hand, transcendental investigation leads to the conclusion that the demand that we be given the matter for thinking is justified. For our finite intellects, at any rate, there is no way to determine which of many possibilities is actual except by letting the world tell us by affecting us sensuously. No matter how much intellectual control we exercise over our understanding of the world through deliberate experimentation and mathematical theorization, we will always remain subservient to the world for the final determination of what is actual. To that extent, there will always be a limit to our intellectual control, a defect in our thinking. For we cannot explain, on the basis of rational principles, why just that possibility is actualized, why our concepts should be applied to the object which is, as a matter of brute fact, given. But we cannot just accept this limitation. We cannot satisfy ourselves with finitude. For transcendental investigation leads just as inexorably to the conclusion that the demand for the elimination of the given is justified. If we depend upon the given for the matter of thinking, then something is lacking in the *form* of our thinking, in our employment of rational principles to make things intelligible. For something remains unexplained, without reason. There must be, somewhere, a lack of rationality on our part: either in our principles, or in our applications of them.

Transcendental investigation of the human condition leads Maimon, then, to the conclusion that what he calls thinking as such necessarily presupposes the simultaneous satisfaction of two incompatible demands. In the face of this antinomy, the best we can do, Maimon thinks, is to commit ourselves to infinite sci-

---

**90** Maimon 2000a, V 24: "Arbitrary thought has no ground at all, and is therefore no thought at all."
**91** However, Maimon uses these terms in his own way.

entific progress, in which the materiality of the given is increasingly subsumed under formal rules, but some residue always remains.

At this point, I may seem not to have kept my earlier promise. For I said earlier that Kant's refutation of idealism leaves logical room for a skeptical antinomy, in which both (empirical) idealism and realism are reduced to absurdity. But Maimon's skeptical antinomy seems to be between, say, rationalism and empiricism, not between realism and idealism.

In fact, I think that I have kept my promise, provided that one takes seriously Maimon's claim to lay out a "general antinomy." Although Maimon himself never spells out his claim to generality, the suggestion is that other philosophical conflicts should be seen as instances of the conflict between the demand for given matter and the demand for intelligible form. Even after one frees oneself from the confusions about the mind presupposed by both empirical idealism and empirical realism, a genuine conflict remains and may be more adequately expressed. The idealist limits knowledge to "that which is within the mind," while the realist demands knowledge of "what is outside the mind." The problem with both positions is that they take those expressions *empirically*. If, instead, one intends those expressions *transcendentally*, then one will find that one has expressed just the contradictory demands of Maimon's "general antinomy."

Now, Maimon never develops this suggestion for a general schema for post-Kantian skepticism involving transcendental antinomy. But Fichte, one of Maimon's greatest admirers, does. In his most famous work, solutions to the antinomy of finitude and reason are repeatedly proposed. Each time the result is a more refined philosophical position. But each time, dissatisfaction with the position calls forth an opposing view, and the antinomy turns out to be unresolved. The conflict between empirical idealism and empirical realism is a less adequate expression of the conflict between the transcendental demand for intelligibility and the transcendental demand for the given.[92] Indeed, the conflict turns out to be an antinomy. We cannot escape the antinomy, so we cannot rationally escape skepticism. Or, rather, we cannot escape the antinomy so long as we remain within the framework of all previous philosophy, including Kant's, if it is taken according to its letter. But we can recover from skepticism if we follow Kant's spirit by reconceiving the age-old distinction between the theoretical and the practical.

---

92 See "Foundations of the Entire Science of Knowledge," in Fichte 1982, 89–287. Dogmatic versions of idealism and realism are distinguished from critical versions (Fichte 1982, 160). New idealisms emerge (Fichte 1982, 169–71), but only to call forth new realisms (Fichte 1982, 188–90). Fichte calls his own position real idealism or ideal realism (Fichte 1982, 246–7).

There are at least two different versions of Fichte's proposal. In what is known as his first Jena presentation, the reconception appears mainly to be a matter of *priority*. Within the theoretical quest for genuine experience, skepticism can never be overcome, for necessary conditions of finite rationality cannot be simultaneously satisfied. But we need not despair, for those conditions can be satisfied within the practical realm of moral agency. There can be no capacity for knowledge without a capacity for moral action, and the actualization of the latter capacity satisfies the demands of finite reason.[93] In what is known as Fichte's second Jena presentation, however, the reconception of the theoretical and the practical seems deeper.[94] The distinction between knowledge and action is a distinction between two—to be sure, necessary—abstractions. In fact, every cognitive act involves the will and every volitional act involves the intellect. Within traditional epistemology, skepticism is inescapable, because traditional epistemology considers cognition in abstraction from volition. The philosophical demand for justification can only be raised if the commitment of the will is abstracted, and once that withdrawal or disinvestment has occurred, conviction cannot be sustained. No purely epistemic ground can repair the loss.[95] But when the cause of our vulnerability to skepticism is seen, a new prospect emerges.[96] We may philosophize anew, reconceiving human experience as a unity from which knowledge and action are abstracted, and we may then find reason to believe that our needs for both passivity and unlimited rationality are not only compatible but actually met.[97]

---

**93** See Fichte 1982, 147–8, 232–3.

**94** For Fichte's own formulation of the relationship between the two presentations on this score, see Fichte 1992, 85–6. I discuss the relationship in Franks 1997 and in Franks 2000b.

**95** See Fichte 1987, 67: "'Nothing exists anywhere outside my mind' is a thought which natural sense considers ridiculously stupid, a thought which no human being could assert with complete seriousness and which requires no refutation. For the educated judgment which knows the deep reasons for it, reasons irrefutable through mere ratiocination, it is a crushing and annihilating judgment."

**96** See Fichte 1987, 71: "No knowledge can be its own foundation and proof. Every knowledge presupposes something still higher as its foundation, and this ascent has no end. It is faith, this voluntary acquiescence in the view which naturally presents itself to us because only on this view can we fulfill our vocation; it is that which first gives approval to knowledge and raises to certainty and conviction what without it could be mere deception. Faith is no knowledge, but a decision of the will to recognize the validity of knowledge." Fichte acknowledges the clear influence of Jacobi on his position. But he differs significantly from Jacobi, notably insofar as he recommends not only a return to the natural standpoint of everyday life, but also a new mode of philosophy.

**97** In his second presentation, Fichte argues that "[t]he 'ought', or the categorical imperative, is also a theoretical principle." See, e.g., Fichte 1992, 437. That is, reason's demand for the un-

This is not the place to reconstruct in greater detail the views of Maimon or Fichte. What I have said should suffice to delineate the structure of a general schema for a post-Kantian skepticism about the very possibility of experience, according to which two conditions are seen both as equally necessary and as incapable of simultaneous satisfaction. A contemporary analogue may be found in McDowell's Locke lectures, which might almost have taken the passage from Maimon as its motto. For McDowell describes himself as responding to "an antinomy: experience both must... and cannot... stand in judgment over our attempts to make up our minds about how things are."[98] On the one hand, experience must stand in judgment, because there seems to be no other way to make sense of the idea that "thinking that aims at judgment is answerable to the world —to how things are—for whether or not it is correctly executed."[99] This requirement, which McDowell calls "minimal empiricism," easily expresses itself in various versions of the Myth of the Given: the idea that experience can play its role as ultimate tribunal only if it is unmediated by any judgment or conceptualization. On the other hand, experience so conceived, as a non-conceptual sense impression, cannot play that role. For "thinking that aims at judgment" must also be answerable to reasons, and what is not conceptual cannot be a reason: "In effect, the idea of the Given offers exculpations where we wanted justifications."[100]

The antinomy to which McDowell is responding is intended to be general, in particular to provide a more adequate expression of the pre-Kantian conflict between empirical realism and empirical idealism over the extent of knowledge.[101] And it is easy to see that the antinomy in question is in some sense transcenden-

---

conditioned, which expresses itself practically as the categorical imperative, is at the same time a constitutive principle of the empirical world.

**98** McDowell 1996, xii–xiii. (This passage is from an introduction that was not included in the earlier hardback edition of 1994.)

**99** McDowell 1996, xii.

**100** McDowell 1996, 8.

**101** McDowell 1996, xiii–xiv: "It is true that modern philosophy is pervaded by apparent problems about knowledge in particular. But I think it is helpful to see those apparent problems as more or less inept expressions of a deeper anxiety—an inchoately felt threat that a way of thinking we find ourselves falling into leaves minds simply out of touch with the rest of reality, not just questionably capable of getting to know about it. A problem about crediting ourselves with knowledge is just one shape, and not the most fundamental, in which that anxiety can make itself felt." Empirical realism and idealism are conflicting answers to the question whether minds are incapable of knowing the rest of reality, that is, capable of knowing themselves alone —if that question is understood empirically. McDowell is suggesting, in effect, that there is a more fundamental, transcendental sense of the question: are minds out of touch with reality altogether, hence capable of directing thought at reality at all?

tal, without an investigation of McDowell's complex relationship to Kant that is out of place here. For the antinomy expresses itself as the question, "How is thinking that aims at judgment possible?", a question "whose felt urgency derives from a frame of mind that, if explicitly thought through, would yield materials for an argument that... [thinking that aims at judgment] is impossible."[102] Furthermore, McDowell all but calls the anxiety to which he is responding "skepticism," for example when he contrasts "the shallow" that Davidson takes to motivate the Myth of the Given—a skepticism "in which, taking it for granted that one has a body of beliefs, one worries about their credentials"—with the "deeper motivation" that the Myth has in McDowell's view: "the thought that if spontaneity is not subject to rational constraint from the outside... then we cannot make it intelligible to ourselves how exercises of spontaneity can represent the world at all."[103] The anxiety that some necessary condition for the possibility of "thinking that aims at judgment" may not be satisfiable—say, because it conflicts with another equally necessary condition—seems to merit the characterization: a deeper, post-Kantian skepticism.

As a final point of analogy, McDowell's intention is neither to dismiss nor to refute skepticism, but to escape from its anxiety while acknowledging its deep source: "The aim here is not to answer sceptical questions, but to begin to see how it might be intellectually respectable to ignore them, to treat them as unreal, in the way that common sense has always wanted to."[104] As he explains, once it becomes clear that skeptical questions express an underlying conflict between two equally necessary conditions of possibility, answering them ceases to be an option: "we need to exorcize the questions rather than set about answering them."[105] The exorcism involves rethinking fundamental presuppositions that render the conditions incapable of simultaneous satisfaction. For McDowell, it is primarily the distinction between the space of reasons and the space of nature that must be rethought. But it is easy to apply an abstract description of McDowell's procedure to Fichte's rethinking of the theoretical–practical distinction, sketched above.

---

102 McDowell 1996, xxiii.
103 McDowell 1996, 17.
104 McDowell 1996, 113.
105 McDowell 1996, xxii–xxiv.

# VI Conclusion

The emergence of post-Kantian skepticisms must have struck Kant as perverse. But their emergence should not be surprising. Elicitation of more radical forms of skepticism is a risk that transcendental philosophy cannot help but run. For transcendental philosophy, as practiced by Kant, aims not to refute skepticism but to domesticate it: to turn skeptical doubts into the founding questions of a philosophical science within which the intellect can live in peace. And the anxiety of skepticism is alleviated, for Kant, because of the established facts of mathematical and natural science. If there are grounds for anxiety about those putative facts, or about the relevance of those putative facts to everyday practices of judgment, then skepticism is bound to emerge, shedding any domestic habits it may have acquired. And if transcendental philosophy has succeeded in exposing conditions for the possibility of *experience* that are at the same time conditions for the possibility of *objects* of experience, then the newly emergent skepticism will now concern the very possibility of experience, or the very possibility of there being any objects to experience.

I have not sought in this paper to assess the grounds for any of the post-Kantian skepticisms discussed, or to assess the prospects for any Kantian or post-Kantian response to those skepticisms. My goal has been to show how Kant's transcendental idealism and the logical structure of some of the arguments in the Analytic of the first *Critique* leave room for several possible post-Kantian skepticisms, how those possibilities are actualized in the 1780s and 1790s, and how some contemporary philosophers may be seen as responding to analogues of those eighteenth-century actualizations. A more detailed investigation of those contemporary skepticisms would have to acknowledge the fact that they are not only post-Kantian but, say, post-Fregean and post-Wittgensteinian as well. Still, the post-Kantian transformation of the skeptical problematic is not only an episode in philosophy's past. Its traces remain visible.[106]

# Bibliography

Allison, Henry E. (1996), *Idealism and Freedom: Essays on Kant's Theoretical and Practical Philosophy*, Cambridge: Cambridge University Press.

Ameriks, Karl (1978), "Kant's Transcendental Deduction as a Regressive Argument," *Kant-Studien* 69 (1978)

Ameriks, Karl (2000), *Kant's Theory of Mind*, Cambridge: Cambridge University Press.

---

**106** For other reflections on varieties of post-Kantian skepticism, see Franks (2005), 146–200.

Anscombe, G.E.M (1971), *Causality and Determination*, Cambridge: Cambridge University Press.

Beck, Lewis White (1978), *Essays on Kant and Hume*, New Haven: Yale University Press.

Beiser, Frederick C. (1987), *The Fate of Reason*. Cambridge, MA: Harvard University Press.

Bergmann, Samuel Hugo (1967), *The Philosophy of Solomon Maimon*, Noah J. Jacobs (trans)., Jerusalem: Magnes Press.

Buchdahl, Gerd (1969), *Metaphysics and the Philosophy of Science*, Cambridge, MA: MIT Press.

Cavell, Stanley (1972), *The Senses of Walden*, San Francisco: North Point Press.

Cavell, Stanley (1976), *Must We Mean What We Say?*, Cambridge: Cambridge University Press.

Cavell, Stanley (1979), *The Claim of Reason: Wittgenstein, Skepticism, Morality, and Tragedy*, Oxford: Oxford University Press.

Cavell, Stanley (1988), *In Quest of the Ordinary: Lines of Skepticism and Romanticism*, Chicago: University of Chicago Press.

Cavell, Stanley (1987), *Disowning Knowledge In Six Plays of Shakespeare*, Cambridge: Cambridge University Press.

Cavell, Stanley (1990), *Conditions Handsome and Unhandsome: The Constitution of Emersonian Perfectionism*, Chicago: University of Chicago Press.

Chisholm, Roderick M. (1966), *Theory of Knowledge*, Englewood Cliffs, NJ: Prentice Hall.

Collins, Arthur (1999), *Possible Experience*, Berkeley, Los Angeles, and London: University of California Press.

Diogenes Laertius (1925), *Lives of the Philosophers*, R. D. Hicks (trans.), London: Heinemann.

Engstrom, Stephen (1994), "The Transcendental Deduction and Skepticism." In: *Journal of the History of Philosophy* 32, 359–80.

Ewing, A.C. (1996), *A Short Commentary on Kant's* Critique of Pure Reason, Chicago: University of Chicago Press.

Fichte, Johann Gottlieb (1982), *The Science of Knowledge*, Peter Heath and John Lachs (trans.), Cambridge: Cambridge University Press.

Fichte, Johann Gottlieb (1987), *The Vocation of Man*, Peter Preuss (trans.), Indianapolis: Hackett.

Fichte, Johann Gottlieb (1992), *Foundations of Transcendental Philosophy*, Daniel Breazeale (trans.), Ithaca: Cornell University Press.

Fogelin, Robert J. (1994), *Pyrrhonian Reflections on Knowledge and Justification*, Oxford: Oxford University Press.

Förster, Eckart (2000), *Kant's Final Synthesis*, Cambridge, MA: Harvard University Press.

Franks, Paul (1997), "Freedom, *Tatsache*, and *Tathandlung* in the Development of Fichte's Jena *Wissenschaftslehre*." In: *Archiv für Geschichte der Philosophie* 79, 331–44.

Franks, Paul (2000a), "All or Nothing: Systematicity and Nihilism in Jacobi, Reinhold, and Maimon." In: Karl Ameriks (ed.), *The Cambridge Companion to German Idealism*, Cambridge: Cambridge University Press, 95–116.

Franks, Paul (2000b), "Review of Wayne Martin, *Idealism and Objectivity: Understanding Fichte's Jena Project*." In: *European Journal of Philosophy* 8, 213–7.

Franks, Paul (2003), "What Should Kantians Learn from Maimon's Skepticism?" In: Gideon Freudenthal (ed.), *Salomon Maimon: Rational Dogmatist, Empirical Skeptic*, Dordrecht: Kluwer, 200–32.

Franks, Paul (2005), *All or Nothing: Systematicity, Transcendental Arguments, and Nihilism in German Idealism*, Cambridge, MA: Harvard University Press.

Freudenthal, Gideon (2003), "Maimon's Subversion of *Kant's Critique of Pure Reason:* There Are No Synthetic A Priori Judgments In Physics." In: Gideon Freudenthal (ed.), *Salomon Maimon: Rational Dogmatist, Empirical Skeptic,* Dordrecht: Kluwer, 144 – 75.

Friedman, Michael (1992a), "Causal Laws and the Foundations of Natural Science." In: Charles Parsons (ed.), *The Cambridge Companion to Kant,* Cambridge: Cambridge University Press, 161 – 99.

Friedman, Michael (1992b), *Kant and the Exact Sciences,* Cambridge, MA: Harvard University Press.

Gillespie, Michael Allen (1996), *Nihilism before Nietzsche,* Chicago: Chicago University Press.

Guyer, Paul (1987), *Kant and the Claims of Knowledge,* Cambridge: Cambridge University Press.

Harré, R. / Madden, E.H. (1975), *Causal Powers,* Oxford: Blackwell.

Hatfield, Gary (2001), "The *Prolegomena* and the *Critiques of Pure Reason.*" In: *Kant und die Berliner Aufklärung: Akten des IX. Internationalen Kant-Kongresses (Vol. 1),* Volker Gerhardt, Rolf-Peter Horstmann, and Ralph Schumacher (eds.), Berlin and New York: Walter de Gruyter, 185 – 208.

Henrich, Dieter (1989), "Kant's Notion of a Deduction and the Methodological Background of the First *Critique.*" In: *Kant's Transcendental Deductions,* Eckart Förster (ed.), Stanford: Stanford University Press, 29 – 46.

Jacobi, Friedrich Heinrich (1994), *The Main Philosophical Writings and the Novel* Allwill, George di Giovanni (trans.), Montreal and Kingston: McGill-Queen's University Press.

Kant, Immanuel (1900– ), *Kants gesammelte Schriften,* Royal Prussian Academy/German Academy of Sciences (ed.), Berlin: Georg Reimer/Walter de Gruyter.

Kant, Immanuel (1998), *Critique of Pure Reason,* Paul Guyer and Allen Wood (trans.), Cambridge: Cambridge University Press.

Kripke, Saul A. (1982), *Wittgenstein on Rules and Private Language,* Cambridge, MA: Harvard University Press.

Langton, Rae (1998), *Kantian Humility: Our Ignorance of Things In Themselves,* Oxford: Oxford University Press.

Lear, Jonathan (1998), *Open Minded,* Cambridge, MA: Harvard University Press.

Longuenesse, Béatrice (1995), "The Transcendental Ideal and the Unity of the Critical System." In: Hoke Robinson (ed.), *Proceedings of the Eighth International Kant Congress,* Milwaukee: Marquette University Press, 521 – 39.

Longuenesse, Béatrice (1998), *Kant and the Capacity to Judge,* Princeton: Princeton University Press.

Maimon, Salomon (2000a), *Gesammelte Werke,* Valerio Verra (ed.), Hildesheim: Georg Olms.

Maimon, Salomon (2000b), *Giv 'at Hammore,* S.H. Bergmann and N. Rotenstreich (eds.), Jerusalem: Israel Academy of Sciences and Humanities.

McDowell, John (1996), *Mind and World,* Cambridge, MA: Harvard University Press.

Pöggeler, Otto (1974), "Hegel und die Anfänge der Nihilismus-Diskussion." In: Dieter Arendt (ed.), *Der Nihilismus als Phänomen der Geistesgeschichte,* Darmstadt: Wissenschaftliche Buchgesellschaft.

Putnam, Hilary (1999). *The Threefold Cord: Mind, Body, and World,* New York: Columbia University Press.

Quine, W.V.O. (1969), "Epistemology Naturalized." In: W.V.O. Quine, *Ontological Relativity and Other Essays,* New York: Columbia University Press, 69 – 90.

Rorty, Ricahrd (1979), *Philosophy and the Mirror of Nature*, Princeton: Princeton University Press.

Russell, Bertrand (1917), *Mysticism and Logic*, London: George Allen and Unwin.

Stäudlin, Karl Friedrich (1794), *Geschichte und Geist des Skepticismus*, Leipzig: Crusius.

Sassen, Brigitte (ed.) (2000), *Kant's Early Critics: The Empiricist Critique of Kant's Theoretical Philosophy*, Cambridge: Cambridge University Press.

Spinoza, Benedict de (1925), *Tractatus de Intellectus Emendatione*. In: Benedict de Spinoza, *Spinoza Opera, Volume 3*, Carl Gebhardt (ed.), Heidelberg: Carl Winter. (In English translation, see: Benedict de Spinoza [1985], *The Collected Works of Spinoza*, Edwin M. Curley [trans. and ed.], Princeton: Princeton University Press.)

Strawson, P.F. (1966), *The Bounds of Sense: An Essay on Kant's* Critique of Pure Reason, London: Methuen.

Stroud, Barry (1983), "Kant and Skepticism." In: Myles Burnyeat (ed.), *The Skeptical Tradition*, Berkeley: University of California Press.

Stroud, Barry (1984), *The Significance of Philosophical Scepticism*, Oxford: Oxford University Press.

Süss, Theobald (1974), "Der Nihilismus bei F. H. Jacobi." In: Dieter Arendt (ed.), *Der Nihilismus als Phänomen der Geistesgeschichte*, Darmstadt: Wissenschaftliche Buchgesellschaft.

Walker, Ralph C.S. (1978), *Kant*, London: Routledge and Kegan Paul.

Williams, Michael (1996), *Unnatural Doubts: Epistemological Realism and the Basis of Scepticism*, Princeton: Princeton University Press.

Wolff, Robert Paul (1963), *Kant's Theory of Mental Activity*, Cambridge, MA: Harvard University Press.

Michael Williams
# Knowledge, Reasons, and Causes: Sellars and Skepticism

1. I want to discuss the implications for our understanding of philosophical skepticism of some central arguments in Wilfred Sellars's classic essay "Empiricism and the Philosophy of Mind" (henceforth: EPM).[1] Surprisingly, perhaps, Sellars appears to take little interest in skeptical problems. There is a reason for this. Sellars thinks that "narrowly" epistemological questions about skepticism or the character of epistemic justification can be addressed only in a broader philosophical context of "explicating the concept of a rational animal or... a language using animal whose language is about the world in which it is used."[2] Since Sellars connects thought and language with participation in the "game of giving and asking for reasons," questions about meaning are broadly epistemological. But they cut deeper than standard narrowly epistemological issues about knowledge and justification. Nevertheless, Sellars's comparative lack of interest in narrowly epistemological questions notwithstanding, concern with skepticism is a powerful subterranean current in EPM, and Sellars would have done well to have made skepticism more explicitly an object of investigation. As we shall see, Sellars's account of the special epistemic role played by observation-reports leads him into an impasse. And the only way out is by way of linking his account of perceptual knowledge with a suitable account of the structure of epistemic justification.

That skepticism is never far below the surface of Sellars's arguments can be seen from this: that one of Sellars's principle aims in EPM is to offer a way between the horns of a fundamental dilemma in the theory of knowledge—the apparently forced choice between foundationalism and the coherence theory. He writes: "One seems forced to choose between the picture of an elephant which rests on a tortoise (What supports the tortoise?) and the picture of a great Hegelian serpent of knowledge with its tail in its mouth (Where does it begin?). Neither will do" (EPM 170). The choice is between a broadly foundational and broadly coherentist conception of knowledge. The appearance of our being forced to make this choice grows out of one of the oldest forms of skeptical argument: the "Agrippan" argument.

---

1 Sellars 1963a. (This edition of EPM contains some new footnotes not available in other editions.)
2 Sellars 2000, 132.

If I represent myself as knowing this or that, rather than simply assuming that it is so, I appear to invite the question "*How* do you know?" In claiming knowledge, then, I seem to commit myself to providing some kind of backup: my evidence, my credentials, whatever. But whatever I appeal to as backup cannot itself reflect a mere assumption: it must be something that I know. It will therefore itself need backup, and so on. This regress of justification is vicious because—so it appears—I can be justified in making any claim or holding any belief only if I have gone through an infinite number of prior justifying steps.

How can the regress be blocked? One way is to refuse at some point to entertain any further requests for justification, in which case the skeptic will say that I am simply making an assumption; and knowledge cannot be based on ungrounded assumptions. Alternatively, I might find myself recurring to some claim already entered, but then the skeptic will say that I am reasoning in a circle, and circular reasoning cannot provide justification. Assumption, circularity, and regress: this is Agrippa's trilemma. It seems to be fatal to our pretensions to knowledge, or even justified belief.

Since the Agrippan problem can be raised with respect to any arbitrary knowledge-claim, Agrippan skepticism is completely universal. The Agrippan skeptic is not just claiming that anything we think we know can be called in question. His suggestion is rather that nothing we believe is ever justified, even to the slightest degree.

Conceding the viciousness of the regress, we are left with two strategies for escaping the trilemma. One is to identify beliefs that are somehow credible without requiring backup. If there are such "basic" beliefs, they will bring requests for justification to a halt without being mere assumptions. They will be the tortoise supporting the elephant. The other strategy is to argue that our beliefs about the world constitute an extensive and complicated *system*, the members of which give each other a kind of mutual support that is not to be equated with simple circularity. Here we meet the serpent with its tail in its mouth.

But do we really have a forced choice here? A natural reaction to the Agrippan problem is that there is something artificial about it. After all, although disputes sometimes get bogged down, or peter out through exhaustion, they can also come to a satisfactory end. When they do, it will be because whoever is on the defensive is able to cite evidence that is acceptable and convincing to all parties to the discussion. Claims that everyone finds too obvious to be worth discussing are not ordinarily called "assumptions." Indeed, what we ordinarily call "justification" just is the production of such evidence.

While not denying this, the Agrippan skeptic will caution against reading too much into it. When we say that justification proceeds from "acceptable" claims, what we really mean is claims that are in fact *accepted*. This "acceptability" is entirely psychological and person-relative: it signals no special epistemological status. The same goes for terms like "evident" or "obvious." So the "common knowledge" that terminates everyday justificational procedures can be seen, on reflection, to be nothing more than a body of common assumptions (and maybe not so common, if we broaden our imagined audience). We can put the point like this: the reply to the skeptic just envisaged represents ordinary justification as entirely *dialectical*. We can all see on reflection that knowledge and justification demand more.

Agrippa's trilemma calls attention to the need for beliefs that meet two conditions. First, they must be non-inferentially credible: justified without deriving their justification inferentially from further beliefs. Second, given that justification cannot be seen as a purely dialectical exercise, they must be credible in a way that reflects some kind of *external constraint*. Empirical knowledge cannot just be a matter of bandying words about: it must have something to do with the objective world.

Sellars accepts the requirement of external constraint, justification that is more than dialectical. Thus, although he rejects traditional foundationalism, he accepts the legitimacy of the demands to which empiricism responds. He writes:

> If I reject the framework of traditional empiricism, it is not because I want to say that knowledge has *no* foundation. For to put it this way is to suggest that it is really 'empirical knowledge so-called', and to put it in a box with rumours and hoaxes. There is clearly *some* point to the picture of human knowledge as resting on a level of propositions—observation reports—which do not rest on other propositions in the same way as other propositions rest on them. (EPM 170)

Observation is the source of external constraint. Accordingly, Sellars's response to the Agrippan problem is found in his account of observational knowledge in Section VIII of EPM: "Does Empirical Knowledge Have a Foundation?" Sellars's exposition may charitably be described as compressed, and less charitably as cryptic. It is far from obvious that Sellars is successful in his attempt to chart a course between foundationalism and the coherence theory. My first task is to explain why. Then I shall try to show that Sellars does, or perhaps can, succeed. Whether Sellars himself is entirely clear either about the problem he faces, or about how best to deploy his resources to cope with it, is a further question. I suspect that he was not.

2. One way to respond to the demand for external constraint is to adopt an externalist-reliabilist (e.g., causal) theory of perceptual knowledge. According to reliabilists, knowledge is simply belief formed by some kind of reliable cognitive

process and so has no essential connections with justification. Justification, in the sense of inference from evidence, is at best one example of such a process and may not be among the most fundamental. A lot of knowledge—and perceptual knowledge is a prime example—results from the unreflective exercise of basic cognitive capacities.

Sellars begins by considering a suggestion along theses lines. Thus:

(a) "An overt or covert token of 'This is green' in the presence of a green item... expresses observational knowledge if and only if it is a manifestation of a tendency to produce overt or covert tokens of 'This is green'—given a certain set—if and only if a green object is being looked at in standard conditions." (EPM 167)

However, pure reliabilism is not an option available to Sellars. According to Sellars, "in characterizing an episode or state as that of *knowing*, we are not giving an empirical description of that episode or state; we are placing it in the logical space of reasons, of justifying and being able to justify what one says" (EPM 169). For Sellars, the connection between knowledge and justification cannot be dispensed with.

Sellars is making more than a narrow epistemological point here. As Robert Brandom explains, the question that Sellars encourages us to ask first is: What distinguishes conceptual from non-conceptual activity? How does the human being who says "That's green" differ from the parrot trained to utter the same vocables in response to the presentation of a green card? Sellars's answer is that the human reporter, unlike the parrot, has the concept "green" and so understands what he is saying in a way that the parrot does not. This understanding consists in the human reporter's grasp of what follows from his reports, what is evidence for them, how they might be challenged, how various challenges might be met, and so on.[3] The reliability condition fails to state a sufficient condition for knowledge because a mere conditioned response does not even express a belief. Lightning does not, in the relevant sense, "mean" thunder.

Supposing that Sellars is right and inferential embeddedness is the hallmark of conceptual content, we can conclude that, to express knowledge, a sentence-token needs more than reliability: it needs authority. According to Sellars, this authority is constituted by:

(b) "... the fact that one can infer the presence of a green object from the fact that someone makes this report." To be correctly made, the reporter need not "follow a rule" in anything other than a "lightning-thunder" sense. Rather, such a report can be "correct as being an

---

3 Brandom 2000. See esp. Section 1.

instance of a general mode of behaviour which, in a given linguistic community, it is reasonable to sanction and support." (EPM 167–8).

This is the "reliability inference." Sellars says that the relevant mode of behavior is one that, in a given linguistic community, it is *reasonable* to sanction and support. He does not say one that, in a given community, *is regarded* as reasonable to sanction and support, or one that is, as a matter of fact, *sanctioned and supported*. He is not attempting to reduce justification to dialectical acceptability. Acceptability supplements reliability: it does not replace it. Non-inferential reporting is reasonably accepted *because* it is reliable.

Given (a) and (b), we get the following results:
(i)  Observational knowledge is a source of external constraint because it is keyed (causally) to features of the environment.
(ii)  It is non-inferential because produced spontaneously, without the self-conscious application of rules or criteria.
(iii)  Non-inferential reports are contentful—more than mere responses—because they are inferentially embedded in a socially enacted reason-giving practice.
(iv)  Because of this embedding, observational knowledge is also dialectically constrained, thus in the space of reasons.

Is our account complete? Not according to Sellars. The "decisive" problem to be solved is that "to be the expression of knowledge, a report must not only have authority, this authority must *in some sense* be recognized by the person whose report it is" (EPM 168). It is not enough that, with respect to my non-inferential reports, someone or other must be able to make the reliability inference. I must be able to do this for myself. Here Sellars appears to take his insistence on connecting knowledge with justification to commit him to a very strong form of epistemic internalism, the doctrine that knowledge cannot depend on factors of which we are unaware. Following through on this thought, Sellars suggests:

> (c) "[F]or... 'This is green' to 'express observational knowledge', not only must it be a *symptom* or *sign* of the presence of a green object in standard conditions, but the perceiver must know that tokens of 'This is green' *are* symptoms of the presence of green objects in conditions that are standard for visual perception." (EPM 168)

Let us call this knowledge of symptomatic relations "reliability-knowledge."

Since knowledge is factive, (c) makes (a) redundant. But swapping (a) for (c) raises the question of whether Sellars has really found a way between the horns of the dilemma between foundationalism and the coherence theory. Observational knowledge presupposes reliability-knowledge and *vice-versa*. This looks like coherentism.

Sellars notes that (c) implies some kind of holism. Thus:

> [I]f the authority of the report 'This is green' lies in the fact that the existence of green items appropriately related to the perceiver can be inferred from the occurrence of such reports, it follows that only a person who is able to draw this inference, and therefore who has not only the concept *green*, but also the concept of uttering 'This is green'—indeed the concept of certain conditions of perception, those which would be correctly called 'standard conditions'—could be in a position to token 'This is green' in recognition of its authority.

From this, "it follows, as a matter of simple logic, that one could not have observational knowledge of *any* fact unless one knows *many* other things as well." Sellars also notes that "the point is not taken care of by distinguishing between *knowing how* and *knowing that*" (EPM 168). Perceptual knowledge of any fact presupposes explicit reliability-knowledge, not just "know how." But what supports reliability-knowledge, if not perceptual knowledge of particular facts? Again, it looks as if Sellars's commitment to internalism has driven him to accept coherentism.

3. Sellars is aware of this objection, or something like it. In EPM, he offers two replies, neither of which is obviously satisfactory.

*First Reply: epistemic versus genetic questions.* Sellars notes that there might seem to be "an obvious regress" in the view he is defending: reliability-knowledge presupposes prior observational knowledge, which presupposes other reliability-knowledge, and so on. Sellars says that this objection rests on "a radically mistaken conception of what one is saying of Jones when one says that he *knows* that p" (EPM 169). Indeed, it is to correct this mistake that Sellars makes his famous remark that "in characterizing an episode or state as that of *knowing*, we are not giving an empirical description of that episode or state; we are placing it in the logical space of reasons, of justifying and being able to justify what one says" (EPM 169). This remark allows Sellars to distinguish the (synchronic) epistemic question about the *authority* of Jones's non-inferential reports from the (diachronic) genetic question about how Jones came to be in a position to report authoritatively. Thus:

> [N]o tokening by S *now* of 'This is green' is to count as 'expressing observational knowledge' unless it is also correct to say of S that he *now* knows the appropriate fact of the form *X is a reliable symptom of Y*... [W]hile the correctness of this statement about Jones requires that Jones could *now* cite prior particular facts as evidence for the idea that these utterances *are* reliable indicators, it requires only that it is correct to say that Jones *now* knows, thus remembers, that these particular facts did obtain. It does not require

that it be correct to say that at the time these facts did obtain he *then knew* them to obtain... Thus, while Jones's ability to give inductive reasons *today* is built on a long history of acquiring and manifesting verbal habits in perceptual situations... it does not require that any episode in this prior time be characterisable as expressing knowledge. (EPM 169)

Unpacking Sellars's argument, we can say that the foundationalist interprets the genetic argument in the light of the principle that knowledge can come only from knowledge. However, this principle runs together causal and epistemic questions. Keeping them properly separate, we can give a purely causal-externalist answer to the genetic question.

While this may be true, it doesn't help. The objection is that Sellars's internalism commits him to giving a coherentist response to the epistemic question. It is not to the point for him to reply that he can give an externalist answer to another, non-epistemic question. Nor does it make a difference that some forms of the objection confuse the two sorts of question: the confusion is inessential to the difficulty in Sellars's own position.

Sellars's lack of explicit attention to the Agrippan problem hurts him here. The assimilation of the epistemic to the genetic question is important only to those who want to break the regress by recognizing a first episode of knowing, i.e., foundationalists, advocates of encapsulated knowledge. If anything, Sellars's argument strengthens the suspicion that the only real alternative to foundationalism is holistic coherentism.

*The Second Reply: two dimensions of dependence.* As we have seen, Sellars agrees that there is "*some* point to the picture of human knowledge as resting on a level of propositions—observation reports—which do not rest on other propositions in the same way as other propositions rest on them." However, he continues, "the metaphor of 'foundation' is misleading in that it keeps us from seeing that if there is a logical dimension in which other empirical observations rest on observation reports, there is another logical dimension in which the latter rest on the former" (EPM 170). What are these two logical dimensions, and what kind of "resting" is involved in each?

The remark just quoted comes towards the end of section VIII of EPM, "Does Empirical Knowledge Have a Foundation?" Section VIII opens with the claim that

one of the forms taken by the Myth of the Given is the idea that there is, indeed *must be*, a structure of particular matter of fact such that (a) each fact can not only be non-inferentially known to be the case, but presupposes no other knowledge either of particular matter of fact, or of general truths; and (b) such that the non-inferential knowledge of facts belonging to this structure constitutes the ultimate court of appeals for all factual claims—particular and general—about the world. (EPM 164)

He then adds an important gloss:

> It is important to note that I characterized the knowledge belonging to this stratum as not only non-inferential, but as presupposing no knowledge of other matter of fact, whether particular or general. It might be thought that this is a redundancy, that knowledge (not belief or conviction) that presupposes knowledge of other facts *must* be inferential. This, however... is itself an episode in the Myth. (EPM 164)

These remarks look forward to the point about the two dimensions of dependence. Sellars's thought, I take it, is this:

- The practice of making non-inferential reports must be mastered as a whole. This will involve learning lots of general facts: about one's reliability as a reporter, about standard and non-standard conditions, and so on. Making authoritative reports on particular matters of fact and acknowledging a wide range of facts about one's reliability are part of a single conceptual package.
- Nevertheless, within our practice of giving and asking for reasons, non-inferential observation reports play a distinguished epistemic role. They control our general commitments in a way that our general commitments do not control them.

Sellars's two logical dimensions are the conceptual and the epistemic; and his thought is that conceptual interdependence is compatible with a fundamental epistemic asymmetry. But while this is suggestive, it is hardly obviously correct. Sellars asserts an epistemic asymmetry, but does not show that he is entitled to do so. And it is not clear that he is, for he appears to have argued:

- Knowledge requires justification: authority.
- Authority demands more than *de facto* reliability.
- This "more" is the subject's own recognition of his reliability.
- Therefore, justification presupposes reliability-knowledge.

This presupposition is not "merely conceptual." If particular observation-reports depend for their *authority* on reliability-knowledge, this dependence is epistemic. Sellars's attempt to distinguish two dimensions of dependence won't bear the weight he puts on it: knowledge of particular facts and knowledge of general facts turn out to be both conceptually *and* epistemically interdependent, as coherence theorists have always thought.

It looks as though Sellars has forgotten his own distinction between the genetic and the epistemic. Observation reports are at best *genetically* non-inferential. They are "cognitively spontaneous" in that they are not consciously inferred from more primitive evidence. But they are *authoritative* because backed by reliability-knowledge. By Sellars's own standards, genetic and epistemic considerations must be kept rigorously apart. Epistemically speaking, observation reports are inferential, i.e., they are justificationally and not merely conceptually dependent on further knowledge. Again, Sellars's internalism seems to force him to adopt the coherence theory.

Writings subsequent to EPM confirm the impression of a drift towards the coherence theory. In his essay "Phenomenalism," composed three years after the first publication of EPM, Sellars discusses "direct" perceptual knowledge in terms of a distinction between "same-level" and "trans-level" inference.[4] Traditional empiricism treats knowledge of physical objects as "indirect" in the sense of depending on a "same-level" inference from basic knowledge of appearances or sense-data. This is a mistake: if direct realism is the claim that we can have perceptual knowledge of physical objects that does not depend on inference from sense-data, direct realism is correct. Nevertheless,

> ... one only knows what one has a right to think to be the case. Thus to say that someone directly knows that-p is to say that his right to the conviction that-p essentially involves the fact that the idea that-p occurred to the knower in a specific way. I shall call this kind of credibility 'trans-level credibility', and the inference schema
>> X's thought that-p occurred in manner M
>> So, (probably) p
> to which it refers, as trans-level inference.[5]

Sellars seems to be arguing here that even "direct" knowledge of physical objects in inferential, in the sense of involving a "trans-level" or "reliability" inference. We saw in considering the second reply that Sellars does not really explain how the conceptual interdependence of perceptual knowledge of particular matters of fact and reliability-knowledge is compatible with an asymmetry in respect of epistemic status. In the passage just cited, however, Sellars appears to abandon the idea of an epistemic asymmetry altogether.

4. Even some of Sellars's warmest admirers, John McDowell and Robert Brandom, think that he goes too far in insisting on reliability-knowledge as a precondition of perceptual knowledge of particular matters of fact, though they offer radically different suggestions for repairing the damage.[6]

---

4 Sellars 1963b, 87–9.

5 Sellars 1963b, 88.

6 McDowell 1996, 129–61. McDowell modifies his criticism, while developing some new ones, in McDowell 1998. For Robert Brandom's views of Sellars on observational knowledge, see Brandom 1994, 215–7.

McDowell thinks that Sellars goes wrong in assuming that the world constrains our thinking only causally. Let us recall once more Sellars's claim that "in characterizing an episode or state as that of *knowing*, we are not giving an empirical description of that episode or state; we are placing it in the logical space of reasons, of justifying and being able to justify what one says" (EPM 169). According to McDowell, "Sellars's thesis is that the conceptual apparatus we employ when we place things in the logical space of reasons is irreducible to any conceptual apparatus that does not serve to place things in the logical space of reasons. So the master thought draws a line: above the line are placings in the logical space of reasons, and below it are characterizations that do not do that."[7] Sellars is attracted to reliabilism, with regard to perceptual knowledge, because it offers the necessary element of external constraint. However, to suppose that the authority of observation reports could be reduced to mere *de facto* reliability would be to suppose that knowledge could be characterized wholly in terms that belong below the line, in violation of the master thought. To bring reliability considerations above the line, Sellars *must* insist that reliability be recognized.

What is the alternative? For McDowell, it is to recognize that perception puts us in direct touch with facts about the world. Recognizing this, we can have external constraint in the form of rational control by the world itself, the layout of reality. All Sellars gives us is causal constraint, and to treat causal constraint as epistemic constraint would be to recoil to the Myth of the Given. To avoid this, Sellars insists on *reliability-knowledge*, thereby recoiling to frictionless coherentism. Presumably, McDowell thinks that Sellars has not freed himself from the spell of modern naturalism, which equates Nature with the Realm of Law. This equation entails that the only possible form of external constraint on our thinking is causal, leaving no room for constraint that is both external and rational. But this means that there is no way of avoiding the choice between foundationalism, i.e., the Myth of the Given, and the coherence theory.

I will not comment at length on McDowell's challenging views. Let me just say this: it is true that, for Sellars, the only way that the world constrains our thinking is causally. So even if McDowell is right about perceptual knowledge, his ideas represent a fundamental break with those of Sellars.

Robert Brandom makes a quite different proposal: that reliability-knowledge can be socially distributed.[8] We can attribute observational knowledge to a subject on the basis of *our* assessment of the subject's reliability. It is not necessary

---

7 McDowell 1998, 433.
8 Brandom 1994, 217–21. See also Brandom 2000 and Brandom 1998.

that the subject herself be in possession of the relevant reliability-knowledge. Monique may be able reliably to identify hornbeams, even if she is diffident of her abilities. Recognizing her reliability, *we* can treat her tentative identifications as expressing knowledge, even she herself hesitates to do so. So whereas McDowell resolves the apparent tension in Sellars's thought by eliminating its causal-reliabilist element in favor of rational control by the world, Brandom retains that element by moving Sellars towards a starker externalism, at least as far as third-person knowledge-attributions are concerned.

I used myself to favor a view along the lines of Brandom's proposal. According to Sellars, a child's early verbal responses to its environment are only "superficially like" genuine observation reports. Discussing this claim in *Groundless Belief*, I wrote that "we might count a child's early observation reports as expressing knowledge because they are *in fact* reliable (and are justifiable by a fully-fledged language-user, thus making the child a *potential* justifier) even though the child could not be expected to marshal facts about his linguistic capabilities in support of his observational claims."[9] I suggested treating children the way Brandom treats Monique.

I still think that this point is correct, as far as it goes. I just no longer think that it goes very far. The problem is that it does not generalize. We can be generous to Monique, with respect to knowing a hornbeam when she sees one, only because she is a full-fledged justifier with respect to lots of her other reporting capabilities. We can be generous to children because we expect them to mature. But if Monique stood to all observable features of her environment as she stands to hornbeams—even things as elementary as green things—or if a child never got beyond the "parroting" stage, our generosity would be misplaced. A subject wholly lacking in the reliability-knowledge that Sellars claims is presupposed by observation-reporting would not be in the game of giving and asking for reasons. Such a subject would not be a knower, even by courtesy.

It is significant that Brandom chooses an object that we do not expect everyone to be able to recognize: the sort of object that activates the division of linguistic labor. (This is also the sort of object that we can start to be able to recognize without being able to say how we do it.) Choosing an object like this foregrounds the undeniable fact that lots of epistemic entitlements are distributed socially via mechanisms like deference. But we should not conclude from this that all a person's observational entitlements could be externally authorized. So I do not think that Brandom has shown us a way of extricating Sellars from the predicament we have placed him in.

---

9 Williams 1999, 94.

5. There is evidence that Sellars did not find his position in EPM altogether satisfactory. In "Epistemic Principles," he considers Chisholm's view that "epistemic principles pertaining to perception and memory are themselves justified... by the fact that unless they, or something like them, are true, then there could be no such thing as perceptual knowledge to the effect... that there is a cat on the roof."[10] What Sellars here calls "epistemic principles" are the reliability-commitments involved in authority-conferring trans-level inferences. Sellars sees Chisholm as offering a Kantian "this or nothing" justification for such principles. But he remarks that Chisholm also seems, on occasion, to treat his principles as synthetic *a priori* or even self-evident truths. Such an approach is less than fully satisfactory.

Although Sellars does not press the issue, it is easy to see how this temptation arises. In the face of a simple, powerful, and apparently intuitive argument for skepticism, "This or nothing" looks more like a restatement of the problem than a solution. After all, the skeptic's question just is "Why not nothing?" The temptation is to say, "Because some epistemic principles are self-evidently true." This is, of course, a foundationalist response.

Given his antipathy to foundationalism, it is not surprising to find Sellars suggesting that the required epistemic principles can be defended in a different way. Thus: "[they] can be placed in a naturalistic setting and their authority construed in terms of the nature of concept-formation and the acquisition of the relevant linguistic skills."[11] But if Chisholm's strategy founders on the Mode of Assumption, why doesn't Sellars's approach invite the charge of circularity? Sellars anticipates the question:

> But surely, it will be urged, facts about learning languages and acquiring linguistic skills are themselves empirical *facts*; and to know these facts involves perception, memory, indeed, all the epistemic activities the justification of which is at stake. Must we not conclude that any such account as I give of the principle that perceptual beliefs occurring in perceptual contexts are *likely to be true* is circular?[12]

This is the question addressed in EPM. But it is not clear that it gets the same response. Sellars writes:

> It must, indeed, be granted that principles pertaining to the epistemic authority of perceptual and memory beliefs are not the sort of thing which *could* be arrived at by inductive

---

10 Sellars 2000, 131.
11 Sellars 2000, 131.
12 Sellars 2000, 132.

reasoning from perceptual belief. But the best way to make this point is positive. *We have to be in this framework to be thinking and perceiving beings at all.*[13]

Whereas in EPM Sellars allows Jones's history of language-acquisition to have furnished him, when fully competent, with the ability to give inductive reasons for his reliability commitments, Sellars could be taken now to concede that inductive justification is never in the cards. On the other hand, the reference to the impossibility of "arriving at" authoritative principles via inductive inference contains echoes of the distinction between genetic and epistemic questions.

Nevertheless, the passage suggests a different justificational strategy. Sellars now seems to be suggesting that fundamental epistemic principles are justified because they are essential elements in anything that could be recognized as a linguistic practice. Hence, given Sellars's commitment to the essential connection between language-mastery and full-fledged intentionality, they are essential commitments on the part of any thinking being. This means, I take it, that there can be no question of a thinking being's not being entitled to such commitments: without them, he would not be a thinking being.

If this is Sellars's argument, it fits in well with his lack of interest in "narrowly" epistemological questions. The argument just given implies that the skeptic arrives on the scene too late. The skeptic takes thought for granted. He allows us to enter claims, make judgments, and hold beliefs, inquiring only why any of them are justified. If, in responding to the skeptic's question, we appeal to epistemic principles, the skeptic asks how they are justified. But simply in allowing us to be thinking beings, the skeptic has conceded our entitlement to epistemic principles, defeating his own purpose.

Sellars sees this argument as reinforcing his thought that questions about meaning are theoretically prior to questions about knowledge and justification. Since actions, as much as thoughts and perceptions, exist in the logical space of reasons, we have to be in the framework of epistemic principles to act as well as to think and perceive. According to Sellars, this makes it clear that "the exploration of these principles is but part of the task of explicating the concept of a rational animal or... of a language-using organism whose language is *about* the world in which it is *used*."[14] Given what Sellars calls his "verbal behaviourist" approach to thought and meaning, skepticism no longer commands our attention. The skeptic is not so much refuted as bypassed.

---

**13** Sellars 2000, 132 (emphasis in original).
**14** Sellars 2000, 132 (emphasis in original).

While I think that there is a lot to what Sellars says here, I do not think that it is the last word. To echo a point made by John McDowell and Barry Stroud, the problem is that the skeptic's question still looks like a good one. Sellars may have shown that our entitlement to epistemic principles cannot be impugned. However, by Sellars's own lights, the problem is not just to defend our entitlement to reliability-commitments but to argue that they are likely to be true. Just how Sellars takes his argument to bear on this question is not easy to make out.

Much depends on what Sellars means by the claim that, to be thinking beings at all, we must be "in the framework" constituted by epistemic principles pertaining to the reliability of perception and memory. If he means only that we must be committed to such principles, he invites the reply that he has not addressed the question of their truth. So perhaps he means that, if we are thinking beings, some such principles must be *true*. However, since he never denies that reliability-commitments concern matters of empirical fact, this would amount to attributing to Sellars an argument for treating them as synthetic *a priori* principles, and his critical remarks on Chisholm indicate that he repudiates this idea. His strategy of placing such principles in a "naturalistic setting" is meant to be an alternative to Chisholm's approach, not an endorsement of it.

Now, at the conclusion of "Epistemic Principles," Sellars suggests that, in the light of his conception of thought and meaning, "the metaphor of 'foundation and superstructure' is seen to be a false extrapolation... from specific 'problematic situations' with respect to which it *is* appropriate."[15] He then quotes himself, reminding the reader of the conclusion he drew at the end of Section VIII of EPM, where he explains why neither foundationalism nor the coherence theory will do. He writes: "empirical knowledge, like its sophisticated extension, science, is rational, not because it has a *foundation* but because it is a self-correcting enterprise which can put *any* claim in jeopardy, though not *all* at once" (EPM 170). The skeptic wants to know why anything that we believe amounts to knowledge. The counterpart of this global question is a project of global legitimation: the project within which the choice between foundationalism and the coherence theory appears forced. I take Sellars to be suggesting that his conception of thought and meaning allows us to see the whole skeptical problematic as a false extrapolation from "specific problematic situations." If this can be made out, skepticism is not just bypassed but successfully diagnosed, and any lingering sense of dissatisfaction evaporates.

---

15 Sellars 2000, 132 (emphasis in original).

Unfortunately, perhaps as a result of his lack of interest in narrowly epistemological questions, Sellars does little to spell out the link between his view of
thought and meaning and his anti-skeptical conception of justification. In the remainder of this paper, I shall attempt to fill the gap.

6. Justification is a matter of epistemic authority: the epistemic status of one's
beliefs. But there are two ways of looking at epistemic status:

> *Personal justification:* whether a *person* is justified in believing a particular proposition to
> be true. Personal justification is a matter of *responsibility.* One is personally justified in be-
> lieving that P iff, in coming to believe that P, one has behaved in an epistemically respon-
> sible way: for example, if one has not carelessly overlooked counterevidence that ought to
> have been taken into account.

> *Epistemic Grounding:* whether the process or procedure (let us say, "epistemic procedure")
> in virtue of which a person comes to hold a particular belief makes the proposition *believed*
> to be true likely to *be* true. Epistemic grounding is a matter of *reliability.* A belief is epistemi-
> cally well-grounded (from here on, grounded) iff it is formed via a process that in fact
> makes it likely to be true.

I am inclined to think that "justification," in its primary sense, answers to personal justification. However, I also think that ordinary talk about "justification"
is poised uneasily between responsibility and grounding. So, for example, "inter-
nalists" and "externalists" tend to use "justification" in different ways, though
neither party thinks that it is doing serious violence to ordinary justification-
talk. From here on, as a way of keeping straight the distinction between justifi-
cation-as-responsibility and justification-as-grounding, I shall use "justification"
exclusively in the sense of personal justification. Justification-as-grounding will
be called simply "grounding."

Knowledge requires justification and grounding. This is the lesson of Gettier's problem. In Gettier examples, a person non-culpably forms a belief via an
unreliable method: for example, he is guided by misleading evidence, which
he has no reason to suspect is misleading. Accidentally, the conclusion he is
led to accept is true. Such cases are supposed to illustrate justified true belief
without knowledge. But they could be better described as illustrating responsibly formed beliefs that are not, in fact, well-grounded.

The epistemological tradition has not paid much attention to the distinction
between justification and grounding because it has tended to take for granted a
certain view of the relation between them. This view is summed up in W.K. Clifford's aphorism: "It is wrong always, everywhere and for anyone, to believe anything upon insufficient evidence." Clifford's claim can be broken down into three
sub-theses:

(C1) *No Unearned Entitlements*. Entitlements do not just accrue to us: they must be earned by epistemically responsible behavior.

(C2) *Responsibility Presupposes Grounding*. It is never epistemically responsible to believe a proposition true when one's grounds for believing it true are less than adequate.

(C3) *Grounds Are Always Evidence*. A belief is adequately grounded iff the believer possesses (and makes proper use of) evidence that makes the proposition in question (very) likely to be true.

The normative epistemic principle articulated by (C1)–(C3) can be called the *Prior Grounding Requirement*. This requirement leads readily to the demand for self-grounding, intrinsically credible beliefs. It is one of traditional foundationalism's deepest commitments.

The way to escape the choice between foundationalism and the coherence theory is to reject the Prior Grounding Requirement. Some philosophers reject it by objecting to one of the sub-theses that make up the requirement. For example, pure externalists reject (C3). They deny that grounding must always take the form of inference from evidence. Sometimes beliefs are well-grounded if they result from the unselfconscious use of *de facto* reliable discriminative abilities. Sellars can agree with them up to a point, though he cannot agree that such grounding is sufficient for knowledge. The way to defend Sellars's hybrid conception of observational knowledge is to deny all three theses. Or rather, to see that, while none is entirely without point, all are false as the foundationalist understands them.

The foundationalist understands (C1), the "No Unearned Entitlements" principle, to require that epistemic entitlements be earned by taking *specific positive steps* in *each* situation in which entitlement is claimed. But there is another way of understanding the relation between entitlement and justification. We can see justification as conforming to what Robert Brandom calls a "default-and-challenge structure."[16] The difference between the "Prior Grounding" and the "Default-and-Challenge" conceptions of justification is like that between legal systems that treat the accused as guilty unless proved innocent and those that do the opposite, granting presumptive innocence and throwing the burden of

---

16 The phrase is Brandom's. There are, however, many prior articulations of this general conception. One of the most important is to be found in J.L. Austin's seminal essay "Other Minds" (Austin 1961b). I believe that this conception of justification is very ancient, originating in Academic theories of "skeptical assent," particularly Carneades's doctrine of the "tested impression."

proof on the accuser.[17] Adopting the second model, justification, hence entitlement, is the default status of at least some person's beliefs and assertions. One is responsible, thus justified, unless there is some definite defect in one's epistemic procedure.

The Default-and-Challenge conception of epistemic responsibility does not imply that personal justification is completely independent of the ability to give grounds for what one believes. What it rejects, rather, is the idea that a responsible believer's commitment to provide grounds is *unrestricted*. A claim to knowledge involves a commitment to respond to whatever appropriate challenges emerge, and to withdraw the claim should no effective defense be available. In claiming knowledge, I commit myself to my belief's *being* adequately grounded—formed by a reliable method—but not to my having *already established* its well-groundedness. Explicit defense is necessary only given a positive reason to think that I reached my belief in some unreliable manner.

Let us recall—yet again—Sellars's master thought that "in characterizing an episode or state as that of *knowing*, we are not giving an empirical description of that episode or state; we are placing it in the logical space of reasons, of justifying and being able to justify what one says" (EPM 169). On the view I am defending, it is critical that Sellars writes of "justifying and being able to justify." I take "being able to justify" to mean "being able to justify, should the need arise." But the need does not always arise.

Of course, not everything we say has the status of default entitlement. Many things worth saying do not. They face standing objections; they invite questions: this is what makes them worth talking about. But not everything we say is like this. Default entitlements halt the regress of justification. But default entitlement has nothing to do with intrinsic credibility. Sellars is not a foundationalist.

On the "Prior Grounding" conception of knowledge and justification, merely making a claim is sufficient to make reasonable the question "How do you know?" The automatic reasonableness of this question is what gets the Agrippan argument off the ground. On the Prior Grounding conception, the burden of proof is always on the claimant. By contrast, on the Default-and-Challenge conception, challengers, as well as claimants, are subject to justificational obligations. There is no standing entitlement to ask, "How do you know?" To be entitled to ask such a question, a challenger must have specific reasons for

---

17 Default-and-challenge structures show up in non-epistemological accounting practices too. Consider a different sense of "responsibility": accountability for one's actions. Here, again, "responsibility" is the default position: one is accountable unless in possession of an appropriate excuse. This view of responsibility is taken up by Austin in his famous paper "A Plea for Excuses" (Austin 1961a). Austin's views on knowledge and freedom are importantly connected.

questioning either the truth of the target belief or the claimant's entitlement to hold it.

The Default-and-Challenge conception explains and defends Sellars's rejection of "global" skeptical doubt. If claimants and challengers are both subject to justificational commitments, justifying—as responding to motivated challenges—always takes place *in some definite informational context*. It follows, as Sellars would say, as a matter of simple logic that while *any* belief may be challenged, given appropriate stage-setting, there is no possibility of judging our beliefs in the *collective* way that the philosophical skeptic aspires to. Sellars is therefore a "coherentist" only in the innocuous sense that, if an epistemic challenge has arisen, it must be dealt with by giving reasons. But the classical coherence theory—the Hegelian serpent of knowledge with its tail in its mouth—is radically holistic: its *raison d' être* is to give a global legitimation in response to skepticism's global doubts. Since Sellars properly rejects the reasonableness of such global questioning, he has no need for such global legitimation.

7. There is a final hurdle to clear. We might wonder whether the authority of observation reports can be assimilated to default entitlement, given that this authority is backed by reliability-knowledge.

We saw that Sellars distinguishes two logical dimensions in which observational knowings of particular facts and relevant items of reliability-knowledge depend on each other. I argued that these dimensions are not easily kept apart. I think that, if we acquiesce in the Prior Grounding conception of knowledge, they cannot be kept apart. But given a Default-and-Challenge conception, things stand very differently. There is no observational knowledge of particular matters of fact in the absence of relevant reliability-knowledge. The relevant reliability-knowledge must be present. But it does not have to be present in a justifying role.

Sellars says that, to express observational knowledge, a token of "This is green" must be "a manifestation of a tendency to produce overt or covert tokens of 'This is green'—given a certain set—if and only if a green object is being looked at in standard conditions" (EPM 167). However, the knowledge that one's tokening of "This is green" is symptomatic of the presence of a green object would not justify one's claim were it subject to a reasonable doubt: for example, a doubt prompted by reasons to suspect that conditions are non-standard. Knowing that, in standard conditions, one's tokenings of certain sentences are reliable indicators of worldly circumstances does not imply that, in the case of a given tokening, one knows that conditions are standard. True, Sellars himself was inclined to think that seeing that an object is red does require knowing that conditions are standard.[18] But here Sellars does go too far, confusing the conditions for perceptual knowing with those for knowing that one knows.

Why, then, on the Default-and-Challenge conception, is reliability-knowledge essential for observational knowledge of particular matters of fact? This is a good question, for it is natural to think that, by abandoning the Prior Grounding Requirement, we sever what Sellars regards as a necessary conceptual link. The answer is that, without a complex body of reliability-knowledge, a person cannot recognize either legitimate challenges to nor appropriate defenses of his claims to observational knowledge. Such a person would not be a participant in the game of giving and asking for reasons and so would not be a knower. Accordingly, the Default-and-Challenge conception explains and defends Sellars idea of there being two logical dimensions of dependence. Reliability-knowledge is conceptually essential, but not always justificationally relevant.

Here we can return briefly to the "No Unearned Entitlements" principle. We have seen that the principle need not be accepted on the reading that foundationalists and skeptics give it. However, the principle is not entirely without point. Although individual entitlements do not have to be earned anew on every occasion they are claimed, the *status* of epistemic subject must be earned through education and training. This status does not come with mere sentience. Its achievement involves mastering a range of epistemic practices, all of which involve extensive general knowledge. Acquiring this general knowledge is necessary if a person is to have the status of knower. This does not mean that such knowledge is justificationally relevant to every individual knowledge-claim. Rather, the default entitlement attaching to observation reports is grounded in the status or credentials of the reporter. No one who lacks the relevant reliability-knowledge can enjoy that status. But that knowledge does not function as evidence underwriting the credibility of particular reports.

With these remarks in mind, we can take a second look at the Genetic Argument. Sellars is not, in fact, committed to a blanket rejection of the principle that knowledge can only come from knowledge. He is committed only to rejecting it under the radically individualist reading of the principle that foundationalism takes for granted. We attain the status of epistemic subject through being *trained* in epistemic practices by others who are *already* competent in them. Knowledge emerges out of knowledge, not because all knowledge can be individually generated, but because the capacity for knowledge is socially transmitted.[19] The

---

**18** EPM, 151 n., 152 n. These are the notes, referred to in note 1 above, that were added to the 1963 reprinting.

**19** For more detailed discussion, see Williams 1999, Chapter 3.

thought that all knowledge must in principle be capable of generated "from within"—that the first-person perspective is the right one for epistemology—is another episode in the Myth of the Given, though one that Sellars himself does not emphasize.

So far, I have concentrated on (C1). Let me say something very brief about (C2) and (C3).

As for (C2)—responsibility implies grounding—it is clear that we can behave responsibly yet, through no fault of our own, follow an epistemic procedure that is not reliable in the specific circumstances that we employ it in. In such a case, we will have epistemic entitlement without knowledge. But, like (C1), (C2) is not altogether pointless. If we were not generally reliable reporters on lots of things, we could not attain the status of epistemic subject, and so, epistemically speaking, could not be responsible or irresponsible. In this sense, responsibility does imply a degree of reliability—and to that extent a degree of grounding.

Similarly for (C3). Grounding does not always have to be evidence: it can be the unselfconscious exercise of recognitional capacities. It is true that, as epistemic subjects, we know a lot about the reliability of such capacities, but this knowledge is not the ground for the authority of the reports they lead us to make. On the other hand, if we find ourselves faced with a properly motivated challenge, thus obliged to give grounds, we will need to marshal evidence.

If I am right about all this, Sellars's account of perceptual knowledge allows us to chart a course between foundationalism, including externalist foundationalism, and the coherence theory. How far Sellars himself had thought through this issue is unclear to me. But I have no doubt that he points us in the right direction.

# Bibliography

Austin, J.L. (1961a), "A Plea for Excuses." In: J.L. Austin, *Philosophical Papers*, Oxford: Oxford University Press, 175–204.

Austin, J.L. (1961b), "Other Minds." In: J.L. Austin, *Philosophical Papers*, Oxford: Oxford University Press, 76–116.

Brandom, Robert (1994), *Making It Explicit: Reasoning, Representing, and Discursive Commitment*, Cambridge, MA: Harvard University Press.

Brandom, Robert (1998), "Insights and Blindspots of Reliabilism." In: *The Monist* 81, 371–92

Brandom, Robert (2000), "Knowledge and the Social Articulation of the Space of Reasons." In: Ernest Sosa and Jaegwon Kim (eds.), *Epistemology: An Anthology*, Oxford: Blackwell, 424–32.

McDowell, John (1996), *Mind and World*, Cambridge, MA: Harvard University Press.

McDowell, John (1998), "Having the World in View: Sellars, Kant, and Intentionality." In: *Journal of Philosophy* 95, 431–91.

Sellars, Wilfred (1963), "Empiricism and the Philosophy of Mind." In: Wilfred Sellars, *Science, Perception and Reality*, London: Routledge, 127–96.

Sellars, Wilfred (1963b), "Phenomenalism." In: Wilfred Sellars, *Science, Perception and Reality*, London: Routledge, 60–105.

Sellars, Wilfred (2000), "Epistemic Principles." In: Ernest Sosa and Jaegwon Kim (eds.), *Epistemology: An Anthology*, Oxford: Blackwell, 125–33.

Williams, Michael (1999), *Groundless Belief*, Second Edition, Princeton: Princeton University Press.

Andrea Kern
# Why Do Our Reasons Come to an End?

## 1

Our actions are not occurrences that simply run their course in us as does the process of digestion. In acting as we do, we claim to be acting well. Nor do the judgments we make strike us as would a headache. When we judge, we claim that our judgment is true and justified. In acting and in judging, we refer to an ideal standard, to the good and the true, to virtue and knowledge. Human life, one might say, proceeds in the light of these ideals. And this means that human life is essentially finite. We do not possess knowledge and virtue by nature; we are not angels. In order to attain knowledge and virtue, we have to exert ourselves, and this is why knowledge and virtue are ideals for us. That our life is finite and that it proceeds under these ideals are two sides of the same coin.

In this essay, my topic will be the ideal of knowledge. Knowledge is an ideal standard for us because we are finite beings, and this means that we do not by nature satisfy this standard. An effort is required of us. To the skeptic, however, the matter seems otherwise. He believes that our nature is such that we cannot satisfy the standard of knowledge, and that, therefore, there is no point even in trying. It seems to him that, since we are finite beings, we are entirely unable to ascertain whether things really are as we believe them to be. Hence, we can never satisfy the ideal of knowledge. In his view, our finitude is an obstacle which makes it impossible for us ever to meet the ideal of knowledge.

One has to reply that this cannot be so. If we declare the ideal of knowledge to be unattainable in principle, then we would no longer be able to understand ourselves, for we would no longer know what it is we are doing when we judge. But this means that the skeptic has a mistaken conception either of the ideal of knowledge or of our finitude.

Now, in contemporary philosophy the suggestion has been made (sometimes traced back to Wittgenstein) that the misstep which leads the skeptic into doubt consists in his misconceiving the ideal of knowledge. The skeptic, according to this line of criticism, thinks of it as an ideal of absolute certainty and indefeasible justification. In truth, however, our ideal of knowledge is to be understood— for example—in a contextualistic manner.

In what follows, I would like to show that one cannot overcome philosophical skepticism by correcting its conception of the ideal of knowledge. I will do so by discussing one of the most prominent versions of this strategy, namely, epistemic contextualism. As long as one continues to believe that the skeptic's mistake is to entertain a false conception of the ideal of our knowledge, Hume will have been right to insist that skeptical doubt is the fate of our human condition, "a malady, which can never be radically cured."[1]

To break free of skepticism, we must travel down a different road, one which, I believe, Kant pointed out to us. Kant's decisive insight consists in his having grasped what it is that the skeptic misunderstands. According to Kant, the skeptic does not entertain a false conception of our *ideal* of knowledge. Rather, he is wrong in his conception of our *finitude*. The skeptic is a skeptic not because he overestimates our ideal of knowledge, but because he underestimates our finitude.

# 2

The skeptic reflects upon the conception we have of ourselves in everyday life, and he asks whether this conception is actually justified. We think of ourselves as being capable, at least in principle, of attaining knowledge. The skeptic, however, believes that to be an illusion, an illusion in which we remain entangled until we begin to reflect philosophically upon our knowledge. A philosophical reflection on our knowledge, however—and this is a reflection guided by reason alone—leads us ineluctably to the discovery that it is impossible for us to have knowledge of the world at all, not merely here and now, but always and everywhere. The skeptic thinks of his doubt concerning our knowledge as a result with which anyone who reflects rationally on the matter will inevitably end. "[S]ceptical doubt arises naturally," writes Hume, "from a profound and intense reflection on those subjects."[2] And the doubt he comes up against does not indicate that we, upon closer examination, have less knowledge than we are generally inclined to believe; rather, it reveals that the very attempt to acquire knowledge is *intrinsically* problematic. The skeptic's discovery is not that, in certain regions of knowledge, we do not meet the requisite standard; rather, he discovers that we are in principle unable to satisfy this standard at all.[3]

How does the skeptic arrive at this surprising discovery? Michael Williams represents the skeptic's argument as follows:

---

1 Hume 1978, 218.
2 Hume 1978, 218.
3 Cf. Williams 2001, 59.

Suppose [...] that I make a claim—any claim. You are entitled to ask me whether what I have said is something that I am just assuming to be true or whether I know it to be the case. If I reply that it is something I know, you are further entitled to ask me *how* I know. In response, I will have to cite something in support of my claim: my evidence, my credentials, whatever. But now the question can be renewed: is what I cite in defense of my original claim something that I am just assuming or something that I know? If the former, it will not do the job required of it: you can't base knowledge on a mere assumption. But if the latter, it will in turn need to be backed up, and so on.[4]

The skeptic becomes a skeptic because he discovers that every attempt to vindicate a claim to knowledge gets caught up in an infinite regress. I agree with Williams that the problem of an infinite regress is crucial to the strategy of most skeptical arguments. Yet Williams's characterization is imprecise; it does not identify the thought which leads the skeptic to consider the infinite regress to be a discovery to which reason compels him. For he is forced into an infinite regress only if he has a reason to believe that citing a reason in support of a claim never suffices to provide a definitive answer to the question whether the claim is true. He must have a reason to believe that citing a reason does not answer this question and that therefore he must renew his question. Without such a reason, the skeptic seems like a not-yet-fully-educated child pestering its parents with a barrage of questions, or a rather unimaginative sophist attempting to confuse us with transparent rhetorical maneuvers. In neither instance would we need to take him seriously as a philosopher.[5] If we are to be confronted with a philosophical problem at all, we cannot conceive of the skeptic as someone who arrives at his skeptical conclusions because his reason is not yet fully developed or because, like the sophist, he misuses it. Rather, we must think of the skeptic as believing that he cannot avoid the results of his reflections, as it is reason itself which reveals them to him. We would do well, then, to formulate the skeptic's line of thought somewhat more precisely. The skeptic arrives at his surprising discovery by way of the following reflection:

---

4 Williams 2001, 62.

5 Later on, we shall see that Williams's lack of precision in characterizing the skeptic's position is no accident. His diagnosis of the skeptical condition is dependent on this imprecise characterization. The root of this lack of precision seems to me to be Williams's idea that we need to distinguish between two different though equally deep-seated kinds of skepticism, namely, between Agrippan and Cartesian skepticism. In my view, this distinction represents a serious misunderstanding, since (as I shall show) it is a specifically Cartesian line of thought which constitutes the presupposition of the so-called Agrippan problem of infinite regress. Without that presupposition, such a regress does not pose a serious philosophical problem at all; it would represent nothing more than a rhetorical maneuver.

Let us assume that I know something. If I do, this means I am in a position to rule out the possibility that my belief is wrong. This is the difference between knowledge and mere belief. If I merely belief something, I consider myself lucky when my judgment proves to be true. If, on the other hand, I know something, the truth of my judgment is something I have made sure of, namely, by excluding the possibility of its being false. But how do I exclude this possibility? I exclude it by providing a reason for my belief. Let us imagine I claim to know that there is a chair in front of me. When I claim to know this, then according to what we said above, the question arises of how I exclude the possibility that it is *not* the case that there is a chair in front of me. In the given case, I would cite my perception of the chair as a reason. I know that there is a chair in front of me because I see that there is a chair in front of me. But does this answer suffice? Is my perception a *sufficient* reason, that is, a reason which excludes the possibility that things are not as I believe them to be? No, we have to say: a mere perception is not sufficient, since it could be illusory. It is possible to have the impression that there is a chair in front of one without this actually being so. This represents an essential characteristic of finite beings: finite beings are capable of error. If we take account of this susceptibility to error, we have to say that our reason can be either veridical or non-veridical, meaning that our reason is of such a nature that, given any reason for believing that p, it may be either true or false that p. If I have the impression that there is a chair in front of me, it can happen either that the truth of my belief is established (when I am in fact perceiving the chair) or not (when I erroneously take myself to be perceiving it).

No reason *as such*, therefore, can rule out the possibility that my belief is false, but only a reason that is veridical. Accordingly, I have to rule out the possibility that the reason I adduce is non-veridical. How do I do this? In just the way I did before: I need to provide a reason for my reason. Yet what happens now? At this stage, we discover that the attempt to rule out the possibility that my belief is false leads into an infinite regress, because the very problem this further reason was brought in to solve by ensuring that the first one actually rules out the possibility of the belief being false recurs, now with respect to this further evidence, and so on ad infinitum. This compels us to conclude that we can never know anything, for as finite beings we will have to break off this regress arbitrarily at some point, without ever reaching a reason that would exclude the possibility that our belief is false.

So much for the skeptic's line of thought. The skeptic assumes it to be a compelling one. That is, it seems to him to rest not on arbitrary assertions about the concept of knowledge, but only on reflections to which reason itself compels us. Contrary to Williams's short version, the above representation of the skeptical argument clarifies why the skeptic feels compelled to renew his question with respect to the evidence one has first cited to justify one's claim: the mere provid-ing of a reason does not suffice to establish the truth of any belief, because it is the mark of finite beings to be susceptible to error. The reasons available to finite beings are not *as such* veridical (for if they were, finite beings would be infalli-ble), but can be either veridical or non-veridical. Therefore, we—in contrast to be-ings incapable of error—have to vindicate our reasons. Thus, our inquiry into the concept of knowledge leads into a peculiar paradox: the paradox that we are forced to conclude, in the end, that we now know that we cannot know anything at all.

In what follows, I shall designate as *diagnostic* those objections to the skep-tic that do not attack him directly (e. g., by showing his position to be incoherent or self-contradictory), but rather refute him by uncovering a premise of his rea-soning which they hold to be less than compelling. According to such a diagno-sis, there is in the skeptic's reflections upon the concept of knowledge something one can call a mistake in the broadest sense of the word: the skeptic begins from some premise (which premise it is depends on the specifics of the diagnosis) that can be shown to be unconvincing.

Here one might think, however, that this diagnostic stance is condemned from the beginning to fail, since it could never suffice. In order to refute the skeptic, one would have to show that his position is *false*, not merely that it is *unconvincing*. This is how Crispin Wright, for instance, argues. He claims it does not suffice to tell this or that diagnostic story about some presupposition of the skeptic's argument and then to show that we can explicate the concept of knowledge without this presupposition. "We have to know," Wright insists, that "the [alternative] story is true. Otherwise the case is not proven, and skep-ticism triumphs at second order."[6]

I believe this is wrong. In order to refute the skeptic, it does actually suffice to show that his argument rests upon a premise nothing compels us to accept. There is from the very beginning an asymmetry between a philosophical position that leads us into skeptical doubt and one which does not leave room for such doubt. This is because it is not open to the skeptic to conceive of the doubt he discovers as merely a *possible* doubt. He must consider his doubt to be *unavoid-able*, i. e., as a doubt which any attempt to comprehend our concept of knowl-edge necessarily encounters. Only then can he think of his skeptical conclusion as one arrived at by *reason* and not as indicating his reason's *weakness*.[7] For this

---

6 Wright 1985, 461.

7 Compare on this point Descartes's argument in the fourth paragraph of the First Meditation, where he claims that he would already have had to imagine himself akin to a madman with a diseased brain were he now to want to doubt—without any plausible reason—that he is sitting at

is precisely what the diagnosis claims to be the case: that the skeptic's failure to understand how we can know anything has its cause not in the matter itself, but is expressive of an incapacity on the side of the skeptic. This means that any non-skeptical position at which we arrive by rejecting as unconvincing a particular premise of the skeptic as such represents a rejection of skeptical doubt. Skeptical doubt is reasonable only if such a position is impossible. Hence Wittgenstein is right to suggest, "In philosophy we must always ask: 'How must we look at this problem for it to become solvable?'"[8] In order to defend the rationality of his doubt, the skeptic has to insist that it is not only impossible for him but impossible in general to look at the problem in such a way as to allow it to be solved. Either the skeptic's doubt is unavoidable, or it simply does not exist.[9]

To confront the doubt of the skeptic seems therefore to be, one might think, surprisingly simple.

## 3

The skeptic is unable to see how human knowledge is possible. What accounts for his blindness? The skeptic insists that in order to be entitled to make a knowledge claim, we *must* adduce a reason which excludes the possibility of our belief's being false. And he claims that we *cannot* produce any such reason. The skeptic does not see any way to escape from skepticism because he does not see how he could abandon either of these two premises. He cannot abandon either the first premise, as it represents a compelling conceptual explication, nor the second, as it is expressive of an indisputable characteristic of our finitude.

We might straightaway challenge the correctness of the second premise. We might claim that we certainly are in a position to adduce a reason that excludes the possibility that our belief is false. The epistemic contextualist takes this to be impossible. The contextualist thinks: The skeptic is blind to what is most obvious, namely, that we are indeed able to have a wide variety of knowledge, but he sees something nonetheless, namely, our human finitude, which consists in our inability to establish the truth of our beliefs by adducing reasons. So, according to the contextualist, we cannot dispute the skeptic's second premise, for then

---

his fireplace, clad in a winter dressing-gown, etc. (Descartes 1984, 13). Also compare Hume 1978, 267–8, and the commentary in Cavell 1979, 129 ff.

**8** Wittgenstein 1977, §11.

**9** Michael Williams makes the same point: "[I]f a coherent, non-skeptical epistemology can be developed from within our ongoing theories of the world, we have everything we need" (Williams 2001, 197).

we would be contesting the fact of our finitude. We would presume ourselves capable of traversing the infinitely long road of justification. We do not know, perhaps, whether a divine intellect would be able to do this. Yet if we consider ourselves to be finite beings, we do know that such a maneuver is beyond *our* intellect. Our justifications come to an end at some point, without having reached the goal. This insight is one which, the contextualist believes, Wittgenstein continuously impresses upon us. "If I have exhausted the justifications I have reached bedrock, and my spade is turned," Wittgenstein says, "then I am inclined to say: 'This is simply what I do.'"[10]

Hence, according to the contextualist, we will emerge from the skeptic's problem only by contesting his first premise, which states that the normative status enjoyed by someone who is entitled to make a knowledge claim depends upon his ability to produce a reason for his claim. The contextualist's strategy now is to argue that the skeptic illegitimately deduces the impossibility of knowledge from the limitations of our ability to justify our claims because he links together, in his first premise, the concepts of knowledge and justification in a manner that is not compelling. In other words, the contextualist does not outright deny that knowledge is for us an ideal that requires us to justify our beliefs, but he suggests that the skeptic relies on an uncompelling interpretation of this ideal.

In this, the contextualist differs from an *externalist* diagnosis of the skeptic's mistake. According to this kind of diagnosis, it is not only the skeptic's *interpretation* of the link between knowledge and justification that is uncompelling, but the assertion of this link as such. To connect knowledge and justification is, rather, to confuse two distinct levels which one needs to keep separate: on the one level are the conditions under which a particular belief has some particular epistemic status; on the other level are the conditions under which an individual subject is conscious of this status. For the externalist, to know that p means nothing more than that a truth-reliable method *in fact* engendered the belief that p. It is not required that I *know* that my belief was engendered by means of such a method. I would require knowledge of the justification of my knowledge only if I wanted to attain second-order knowledge, that is, if I wanted to know whether I know that p.

The externalist claims that the skeptic becomes a skeptic because he sets much too high a standard for knowledge. The externalist believes we can devise a more moderate standard in such a way that fulfillment of it is no longer something for which we have to *exert* ourselves, but something which either is or is

---

10 Wittgenstein 1998, §217.

not the case. But with this, he does not so much cut the standard down to size as redefine its character. The standard of knowledge would no longer have the character of an *ideal* one might fail to satisfy, but rather the character of a *fact* that might or might not hold. If my belief that there is a chair in front of me is knowledge, this expresses not my successful effort at satisfying an ideal, but the fact that my perceptual system is in proper working order.

Such a proposal is—at least for the skeptic—completely aberrant. I mentioned Kant's idea that the mistake of the skeptic consists in his inability to see our human finitude as being anything other than an obstacle preventing us from attaining the ideal of knowledge. The revelation that our finitude represents no obstacle because knowledge is not something over which one has to exert oneself is worth about as much as the attempt to reassure a professional sprinter who is nervous that a knee injury he has suffered will narrow his chances of winning a competition by telling him that the race won't be decided by the exertions of the competitors but by the umpires' drawing lots. If we wish to understand how, as beings whose reason is finite, we are capable of knowing, surely it will not help us to be told that knowledge is not an attainment of reason.

# 4

As Robert Brandom puts it, knowledge is a matter of our "sapience," not our "sentience."[11] We might also say: knowledge is an ideal we seek to attain, not something that simply happens to us. In other words, the concept of knowledge has a *normative* character: one must acquire an *entitlement* to claim knowledge. The skeptic, I said, does not see any way of escaping from skepticism because he does not see how he could give up either of the two premises of his argument. As the contextualist believes we cannot contest the skeptic's second premise (which holds that on account of our finitude we are incapable of providing a reason that would exclude the possibility that our claims are false), he must consider it possible to contest the first: namely, the premise that to be entitled to claim knowledge we must cite a reason that rules out the possibility that our assertion is false. The contextualist seeks to provide a diagnosis of the justification-requirement formulated by this first premise, one that will reveal the requirement to be pure invention.

What is it, the contextualist asks himself, that brings the skeptic to believe that one always has to earn the entitlement to make a knowledge-claim by way

---

11 Brandom 1994, 5. See also Williams 2001, 149.

of providing reasons for it? The answer given by the contextualist's diagnosis runs as follows: The skeptic can believe this only if he presupposes that doubting a knowledge claim does not itself need to be justified in order to be legitimate. The skeptic assumes that such a doubt is, in any situation whatsoever, a *justified* doubt. Only on this basis can he demand that one needs to cite a ground that dismisses this doubt for *any* belief of which one claims knowledge. Thus, the diagnosis insists that the skeptic's justification-requirement rests upon a conception that releases doubt from the burden of itself requiring justification. According to Williams, the skeptic "must deny that, to be reasonable, a challenge to a knowledge-claim itself needs to be motivated by reasons."[12]

Yet the contextualist thinks that we can reject this conception. It is by no means compelling, he will argue. In fact, it represents nothing other than a tenacious prejudice. As Brandom writes: "One of the lessons we have learned from thinking about hyperbolic Cartesian doubt is that doubts too sometimes need to be justified in order to have the standing to impugn entitlement to doxastic commitments."[13] If we wish to act upon the lesson contextualists think we have learned from our dealings with skeptical doubt, then we will have to interpret the standard for knowledge differently from the skeptics—namely, in such a way that the justification-requirement no longer applies to any belief independent of context, but rather depends upon whether, in a given context, there exists a justified doubt about a particular belief. Entitlement to a knowledge-claim is not something one has to *attain* by adducing a reason; it is something one must merely *defend* whenever reasons are adduced which render it doubtful.

Thus, the contextualist arrives at the following explication of the concept of knowledge: someone has knowledge only when, firstly, his belief is in fact true and, secondly, there is in the given context no reason to doubt that it is.

The standard for knowledge is thus defined as essentially dependent upon context. What one has to do in order to meet the standard is not defined independently of context, but differs according to the particular context. Thus, it could be that in a particular context one may legitimately claim knowledge of a belief p only if one can justify p, for in this context there exists a justified doubt about the truth of p, while in a different context, one could be entitled to claim knowledge of p without having to undertake any justification, for in this different context there is no justified doubt about the truth of p.

With this, the contextualist believes he has found a way around the skeptical problem. He believes himself able to show that the ideal of knowledge we strive

---

12 Williams 2001, 150.
13 Brandom 1994, 117.

to fulfill actually requires less from us than the skeptic assumes. The skeptic interprets this ideal such that it demands something impossible. However, the skeptic's first premise by no means contains an indisputable conceptual clarification; rather, it gives expression to a prejudice that we can easily dispense with. If we render the standard for knowledge dependent upon context in such a way that the justification-requirement, in contrast to the truth-requirement, represents a context-dependent element that becomes operative only in those contexts in which a justified doubt exists, then we can conclude that our finitude is not an obstacle to knowledge. For we do not have to follow the road of justification to infinity in order to reach our goal, but rather only until there no longer is, in the given context, a justified doubt about our belief. That at some point our reasons "give out," as Wittgenstein remarks, does not by any means compel us to believe that knowledge is unattainable for us.[14]

# 5

Let us ask ourselves whether the contextualist is actually successful in construing the ideal of knowledge in such a way as to allow us to see how we are able to attain knowledge. According to him, a belief must be both true and adequately justified if it is to amount to knowledge. But what is, in the contextualist's view, the significance of the justification? The justification does not, as he explains the matter, aim positively to establish the truth of the belief. Rather, its purpose is the dialectical or defensive one of carrying out liquidation of any doubt concerning that truth. We have to justify our belief only if there is, in the given context, a justified doubt about it. Consequently, the contextualistic construal of knowledge reduces the requirements of justification by defining *the significance of the justification* differently from how the skeptic does: the justification is not linked internally to the truth-requirement for knowledge, but rather represents an *additional* requirement alongside it.

For the skeptic this is not so. For him the justification-requirement is not an additional requirement alongside the truth-requirement; rather, the latter determines the significance of the former. For why does the skeptic believe that one needs, in each and every context, to earn the entitlement to a knowledge-claim by adducing reasons? He thinks so because, in his view, to be entitled to a knowledge-claim is to be in a position to rule out the possibility that the claim is false. And the function of justification is to do precisely this—to rule

---

14 Wittgenstein 1998, §211.

out the possibility that the claim is false, and thereby to establish that it is true. Thus, for the skeptic, justification is linked *internally* to truth. And it is, he insists, precisely for this reason that one must always justify one's statements if one wants legitimately to obtain the status of knowledge for them.

Let us ask what is achieved by the contextualist's reduction of the extent to which justification is required. Let us suppose that I have liquidated every justified doubt concerning some belief of mine. Then in the eyes of the contextualist I have done all that I need and can do in order legitimately to claim the status of knowledge for that belief. And yet what is it that I have actually done? I have satisfied the justification-requirement for knowledge. In meeting the justification-requirement, however, I have not yet met the truth-requirement. This is precisely the point of disputing the internal connection between truth and justification—as one must if one wants to assert that it is possible to be entitled to a knowledge-claim without having earned this entitlement by providing reasons.[15] It is just because the justification, for the contextualist, is not meant to establish the truth of the claim at hand but only functions in a dialectical or defensive manner that the truth-requirement can be unmet even if the justification-requirement has been fulfilled. If I have satisfied the justification-requirement, then for my part I have done everything I can legitimately to claim knowledge. Yet whatever I can do, there will remain a gap between my judgment's being justified and its being true. But then the fact that I am entitled to claim knowledge is, *in every instance*, compatible with the fact that the object of my knowledge is actually other than as I know it to be. And this is simply incoherent. For a belief cannot represent knowledge for me if at the same time I have to concede that it might be untrue.

Whether my judgment is not only justified but also true is something which always remains an open question for the contextualist. If the world wishes to favor me, it will take care to ensure that precisely those judgments that are best supported by reasons are actually true. Yet whether the world in fact does so favor me will always remain a mystery. Even the slightest gap between a belief's justification and its truth will become infinitely large when we face the challenge of deciding whether we know something or not. If in no case my reasons decide whether things are as I believe them to be—and this means: if in every case things could, despite my reasons, be otherwise—then I can never know anything at all.[16]

---

15 To assert, in other words, that there exist some beliefs having so-called "default-status." Cf., Williams 2001, Chapter 13, and also Williams 2013 (in this volume). Also see Brandom 1994, 117 ff.

16 Cf., McDowell 1998b, esp. 402–6.

It seems to me that contextualism turns out to be a version of skepticism and not a response to it. This entails, negatively, that the contextualist's diagnosis, according to which the skeptic is driven to his conclusion because he proposes an exaggerated justification-requirement for knowledge, is revealed as false. Giving up the skeptic's justification-requirement in favor of a contextualistic conception of justification does not yield the desired result: the skeptical problem is not dispelled, but reappears elsewhere.

# 6

Our finitude turns out to be an insurmountable obstacle to knowledge on the contextualist's conception as well as on the skeptic's. Although the separation of the requirements for justification and for truth would allow us to fulfill the former, the price to be paid is our inability to establish the truth of our beliefs by adducing reasons.

At this point, I would like to claim that the contextualist remains blind to the incoherence of his position because he vacillates between two different, mutually exclusive conceptions of the skeptic. The contextualist must entertain both conceptions at once if he is to find his diagnosis of the skeptical problem satisfactory.

The contextualist's *first* conception suggests that the skeptical conclusion rests on the fact that the skeptic endlessly repeats the question "How do you know?" even when he has no reason for raising the question. The skeptic takes himself to be entitled to repeat the question without having earned that entitlement by way of giving reasons. If the contextualist understands the skeptic in this way, then his diagnosis is indeed correct—the diagnosis according to which the skeptic's requirement that one has to give reasons in order to be entitled to have knowledge rests on the prejudice that one does not need to give reasons in order to be entitled to raise doubts. We can very well abandon this prejudice and assert instead that we do not need to exclude every doubt concerning the truth of our beliefs, but only doubts that are justified. And this constraint, so it seems, makes it possible for finite beings to satisfy the conditions of knowledge.

However, I have already indicated above that this understanding of the skeptic makes no sense; it represents the skeptic as though he were a child who, without understanding, pesters his parents with an endless series of "But why?" questions. If the skeptic were simply to repeat his question without understanding and without any reason for doing so, there would be no *philosophical* problem for which contextualism would provide a solution, for in that case, the skeptic's infinite regress would result not from a "profound and intense reflection" on the concept of knowledge, but rather from a perhaps amusing play with words which would have no philosophical significance.[17] One does not need philosophy to stop such a regress.

To this objection, the contextualist would probably respond that *of course* we have to understand the skeptic as someone who *believes* he has a good reason for his doubt. We need, then, to reconstruct the skeptic's discovery as proceeding in two steps—that is, precisely in the way I did when I substituted Williams's vague description of the skeptical thought with a more detailed description that was supposed to reveal the reason which forces the skeptic to repeat his question infinitely. Given this two-step reconstruction, however, the contextualistic diagnosis of the skeptic's mistake cannot be accepted. Let us see why. The skeptic's first move, according to this diagnosis, consists in claiming (a) that in order to know that something is the case, one has to rule out the possibility that one's belief is false, and (b) that the only manner in which one can do that consists in justifying one's belief. The justification-requirement proposed by the skeptic is put forward only in order to establish the truth of one's belief. That is what has to be established, and it is for this reason alone that the skeptic claims we need to justify our beliefs. The purpose of the justification is to exclude the possibility that one's belief is false. The skeptic thinks of this connection between truth and justification as simply providing an unobjectionable conceptual explication of what it means for a belief, in contrast to a mere opinion, to count as knowledge.[18]

The skeptic, in a second move, discovers that it is impossible to rule out the possibility that a belief is false by way of giving reasons for it. This he does by virtue of interpreting an indisputable metaphysical insight, namely, that we human beings are essentially susceptible to error, as expressing an *epistemological* point: our susceptibility to error derives from the nature of the reasons we are able to give for our beliefs. It lies in the nature of these reasons that it is possible for us to have a reason for believing our belief is true while in fact it is false.

---

**17** Concerning reasonableness as representing an essential characteristic of the skeptic's self-understanding, see Cavell 1979, 130 ff.

**18** This distinction between knowledge and mere opinion is so generally acknowledged and obvious that Kant considered it virtually a waste of time to discuss the matter. In a passage in the third section of the "Canon of Pure Reason" in the first *Critique*, where he briefly outlines the differences among the three modes of holding something to be true (namely opinion, knowledge, and belief), he concludes by informing us that "I shall not linger upon the elucidation of such readily comprehensible concepts" (Kant 1996, A822/B850). See also *The Jäsche Logic*, in Kant 1992, ix, esp. 570 ff.

For instance, I can perceive that there is a chair across from me, and thus have a reason to believe it is there; but my perception can be wrong because I am hallucinating, for example, or because I am dreaming, or because I am a brain in a vat made to think that on the other side of the room there is a chair. Consequently, it does not suffice, on account of our susceptibility to error, simply to perceive that something is the case in order to know that it is true; rather, one must also know that one's perception is veridical. Whether something is actually the case can be known only once one knows that one's perception is veridical.

Only in this second, self-reflexive move are the so-called skeptical error-possibilities brought into play. The skeptic raises these error-possibilities when he poses himself the question whether the reasons we cite in support of our beliefs are actually capable of ruling out the falsity of those beliefs. The skeptical error-possibilities enter the skeptic's argument precisely at the point where he raises the question of whether our reasons are capable of establishing the truth of our beliefs.

Thus, the role of the skeptical error-possibilities consists in making clear to us that our reasons are worth nothing by themselves, because as finite beings, our reasons have the characteristic that they can be either veridical or non-veridical. The error-possibilities are supposed to *illustrate* that it is characteristic of our finitude that our reasons as such can be either veridical or non-veridical.[19] And this means that they first become valuable once we have ascertained their veridical character. However, that is precisely what the skeptic's discovery shows us to be incapable of accomplishing.

Properly speaking, therefore, the regress of justification the skeptic discovers is not so much a regress in the attempt to *justify one's belief* (we endlessly require further and further reasons) as a regress in the attempt to *justify one's justification*, because it represents a demand that one produce reasons for one's reasons. It is a regress that arises at the precise moment when the justification turns upon itself and requires that it be justified as well.

If, however, the skeptic's discovery cannot be understood otherwise than as a discovery of the impossibility of justifying justification, then the contextualist is simply wrong to issue the diagnosis that the requirement of the skeptic that one always has to justify one's belief in order to be entitled to have knowledge

---

**19** I find that the question of closure (i.e., whether our knowledge is closed under known entailment) represents, with respect to skepticism, a thoroughgoing misunderstanding, for it is based upon the mistaken assumption that the role of the skeptical error-possibilities is to define some particular possibility of error that we then have to rule out if we are to attain certain knowledge. Compare, for instance, the debate among: Nozick 1991; Dretske 1999; Stine 1999; and Williams 1996, Chapters 5 and 8.

depends upon a conception of doubt as itself not needing to be justified. The skeptic does not propose the justification-requirement for knowledge because he has absolved his doubt from the obligation of being justified. Rather, it is just the reverse: his justification-requirement represents the premise that makes the doubt he insists must be overcome meaningful in the first place— the doubt concerning the capacity of our reasons to establish the truth. That is, the skeptic's justification-requirement is the very *presupposition* needed if that doubt, which the skeptic claims must be surpassed, is even *to arise* at all. And what directly provokes this doubt is nothing other than the skeptic's *metaphysical insight* into our finitude. Accordingly, the skeptic's doubt is understood by him to be nothing but an expression of that insight. There then remains merely a simple alternative: either this doubt about the capacity of our reasons to establish truth must be excluded, or we are able to clarify the capacity of our reasons to establish truth in such a way as to reveal the doubt to represent not an expression but rather a profound misunderstanding of our finitude. At this juncture, it is senseless to say that only *justified* doubt need be overcome, because the doubt with which the skeptic is concerned has, in his view, a metaphysical reason: namely, our finitude.[20]

With this, the following problem is posed for the contextualist's diagnosis. On the one hand, if he conceives of the skeptic solely in the first way, then a conception of knowledge that requires doubt to be justified would indeed provide a solution to the skeptical problem. But in that case, the contextualist would be attacking a mirage, not a philosophical problem. On the other hand, the contextualist might concede that the skeptic's discovery cannot be summarized in this manner and accordingly adopts the second conception. But then the contextualist's diagnosis—namely, that the skeptic's justification-requirement for knowledge depends upon a conception of doubt as itself exempt from the justification-requirement—turns out to be mistaken. The skeptic has a reason for his doubt, namely, our finitude. Consequently, the contextualist's strategy of establishing the possibility of knowledge by claiming that the justification-requirement comes into play only in certain contexts, depending on whether some justified doubt exists, would seem to be an aberrant undertaking.[21]

---

20 In the Fourth Meditation, Descartes expressly claims that his doubt has a metaphysical basis. Cf., Descartes 1984, 38 ff. A doubt of this kind cannot be countered by claiming that it is unjustified, but only by overturning the metaphysical foundation it is based upon.

21 Equally aberrant, therefore, are the attempts to limit skeptical doubt by establishing criteria of relevance, as undertaken (among others) by Putnam 1998 and Lewis 1999. Putnam and Lewis comprehend neither the self-reflexive character of the doubt with which the skeptic is concerned, nor his claiming a metaphysical foundation for it, because they take this foundation to be

The contextualist does not see the incoherence of his own position, for he fails to perceive that he simultaneously entertains two different, mutually exclusive conceptions of the skeptic and his doubt. He fails to see that there is a difference between (a) the claim that in order to know something, one must exclude the possibility that one is mistaken by justifying one's claim, and (b) the claim that in order to know, one needs to rule out the possibility of one's justification being mistaken by justifying one's justification. The skeptic, for his part, believes that, for finite beings, the first of these claims necessarily entails the second. The contextualist notices no difference between them, which is why he thinks that making the justification-requirement dependent upon the context represents the only way to escape the skeptic's conclusion.[22]

# 7

The contextualist believes (as does the externalist) that skeptical doubt has its source in the skeptic's having proposed a standard for knowledge that makes demands upon human beings so great as to render their fulfillment impossible for us. This standard, he thinks, can be moderated.[23] However, the only thing which has been shown so far is that there are two explications of the ideal of knowledge, one which is knowingly skeptical, and one which cherishes the illusion of being not skeptical. We are confronted with, to borrow a phrase from Stroud, a "familiar pattern in the theory of knowledge": we seem to have a choice between an unsatisfactory skepticism and one or another theory of knowledge that, as soon as we consider it more carefully, no longer satisfies us any more than does the skeptical position it was meant to refute.[24]

---

so self-evident that they no longer even recognize that the skeptic has based his doubt entirely upon it alone.

**22** For a more detailed criticism of the contextualist's position, see Kern 2006, 107–32.

**23** The strategies of those who wish to moderate the standard for knowledge always argue that the skeptic sets this standard higher than is needed to understand the concept of knowledge. De Rose's argument exemplifies this view: the skeptic, he writes, imposes "very high standards that we don't live up to." That we cannot satisfy these standards, according to De Rose, does not mean, however, that we cannot fulfill "the more relaxed standards" established by the concept of knowledge that has its place in our "more ordinary conversations and debates" (De Rose 1999, 207). Regardless of such distinctions, however, it seems to me that any claim that the skeptic arrives at his conclusion "by raising the standards for knowledge" will come to naught, for it rests upon the same misunderstanding in which the contextualist is entangled.

**24** Stroud 1984, 168.

I think that this uncomfortable conclusion is unavoidable so long as we continue to believe that the skeptic's mistake consists in demanding, in one way or another, *too much* from us. When Kant suggested that the mistake of the skeptic's philosophy consists in thinking of our finitude as an obstacle, he did not mean that the source of the skeptic's doubt should be sought in the skeptic's having formulated an ideal of knowledge that is unattainable for finite beings. He did not, in other words, mean that the skeptic entertains a false conception of the ideal of knowledge; rather, he meant that it is the skeptic's conception of our finitude that is false: the conception that it is a basic characteristic of our finitude that our reasons can be either veridical or non-veridical such that, in order to justify the truth of our beliefs, we have to set out on an infinite road we cannot but abandon at some point without the goal of the justification having been attained.

According to Kant, it is this false picture of our finitude that represents the actual root of the skeptic's doubt. A way out of skepticism opens up only if we acknowledge that the skeptic's second premise (the premise that our reasons do not suffice to establish the truth of a claim) is by no means an expression of our finitude but rather an indication of its having been thoroughly misjudged. The skeptic becomes a skeptic, Kant thinks, because he underestimates our finitude. The skeptic (and the contextualist with him) considers our susceptibility to error to be the deepest feature of our finitude. Thus, he is able to comprehend this feature as being only *epistemological* in nature: we are finite in that our reasons are either veridical or non-veridical. This is precisely why he thinks that we must set out on an infinite road of justification. The skeptic discovers a regress of justification because he has given a specific epistemological interpretation to the indisputable metaphysical insight that we human beings are essentially prone to error: he attributes this susceptibility to the nature of the reasons we are able to offer for our beliefs.

Yet our beliefs' susceptibility to error is not the most fundamental characteristic of our finitude. It itself is, Kant suggests, the result of a much more deep-seated finitude located in the essential structure of our knowledge itself.[25] Kant clarifies the finitude of our knowledge by distinguishing it formally from infinite knowledge. Infinite knowledge, according to Kant, is the knowledge that is not in any way limited by that which it knows.[26] That can only be the case if this knowledge first creates its own contents by knowing them. Infinite

---

25 For what follows, compare Heidegger 1997a, 18 ff (German edition: Heidegger 1991, 25 ff); and Heidegger 1997b, 56 ff (German edition: Heidegger 1988, 81 ff).
26 See Kant 1996, B72f. and B138f.

knowledge, therefore, is fundamentally knowledge-creating. Finite knowledge, by contrast, is incapable of producing by itself the contents which it knows; it depends upon the contents of its knowledge being given to it. Hence, finite knowledge is (in the best case) objective knowledge. This, according to Kant, is the real reason for the finitude of our knowledge: that knowledge is possible at all only "insofar as the object is given to us."[27] We are not finite because we, in contrast to the divine mind, are able to err and thus have to support our beliefs with a sequence of reasons that terminates without their goal having been reached. Rather, that we can err represents an "essential consequence" of the fundamental finitude of our knowledge.[28] And this fundamental finitude consists in our "being dependent" (*Angewiesensein*) upon the contents of our knowledge being given to us, in our having to "take them in stride" (*hinnehmen*).[29]

It is obvious that a being whose knowledge is creative does not have to support his beliefs by reasons in order to be certain of their truth. Creative knowledge as such is true. Hence, not only is it not necessary to justify creative knowledge, it is pointless to do so. If the knowledge is itself the origin of that which is known, the idea of an independent justification makes no sense. By contrast, the beliefs of a being whose knowledge is objective—that is, a being to whom the content of his knowledge must be given—can either be true or false. Hence, such a being must justify his beliefs in order to be certain of their truth. This is precisely what the skeptic claims, and here he is completely right.

Yet the real question to be asked in view of our finitude is not the one in which the skeptic and after him the contextualist are entangled: the question of how a being that is finite can give his beliefs the epistemic status of knowledge. For that question takes for granted what, in view of our finitude, must first be clarified, namely, that our beliefs have a *content*. Hence, the real question put before us in view of our finitude is this: in the case of a being whose finitude consists in his having to let the contents of his knowledge be *given* to him, how are his beliefs able to have content? To understand that human knowledge is in essence finite means, for Kant, to comprehend how this "taking in stride" (*hinnehmen*)— in virtue of which alone our knowledge can have content—is possible. Kant's answer is that it is only possible if the objects of the world "stir" our senses and thus are given to us to intuit, and this, for its part, can only happen when our intellect, which shows us how things are, is being "set in motion."[30] Thus, Kant's inquiry into the essence of our finitude leads him to the discovery

---

27 Kant 1996, B33.
28 See Heidegger 1997a, 17 (German edition: 25).
29 Heidegger 1997b, 59 (German edition: 86), and Heidegger 1997a, 18 (German edition: 26)
30 Kant 1996, B1.

that our knowledge can only have a content when it lets one be provided in a sensuous experience of the world—an experience that is not neutral with respect to the question whether things are this or that way, but rather contains an answer to this question, an answer the world itself impresses upon us by means of our senses.[31] Our knowledge can have content, according to Kant, only if it is based upon a sensuous experience that contains a claim about the world, a claim sensuously impressed upon us by the world itself. Beliefs about the world that have not let content be given to them in that way are not unjustified, according to Kant, but rather are without any content at all.

The skeptic thinks that a finite intellect can give its beliefs the epistemic status of knowledge only by furnishing a justification. This thought is not the origin of his mistake, however, but embodies his deepest insight. Yet the skeptic is mistaken when he thinks a justification is as such unable to give a belief the status of knowledge. He is mistaken because he fails to see that a belief of a finite intellect only has the *content* that it does when it lets that content be given to it through a sensuous experience in which the world impresses the content upon it. That the human intellect has finite knowledge does not mean that he can only finitely justify his beliefs; it means that his beliefs have the content they do only by virtue of a justification that ends in a claim about the world that the world itself has sensuously impressed upon him.

# 8

And yet, one might be inclined to respond, in essence we are prone to error. This cannot be denied. Not at all. Of course we can err. However, our susceptibility to error has to be understood differently. The skeptic is only able to understand it as an epistemological matter, for he considers it to be the real basis of our finitude. But when we see that, on the contrary, the basis of our finitude actually consists in our depending upon the world's giving us the contents of our knowledge, then we have to think of our susceptibility to error as arising from this deeper source of the finitude of our knowledge. When we err, it is not because our reasons are, with their narrow scope, as such unable to tell us whether a belief is true or false, but rather because our reason in this particular instance was only an *apparent* reason. It only seemed to us as though the world were impressing a particular claim sensuously upon us, whereas in fact the world did not do so. If we err, we were not simply wrong to have considered a particular belief to be true;

---

31 Cf., McDowell 1998a, 440.

we erred in trusting the reason for that belief. When we acknowledge our mistake, this does not mean what the skeptic thinks it does, namely, that we recognize that we did indeed have reason to believe that such-and-such was the case although in fact it was not; it means we recognize that it only looked as though we had a reason to believe it to be the case. Whenever we are in error, we are entirely in error—with respect not only to the *truth* but also to the *content* of our beliefs. When we discover an error, we recognize not only that our judgment was false, but that the content of our judgment (or of some part of it) was not given to us by means of the senses at all, although it had seemed that way to us.

Our beliefs' susceptibility to error is a consequence of our needing to have the claims that constitute the content of our judgments impressed upon us by means of the senses. It is because they have to be impressed upon us that error is possible: error occurs when it seems to us as though a particular claim had been impressed upon us and yet that was not in fact the case. Yet for this to happen presupposes that the circumstances were unusual. Unusual circumstances are those in which we believe we experience something sensuously when in fact we do not. For instance, when the stick whose form we are judging is partially immersed in water and therefore appears to be crooked when in truth it is straight; or when the necktie whose color we are trying to determine is viewed in artificial light and therefore seems to be blue, although in fact it is green. Under unusual circumstances such as when the stick is half submerged in water, we cannot *see* that the stick really is straight. We may stare as intensely as we like; we do not manage to take in the form of the stick through our eyes.

There are other circumstances of which we know in advance that, in such circumstances, we are unable to perceive how things are, as when, for instance, it is pitch black and we try to read a book. In such a case it is obvious that we cannot even see what is written in the book. But this comes as no surprise, whereas the appearance of the stick immersed in water may well astonish us. We believe we see its form but in fact we do not. This is a deception that, had we never before experienced or been informed of it, we would be powerless to prevent. On the other hand, under normal circumstances nothing is easier, when a stick is in front of our eyes, than to perceive it and thus to know its form.

At this point, it is easy to succumb to a skeptical panic and, like Sellars, ask oneself whether the consequence is that in order to know something I not only have to perceive it, but also have to know that the circumstances of perception are normal.[32] But then the question would arise of how I could know that. And it seems clear that I can know it only by way of perceiving it. But such a perception

---

32 Cf., Sellars 1963, §22. On this, see also McDowell 1998a, 474.

can only reliably inform me that the circumstances are normal if I not only perceive that they are normal, but also know that the circumstances under which I perceive this are in turn normal, and so on infinitely. It would appear, then, as though all has been for naught, for evoking normal circumstances suddenly confronts us yet again with a regress seemingly as unstoppable as the original skeptical regress.

Yet the idea that we have to know that the circumstances are normal if we are to have knowledge can only occur to someone who has misunderstood the point of the foregoing discussion of our susceptibility to error. Only someone who continues to think of this susceptibility in a solely epistemological way, as deriving from the nature of our reasons, can still fall prey to this misunderstanding. It is precisely such a merely epistemological understanding of our susceptibility to error that becomes impossible once we conceive of our knowledge as being finite in essence. For then we can no longer think of a sensuous experience as something that is neutral with respect to the world; rather, the very idea of sensuous experience implies the idea of our having a relation to the objects in the world such that, in this relation, they reveal themselves to us. The idea of "normal circumstances" is then no longer an *additional* idea with which the idea of sensuous experience needs to be supplemented in order to clarify when a sensuous experience has a world-revealing character and when not. Rather, the idea of normal circumstances articulates an *inner characteristic* of sensuous experience itself—a characteristic one cannot extricate from the idea of sensuous experience without dissolving this idea altogether.[33]

# 9

Our reasons for our beliefs come to an end, yet they do so neither because, in the unending process of justification, we run out of time, interest, or imagination, as the skeptic thinks, nor because in a moment of need the context heeds our call for help and ensures that there is no further reason for doubt, as does the contextualist, but rather simply because there is an end to the sequence of reasons we need to give. This end is reached precisely whenever we come up against the experience responsible for our belief's having just the content it does. The sequence of reasons does not terminate indifferently here or there, but concludes

---

33 The relation between normal circumstances and the idea of perception is developed in more detail in Kern 2006, 276–313, as well as in Kern 2011.

precisely whenever we cite as the reason for a belief the reason that gives it its content. And then any further justification is not only unnecessary, but pointless.

Both the skeptic and the contextualist consider our susceptibility to error to be the deepest characteristic of our finitude and therefore think of our finitude as an epistemological matter, as characterizing the nature of our reasons. These, they believe, do not reveal the world *as such* to us, but permit us at best only a glimpse of how things out there might look. Hence, while I might collect any number of reasons that license the belief that such-and-such is the case, I will advance no further. I can pace up and down in the space of reasons, the contextualist and the skeptic think; yet to answer the question of *truth*, the world must meet me halfway. I cannot take the last step to knowledge alone: the world must come to me. Kant saw that our finitude runs deeper than the skeptic suspected. When we clarify our faculty of knowledge in light of human finitude as seen by Kant, then it becomes clear that the idea that drives the skeptic into his regress represents not a heroic recognition of our finitude, but rather the most thoroughgoing denial of it. We are finite not because we are capable of error, but because we depend upon the world to provide us with the appearances we must take up by means of our senses if we are to have even a single belief about the world.

Yet what if, someone might object one last time, we are delivered over to nothing more than mere appearances? What if the unusual circumstances in which we believe we see something—although in fact we do not—are indeed our normal condition? Whoever would like to ask this may do so. But he does not confront us with a skeptical problem. The problem of the skeptic, I stated at the outset, only arises when we, by means of reflections to which reason appears to compel us, are no longer able to understand how it is possible for us to know that, for instance, there is a chair standing here. Metaphysical considerations were meant to resolve a problem *of this type*, one in which our reason can entangle us. My objective has not been to respond to questions with regard to which it cannot be seen how anyone's reason could have led them to be posed. No skeptic conceives of his doubt as resulting from an arbitrarily raised question.

And yet the impossibility of answering such a question allows us to view our finitude, as it were, from the other side. For it makes clear that if the world never allowed itself to be seen by us—that is, if all we were ever given were mere appearances—we could do nothing about it. We would be condemned never to have even the slightest reason for any belief whatsoever about the world. That we are finite means that our existence as rational thinking beings depends, metaphysically speaking, upon the world's actually being, at times, as it appears to us to be.

Thus, the world actually does have to meet us halfway, yet not where the skeptic suspects, namely, in order to make our beliefs true. The world does not make the last move; it makes the first. It has to advance toward us if we are to enter the space of reasons at all. But once it has done so, then whenever we enter the space of reasons, we enter at the same time the space of the world.

*Translated from German by Jack Ben-Levi*
*(Revised by Roger E. Eichorn)*

# Bibliography

Brandom, Robert (1994), *Making It Explicit: Reasoning, Representing, and Discursive Commitment*, Cambridge, MA: Harvard University Press.

Cavell, Stanley (1979), *The Claim of Reason: Wittgenstein, Skepticism, Morality, and Tragedy*, Oxford: Oxford University Press.

Descartes, Réne (1984), *Meditations on First Philosophy.* In: Réne Descartes, *The Philosophical Writings of Descartes, Volume II*, John Cottingham, Robert Stoothoff, and Dugald Murdoch (trans.), Cambridge: Cambridge University Press.

De Rose, Keith, "Solving the Skeptical Problem." In: Keith De Rose and Ted A. Warfield (eds.), *Skepticism: A Contemporary Reader*, Oxford: Oxford University Press, 183–219.

Dretske, Fred (1999), "Epistemic Operators." In: Keith De Rose and Ted A. Warfield (eds.), *Skepticism: A Contemporary Reader*, Oxford: Oxford University Press, 131–44.

Heidegger, Martin (1988), *Phänomenologische Interpretation von Kants Kritik der reinen Vernunft*, Frankfurt am Main: Klostermann.

Heidegger, Martin (1991), *Kant und das Problem der Metaphysik*, Frankfurt am Main: Klostermann.

Heidegger, Martin (1997a), *Kant and the Problem of Metaphysics*, Fifth Edition, Richard Taft (trans.), Bloomington and Indianapolis: Indiana University Press.

Heidegger, Martin (1997b), *Phenomenological Interpretation of Kant's Critique of Pure Reason*, Parvis Emad and Kenneth Maly (trans.), Bloomington and Indianapolis: Indiana University Press.

Hume, David (1978), *A Treatise of Human Nature*, L.A. Selby-Bigge (ed.), Second Edition, revised by P.H. Nidditch, Oxford: Oxford University Press.

Kant, Immanuel (1992), *Lectures On Logic*, J. Michael Young (trans.), Cambridge: Cambridge University Press.

Kant, Immanuel (1996), *Critique of Pure Reason*, Werner S. Pluhar (trans.), Indianapolis: Hackett.

Kern, Andrea (2006), *Quellen des Wissens. Zum Begriff vernünftiger Erkenntnisfähigkeiten*, Frankfurt am Main: Suhrkamp.

Kern, Andrea (2011), "Knowledge as a Fallible Capacity." In: Stefan Tolksdorf (ed.), *Conceptions of Knowledge*, Berlin: Walter de Gruyter.

Lewis, David (1999), "Elusive Knowledge." In: Keith De Rose and Ted A. Warfield (eds.), *Skepticism: A Contemporary Reader*, Oxford: Oxford University Press, 220–39.

McDowell, John (1998a), "Having the World in View: Sellars, Kant, and Intentionality." In: *Journal of Philosophy* 95, 431–91.

McDowell, John (1998b), "Knowledge and the Internal." In: John McDowell, *Meaning, Knowledge, and Reality*, Cambridge: Harvard University Press, 395–413.

Nozick, Robert (1991), *Philosophical Explanations*, Cambridge: Harvard University Press.

Putnam, Hilary (1998), "Skepticism." In: Marcello Stamm (ed.), *Philosophie in synthetischer Absicht*, Stuttgart: Klett-Cotta, 239–68.

Sellars, Wilfred (1963), "Empiricism and the Philosophy of Mind." In: Wilfred Sellars, *Science, Perception and Reality*, London: Routledge, 127–96.

Stine, Gail (1999), "Skepticism, Relevant Alternatives, and Deductive Closure." In: Keith De Rose and Ted A. Warfield (eds.), *Skepticism: A Contemporary Reader*, Oxford: Oxford University Press, 145–55.

Stroud, Barry (1984), *The Significance of Philosophical Scepticism*, Oxford: Oxford University Press.

Williams, Michael (1996), *Unnatural Doubts: Epistemological Realism and the Basis of Scepticism*, Princeton: Princeton University Press.

Williams, Michael (2001), *Problems of Knowledge: A Critical Introduction to Epistemology*, Oxford: Oxford University Press.

Williams, Michael (2014), "Knowledge, Reasons, and Causes: Sellars on Skepticism." In: James Conant and Andrea Kern (eds.), *Varieties of Skepticism: Essays After Kant, Wittgenstein, and Cavell*, Berlin and New York: Walter de Gruyter.

Wittgenstein, Ludwig (1977), *Remarks on Colour*, G.E.M. Anscombe (ed.), Linda L. McAlister and Margarete Schätte (trans.), Oxford: Basil Blackwell.

Wittgenstein, Ludwig (1998), *Philosophical Investigations*, G.E.M. Anscombe (trans.), Oxford: Blackwell.

Wright, Crispin (1985), "Facts and Certianty." In: *Proceedings of the British Academy* 71, 429–72.

Hilary Putnam

# Skepticism, Stroud, and the Contextuality of Knowledge

In my previous writings on the subject of skepticism,[1] I have relied on what might be called a contextualist view of language in general and of the verb "to know" and its counterparts in other languages in particular. A contextualist view of language (the view that, as Charles Travis has so brilliantly explained, lies at the heart of the views of language of J.L. Austin as well as of the later Wittgenstein),[2] does not, of course, claim that the *meanings* of sentences vary from context to context, or at least it does not claim that in *every* sense of that multiply ambiguous word "meaning," the meaning of a sentence that one understands changes whenever one finds oneself in a new context. In some sense it must be true that a speaker (as we say) "knows the meaning" of each sentence that he or she is able to use *prior* to using it or understanding another speaker's use of it in a new context and that this "knowledge of its meaning" plays an essential role in enabling the speaker to know what the sentence is being used to say in the context.

(Let me also say here that I do not think of meanings as either platonic objects or as mental objects; in my view, talk of meanings is best thought of as a way of saying something about certain world-involving[3] competences that speakers possess. And corresponding to those competences, there are constraints on what can be done with sentences without, as we say, "violating," or at least "extending" or "altering," their meaning.)

What contextualism *does* deny is that the "meaning" of a sentence in this sense determines the *truth-evaluable content* of that sentence. The thesis of contextualism is that in general *the truth-evaluable content of sentences depends both on what they mean (what a competent speaker knows prior to encountering a particular context) and on the particular context, and not on meaning alone.*

The easiest way to explain what I just said is with the aid of examples. Here is one that I used in a recent book:[4] every competent speaker of English knows

---

1 In particular, Putnam 1998a and 1998b.
2 See Travis 1981, Travis 1989, and Travis 2000.
3 My reasons for saying "*world-involving* competences" are, of course, the by-now-familiar reasons for "semantic externalism" that I laid out in "The Meaning of 'Meaning,'" (Putnam 1975) and in Chapter 2 of Putnam 1988.
4 Putnam 2000.

the meaning of the sentence, "There is a lot of coffee on the table." But *consistently with what it means*, it is possible to *understand* that sentence as saying:

(1) There is a lot of (brewed) coffee on the table (e.g. in cups or mugs).
    *Sample context:* "There is a lot of coffee on the table. Help yourself to a cup!"
(2) There are dozens of bags full of coffee beans on a table standing near a place where trucks come to get them and take them to a warehouse.
    *Sample context:* "There is a lot of coffee on the table. Load them in the truck."
(3) A lot of coffee has been spilled on a table.
    *Sample context:* "There is a lot of coffee on the table. Please wipe it up."

Note that in one and the same context, the *truth-value*—the truth or falsity—of the sentence, "There is a lot of coffee on the table" (or of the "content" that the speaker means to convey by uttering the sentence) will be quite different if the appropriate understanding of the sentence is as it is in the first example or as it is in the second or in the third (and the number of possible non-deviant *understandings* of the sentence is much greater than three—in fact, it is literally endless).

For example, if a speaker intends the first understanding and a hearer thinks the third understanding is meant, they will seriously misunderstand each other. Yet neither speaker nor hearer can be said *not to know the meaning* of the English sentence, "There is a lot of coffee on the table." Nor can the speaker be accused of misusing the sentence, or the hearer of understanding it in a way that would be a violation (or extension, etc.) of its meaning. Thus, there are at least three (in fact, as we just said, there are an endless number of) possible understandings of this sentence. And if the view Travis ascribes to Austin and Wittgenstein is right, this is typical of sentences in any natural language. I call these understandings "truth-evaluable contents" (this is my terminology, not Travis's) because in the contexts we (very roughly) described, they are typically sufficiently precise to be evaluated as true or false. (Note that even a vague sentence—"He stood roughly there—can often be evaluated as true or false *given an appropriate context*. But it is also the case that these "contents" themselves admit of further specification, i.e., admit of different understandings in different contexts.)[5]

I have just given a rough description of a kind of contextuality—the dependence of the truth-evaluable content of a sentence on features of the context of

---

**5** This point is stressed by Travis in Travis 2001.

use that are not determined simply by the sentence's meaning.[6] If this is indeed ubiquitous, it will follow, of course, that the truth-evaluable content of a sentence of the form *X knows that p* will depend on the particular context of utterance (or inscription) of the sentence. In the present essay, I will suggest that one way of reading Barry Stroud's extremely influential *The Significance of Philosophical Scepticism*[7] is as an attack on the idea that "know" is a context-dependent verb and that Stroud's attack must, in the end, be rejected as misguided. My procedure will be, first, briefly to summarize some of the ways in which it has been suggested that *know* is context-dependent, and to explain how this context-dependence has been claimed to be relevant to the problem of skepticism; and, secondly, to explain how I read Stroud as attacking this whole approach to skepticism—not just in the few pages in which he briefly considers (and quickly dismisses) it, but in the whole of the first three chapters of his book—and, simultaneously, to criticize his attack.

# The context-dependence of "know"

One of the ways (by no means the only way) in which "know" has been claimed to function as a context-dependent verb is the following: typically, it has been claimed, when one says, "I know that *p*," one is claiming that one is in a position to exclude a possible doubt concerning the truth of *p*.[8] This is not, in itself, a contextualist claim, but it becomes a contextualist claim if one adds that not

---

**6** Of course, certain sorts of context-dependence are recognized by all semantic theorists: for example, the dependence of the truth-value of a sentence containing a pronoun on the (contextually determined) bearer of the pronoun, the dependence of the truth-value of a sentence containing a demonstrative on the (contextually determined) reference of the demonstrative, and the dependence of the truth-value of a sentence containing a finite verb on the time at which the sentence is uttered. But the thesis defended by Wittgenstein, Austin, Travis, myself, and others is more radical, as the "coffee" example illustrates: the very *extension of common nouns and verbs* is (we hold) context-dependent.

**7** Stroud 1984.

**8** I believe that, in fact, the so-called "causal theory of knowledge" introduced by Peter Unger and later made popular by Robert Nozick, according to which "X knows that *p*" is true *even if X can in no way justify the claim that p* just as long as X's belief that *p* was caused by a process which reliably produces true beliefs (details vary from causal theorist to causal theorist), is wrong if regarded as a description of the most typical uses of "know," but does point to the fact that in some contexts we may say that someone "knows" even though there is no question of *their* being in a position to rule out relevant doubts at all.

every *conceivable* way in which *p* might be false is a "possible doubt"; a "possible doubt" must satisfy context-sensitive standards of *relevance.*[9]

The relevance to external-world skepticism is immediate, since the contextualist will point out that it is only in exceptional contexts that "I might be dreaming" (the skeptical possibility that is introduced by Descartes in the First Meditation and strongly emphasized by Stroud) counts as a relevant possibility, and if the skeptics were to concede that this shows that in a normal context the mere conceivability that "my experiences might be a dream" does not *contradict* my claim to know whatever it is I claim to know, they would have to abandon the most famous arguments that they have hitherto used to "show that we don't know that there is an external world."[10]

## Stroud's criticisms of contextualism

Here is an example which may illustrate what is at issue in the dispute between Stroud and the "contextualists":

Suppose my wife and I are on our way home, and she asks me, "Do you know if we have enough milk for breakfast?" I reply, "Yes, we do." (I was the one who put the milk bottle back in the refrigerator, and I remember it was more than half full.)

Now, imagine that a student who knows my family well and who is impressed by Stroud's arguments overhears this and immediately raises the following objection:

> "I know," the student says, "that your son has a key to your house. Isn't it possible that he stopped by your house today in your absence?"
> "But he would have been at work," I object.
> "Couldn't he have taken a day off?" the student says.
> "Well, he *could* have," I admit. "But I very much doubt that he did."
> "Still, you admit that he could have," the student continues. "And couldn't he have been thirsty and drunk up most or all of the milk?"

---

**9** When Stroud first (rather obliquely) refers to this sort of position, his formulation is that "there must be some 'special reason' for thinking a certain possibility might obtain" (63). This seems to me to be already loading the dice against the contextualist. Normally, we are not required to give reasons at all, let alone "special" reasons, for taking what are *obviously* relevant possibilities to be so. Stroud would perhaps reply that he didn't say we are required to *give* the reason that a given possibility is relevant in a given context; it is just that there has to *be* such a reason (one that a theorist could give, if not the ordinary speaker herself).
**10** See Chapter 1 of Stroud 1984.

"Of course he could have," I say, "*if* he was at my house. But there is no reason at all to think he was."
"Still, you don't *know* that he wasn't, do you?" (The student closes in for the "kill.")
"No, I don't," I admit.

The student will now conclude that I *don't* know that there is enough milk in the refrigerator for breakfast, and in fact that I never know any such thing (since this argument can be run on just about any day—even if I think my son is away in California, "Couldn't he have come back from his trip a day early?", etc.) But what I will tell my student is that I do not regard the logical (indeed the physical) possibility that my son did such an unusual thing as a "relevant possibility" and that I regard what I said to my wife as appropriate and, indeed, as *true*.

This is a case in which it is features of the context that the person who is said to know/not-to-know is in that determine which logical/physical possibilities are relevant; but in the general case, it may be features of the context of someone who hears the knowledge-claim, or even someone who later hears *of* the knowledge-claim, that determine this, on a contextualist view—so that one speaker may be entitled to regard the utterance as true and another as false, because they appropriately assign different truth-evaluable contents to the utterance. (Whether in such a case the persons are correctly said to *contradict* each other is itself a context-dependent matter, or so at least one contextualist—Charles Travis, *op. cit.*)—would claim, I believe.)

That Stroud is inclined to disagree with all this may be fairly inferred from a passage in *The Significance of Philosophical Scepticism* (61–62). Stroud imagines a case in which he has "just about the most favorable grounds one can have" for saying that John would be at the party. We imagine that John fails to come, nonetheless, because he was struck by a meteorite just as he stepped out of his front door. After pointing out that his failure to know in this case can be correctly described as "due to the falsity of what [he] claimed to know," and so a "necessary condition of knowledge was unfulfilled even though no one was in a position at the time appropriately or reasonably to criticize [his] claim on that basis," Stroud says, "Perhaps the same is true of other necessary conditions of knowledge."

To set the stage for his answer—*that he would ("perhaps") have been wrong to claim that he knew that John would be at the party even if there had been no meteorite and John had come just as Stroud said he would*—and for his further claim *that the mere conceivability that John would be hit by a meteorite "perhaps" defeats Stroud's claim to know that John was coming to the party*—Stroud first imagines an unreasonable host raising that very possibility:

Suppose that, as soon as I had hung up the telephone from talking with John and had said that I knew he would be at the party, the boorish host had said 'But do you really know he'll be here? After all, how do you know he won't be struck down by a meteorite on the way over? You don't know he won't be'... Not only is this 'challenge'... unfair and inappropriate... it is difficult to understand why he even brings up such a consideration at this point and thinks it is a relevant criticism. His doing so would normally suggest that there have been a lot of meteorites hitting the earth lately in this general area, some of them rather big and capable of causing harm. If that were so, perhaps I should have thought of it and considered it—or at least if I didn't know about it my ignorance might threaten my claim to know John would be there. But in the absence of any such special reason, the 'challenge' seems... outrageous. (61)

Now Stroud is by no means a philosopher who despises the work of the later Wittgenstein; indeed, he is a serious scholar of that work. In particular, he by no means wants to ignore or treat as irrelevant the ordinary employment of words. In particular, he attempts to do justice to the ways in which one might actually employ the sentences the "boorish" host is described as uttering. But he fails to note that the "boorish host" in his little story is not merely speaking outside the language-games that we normally play in uttering such a sentence as "I know Jones is coming to the party," but is speaking outside of *any* definite language-game—outside of any linguistic practice that determines, given the context, criteria for "knowing" and "not knowing," criteria that masters of the language can project from the context. Indeed, *unlike* all other philosophers influenced by Wittgenstein that I know of, Stroud does *not* think that the fact that the "boorish host" is speaking outside of language-games *shows* that the "challenge" is unintelligible; Stroud thinks it can be assigned a truth value, and that what the "boorish host" says may well be *true*. For he immediately goes on to write:

> My act of asserting that John would be at the party was made on just about the most favourable grounds that one can have for saying such things. It is no reflection on me or on my saying what I did that I had not ruled out or even thought of the meteorite possibility. But once the question is raised, however inappropriately, can it be said that I do know that that possibility will not obtain? It seems to me that it cannot... I do not think it was true when I hung up the telephone that I knew John would not be hit by a meteorite. So again, part of what the host says is true. I did not know any such thing. But still I said I knew John would be at the party. (61–2)

We should note carefully that Stroud does not say that the skeptical possibility raised by the "boorish host" *shows* that Stroud's claim to know that Jones was coming to the party was false. What he claims is that it *may* show this, that the contextual irrelevance of the meteorite possibility *may* only show that it is *inappropriate* to say that Stroud didn't know, and not that it was *false* that he didn't know. But after many rereadings of *The Significance of Philosophical Scep-*

*ticism*, it has become clear to me that the gravamen of the first three chapters is that this is, in fact, the most plausible line to take. I cannot present all the textual evidence for this claim in one paper, but I shall try to make it plausible in what follows.

That it is at least *open* whether the "inappropriateness" of the boorish host's remark counts against its *truth* is something Stroud himself immediately claims:

> All I am saying at the moment is that it does not follow directly from the admitted outrageousness of [the boorish host's] introducing that possibility that my ruling out the meteorite possibility is simply *not* a condition of my knowing that John will be at the party. Its being a necessary condition of my knowledge is so far at least compatible with the host's remarks' [sic] being inappropriate or outrageous, just as John's being at the party is a necessary condition for by knowing he will be there... (62)

In fact, however, Stroud's discussion of contextualism, even at this early point, is not as "neutral" as his "perhaps" and "all I am saying at the moment" might suggest. Let us briefly go back to some sentences we already quoted:

> ... once the question is raised, however inappropriately, can it be said that I do know that that possibility will not obtain? It seems to me that it cannot... I do not think it was true when I hung up the telephone that I knew that John would not be hit by a meteorite. So again, part of what the host says is true. I did not know any such thing. But still I said I knew John would be at the party.

What Stroud is saying is that the skeptical possibility raised by the host *does* show that "Stroud did not know that John would not be hit by a meteorite" is true. All that is left open is whether the supposed fact that Stroud does "not know" that the meteorite possibility does not obtain *shows* that Stroud also does not know that John will be at the party. ("I want to be careful here. I want to emphasize that I am not saying that in this second case I do not know that John will be at the party because I do not know when hanging up the telephone that he will not be struck down by a meteorite on the way over.") But the step (which Stroud evidently thinks is obvious) from "it is not true that I knew" to "I did not know" *already assumes* the falsity of contextualist (specifically, of Wittgensteinian) critiques of skeptical arguments. For what contextualists maintain—or at least, what Wittgenstein teaches us[11]—is that in the sort of context Stroud describes, both "Stroud knows that John will be struck by a meteorite on his way to the party" and "Stroud does not know that John

---

11 Here I am following Stanley Cavell's interpretation of Wittgenstein's *Philosophical Investigations* in Cavell 1979.

will be struck be a meteorite on the way to the party" presuppose some definite *question*, and if the question whether John will be struck by a meteorite is one that does not remotely arise, then we have no space of relevant possibilities to speak of as excluded or not excluded. *Here and now*, if you ask, "Hilary, do you know or not know that Jim will not be struck down by a meteorite tomorrow," I would not say either "I know" or "I do not know"; I would say, "I don't know what you mean to be asking me." If it is "not true" that "I know that Jim will not be struck down by a meteorite tomorrow," that is because, uttered here and now, with no specified context other than the empty context of "it's a logical possibility," "I know that Jim will not be struck down by a meteorite tomorrow" isn't *merely* something that is "not true," it is something that *hasn't been given a determinate content in the context*. By assuming that the negation of the knowledge-claim "Stroud knows that John will not be struck down by a meteorite on his way to the party" is true, Stroud has assumed that that knowledge-claim has a truth-evaluable content, and this is precisely what I think we should deny.

The point I am making might also be put in pragmatist rather than "contextualist" language. As I interpret Peirce's celebrated distinction between "real" and "philosophical" doubt, the point Peirce is making is that *doubt must be capable of justification just as much as belief.* Both pragmatists and "Wittgensteinians" think that *not all questions of the form "Does X know that p?" make sense.* If we cannot tell from the context what a justified doubt that *p* might be, then no definite question has been asked.

## "Non-claim contexts"

It is obvious that Austin's arguments in *Sense and Sensibilia* and in "Other Minds" are of the contextualist variety. In *The Claim of Reason*, Stanley Cavell makes a far more nuanced employment of contextualist considerations, one which criticizes Austin for missing important distinctions, and also offers a reading of Wittgenstein's *Philosophical Investigations* which puts skepticism at the heart of Wittgenstein's concerns. Here I have room to mention just one of Cavell's notions, the notion of a *non-claim context.*

Cavell's point, whose connection with the preceding will be apparent, is easiest presented with the aid of an example. I am sitting alone in my office writing these words on a computer. If someone were to telephone and ask me, "What are you doing now?", I might, in fact, mention that I am working on the computer. But if the person were to ask, "How do you know?", I would be nonplussed. I am, unquestionably, in a position to *say* what I am doing: I am working on the computer. But that does not mean that I can intelligibly say that "I know I am working on the computer" when the question does not even arise. In Cavell's terms, "I am working on the computer" is not a *claim*, and defending it, justifying it, etc., are demands that do not arise any more than the question "how do you know?" arises.

If the sort of treatment of skeptical doubt that I have described is sound, then the skeptic is wrong to say, "You do not know..." (that you are not dreaming, that there is a computer in front of you, that your name is, etc.). But does failing to discover that the skeptic is wrong for *these* reasons not leave us, in the end, with a feeling of disappointment? Not disappointment with the reasons, but disappointment with *human knowledge as such?* This is the large (and strikingly original) question which Cavell presses with amazing depth in *The Claim of Reason.* To discuss this question here would take me far from my topic, which is Stroud's *Significance.* But I cannot speak of Cavell's work, even in passing, without mentioning it. To see why such disappointment can arise at all, it perhaps suffices to reflect that it is just the sort of things that we are entitled to say without justification, the things we rely on without "knowledge," that we appeal to when there *is* a question of justification. "Our relation to the world is not one of knowledge," Cavell tells us. (He calls this "the truth of skepticism.") The language-game rests on *trust*, Wittgenstein tells us.[12] The notion of resting the language-game on knowledge, or on certainty, or on demonstration, is ultimately unintelligible: there is no coherent possibility that we have discovered not to obtain. But one can be disappointed when something turns out to be meaningless as well as when it turns out to be false. And Cavell's perhaps deepest insight is that such disappointment is not always childish, or something to be gotten over; it may be that *not* feeling it (or pretending—to oneself, at that—not to feel it) is one form that failure to grow up can take. But now I must return to Stroud.

# The "airplane-spotters"

A few pages after discussing the question as to whether he (that is to say, anyone) can know that Jones will come to the party (that is to say, just about any empirical fact), Stroud writes,

> One way to bring out what I think is the sceptical philosopher's conception of everyday life in relation to his epistemological project is to consider in some detail the following story

---

12 Wittgenstein 1969, §§508–9: "What can I rely on? I really want to say that a language-game is only possible if one trusts something (I did not say 'can trust something.')."

adapted from an example of Thompson Clarke's.[13] Suppose that in wartime people must be trained to identify aircraft and they are given a quick, uncomplicated course on the distinguishing features of various planes and how to recognize them. They learn from their manuals, for example, that if a plane has features $x$, $y$, and $w$ it is an E, and if it has $x$, $y$, and $z$ it is an F...

Suppose there are in fact some other airplanes, Gs say, which also have features $x$, $y$, $z$. The trainees were never told about them because it would have made the recognition of Fs too difficult; it is almost impossible to tell an F from a G from the ground. The policy of simplifying the whole operation by not mentioning Gs in the training manual might be justified by the fact that there are not many of them, or that they are only reconnaissance planes, or that in some other ways they are not as directly dangerous as Fs; it does not matter as much whether they fly over our territory.

When we are given this additional information I think we immediately see that even the most careful airplane-spotter does not know that a plane he sees is an F even though he knows that it has $x$, $y$, $z$. For all he knows, it might be a G. (67–8)

Two paragraphs later Stroud draws his conclusion:

I think the sceptical philosopher sees our position in everyday life as analogous to that of the airplane-spotters. There might be very good reasons[14] why we do not normally eliminate or even consider countless possibilities which nevertheless strictly speaking must be known not to obtain if we are to know the sorts of things we claim to know. We therefore cannot conclude simply from our having carefully and conscientiously followed the standards and procedures of everyday life that we thereby know the things we ordinarily claim to know. (69)

And further:

The point is worth stressing. Many people [e.g., contextualists] are apparently disposed to think that if the philosopher holds that a certain condition must be met in order to know something, and we do not insist on that condition's being met in everyday life, then the philosopher simply *must* be imposing new or higher standards on knowledge or changing the meaning of the word 'know' or some other word. But if our position in everyday life is like that of the airplane-spotters that is not so (69–70)

While this seems clear at first reading, on reflection it is harder and harder to see what Stroud is claiming. While Stroud's official position is only that the contextualist has not proved his case, that the alternative suggested by the airplane-spotter analogy—that is, that context is relevant only in fixing what it is practically useful "for very good reasons" to say we know, to treat as appropriate to say

---

**13** Clarke 1972, 759 ff.
**14** Can a "skeptical philosopher" grant that there are such things as "good reasons"?

we know, and the like, but not to fixing what it is *true* to say we know—he so insistently presents this alternative that one can hardly avoid the conclusion that he simply thinks the position(s) I have lumped together as "contextualism" are *wrong* (and this is also my impression from a recent, unfortunately brief, conversation with him). At the same time, he refrains from saying flat out that the skeptic is *right*. Whether the skeptic is right is supposed to be a deep and presently unsolved philosophical problem. But if contextualism is wrong to *this* extent—namely, that the possibility that Descartes is dreaming is enough to show that Descartes doesn't know that there is a fireplace or a room or a dressing-gown in his vicinity, and the fact (as we have seen, Stroud takes it to be such) that Stroud doesn't know that John will not be struck down by a meteorite is enough to show that Stroud doesn't know that John will come to the party (right after talking to John on the telephone), etc.—then why *doesn't* Stroud just conclude that skepticism is true? In many ways, *The Significance of Philosophical Scepticism*—or at least its opening chapters—makes more sense as a demonstration of the *truth* of skepticism rather than (as it sees itself as being) a demonstration that there is a "deep problem." If I jump out of a fourteenth-story window, there is not a "deep problem" as to whether I will fall; yet Stroud has jumped out of the skeptical window, but seems to be unsure as to the fate he faces.

Indeed the airplane-spotter analogy itself seems to be problematic in more than one way. Presumably, the idea *isn't* that the people who wrote the manual and omitted the information that "there are in fact some other airplanes, Gs say, which also have features *x*, *y*, *z*" definitely *knew* that this was the case; for in that case, how could this be an analogy that a "skeptical philosopher" might use? (A skeptical philosopher would say that the writers of the manual might have been dreaming or hallucinating.) Rather, the idea must be that the relation in which the airplane-spotters' use of "know" stands to the manual-writers use of "know" is *analogous* to the relation that our "everyday" use of "know" stands to... what? Hardly the skeptics' use of "know"! For it was essential that the manual-writers are supposed to know *more* than the airplane-spotters, but according to the skeptic's use of "know" (which may be the literally correct use, if I understand Stroud's worry), the skeptic, like everyone else, knows nothing. (This unclarity in the nature of the analogy is connected to the casual use of expressions like "very good reasons" by Stroud in explaining what is supposed to be the skeptic's view.)

Finally, look at the following sentence closely:

> The policy of simplifying the whole operation by not mentioning Gs in the training manual might be justified by the fact that there are not many of them, or that they are only recon-

naissance planes, or that in some other way they are not as directly dangerous as Fs; it does not matter as much whether they fly over our territory. (67–8)

These are, in fact, very different cases. If, on the one hand, Gs are extremely rare, then it could well be that even someone as knowledgeable as the manual-writers would feel justified in saying he "knew" that what he had spotted was an F on the basis of features *x*, *y*, *z*—just as we normally feel justified in ignoring the rare event of someone being struck down by a meteorite. Of course, Stroud can explain this away as a case of saying what it is convenient-but-not-true to say, but since the whole point of the airplane-spotter story is that it is supposed to support this very move by being a *clear case* of something's being convenient to say but not true, this would make the entire argument circular. On the other hand, if Gs are common but the manual writers ignored them because they cause little harm, then we would very likely say (on learning this) that the airplane-spotter did not know that a given plane he identified as an F really was an F (given the low reliability of the method he relied upon); but this reliability consideration can also point in an anti-skeptical direction (the direction taken by "causal theories of knowledge"). So it is natural to ask why Stroud treats these very different cases as equivalent. It seems that, for Stroud, the only relevant feature of the cases is that they show that there is a *possibility* that something which meets the criteria the airplane-spotter is relying upon (namely, the features *x*, *y*, *z*) does not have the relevant property (namely, being an F); and Stroud must be assuming that any reader who sees this will agree that the spotter does not *know* that it is has the property. Stroud expects the reader to think that it is *irrelevant* whether the possibility is one that is frequently or very infrequently realized. Only the status of possibility is relevant. But the assumption that *bare* possibility is enough to defeat a knowledge-claim is precisely the one that the skeptic's argument turns upon!

## Stroud contra Malcolm

The principle defender of a contextualist view whom Stroud directly rebuts is Norman Malcolm (97 ff.) From my own point of view, Malcolm's contextualism suffers from his unwise insistence that there is such a thing as *the* proper use of the word "know." In the spirit of and under the inspiration of Stanley Cavell's work,[15] I have argued elsewhere that in general we should not expect to capture

---

15 I discuss Cavell's work in Putnam 2001.

the cases in which competent speakers will find that we have used a word in a way that is a "natural projection" of uses previously accepted as perfectly in order by a closed set of "rules." This insistence on the openness of our possible projections certainly seems more in keeping with the spirit of contextualism. (Think how hard it would be to capture all the present and possible future uses of "There is a lot of coffee on the table"!)

In any case, in "Defending Common Sense"[16] Malcolm claimed that, for a use of the word "know" to be proper, there must be some question at issue or some doubt to be removed; the person saying he knows something must be able to give some reason for his assertion; and there must be some investigation that, if carried out, would settle the question. Since Moore's celebrated "proof of the external world"[17] uses "know" in a way that violates these criteria, Malcolm concluded that he had exposed Moore's argument as fallacious (as turning on a violation of the correct use of "know").

Stroud contends, against Malcolm, (1) that there are uses of "know" that are *not* misuses but which violate all three of Malcolm's criteria; but, against Moore, (2) that such uses may not be relevant to "the philosophical problem of the external world." Stroud's example is borrowed from Thompson Clarke:[18]

> To see that it is possible to use Moore's very words in contexts that appear nowhere in Malcolm's list of correct uses of 'know', we can recall Thompson Clarke's example[19] of the physiologist lecturing on mental abnormalities. Near the beginning of his lecture he might say:
>
> > Each of us who is normal knows that he is now awake, not dreaming or hallucinating, that there is a real public world outside his mind which he is now perceiving, that in this world there are three-dimensional animate and inanimate bodies of many shapes and sizes... In contrast, individuals suffering from certain mental abnormalities each believes that what we know to be the real world is his imaginative creation.
>
> Here the lecturer uses the same words often used by philosophers who make or question general statements about the world and our knowledge of it. When he says that each of us knows that there is a public world of three-dimensional bodies, he is stating what can only be regarded as straightforward empirical fact. Most of us do know the things he mentions, and those with the abnormalities he has in mind do know. That is a real difference between people that can be observed or ascertained. (100–1)

As I mentioned, Stroud does *not* think that the "physiologist's" use of "know" is philosophically relevant. "I think we do not regard the lecturer in this context as

---

**16** Malcolm 1949.
**17** Moore 1959, 127.
**18** Clarke 1972, 756.
**19** The example, it is worth noting, is made-up.

having settled affirmatively the philosophical problem of our knowledge of the external world" (101). Presumably, then, the "physiologist's" use is analogous to the "airplane-spotters'" use in some way. But equally clearly, Stroud does think that, having shown to his own satisfaction that Malcolm has not listed *all* the "proper" uses of "know,"[20] he can take it that there *is* a proper use which is the one involved in the "philosophical problem of our knowledge of the external world." But what is that use?

Stroud is extremely coy on this crucial point. Consider what he writes in a lengthy footnote concerning Peter Unger's defense of skepticism. After explaining with the aid of the "boorish host" and the "airplane-spotter" examples that it is possible that the facts about our everyday use only reveal *appropriateness-conditions* for our utterances, and do not tell us what their *truth-conditions* might be, Stroud writes that (if this possibility obtains):

> ... [o]ne would then be in a strong position to defend the sceptical conclusions against any objection to the effect that it distorts the meaning of the very words in which it is expressed since it conflicts with obvious facts about how those words are ordinarily used. The evidence from usage would not support that conclusion about meaning on the conception of the relation between meaning and use that I have tried to identify. (75)

The footnote to Unger's work is a footnote to this last sentence, and reads in part as follows:

> Peter Unger rightly insists on the importance of this distinction in the defense of scepticism. He identifies a class of terms he calls 'absolute terms' (like 'flat' and 'empty') which are appropriately applied on many occasions even though they are never literally true of any of the things to which they are applied... For Unger the same holds for 'certain' and, since knowledge implies certainty, for 'know' as well... I do not agree that Unger can *establish* scepticism on the basis of his theory of 'absolute terms' alone. I think his argument to show that no one is ever undogmatically certain of (and hence doesn't know) anything about the world makes essential use of a step that is equivalent in force to Descartes's requirement that we must know we are not dreaming if we are to know anything about the world around us. Without that requirement, the 'absoluteness' of 'certain' and 'know' will not yield the sceptical conclusion. And I have tried to show here that with that requirement we have all we need to generate the sceptical conclusion, so the doctrine of 'absolute terms' is not needed. (75)

---

**20** Actually, the "physiologist" does not talk like any neural scientist *I* have ever heard. One of the peculiarities of his odd little speech is the claim that "each of us who is normal" knows that he is now awake. Aren't any normal people now *sleeping*?

Now, Stroud believes that if Descartes is right about "that requirement," then we do not even need to employ the empirical fact that people dream to argue for external-world skepticism. Early on, for example, when Stroud summarizes Descartes' argument in the First Meditation, he writes:

> When he first introduces the possibility that he might be dreaming Descartes seems to be relying on some knowledge about how things are or were in the world around him... [H]e seems to be relying on some knowledge to the effect that he has actually dreamt in the past and that he remembers having been 'deceived' by those dreams. That is more than he actually needs for his reflections about knowledge to have the force he thinks they have. He does not need to support his judgement that he has actually dreamt in the past. The only thought he needs is that it is now *possible* for him to be dreaming that he is sitting by the fire, and that if that possibility were realized he would not know that he is sitting by the fire. (17)

So the threat of skepticism turns out to be the threat that the philosophically relevant use—or rather, given the way Stroud distinguishes between meaning and use, the philosophically relevant *meaning*—of "know" might be such that *the mere logical possibility of dreams establishes that we do not and could not have any knowledge of "external" objects.* Such a "meaning" *would* make "know" behave the way Unger thought "flat" behaves"—that is, as a term that never applies (at least, not to any empirical claims about "external" objects). It *would* make "know" an "absolute" term in Unger's sense. Like Unger's semantics for "flat," it would violate the Principle of Charity to the maximum possible extent.[21] But the question that neither Unger nor Stroud face is this: why should the language contain a term for "knowing" in a sense in which it is an *obvious* logical truth that we have no empirical knowledge?

Stroud would, of course, reply that he doesn't say that it is an *obvious* logical truth. After all, Descartes's argument depends on more than the premise that I don't know that I am not dreaming (which Stroud appears to accept, just as he accepts that he doesn't know that John won't be struck down by a meteorite). It depends, as Stroud reminds us in the footnote I just quoted, on the further premise that to know I am in front of the fire, or whatever, I need to know that I am not dreaming (or: to know John will come to the party, I need to

---

**21** The context-*insensitivity* of such "absolute" terms as "flat" was defended by Unger in Chapter 2 of Unger 1975. David Lewis, in response, advocates a context-sensitive approach in Lewis 1979. Incidentally, Unger no longer endorses the view that "flat" context-insensitively expresses a property only ideal geometric surfaces possess. In Unger 1984, he hypothesizes that there's no fact of the matter as to whether his earlier view or Lewis's view is correct. (Thanks to Steven Gross for these references.)

know that he will not be struck down by a meteorite). And it is a deep problem, Stroud claims, whether this is right or wrong.

With all my respect for Barry Stroud's scholarship, intelligence, intellectual integrity, and unbelievable willingness to follow this investigation to the very end, I have to say that at the end of the day I feel, in reading *The Significance of Philosophical Scepticism*, as if I am in Jabberwock Forest. Stroud has separated "meaning" and "application" (on the basis of what seems to me an overestimation of the value of Grice's arguments);[22] then he asks whether the "meaning" of "know" is such that the skeptical "requirement" holds—and apparently nothing but a conclusive demonstration will satisfy him one way or the other; and finally, having failed to specify any procedures (let alone a justification) for determining this application-transcendent "meaning," he finds that he is unable to say whether the skeptic is right or wrong!

# Bibliography

Cavell, Stanley (1979), *The Claim of Reason: Wittgenstein, Skepticism, Morality, and Tragedy*, Oxford: Oxford University Press.

Clarke, Thompson (1972), "The Legacy of Skepticism." In: *Journal of Philosophy* 69, 754–69.

Lewis, David (1979), "Scorekeeping In a Language Game." In: *Journal of Philosophical Logic* 8, 339–59.

Malcolm, Norman (1949), "Defending Common Sense." In: *Philosophical Review* 58, 201–11.

Moore, G.E. (1959), "Proof of an External World." In: G.E. Moore, *Philosophical Papers*, London: George Allen & Unwin, 127–50.

Putnam, Hilary (1975), "The Meaning of 'Meaning.'" In: Hilary Putnam, *Mind, Language and Reality: Philosophical Papers, Volume 2*, Cambridge: Cambridge University Press, 215–71.

Putnam, Hilary (1988), *Representation and Reality*, Cambridge, MA: MIT Press.

Putnam, Hilary (1998a), "Skepticism." In: Marcello Stamm (ed.), *Philosophie in synthetischer Absicht*, Stuttgart: Klett-Cotta, 239–68.

Putnam, Hilary (1998b), "Strawson and Skepticism." In: Lewis Edwin Hahn (ed.), *The Philosophy*, Chicago and La Salle, IL: Open Court, 273–87.

Putnam, Hilary (2000), *The Threefold Cord: Mind, Body, and World*, New York: Columbia University Press.

Putnam, Hilary (2001), "Rules, Attunement, and 'Applying Words to the World': The Struggle to Understand Wittgenstein's Vision of Language." In: Chantal Mouffe and Ludwig Nagl (eds.), *Deconstruction and Pragmatism*, Bern and New York: Peter Lang Press.

Stroud, Barry (1984), *The Significance of Philosophical Scepticism*, Oxford: Oxford University Press.

---

**22** For a criticism of those arguments, see Travis 1991 and Travis 1989.

Travis, Charles (1981), *The True and the False: The Domain of the Pragmatic*, Amsterdam: J. Benjamins.

Travis, Charles (1989), *The Uses of Sense: Wittgenstein's Philosophy of Language*, Oxford: Clarendon Press.

Travis, Charles (1991), "Annals of Analysis." In: *Mind* 100, 237–63.

Travis, Charles (2000), *Unshadowed Thought: Representation In Thought and Language*, Cambridge, MA: Harvard University Press.

Travis, Charles (2001), "Mind Dependence." In: *Revue Internationale de Philosophie* 55, 525–33.

Unger, Peter (1975), *Ignorance: A Case for Scepticism*, Oxford: Oxford University Press.

Unger, Peter (1984), *Philosophical Relativity*, Minneapolis: University of Minnesota Press.

Wittgenstein, Ludwig (1969), *On Certainty*, Denis Paul and G.E.M. Anscombe (trans.), Oxford: Basil Blackwell.

Sebastian Rödl
# Finite Knowledge

## 1 Introduction

The skeptic holds that it is impossible to know anything. In his article "Skepticism"[1], Hilary Putnam seeks, he says, "to provide... an argument *that convinces me* that *the skeptic cannot provide a valid argument from premises I must accept to the conclusion that knowledge is impossible*" (255). I shall discuss Putnam's treatment of one such argument. I do not think Putnam succeeds in showing that this argument is unconvincing. I shall argue in sections 2–4 that, on the contrary, his position reinforces its conclusion. Putnam claims that the skeptic disregards the structure of human knowledge, failing to realize that doubt requires justification. In sections 5–10, I shall describe the structure of human knowledge in virtue of which doubt sometimes requires justification. It will turn out that Putnam misconceives this structure and, hence, misconstrues where and how the skeptic fails to acknowledge it. Skepticism responds to the finitude of human knowledge, and so does every response to skepticism. I shall end, in section 11, by explaining how Putnam's view and the one I shall develop differ in how they conceive of this finitude.

## 2 An Argument for Skepticism

The following argument intends to show that knowledge is impossible. It proceeds from two premises. The first premise is: One knows something if and only if one is in a position to give sufficient grounds for it, that is, grounds that rule out that one is mistaken. The second premise is: No matter what one's grounds are, there is a possible circumstance such that, if it obtained, one's grounds would not rule out that one is mistaken. It follows from these two premises that it is impossible to know anything. According to the second premise, whatever one's grounds, they do not rule out a circumstance such that, if it obtains, one is mistaken. And this means that, given one's grounds,

---

1 Putnam 1998. Bare numbers refer to the pages of this article.

it is possible that one is mistaken. One's grounds do not, after all, rule out the possibility of error. Hence, according to the first premise, one does not know.[2]

# 3 Lowering the bar

Putnam wants to show that the above argument is invalid. As its reasoning seems impeccable, the fault must lie with its premises. Putnam rejects the first premise, according to which one knows if and only if one is in a position to rule out that one is mistaken. One must be able to exclude the possibility of error. Putnam objects that, in order to know, it is not necessary to be in a position to rule out *all* circumstances in which one would err, but only those that are *relevant*. He writes:

> As we actually use the word "know", a statement of the form "X knows that so-and-so" does not claim that... X... is in a position to defuse *every* conceivable "doubt" (or "possibility of error")... When we say "I know", what we mean is that we can rule out certain relevant "doubts", but *not* all possible "doubts". (249)

I do not think that this is how we use, or could use, the word "know". That someone cannot rule out that circumstances obtain under which his claim is false, Putnam maintains, need not prevent him from knowing what he claims to know. For the possibility that these circumstances obtain may be irrelevant, in which case he is not required to be in a position to exclude it in order to know. But this means that someone may know something while, given his grounds, it is possible that he is mistaken. He may know something while, for

---

**2** A standard response to this argument is to accuse it of a level confusion, of failing to distinguish knowing and knowing that one knows. The second premise states that it always remains possible that one's grounds do not rule out the possibility that one is mistaken. But according to the first premise, in order to know something, it is required only that one's grounds rule out this possibility. It is not required that one *be in a position to establish that they do*. One knows something if and only if one has grounds that rule out the possibility of its being otherwise. And one knows that one knows it if and only if one has grounds that rule out the possibility that one's grounds are insufficient. So the argument treats a condition of knowing that one knows something as a condition of knowing it. It is then no wonder that one can never know anything.

I shall not, in this essay, discuss this line of reasoning. For if it is correct, both Putnam's and my responses to the skeptical argument are unnecessary and misleading. Putnam ignores it (justly, I think); as it is my objective to discuss Putnam's critique of the skeptical argument, so shall I.

all he knows, it is possible that things are not as he knows them to be. This seems incoherent.[3]

Putnam holds that, in order to know, one need not, as the skeptic claims, be in a position to exclude all possibilities of error. It suffices that one be in a position to exclude some. "All" implies "some," but "some" does not imply "all." So the skeptic's condition is more demanding than Putnam's. Knowing, as Putnam understands it, is *less* than knowing as the skeptic understands it. The requirements are not so stringent, Putnam tells the skeptic. Less is enough: not all, only some.[4] A response of this form fails to engage the skeptic. The skeptic will not be surprised to hear that we can declare ourselves knowers by easing the burden of justification. Nor will it be new to him that we in fact often so ease the burden. This is an implication of his view, given that he is aware that we often think and say that we know things. In a later passage, Putnam argues that the skeptic's concept of knowing can serve no purpose, since nothing falls under it. But what if it is our fate to live under an unapproachable ideal that humbles our pretensions? It seems a shallow pragmatism that says that such an ideal serves no purpose.[5]

---

3 Compare McDowell 1998, 371.

4 Putnam sometimes seems to maintain that "knowing", used in accordance with the first premise of the skeptical argument, fails to express any concept. But this cannot be Putnam's meaning. If we understand what it is to rule out some possibilities of error, then we understand what it is to rule out all. It is impossible that, of the phrases "all X" and "some X", only one bears a sense.

5 "That the language game is not played the way the skeptic plays it is a fact about the *structure* of our concepts. It is not a mere contingent fact about our psychology that we do not use 'know' in such a way that the only knowledge-statement we can make is the one negative statement that we do not know anything; for such a use of 'know' would defeat the purposes for which we have the concept, and *that* is as much a logical fact as is the fact that if we have one contradiction in a logical calculus (whose rules include the standard use of two-valued logic) we can derive every statement as a theorem in the calculus, and then the calculus would be useless (if intended as a formalization of some branch of discourse)" (254).

Putnam seems to claim that the word "know" cannot be used in accordance with our first premise, because this would in some way be counter to logic. I do not see why. I presume it is a logical fact that, in a calculus the rules of which license inference *ex falso quodlibet*, if a contradiction is derivable, every formula is derivable, just as it is a logical fact that in a calculus without ex falso quodlibet, this is not so. Those are logical facts on the assumption that it is the office of logic to study the properties of calculi. It does not seem to be a logical fact that a calculus in which every formula is derivable is useless. Logic does not attend to the question, I think, of what is useful and what is not. Similarly, I do not see how it can be a logical fact, if it is one, that the skeptic's concept of knowledge would serve no purpose.

# 4 Justification for doubt

Putnam accuses the skeptic of failing to realize that *doubt requires justification.*

> Doubt requires justification as well as belief. And pointing to remote possibilities of error, mere logical possibilities or even far fetched empirical possibilities, does not, in itself, justify doubt... [This is] a fact about the *structure* of our concepts. (254)

The skeptic demands that *every* possibility be excluded. Putnam thinks this is wrong because doubt requires justification. One need exclude that things are a certain way only if there is some justification for thinking they indeed are that way. That doubt requires justification thus limits the range of possibilities one must exclude in order to know. It undermines the first premise of the skeptical argument. Now, I do not deny that doubt sometimes requires justification. What I deny is that this lends support to the idea that grounds may be sufficient for knowledge while failing to exclude error. Grounds are sufficient, Putnam claims, if they exclude not all, but only all *relevant* possibilities of error. A possibility is irrelevant if it is remote or far-fetched. And this is explained as meaning that there are no grounds for thinking it obtains. On this view, then, one knows something if there are no grounds for thinking otherwise. But this is false. Suppose someone claims to know that the roulette ball will land on a red number. One would want to tell her that the ball may just as well land on a black number and that he is not in a position to rule out this possibility. It does not seem that he may respond that there are no grounds for thinking that it will land on a black number and that, hence, this possibility is irrelevant. It is not the case that one knows that things are so simply because there are no grounds for thinking otherwise. *One must have grounds for thinking that things are so.* Accordingly, one might attempt to rectify the account by saying that one knows something if one has some grounds for thinking it and no grounds for thinking otherwise. But this is just as false. Think of someone who claims, and has some reasons for claiming, that the stocks will go up next week. However, her reasons leave it open that the stocks may go down. Then she does not know that the stocks will go up. It is immaterial whether or not there are grounds for thinking that they will go down. There may be none. Still, she does not know, not because there are grounds for thinking otherwise, but because her grounds for thinking so are insufficient. One does not know something just because *something* speaks in its favor. In order to know, one must have *sufficient* grounds. It seems, then, that we must say that one knows if and only if one has sufficient grounds and there are no grounds for thinking otherwise. But now the account can no longer serve as an account of what it is for grounds to be sufficient.

# 5 What Putnam can exclude

I agree that doubt sometimes requires justification. And I agree that this is definitive of the structure of human knowledge. I shall now inquire into this structure. Putnam thinks one's grounds may be sufficient even if one is not in a position to exclude that one is mistaken, because he believes that, very often, when—according to ordinary parlance—one would be said to know, one is not in a position to exclude this. This is his example:

> Here is a relevant example: (1) I know (for example) that the color of my house is "off-white." (2) I know the (obvious) implication: If some pranksters painted my house blue this morning, then the color of my house is now blue, and not off-white. (3) But I do not know that some pranksters did not paint my house blue this morning (I have been at the office all day). (249)

It seems to accord with our ways of speaking to say that Putnam knows that his house is white, but—so Putnam thinks—he is not in a position to rule out that someone has painted it blue. Putnam suggests that he does not know whether someone has painted his house, because he has been at the office all day. But why would that prevent him from knowing that nobody has painted his house? Putnam seems to assume that he could only be in a position to rule out that someone painted his house had he continuously observed his house. But this is not the only way he can be in this position. Putnam can know that nobody has painted his house on the grounds that he has not asked or hired anyone to do it. He can know it on the grounds that, in general, people do not paint other people's houses unless they have made some arrangement with the owner.[6] In general, one may be in a position to rule out that someone *has done* such-and-such or that such-and-such *has happened* not by way of having relentlessly kept one's eye on the object, but by way of knowing what people *do* and what they do not do and what *happens* and what does not happen. One may be in a position to exclude a possibility of error not on the grounds of one's sensible experience of what has happened *there and then*, but on the grounds of one's understanding of what, *in general*, happens and is done. In

---

6 In discussion, Putnam objected that, even given that, in general, people do not paint other people's houses unless they have been asked to do it, it is still *logically* possible that someone painted Putnam's house this morning. So it is, but this is immaterial as to whether Putnam knows the color of his house. In order to know, one must be in a position to exclude error. It is not required that one be in a position *logically* to exclude error. If this were a condition on knowledge, what is known would by definition be logically true. The concept of possibilities-relevant-to-knowledge cannot be explained in terms of logical laws.

this case, the excluding proposition *differs in logical form* from the proposition it excludes. What excludes is general and atemporal; its expression is tenseless— one's house gets painted by someone only if one asks or hires him to paint it. What is excluded is particular and dated; its expression bears a tense—someone painted Putnam's house.

Knowing that such-and-such happens only when __, or that people do not do this-and-that unless __, may put one in a position to exclude the possibility that such-and-such happened yesterday or that someone has done this-and-that this morning. The general statement supports *modal* particular statements. I shall therefore call these general statements laws.[7] It is clear that the atemporal and tenseless statements that enter into the justification of ordinary claims never hold without exception. They are about what happens or is done in general. And what happens in general is not what happens always. If true statements about what happens in general are laws, they are not strict laws. Some may want to call them *ceteris paribus* laws. I shall call them *sublunary* laws in deference to Aristotle, who holds that the laws that govern perishable substances composed of form and matter do not determine what happens always, but only what happens in general.[8]

Putnam thinks he does not know whether someone has painted his house this morning since he has not observed his house in the interim. He thus denies that he may know this in virtue of his understanding of the ways in which it comes about that someone paints someone else's house. But why would Putnam deny this? One may want to say: Sublunary laws do not hold without exception. A given situation may deviate and fail to exemplify the law. People do not paint someone else's house, unless they have arranged with the owner to do so. So it is, but not without exception. Harry, in a fit of madness, may have painted Putnam's house. But Putnam cannot exclude Harry. Hence, Putnam cannot exclude the possibility that someone has painted his house. I shall say that a law does not bear on a given situation if and only if the situation is an exception. A sublunary law, then, may or may not bear on the given situation. So Putnam reasons

---

7 Compare Donald Davidson's conditions for law-like statements: "Lawlike statements are general statements that support counterfactual and subjunctive claims, and are supported by their instances" (Davidson 1980, 217).

8 See *Metaphysics* E, 1027a8 – 19. Aristotle's term "*hos epi to polu*" is sometimes translated "for the most part". I render it "in general" in order not to encourage what I take to be a misunderstanding, namely, the view that judgments about what happens *hos epi to polu* are judgments of frequency. Obviously, judgments of frequency do not constrain what is possible. (For the most part, the roulette ball lands on a number within the first two dozens. This does not exclude the possibility that it will land on a number within the third dozen.)

thus: One is never in a position to exclude the possibility that one is mistaken simply in virtue of knowing a sublunary law. One must, in addition, have grounds excluding the possibility that the law does not bear on the situation.

This line of reasoning is parallel to one which moves from the fallibility of the faculty of sense-perception to the defeasibility of the grounds it may provide in a given situation.[9] The faculty is fallible in that, in a given situation, it may fail to yield knowledge. I shall say that, in such a situation, the faculty does not bear on the situation. A fallible faculty, then, may or may not bear on a given situation. So one reasons: One is never in a position to exclude the possibility that one is mistaken simply in virtue of exercising one's faculty of sense-perception. One must, in addition, have grounds sufficient to exclude the possibility that this fallible faculty does not bear on the situation.

# 6 Seeming to know

Putnam thinks he is not in a position to exclude the possibility that someone painted his house blue this morning. I suggested that he thinks so because he is in the grip of a certain conception of what can constitute being in such a position: in order to know whether or not someone has painted his house this morning, Putnam thinks, he must have kept a watch on his house throughout the morning. But, I claimed, one may be in a position to exclude house-painting in virtue of knowing something general: people do not paint someone else's house, unless __. I then imagined a line of reasoning to the effect that knowing something general that does not hold without exception can never amount to being in a position to exclude things that do not conform to it. And I observed that this line of reasoning is parallel in structure to an infamous line of reasoning which argues that exercising a fallible faculty can never amount to being in a position to exclude that one is mistaken. Knowing through a fallible faculty and knowing through a sublunary law have the same structure. It is a structure fundamental to human knowledge, and as I will try to show now, it is in virtue of this structure that doubt sometimes requires justification.

When does doubt require justification? Someone claims to know that the roulette ball will land on a red number. Someone who doubts that this will happen need not justify his doubt. He need not give a reason to believe that the ball will land on a black number. Or someone claims that stocks will go up. Someone may doubt this, and he need not justify his doubt. There may be no grounds for

---

**9** Compare McDowell 1998.

thinking that the stocks will go down. But it is a possibility. If one cannot exclude this possibility, one does not know. So in general, doubt does not require justification. It requires justification in cases such as these: One thinks one knows that this tie here is green on the grounds that one's senses tell one so. Someone raises a doubt and says, "What if the lights are falsifying the colors?" Or one thinks one knows that nobody has painted one's house this morning on the grounds that, in general, one's house does not get painted unless one asks or hires someone to do it. And someone raises a doubt and says, "What if Harry has gone mad and painted your house?" These doubts have no force *unless there is reason to think that the light is misleading and that Harry has gone mad*. In the absence of reasons to think this, one's claim to know stands fast.

If it turns out that the light is falsifying or that Harry has gone mad, it turns out that one only *seemed to know*, but did not know. One only seemed to have sufficient grounds, but did not; one only seemed to be in a position to exclude error, but was not. A case of seeming to know has a specific logical structure. Not everyone who does not know seems to know. Someone predicting the roulette ball or the stocks does not even seem to know. Nor is seeming to know the same as thinking one knows. Someone may think he knows where the roulette ball or the stocks will go, but he will not for that reason seem to know it. One seems to know when one would know were it not for something that *intervenes*. Something intervenes in relation to something general: it intervenes in that it prevents the general from bearing on the given situation. So one seems to know on grounds consisting in the application of something general to the given situation: one seems to know that this tie here is green on the basis of one's faculty of sense-perception, and one seems to know that nobody has painted one's house on the basis of a sublunary law. But something intervenes, something particular and temporal, something here and now or there and then: the lights here are falsifying the colors, Harry went mad with his new paint. It is not that one lacks the sense of sight, or that it is a custom around here to paint one's neighbors' house at Easter. In that case, one would not seem to know that this tie was blue or that nobody had painted one's house this morning. The logical structure of seeming to know is this: One seems to know something particular in virtue of something general that is brought to bear on the given situation, but something particular intervenes and prevents the general item from bearing on this situation.

One seems to know if one would know on the basis of something general were it not for the intervening particular. A doubt requires justification when it questions whether one only seems to know what one thinks one knows. It requires justification if and only if it relates to an intervening particular. One would know that this tie is green were it not for the falsifying light. And one would know that nobody painted one's house were it not for Harry's unruly desire to paint.[10] If one does know—if the light is right and Harry stays at home—one knows in virtue of something general. One knows that the tie is green in virtue of one's faculty of sight. One knows that nobody has painted one's house in virtue of one's knowledge that people do not paint someone else's house unless __. One knows in virtue of something general: a faculty, a law, that is, in virtue of something in virtue of which one may know an unlimited number of things. And this general item is one that may fail to bear on the situation. The faculty is fallible, the law is sublunary.

# 7 Why doubt requires justification

Doubt requires justification in this case: One ostensibly knows something particular through something general, which nevertheless is such that it may fail to bear on a given situation. Putnam claims that it is definitive of the structure of human knowledge that doubt requires justification. If this is right, then the structure of human knowledge is this: *one knows the particular through the general*. In order to vindicate Putnam's claim, then, we need to show that this structure—knowing the particular through the general—would break down if doubt never required justification. And indeed this can be shown.

The ball may land on red, and it may not. The stocks may go up, and they may not. It is possible that the ball will not land on red or that the stocks will not go up. Someone does not know unless he has grounds that exclude these possibilities. This is so even if there are no grounds for thinking that the ball will land on black or that the stocks will go down. In these cases, doubt does not require justification. Now, the general may bear on the given situation, and it may not. If doubt does not require justification here as well, then things are here as they are with the ball and the stocks: since it is possible that, in the given situation, one's faculty of sight fails to operate properly, one does not know unless one has grounds excluding this possibility. Since it is possible that, in the given situation, the sublunary law fails to hold, one does not

---

**10** A doubt requires justification if it questions whether someone only seems to know. It questions whether someone only seems to have sufficient grounds. Putnam seeks to explain what it is for grounds to be sufficient by reference to the fact that doubt requires justification: One's grounds are sufficient if and only if they exclude all and only justified doubts. This explanatory strategy is doomed. The notion of sufficient grounds is prior to the notion of grounds for thinking that someone only seems to know, since "seeming to know" is "seeming to have sufficient grounds".

know unless one has grounds that exclude that. In general: since it is possible that the general will fail to bear on the particular, one does not know unless one is in a position to exclude this possibility. It is insignificant whether or not there are grounds for thinking that the general does not bear on the situation.

If doubt never requires justification, then one never knows simply by way of exercising a fallible faculty in a given situation or by way of applying a sublunary law to a given situation. One knows only if one has sufficient grounds for thinking that one's fallible faculty or the sublunary law bear on the given situation. Now, let us contemplate the logical consequences of this. Grounds for thinking that the general bears on the given situation must relate to something particular; they must be about what is here and now and there and then. (Otherwise, the question would arise whether they bear on the situation, and grounds would have to be given to exclude that they fail to do so.) It is never the case, then, that one knows something particular through something general. One knows in virtue of something general if and only if one may, on the same grounds, know an unlimited number of things in suitable situations. But if grounds concerning the particular situation must establish that the general bears on the situation at hand, then there is no such thing as knowing something on grounds on which one may know other things as well. One comes to know that this tie is green. Later, one comes to know that it is actually blue. It would seem that one knows the one and the other on the grounds that, in each case, one exercised one's faculty of sight. But suppose one knows only if one has grounds that exclude the possibility that one's faculty is failing to bear on the situation. The grounds that exclude this in the one situation are not the grounds that exclude it in the other situation. (If they were, they would be general, and one would need to exclude that they fail to bear on the situation.) One knows that one's house has not been painted this morning. And one knows that it has not been painted this evening. It would appear that one knows both on the grounds that one paints someone else's house only if one has been asked or hired to do it. But now, one knows only if one has grounds that exclude that this law fails to bear on the given situation. These grounds will be different in the morning and in the evening.

It is essential to the notion of a faculty of perception that resting a claim on what it delivers may be a way of excluding that one is mistaken. And it is essential to the notion of a law that it delimits what is possible and, hence, may play a role in excluding possibilities of error. If something is such that the fact that one's claim conforms to what it delivers leaves untouched the question as to whether it is as one claims it to be, then it is not a faculty of sense-perception. It may be a machine that prints out sentences. It may turn out that the sentences it prints are often true. But clearly, one does not know that things are so on the grounds that the machine has printed a sentence saying it is so. Equally, a general judgment is not a law if it is such that the fact that some particular thing fails to conform to it does *not* speak to the question as to whether that particular thing is possible. It may be a judgment of frequency. And one cannot exclude something on the grounds that it happens rarely. Now, if doubt never requires justification, then it is an open question whether, in the given situation, things are as one's senses say; it is an open question whether, in the given situation, things conform to the law. One needs grounds—in the end, sufficient grounds—for thinking so. Hence, if doubt never requires justification, then there is no such thing as a fallible faculty of sense-perception, but only machines that print out sentences. There is no such thing as a sublunary law, but only judgments of frequency. There is no such thing, that is, as knowing the particular through the general.

One cannot simply doubt that the general—a fallible faculty, a sublunary law—bears on the given situation. There must be grounds for thinking so. Doubt, here, requires justification. One may be tempted to think that this makes doubting more difficult and knowing easier. One may think that, since doubt requires justification, one need not give sufficient grounds for thinking that, in the given situation, one's faculty of sense-perception does not fail. And one need not give sufficient grounds for thinking that the given situation is no exception from a certain sublunary law. It is enough if there are no grounds for thinking that one's faculty fails or that the situation is an exception. This would be a fatal misunderstanding. It is not the case that one need not give grounds for thinking that the general bears on the given situation. Rather, in the absence of a justified doubt, there is no such thing as giving grounds for thinking that the general bears on the given situation. Giving grounds for thinking that the general bears on the situation *is* responding to grounds for thinking it does not. In the absence of such grounds, *no activity is identified by the words* "giving grounds for thinking that the general bears on the given situation". If there were such an activity, then there would be no such thing as knowing the particular through the general. I said one might think that one need not give grounds to establish that one's fallible faculty bears on the situation or that a sublunary law holds. But in fact, there is no such thing as thinking this. The words following the phrase "one might think" do not identify a thought. Their sense self-destructs, as they undermine the notions of "faculty" and "law" that they attempt to employ.

# 8 How we know

Doubt requires justification. Putnam thinks this speaks in favor of his idea that we can know things in spite of the fact that we are never in a position to exclude the possibility of error, because we must exclude *only relevant* possibilities. But in fact, it has a very different significance. We see how we can be and often are in a position to exclude error when we understand why it is and what it means that doubt requires justification. Remember Putnam's example. Putnam maintains that he does not know that no one painted his house blue. However, he has no grounds for thinking someone did paint his house blue. Hence, even though he cannot rule out that someone painted his house blue, Putnam argues, he is entitled to dismiss the possibility as irrelevant. But Putnam here disregards an essential element: his knowledge of what, in general, people do and do not do. Putnam knows that, in general, no one paints a house unless he owns it or the owner asked or hired him to paint it. And he has no grounds for thinking that the situation is an exception. So it is not just that he has no grounds for thinking that someone painted his house, in the way in which he has no grounds for thinking that the roulette ball will land on a red number. Rather, he has *no grounds for thinking himself prevented from excluding the possibility that someone painted his house in a way in which he would otherwise be able to exclude it.* Given that he has no grounds for thinking this, he is, in virtue of his knowledge of the sublunary law, in a position to exclude that someone painted his house. If there are no grounds for thinking that a sublunary law fails to bear on the given situation, then, if the law does not fail to bear on it, one is, in virtue of knowing the law, in a position to exclude things that do not conform to it.

One may be tempted to think that this differs only verbally from what Putnam says. If there are no grounds for thinking that the law fails to bear on the given situation, then one knows through this law, given that the law in fact does not fail to bear on the given situation. And Putnam says that one need not give grounds to exclude the possibility that the law fails to bear on the given situation, since this possibility is remote or far-fetched and, hence, irrelevant. But this is not a verbal variant of, and is in fact incompatible with, what was said above. It is not that, as long as there are no grounds for thinking that the general fails to bear on the given situation, one need not exclude this possibility. Rather, as long as there are no such grounds, the words "excluding the possibility that the general fails to bear of the given situation" have no meaning. *It is not that something is not required for knowledge, but that the term that allegedly identifies that thing is void.*

# 9 Default and coherence

Human knowing has this structure: one knows the particular through the general. That doubt requires justification, then, is not a structure of rules of a dialectical game—of who must do what, and who wins out when. It is *a structure of the contents of knowledge*. It is a remarkable feature of analytic epistemology that it abstracts from all distinctions regarding the logical form of things known. Without reflecting upon it, it presupposes that it is possible to understand what it is to know something while disregarding the logical category of what is known. This is a strange assumption. One of its consequences is an incapacity to understand why, and what it means that, doubt requires justification. That doubt sometimes requires justification has been described as a "default and challenge structure of justification".[11] Now, when it is recognized that knowing is knowing the particular through the general, it is clear why some claims have default status. Given that one's senses tell one that this tie is green, the claim that it indeed is has default status: someone who challenges it must give grounds for thinking one's faculty of perception disturbed. And given that there are certain ways in which it comes about that one's house gets painted, the claim that no one painted Putnam's house this morning has default status. A challenger must give grounds for thinking the situation exceptional. But when one abstracts from the fact that one may know the particular through the general, it becomes mysterious how it is that certain claims enjoy a default status. A claim and its negation cannot both enjoy default status. Otherwise, justification would be impossible. Why is it, then, that of two opposing claims, one is default-justified, and the other is not? What makes the one claim, and not the other, deserving of this privilege? Within the confines of an epistemology that pays no attention to the logical category of what is known, this question has no answer. It is inevitable, then, that one hold that the distinction in virtue of which one claim is privileged over its negation is not objective, not *in* what is claimed. One is bound to think it subjective, as consisting in our attitudes toward the claims. We privilege one claim against the other; we institute its default status and exempt ourselves from the duty of justifying it.[12] The partisans of this view are less outspoken than Hume when they refrain from calling it a skeptical response to skepticism.

---

11 See Brandom 1994, 176–9; and Williams 2001, Chapter 13.
12 See Brandom 1994, 177: "One of the lessons we have learned from thinking about hyperbolic Cartesian doubt is that doubts too sometimes need to be justified in order to have the standing to impugn entitlement to doxastic commitments. Which commitments stand in need of vindication... is itself a matter of social practice—a matter of the practical attitudes adopted toward them by the practitioners."

Someone in the grips of an epistemology that abstracts from the category of the things known may think that the account I have tried to develop begs the question against the skeptical doubt. It explains that one may know something particular in virtue of knowing a suitable sublunary law. It thus explains how one can know one thing given that one knows some other thing. So the view is, at best, a version of a coherence theory of knowledge according to which things are known if they fit with what one already takes oneself to know.[13] Now, it is indeed a consequence of the account that, in order to know a particular thing, one must have general knowledge. This implies that it is wrong to think of knowledge about what, in general, people do or what, in general, happens as *abstracted from* knowledge about what this-and-that person did or what happened here-and-there. Of course, one's finding what he or she has done will inform one's conception of what people do. But it is not founded upon it, since general knowledge is always already invested in knowledge of particulars. Particular knowledge depends on general knowledge, as general knowledge depends on particular knowledge.[14] However, this does not express a coherence theory of knowledge. It does not even have the right form to specify a sufficient condition on knowledge. *It describes a structure of things known that is in place whenever anything is known in the way in which humans know things.* It describes an order of contents of a mind, an order that is in place if the mind in question is that of a human knower. The concept of knowing does not apply to everything whatsoever. It applies neither to stones nor to animals nor to newborns. A subject concerning whom there is a question as to whether she knows or not must possess certain capacities. She must be capable of giving grounds for what she says or thinks. But giving grounds means resting the particular on the general. It follows that a being who has the capacity to give grounds has knowledge of sublunary laws. I have followed Putnam in claiming that giving grounds in this way is the structure of human knowing. Thus, someone who lacks such knowledge neither knows nor does not know, but rather is not a proper subject of predications of knowledge in the sense in which such predications apply to humans. Objecting to the mutual dependence of particular and general means denying the

---

13 Michael Williams raised this objection in discussion.

14 This may sound reminiscent of Sellars's famous claim: "If there is a logical dimension in which other empirical propositions rest on observation reports, there is another logical dimension in which the latter rest on the former" (Sellars 1963, §38). However, the general knowledge of which Sellars speaks is what is sometimes called "reliability-knowledge": knowledge of a lawful covariation of utterances with what they are about. Nothing of what I say speaks in favor of thinking that particular knowledge rests on reliability-knowledge.

structure of human knowledge. It is to employ a concept of knowledge that does not apply to human beings.

# 10 The skeptic's conception of knowing

Above, I presented an argument to the effect that we cannot know anything. Its first premise is that one knows something if and only if one is in a position to rule out that one is mistaken. Its second premise is that, regardless of one's grounds, there are circumstances such that, if they obtained, one's grounds would not rule that out. Putnam claims that the skeptic fails to acknowledge the structure of human knowledge. The skeptic's argument distorts the concept of knowledge as it applies to humans. It is natural to locate this distortion in the first premise of the argument, for it appears to be conceptual: it articulates what it is to know. The second premise, by contrast, seems factual; it seems to express a discovery about the limited powers of our grounds. And it is in the first premise that Putnam locates the skeptic's mistake, whereas he thinks the second premise is true—his example is intended to illustrate its truth. I agree with Putnam that the skeptic fails to acknowledge the structure of human knowledge. I identified this structure as one of knowing the particular through the general. If the skeptic denies that this is how one may know, then this denial must be expressed in his argument. Since it is not be expressed by its first premise—there is no concept of knowing which does not conform to this first premise—it must be expressed by the second premise. Then the second premise is not factual, much less true, but imposes a condition on knowledge that is beyond the human.

One knows that things are so on the ground that one's senses reveal them to be so. And one knows that things are so because a sublunary law excludes that they are otherwise. However, the faculty is fallible; the law is not without exception. It may be, then, that the faculty and the law fail to bear on the situation. It may be that, in the given situation, one is prevented from knowing in virtue of one's fallible faculty or one's knowledge of a sublunary law. I shall say that, in this case, the situation is unfortunate. The second premise of the skeptical argument says that no matter what one's grounds, there is a possible circumstance such that, if it obtained, one's grounds would not be sufficient. The circumstance in question is one that would make the situation unfortunate. Now, it is clear that, if the situation were unfortunate, *one would not have sufficient grounds*. However, the second premise says something different. It says that if the situation were unfortunate, *one's grounds would not be sufficient*. This way of putting it implies, as the other does not, that the grounds on which one knows in a situation that is not unfortunate would be available even if the situation were unfortunate. In general, it implies that grounds on which one knows in one situation can be available in any situation. I shall call grounds satisfying this condition, and knowledge based on such grounds, asituational. It is crucial to the skeptical argument that grounds be asituational. The argument is a reductio of the assumption that one may have sufficient grounds: If someone, in a certain situation—a situation that is not unfortunate—has sufficient grounds, then there is a situation—an unfortunate situation—such that, in this situation, these grounds would not exclude that one is mistaken. But then one's grounds are not sufficient even in the fortunate situation. For grounds cannot be sufficient in one situation and insufficient in another. Whether something excludes something is not a feature of the situation in which it is called upon as a ground.[15] Now, this argument would not get going if the fortunate and the unfortunate situation differed in that, in the former, one has access to grounds that are out of reach in the latter.

The second premise of the skeptical argument imposes a condition on the nature of grounds on which one may know. *It requires that grounds for knowledge be asituational.* But if grounds are asituational, then there is no such thing as knowing the particular through the general. One knows the particular through the general when one knows that things are so on the ground that one perceives that they are. And one knows the particular through the general when one knows that things are so on the ground that a sublunary law excludes that they are otherwise. In an unfortunate situation, however, one's faculty of perception does not operate properly and the sublunary law does not apply. In such a situation, one does not perceive that things are a certain way, nor does the sublunary law exclude that they are a certain way. If it is required that grounds on which one knows in one situation be available in any situation, then neither the fallible faculty nor the sublunary law can be grounds on which one knows. Rather, one's grounds must consist, say, in one's senses letting one believe that

---

15 One may want to object that this thought is one Putnam attacks. (Compare 245–6 and n. 23.) It assumes that inferential relations are not "occasion-sensitive". But this would be a confusion. It may, of course, be that what in one situation is said with a certain sentence entails what, in the same situation, is said with another sentence, while this relation of *sentences* does not hold in another situation. But what excludes or entails something is not a sentence, but something said in using a sentence. It may be that things said in one situation are not available to be said in another, be it using the same or another sentence, and that, consequently, what can be excluded in one situation by speaking truly using a certain sentence cannot be excluded in another situation using the same or another sentence. This insight into the occasion-sensitivity of what is said—and, hence, excluded—in using a sentence does not call into question, but rather presupposes, that there is no such thing as something's excluding or entailing something in one situation but not in another.

things are so-and-so in a way that may or may not be a case of one's exercising one's faculty of perception. And they must consist in the fact that a certain state of affairs does not conform to a law that may or may not apply in the given situation. But these are not insufficient grounds, but *no grounds at all.* Grounds appear on the scene only when there are some grounds for thinking that the law applies and that the faculty operates. And as we saw, the idea that there are such grounds undermines the notions of a fallible faculty and of sublunary laws. It undermines the notion of knowing the particular through the general.[16]

The second skeptical premise requires that grounds for knowledge in one situation be available in any situation. It requires that, for any situation, there is something which, in this situation, would be those grounds. The situation in which the grounds suffice for knowledge must be inessential to the being of these grounds. As conceived by the second premise, *knowing something on certain grounds is not a way of being in a situation.* A knower, as such, is in no situation. The traditional paradigm of asituational knowledge is knowledge of geometrical forms. Geometrical knowledge is asituational because its subject matter is asituational. The general must not be brought to bear on the particular because what is known itself is general. Geometrical forms are the paradigm forms, the paradigm general or structural. As long as thought moves in the realm of the general or structural, it can achieve asituational knowledge. Hence, the second premise of the skeptical argument imposes a condition on knowledge which is not satisfied by a human intellect, which must return to the particular, the here-and-now and there-and-then. It is satisfied only by a divine intellect, which enjoys pure contemplation of the forms, of the general or structural. A divine intellect is in no situation—he is nowhere-and-nowhen—as is the object of his knowledge.

# 11 Two conceptions of finitude

The skeptical argument does not recognize that doubt requires justification. It thus imposes conditions on knowledge that are beyond human beings, but fit only for a divine intellect. I have argued that Putnam misidentifies the premise expressive of the skeptic's failure to acknowledge the structure of human knowledge. I now wish to argue that, in consequence, Putnam agrees with the skeptic in how he conceives of the finitude of the human mind.

---

16 I suppose that this generalizes John McDowell's disjunctive conception of experience.

Putnam believes the first premise of the skeptical argument to be faulty. However, its fault, as he sees it, does not lie with its concepts. It is beyond the human intellect to rule out all possibilities of error, Putnam thinks. Human knowing involves being in a position to rule out *some* of them. The condition definitive of divine knowledge (as expressed by the first premise of the skeptical argument) and the condition definitive of human knowledge (as expressed by Putnam's rectified version of it) are conceptually homogenous. There is no conceptual break in the passage from the human to the divine. In consequence, a human being and the concept of divine knowledge combine to yield a thought. But such a thought is necessarily false. This idea seems to be the essence of skepticism.

I have argued that the second premise of the skeptical argument is what is at fault. The premise requires that grounds for knowledge be asituational. Situational grounds are not weaker than asituational grounds. They differ in the way in which having a ground relates to being in a situation. That human grounds are situational means that the notion of a ground, as it applies to humans, includes the notion of a situation. Human knowing—knowing the particular through the general—is, essentially, knowing on situational grounds. The notion of an asituational ground does not apply to the human intellect. It is not the case, then, that human knowing is less than divine knowing. And it is not the case that a human being and the concept of divine knowledge combine to yield a—necessarily false—thought. There is no such thing as a thought that joins a human being with this concept.

Putnam's critique of the skeptical argument and the argument I have presented exemplify two opposing ways of conceiving the finitude of the human mind. Our finitude can be understood as lack or privation, or it can be understood as form or essence. I have tried to bring out that skepticism is, fundamentally, an expression of the former way of understanding human finitude, and I have tried to sketch a response to skepticism that questions this way of understanding it.

# Bibliography

Aristotle (1984), *Metaphysics*. In: Aristotle, *The Complete Works of Aristotle, Volume 2*, Jonathan Barnes (ed.), Princeton: Princeton University Press, 1552–728.

Brandom, Robert (1994), *Making It Explicit: Reasoning, Representing, and Discursive Commitment*, Cambridge, MA: Harvard University Press.

Davidson, Donald (1980), "Philosophy as Psychology." In: Donald Davidson, *Essays on Actions and Events*, Oxford: Oxford University Press, 229–38.

McDowell, John (1998), "Criteria, Defeasibility, and Knowledge." In: John McDowell, *Meaning, Knowledge, and Reality*, Cambridge, MA: Harvard University Press, 369–94

Putnam, Hilary (1998), "Skepticism." In: Marcello Stamm (ed.), *Philosophie in synthetischer Absicht*, Stuttgart: Klett-Cotta, 239–68.

Williams, Michael (2001), *Problems of Knowledge: A Critical Introduction to Epistemology*, Oxford: Oxford University Press.

Sellars, Wilfred (1963), "Empiricism and the Philosophy of Mind." In: Wilfred Sellars, *Science, Perception and Reality*, London: Routledge, 127–96.

Part II: After Wittgenstein

Cora Diamond
# The Hardness of the Soft: Wittgenstein's Early Thought About Skepticism

## I Introduction: A Question

I shall look at some ideas about skepticism that I think are those of Wittgenstein at the time he was writing his early Notebooks and the *Tractatus*. Wittgenstein is usually read as distinguishing sharply between the method of philosophy and that of science; what the method of science is is not usually taken to be problematic on that sort of reading. I shall be arguing that his treatment of skepticism shows that he is concerned with misunderstanding the method of philosophy on the model of the method of science as the latter method may be misunderstood. (This is not to suggest that if you got right the method of science, you could do philosophy using that method; rather, the temptingness of science as a model for philosophy is connected with misconceptions of how scientific thought is connected with the world.)

On the first of May, 1915, Wittgenstein wrote in his notebook:

> Scepticism is *not* irrefutable but *obvious nonsense* when it tries to doubt where no question can be asked.
>
> For doubt can exist only where a question exists; a question can exist only where an answer exists, and this can exist only where something *can* be said.[1]

He repeated this almost verbatim in the *Tractatus* (6.51).[2] We ought to find the passage puzzling. Skepticism is supposedly nonsensical if it tries to raise doubts where no questions can be asked. *Why* are the questions the skeptic tries to raise supposed to be non-questions? Why is the skeptic described as trying to doubt where no questions can be asked? Wittgenstein's answer to that is that there can be a question only where an answer exists, and an answer only where something can be said. But *why* can't it be said that the answer to the question, for example, whether physical objects—things like chairs and tables—exist independently of experience is "No, they do not?" Why would that not be something that can be said? Or if the skeptic raises doubts about other minds, why can't we answer the skeptic by saying, for example, that other people do have thoughts

---

**1** Wittgenstein 1961a, 44. I have slightly changed the wording of the translation.

**2** Wittgenstein 1961b.

and feelings? Why would that not be an answer? Why is it not something that can be said? If skepticism is supposed to be obviously nonsensical in trying to raise doubts where no questions can be asked, where is the obviousness? Why does Wittgenstein think that the questions and answers here are attempts to say something where there is no saying anything?

When we read the *Tractatus*, and we think about Wittgenstein's remarks about what can't be said, we usually take quite a different sort of example of unsayable things. Indeed, usually we focus on the propositions of the *Tractatus* itself and propositions closely related to them. But the case of skepticism seems to be somewhat different. For the skeptic is not attempting to speak about the relation between language and reality, or about logical form, or about whether or not there have to be simple objects. Why should he not be understandable as denying or doubting some genuine hypothesis?

If you read the *Tractatus* as containing or implying some form of verificationism, you can answer the questions I have been asking. If skepticism is supposed to be nonsensical because it attempts to raise doubts where no questions can be asked, and questions can be asked only where something can be said, you could explain those ideas as reflections of verificationism. The skeptic, we might say, is dissatisfied with the verification procedures for our claims about other minds (for example); he may argue that the behavior we observe might be just what it is, but might have nothing—no pain, no feelings, no thoughts—behind it. He may insist that, whatever ways we have for establishing our claims about what someone is feeling, the evidence doesn't give us the fact itself; the facts could be totally different from what we take them to be. And so we cannot know about others what we claim to know. A verificationist reading of the *Tractatus* could be used to explain why such skepticism could be called nonsensical. For the skeptical position just outlined depends on rejecting any understanding of our claims about the minds of others that limits itself to what we can verify. In fact, one might say that those readers of the *Tractatus* who have argued that it is not verificationist in character owe us an alternative explanation of why skeptical doubts are supposed to be obviously nonsensical. Here I'd make a stronger claim. The *Tractatus* claims to provide a way of dealing with philosophical problems all at once, and once for all; and we may take the problems of skepticism as intended to illustrate the nonsensicality of philosophical problem-mongering, as revealed by the *Tractatus*. So about the question "If the *Tractatus* is not verificationist, how is it that skepticism is supposedly shown to be nonsensical?", we can say that, if you don't have an answer to *that*, you don't have a reading of the *Tractatus* connecting what it takes to be its achievement with a particular example which it gives of the application of its central ideas—an application given a prominent position in the text in the concluding sections. Your reading is broken-backed.

## II Wittgenstein and Russell on Skepticism

There are various ways in which one might try to answer the question I have asked. There are interpretations of the *Tractatus* which take the 'simple objects' of which Wittgenstein speaks to be material points; and on such a reading the nonsensicality of skepticism about the external world might be taken as a straightforward consequence of the character of the simple objects. Another answer to my question might be given by looking at Wittgenstein's discussion of claims such as "There are objects" (4.1272). This is supposedly nonsensical because it gives to the word "object" (which is a word used as a variable, according to the *Tractatus*) the use of a proper concept-word. Wittgenstein provides a short list of other words which may lead to philosophical problems in similar ways: "complex," "fact," "function," and "number." It is not meant to be complete. One might ask whether the skeptic's expression of doubts involves a use of language of the same sort as those specified (and whether the doubts cannot be reformulated in language which avoids the use of formal concepts as proper concepts). If one explored that line of argument, one would be looking at Wittgenstein's claims about skepticism as applications of a quite general approach to metaphysical uses of language. I shall go in a different direction, and consider the particular case of the sort of skepticism Wittgenstein had in mind. I think it is clear that he had in mind Russell on skepticism, and I shall turn now to Wittgenstein in relation to Russell's ideas about skepticism.

What, then, is Wittgenstein responding to? In *The Problems of Philosophy*, a book with which Wittgenstein was familiar, and of which he had a low opinion, Russell had remarked that skepticism cannot be refuted, although he thought that the adoption of a skeptical view of the possibility of knowledge would not, merely on that account, be reasonable.[3] Russell also explicitly took the view in that book that philosophy cannot answer all the questions it asks, and there he is plainly including skeptical questions as among the questions asked by philosophy. His introductory chapter on appearance and reality in fact begins with the quest for certainty, described in terms that come from post-Cartesian skepticism about the external world. And so it is possible that Wittgenstein's remarks about skepticism in 1915 are responses to Russell's *Problems of Philosophy*.

---

3 Russell 1967. The irrefutability of skepticism is discussed on 87.

But I think it likely that he had in mind a later work of Russell's, *Our Knowledge of the External World*. In January of 1915, Wittgenstein received a letter from Keynes, referring to Russell's book as having recently been published; in his reply, Wittgenstein asked Keynes to send it to him.[4] I think Keynes sent it to Wittgenstein together with Russell's essay "On Scientific Method in Philosophy," and that Wittgenstein received the book and the essay some time in March or April. My argument is going to be that we can see how Wittgenstein was thinking about skepticism if we see how his ideas are connected with the rest of his response to Russell; and so I'm going to include here the rest of the passage from the Notebooks that I quoted earlier, from May 1st. After the remark that skepticism is not irrefutable but obvious nonsense when it raises doubts where no question can be asked, and the comment that doubt can't exist where our questions have no answers because in such cases nothing can be said, Wittgenstein continues this way:

> All theories that say: "This is how it must be, otherwise we could not philosophize" or "otherwise we surely could not live," etc., etc., must of course disappear.
> My method is not to sunder the hard from the soft, but to see the hardness of the soft. It is one of the chief skills of the philosopher not to occupy himself with questions which do not concern him.
> Russell's method in his "Scientific method in philosophy" is simply a retrogression from the method of physics.[5]

I shall not discuss in detail all the connections between that passage and the writings that I believe were sent to Wittgenstein by Keynes, but every remark in the passage appears to refer to something Russell says and to bear on the issue of skepticism. I shall list here the apparent connections, since there is no external evidence that I know of for Wittgenstein's having received this material.[6] Wittgenstein's remark about skepticism not being irrefutable refers to Russell's saying that universal skepticism is irrefutable.[7] Wittgenstein's remark

---

4 Wittgenstein 1974, 111. Cf. also Wittgenstein 1991, 55.

5 Wittgenstein 1961a, 44.

6 Page references are to Russell 1929. See also Baker/Hacker 1980, 464 n. 7, and 465 n. 8; Baker and Hacker raise the question whether Wittgenstein was likely to have been able to refer to Russell's Spencer Lecture, "On Scientific Method in Philosophy" (given in late 1914), as contrasted with the earlier Lowell lectures, a question which arises if Wittgenstein got hold of the relevant writings of Russell's either before the War or relatively early during the War. If, as I think, Wittgenstein received some writings of Russell's from Keynes in the spring of 1915, the respective dates of the Lowell and Spencer lectures would not be relevant to the question of what he was referring to in May of 1915.

7 Russell 1929, 71, 75.

about theories that say what we have to do in order to philosophize refers to Russell's discussion of skepticism: Russell says that, if we are to continue philosophizing we have to make our bow to the skeptical hypothesis and proceed to the consideration of other hypotheses which, though perhaps not certain, have at least as good a right to our respect as has that of the skeptic.[8] (Russell also speaks, elsewhere in the chapter, of what we cannot help believing.) Wittgenstein's remark about separating the hard from the soft refers to the same passage in Russell; Russell's distinction is between data that stand up to philosophical–critical reflection, and data that can be made to appear more or less doubtful by such reflection. And it seems likely that Wittgenstein's remark about its being one of the chief skills of the philosopher not to occupy himself with questions that do not concern him concerns Russell's use, in this same passage, of psychological notions in his discussion of skepticism. What Russell terms "hard" data are data resistant to doubt; and greater or lesser resistance to doubt is a psychological matter. That is what the philosopher ought not to occupy himself with. The final remark in the passage, about Russell's method, may refer directly to Russell's essay, not to *Our Knowledge of the External World*;[9] but I believe the remark is linked to the others through Wittgenstein's thinking that what is wrong with Russell's treatment of skepticism in *Our Knowledge of the External World* depends on Russell's faulty method in philosophy. Wittgenstein's remark about Occam's razor, on April 23rd of 1915 (repeated in the *Tractatus*), appears to be a response to Russell's talk of Occam's razor in *Our Knowledge of the External World*.

---

**8** Russell 1929, 71, 75–6.

**9** The matter is subject to some uncertainty. *Our Knowledge of the External World* originally included in its title the words "Scientific Method in Philosophy"; the American edition of the book had the title "Scientific Method in Philosophy" on the spine. If Wittgenstein did receive the material from Keynes, it is possible that Keynes sent only the book, not the essay, and possible also that it was easier for him to arrange for the book to be sent from a neutral country and that the American edition was sent. For these reasons it is possible that Wittgenstein's remark about "Russell's method in his 'Scientific method in philosophy'" refers to *Our Knowledge of the External World*. See also Baker/Hacker 1980, 465 n. 8; they take it that it is more likely that Wittgenstein's reference is to *Our Knowledge of the External World*. But they appear to assume that, if Wittgenstein had access to either work, he had received the material before the War or at any rate before 1915. I think the sudden appearance in Wittgenstein's notes of very direct references to Russell's book a few months after he had heard from Keynes about the book and asked Keynes to send it to him suggest instead that he received a parcel from Keynes some time during 1915. I don't know of any reason to think that Wittgenstein had received a version of the Lowell lectures at any earlier time. The lectures were given before the War, but Wittgenstein and Russell were no longer in regular contact. The existing letters between Russell and Wittgenstein don't suggest that Wittgenstein received the Lowell lectures from Russell before or during the War.

A further connection between *Our Knowledge of the External World* and the *Tractatus* can perhaps be seen at 5.135, which may be a response to Russell's statement that causal laws simply are those propositions which allow us to infer the existence of one thing or event from the existence of another or of several others,[10] but (as Peter Hylton has pointed out) Russell had accepted at least as early as 1912 the view Wittgenstein rejects, namely that we can make such inferences.[11] The propositions about causality at 6.32–6.34 may be responses to Russell's discussion of causation; they date originally from March 29th and April 23rd of 1915. Wittgenstein's remarks on freedom of the will on April 27th may also be a response to Russell on freedom of the will in *Our Knowledge of the External World*. Although I think it likely that Wittgenstein's discussion of causation in the Notebooks and the *Tractatus* is intended to bear on Russell's views about causation and about skepticism, I shall not discuss causation in this essay.

Wittgenstein's response to Russell on skepticism is linked to his rejecting, in its entirety, Russell's conception of philosophical method. Here is a specification of the central features of Russell's conception, as expressed in the essay on "On Scientific Method in Philosophy."[12]

1. According to Russell, philosophical propositions are general in the sense of being true of everything, "of each individual thing" (SMIP, 110).

2. Russell took philosophical propositions to be concerned with what is true in every possible world, not with what is merely and accidentally true in this one (SMIP, 111).

Those two ideas together lead Russell to characterize philosophy as *the science of the possible* (SMIP, 111).

3. Philosophy, as the science of the possible, investigates logical forms. It is thus able to deal with its problems piecemeal, to make progress as other sciences do, bit by bit, building on previous results. Philosophy, like other sciences, should achieve successive approximations to the truth (SMIP, 112–13).

4. There are problems which cannot be decisively dealt with in the way described. We may be capable merely of showing that a particular philosophical theory accounts for the facts in a natural and relatively simple way, and such a demonstration would not decisively refute alternative hypotheses (SMIP, 120, 124).

---

10 Russell 1929, 231.
11 Hylton 1990, 384.
12 References to "On Scientific Method in Philosophy" (hereafter: SMIP) are to the essay as printed in Russell 1917, 97–124.

Wittgenstein rejects all four of these points. I shall be concerned in this essay with the first, third and fourth. (Part III has some remarks bearing on the second point.)

Russell had argued that progress in philosophy, as in the other sciences, should be piecemeal, little by little, incremental. In the Preface to the *Tractatus*, Wittgenstein says, "No." He believes himself to have found, on all essential points, the final solution to the problems.[13] And, interestingly, he continues: If he is not mistaken in this belief, part of the value of his book consists in its showing how little is achieved when these problems *are* solved. And that last point too marks a disagreement with Russell. For if you conceive philosophy as the science of the possible, the solution of all of the problems of philosophy at once would be a huge achievement, analogous to a solution all at once of all the problems of physics, but on an even grander scale. The Russellian picture of incremental progress goes, that is, with a grand conception of the whole philosophical project; Wittgenstein announces an all-at-once solution of the problems, and puts with that a statement implying that the Russellian conception of the grand philosophical long-term project is illusory: the incremental progress idea is tied closely to a false conception of the problems.

In the Notebook remarks quoted above, Wittgenstein rejects Russell's conception of scientific method in philosophy as a retrogression from the method of physics, a step backwards from what that method is (a step backwards presumably in the sense that, before the development of physics as a genuine science, there was a stage of thought involving the method, or something like the method, that Russell takes to be 'scientific method'). So Wittgenstein is not criticizing Russell merely for modeling philosophical method on that of the sciences, but for modeling philosophical method on the method of physics as he misunderstands *that*. In late 1914 (that is, some months before receiving Russell's book or essay, on the chronology I am assuming) Wittgenstein had described the method of physics as he understood it; there is an obvious contrast with Russell's understanding. Thus, Russell takes it that the laws of physics are uniformities which we have discovered. It is clear, he says, that there must be some uniformity that will fit the data, however complicated the data may be. The uniformities that we have discovered have been relatively simple, but we may then come to find that they do not fit accurately when we consider new

---

13 While Wittgenstein rejected Russell's idea of piecemeal progress in philosophy, his idea of philosophical method nevertheless involved a kind of piecemeal approach to the things that philosophers say. See Diamond 2004. See also Anscombe 1963, 151 (on the *ad hoc* character of the criticism of sentences that express no real thought).

data.[14] Wittgenstein's contrasting view comes out sharply here: "[I]t asserts nothing about the world that it can be described by means of Newtonian mechanics; but *this* asserts something, namely, that it can be described in that particular way by means of Newtonian mechanics in which indeed it is described."[15] And Wittgenstein adds that we are told something about the world by this too: that the world can be described more simply by means of one mechanics than by means of another. The 1914 account of how mechanics is related to the world is repeated in the *Tractatus*, and is very different from one which takes the laws of mechanics to give us uniformities that we have so far found to hold. For if they did give us uniformities of that sort, it *would* assert something about the world that it can be described by means of Newtonian mechanics.[16]

When Russell says that skepticism is irrefutable, he is thinking of it on the model of a hypothesis considered within the sciences and as an alternative to other philosophical hypotheses about experience and what lies beyond it. It may be difficult to give an account of what entities, exactly, a statement concerns; this applies to the laws and hypotheses of physics and to the hypotheses of philosophers. But Russell's conception of how the laws and hypotheses in both cases connect with the world is ultimately the same. Their connection with the world is not different in kind from that of ordinary generalizations. Wittgenstein's view about skeptical problems was tied to his idea that skeptical doubt doesn't put before us a hypothesis that is difficult or impossible to prove false. The skeptic hypothesizes *nothing*. The skeptic fools us and himself into taking nonsense for a hypothesis. Wittgenstein's account depends on his view of a contrast between ordinary generalizations and other types of general-

---

**14** See especially SMIP 101–105.

**15** Wittgenstein 1961a, 6.12.14. The translation is based on Wittgenstein's suggestions about the translation of the corresponding passage in the *Tractatus*.

**16** The account I am giving here and in the rest of this essay can be contrasted with that of Hacker 1996, 35. Hacker says that, on Wittgenstein's view, the task of physics is to discover the most general truths about the universe. If this is supposed to imply that, on Wittgenstein's view, the laws of physics are general truths about the universe, it seems inconsistent with Wittgenstein's remark that it asserts nothing about the world to say that it can be described by means of Newtonian mechanics. That seems clearly to imply that "F = ma," for example, is not a very general truth about the universe. On the kind of account Hacker gives, Wittgenstein thinks that the trouble with Russell's philosophical method is that it is modeled on that of science; on my account, he thinks that the trouble is that it is modeled on a misconception of the method of science. I believe Wittgenstein also thought that clarity about the method of science could help us to see that what we want to do in philosophy is not the kind of thing that is done in physics, properly understood. See also Baker/Hacker 1980, 465, for another statement that seems to suggest that Wittgenstein took the laws of physics to be propositions which are true or false in the way that ordinary generalizations about the world are.

ity: the generality of logic, of mathematics and of the sciences, or rather of physics.

# III Looking At the Use: A Few Notes

I want to see the *Tractatus* as exhibiting a kind of tension. Wittgenstein says in the Preface that he thinks he has "*die Probleme im Wesentlichen endgültig gelöst.*" That is, he sees himself as having, in it, completed a task. On the other hand, we can see the book, as Michael Kremer has argued, as a kind of transitional work, in which themes which are familiar from the later work are already making their appearance, and in which some of Wittgenstein's earliest ideas about the relation of language and the world have already been subjected to criticism.[17] In this section of my essay, I want to consider a feature of the *Tractatus* as a work in transition. At remark 6 of the book, Wittgenstein gives us the general form of a proposition. In the remarks that begin at 6.1, he considers a kind of proposition, logical propositions, the use of which is radically different from that of ordinary senseful propositions. Logical propositions are not generalizations over everything; their connection to the world is very different from that of general propositions that say things stand this way or that. In the remarks beginning 6.2, Wittgenstein considers mathematical equations. Their use, too, is different from that of general propositions that say things stand in such-and-such a way; their connection to the world is different. In the remarks beginning 6.3, Wittgenstein considers a quite different range of propositions, the principles of physics, and in particular the principles of Newtonian mechanics. These principles (as we have seen) do have a connection to the world; it is not that of logic, and it is equally not that of ordinary descriptions of how things are. Such principles provide a form in which descriptions of the world can be cast. Their generality is not that of ordinary general propositions. In the 6.4s, Wittgenstein considers yet another type of use of language, which he describes in language the use of which has resemblances to the use about which he is speaking.[18] He speaks of the relation of such language to the world as being a relation to the world as a whole. (In the later "Lecture on Ethics" he elaborates the idea that, when we speak in the kind of way he had in mind, it is essential to what we are doing that no account can be given of what it is such sentences say; what is said is not a description of some sort of fact the correct logical analysis of

---

**17** Kremer 1997, Part 7.
**18** For a discussion of the resemblances and differences, see Diamond 1991.

which has not yet been found.)[19] We have him, then, in the 6.1s, the 6.2s, the 6.3s, and the 6.4s, speaking of different uses of language: all four sets of remarks are about uses of language which are different from the saying-things-are-so use. All four concern forms of language that might be taken to express a priori truths about the universe, truths having total generality or absolute necessity; and it is Wittgenstein's concern in the 6s to show how misleading such an understanding of them would be. What sets them apart is not that they are or must be true of everything or that they are or must be true under all conditions; it is rather that they have very different uses from propositions which are true of this or that thing or many things or everything or nothing. The 6s begin, then, to give prominence to the idea of there being quite distinct kinds of use of sentences; there is also the implication that sentences that seem to be generalizations over things may in particular have quite different functions. (I believe that the account of these functions of language in the 6.1s, 6.2s, 6.3s, and 6.4s is meant to bear on the question of the method of philosophy, to which Wittgenstein turns in the 6.5s. What the correct method in philosophy is can be seen once wrong ways of conceiving the method are ruled out by correcting the misconceptions on which they rest. Thus, first, the relation of philosophy to the world might be taken to be like that of logic, logic itself being conceived as a science of general necessary truths, or philosophy might be taken to be part of such a science; in either case the conception of philosophy would rest on misconceptions about logic. Or, secondly, philosophy might be taken to be related to the world in something like the way mathematics is, mathematics being taken to express a priori truths about mathematical objects and their relations; again such a conception of philosophy would rest on a misconception of mathematics. I shall discuss the bearing of misconceptions about science on our understanding of philosophy below. Philosophy might also be conceived as providing answers to questions about life, might, that is. be thought to be continuous with ethics, where ethics is thought of as providing knowledge of non-accidental truths about value. A misconception of ethics can thus also provide the basis for misunderstanding philosophy.)

When Wittgenstein returned to philosophy in the 1930s, he gave considerable attention to what he then spoke of as 'hypotheses.' Hypotheses are laws for constructing statements; they are not true or false, but provide modes of description that are more or less simple and convenient. The account of hypotheses is obviously very close to the Tractatus account of the principles of mechanics as providing forms of description; an example (which may be Waismann's) is

---

**19** Wittgenstein 1965, 11.

that of the application of Boyle's law in constructing descriptions of the behavior of gases.[20] In Wittgenstein's 1930's way of thinking, sentences about chairs and tables and other ordinary physical objects are described as hypotheses; that that is their use is evident in the complex relation of our sentences about such things to verification.[21] In this account of sentences about physical things, Wittgenstein is developing further the idea that is present in the 6s in the Tractatus, of various uses of sentences distinct from the use of saying such-and-such is so. And in particular he develops the idea that the law-character of physics is evident in what he speaks of as its incompleteness. There isn't such a thing as getting to the end of what a law of physics says or of what is said by, say, a statement about a bird's laying eggs, thereby completing its verification. Wittgenstein makes use of the image of a cross-section: what is verified is cross-sections through the hypothesis or law.[22] I shall return to this issue of *completeness of sense*, which surfaces in a different way in Wittgenstein's earlier discussions of physics.

# IV Separating the Hard from the Soft: Some Comments

Here I should like to move back to Wittgenstein's initial response to Russell on skepticism, in 1915. What did he have in mind by the mysterious remark that his method is not that of separating the hard from the soft, but that of seeing the hardness of the soft? In this section, I begin to discuss the questions: What is hard and what is soft? And what has it all to do with skepticism?

Russell's idea of distinguishing the hard from the soft is central to his conception of philosophical method. We start with the data of what we take ourselves to know in ordinary life, and we see how resistant the various sorts of data are to dissolution by the critical reflection of philosophy. We find that there are two sorts of data that stand up best to the attempt to subject them to doubt: the particular facts of sense and the general truths of logic. These two sorts of data share two features. We find that we simply cannot doubt them; real doubt would be pathological. And it is also the case that we need to assume that these data do represent genuine knowledge or we should not be able to philosophize. Wittgenstein treats both points as examples of Russell's

---

**20** Waismann 1979, 255. Cf., also Wittgenstein's use of kinetic versus caloric theories of heat, at Wittgenstein 1961a, 23.12.14.

**21** See, e.g., §8 of "Theses" in Waismann 1979.

**22** Waismann 1979, 100, 259.

introduction into philosophy of what does not belong there. The psychology of doubt, the psychological facts of what is evident to us, or not doubtable by us, are irrelevant to philosophy. This criticism of Russell enters the *Tractatus* at a quite different point, as a criticism of Russell on logic (5.4731), but it is equally relevant to Russell on skepticism, as the Notebook entry makes clear. It is relevant too to Wittgenstein's later ideas about skepticism and certainty; there too the issue of the psychology of doubt and certainty is separated from the question where, logically, there is room for doubt. If we approach the question of skepticism by taking it that what is the matter with skeptical doubt is that it is psychologically out of reach, or that it would make it impossible for us to do certain sorts of thing, like philosophize, or that we have to assume the doubts to be unreal in order to live, we leave intact the fundamental skeptical conception of our relation to the world, the conception shared by Russell and the skeptic. We see that conception when Russell, after taking it that he is entitled in his philosophical treatment of knowledge to take as indubitable the data of sense and the general truths of logic, proceeds to respond to skepticism about the external world by giving a representation of our knowledge of physical objects and of the laws of physics that abstains from inferences to the kinds of entities belief in which would be 'soft.' Russell attempts to show that an explanation of the 'hard' data of sense is available which has a naturalness and simplicity which make it preferable to the hypothesis of the skeptic; he makes clear, too, that his account avoids the risk of introduction of metaphysical entities. The skeptic and Russell share a conception of risk and of the avoidance of risk in relation to our knowledge of the world. Russell sees skeptical questioning and skeptical doubt as demonstrations of the risks; he sees responses to such questioning and doubt as risk-avoidance strategies, his own strategy being one of showing that our knowledge of the external world doesn't need to be conceived as going quite so far out on a limb as the skeptic thinks it does.

What is it, then, in response to Russell's approach to our knowledge of the world, to look for, or to try to see, the hardness of the soft? What is supposedly soft is belief in the kinds of thing the skeptic can get us to doubt. In *Our Knowledge of the External World*, the main soft thing is our knowledge of physical objects, where these are taken (at any rate, as we first conceive them) to be objects independent of the self. This 'softness' is evident in post-Russellian approaches too, such as that of Thomas Nagel. He begins his Introduction to philosophy by telling students that, if you think about it, the inside of your own mind is the only thing you can be sure of. Ordinarily, you have no doubts about the existence of the floor under your feet, but how do you know it really exists?[23] Nagel attempts to lead you down a path towards taking your belief in the existence of the floor to be 'soft' in Russell's sense. So what is it to try to see the hardness there? To see the hardness of the soft would be to see that it isn't soft at all, that its looking soft had been a matter of misunderstandings of the use of language. The resistance to skeptical doubt, the 'hardness,' that concerns Wittgenstein is logical, not psychological.

# V Russell, Wittgenstein, and Things: a Beginning

The apparent softness is that of our beliefs about ordinary things like tables and chairs; and what we need to look at in more detail now is how Russell and Wittgenstein think of our thought about *things*. Russell held that our ordinary beliefs about familiar things like chairs lead us to a natural but 'audacious' metaphysical theory.[24] We naturally come to think of sense-appearances as caused by objects that are independent of our minds and that persist when not perceived; we naturally, at first, take these inferred objects to be at least similar to the sense-appearances they cause, for example, in being colored. This form of realism about the character of physical things and of their relation to the senses is soft; Russell had earlier argued that, even if it could not be definitively refuted, it could be shown to be groundless.[25] Russell's alternative account takes the ultimately real constituents of the world to be quite different from physical objects conceived on that 'natural' metaphysical view. His account takes to be real only sense-data and particulars that resemble sense-data (except that they are not actually perceived). The account is open to skeptical doubt so far as it does involve inference to entities with which one is not acquainted: inferences to sense-data not had by oneself and to particulars resembling sense-data but not had by anyone. So on his own view, it cannot be entirely certain that the theory does correctly describe the ultimate constituents of reality. It involves quantifying over particulars most of which are inferred entities, and its own openness to skeptical doubt arises because the entities that have to exist for the theory to be true may not exist, and if they do exist, they may nevertheless not have the properties ascribed to them. The theory does, though, provide an explanatory account that is intended to be superior to the alternatives Russell has in view (including ideal-

---

23 Nagel 1987, 8–9.
24 Russell 1929, 108.
25 Russell 1967, 17.

ism, skepticism, and various non-Russellian forms of realism). As Peter Hylton makes clear in his account of Russell's method, Russell's conception of philosophy as capable of incremental progress is tied closely to his understanding of how such progress will diminish the plausibility of the skeptic's hypotheses. A complete or ideal response to the skeptic would enable one to represent the things one claims to know entirely in terms of logical constructions from one's own objects of acquaintance. And so progress in philosophy, in representing different sorts of thing we claim to know through the method of logical constructions, would leave progressively fewer areas of thought within which skepticism could seriously challenge our beliefs.[26] Russell gave two slightly different formulations of the basic maxim of scientific method in philosophy as he understood it: "Whenever possible, logical constructions are to be substituted for inferred entities,"[27] and "'Occam's razor': *Entities are not to be multiplied without necessity.*"[28] In choosing these ways of putting in a nutshell his conception of scientific method in philosophy, Russell was at the same time expressing the significance of responding philosophically to skepticism by the avoidance, so far as possible, of commitment to entities belief in which is 'soft.'

Wittgenstein discusses the relation of the propositions of physics to ordinary propositions in an inconclusive and difficult passage in the Notebooks, in late June of 1915 (20.6.15). He had earlier (in the passage I discussed in Part II) taken the laws of mechanics to speak about the world only through the logical apparatus that connects them to propositions which describe the world and which are constructed in accordance with the ground-plan the laws in question provide. The two passages together enable us to see, then, that such a law has a different sort of relation to the world from that of a proposition in the full sense, where the proposition-in-the-full-sense might belong to physics (might form part of a description explicitly formulated on the 'ground-plan' provided by physical laws) or might be part of our ordinary talk of things.[29] A proposition such as "The

---

26 See Hylton 1990, Chapter 8, esp. 384–90.

27 Russell, "The Relation of Sense Data to Physics," in Russell 1917, 145–179, at 155.

28 Russell 1929, 113.

29 I can only very briefly indicate how the reading I am giving of Wittgenstein on physics differs from that of Anthony Kenny (see Kenny 1975, 99). Kenny takes Wittgenstein to be working with a contrast between two sorts of laws within physics, laws like the fundamental principles of mechanics, which do not speak about the world directly or indirectly, and particular laws which do speak, but indirectly, about the world and are propositions in the full sense. I think that Wittgenstein's idea was that the general principles and the less general principles give ways of constructing senseful propositions on a 'ground-plan' and, so far as they speak about the world, they do it in the same way, by providing ground-plans which will then enable us to give descriptions of the world with greater or lesser ease compared with competing ground-plans. A

book is on the table," Wittgenstein says, has a relation to reality such that *whatever* is the case, we must be able to see whether the proposition is true or false. There you see expressed an idea that Wittgenstein repeatedly emphasizes in the Notebooks: that, if an ordinary proposition has a sense, the sense is *complete*. Thus he had said, a few days earlier, "Every proposition that has a sense has a COMPLETE sense, and it is a picture of reality in such a way that what is not yet said in it simply cannot belong to its sense."[30] The laws of physics are not propositions in that sense; the very fact that their bearing on the world goes through the use they have in providing a plan for the construction of propositions *with* sense indicates their 'incompleteness' in the relevant regard. They speak of the world only *through* something external to themselves, unlike a proposition-in-the-full-sense.[31] I am not here suggesting that Wittgenstein took the sense of ordinary propositions not to depend on use. The issue is rather the difference between two sorts of use, and I shall turn to that difference in Part VI.

# VI Wittgenstein's 1915 Philosophy of Things: More Notes on Looking at the Use, and More About the Hard and the Soft

Wittgenstein's remarks about physics are, as I said, difficult to construe, and, further, they are clearly a reflection of ideas in flux. The ideas are questioned and rethought even in the notes from a single day. Nevertheless, I think it is possible to see the kind of implication they have for Wittgenstein's 1915 philosophy of Things. Consider an example that Wittgenstein uses several times, that of propositions about his watch, e.g., that it is not in the drawer, or that it is lying on the table. He says: "If... I say that this watch is not in the drawer, there is absolutely no need for it to FOLLOW LOGICALLY that a wheel which is in the watch is not in the drawer, for perhaps *I had not the least knowledge* that the wheel was in the

---

more particular ground-plan is still a ground-plan, not a proposition-in-the-full-sense. The reason Wittgenstein says little about more particular ground-plans is that it is unnecessary to do so, since they represent a stage in the construction of propositions-in-the-full-sense from the overall ground-plan. For an account of Wittgenstein's view of scientific theories, see also Griffin 1964, 102–8.

**30** Wittgenstein 1961a, 15.6.15.

**31** See the development of this idea of completeness of sense of genuine propositions in the notes of 15.6.15, e.g., the statement that if a proposition tells us something, then it must, just as it is, be a picture of reality.

watch, and hence could not have meant by 'this watch' the complex in which the wheel occurs."[32] Here, the complexity of the proposition about the watch includes the complexity of the cases the speaker would count as relevant to the truth or falsity of the claim; and, in the case Wittgenstein considers, the speaker does not count as relevant to truth or falsity anything about the innards of the watch. It might have no wheels inside, or wheels made out of butter, as far as the sense of this proposition is concerned. Wittgenstein says nothing about alternative ways of talking about the watch. We should not, though, take him to be suggesting that what he has described is the only way in which language connects with the watch. But if we give an account of how the hands move from having such-and-such angle between them to having such-and-such other angle between them—if we talk about watches as *machines*—the relation of our talk to the world is different; the kind of proposition is different, and the proposition is not in the same full sense a proposition; it does not have a complete sense of its own. We can give the mechanics of watches, but this will not be a matter of our having propositions about watches that are just more complicated than the proposition about this watch not being in the drawer; it will not be a matter of our watch-propositions (in the machine-case) containing more conjunctions or generalizations.[33] If that were the case, the propositions would still be propositions with their own 'complete' sense; but, where physical laws are involved, the propositions are no longer complete specifications of truth-conditions; they are in a sense then 'not propositions.' (This is not to deny that we could conjoin

---

32 Wittgenstein 1961a, 18.6.15.

33 The difference can be seen if we consider a diagram of the mechanics of escapement watches. Such a diagram is not, in Wittgenstein's sense, a picture or model of any situation, but we can use it to construct propositions about the position or the movements of hands of actual watches. The diagram provides a simple mode of description for watches. What tells us something about the world is not the diagram, but the exact way in which it is possible for us to describe watches using the diagram. The diagram could be used in other ways, as, for example, a representation of the insides of a particular watch. Compare the various other cases in which the *Tractatus* recognizes different possible uses for the same picture or proposition, as at 4.062 and 4.0621, where Wittgenstein speaks of reversing the sense of a proposition, and at 3.315, where he speaks of turning a constituent of a proposition into a variable. This is not a matter of replacing an 'a,' say, by an 'x,' but of using a sign as a variable, giving it a use different in kind from that of the constituent it replaces. In one sense, the proposition-as-picture might remain unchanged, but in its new use it no longer pictures or represents that anything is the case. A picture of a watch can similarly function as a picture of a particular watch, as part of a generalization about watches, or alternatively, as a mechanical diagram. The kind of generality it has in the latter case is entirely different from that of an empirical generalization. See also Juliet Floyd's discussion of Wittgenstein on generality, in Floyd 2005, 92, where she discusses the difference in use between a genre picture and a picture of a concrete situation.

propositions describing the insides of a watch with propositions about the position of the watch to make more complex propositions that have a complete sense of their own; the point is rather that that is not what a proposition about watches-as-machines is.) I am suggesting that Wittgenstein's treatment in the 1930s of the laws of physics and of hypotheses is a development of the contrast in the Notebooks between a proposition in the full sense (a proposition whose sense is 'complete') and a proposition the connection of which to reality goes through the construction of other propositions, where that application is not itself a part of the proposition in question. In the latter case, the proposition does not have a 'complete' sense.[34] My suggestion, then, is that Wittgenstein in the Notebooks and the *Tractatus* enables us to distinguish two different sorts of use: a law-use of propositions most clearly exemplified by the equations of physics, and a non-law use of propositions exemplified by the statement that one's watch is on the table, where that is non-committal about anything beyond these-or-those positions of a certain thing. (The logical point is not that the latter sort of proposition is about the watch as something I can see or point to, but that the sense of the latter sort of proposition can be laid out completely. It is non-committal about many things, which would come out, in analysis, in the role of disjunctions and quantifiers in its structure, but it is fully determinate what it is committed to and what it leaves open.)[35] The possibility of a law-use of propositions about watches and about persistent physical objects of all sorts is implicit in the character of mechanics as (supposedly) providing forms of description for anything we might wish to describe. Mechanics will provide derivative law-forms for the calculation of the tides, for example; and similarly it will enable us to arrive at derivative law-forms which can be used in describing machines like watches, or indeed persistent objects like chairs. "Mechanics is an at-

---

**34** See also Wittgenstein 1961a, 67, where Wittgenstein speaks of the typical form of equation in physics as "sinnlos." As far as I know, he had not at that time made use of the word 'sinnlos,' and the contrast with 'unsinnig,' in describing the function of tautologies and contradictions. But the 1915 use of the word 'sinnlos' for the equations of physics is interesting in the light of Wittgenstein's later use of the term for tautologies and contradictions; the equations of physics are like tautologies and contradictions in lacking genuine truth-conditions, but they have a use through which they are connected to the world.

**35** Completeness of sense is a logical matter. Wittgenstein is not, like Russell, working with an independent notion of experience. *Erfahrung*, or experience, is *that something is so* (5.552). So the general form of fact provides a general variable fixing 'experience.' The general form of fact is the same as the general form of proposition. Since propositionhood is explicated in terms of full definiteness of sense, *that* logical notion provides a 'logicized' notion of experience. The contrast, then, between laws and propositions-in-the-full-sense cannot be thought of as defined in terms of an independent understanding of some relation to experience.

tempt to construct according to a single plan all the *true* propositions that we need for the description of the world."[36] (Note here that propositions about the future are not taken by Wittgenstein to be inferable from propositions about the past; they are, however, constructible in accordance with the laws of mechanics. What Wittgenstein has in mind would include the constructability of propositions about the position of the hands of this watch n seconds after t from a proposition about the position of the hands at t. The propositions in accordance with which we make such constructions aren't themselves propositions-in-the-full-sense; their generality isn't that of propositions-in-the-full-sense containing quantifiers.)

The skeptic with whom Russell had been concerned raised doubts about the existence of objects independent of our experience. How, then, is Wittgenstein's philosophy of Things relevant to skepticism? Wittgenstein said in the Notebooks and repeated in the *Tractatus* that we are told something about the world by the way in which we can describe the world using a particular system of physical laws. In the Notebooks, he gave the case of the two conceptions of heat to illustrate his theory of the meaning of the description of nature given by physics: heat conceived as a stuff, heat conceived as motion.[37] His idea was that we are told something about the world by the fact that, conceiving of heat in the latter way, we are able to describe the world more simply. One can then ask how well we do, not conceiving of heat this way rather than that, but conceiving of watches as machines with wheels and gears and springs made of metal with such-and-such properties, or conceiving of chairs as persistent objects. The familiar everyday physics of persistent objects is simpler than a physics of objects that disappear when not observed; and conceiving of watches as machines with rigid wheels and gears and pins is *great!* So how exactly would the skeptic be able to lead us to doubt the existence of persistent objects? On Wittgenstein's view, a philosophical clarification of an assertion about a watch or about watches might show that it described a particular situation or situations; it says something with determinate truth-conditions. Alternatively, we might be speaking about watches as machines, and this would be a different use altogether. This sort of proposition allows us to give descriptions of particular watches, descriptions cast in a certain form, the form given by the mechanics of such machines. Skepticism about what lies beyond experience gets no foothold in either sort of case. The *Tractatus* notion of experience can be seen at 5.552:[38] experience

---

36 Wittgenstein 1961b, 6.343; cf., Wittgenstein 1961a, 36.
37 Wittgenstein 1961a, 37.
38 Cf., Wittgenstein 1961b, 5.634: experience is whatever may be describably the case. See also note 35 above.

is that something or other is so, something that can be said to be the case in a senseful proposition; a proposition the sense of which is 'complete.' If our proposition about a watch or about watches is a genuine proposition—if it says this or that is the case—it is experiential in the *Tractatus* sense. The skeptic's would-be challenge is not a challenge to what we say using such propositions, for the skeptic wants to say something about what might be the case even if our experience is just as it is. But now consider the case of assertions that treat watches as machines. These are tied to derivative laws of physics, and such assertions are connected with the world through their application, through the propositions that are constructed in accordance with them. The latter sort of propositions concern things we can observe, like the position of chairs, like their staying put, like the movement of the hands of the watch, like the times of occurrence of tides, the observable position of planets, and so on. Physical-object statements, used in the 'law' way, speak about the world through their application. The skeptic about the external world is not putting forward an alternative to these laws in the same business as the laws. He is not putting forward an alternative physics, in the sense in which the conception of heat as motion is an alternative to the conception of heat as stuff. It is indeed essential to the situation of the skeptic that the laws of mechanics and all the derivative laws, including those of watches and chairs, do work, and work reasonably well. The skeptic wants to argue that, even given the obvious usefulness of the procedures we use in describing the world, we have no guarantee that there are Things external to what we observe. Since he admits the usefulness of our procedures, his suggestion that there may be no Things is not being given the use of a suggested alternative to those procedures. So what is its use? Putting this question another way: the laws of physics say something about the world through their application. If the skeptic were putting forward a possible 'theory of Things,' if he were calling into question ordinary thought about Things, what he said would have a connection with the world through its application. But it is plain that he does not want to make a statement that has that kind of connection with the world; for, in order to do so, he'd have to make plain the *difference* at the level of application between his 'hypothesis' and our ordinary thought. But that is not where he wants there to be a difference between what he is suggesting and what he takes us to believe. So again the question is, if he is not giving his 'hypothesis' a use like that of law-statements in physics, what is its use supposed to be? The question arises acutely precisely because the use of law-statements is not that of making very general statements about the world. If one understands physics itself to be putting forward very general statements about the world (as Russell does), then it is natural to conceive philosophical theories as having the same sort of generality. But if one recognizes that scientific theories do not have that sort of generality, one no longer has the same model available to provide an understanding of what philosophical theories say, or of what one is oneself saying in putting forward a philosophical account of reality.

Russell's understanding of what the skeptic is up to depends on his belief that we naturally accept an audacious metaphysical theory about persistent objects as constituents of reality; his recognition of the vulnerability of his own account to skeptical doubt depends on his taking his account to involve belief in sense-data-like particulars as ultimate constituents of reality. Now what about Wittgenstein's philosophy of Things? You could, on his view, give to a proposition that says, "The ultimate constituents of reality are thus-and-so," the use of a physical law. But if you did so, its way of saying something about the world would be the law way; it would be justified through its usefulness in providing forms in which propositions about things we observe could be put. If it is given that use, it is not the kind of statement that the skeptic really wants to challenge. For the skeptic to challenge something, there must be something for him to challenge; there must be some other way of using statements about the ultimate constituents of reality, or any other statement the skeptic wishes to challenge. At this point, Wittgenstein's philosophical approach is, as one might put it, invitational: it invites the philosopher to specify a use for the kind of sentence that attracts him. Wittgenstein is not, that is, saying that *what the skeptic says* is something that lies outside the boundary of sense. Rather, the idea is that the skeptic takes himself to be doing something like (in some respects) what is done in putting forward or calling into question a scientific claim about the nature of things, and yet if he were putting forward or calling into question a scientific claim, that would not really be what he wanted: he does not want his statement to have the kind of relation to the world that scientific claims really do have. That is, he does not want what he says to speak about the world through its application to propositions like those about the measurements we make of such-and-such distances. He does not want *that*; but then what does he want?

The argument I have given is not the end of the matter, but what I wish to bring out is the ground on which the discussion proceeds, if it goes on as Wittgenstein wants it to. It is the ground provided by Wittgenstein's reinterpretation of Occam's razor. The fundamental maxim of philosophical method as Russell understood it, of the scientific method in philosophy, was: reduce as far as possible the dependence of your philosophical account of reality on inferred entities. Entities aren't to be multiplied without necessity; keep the entity-count down, and keep the entities that you do admit as much as possible like entities with which you are acquainted. Wittgenstein substitutes for Russell's "Entities aren't to be multiplied beyond necessity" the maxim: "Signs that serve *one* purpose are logically equivalent, and signs that serve *none* are logically meaningless." Talk about the ultimate constituents of reality may serve the same purpose as physical-law-talk, in which case such talk speaks of the world in the way such laws do and has the kind of justification that such laws have. Or it may serve *no* purpose, and be logically meaningless.[39] If it is supposed to serve some other purpose, what is that? What I have spoken of as a shift in the ground is then a shift away from the Russellian conception of the dispute between realism and skepticism as a dispute about what entities there are. The shift is to: If you are talking about what entities there are, what use are you giving your talk? Wittgenstein's challenge to metaphysical realist and skeptic alike is to specify the use of the statements they make.[40]

I have reached a point where I can answer the question of what it is to see the hardness of the soft. The 'soft' is made to appear subject to doubt because the use of law-language, its kind of relation to the world, is misunderstood. To see the hardness of the soft is to see the use of supposedly 'soft' statements or beliefs, to see how propositions with the type of use of the laws of mechanics (including derivative laws) speak about the world through their application. You can perfectly well say that we do believe in the existence of things beyond expe-

---

39 Compare Baker/Hacker 1980, 465, on the use to which Wittgenstein puts Occam's razor. My account differs from theirs in seeing Wittgenstein's treatment of the principle as tied to his understanding of scientific method and, in particular, to his understanding of the functioning of physical laws.

40 My argument so far puts me into disagreement with Witherspoon 1996. Speaking of the remarks on skepticism in the *Tractatus*, Witherspoon describes Wittgenstein as having disposed of skepticism in one grand gesture. I don't think that Wittgenstein took the remarks in the *Tractatus* to have disposed of skepticism. The work of seeing how the remarks connect with skepticism was left for the reader to do. In this case the reader whom Wittgenstein had primarily in mind was Russell, and I don't think Wittgenstein believed that there was some way the relevance of the *Tractatus* remark about skepticism to Russell's views could be seen without examination of the issues he had picked out in the Notebooks passage, that is, the issues which I have been discussing. Skepticism is, for Wittgenstein, an issue intimately connected with questions of philosophical method, and no 'gesture' could disentangle the issues there; the idea was that the reader had to do the disentangling for himself, after having been given an initial kick, as it were, by the *Tractatus*, and in particular by the (to Wittgenstein's mind obvious) hint of the remark about Occam's razor. I think the structure of the 6 s in the *Tractatus* was intended to bring out their bearing on philosophical method; the bearing of the 6.3 s on the remark about skepticism was meant to be intelligible to a reader familiar with Russell's views about skepticism and method. Wittgenstein had originally put the remark about skepticism much earlier in the 6 s; he may have become clearer, during the course of working on the *Prototractatus*, how the remarks should be organized to give a reader what he thought of as a fair chance of seeing the point about skepticism. (The number of the remark about skepticism was plainly not originally 6.51; it looks to me as if it may have been 6.001, but it is hard to say.)

rience; chairs are not 'reducible' to appearances (not if chairs are being spoken of in our familiar ways of talking and thinking about them). But to say that chairs are not reducible to appearances is not yet to say how talk about persistent objects like chairs is used.

My account of Wittgenstein's early response to skepticism is meant to play down the significance of the *particular* account he gives of physical laws. (That account was subsequently elaborated by W.H. Watson, Stephen Toulmin, and others, and has been subjected to various sorts of criticism, including criticism by N.R. Hanson, who emphasized the variety of kinds of use that even the statement of a law such as the second law of motion can have.) What is important in this early response is the idea that law-propositions have a relation to the world through their application. Wittgenstein's method of treating physics thus has obvious parallels with his treatment of mathematics, early and late. There is, in the case both of mathematics and physics, the possibility of philosophical misunderstanding arising from failure to consider the kind of application the propositions in question have, and failure to see the kind of generality the propositions have. Physics, philosophically misunderstood, resembles mathematics, philosophically misunderstood, in that it may be taken as a model for philosophical method, as Wittgenstein's remark about Russell's 'retrogression' from the method of physics brings out. The idea is not that physics-wrongly-understood gives us a bad model for philosophy, but that physics-rightly-understood would give us a better model. Rather, if we were to see clearly what the method of physics is, what the generality is of the laws of physics, what the application really is of the laws, we should not be tempted to take physics as a model for philosophy.[41]

# VII Skepticism and the Appearance of Sense: First Approach

I referred earlier to the *Tractatus* as a work in transition, following in this description Michael Kremer's discussion. Obviously. Wittgenstein's response to

---

41 The differences between Russell's account of physics and Wittgenstein's could be examined in more detail. There is a question how far Russell is committed to the reality of the 'ideal elements' we accept as logical constructions in the philosophical account of the laws of physics. But it seems to me clear that he is committed to the laws being true or false, although we are not in a position to come to know the truth of the laws. The method of logical construction, as described by Russell, does not close off the possibility of the skeptical position being correct. See Russell 1929, 116–9.

skepticism changed later in important respects; it went far beyond where he was in 1915 or in the *Tractatus* in various important ways. But some of the central features of his response to skepticism are already present, I think, in 1915, including the insistence that we may have failed to say anything, without realizing that that is so. Here I want to quote Stanley Cavell on Wittgenstein's later thought. Cavell writes about how it is possible for us, in philosophy, to fail to say anything:

> "Not saying anything" is one way philosophers do not know what they mean. In this case it is not that they mean something *other* than they say, but that they do not see that they mean *nothing* (that *they* mean nothing, not that their statements mean nothing, are nonsense). The extent to which this is, or seems to be, true, is astonishing.[42]

The view that I am ascribing to Wittgenstein does hold that the skeptic and the philosophical realist are uttering nonsense; but it is also the case on that view that *they* mean nothing. They want their statements to be like those of physics in their capacity to speak about reality in general terms and to go beyond what we observe; they do not, however, want their statements to bear on the world through their application. They have not thought through, got to the bottom of, those desires.

What can be said, then, about the philosophical conviction that skepticism *is* intelligible? If I am right that the central point in Wittgenstein's early response to skepticism is the insistence that the skeptic has not given any use to the supposed 'hypothesis' that there may be nothing beyond experience, no objects of the sort we (supposedly) believe there to be, why is the skeptic so convinced that he does mean something?

Here I should like to look briefly at two recent defenses of the intelligibility of skepticism. Both Barry Stroud and Thomas Nagel, in discussing skepticism, try to show that a verificationist response to skepticism is inadequate and ultimately unconvincing.[43] What is interesting is how they see the kind of response to skepticism which they (quite rightly) find unconvincing. They take the skeptic to put forward a claim about reality external to our minds, a claim that is apparently intelligible, but which supposedly, on the verificationist account of the matter, runs foul of a principle: the principle that, in order to be meaningful, what one says must be capable of verification. So on that sort of understanding of verificationism, the verificationist takes statements or questions that we make—statements or questions that appear to us to be intelligible—shows that they run foul of a principle, and concludes that nothing has really been stated

---

42 Cavell 1979, 210; cf., also 206–9.
43 Stroud 1984, Chapter 5; Nagel 1987, 15–7.

or that nothing has really been asked. It is then possible to defend the intelligibility of skepticism by arguing that the initial appearance of intelligibility can be challenged only by demonstrating that the verifiability-principle has philosophical credentials strong enough to overcome our initial conviction that we mean something. (The argument against the verificationist response is laid out by Stroud; Nagel's treatment is briefer.) Stroud in fact argues that the verificationist understands the statements made by metaphysical realists and by skeptics perfectly well. In order to make a verificationist argument against the realist, a verificationist must take the realist to be asserting that such-and-such is the case, though it cannot be experientially verified that it is the case.[44]

My description of Wittgenstein's response in the *Tractatus* to the skeptic is meant to make clear that he is not doing what the verificationist is taken to do in arguments like that of Stroud or Nagel. Wittgenstein's philosophical method allows, as a response, a description of the way one is using an expression or a proposition or proposition-like construction. If there is a justification for thinking that the skeptic or the realist owes us a story about the use of his statements, the justification lies in the suspicion that he wants his statements to resemble in their capacity to speak about the world those of physics, but does not want that *fully*, in that he does not want his statements to speak about the world *through* their application to propositions about things we can observe. I shall discuss this further in Part VIII, but I can get to the issues here only by returning to questions that came up earlier.

# VIII Skepticism and the Appearance of Sense: More

I need to return here to two points discussed earlier: Wittgenstein's claim that Russell's 'Scientific Method in Philosophy' is a retrogression from the method of physics, and Wittgenstein's discussion, in the 6s of the *Tractatus*, of the uses of forms of language which might be taken to express truths having total generality or absolute necessity. In the 6.3s, Wittgenstein's account of the method of physics is meant to contrast with any account that takes the laws of physics to be straightforwardly general propositions, constructed from elementary propositions, and having the sense they have through being such constructions. The laws of physics do not have the sort of generality that is marked by the occurrence of the quantifiers, understood in the way Wittgenstein had explained in

---

**44** Stroud 1984, 179, 205 – 6. See also Witherspoon 2000.

the remarks beginning at 5.52. Wittgenstein's rejection of Russell's approach to skepticism depends on taking Russell to have got wrong the kind of generality that physics has and to be working with that wrong conception of the generality of physics in his understanding of the kind of generality involved in his own response to skepticism through logical constructions involving inferred entities. Using the language of Wittgenstein's later philosophy, I would say that there is a kind of picture of generality that Wittgenstein takes to be a misleading picture and to be a picture that underlies Russell's understanding of skepticism and his response to it. It is a picture that we could say is a picture of truth-conditions, abstracted from the ways in which truth-conditions are given through the use of our propositions.

Russell's response to skepticism in *Our Knowledge of the External World* is a kind of realism in that it provides a conception of the external world as containing things outside one's own experience, but it is intentionally a relatively non-risky realism, or as we might say, a *scared* realism. It involves quantifying over entities taken to resemble the entities about which there can (on Russell's view) be no doubt, namely, one's own sense-data, belief in the existence of which cannot be believably challenged by skepticism. It involves no quantifying over the traditional entities of metaphysical realism, external objects that are of a character quite unlike sense-data. As Peter Hylton notes in a discussion of the development of Russell's method, Russell's earlier account of our beliefs about the external world did involve quantifying over entities unlike sense-data. One speaks of these entities, on that earlier view, through descriptions roughly of the following sort: "There is one and only one object that causes such-and-such sense-data and which has such-and-such further properties." Hylton comments that such an account seems to be incompatible with *Principia Mathematica*, in which Russell appears to suggest that one cannot make judgments quantifying over some kind of object unless one can make a (genuinely) singular judgment about objects of that kind.[45] But Russell's own view about acquaintance and about the relation between acquaintance and judgment preclude our making such genuinely singular judgments about external objects as Russell then conceived them. Hylton notes that this problem plays no overt role in Russell's development of his new method, but the new method does avoid quantification over entities unlike sense-data. Although the problem is not discussed by Russell, Hylton's account puts before us a question which the Stroud and Nagel approaches ignore, a question that I believe is extremely important in Wittgenstein's thought.

---

**45** See, e.g., Whitehead/Russell, *12. For Hylton's discussion, see Hylton 1990, 379.

The *Tractatus* describes, as I've said, various different ways of using the language of generality. In the 5.52s, Wittgenstein describes the possibility of constructing propositions with quantifiers, a possibility given with the elementary propositions themselves. (Elementary propositions are given with logical operations, that is, with the possibility of construction of propositions from them, all of which stand in determinate logical relations to each other.) For a sign to be used as a quantifier (in the 5.52s' sense) is for propositions constructed with that sign to be so used that they stand in such-and-such inferential relations to propositions constructed without quantifiers, propositions that are in the inferential space of the speaker. (Propositions so constructed have a sense that is 'complete' in the Notebooks' sense of that term. The issue of 'completeness of sense' appears in the *Tractatus* as the issue of full determinacy of sense.[46]) This description of a use of the language of generality thus includes only those cases in which what we quantify over we can (or could in principle) also name. Any kind of case in which there is a use of general language such that, if we tried to construe it as involving quantification, the quantification would be over entities about which we could not speak without quantifiers is a use that needs some alternative description. I have argued elsewhere that this description of the use of quantifiers constitutes a criticism of Russell's view of other minds, which involves quantifying over objects which cannot be spoken of in genuinely singular propositions by anyone except the person within whose experience the objects in question lie.[47] My point now is that Wittgenstein's account of the laws of physics is an example of his responding to the issue of 'the limits of quantification' through an account emphasizing that not all generality is the generality of the quantifier. The generality of the quantifier isn't a matter of our intending *all* or *some* or *none* by "all" or "some" or "none." It's not a matter of a picture we may have of what the truth-conditions of our propositions are. It's a matter of how our quantified propositions hang together inferentially with other propositions of our language, as that language is used. Any impression we might have of meaning the same by "all" or "some" or "none" in other cases involves our attending to a picture of supposed truth-conditions rather than looking at use. Putting the point another way: there is a use of signs, the signs we call quantifiers, in which propositions with those signs stand in such-and-such inferential relations to propositions without them, all the propositions in question lying within the inferential space of our use of lan-

---

**46** See Wittgenstein 1961b, 3.23, which picks up the discussion in Wittgenstein 1961a, 17.6.15 and 18.6.15.
**47** Diamond 2000.

guage, of our thought. If we claim that there are certain objects that can be known only as those which stand in certain causal relations to things we do experience, or if we claim that there are not such objects, or that there may be no such objects, we are using "there are" in a different way, since the propositions we make are supposed to stand in no inferential relations to propositions that we ourselves can use, speaking of the objects supposedly quantified over, but speaking of them without quantifiers.

We may think of there being a position, unavailable to us, from which one could speak of the objects in question both with quantifiers and without quantifiers, a position from which the objects in question would not be on the far side of a sort of barrier. The idea is that *we* cannot frame and use propositions directly about these objects because we are 'within' the world of experience, while the objects (which we can speak of through descriptions as the cause of this-or-that within experience) are 'outside' it, acting on us; but from an 'ideal' position, propositions directly about these objects would be accessible. This is a kind of image of a language that we do not ourselves speak; it may seem to explain our own use of the language of generality in our talk of the objects in question. It is a picture in which the language of generality, as used of objects outside experience, appears to mean what it usually does: the truth-conditions appear to be what they usually are for sentences with "there is" and similar expressions. This kind of image of an ideal position for the use of talk of this-or-that sort of object is discussed by Wittgenstein in *Philosophical Investigations* at §426. In treating closely related questions, Michael Dummett also discusses this sort of imagery of the hypothetical mental operations of a being or beings not subject to our 'limitations.' Ramsey also has a related discussion.[48] It may seem anachronistic to introduce this kind of point in an account of the *Tractatus* view of skepticism. I have argued elsewhere that Wittgenstein's use of the image of 'logical space' shows his concern with the misleadingness of a picture of generality that has, central to it, the idea of propositions that stand in inferential relations to ours, but which are beyond our direct reach.[49] Here I want only to note that such a picture can stop us noting an indubitable difference in use. You use the generality notation one way when you make with it propositions that stand in such-and-such determinate relations to propositions without quantifiers of your own language, propositions referring without quantifiers to objects of the sort quantified over. You are not using the generality notation in that way, if, on your own account, the propositions with the generality sign do not stand in such

---

48 Wittgenstein 1958; Dummett 1973, 119; Ramsey 1965, 237–8.
49 Diamond 2000.

logical relations to singular propositions in the language you use. Your propositions involving generality do not have the use of constructions from singular propositions. That point, as it stands, does not apply to Russell's account of the external world, which involves no quantification over entities that could not be the subject of singular judgments by us. On my reading of the issue, Russell may be responding, but in a quite different way from Wittgenstein, to the problem of the relation between propositions with quantifiers and propositions without quantifiers; that, then, would mark a contrast between both of them on the one hand and, on the other, most discussions of skepticism, which do not engage with the problem.

The *Tractatus* says that a proposition is the expression of its truth-conditions (4.431). Any statement of the truth-conditions of a proposition—any giving of its truth-conditions through a truth-table, or whatever—repeats the proposition, *is* the same proposition. Repeating a proposition, putting it in other ways, for example, using a truth-table, or rewriting it using a Russellian analysis, may clarify it, but such puttings-in-other-words don't necessarily clarify it. If I say of a philosophical proposition about what is responsible for experience, "It is true if and only if at least one object $x$ in the domain of extended objects independent of minds stands in such-and-such relation to so-and-so," I have repeated the proposition without genuinely making it clearer. If it is a proposition in the full sense, its clarification makes it easier to see how, through its construction, it has its logical relations to other propositions in logical space. Wittgenstein plainly allows for a different sort of clarification of propositions that do not have the use of propositions-in-the-full-sense, such as the laws of mechanics. Truth-conditional clarification is one kind of clarification, but there is no such clarification for 'propositions' that are supposed to stand in logical relations to propositions outside of the inferential space of the language we speak; repeating them in a truth-conditional *style* ("It is true if and only if...") moves nowhere.[50] The extremely strong impression that a philosopher may have that she is saying something, that she is making sense, may reflect the idea she has of *what the truth-conditions are* of what she is saying. She has such a conception vividly in front of her mind. The idea we get from Wittgenstein is that exactly such an impression is consistent with failure to see that the use of the proposition she is asserting has been left unclear and that she may indeed have given it no use. If, indeed, a philosopher were to set against the impression we have that we are saying something intelligible a principle that what we say cannot be intelligible if it

---

50 The argument in this paragraph picks up Ramsey's argument in Ramsey 1965. See note 48 above.

has a certain character, one might well argue as Stroud does that the very strength of our persuasion of the intelligibility of what we are saying is a reason to reject the principle. But Wittgenstein's argument does not depend on a principle that propositions quantifying over objects we cannot observe are meaningless, or on any other principle. It depends on laying out different uses of generality, including that of the quantifiers, and leaving the skeptic to make clear what she wants to say.

One can describe the *Tractatus* as having a truth-conditional view of meaning, but that is somewhat misleading, since propositions such as the laws of physics are not nonsensical, not tautologies or contradictions, and not constructed truth-functionally from elementary propositions. (Some of them are equations, but the use of those equations is different from that of equations in pure mathematics.) They don't have what counts as truth-conditions in the *Tractatus* sense. They do speak of the world, though indirectly through their application. If what counts as truth-conditional clarification on the *Tractatus* account is not available for propositions with some type of use, that does not imply that no other sort of clarification of their use is available. It's not, I think, an objection to the *Tractatus* response to skepticism that Wittgenstein is simply limiting the title of 'proposition' to a limited class of propositions and that we can understand lots of propositions that do not belong to that class. To think that that would be an objection to his view would be to ignore the structure of the book, which suggests clearly that we can *go on* with the work of clarification of the use of propositions, even when we are not dealing with propositions-in-the-full-sense.

In his discussion of the intelligibility of skepticism, Stroud tries to head off any kind of objection to skepticism that is tied to the generality of the claims made by the skeptic. In response to such an objection, he refers to the view (to which he takes Carnap to be committed) that statements like "There are external objects," though totally general, can be intelligible if taken as internal to a linguistic framework.[51] As part of his response to the same objection, he mentions the Cartesian type of example in which beliefs about particulars, rather than general claims about the external world or our knowledge of it, are subjected to skeptical doubt.[52] But we should note that the judgments involved in such cases are not singular judgments. The Cartesian cases discussed by Stroud are cases of inference to objects that we believe are the causes of representations in our minds. If I am to be possibly wrong about there being a piece of paper

---

51 Stroud 1984, 206.
52 Stroud 1984, 206 – 7.

in my hand (in a case of the sort Descartes invites us to imagine), it is because I am supposedly judging something of some such form as, "There is an extended body with such-and-such nature that..." The inference to there being such an object would itself be based on a general judgment about objects that cause such representations; and Descartes's own argument in the First Meditation makes plain that these general judgments themselves are open to doubt. For all I know, God may have brought it about that I have exactly the sort of representations I am having despite there being no extended bodies at all—so Descartes tells himself. The questions I have been discussing arise concerning the understanding of the generality in both the judgments about there being such-and-such an extended body in a specific case like that of the impression of a piece of paper in my hand, and the judgments on which they are supposedly based, about the source of such impressions. The judgments may be pictured as involving a sort of quantification over objects which are reachable by our thought (supposing the sort of objects in question do exist) only through inferences to the supposed causes of what we observe. The philosophical problems about generality arise even when our explicit concerns are a particular dressing gown, a particular hand, and a particular piece of paper, in the Cartesian style.

I have argued that Wittgenstein's treatment of skepticism is not open to the kind of objection raised by Stroud and Nagel to verificationist responses to skepticism. Wittgenstein's response does not involve first understanding the skeptic to be making or attempting to make a claim that goes beyond experience, and then objecting to such claims on principle. Rather, what he wants us to see is that an empty idea of the truth-conditions of what we have said can obscure from us the fact that we have given no use to a would-be proposition. No full account of Wittgenstein's response to skepticism in the *Tractatus* could avoid the topic of his treatment of causation (especially 6.36 and 6.361). I think he held that various forms of philosophical realism, and the challenges to them by skeptics, involve confusions about causation. But I cannot examine these issues here.

# IX Skepticism and Twentieth-Century Philosophy

I have argued that we can understand Wittgenstein's response to skepticism if we consider it along with his ideas about Russell's conception of scientific method in philosophy: Russell takes as a model for philosophical method what is actually a misunderstanding of scientific method. And I have argued that Wittgenstein's remark that skepticism is not irrefutable but nonsense should not be seen as a conclusion about skepticism from some general principle about meaningfulness, allegedly violated by skeptical questions and statements. Rather, the skeptic is not doing with his words this-or-that; what use, then, does he want his words to have? That's what he hasn't determined. You can see Wittgenstein's point in that way only if you see the importance of the issue of the misconception of science. My reading of Wittgenstein, that is, takes him to treat Russell's philosophical conception of science as itself an expression of the view that skepticism and metaphysical realism share. Only by looking to see what the method of science is can we see the point of Wittgenstein's remark that skepticism is nonsensical. For only then can it become clear to us that we may really be saying nothing at all in expressing skepticism or responding to it.

In the final part of this essay, I want to connect these points with questions about how we read the history of philosophy during the last hundred years. The way we read the history of analytic philosophy is tied to our understanding of what is at stake in skepticism. I shall look at a particular reading of the history of analytic philosophy, that of Barry Stroud, and I shall try to show how it is related to an understanding of skepticism.

Here, then, is Stroud's reading of the history.[53] Analytic philosophy, as we see it in its beginnings, especially in the work of Russell in the early years of the century, did involve criticism of much past metaphysical thought. But it did not involve a rejection of the idea that philosophy should try to give a general account of the world. Russell's idea was rather that past philosophers had given incorrect accounts; he did not think that philosophy should reject the task of giving a complete account of the world. Philosophy on Russell's view (as summarized by Stroud) would be continuous with science. It would be more general than particular sciences; it would attempt to discover the most general features of the world. In the middle period of analytic philosophy, which Stroud takes as going from the publication of the *Tractatus* to roughly the middle of the 1960s, there is a totally different conception of the character and aims of analytic philosophy. The *Tractatus* itself, which marks the beginning of this new phase, is read by Stroud as calling into question the possibility of philosophy itself. He reads the *Tractatus* as disallowing philosophical propositions because they violate the conditions of making sense; and he sees the logical positivists as following Wittgenstein in specifying the conditions of sense, conditions which traditional metaphysical propositions allegedly violate. A similar concern to delimit what can meaningfully be said can supposedly be discerned also in Wittgenstein's later work.[54] While Stroud treats the work of Austin and of those influenced by him as significantly different from Wittgenstein's, he emphasizes the far great-

---

53 Stroud 1986.
54 Stroud 1986, 64.

er difference that there is between all the analytic philosophers of the middle years of the century and analytic philosophy as it was before and after that period. For he takes recent analytic philosophy to have returned, in important respects, to a Russellian approach: to a conception of philosophy as seeking general truths about the world, to a conception of philosophy as continuous with science, and as unapologetically concerned with getting metaphysics right, not with questioning the enterprise itself. Taking Quine's views as exhibiting the relevant features in an exemplary manner, Stroud gives a description of contemporary analytic philosophy in terms drawn from Russell's early thought: Philosophy, like science, "asserts the existence of those things it needs to posit in order to account for what it wants to explain."[55] Philosophical theorizing is thus like that of science, but at a higher level of generality. "It tries to find the simplest and most general framework within which to say what there is. In that way it follows Russell's plan: 'find out what entities are undeniably involved, and state everything in terms of those entities.'"[56] Stroud sees this giving-up of the approach of the mid-century as a return to what has for centuries been recognized as the basic task of philosophy.[57]

How is that picture of the history of analytic philosophy related to thought about skepticism? I mentioned in Part VII Stroud's argument against a 'verificationist' critique of skepticism. The verificationist he has in mind is Carnap; I cannot examine the question whether the views he ascribes to Carnap are genuinely Carnap's.[58] Although his Carnap takes both realism and skepticism to be nonsensical, Carnap actually, according to Stroud, understands both; Carnap has to understand the realist's view well enough to be able to conclude that the realist is putting forward an unverifiable claim. The realist's claims violate the conditions of meaningfulness, and hence neither his claims nor the doubts of those claims by the skeptic are meaningful. Interestingly, when Stroud explains the response of Stanley Cavell to skepticism, he gives Cavell's views the same structure.[59] He takes Cavell's response to skepticism to be deeply aware of the sources of skepticism, and deeply promising, but it seems to me that his reading of Cavell aligns Cavell's thought too closely with the overall pattern he sees in mid-twentieth-century analytic philosophy. He sees Cavell as putting forward, following Wittgenstein, a story about what the conditions are for claiming something and as saying that, since the philosopher attempts to claim something when the condi-

---

55  Stroud 1986, 69.
56  Stroud 1986, 69–70.
57  Stroud 1986, 74.
58  See Witherspoon 2000.
59  Stroud 1984, 255–63.

tions are not met, he fails to make any claim. The claim the philosopher wants to make cannot be made. And Stroud then argues that we should need some general account from Cavell explaining why the general conditions for claiming anything cannot be met in the kinds of cases that are central for the philosopher who is attempting to reply to the skeptic by claiming that we do know the things the skeptic has said we don't.[60] The philosopher, as Stroud's Cavell sees him, is aspiring to assert that something is so, outside the conditions for asserting that something is so. Now, although Cavell does speak of conditions in which, if we say such-and-such, we can be taken to be asserting something, or remarking something, he explicitly notes that he is not saying that certain statements cannot be made; and he tries to make clear the only sense in which he is saying that something 'cannot' be done: "you cannot say something, *relying on what is ordinarily meant in saying it*, and mean something other than would ordinarily be meant."[61] As I read Cavell, he is not trying to show us that we cannot make a certain kind of sense except when certain conditions are met. He isn't showing that there is something we cannot do; rather, his aim is to lead us to see what we are doing in a different way, to see that it isn't recognizable (even by ourselves) as a claiming, or telling, or asserting, of anything. Here I cannot go further into the issue of Stroud's reading of Cavell and the way that he shifts Cavell's thought (as I think) into a key different from that of *The Claim of Reason*. What interests me is the structure of Stroud's reading of two analytic philosophers: he sees the philosopher who questions the traditional self-understanding of the realist and skeptic, whether it is Carnap or Cavell, as putting forward, or as committed by his approach to putting forward, general principles of meaningfulness, conditions of our meaning something (in Carnap's case) or conditions of our claiming or asserting something (in Cavell's), which the skeptic or the realist has failed to heed. His Carnap and his Cavell tell us there is something we cannot do. And that's where I want to make the connection to Stroud's reading of the history of analytic philosophy. The analytic philosophy of the mid-century takes off, on his view, from Wittgenstein's telling us in the *Tractatus* that there are limits to what can be said and that the trouble with traditional philosophy is that the things it says, or tries to, are things that can't be said. And Wittgenstein's later philosophy, on Stroud's account of the history, works in the same way, but gives a different account of the conditions of saying something meaningful.[62]

---

**60** Stroud 1984, 261.
**61** Cavell 1979, 212.
**62** See Stroud 1986, 64: "Wittgenstein never deviated from his original idea that a philosophical doctrine or theory is an attempt to say what cannot be said. What changed was his idea of what determines what can and cannot be said."

Stroud sees us as having gone back (in post-1960s philosophy) to an older understanding of the aim of philosophy, the aim of getting a true view of the most general features of the universe. We were told by all those mid-century analytic philosophers that we could not do *that*. But we no longer take seriously their "You
can't do that." Both Stroud's reading of the history of analytic philosophy and
his reading of Cavell on skepticism draw on the idea that, when philosophy questions the intelligibility of what we say, it does so by taking us to mean something
beyond the conditions of meaning. Philosophy can then say, "You can't do that,"
or "You can't say what you are trying to say," or "You can't mean what you take
yourself to mean." I am suggesting that Stroud doesn't see, not fully, the possibility of a different sort of philosophical response to skepticism or realism, one
which can be mis-seen (I'm suggesting) as belonging in the general family of
"You can't say what you're trying to say." What I've tried to lay out as Wittgenstein's response in the *Tractatus*, and what I think is Cavell's response in *The
Claim of Reason*, do not involve the idea that such-and-such can't be said, or
can't be meant; and if these responses suggest that you aren't doing with your
words what you take yourself to be doing, they try to do so through *making
live for you the question* what you are doing, *making live for you the possibility*
that your own words are empty. There is no setting forth in advance a set of conditions, or anything else, that will, in a particular case, make that a live question.
Further, it seems to me that Stroud's reading of the history of analytic philosophy, and his reading of responses like those of Carnap and Cavell to skepticism,
take for granted a conception of scientific generality. It's because philosophers
are understood as trying to do what scientists do in their general talk about
the world that the intelligibility of philosophical descriptions of the world
seems so unquestionable. So it looks as if the intelligibility of traditional philosophy could have been questioned by analytic philosophy only if what analytic
philosophy had been saying was, "You can't do *that*."

Now, in fact, Stroud's conception of analytic philosophy of the period between 1918 and the mid-60s—the conception of analytic philosophy as saying,
"You can't do that," or "You can't say that"—does fit many analytic philosophers
of the period. And indeed many readers of Wittgenstein also see him, early and
late, as setting out the conditions for making sense, conditions the specification
of which puts us into a position to say to traditional philosophers, "You can't say
that," because they would supposedly be violating the conditions of sense. Such
readers of Wittgenstein see him as giving one account of the conditions of sense
in the *Tractatus* and another later on. What I have tried to suggest is that Wittgenstein's appeal to Occam's razor in the *Tractatus* functions in an altogether different way. Signs that have *no* use are meaningless. The laws of physics have a
use, though it isn't the use of ordinary generalizations. What the skeptic says,

what the realist says, isn't meant to have that use, isn't meant to speak about the world through its application. So Occam's razor, together with the understanding provided in the 6.3s of what the use is of the laws of physics, puts pressure on the skeptic to examine his own intentions. Is there a use he wants to give to his words? The point is not that he is saying something, or trying to say something, where the 'something' he says or tries to say runs foul of a principle. (I am suggesting, then, that we can see what Wittgenstein's own method is only if we do not assume that there is no real problem what he is *doing* with talk of the limits of language. I have argued elsewhere that it is not his view that 'outside the limits' there are various sorts of interesting things we can grasp but cannot say.[63] My point in this essay is that we can be helped to see the significance of the idea that there is nothing but plain nonsense 'outside the limits,' the idea that the 'limits' are not *limiting us* in our saying, if we see how we can work from 'inside' language to an understanding of what sort of relation to reality the laws of physics have and thus to an understanding that there is nothing we wanted to say when we were putting forward the 'audacious' metaphysical theory of the external world or the skeptical doubt of that theory or the Russellian alternative to the audacious theory and to skepticism. Working from 'inside' language is becoming clearer about what making sense is *like*, e.g., in applying the laws of physics in talk of watches or chairs. Being clearer about various uses of language can help us to recognize that some impression we had of saying something was empty. The idea that philosophy tells us what we *cannot* say is, alternatively, a picture of what philosophy does that no longer works from 'inside'; and my difference from Stroud about Cavell reflects the idea that ultimately he does not see, or does not fully see, Cavell as working from 'inside' in this sense.[64])

I have argued that Wittgenstein's response to Russell on skepticism has at its heart the idea that Russell misunderstands the kind of generality that physics has. The idea—Stroud's idea—that analytic philosophy in the mid-twentieth century attempted to tell us that we couldn't go on with the old project of giving the most general features of the world conceives the forbidden project in terms of its

---

**63** Diamond 1991.

**64** See, on this matter of working from 'inside' as contrasted with the philosophical laying down of conditions for making sense, the discussion of Barry Stroud's criticism of John Austin by Mark Kaplan, in Kaplan 2000. Kaplan shows 'from inside' the kind of degeneration of epistemological thought that there can be as it departs from ordinary practice. He shows us how, following out an Austinian argument, we can recognize a kind of failure to make the kind of sense we take ourselves to be making as philosophers. Kaplan's argument responds to Stroud's attempt to show that Austin illegitimately takes conditions governing the ordinary assertion of claims to know to govern contexts of philosophical investigation of knowledge and its limits.

similarity to and connection with science, understood in just the way Wittgenstein thought reflected Russell's misunderstandings. Stroud sees mid-twentieth-century analytic philosophy as having tried to make us confront the question of what we are doing with our words in putting forward metaphysical theories; my disagreement with him is about what was involved, for Wittgenstein, in making that a live question in any particular case. It is just there, I think, that we should see what was genuinely radical in Wittgenstein's philosophy, even as early as the *Tractatus*.[65]

# Bibliography

Anscombe, G.E.M. (1963), *Introduction to Wittgenstein's* Tractatus, London: Hutchinson.

Baker, G.P. / Hacker, P.M.S. Hacker (1980), *Wittgenstein—Understanding and Meaning*, Chicago: University of Chicago Press.

Cavell, Stanley (1979), *The Claim of Reason: Wittgenstein, Skepticism, Morality, and Tragedy*, Oxford: Oxford University Press.

Diamond, Cora (1991), "Ethics, Imagination, and the Method of Wittgenstein's *Tractatus*." In: Richard Heinrich and Helmut Vetter (eds.), *Bilder der Philosophie: Reflexionen über das Bildliche und die Phantasie*, Wiener Reihe vol. 5, Vienna: Oldenbourg, 55 – 90.

Diamond, Cora (2000), "Does Bismarck have a Beetle in His Box?" In: Alice Crary and Rupert Read (eds.), *The New Wittgenstein*, London: Routledge, 262 – 92.

Diamond, Cora (2004), "Criss-cross Philosophy." In: Erich Ammereller and Eugen Fischer (eds.), *Wittgenstein at Work: Method in the Philosophical Investigations*, London: Routledge.

Dummett, Michael (1973), *Frege: Philosophy of Language*, London: Duckworth.

Floyd, Juliet (2005), "Wittgenstein on Philosophy of Logic and Mathematics." In: Stewart Shapiro (ed.), *The Oxford Handbook of Philosophy of Mathematics and Logic*, Oxford: Oxford University Press.

Griffin, James (1964), *Wittgenstein's Logical Atomism*, Oxford: Clarendon Press.

Hacker, P.M.S. (1996), *Wittgenstein's Place in Twentieth Century Analytic Philosophy*, Oxford: Blackwell.

Hylton, Peter (1990), *Russell, Idealism and the Emergence of Analytic Philosophy*, Oxford: Clarendon Press.

---

65 I am very grateful to have had the opportunity to read an earlier version of this paper at the Amsterdam conference on skepticism in 2000, at the Delphi conference on Wittgenstein in 2001, and at Texas A&M University. I am particularly grateful to Barry Stroud for his comments at the Delphi conference, at which he argued that I had seriously misread him, and I hope that this present version is closer, at any rate, to getting his views right. I am also very grateful to Sandra Laugier for her illuminating commentary on the original version of the paper and for showing how one might see the connections with Wittgenstein's later thought. I am very glad also to have had comments and suggestions from Gordon Baker, James Conant, and Matthew McGrath.

Kaplan, Mark (2000), "To What Must an Epistemology Be True?" In: *Philosophy and Phenomenological Research* 61, 279–304.

Kenny, Anthony (1975), *Wittgenstein*, Harmondsworth: Pelican Books.

Kremer, Michael (1997), "Contextualism and Holism in the Early Wittgenstein: From *Prototractatus* to *Tractatus*." In: *Philosophical Topics* 25, 87–120.

Nagel, Thomas (1987), *What Does It All Mean? A Very Short Introduction to Philosophy*, Oxford: Oxford University Press.

Ramsey, F.P. (1965), "General Propositions and Causality." In: R.B. Braithwaite (ed.), *The Foundations of Mathematics*, Totowa, NJ: Littlefield, Adams.

Russell, Bertrand (1917), *Mysticism and Logic and Other Essays*, London: Allen and Unwin.

Russell, Bertrand (1929), *Our Knowledge of the External World*, New York: Norton.

Russell, Bertrand (1967), *Problems of Philosophy*, Oxford: Oxford University Press.

Stroud, Barry (1984), *The Significance of Philosophical Scepticism*, Oxford: Oxford University Press.

Stroud, Stroud (1986), "Analytic Philosophy and Metaphysics." In: L. Nagl and R. Henrich (eds.), *Wiener Reihe* 1, *Wo steht die Analytische Philosophie heute?*, Vienna: R. Oldenbourg, 58–74.

Waismann, Friedrich (1979), *Ludwig Wittgenstein and the Vienna Circle*, Joachim Schulte and Brian McGuinness (trans.), Oxford: Blackwell.

Witherspoon, Edward (1996), *Nonsense, Logic, and Skepticism*, Ph. D. dissertation, University of Pittsburgh.

Witherspoon, Edward (2000), "Conceptions of Nonsense in Carnap and Wittgenstein." In: Alice Crary and Rupert Read (eds.), *The New Wittgenstein*, London: Routledge, 315–347.

Whitehead, Alfred North / Russell, Bertrand (1973), *Principia Mathematica*, Cambridge: Cambridge University Press.

Wittgenstein, Ludwig (1958), *Philosophical Investigations*, G.E.M. Anscombe (trans.), Oxford: Blackwell.

Wittgenstein, Ludwig (1961a), *Notebooks: 1914–1916*, G.H. von Wright and G.E.M. Anscombe (eds.), G.E.M. Anscombe (trans.), Oxford: Blackwell.

Wittgenstein, Ludwig (1961b), *Tractatus Logico-Philosophicus*, D.F. Pears and B.F. McGuiness (trans.), London: Routledge.

Wittgenstein, Ludwig (1965), "A Lecture on Ethics," *Philosophical Review* 74, 3–12.

Wittgenstein, Ludwig (1974), *Letters to Russell, Keynes and Moore*, G.H. von Wright (ed.), Oxford: Blackwell.

Wittgenstein, Ludwig (1991), *Geheime Tagebücher: 1914–1916*, Wilhelm Baum (ed.), Vienna: Turia & Kant.

Albrecht Wellmer
# Skepticism in Interpretation

The kind of skepticism I shall discuss in this essay may be called "hermeneutic" skepticism. It is a skepticism concerning the possibility of a "true" or "genuine" understanding of what other people have said or written. What I shall try to show is that hermeneutic skepticism, like the skepticism concerning meaning and understanding that Wittgenstein discusses in his *Philosophical Investigations*, rests on a misconception of the grammar of "meaning." To show this, however, will not just be to restate Wittgenstein's dissolution of the skeptical paradox concerning rule-following; it rather needs new arguments, even if Wittgenstein's arguments are still to play an important role.

1. I shall start with a quote from Wittgenstein (*Philosophical Investigations* §§201 and 219):[1]

> What this shews is that there is a way of grasping a rule which is *not* an *interpretation*, but which is exhibited in what we call "obeying the rule" and "going against it" in actual cases. Hence there is an inclination to say: every action according to the rule is an interpretation. But we ought to restrict the term "interpretation" to the substitution of one expression of the rule for another... When I obey a rule, I do not choose. I obey the rule *blindly*.

With these passages, Wittgenstein reaches the culmination of a long series of reflections that at first seemed to lead to a radically skeptical conclusion. The apparent skeptical conclusion was that rule-following could only be possible via an infinite process of interpretation, which in the end would imply the impossibility of distinguishing between "right" and "not right" (false, incorrect), thereby invalidating the concept of rule-following as such. This conclusion, however, Wittgenstein says, is the sign of a confusion. "We ought to restrict the term 'interpretation' to the substitution of one expression of the rule for another" (§201). Interpretations in this sense are sometimes necessary and helpful, but the comprehension of a rule cannot solely consist in the ability to interpret it in this sense; in the end it can *show* itself only in the practice of applying the rule, i. e., in the *practical* capacity to obey it; and this practical capacity is in an essential sense the capacity to obey the rule "blindly." Wittgenstein had pointed to the aspect of "training," which first enables us to follow rules; and he shows that rule-following is part of a praxis, of a "language-game," a "form of life." Without

---

1 Quotes are from Wittgenstein 1958.

this background of a complex praxis, of a "language-game," in which verbal and non-verbal activities are intertwined, the concept of rule-following, and therefore the distinction between "right" and "false" (correct, incorrect)—and with it the concept of meaning itself—would become unintelligible.

Following the first two sentences quoted above, Wittgenstein says: "And hence also 'obeying a rule' is a practice. And to *think* one is obeying a rule is not to obey a rule. Hence it is not possible to obey a rule 'privately'; otherwise thinking one was obeying a rule would be the same as obeying it" (§202). This section has divided commentators on Wittgenstein. Does Wittgenstein say that speaking a language requires a plurality of speakers through which the essential *publicity* of rule-following can be constituted; or does he only anticipate the results of the so-called Private Language argument (PLA) in the narrower sense of §258 ff.? I am inclined to follow Kripke, Davidson, and others, who have argued for the former, stronger thesis—at least in the sense that, according to the logic of Wittgenstein's arguments, the stronger thesis should follow. To be sure, I believe that a sufficient justification of the stronger thesis can be found neither in Wittgenstein nor in Kripke's interpretation of Wittgenstein. Nevertheless, I think that Kripke has put forward an interesting argument, one that I wish to take up, not primarily to defend a strong version of PLA, but to prepare a distinction I shall make use of later on: namely, the distinction between the roles of the first- and the second-person in linguistic communication. With this distinction, I aim to develop a way of understanding language such that "understanding" and "interpreting" can no longer be separated in the manner suggested by Wittgenstein in his remarks on rule-following. We can in Wittgenstein find important hints of the view I develop here. I believe, however, that these hints can be made productive only if they are, as it were, "recontextualized," i. e., if they are related to a context of questions that Wittgenstein was not *primarily* interested in.

2. I shall reformulate Kripke's argument rather freely, ignoring what I take to be its problematic empiricist background. I begin by quoting two passages from Kripke, which I think contain the core of his argument. The first is: "The relation of meaning and intention to future action is normative, not descriptive."[2] And the second: "It turns out that the sceptical solution does not allow us to speak of a single individual, considered by himself and in isolation, as ever meaning anything."[3] I shall ignore the term "skeptical" for now, since I do not believe that Wittgenstein's dissolution of the—apparent—paradox of rule-following is a

---

2 Kripke 1982, 37.
3 Kripke 1982, 68–9.

*skeptical* one. Rather, I am interested in the kind of justification Kripke suggests for the passages I quoted. As is well known, Kripke phrases his exposition of the skeptical paradox, as well as his solution of it, in terms of the question, "How can sentences like 'X means addition by "plus"' can have a justified use?" His answer is that the use of such sentences implies reference to a linguistic community. This thesis, I think, has been misunderstood by many commentators (including Kripke himself). What the thesis really says is, I believe, that a justifiable and criticizable use of "meaning-sentences" (as I shall call them) presupposes a difference between at least two speakers. Kripke's basic idea (or what I take it to be) will become clearer if we allow for a certain variation of his examples. Kripke's own formulations conceal the fact that, normally, when a "meaning-sentence" is used, a term employed by X is *mentioned* and a corresponding term is *used* in a peculiar way by the speaker who utters the sentence. For instance: "By (the term) 'and,' X means *plus*"; or "By 'it is pouring,' X means *it is raining hard.*" The expression on the right side of these sentences are not only *mentioned* by the speaker, but are used in a peculiar way; otherwise, the sentences could not have the empirical content they do. But since they are used in a peculiar way, I have emphasized them. "Meaning-sentences" of this kind evidently function in a way similar to that of ordinary meaning-sentences, such as: "'Nonsense' (in English) means *Unsinn*" (uttered by a German speaker). Formulating Kripke's "meaning-sentences" in this way clarifies the meaning of the claim that "the relation of meaning and intention to future action is normative, not descriptive." To say of X that she means *plus* by "and" is to say that X—within certain limits—will use the sign "and" as a sign of *addition* in the *right* way. And in saying this, I use *my* understanding of the sign "plus" as a standard of rightness. Should I discover (Kripke's "contrapositive") that X does *not* use the sign in the "right" way (according to the meaning I imputed to her)—a special case would be the one in which, e.g., X has not yet learned to add—I would have to withdraw my ascription of a meaning-intention to X. It now becomes clear why a *primary* use of "meaning-sentences" requires at least *two* speakers: For these sentences to have an empirical content and a justified use, there must be a difference of perspective between two speakers, one of whom uses a term of her own language as a standard of correctness with respect to the fact of "meaning something by a word" that she ascribes to the other speaker. The "interpreter" must use the terms of her own language as a norm of correctness to intelligibly say what another speaker *means* by a word. Even if both speakers use an expression in the same way, a corresponding "meaning-sentence"—"By 'plus,' X means *plus*"—still has an empirical content (namely, that X uses the term "plus" in the same way I do). In contrast, such sentences would lose their point, as well as the possibility of being justified or criticized, in the case of a solitary speaker who is not an interpreter of other speakers: they could not have empirical content, nor could the fictional speaker use them or withdraw them on reasoned grounds. That means, however, that at *this* point the "community" is only the minimal community of two speakers who can ask of each other. "What does X mean by 'Q'?" Naturally, then, this use of meaning-sentences also implies the possibility of their being used in a first-person manner ("I mean," "I meant..."), whereby a speaker becomes her own interpreter. I shall return to this point in section 9, below.

3. As I indicated already, I am not primarily interested in defending a strong version of PLA. However, it follows from what I have said that the grammar of words like "understanding" or "meaning"—in its verbal and its substantive use—presupposes a plurality of speakers, i.e., it follows that these words could have no intelligible place in the practice of a solitary speaker. And I do not believe that we can call anything that has no place for such words a full-blown "language." (Note that I believe that Kripke's basic argument as I have characterized it would be a good starting point for reformulating Davidson's idea of "triangulation," of which Davidson himself has never provided a plausible account.[4] And it is of course no accident that the significance that I have attributed to the difference between the *mentioning* and the *use* of expressions in "meaning-sentences" has an exact correlate in Davidson's use of Tarskian T-sentences. However, I am interested in something else at this point: I want to try to analyze somewhat more extensively the role of the second-person, i.e., that of an interpreter, with regard to the grammar of words like "meaning" and "understanding.")

So far I have talked about "meaning something" (in the "active" sense of *etwas meinen*) as the correlate of a certain understanding of a word by the speaker who uses the word (and to whom this "meaning something" may then be ascribed by another speaker). To say that X means addition by "plus" is to say that X *uses* the word "plus" in a certain way or that she understands the word "plus" as the addition sign. So it seems that my reflections still moved within the conceptual plain of Wittgenstein's considerations concerning the meaning and understanding of words and other linguistic expressions, a conceptual plain, therefore, to which Wittgenstein's remarks about the relationship between "meaning," "use," and "rule-following" belong. However, Kripke's arguments as I have tried to reconstruct them already concern the problems of "meaning" and "understanding" in a more specific sense; for what is at stake here is the understanding by a hearer (a "second person") of what a speaker has meant by an utterance.

---

4 A compelling critique of Davidson's view of triangulation has been put forward by Thomas Hoffmann in Hoffman 2000.

"Meaning" and "understanding" are here correlative terms—related to a speaker, on the one hand, and to a hearer (an "interpreter") on the other. What is said by a speaker (what she meant to say, her "meaning-intention") is understood or misunderstood by a hearer (an "interpreter"). So what is at stake here is the understanding by a hearer of what, in a concrete situation, a speaker meant to say with her utterance. Kripke's "meaning-sentences," therefore, in fact point already to a Davidsonian problematic. Perhaps one could say: While Wittgenstein analyzes the concepts of meaning and understanding primarily from the "performative" perspective of a speaker (the first-person), Kripke and Davidson thematize these concepts from the "interpretative," second-personal perspective of a hearer. How are these two perspectives related?

A first answer to this question might be (and I think this is the answer primarily suggested by Wittgenstein): Understanding a language determines the possible uses that a speaker can make of words and sentences in specific situations and what, therefore, a speaker can *mean* by using these words and sentences in specific situations; and inasmuch as speaker and hearer understand words and sentences in the same way, understanding a language determines the possibilities of *understanding* a speaker's utterances by a hearer. Indeed, very often the situation in which two speakers find themselves, together with the meaning of the linguistic expressions they use, leaves practically no choice as to how a hearer understands a speaker's utterance: in such cases, the communicative intentions of a speaker are "embedded"—as Wittgenstein once put it—in such a way that the understanding of an utterance becomes "automatic." When the woman at the cash register says, "That'll be $5.50," I understand her utterance and duly pay my five dollars and fifty cents. It is tempting to speak—analogously to Wittgenstein's phrase about "blind" rule-following—of a "blind" understanding of the woman's utterance. However, I think that doing so would be misleading. I shall therefore speak instead of an "automatic" understanding; and I want to argue now that such an automatic understanding should be seen as the limiting case of an *interpretative* understanding by a hearer (whereas a "blind" rule-following is not a limiting case of an interpretative comprehension of a rule, but rather is always—in actual cases—its very precondition).

4. Why should we speak of an "interpretative" understanding of utterances by a second person (the "interpreter") in the general case? The basic idea is simple. Whereas Wittgenstein's investigations are focused upon the commonality of a linguistic practice, now the plurality of perspectives—the very correlate of a common language—moves into the foreground. Whereas, for Wittgenstein, the destruction of an intentionalist conception of meaning is the central concern, now what is at stake is the unforeseeable plurality of intentions that a common

language reveals to us (at the same time that it reveals infinite possibilities of misunderstanding, by which understanding one another becomes a practical problem for adult speakers). And whereas Wittgenstein thematizes understanding as, above all, a "knowing-how" from the first-personal perspective of a speaker (i.e., as the capacity to follow rules and to participate in a common practice), this "knowing-how" is now thematized from the second-personal perspective of a hearer, which means, at the same time, that understanding is thematized with regard to the "occasionalistic" aspects of the understanding of utterances-in-situations. "Understanding" now means the correct comprehension of the communicative intentions of a speaker by a hearer—communicative intentions that in more interesting cases are not yet clearly determined by a common understanding of words and sentences plus the situation in which they are used.

Let me first explain the sense in which I consider cases of "automatic" understanding to constitute limiting cases of an *interpretative* understanding and, therefore, as cases of an implicitly interpretative understanding. Generally speaking, the interpretative character of the understanding of utterances by a hearer becomes manifest in the hearer's—the "interpreter's"—ability to give an account of what a speaker said in the hearer's own words and from her own perspective, i.e., in her ability to *say* what it is she has understood or grasped as the communicative intention of the speaker. To speak of an *ability* means, at the same time, that in cases of "automatic" understanding there is, of course, no psychological *act* of interpretation involved. What is important is only that a hearer could make her understanding of an utterance explicit in her own words and from her own perspective; and this ability has no correlate in cases of "blind" rule-following. Understanding utterances means grasping what a speaker wants to say. Such grasping, however, entails occupying a place in the space of *possible* interpretations; it is a *making-sense* of what another says.

Let me next point to some elementary—and rather trivial—aspects of what I have called an "interpretative" understanding. The first aspect is the most inconspicuous one. It concerns the referential system of personal pronouns and indexical expressions. "I shall not come tonight," X tells me, and the next day I tell someone else, "X told me yesterday that he would not come this evening." To be sure, one might still say that the ability to substitute personal pronouns and indexical expressions for each other is merely the expression of our understanding of the *meaning* of personal pronouns and indexical expressions. However, consider demonstrative terms, or definite descriptions used in a demonstrative way: here, a misunderstanding is always possible—and it could be made *explicit*, due to our ability to substitute de-re ascriptions for de-dictu ascriptions in interpreting a speaker's reference. "The man at the bar who is talking with the bartender is Günter Grass," my friend tells me. And I, who knows that the alleged bartender is not a bartender at all but is rather the owner of the bar, may say to someone else, "My friend told me that the man at the bar who is talking with the owner is Günter Grass," thereby replacing my friend's mistaken definite description by a correct one and at the same time *correcting* and *preserving* my friend's reference to "that man at the bar." And if later on, at the theater, I recognize "the man at the bar" sitting in front of me, I might say to my girlfriend, "My friend told me that the man sitting next to the lady with the pink dress is Günter Grass," thereby correctly reporting who it was that my friend had claimed to be Günter Grass. However, it is possible that "the man at the bar"—the one my friend meant when he said it was Günter Grass—was in fact talking with the bartender (whom I could not see) while *another* man was talking with the bar's owner. In this case, I would have *misunderstood* what my friend was telling me. Robert Brandom, from whom I take this type of example,[5] claims—correctly, I think—that without the possibility of such a transition from de-dictu to de-re ascriptions, no *intersubjective* content of assertions would be possible. Such transitions, however, amount to substituting one expression (of a speaker's reference, not of a rule) by another; and in contrast to the case of substituting indexical expressions or personal pronouns for each other, the substitution of de-re for de-dictu expressions is not simply regulated by the meaning of the linguistic expressions used. So we can speak here of "interpretation" in Wittgenstein's sense—with the always-open possibility of *mis*interpretations.

Finally, the third aspect under which we can talk, in an elementary sense, of an "interpretative" understanding concerns the "pragmatic" embeddedness of utterances in situations: not only their illocutionary force, but—more generally—the way a speaker wants her utterance to be taken by an audience. (Is the utterance a proposal, a request, a warning, or a quotation? Is it meant seriously or ironically, literally or part of a performance, such as a theatrical play, etc.?) Obviously, even from the viewpoint of the 'pragmatic' or 'conversational' embeddedness of utterances in situations, understanding will often be "automatic." However, an implicit interpretative aspect of such understanding will make itself manifest in the very moment in which misunderstandings become apparent. Davidson's famous example is of an actor who, from the stage, screams, "Fire!" Even when he means it seriously (the theater is actually on fire), the audience may still take it to be part of the play. And this might even happen when the actor adds: "This is not part of the play—I mean it seriously!"

The difference between the problem of a hearer's understanding of utterances and the problem of understanding—that is, *knowing*—the meaning (in Witt-

---

5 See Brandom 1994, Chapter 8.

genstein's sense) of words or sentences in a language could also be put in the following way: If, as someone who is learning a language, I do not (yet) understand (know the meaning of) a word or sentence, I will be unable to *apply* this word or sentence correctly *to* and *in* specific situations (e.g., I will not have learned to use words in the right way). If, however, I do not understand the utterance of another speaker even though I have learned to use the words or sentences that this speaker uses, I do not understand the way in which the utterance is related to the situation. There are a number of possibilities of why this might happen: I might misunderstand the speaker's reference; I might misunderstand what he is up to; I might misunderstand the situation *from* which and *in* which somebody is speaking and, therefore, fail to grasp the communicative intention of the speaker; etc. Understanding someone else's utterances usually presupposes a shared understanding of the "situation" or "context" of speech; understanding a language, however, is only a *necessary*, not a *sufficient* condition of such "situational" understanding, since often different people understand the same situation in different, conflicting ways. When Wittgenstein says that an intention is "embedded" in its situation and only as such can *be*—and can be *understood as*—the intention it is, he certainly points to an important precondition of having and understanding intentions. What has to be added, however, is not only that specific situations usually allow for many different intentions, but also—more importantly—that situations may be perceived and understood differently from different perspectives. Although it is true that by sharing a language—a form of life—we necessarily also, in many cases, share an understanding of situations, sharing a language also opens up the possibility of a plurality of perspectives *on* situations. So if we talk about "the" situational context of utterances, we have to keep in mind that situations can always be variously and controversially understood. Certainly, our understanding of situations can be negotiated with arguments—that much is implied in the idea of *understanding* a situation in a specific way. However, *the* situational context of an utterance can be what it is only *as* being understood—or interpreted—in a certain way.

Obviously, my distinction between two different dimensions of understanding must be understood as a merely analytic one. *De facto* the two dimensions—the ability to "follow rules," and the ability to communicate with and to understand other speakers—are inseparable. Our ability to speak does not exist prior to and independently of our ability to successfully communicate with and to understand other speakers. In this sense, the two abilities are one. In another sense, however, speaking a common language opens up infinite possibilities of misunderstanding and non-understanding, and these possibilities are primarily located at the level of what I have called "interpretative" understanding. From the perspective of a "second person," even the understanding of words and sentences may be seen as—at least potentially—an "interpretative" understanding. For when we do not understand the words and sentences used by another speaker "automatically,"—i.e., as words and sentences of our language as we understand it—we are forced to interpret them. Kripke's "meaning-sentences" give us the most primitive idea of such interpretation, which amounts to a "translation" of words to sentences used by another speaker into "our own" language. Kripke's "meaning-sentences," then, signify a further dimension of "interpretative understanding." That such a dimension of interpretative understanding exists even within a common language is due to the essential *openness* of the rules of meaning, which in a Wittgensteinian conception of language is but the other side of his conception of rule-following. If we take this other side of rule-following into account, it becomes clear that a language can never be *quite* a *common* language. The commonality of language is as much a precondition of communication as it is something always again to be achieved through communication. (The latter aspect is what Davidson has made the exclusive and one-sided focus of his theory of interpretation.)

If, however, the understanding of utterances is always—implicitly or explicitly—an *interpretative* understanding, the threat of a skeptical argument seems to reappear, as it were, on the backside of the linguistic practices as they were analyzed by Wittgenstein. For at this point a famous rebuttal of skepticism—one which Wittgenstein puts forward in the form of a question meant to disarm the skeptic by means of a pun—seems no longer sufficient. In §504 of the *Philosophical Investigations*, Wittgenstein says: "But if you say: 'How can I know what he means, when I see nothing but his signs?' then I say: 'How is *he* to know what he means, when he has nothing but his signs either?'" This reply, I said, seems no longer sufficient as a rebuttal to the skeptical question; this is because Wittgenstein seems to ignore the infinite possibilities of *misunderstanding* and *non-understanding* that characterize linguistic communication, even in cases of communication in a common language. I think that, on this point, some of Derrida's arguments can be seen as supporting the skeptical question as a *skeptical* one. I am thinking in particular of what Derrida calls the "force" of linguistic signs to "break" with their (real or semiotic) context and of the possibility of their being "grafted" into new contexts.[6] Something of this sort seems indeed to be involved in what I have called "interpretative understanding." Obviously, the clearest example would be the interpretation of texts, which always goes along with a "decontextualization" and "recontextualization" of written signs. Think of my interpretation of Kripke: I took the few sen-

---

6 See Jacques Derrida, "Signature Event Context," in: Derrida 1998, 1–24, at 9.

tences I quoted out of their semiotic context and "grafted" them into the context of my own arguments. I am sure that many people would say that my interpretation did *violence* to Kripke's text, that what Kripke tries to say must be understood differently. But what are the criteria of "rightness" here? Kripke's "meaning-sentences" certainly won't do. But then what *will* do? We all know from our practice of reading philosophical texts that the problem won't disappear when we read texts "word for word" or try to do what philologists or historians of philosophy often do, namely, to reconstruct the context—the "real" and the philosophical one—of those texts. The problem I am talking about will reappear with every step we take: we will never get at *the* meaning of a text, a meaning that would not be tainted by our own language, prejudices, and expectations and by the linguistic context of *our* interpretation of the words and sentences of the text. The intention of the author, so it appears, remains hidden behind a veil of signs. One might suspect, as Nietzsche occasionally did, that interpretation—at least if we leave the immediate practical concerns and practical certainties of everyday interaction aside—can only be a *making-sense* of utterances or texts for which no criteria of "rightness" exists or can exist. I do not say that this is Derrida's conclusion.[7] What I would say, however, is that Derrida has hardly shown convincingly why this should *not* be his conclusion.

5. As I said, to give a non-skeptical answer to the skeptical question, "How can I know what he means?", it is not sufficient to point to Wittgenstein's dissolution of the paradox of rule-following. Although in my own answer I shall come back to Wittgenstein's answers to skeptical questions, these answers will now be answers to a new question.

Let me return to Kripke for a moment. Kripke has interpreted his reconstruction of Wittgenstein's PLA as the skeptical dissolution of a skeptical paradox. However, this dissolution of a skeptical paradox can be called a *skeptical* dissolution only if an empiricist ideal of "facticity" or "objectivity" is presupposed. Since Kripke shares such a presupposition, he himself has provoked unnecessary misinterpretations of his basic argument. What Kripke—or what Kripke's Wittgenstein—really shows is that the idea of "objective facts" leads us astray where the grammar of words like "meaning" and "understanding" are concerned. But if this is true, it does not make sense to call Wittgenstein's dissolution of the paradox a "skeptical" one. I think something similar holds with regard to the present skeptical question. Bishop Berkeley may provide an analogy here, not (as for Kripke) Hume. Berkeley's "esse est percipi" can be

---

7 See Jacques Derrida, "Afterword," in: Derrida 1998, 111–60, at 146.

seen as a somewhat queer anticipation of what might intelligibly be said about the being of linguistic meaning: its "esse," one might say, is "interpretari." Linguistic meaning has its being in a process of interpretation. As far as the meaning of utterances (or of texts) from the perspective of a "second person" (i.e., of an interpreter) is concerned, the question of a meaning "in itself" (beyond interpretation) is senseless; and from the "performative" perspective of the "first person" (of a speaker), the question does not arise, because a speaker, while speaking, need not interpret herself (she simply follows the rules, or else applies or violates them in an innovative way, depending on the situation). The question of what a speaker means to say by her utterances poses itself essentially from the perspective of a second person; the grammar of the expression "meaning something" has to be construed from the second-personal perspective. To be sure, this is not yet a rebuttal of the skeptical question; however, I shall try to show that it is at least the beginning of such a rebuttal.

6. To show this, I next want to discuss how the concept of truth is involved in the interpretation of texts and utterances. The relationship between truth and interpretation has been a central concern of both Gadamer's and Davidson's. Speaking generally, the thesis of the "truth-relatedness" of interpretation states that, in the interpretation of texts or utterances, we necessarily must raise—either explicitly or implicitly—a question concerning the truth (relevance, appropriateness, sincerity, etc.) of *what* is interpreted.[8] We can do this, however, only by bringing our own current beliefs and prejudices into play via an anticipation of what a speaker or author could intelligibly mean to say. It is this specific involvement of an interpreter with what he is interpreting that Gadamer, following Heidegger, has analyzed as the peculiar structure of the hermeneutic circle. This circle concerns not only the relationship between the parts and the whole of a text, but also—and more importantly—the constitutive role played in the *process* of *interpretation* by the interpreter's beliefs and anticipations concerning the problems that the text is *about*. Furthermore, both Gadamer and Davidson have argued—albeit in different ways—that a "presupposition of truth" is a condition of the possibility of making sense of what other speakers say (Gadamer's "fore-conception of perfection" and Davidson's "principle of charity"). It is these "hermeneutic principles" or "principles of interpretation" that are supposed to delimit the arbitrariness of interpretation. (When I shall talk about "truth" in what follows, I

---

**8** I should emphasize at this point that I shall not talk about *literary* texts in what follows, because I take it that "truth" is not the *basic*—and certainly not the *only*—norm that guides the interpretation of works of art.

shall use the term in a *wide* sense, as applying to all kinds of assertions, beliefs, or presuppositions—not only empirical, but also moral, evaluative, etc., for or against which reasonable argument is possible.)

For reasons that should become clear below, I want to propose at this point a hermeneutic principle that is weaker than Gadamer's as well as Davidson's "presupposition of truth." I call it the "principle of intelligibility." It might be understood as a pragmatic reformulation of Davidson's principle of charity. My claim is that a presupposition of intelligibility is necessary if we want to make sense of texts or utterances *at all*. The presupposition of intelligibility is the presupposition that what a speaker says is intelligibly related to the situation and context, as the interpreter sees them, of her utterances. In a situation of "radical interpretation," such a presupposition will more or less coincide with Davidson's principle of charity, which may then be split into two components: a principle of *coherence* and a principle of *correspondence* (postulating a maximization of truth). But only in such a situation can the principle of correspondence—i.e., the presupposition of truth—play the prominent role that Davidson attributes to it. For in such a situation, the main problem is to learn the meaning of the words and sentences of the foreign language; the presupposition of truth—to put it in non-Davidsonian terms—is here equivalent to the presupposition that the foreign speakers do speak a language and have learned to correctly use the words and sentences of *their* language. ("Coherence" and "correspondence" virtually coincide.) Davidson, however, falsely generalizes the situation of radical interpretation, making it the paradigm of communication in general. (The reason for this false generalization is, I think, Davidson's fixation upon a Tarskian theory of interpretation, from the vantage point of which the differences between "radical" and "ordinary" interpretation may indeed be seen as merely a matter of degree.)

In contrast, the paradigm that I take as my starting point is communication in a more or less common language, where often the problem is *not* to find out the meaning of words and sentences used by a speaker, but to find out the communicative intention with which she uses them. It seems obvious to me, however, that it is precisely in the *sharing* of a language that a multi-dimensional space of truth is opened up, a space in which the possibilities of *disagreement*—i.e., of possible errors and false beliefs and, therefore, the possibilities of debate about questionable truth-claims—grow indefinitely. And with the possibilities of disagreement, the possibilities of misunderstanding grow indefinitely as well. Although disagreement and misunderstanding are different, they are also related; this is because of the "truth-relatedness" of interpretation. Precisely because, as interpreters, we cannot presuppose that other speakers are always correct in what they say or write, understanding what is spoken or written involves a sorting-out of the true and the false—the adequate and the inadequate, the plausible and the implausible, the relevant and the irrelevant—in whatever is said or written. But since the beliefs and presuppositions—which an interpreter must necessarily bring into play in her interpretations of what others say or write—are themselves always a matter of possible disagreement, they can always be a source of possible misunderstanding as well. Therefore, a disagreement about interpretations usually involves either a disagreement about the truth or adequacy of what is said or written, or a disagreement about certain presuppositions made by speaker and interpreter respectively.

Where communication in a common language is concerned, (the presuppositions of) "coherence" and "truth" no longer coincide. But in that case, truth can no longer be generally presupposed. However, a presupposition of intelligibility must be operative in our interpretation of other speakers' utterances; otherwise, we could not locate each other's speech in an intersubjective space of reasons at all, i.e., we could not identify it *as* (intelligible) speech. In cases of doubt, the question that has to be answered is: what could she *possibly*—that is, *intelligibly*—mean to say (given the situation and the relevant context of speech)? Wittgenstein's remark that an intention is embedded in its situation can serve—and usually does serve "automatically"—at least as a principle of exclusion in the process of interpretation, even if we must admit that intentions can be embedded in their situation in numerous different ways. The presupposition of intelligibility may be roughly compared with Davidson's principle of coherence, for it demands a considerable degree of coherence on the part of a speaker as a precondition for an interpreter's being able to make sense of her speech. However, I now want to argue that this presupposition must after all be seen as connected in some way—although not in the way Davidson assumes—with a presupposition of truth. Such a presupposition of truth is not only (morally) necessary in cases where otherwise we would treat another person in an *unjust* way, but also—and more importantly, as Gadamer correctly saw—for the sake of understanding itself. If we do not start with such a presupposition—or, to use a better term, such a *presumption*[9]—with regard, e.g., to difficult texts, we are likely to miss a possible truth-content of such texts; and that means that we *mis*understand them, understand them *falsely*. If to understand what is said or written is to locate it in a multi-dimensional space of truth and reasons, to do so *correctly* means to correctly "sort out" and relate to each other what is true and what is false (illuminating and obscuring, relevant and irrelevant, etc.) in what is said or written. To do this, a presumption of truth is

---

9 Here I follow a suggestion made by Oliver Scholz in Scholz 1999, 148.

necessary, since only with such a presumption could we be said to be open to a full understanding of what is said or written. The presumption of truth is necessary inasmuch as we are concerned at all with the truth of what is said or written as well as with the truth of our own beliefs, the adequacy of the way we see things and of the way we understand ourselves; it is necessary if we are willing to learn from others—regarding our beliefs, our ways of speaking, or our way of seeing things. However, the presumption of truth with regard to our interpretation of what is said or written does not have the same constitutive role for the practice of interpretation as the presupposition of intelligibility does. For the latter presupposition cannot be withdrawn without, at the same time, ceasing to take another person seriously as a person who is accountable for her utterances and actions. In contrast, the presumption of truth can always be withdrawn if we come to the conclusion that a speaker or writer is *mistaken*—for to be mistaken is not a sign of irrationality or of linguistic incompetence. Rather, all of us are, all the time, "mistaken" in at least *some* respect in the eyes of at least *some* people.

7. How does all this bear on the skeptical question I have raised? I have, after all, reaffirmed some of the skeptical question's presuppositions: viz., that interpretation is only possible from the perspective, and within the horizon, of the interpreter, which means that the language, the beliefs, and prejudices of the interpreter will be essentially involved in his interpreting what someone else has said or written. This implies that, while interpreting, we do indeed constantly "graft" the words and sentences of other speakers or writers into new chains of linguistic signs—our own—decontextualizing and recontextualizing them in often wild ways (as might be said about my interpretation of Kripke). What the skeptical question implied was that there are no possible criteria for doing this in the "right" or the "wrong" way, so that the very concept of "understanding"—with the implied distinction between understanding correctly and incorrectly—would lose its point. What sort of anti-skeptical reply could follow from my reflection on "hermeneutic" principles of interpretation?

To show what this reply is, I shall first discuss a simple example. Let us suppose a friend of mine, with whom I am hiking in the mountains, suddenly says, "I would like a steak." The situation seems clear: my friend expresses the—understandable—wish to eat a steak. If we had been in a butcher's shop and my friend had uttered the same sentence, I would have understood his utterance differently, namely, as the expression of his intention to buy a raw piece of meat; and if we had been in a restaurant and my friend had addressed the waiter who just came to take our orders, I would have understood his utterance as the ordering of a fried steak. (It is interesting that the expectations and obligations implied by the utterance of the same sentence in different situations can be so very different.) The justification of my understanding of my friend's utterance in these different situations rests on my understanding of the situation, an understanding that—I have reason to assume—we both share. (How could my friend, during our hike in the mountains, have meant his utterance as the ordering of a steak? Only if he had been, e. g., hallucinating.) So far, Wittgenstein's dictum would be sufficient: an intention must be embedded in its situation. However, I *could* have misunderstood my friend in the mountains: perhaps he did not utter an urgent desire, but only imitated an acquaintance, with whom he had spent the prior evening in a restaurant; or perhaps he had begun to quote a passage from a book that he was occupied with at the moment (perhaps he forgot the next sentence and so fell into silence again); or he tried to start a game that we might call a "chain poem" (one of us begins with a line; then the next person must, first, come up with a line with an end rhyme, then add a new line; and so on). When we focus our attention solely on the moment of the utterance, one has to admit that a number of possible interpretations—and misinterpretations—would be possible, even if we take the tone of voice or any accompanying gesture as additional clues. Things will appear differently if we—as Wittgenstein postulates in analogous contexts—take into account what happened *before* and what happens *after* the utterance, i. e., the "temporal surrounding" or the "narrative context" of the utterance. Intentions are embedded in situations not only with respect to the moment of their utterance, but as part of an ongoing story, and situations may, at the same time, also be occasions for the beginning of a new story. This also means, however, that "intelligibility" can never signify just isolated utterances or actions. Rather, it always signifies, in one way or the other, intelligibility over time, the intelligibility of creatures who are involved in stories, who can learn, who can participate in an ongoing social practice of giving and asking for reasons and who understand themselves as creatures for whom intelligibility and truth have the force of normative demands regarding their speech and action over time. In this sense, intentions are "embedded" in situations always as points of intersection between a "before" and an "after." The reasons for a specific understanding of an utterance, therefore, can never be derived from the moment of the utterance as something cut out of its before and after. Situations are always understood as part of an ongoing interaction or story we are involved in, and each understanding implies the anticipation of a specific continuation of such stories, which may turn out to be wrong. In the case of my friend, his next utterance could dissolve all misunderstanding, e. g., if he said, "I am so hungry," or "Do you remember?" or "Why don't you go on?" So here we have a situation in which we can clearly have reasons to interpret an utterance in one or the other way. And we often lack any reasons to *doubt* such an interpretation. One might hold that a doubt needs a reason as well. When we have reasons to doubt our interpretation of what someone has said, we shall sometimes be able to resolve our doubts, sometimes not. So there is no room for a *skeptical* doubt here, since a skeptical doubt would involve doubting whether we could *ever* correctly understand any utterance of another speaker, whether there is *any* understanding other speakers.

I have tried to show that there are trivial cases where a lack of understanding usually *shows* itself in the further process of interaction or communication. We can say that usually there are reasons for *interpreting* someone in a certain way, and often there are reasons also for *questioning* an interpretation. Interpretations, therefore—to put it differently—are themselves located in a social space of reasons; and wherever we argue for or against an interpretation, we presuppose that there is something to be argued about.

Since the skeptic could hardly deny this, it seems that the skeptical argument must cut deeper if it is to have any force. Obviously, it must intend to show that there is something illusory about our arguing for or against the correctness of interpretations as such. So I come back to the question I raised above: What sort of anti-skeptical reply could be contained in my reflection on hermeneutic principles?

Before I answer this question, let me first distinguish between two possible forms of skepticism. The *first* starts from the idea that a good, correct interpretation ought to capture the intentions of the speaker or writer, together with the insight that nothing but her signs (and perhaps her actions) can provide access to these intentions. The conclusion, then, is that the intention of the speaker or writer must necessarily remain hidden behind a veil of signs and therefore cannot serve as a yardstick of correct understanding. Now, this argument is certainly wrong as it stands. In fact, Wittgenstein already has already provided a sufficient answer. According to this Wittgensteinian response, the argument's mistake lies in the assumption that there is an internal, mental something—the "meaning" or "intention" of the speaker or writer—which, existing prior to the language used to express it, would both determine the meaning of her utterance and remain, in principle, inaccessible to an outside observer, i.e., to an interpreter. Evidently, this is the kind of argument that, after Wittgenstein, we should no longer take seriously, even if we are ready to admit that much of our internal life may remain hidden to an outside observer—or even to ourselves.

The *second* form of skepticism—let me call it "poststructuralist" skepticism—rests on a *critique* of intentionalist conceptions of meaning. It does not take intentions, but rather contexts—"internal," semiotic ones as well as "external," i. e., situational, social, historical, ones—as determining the meaning of texts and utterances. To understand texts or utterances, then, would be to understand them *as* determined by their—narrower and broader—context, by past language-use. etc. It could then be argued, as Derrida has done, that the meaning of a text or utterance can never be fully "present" either to the speaker or writer himself or to an interpreter. It could not be present to the speaker or writer because every context is "limitless" ("the entire 'real history of the world'"),[10] so that "there is an indefinite opening of every context, an essential nontotalization."[11] And while, for the same reason, it could never be fully present to an interpreter, the situation is even more dramatic with regard to interpretation, since every interpretation involves a decontextualization and recontextualization of the spoken or written signs, which makes it all the more impossible to grasp the contextual determination of the meaning of texts or utterances. Now, I take it that Derrida's point is not really skeptical, but is rather concerned to critique "objectivism" about meaning—an objectivism that would necessarily *lead* to hermeneutic skepticism. But the manner in which Derrida makes his point can easily be used (and has been used) to advocate the thesis that the very term "understanding" (of texts and utterances) involves an illusion, because what determines meanings—and therefore the meanings themselves—can never be grasped by an interpreter. If contexts can never be exhausted, and if, in the act or process of interpretation, an interpreter is always entangled in his particular perspective, horizon, and beliefs, and if interpretation, therefore, always involves a decontextualization and recontextualization of linguistic signs—a "grafting" of signs into new contexts—then interpretation can never be a grasping of what is objectively given, of what preexists as "the" meaning of utterances or texts. Consequently, the very distinction between "right" and "wrong" interpretation collapses. If this were true, however, then to argue about the "real" meaning of a text or utterance would rest on an illusion. Moreover, the problem would be reiterated with every new step taken in a debate about interpretations, for arguments must themselves be understood, that is, interpreted. In the end, we would be left with nothing but an untamable play of signs.

What is common to both forms of skepticism is the idea that there *is* a determinate meaning of texts or utterances (somewhere "out there") prior to their interpretation—determined either by intentions or by context—a determinate meaning, however, which is structurally inaccessible to an interpreter. So the only possible ("objective") criterion for distinguishing between "correct" and "incorrect" interpretation lies out of reach of any possible interpreter.

---

10 Derrida 1988, 136.
11 Derrida 1998, 137

Every interpretation would therefore involve an unavoidable shift of meaning between speaker or writer and interpreter.

Now, what my reflections on meaning and (the "conditions of the possibility of") interpretation were meant to show is that to talk about meanings as something objectively given—whether determined by intentions or by a nontotalizable context—misconstrues the grammar of the word "meaning." For the word "meaning," with regard to texts and utterances, can have a *justified* use *only* from the perspective of an interpreter who tries to "identify" this meaning from her particular perspective and horizon. Consequently, interpretation is the only way to identify the meaning of texts or utterances. To speak of a "meaning" of a text or utterance beyond that which may be "identified" as the meaning by an interpreter through her interpretation can only have an intelligible point if what is meant are better, more adequate—perhaps "deeper"—interpretations. So there is nothing beyond interpretations that could serve as an "objective" standard concerning the correctness of interpretations. In this, the skeptic is right; but he misunderstands his own point. For he wrongly assumes that if meanings can only be identified through interpretation, and if no *external* standards of correctness are available, then there can be no standards and criteria *at all* and therefore no way of rationally *justifying* or criticizing interpretations. That this assumption is wrong, however, becomes obvious once we reflect upon how the grammar of "meaning" reflects an internal relationship between meaning and interpretation. I have argued above that an interpreter in an act or process of interpretation is necessarily involved with (a) her own beliefs and prejudices, (b) her current perspective on situations, problems, or areas of concern, and (c) her own language, as a starting point. So far, the skeptic would most likely agree. But what is more important is that the interpreter will also be involved with questions of truth—in the broadest possible sense—concerning that which is said or written. I have called this the "truth-relatedness" of interpretation. What has to be understood, then, is that these hermeneutic preconditions of interpretation define at the same time the very conditions of the possibility of talking about and of "identifying" the meaning of texts and utterances, so that any talk of "the" meaning of texts or utterances prior to or independent of a process of interpretation is empty. To talk about the meaning of texts or utterances presupposes the perspective of an interpreter. Therefore, one might say that the "esse" of meaning is "interpretari." But then the standards and criteria that are always already operative in processes of interpretation are the only *conceivable* ones for a "correct" identification of meaning. That interpretations are often controversial, then, is but another expression of the fact that *truth* is often controversial. It does not mean that there is something illusory about our practice of arguing for or against interpretations. Skepticism with regard to interpretation, then, rests on a false "objectivism" regarding meaning.

Instead of speaking about the "truth-relatedness" of interpretation, one might speak of the *normative* character of interpretation, of the variety of normative dimensions in which interpretations may involve an evaluation of what is said or written. In contrast to the "intentionalist" and "objectivist" conceptions of meaning that I have criticized, a "normative" conception of meaning and interpretation will link the process of interpretation directly with our truth-oriented social practice of giving and asking for reasons. It is this practice that is constitutive of the normative "framework" of interpretation, without which no identification of meanings from the perspective of a second person—i.e., an interpreter —would be possible. This also means that the principles of interpretation I have mentioned above demand an attitude on the part of the interpreter that is quite different from the one suggested by intentionalist conceptions of meaning. For the former imply a normative distinction between more or less adequate, i.e., more or less self-critical, ways of getting involved with questions of truth and adequacy in the process of interpretation. The hermeneutic principles imply a postulate of hermeneutic "openness" as a condition of successful interpretation,[12] and it is only for this reason that the process of interpretation may be understood as part and parcel of a communicative learning process in which the language, the perspective, the beliefs and prejudices of the interpreter may always *change* in unforeseeable ways in the course of interpretation and communication. To have an open mind in the hermeneutic sense means to be prepared to put one's own perspective, beliefs, and prejudices at risk in interpreting what others have said or written. This also means that interpretation, and communication in general, are misunderstood if we "fail to see that here concepts are constantly in the process of being formed."[13] (It is this aspect of interpretation that has no place in Davidson's theory, but which Gadamer focuses upon.)

8. Although I have so far talked about texts *and* utterances, one might object that in the case of textual interpretation things are more complicated than I have presented them here. This objection certainly has a point. I would argue, however, that the complications concern the process of interpretation itself, if it comes to,

---

12 It is notoriously controversial whether such a postulate of hermeneutic "openness"—that is, of openness to the possible truth of what has been said or written by somebody else—is expressive merely of a *rational* or also of a *moral* requirement. It seems obvious to me that, depending on the situation, it *can* be both. But perhaps it is not even possible in the present context to draw a sharp line between "rational" and "moral" requirements in every case.

13 Gadamer 1994, 403.

say, the interpretation of literary or philosophical texts, as well as the resp. role which interpretation plays in our encounter with such texts. As far as literary texts or artworks in general are concerned, interpretation in the hermeneutic sense (as I have discussed it here) plays, I believe, a role quite different from the one it plays in the case of philosophical texts—at least as long as we do not reduce artworks (as I think we shouldn't) to nothing more than special sources of truth (though they may also be that).[14] Therefore, I shall not talk about the interpretation of literary texts (or artworks in general) here, but only about texts where a hermeneutic approach, with its truth-relatedness, is the dominant one we take when confronted with such texts.

Let me distinguish between two different sorts of texts: those that we feel free to criticize while interpreting, on the one hand, and those that are taken as "authoritative" texts—such as the Constitution or, for some people at least, the Bible. Regarding the first kind of texts—let me take philosophical texts as a paradigm case—not much needs to be added to my reply to the skeptical argument. I would again argue (1) that the "identification" of textual meaning—for which, of course, the internal textual context provides the most important clues—is *only* possible from the perspective of interpreters, a class of which the author is just another, though perhaps an important, member; in short, there is no textual meaning "in itself," as though it were a strange entity existing objectively somewhere in the universe; and (2) that an interpreter's understanding of the problems involved—an understanding that may change through her careful reading of the text—will always guide her understanding of what the text says. The interpreter will try to reformulate in her own words—by "recontextualizing" the words of the author—what the text, or what a passage of the text, says, thereby separating, at the same time, what she thinks is true and what false, what is illuminating and what doubtful or confused, what is coherent and what incoherent, etc., in the text. A "correct," i.e., a *good*, interpretation of a text would then be one that had sorted out the true from the false, etc., in the *right* way. And the word "right" here gains its "direction" from all those criteria and standards that, as I have tried to show, are always already operative, because of its truth-relatedness, in the process of interpretation and which also may change in this process whenever we are confronted with new arguments and viewpoints. So the use of the word "right" with respect to interpretation is no more—and no less—"contextual" than our use of the word "true." Therefore, if

---

14 The problem is much too complicated to be discussed here, since it concerns the relative right of hermeneutic, formalist, and deconstructive conceptions of art. For a brilliant attempt to transform these different conceptions of art into legitimate aspects of one single perspective on art, see Sonderegger 2000.

the contextual character of an interpretation should be seen as a new source of hermeneutic skepticism, then skepticism concerning interpretation would now merge with skepticism concerning truth. A skepticism, however, that would be based on the contextual nature of our use of "true" is, I would claim (but cannot argue here[15]), as ill-founded as a more specific skepticism concerning interpretation.

To be sure, interpretations can go wrong in many different ways. For instance, I may have missed an important point the author has made because I did not understand the problems he was dealing with (hence the importance of a "presumption of truth" in such cases); or I may have missed the meaning of certain words or sentences because I am not familiar enough with, say, ancient Greek or current French; or I may have missed the point of an innovative or figurative use of language; or I may just be too impatient, biased, or stupid. However, I would claim that wherever serious conflicts of interpretations exist with regard to the meaning of philosophical texts, there are always *philosophical* disagreements involved—concerning our understanding of the philosophical issues or problems that are dealt with in the text. Even disagreements about what the problem really is that is thematized in a text will often *also* be disagreements about which problems are *worthy* of thematization. What I want to say is that disagreement about the interpretation of philosophical texts is inseparable from disagreement about philosophical problems and theses. The reason why the debate about the "correct" interpretation of philosophical texts is virtually interminable is, I believe, simply that the debate about the hard philosophical questions is interminable. But this, I would argue, is no reason for a *skeptical* doubt concerning interpretation.

What has to be admitted, however, is that there is no clear-cut boundary between what may be called an "adequate" interpretation of a text, on the one hand, and what should rather be called a "strong" or "violent"—though perhaps productive—reading of a text, a reading that only *uses* a text to put forward some interesting new thesis. The question whether an interpretation belongs to one or the other category is notoriously controversial. Although to the extent that we are primarily interested in the *philosophical* problems under debate, this question often seems rather irrelevant. However, this does not mean that we cannot argue such cases. We may, e. g., show that an interpreter has simply ignored important parts or layers of a text, elements that are incompatible with his interpretation—although, of course, such arguments will themselves not be independent

---

15 See, however, Wellmer 2001, where I argue for a view on truth and justification that, I believe, leaves no room for a *skeptical* argument.

of our understanding of the problems the text deals with. Understanding a text, then, means sorting out what is true *and* what is false in it *in the right way.* While from the viewpoint of *philosophical truth*, it may often seem irrelevant whether we understand a text correctly or have merely used it to advance an interesting new thesis, from the viewpoint of hermeneutic truth, we can always ask the *additional* question of whether a text has been adequately *interpreted.* So even if our interpretation of philosophical texts necessarily involves us in questions of truth, we might still distinguish between two forms of involvement in these questions: the form in which philosophical *truth* is our main concern and in which we make a productive *use* of texts; and the form in which the *meaning of a text* is our main concern and in which we make productive use of our philosophical insights in advancing a careful *interpretation* of the text. I think that both ways of dealing with texts are legitimate and necessary, because new philosophical insights often emerge precisely from the interaction of these two forms of involvement.

Regarding the second kind of texts I mentioned—the "authoritative" ones—things are somewhat more complicated, for here the text is considered as a standard of what is to be taken as true or right. What complicates matters here is that, in her understanding of what is true or right, the interpreter must, on the one hand, justify this understanding by reference to what the "authoritative" text is saying, while, on the other hand, her understanding of what is true or right will not only—conversely—guide her interpretation of the text, but will also serve to reinforce the authority of the text. So there is a quite specific kind of "hermeneutic circle" here, one that is typical not only of Biblical exegesis, but—more importantly—of legal interpretation as well. Now, the only case I want to consider here is the case of constitutional interpretation in democratic societies, since it is the only (unproblematic) case *I* know of in which reference to an authoritative text is, at the same time, a reference to how *we* (want to) understand ourselves (namely, as free and equal citizens), whereas the authority of religious texts has always been tainted by the idea of revelation and the power of a clerical hierarchy. If put in this way, however, the interpretation of an "authoritative" text—of the constitution—will not pose an essentially new problem as contrasted to textual interpretation in general. I think this has become clear in the extended debate between Ronald Dworkin and Stanley Fish about constitutional interpretation.[16] A tacit premise of this debate has been that controversies regarding constitutional interpretation take place among interpreters who all affirm the constitutional principles about whose interpretation they disagree. Elsewhere, I have spoken of an unavoidable practical-hermeneutic circle of demo-

---

16 Cf., Dworkin 1985, Chapters 6–7; Dworkin 1986; Fish 1989, Chapters 4, 5, 16.

cratic discourse,[17] which is due to the fact that constitutional principles can never take care of their own interpretation and institutional implementation. Controversies about the correct interpretation of constitutional principles are, therefore, part of their very "being." Seen in this way, however, the case of an interpretation of a—genuine—"authoritative" text seems not so different from that of textual interpretation in general. In both cases, there is no possible access to an "objective" meaning of the text, while at the same time, interpretation—because it always takes place in a social space of reasons—is never an arbitrary imputation of meaning to a text either. Or as Stanley Fish has put it in response to Dworkin's claim that interpretation is "an activity in need of constraints": "... what I have been trying to show is that interpretation is a *structure* of constraints, a structure which, because it is always and already in place, renders unavailable the independent or uninterpreted text and renders unimaginable the independent and freely interpreting reader."[18] What has to be added is merely that the "structure of constraints" can itself at any given point become a topic of debate. There is no Archimedean point for judging interpretations outside the very process of interpretation. But that we go on debating about the meaning of the constitution shows that there is something—our self-understanding as democratic citizens—that is worth arguing about.[19] And of course, situations are always imaginable in which even genuine authoritative texts may lose (some of) their authority. Even constitutions may be changed.

9. Throughout this paper I have argued that questions concerning the meaning of texts or utterances can only be raised from the perspective of an interpreter—so that even a speaker or writer, if she wants to say what it is that she meant to say or write, will become an interpreter of herself, possibly arguing with other interpreters about the correct interpretation of what she has said or written. To this it might be objected that frequently we are willing to concede that a speaker or author may or even must know better than her interpreters what she meant to say or write. Would we not give Wittgenstein a privileged place among the Wittgenstein commentators were he still alive, or to Gadamer, who at the moment in which I am writing this text *is* still alive, among the interpreters of Gadamer's texts?

---

17 See Wellmer 1998, 45f.
18 Fish 1989, 98.
19 This, of course, is not to deny that power relations play a role in debates about the constitution—particularly with respect to *which* interpretation will become effective in the legal system.

Let me first discuss this question with regard to ordinary utterances in every-day communication. So far I have argued that the idea that a speaker must know what she means, even if an interpreter doesn't—an idea that then leads itself to an intentionalist conception of meaning—rests on an optical illusion, because even the speaker, once she is confronted with the *question* of what it is she meant to say, can answer this question only from the position of a second person—that of an interpreter. Therefore, to say, "Only the speaker can know what she means," amounts to saying, "While I am speaking, my 'meaning' is usually no object of a possible doubt for me (although this happens too)." But this "meaning to say" is not a mental event of which I am aware and of which nobody else can be aware. The self-transparency of meaning-something is a *performative*, not a *cognitive* one. Consequently, a speaker can only *say* what she "knows" (her meaning something) by becoming an interpreter of herself.

If this sounds counterintuitive, it is because of the ambiguous role that the verb "to know" plays in such contexts. For in one sense of "knowing," a speaker certainly *can* be in a privileged position with respect to her interlocutors. Often she may have reasons that are unavailable to her interlocutors for saying why she could or could not have meant what she said in one or the other way. And these "additional reasons" usually refer to something that the speaker *knows* about the situation or herself and that the interlocutors don't know (although in principle they *could* know—e. g., by being told by the speaker). So the speaker *might* know better than her interlocutors how her "meaning-intention" was "embedded" in the situation. This "knowing better," however, is misconstrued if it is understood as a privileged access to a meaning-intention behind the words. It is, rather, a "knowing" in an ordinary sense, that is, in the sense in which I might be said to know certain things (e. g., about a situation or about myself) that others don't know. And in any case, this "privileged position" of the speaker (concerning the interpretation of what she said) can only be a *relative* one—and often it is not even that. In more complex cases—think of psychoanalysis or of philosophical discussions—we often learn from the interpretations and reactions of our interlocutors that we do not really know what we meant to say; so it happens that "meanings" may be clarified only in the process of communication. And in such cases, it is usually obvious that the clarification of meaning-intentions is inseparable from a debate about what it would be *adequate* to say. Consequently, the possibility that sometimes I do know better than my interlocutors what I meant to say or *how* I have meant what I said presupposes the grammar of the words "meaning" and "understanding," as I have tried to reconstruct it, and does not run against it.

When it comes to the interpretation of texts—let me again take philosophical texts as a paradigm—it is even more obvious that the author can at best be in a *relatively* privileged position as an interpreter of what he has written, for the simple reason that he is more familiar with the context of his own words, with the ideas, arguments, and alternatives he has tried out, etc. (Sometimes, of course, he may just be better at philosophy than his audience.) But inasmuch a textual interpretation is always a sorting-out of what is true or false, adequate or inadequate, illuminating or confused, etc., the author is *not* in a privileged position, so that here it becomes entirely obvious that a debate about interpretations is inseparable from a debate about truth; and in this debate, the author can only have *a*—stronger or weaker—voice among *other* voices. But of course, authors —except, for instance, in discussions after lectures—usually don't interpret their own writings, but rather continue to talk and write about the questions they have raised in their works, learning from objections and replies, decontextualizing and recontextualizing their former words and sentences and thereby often also criticizing themselves. So if they try to say what they meant to say, they will usually try to reformulate in new words what they think was "right" and what was "wrong" in what they had previously said or written. (Think of Wittgenstein's interpretation and critique of his *Tractatus Logico-Philosophicus* in the *Philosophical Investigations*.) So if we ask what an author could have meant by what she has written, we are not looking for a mysterious "meaning-intention" *behind* her words. Rather, we are trying to discover what interesting, important, or illuminating things she could have meant to say; and these interesting, important, or illuminating things—as well as also the misleading or erroneous things she might have said—can only be reformulated from the interpreter's perspective and in the interpreter's language. What I have tried to show is that this is not merely the only way we can go about interpreting the "meaning-something" of an author, but that to ask for more is to misunderstand the grammar of "meaning."

10. So far I have criticized what might be called a "representationalist" misconception of meaning and understanding, a misconception according to which the understanding of utterances or texts would be like grasping something—their meaning—that, independently of the process of interpretation, exists objectively somewhere in the world "out there." If understanding and interpretation are conceived in this way, the very conditions of the possibility of understanding will appear as conditions of the *impossibility* of understanding. In contrast, I have tried to show that understanding and interpretation should be conceived as a "making-sense-of" texts and utterances; a "making-sense-of" texts and utterances that is by no means arbitrary (as the skeptic would suspect), but which,

as something taking place in a social space of reasons, is "regulated" in its own peculiar way.

At this point, it might be objected that, so far, I have only scratched the surface of the problems that really motivate the skeptical doubt, and that those problems will become visible only if we dig beneath this surface. Metaphorically speaking, one might characterize what lies "beneath the surface" by saying that human beings, as speaking animals, will always be, to a greater or lesser extent, a foreign territory for themselves and for each other; that, therefore, a *real* understanding of other persons will never be possible; and that what we take to be an understanding of each other's motives, attitudes, utterances, and actions might be nothing more than an expression of how we want to see each other, a "wanting to see each other" that might be based on unconscious motives, on power relations, on blind affection, hostility, or distrust. Now, I certainly do not want to dispute that these sources of hermeneutic skepticism are real. However, in my reflections on understanding and interpretation I deliberately stayed on the "surface" of ordinary communication—talking about texts and utterances and how we go about interpreting them—because I think it is here that a *radical* hermeneutic skepticism is to be refuted. And only if it is refuted, I believe, can we see what lies beneath the surface in the right way. To show this, I now want to complement my anti-representationalist account of meaning and understanding by looking at some typical, but still ordinary, situations where hermeneutic doubt and hermeneutic suspicion appear to be insuperable.

I am thinking of, for instance, situations in which it is of utmost importance for us to correctly understand what another person has said or written, and in which we are tortured by an interminable doubt regarding what it *is* that the other person has said or written. A typical situation would be that of an intimate relationship, where the question of what the other person meant or implied concerns, at the same time, the quality of the relationship itself. These are cases of existential uncertainty, where understanding the other is of utmost importance— my whole life, or so it may appear, is at stake—while the problem is that the *situation* of speech, which in ordinary cases of communication often provides unmistakable clues for a correct understanding, is uncertain with regard to what it really is, simply because it is precisely my relationship to the other person that is the most important aspect of this situation. So the utterances, gestures, and actions of the other person have to serve as clues for my understanding of the situation, which therefore cannot serve as an unmistakable clue for understanding the other person's *utterances*, gestures, or actions. A circularity evolves here between the understanding of utterances and the understanding of the "situation" of utterances, while none of the two can provide an unmistakable clue for the other. So for at least one of the parties there may be no way out of uncertainty and doubt, as is also the case in typical situations of "double bind." Or think of the interminable quarrels that sometimes develop between two persons who are close to each other, quarrels revolving around what he or she *meant* to say or *implied* by something said at some earlier moment. In such situations, whatever the other person says or does may become a new source of hermeneutic doubt or hermeneutic suspicion. Or think of all the possibilities of hiding our motives from each other—and even from ourselves—of inauthentic self-understanding and self-presentation, of manipulating each other, etc., which may be a source of radical hermeneutic doubt or suspicion. Could we not say that these situations of radical hermeneutic doubt or suspicion show something illusory about our *ordinary* hermeneutic certainties—and perhaps, by implication, also about our ordinary certainties concerning perception and memory?

I think that, in the first place, what such experiences show is something general about the human condition: that we can never completely control the contingencies of life or the fate of our relationships with other persons, that our memories and intentions are weak and unstable, that our motives are often dubious and not presentable to others—or even to ourselves—and that we may be under the sway of desires, resentments, paranoias, fixations, or obsessions that blind us to who we are as well as to the otherness of other persons, make us incapable of recognizing other persons' legitimate expectations, and distort the perception of our relationships with them. But these facts about the human condition are, I believe, misconstrued if they are taken as justifying a radical hermeneutic skepticism. For, *first of all*, even radical hermeneutic doubt or suspicion always presupposes a background of hermeneutic certainties—as doubts about empirical facts presuppose a background of empirical certainties.[20] Such certainties are the condition of the possibility of radical hermeneutic doubt or suspicion —as a "community of judgment" and the shared certainties that go with it are the conditions of the possibility of radical disagreement and error. *Secondly*, and perhaps more importantly, regarding situations that give rise to radical hermeneutic suspicion and skepticism, the problem should not be primarily construed as *cognitive*, but rather as *practical:* Our life is in disorder, we don't trust each other any more, so that disagreement and distrust are hopelessly confounded. The problem is one of "distorted communication," to use a Habermasian term. There is, however, no "cognitive" solution to such problems, except as the byproduct of a *practical* change: a change in the way we relate to each other, a change in our self-understanding and our practical orientations—in short, a change of *life*. What is lacking in situations of distorted communication are the preconditions for her-

---

**20** As Wittgenstein has shown in Wittgenstein 1969.

meneutic openness, for mutual trust and mutual recognition; only where these preconditions are lacking may hermeneutic doubt and suspicion—a search for hidden meanings and motives, disbelief in the sincerity of the other person—become interminable. My claim that there is no "cognitive" solution for such problems independently of a practical one has a corollary: that hermeneutic doubt or suspicion makes sense only in *specific* contexts, for instance, when understanding each other has become a practical problem. That human beings are never quite transparent to each other and in *this* sense can never "fully" understand each other is *not* a problem but an opportunity, namely, the precondition for our not being fully "objectified" by each other. In this sense, the very idea of a "full" understanding of each other is just a misfire (or, perhaps, the expression of a perverse wish).

Radical hermeneutic skepticism, then, as far as it is not the expression of a representationalist misconception of meaning and understanding, should rather be seen as a skepticism concerning the possibility of mutual trust and sincerity among human beings, i.e., as the possibility of undistorted communication. Now, I believe that *this* skepticism might be understood in two different ways. If understood in one way, a philosophical reply is still possible; if understood in the other way, however, philosophy can offer no consolation. Let me explain.

First of all, one might say that a skepticism concerning the possibility of undistorted communication can have a point only in specific situations, situations in which we don't trust each other or in which we have reasons to suspect that communication is distorted (which may often be the case). But then it should not be called skepticism (in a philosophical sense). What this "skepticism," understood as a *general* one, expresses is but a recognition of the contingencies and the fragility of human relationships, of an element of irresolvable opaqueness that belongs to them, and of the ever-present *possibility* that communication may become distorted—that is to say, however, of those aspects of the human condition that are, at the same time, the very preconditions of speech and of communication between embodied creatures; of our inhabiting a common world; of preserving and changing it for the better; of critique, innovation, and progress; of artistic creation; and not least of all, of the possibility to practically transcend particular situations of distorted communication. So it is "skepticism" only with regard to rationalist illusions. If, in contrast, it is understood as a skepticism regarding the very possibility of "undistorted communication," it cannot—so one might argue—be generalized, since such skepticism, as long as the common world we inhabit has not actually fallen apart, always presupposes some degree of unsuspicious, of trustful relationships between human beings and the practical and hermeneutic certainties that go with them. Without such practical and hermeneutic certainties, we would have lost the common world in which we can communicate with—in which we can understand *and* misunderstand—each other, and would ultimately lose our status as persons who are accountable to each other and who are able to interact with each other in a social space of reasons. To lose this status, however, is not to lose an illusion, but to lose a capacity and to lose a world. So the problem of radical hermeneutic skepticism is that it could only be *lived* at the price of losing one's status as a person, of losing the world that we share with others. The idea, however, that this common world itself is but an illusion makes sense only if we presuppose a point outside the world from which we could see things as they *really* are. And this would be bad metaphysics.

This is about how far a philosophical reply to the kind of skepticism we are considering can go. It accuses the skeptic of something like a "performative self-contradiction," arguing that he could not even articulate his skepticism without presupposing the existence of communicative relationships the possibility of which he is denying. This sort of philosophical reply to skepticism, however, will not work if we understand this skepticism in a different way: no longer as a (general) philosophical skepticism concerning the possibility of undistorted communication, but rather as the expression of a concrete fear—based on specific historical experiences that are articulated in a radical critique of society—that our world has already begun to fall apart. This would not be skepticism any longer, but a "negativism" exemplified by Adorno and Horkheimer's *Dialectic of Enlightenment* or by the later Adorno's *Negative Dialectics*. The fear that our world may already have begun to fall apart—which for the later Adorno became the fear that Auschwitz may be a prefiguration of what is yet to come in the modern world—is here based on a diagnosis according to which the horrors of our time are deeply rooted in social and cultural transformations of modern societies, transformations that point toward an imminent moral and cultural disaster of modern civilization and, not least, tend to make independent thought and genuine communication impossible. Now, it would be easy to accuse Adorno and Horkheimer of a performative self-contradiction in the way they have formulated their radical critique, but this accusation would miss the point of their critique and of their fear. The point of their radical negativism is not that of a general philosophical skepticism that may be philosophically refuted, but rather (a) to point to a mortal danger, the danger that the development of modern civilization might undermine the conditions of genuine communication, and thereby (b) to *strengthen* critical thought and the forces of resistance against what they see as disastrous tendencies of modern civilization. This, of course, is not to say that one could not disagree with Adorno and Horkheimer's—or with the later Adorno's or with Foucault's—critical negativism on many points (as I myself do). It is rather to mark a point where anti-skeptical philosophical arguments would become "ideological," because they would amount to closing one's eyes to problems that are not (merely) *philosophical* problems any longer. No philosophical reassurance or consolation is possible where distorted communication has become a reality, where the preconditions of democratic discourse are undermined, or where the bases of individual autonomy, public liberty, and social solidarity are disintegrating. What is needed in such situations—and are the dangers I mentioned not with us all the time? —is social and political critique as well as a change of practices, self-conceptions, and institutions. In short: a practical improvement of the social and political forms and conditions of communication. Seen in this way, radical negativism, with its correlate of a radical impulse toward transcending a bad status quo (perhaps Derrida's philosophy might be seen as a new form of such negativism), may in the end also be a necessary antidote against the danger of a false self-complacency in the critique of philosophical skepticism.

# Bibliography

Brandom, Robert (1994), *Making It Explicit: Reasoning, Representing, and Discursive Commitment*, Cambridge, MA: Harvard University Press.

Derrida, Jacques (1988), *Limited, Inc*, Evanstan, IL: Northwestern University Press.

Dworkin, Ronald (1985), *A Matter of Principle*, Cambridge, MA: Harvard University Press.

Dworkin, Ronald (1986), *Law's Empire*, Cambridge, MA: Harvard University Press.

Fish, Stanley (1989), *Doing What Comes Naturally: Change, Rhetoric, and the Practice of Theory In Literary and Legal Studies*, Oxford: Clarendon Press.

Gadamer, Hans-Georg (1994), *Truth and Method*, Joel Weinsheimer and Donald G. Marshall (trans.), New York: Continuum Books.

Hoffmann, Thomas (2000), *Der Mythos des Kausalen: Davidson und McDowell über Erfahrung*, Master's Thesis, F.U. Berlin.

Kripke, Saul A. (1982), *Wittgenstein on Rules and Private Language*, Cambridge, MA: Harvard University Press.

Scholz, Oliver R. (1999), *Verstehen und Rationalität: Untersuchungen zu den Grundlagen von Hermeneutik und Sprachphilosophie*, Frankfurt am Maim: Vittorio Klostermann.

Sonderegger, Ruth (2000), *Für eine Ästhetik des Spiels: Hermeneutik, Dekonstruktion, und der Eigensinn der Kunst*, Frankfurt-am-Main: Suhrkamp.

Wellmer, Albrecht (1998), *Endgames: The Irreconcilable Nature of Modernity*, David Midgley (trans.), Cambridge, MA: The MIT Press.

Wellmer, Albrecht (2001), "The Debate About Truth: Pragmatism Without Regulative Ideals." In: William Egginton and Mike Sandbothe (eds.), *The Pragmatic Turn In Philosophy: Contemporary Engagements Between Analytic and Continental Thought*, New York: State University of New York Press.

Wittgenstein, Ludwig (1958), *Philosophical Investigations*, G.E.M. Anscombe (trans.), Oxford: Blackwell.

Wittgenstein, Ludwig (1969), *On Certainty*, Denis Paul and G.E.M. Anscombe (trans.), Oxford: Basil Blackwell.

Martin Stone[*]

# Interpretation: Everyday and Philosophical

> *What we do is to bring words back from their*
> *metaphysical to their everyday use.*
> – Wittgenstein, Philosophical Investigations[1]

I begin by comparing and contrasting some familiar settings in which interpretations are called for: law, literature, and artistic performance. The aim is to clarify the variability and unity of "interpretation" across these settings: How is interpretation of a literary text like and unlike the interpretations that are official applications of the law?

There is today also a distinctively *philosophical* use of the term interpretation. An author speaks, not of the meaning of this or that thing, but rather of interpretation as the condition of the possibility of meaning or understanding *as such*. In the broadest formulations, interpretation is said to be present in every experience of the world. Nietzsche: "There are no facts, only interpretations."[2] No such question—'how is meaning possible?'—seems to be in play when interpretation appears in its more quotidian employments.

Wittgenstein encourages us to ask: Is this a significant use of the term interpretation? Or must the meaning of some things be available *without* interpretation if interpretation is to be possible at all?[3] This question should be taken in connection with one of his larger themes: that of philosophical voice as speech dislocated from——yet still dependent on——its everyday contexts.[4]

The present study is guided by this larger theme. I suggest that the philosopher's motivation in drawing on the word "interpretation" comes into sharper view against the background of the word's everyday settings. This shouldn't be surprising. Someone who wishes to put the term "interpretation" to work for philosophical purposes—in expressing insight into meaning, experience, etc.— isn't merely intending to introduce a new technical term, but is apparently relying on our familiarity with a term we already have. So the everyday settings of

---

[*] Thanks to Matthew Boyle for a discussion of the concept of interpretation, to Richard Moran for his comments on a previous draft, and to Michaela Brangan for helpful corrections in a pinch.
1 Wittgenstein 1958 (hereafter: PI), §116.
2 Nietzsche 2003, 139.
3 PI, §§85; 185–201, esp. §§188, 201.
4 Cf., PI §116. In numerous works, Stanley Cavell provides a reading of Wittgenstein that gives special attention to this theme. See, e.g., Cavell 1979, Parts I and II.

"interpretation" are bound to be relevant to understanding why she is attracted to this expression or what's in it for her.

# Part I: Settings of Interpretation

1. Conversational remarks, laws, poems, dreams, oracles, history, social practices, ideals (e.g., democracy), and forms of relationship (e.g., marriage) all come in for "interpretation." Sometimes the term is used as a synonym for 'scientific hypothesis.' Translators of living speech are 'interpreters,' and performances of an artistic work (a ballet, a play, a sonata, etc.) are 'interpretations' of those works. Logicians speak of the 'interpretation' of a variable—the assignment of a value to it.

Such variation is to be expected. But today, heady conclusions are sometimes reached starting from the thought that a discourse is an 'interpretive' one, without sufficient concern for whether the sense of 'interpretive' is appropriate to the discourse in question. Literary interpretation, for example, is a kind of creative writing, which not only discovers but arguably also creates new meanings in its texts.[5] It obviously doesn't follow, just because judges 'interpret' the law, that they must be similarly creative. This is one reason why a partial survey of settings of interpretation may be useful. I shall be concerned especially with recent misconstructions of literary interpretation on the model of legal hermeneutics and *vice versa*. The point is not that there isn't an analogy between these types of interpretation,[6] but only that they *are* different types. What this means (Part I), and how the philosopher's attraction to "ubiquitous interpretation" is apt to be forgetful of it (Part II), is part of the matter to be developed here.

2. (1) The role of a judge is to interpret the law.
Here, to "interpret" means to *apply*—to say what the law requires in a particular case.[7] Such interpretations aim to preserve meaning: The judge is not to make

---

5 On the distinction between discovering and creating new meanings, and for a defense of critical creativity in the stronger sense, see Joseph Raz, "Interpretation Without Retrieval" and "Interpretation: Pluralism and Innovation" in Raz 2009, 241–64, 299–322. I'm indebted to Raz's account of interpretation at various points in Part I of this paper.
6 On the analogy, see, e.g., Dworkin 2003, Chapter 2; Fish 1989.
7 Classical tradition sometimes distinguishes between interpretation and application, or between statements of a text's meaning and determinations of its contextual significance. The distinction is critically examined by Hans-Georg Gadamer in Gadamer 1975. Everyday, nontechnical usage does not appear to recognize this distinction.

things up. He is not to decide, if the law has already decided, which features of the situation ought to guide his decision. Of course, if this is so, it could be asked why. The law might be bad or unjust. So it might be better if judges didn't have to interpret the law, but could simply revise it, like a legislature. Why should judges say what the law requires when they could change it for the better, or decide each case on its merits apart from the law?[8]

(2)  The volume contains several psychoanalytic interpretations of *Hamlet*. (literary interpretation).

(3)  Branagh's interpretation of *Hamlet* presents a less neurotically conflicted character than does Olivier's. (performing interpretation).

Two contrasts are in view here: (A) between (2) and (3); and (B) between this pair on the one hand and legal interpretation (the application of the law) on the other.

(A) An interpretation isn't always an application (1). Neither is it always a gloss or a *take* on its object (2). Sometimes it is an instance or *token* of it (3). (Perhaps it has other shapes as well.) Such tokenings, like any interpretation, can themselves be interpreted; their meanings can be explained. There may be a temptation to think that performance-tokens are a secondary form of interpretation: i.e., whenever a work is performed, some particular "take" on it must be working behind the scenes. This over-intellectualizes performance—think of musical interpretation. Perhaps it merely remembers that performances can themselves be interpreted, that they can be taken in various ways. But if to interpret a work a performer had first to have some take on it, there would be no end to the takes (and takes on those takes) needed before performance could begin.[9] The critic may explain the meanings in Branagh's *Hamlet*, but this does not mean that Branagh's performance must derive from, or be expressive of, a bit of criticism.

(B) Both (2) and (3) contrast with the use of interpretation in (1)—the application of the law.

All interpretation purports to be in accord with a prior object or text. But there is no implication, in the literary or performing contexts, that one is *following* the text, or carrying its meaning through, in a particular case. Branagh's performance gives us an instance of Hamlet, but not any case of it: He is not working out what the play means or requires here and now. Perhaps artistic

---

8 For one answer—in terms of "respect for authority"—see Joseph Raz, "On the Nature of Law" and "Why Interpret?" in Raz 2009, 91–125, 223–240.

9 This is a version of Wittgenstein's interpretive regress. See PI §§198, 201.

performance is not entirely without some applicative structure: A director might endeavor to make *Oedipus Rex* come alive for an audience today.[10] But "an audience today" is just the present horizon of interpretation, not a special case. Similarly, the relation of criticism to works of literature is not one of "following" or "applying," though some literary works have been followed (e. g., the Bible), just as some laws might be read "as literature."

Does the possibility of "reading *as*" undermine the claim that legal and literary texts call for different types of interpretation? No. It suggests that legal and literary interpretation differ from one other, not because their objects are semantically or ontologically distinctive, but because they are functionally so: We make different uses of these texts. To read something "as literature" is to take a certain kind of interest in it, to give it a special kind of attention. And a partial specification of what this means is that one is not attempting to follow it. The notion of "kinds" of texts (legal, literary, etc.) can be understood in terms of the nature of our interest in them, our reasons for attending to them.[11]

The important point here is that one interprets for a reason. Interpretation isn't something that just happens, like a chemical reaction, when readers and texts come together. It is an intentional activity. Hence, it always makes sense to ask: "*Why* interpret?" And the answers for different kinds of texts are, unsurprisingly, different. So it is only to be expected that interpretation will vary in structure, just as any general activity is apt to vary depending on why one is doing it.[12] Different reasons for interpreting account for differences in the shape of interpretation and in types of text. This has been emphasized recently by Joseph Raz.[13] One important upshot is that it becomes possible to see some theses about interpretation in general (e. g., its relation to authorial intention, its creativity, its ubiquity, etc.) as really highlighting grammatical features of interpretation in one or another of its settings, conceived in terms of reasons for

---

**10** Cf., Gadamer's thesis that all interpretation has an applicative structure and involves a "fusion of horizons" (Gadamer 1994).

**11** This paragraph is meant to indicate the importance of the topic of "literary interest," but not (obviously) to give positive specification of it. For one study, see Knapp 1993. I think Joseph Raz is right to suggest that today the interest in any art (including literature) is an interest in "cultural products," regarded independently of what their authors meant to express. See Raz 2009, 241–64.

**12** Note that one's reasons for interpreting (like one's reasons for doing anything) can always enter into a more extensive specification of *what* one is doing. Thus, we may say that the judge is interpreting the statute of frauds, but we may also say that he is determining the rights of the parties.

**13** See esp. Chapters 9–12 in Raz 2009.

taking an interest in an object.[14] I shall pursue some applications of this idea below.

As an illustration, consider the commonplace thought: There can be more than one good or correct interpretation of a text. The home of this thought— the place of its clearest application—is performance and criticism. Interpretation, in these settings, *always* occupies a space of contrasting interpretations. To speak of "an interpretation of *Hamlet*" is to suggest that, at another time, the play may be performed (or understood) differently. Indeed, that is something to be *encouraged.* Part of the value of interpretation here is that it permits the expression of novel orientations. It follows that an interpreter must engage in some kind of choice or originality, even if she remains responsive to a text and responsible for getting it right. Some theorists are tempted to suppose that critical creativity and pluralism stem from special semantic properties of literary texts (figurality, metaphoricity, absence of illocutionary force, etc.),[15] or from features of language-use in general. But there is a more plausible (and less extravagant) explanation: They are functions of local norms of interpretation, norms that reflect the kind of interest we take in literary texts, the use we have for them.[16]

Contrast the law. Creativity may be needed in saying what the law requires— e. g., the law may be vague, or in conflict with itself or with morality—but it may also *not* be needed. Such hard cases take place against the background of easy ones, where the rules are clear and acceptable, so they afford no reason to suppose that a judge must always be creative.[17] Moreover, judicial creativity isn't always a virtue. Legal (and other) rules allow choices to be made in advance of the situations in which one must act or judge. The advantages of this would be defeated by a general practice of "interpreting" the law to reflect the reasons revealed by the particular case. This is one way the absence of creativity becomes a value in applying the law. Further, when creativity does appear, its point is to improve the law—to make it morally better, clearer, or more coherent—not to exhibit novelty for its own sake. Our interest in criticism and performance lies part-

---

14 Cf., Raz 2009, 232.

15 See, e.g., de Man 1979, 10.

16 Other, related features of literary interpretation would flow from a fuller specification of "literary interest." For example, such interest involves, I think, an interest in a work as a "cultural product" that is relatively autonomous of its author's intentions. See Raz 2009, 241–64. Otherwise put, the general authorial intention relevant to a work of literature is an intention to produce a work that is interpretable independently of what its author meant to express. Ronald Dworkin draws such a distinction between "general" and "specific" authorial intention in Dworkin 1998.

17 See Stone 1995.

ly in the way they introduce something new, and thereby also reveal the interpreter's individuality (hence *"Branagh's Hamlet," "Gould's Goldberg"*); failing this, they are uninformative, hackneyed, or slavish. The merit of judicial innovation, in contrast, is just a matter of whether it has improved the law. And since the law might already be okay, there need be no defect when a judge merely reiterates the established legal concept and saliencies. *Stare decisis et quieta non movere:*[18] Adherence to precedent is the everyday life of the law, but the death of an art (as is often said).

So the shape of interpretation reflects what a text is for, our business with it; this is constitutive of the kind of text it is. Interpretation has a dual aspect: It is both responsive and creative. Literature and the arts aside, interpretation isn't always creative. But it appears that, in many settings, it necessarily *can* be creative; that is one of its essential possibilities.[19] Where instructions are usually mechanically followed—e.g., "add two cups of water and stir" in an unambiguous recipe—we don't ordinarily speak of an interpretation. (In such cases, an agent does not purport to interpret.) Correlatively, where creativity is no longer responsive, it becomes inventive rather than interpretive. The novelist's depiction of a character isn't an "interpretation" of that character, though it may interpret a character *type*. Naturally, these distinctions aren't clear in every case. It suffices if they are clear in some.[20]

3. If judges were never creative—if, for example, when the law was indeterminate, they declared that there was no applicable law—the present contrasts between legal and literary interpretation wouldn't be worth mentioning, for no one would see their likeness to begin with. In fact, judges are usually required to decide non-arbitrarily for one of the parties. Taken together with the well-noted difficulty of codifying appropriate conduct in advance of particular cases,[21] this insures that judges will sometimes have to be creative. Thus, besides (1) above, there is another, related use of "interpretation" in the law:

(4) Common-law judges interpret the standard of "due care" in tort law as "the care which the ordinary person would take under the circumstances." Ac-

---

18 *Spicer v. Spicer*, 79 Eng. Rep 451 (Kings Bench, 1620, Lord Coke).
19 See Raz 2009, 13, 302, 354.
20 The dual face of interpretation suggests that it is apt to be important in those fields that combine an interest in continuity or conservation along with innovation. On this, see Raz 2009, 315 – 8, 117 – 8, 353 – 4, 356 – 7.
21 See, e. g., Hart 1961, Chapter 7.

cording to Cardozo, this means only the "ordinary prevision to be looked for in a busy world."[22]

An "interpretation" here is a *gloss* on the legal standard as an aid to correct, determinate judgment in particular cases. Whether it succeeds depends on its content. (Determinacy and correctness often tend to come apart in the common law, which sometimes shows a preference for impeccable but indeterminate standards like "ordinary care.") Often the need for further glosses, or the rejection of previous ones, is revealed by subsequent cases. Such judicial glosses tend to involve the features of plurality, creativity, and responsiveness to wider values, which characterize criticism:[23] hence the analogy to literary interpretation. But the analogy also has its limits.[24]

First, glossing interpretation could not be all that is meant by "judges are to interpret the law"—they must render verdicts after all. Moreover, when judges do reformulate the law, their activity is controlled by a type of interest—following the law—that is structurally absent from the literary context. Not all legal interpretations are applications of the law, but there would be no point to them unless some were.

This has a further consequence.[25] Just as hard cases have their natural background in easy ones, so glossing interpretations presupposes the possibility of a case in which the rules are clear and no further glosses are required. *Clara non sunt interpretanda; Interpretatio cessat in claro*—such formulas are apt wherever 'following the text' is part of the reason for interpreting.

---

**22** The quotation is from *Greene v. Sibly, Lindsay & Curr Co.*, 177 N.E. 416 (N.Y.1931)

**23** A judge's failure to acknowledge such creativity is one the meanings of the recurring charge of "formalism." See Stone 2002; Schauer 1988.

**24** I discuss only a few of them here, ones that pertain to my broader theme. The contrasting roles of both authority and authorial intention in legal and literary interpretation, as well as the possibility of authoritative determinations and changes of the meaning of the law, though not of the meanings of literary text, might be discussed in a fuller treatment of the topic. On the contrast concerning the role of authority, see Raz 2009, 318–21. On authorial intention, see notes 16 and 25 in this article

**25** Actually, it has a number of further consequences. The constitutive legal interest in "following" is related to law's status as an authoritative source, and a grasp of this would probably reveal interpretation to have different relations to authorial intention in the legal and literary settings. Crudely, our interest in interpreting is often, in the law—though usually not in the case of literature—an interest in what an author thought or meant to express. On this, see Raz 2009, 241–98. I leave this and other contrasts aside in the present context, as they would lead away from my main theme: the contrast between interpretation in its everyday and philosophical settings.

Correspondingly, what is special about literary interpretation appears partly in the inapplicability of such formulae. They are inapplicable not because critics like to make things difficult, but because what it might mean to say of a text that it is "unclear" or "indeterminate" doesn't begin to appear here, apart from an endeavor to follow it. Such terms have their home in applicative discourses, such as the law, where they function to assess a rule's usefulness as a standard of correctness in a range of normal or foreseeable cases. Talk of "indeterminacy" gets its sense from problems of applicative judgment. But when Olivier and Branagh interpret *Hamlet* in incompatible ways, are we to say that Shakespeare's text is indeterminate or uncertain? That makes it sound as if Shakespeare left something out or gave incomplete directions.[26]

Consider how, in Paul de Man's celebrated reading of Keats's "The Fall of Hyperion," terms like "indeterminacy" and "undecidability" have migrated from legal hermeneutics:

> Faced with the ineluctable necessity to come to a decision, no grammatical or logical analysis can help us out. Just as Keats had to break off his narrative, the reader has to break off his understanding at the very moment when he is most directly engaged and summoned by the text.[27]

Whence "the ineluctable necessity" to *decide?* Poets may be "unacknowledged legislators,"[28] but criticism hasn't thereby become a form of judicial review. Is "coming to a decision" an apt description of what readers of literature try to do—as "deciding the party's rights" describes why a judge interprets (and hence *what* he is doing when he interprets)? Moreover, why does de Man take the plurality of meanings he uncovers to indicate that interpretive understanding has *failed* (it must be "broken off")? This assumes that the interpretive aim is to resolve ambiguity. But good interpretation is often ambiguity-*preserving.*[29] Suppose that in a business negotiation, we hear: "You're going to do business with *Williamson?!*"—in that way which is neither clearly a question, a statement, a warning, etc. "No grammatical or logical analysis can help us out." But so what? The good interpreter–translator must use tone and pitch (or punctuation) to make the different possibilities apparent. Psychoanalytic interpretation often seeks to preserve ambiguity as well. These examples remind us that creative in-

---

**26** Or, applied to a literary text (or a painting, a piece of music, etc.), "indeterminate" might suggest that we don't have a definitive manuscript (or canvas, score, etc.).

**27** De Man 1986, 16.

**28** Shelley 2004 and Shelly 1920.

**29** See Raz 2009, 308.

terpretation is never required just because a text is ambiguous or indeterminate. If judges must be creative when the law is indeterminate, this is owing to their reasons for interpreting in the first place. Hence, in view of the *literary* context, should we not say that understanding, in de Man's ambiguity-preserving reading, has not in fact "broken off," but has succeeded just as it should?[30]

A defense of "indeterminacy" in the context of criticism and performance might run: "A literary text is 'indeterminate' just insofar as there are different but equally good ways of exhibiting its meaning."[31] Of course, this is now a *stipulation*. It doesn't change anything. Accepting it, one must grant that *all* literary texts are "indeterminate." And this "all" exhibits the difference between law and literature. A literary text doesn't just *happen* to be "indeterminate," as say, a statute might be. Its availability for different interpretations is rather its birthright, a reflection of the interest we take in it as literature. Nor does interpretation remedy this indeterminacy (or try to): it multiplies readings; it has no authority to resolve them. Calling this a "crisis" seems to suggest that something other than criticism was wanted, and hence seems to forget that it is *literature* one is reading. Or it insinuates that the interpretability of literature is somehow exemplary of how it is with "texts" in general.

This should be taken in light of a further distinction. (1) Different interpretations of a literary work aren't interesting *as such*, since there can be different, but compatible explanations of nearly anything. (Why does John love Mary? Psychoanalysis, sociology, neuroscience, and the lover's discourse all have their two cents here; none occludes the others.)[32] (2) What *is* interesting are *conflicting* interpretations, but (3) interpretive conflict in criticism is not always easy to discern. In law, conflict appears as inconsistent applicative judgments: e.g., under one interpretation of the First Amendment, you have the right to march; under another, you don't. But consider the standard literary situation of good Marxist, psychoanalytic, feminist, new historical, and deconstructive readings of a work. Is there conflict, or just different explanations, emphasizing different aspects of the work? How are we to tell?

---

30 In support of this, consider that the multiplicity present in Keats's poem is presented by de Man as a kind of allegory of reading: "Just as Keats had to break off his narrative, the reader has to break off his understanding..." So there is something self-defeating in de Man's suggestion that the reader is unable to *decide* between the relevant possibilities: If he could decide, then the poem wouldn't bear the interpretation de Man has put on it.

31 Raz employs such an idea of literary indeterminacy in Raz 2009, 307–9.

32 Though the lover's discourse has a certain primacy: If it didn't exist, there would be nothing for the other discourses to explain.

Various writers have pointed to *non-combinability* (into a single interpretation) as the relevant notion in explaining interpretive conflict.[33] This accounts for something we intuitively sense. Take various readings of a text and somehow endeavor to combine their elements: What you would often get is not a more complete view of things, but a mess. Performing-interpretations, as Joseph Raz suggests, offer a good illustration of this.[34] Combining features from, say, Gould's and Landowska's *Goldberg Variations* seems a reliable formula for getting *less* than the sum of the original parts. Non-combinability is obviously a broader notion than logical inconsistency. We find it in the way character traits tend to occlude one another, in the exclusionary character of friendships and intimate relationships (e. g., polyamory doesn't simply multiply the goods of monogamy), and in, say, styles and good ways of life: Not all the elements of these things can be combined to create an even better item of the same kind.

Of course, this isn't a very informative account of interpretive conflict until more is said about what, besides contradiction, makes two interpretations "un-combinable." (Perhaps there isn't more to say in general.) In any case, these reflections help to clarify the differences between relevant notions of legal and literary "indeterminacy." A legal rule will be indeterminate, if it is so, *before* interpretation has begun; remedying this is one reason for interpreting (glossing) it. But insofar as it makes sense to speak of literary "indeterminacy," interpretation plays a constitutive rather than a remedial role; "indeterminacy" appears here only in the fact of interpretations that resist combination. Hence literary "interpretation" doesn't alleviate indeterminacy; it reveals—expresses, celebrates, ramifies—it. And this is related to a further contrast concerning the value of indeterminacy. It is usually of negative value in the law, as in any text (a shopping list, instructions from the flight tower) made to be followed.[35] Not so in criticism. In fact, what the critic does is better than what he sometimes says. For, in practice, different readings are encouraged, and the capacity of a literary work to bear them is seen as part of its value. No one proceeds as if the critical aim were to bring it about that, say, *Paradise Lost* need never be interpreted again. There is no such thing as a definitive piece of criticism.

In light of these contrasts, and thinking of the jurisprudential significance of "*Interpretatio cessat in clara*," one might propose a corresponding maxim for the critic: "*There is no text so clear that it is unavailable for interpretation*," or "*Every*

---

**33** See e. g., Raz 2009, 226, 270–1, 302; Juhl 1980, 199.
**34** Raz 2009, 271.
**35** "Usually of negative value": Exceptions would be standards that can only be explained through examples ("reasonable care"), and the use of indeterminacy as a jurisdiction-shifting device, requiring a local decision-maker to make a judgment. See Stone 1995; Schauer, 1993.

*reading of a text is an interpretation.*" These are grammatical remarks in Wittgenstein's sense: They say 'what kind of thing' an interpretation in a particular setting is.[36] Of course, the ubiquity of interpretation is already stressed by many literary theorists. So all that is needed is to make this thesis acceptable by restricting it to *literary* texts, eschewing any general "linguistic" grounding.[37] Perhaps a misleading implication might be dispelled as well. Suitably restricted, talk of "ubiquitous interpretation" won't be heard as denying that many narrative facts are available without recourse to interpretation. That Hamlet is a man, preoccupied with his father's death and his mother's recent marriage are not interpretations, but immediate facts comprising part of what there is to be interpreted. Where criticism or performance is inconsistent with such facts, it is no longer interpretive, though it may be otherwise provoked or inspired by the text.[38]

4. The discussion has emphasized interpretation as an activity that varies, according to its setting, in ways intelligibly related to the reasons for engaging in it. This emphasis might lead someone to wonder whether, beyond the variation, there is any common "it" to engage in—any "interpretive theory" or "hermeneutics" in general.

Compare "explanation." How something is to be explained is internally related to the kind of thing it is, and different forms of explanation correspond to different reasons for explaining. So the natural focus, in explaining 'explanation,' are the different settings of explanation: e. g., explaining the meaning of a word, a norm, what something is good for, how to do something, what leads to what, why someone acted as they did, etc. Whether there are many interesting truths concerning explanation *as such* seems doubtful. Is there, in contrast, an interesting general concept of interpretation? If to interpret is to apply, to token and to gloss, and if it is sometimes to preserve and sometimes to create meaning, are we dealing with *one* concept? Or is it only by a loose way of speaking that judges, critics, performers, translators, etc., are all said to engage in the same activity? Naturally, other descriptions of what an interpreter is doing are always available: Judges are (*by* interpreting) determining the rights of the parties; literary critics don't do *that*. Up to a certain date, "hermeneutics" was always adjectively qualified——as biblical, legal, etc.: rules of construction for different kinds of texts. Is more recent philosophy (beginning in the nineteenth

---

**36** Cf., PI §373.

**37** See Part II below. Such a restriction would run counter to a strand of thought in both Paul de Man and Stanley Fish. See Stone 2004a.

**38** See Sedivy 2004.

century) right to think of "hermeneutics" as a discrete and unified topic, part of a philosophy of the humanities?[39]

The matter is controversial. I shall conclude this Part with some speculations about this.

One basis for answering "yes" builds upon the intuition that, over a central range of cases, interpretation is a species of explanation.[40] Explanation doesn't appear to be a species of anything more abstract. To say that interpretations are explanations admittedly sounds odd in the case of performance or the judge's application of the law: exposition, illustration, elucidation, determination, etc., might sometimes be more idiomatic. But what matters here is not whether the word "explanation" is always completely natural in place of "interpretation." It is enough to see the resemblance between "interpretation" and the foregoing family of notions.

If we hesitate to call the judge's application of the law an explanation, this is only perhaps because a judicial decision is—by virtue of its other forces (e.g., someone is ordered to do something)—much *more* than an explanation. But everyone knows that a good way to elucidate the law is to say what it would require in hypothetical cases, i.e., to illustrate it. If hypothetical cases can serve to clarify what the law means or requires, then surely real ones must do so too. A similar point pertains to performances: To speak of an "interpretation" is to imply that something is brought to light or revealed, something not otherwise readily seen or heard. This goes beyond the iteration of a score or text. The teacher's calling role isn't any "interpretation" of the class list, for it doesn't purport to shed light on it. Similarly, reading through *Hamlet* just to verify that it will take longer than two hours to perform involves no interpretive purport. Interpretations aim to make the meaning of their objects apparent. (Oracles and dreams are paradigms of things that *always* have to be interpreted.[41] The reason is that it is part of the concept of these things that their meaning is never fully manifest.)

If interpretation is a species of explanation, then a general concept of interpretation is approached by asking how interpretations are different in kind from

---

**39** Cf., Heidegger 1996, 33. The story of the development of a general interest in interpretation is told by Gadamer in Gadamer 1994.

**40** This is central to Raz's treatment of interpretation in Raz 2009, Chapters 9–12. See also Hampshire 1966, 101–8. The point isn't contradicted by the labels—Erklaren and Verstehen (explanation and understanding)—that Droysen used to draw methodological distinctions between the natural and historical (interpretive) sciences. These are best treated as technical terms. In everyday English, it would be natural to say that all explanation aims to bring about understanding.

**41** See Hampshire 1966; cf., Gadamer 1986, 68–9.

non-interpretive explanations. I will indicate one way of developing this contrast, without arguing for it here.[42]

Consider the statement, "According to the table of interpretations, '→' means 'turn right.'" This is of course an explanation (of the use of a sign), but it is clearly unlike the interpretations produced by lawyers, critics, and performers, since it merely sets up a meaning, rather than responding to one already there.[43] Remembering that what is at stake is the unity of a concept (not the use of a word), we might sharpen things by saying: Interpretations are correct or incorrect in light of the meanings of their objects.[44] And a natural further qualification might be: "... in light of the *non-natural* meanings of their objects." This is too imprecise.[45] But the motivation for the further restriction is that such uses as "That's how I interpret the signs: these clouds mean rain," or "On one interpretation, the white area in the x-ray shows an infection" also appear to be different from the interpretations produced by critics, performers, etc., in at least this way: They don't admit of conflicting interpretations, except by way of implication that not all the facts are known.[46] Interpretive conflict here reflects the epistemic position of the interpreters; as that position improves, we expect the conflict to disappear. (Either it will rain or it won't; but the explanation of the "meaning" of the clouds is *inert* with respect to this fact. And if the fact doesn't obtain—if it doesn't rain—then the clouds didn't "mean rain.")[47]

In understanding this, it would be good to remember that merely *different* explanations are always to be expected, even under ideal conditions. This is a

---

**42** My sketch is generally indebted to Raz 2009, especially for its suggestion that "pluralism" and "innovation" are marks of interpretive explanations. See Raz 2009, 299 – 322, esp. 302. Other writers have gestured toward, if not exactly articulated, a concept of interpretation that is proprietary to what are roughly called the humanities. Von Wright 1971, Chapter 1 surveys some of the literature.

**43** The logician's 'interpretation' of a variable is a similar case in this respect.

**44** Are interpretations also guided by the meaning of their objects? Or could one discover that a passage in Marx interprets current political events?

**45** The phrase "non-natural meaning" is due to Paul Grice (Grice 1957). Grice's explanation of the distinction isn't directly serviceable here, however, since it refers to a communicative intention. Many objects that call for interpretation involve meanings that are neither "natural" (in Grice's sense), nor, since they lack authors, analyzable in terms of communicative intentions (e. g., history, customs, rituals).

**46** This is controversial, of course, since many theorists apparently reject pluralism as a mark of the concept of interpretation in any domain. See e. g., Dworkin 1986, Chapter 2; Juhl 1980. I have given no argument for pluralism here beyond the fact that it appears instinctive in the way people talk about literary and performing-interpretation.

**47** Cf., Grice 1957.

feature of the familiar relativity of explanations to the practical context.[48] Why did so many people die? Possible explanations include: the human body cannot withstand such pressure; there was an earthquake; the buildings were badly constructed; the Council repealed the hazard zoning laws; there were only two doctors nearby. It is easy to see that these explanations can be combined. Now, sometimes two *un-combinable* explanations can't both be valid, except as equally reasonable beliefs given the evidence—e. g., the forensic evidence indicates genocide/death by natural causes. But sometimes, we are supposing, they *can* be. And the suggestion is: Where this is so—where conflicting explanations can each be non-epistemically valid—we have a paradigm of an interpretive enterprise. In such cases, interpretation would play a constitutive role in determining the meanings of a text (relative to that interpretation). Typically, it exhibits the text's elements as parts of a larger whole, specified in terms of some general interest or point of that text.[49]

In partial support of this, consider how odd it would be to think of different (un-combinable) portrayals of Hamlet as merely epistemically "reasonable," as if, once all the facts were known, only one performance will remain standing —as if most audiences never saw the real thing. Curiously, when interpretive monism is defended in literary theory, the focus is on criticism.[50] The ideal of a single definitive performance isn't mentioned. But why not? And if non-epistemic pluralism holds for performances, as no one seems to deny, why not for criticism as well?

This line of inquiry begins to suggest why "interpretation" causes philosophical trouble. Armed with a picture of "explanation" based on the "natural-scientific" cases, a philosopher is apt to ask: "How is such a thing as interpretation *possible?* Surely explanations are inert; they don't affect what they explain."[51] So either interpretations aren't all explanations, or the pluralism that surrounds talk of interpretation is mistaken (since, on the assumption that explanations are inert, the validity of conflicting interpretations would imply an object to which contradictory predicates apply); or such pluralism must be understood merely epistemically, i. e., as the reasonableness of different interpretations in cases in which knowledge is imperfect. Various contemporary theories of interpretation endeavor to save some of the commonplaces by denying at least one of the others. But perhaps there is a further possibility. Can't explanations affect their ob-

---

**48** See, e. g., Hart/Honore 1985.

**49** Note that the explanatory fitting of parts into wholes is foreign to the cases of "interpreting" x-rays or clouds.

**50** See, e. g., Nehamas 1981.

**51** Cf., Raz 2009, 304–5, 272.

jects?[52] The philosopher's explanation of "explanation" is apt to beg that question: His examples will not be those of explaining a literary text, or what a metaphor means, or social relations like marriage! Moreover, the everyday explanation of action is an exception to the putative inertness of explanation. For it belongs to the concept of action that an agent's knowledge of "why" he is doing something plays a constitutive role in determining *what* he is doing;[53] actions are thereby explained by exhibiting them as parts of a larger conceptual whole.[54] Unlike x-rays and clouds, the regions where interpretations, as conceived here, are called for have to do with action and its products—roughly speaking, the humanities. So everyday action-explanation may provide a clue that can accommodate us to a concept we make familiar use of, but which, given a certain philosophical set-up, might appear paradoxical.[55]

# Part II: Interpretivism

5. "Interpretation" is called for where explanation or elucidation is wanted. P.G Wodehouse has a joke which depends on our recognizing this:

> 'When you come tomorrow, bring my football boots. Also, if humanly possible, Irish water spaniel. Urgent. Regards. Tuppy.'
> 'What do you make of that, Jeeves?'
> 'As I interpret the document, sir, Mr. Glossop wishes you, when you come tomorrow, to bring his football boots. Also, if humanly possible, an Irish water spaniel. He hints that the matter is urgent, and sends his regards.'
> 'Yes, that's how I read it, too...'[56]

But some philosophers will say it is no joke.[57] "There are no facts, only interpretations," Nietzsche writes. And he adds, "We cannot determine any fact '*in it-*

---

52 A defense of this possibility is offered by Raz in Raz 2009, 299–322; see esp. 313.

53 "Practical knowledge," as Anscombe (following Aquinas) puts is, "is 'the cause of what it understands,' unlike 'speculative' knowledge, which 'is derived from the objects known'" (Anscombe 1957, §48). Anscombe makes clear that "cause" doesn't just mean efficient cause. The thought is also that, but for the agent's knowledge of what he is doing, he wouldn't be doing *that*. On this, see Moran 2004 and Moran/Stone 2009.

54 See Thompson 2008.

55 There are some suggestive remarks about the analogy between the interpretation of texts and the explanation of action in Ricoeur 1973.

56 Wodehouse 1930.

57 On the analytic side, Donald Davidson is an example. See Davidson 1984. But I think that in speaking of "interpretation" as a condition of understanding another speaker, Davidson means

*self.*"[58] Whatever this says, it is not that every fact comes with an explanation of itself. Nor does it make sense to ask here about anyone's reasons for interpreting; the idea rather seems to be that only by way of some interpretation are there any reasons to speak of. It is remarkable that such a thesis is sometimes put forward as a kind of pragmatism or "realism" (in the ordinary sense, which opposes mythology or metaphysics).[59] For what is involved looks like a substantial metaphysical thesis, an account of how it is with the whole world, with everything. "The implications [of the ubiquitous need for interpretation] are almost boundless," Stanley Fish writes, "for they extend to the very underpinnings of the universe."[60] (NB: Is this statement itself supposed to be only an interpretation, where other interpretations are possible?)

The following sections depict a response to this contemporary thesis that neither affirms nor denies it, but confronts it with "interpretation" in its everydayness. The philosopher is moving within this everydayness; he emphasizes a word we have learned to apply in practices like law, literature, and performance. But accounts of "interpretation," based on these practices, are apt to be unsuitable for his purposes; they always render his thesis too *obviously* true or false. So he is apt either to reject them as clues to what he means, or else to require that they be understood in a special 'philosophical' sense, which remains to be explained.

To develop this, I will focus specifically on a line of thought within recent legal theory—*interpretivism*, as I will call it, since it makes a quite unrestricted use of the concept of interpretation. Interpretivism suggests that confusion about interpretation travels in more than one direction: It is not just criticism that sometimes mistakenly grasps itself on the model of legal hermeneutics (§3); sometimes legal judgment is mis-described in terms of the ubiquitous interpretation that belongs constitutively to the domain of literature. Here are some examples:

> [T]he very idea of a rule as a force that pulls us down the track through each new fact situation, determining the outcome of a particular case, is false. Therefore, no line of precedent can fully determine a particular outcome in a particular case because the rule itself is

---

to introduce a technical term. My concern in this Part is with philosophical uses of the term "interpretation" where this is not so.

**58** Nietzsche 2003, 139.
**59** See, e. g., Rorty 1982, xxxix, xli. On "realism" in the ordinary sense, see Diamond 1991.
**60** Fish 1989, Chapter 4. That what is offered by "interpretivism" isn't meant to be, but has become, another metaphysical thesis is the starting point of my response to Fish in Stone 2004b and also Vattimo 1997 (see esp. 1–14). Vattimo's response is to adhere to interpretivism, but to affirm that it is itself only an interpretation. I offer a difference response to the thesis below.

always in the process of reinterpretation as it is applied. It is interpretation that gives us the rule, not the other way around. This insight is what has come to be known as the "indeterminacy thesis.[61]

While there will always be paradigmatically plain cases—Hart is absolutely right to put them at the center of the adjudicative process—far from providing a stay against the force of interpretation, they will be precisely the result of interpretation's force; for they will have been written and rewritten by interpretive efforts.[62]

[T]he *rule itself* [cannot] step forward to claim its own instances. The plain case, where the general terms *seem* to need no interpretation and where the recognition of instances seems unproblematic... are only the familiar ones... where there is general agreement in judgments as to the applicability of the classifying terms.[63]

If law is to be applied by a legal organ, he must determine the meaning of the norms to be applied: he must "interpret" these norms. Interpretation, therefore , is an intellectual activity, which accompanies the process of law application in its advance from a higher to a lower level.[64]

Each case is other, each decision is different and requires an absolutely unique interpretation, which no existing, coded rule can or ought to guarantee absolutely.[65]

[T]here can be no law without interpretation... [Legal doctrine] means nothing until it is interpreted, and although it will always have meaning, its meaning will be determined by those who interpret .[66]

6. Part I located the point of legal interpretation against the background of a distinction between hard (where creative glosses are needed) and easy cases (where they aren't: §3). The interpretivist's burden is evidently to suggest that these distinctions lack the substance we are apt to credit them with. For the way they are drawn in any particular case is already an effect of interpretation ("It is interpretation which gives us the rule, not the other way around"). His striking claim is that in order to say what the law requires, the judge must make an interpretation. This doesn't mean there are no easy cases. Rather, an "easy case" is considered to be one in which the presence of interpretation is, on account of a prevailing social consensus, hidden from view. (The rule only "*seems* to need no interpretation.")[67] So an easy case, the interpretivist is apt to say, is really a special instance of a hard one: It exhibits the success or hegemony of a particular interpretation (it is "the result of interpretation's force"), not the absence or superfluity of interpretation as such.

---

**61** Drucilla Cornell, *The Philosophy of the Limit*, New York: Routledge, 1992, 101–2.

**62** Fish 1989, 153.

**63** Hart 1994, 126.

**64** Kelsen 1967, 348.

**65** Derrida 1992, 23.

**66** Hutchinson 1989, 558–59.

**67** Hart 1994, 126

What can be made of this? There is a good sense in which, whenever the law is officially applied, some official "interprets" it—i. e., makes a determinate judgment. This commonplace might suggest the interpretivist thesis, but it really only touches its surface; for the thesis is evidently meant to explain how such determinate judgment is possible, not merely to observe that it occurs. Could it be rather the *glossing* sense of "interpretation" that the interpretivist needs? No: The interpretivist would reject such an account of what he means, for then endless glosses would be needed prior to judgment.[68] Perhaps the interpretivist only means to describe the law as we find it: "All appellate cases involve legal uncertainty and therefore require interpretation; why else would the parties prefer litigation over settlement?" But this empirical hypothesis depends on an unanalyzed distinction between legally easy and hard (or uncertain) cases, and it confines "interpretation" to a remedial role in hard ones. That interpretation plays a remedial role when the law is uncertain is hardly a revelation.

The possibility of hearing the interpretivist's thesis in these straightforward ways might lead us to imagine that we understand him. But as soon as these readings are identified, their failure to account for what the interpretivist intends to say becomes apparent. This pattern will repeat itself with each philosophical step.

7. A common way of expressing the interpretivist's insight refers to the impotencies of a rule *itself:* "The rule itself cannot step forward to claim its own instances," "The rule itself is always in the process of reinterpretation as it is applied." Talk of ubiquitous interpretation and of the impotency of some meaning-carrying item when considered just *in itself* apparently go hand in hand.[69]

Well, *do* rules *themselves* ever determine their own applications? Every jurist knows that sometimes they do and sometimes they don't: Sometimes attention to the rule is sufficient to resolve the case, and sometimes you need other materials. That is, if the jurist has a use for the expression "the rule itself," the situation is one where it is significant to distinguish a rule, on the one hand, from what someone has said about it on the other. Looking at random:

---

68 This was first noticed by Kant (Kant 1929, A133/B172); and it reappears in Wittgenstein's discussion of following a rule: PI §§198, 201.

69 When Nietzsche writes, "There are no facts, only interpretations," he immediately adds, "We cannot determine any fact *'in itself'*" (Nietzsche 2003, 139). Or again: "[O]ne must first interpret this set of facts: in itself it stands there, stupid to all eternity, like every 'thing-in-itself'" (Nietzsche 1998, 75).

(A) In 3.1, the parenthetical remark is a bit strange (why is that discussion relevant to that rule?), but the *rule itself* is clear.[70]

(B) In addition, the board will update a "regulatory assessment" (a cost-benefit analysis) on the final rules which, along with *the rule itself*, will be submitted to the Office of Management and Budget for clearance.[71]

(C) It is not disputed that advisory comments are not binding. Rather, the comments are recognized as providing guidance which courts may follow. This is especially true when, as in the present case, *the rule itself* is clear and unambiguous.[72]

(D) This guide, produced in cooperation with the FTC [Federal Trade Commission] explains the requirements of the "30-day Rule" in plain English. How to comply with the Rule, examples of delay notices, a Question and Answer section and the *Rule itself* are included.[73]

(E) Although the *rule itself* is clear, the source of the rule is not completely apparent. Compare Artis, 967 F. 2d at 1137 (basing rule on 7th Amendment) with Snider, 973 F. 2d at 559 (grounding rule in collateral estoppel and not 7th Amendment).[74]

It emerges here that a "rule itself" isn't any mysterious, liminal entity, but rather one with which lawyers have been enjoying direct contact—citing it, reprinting it, even sending it through the mail. For them, the expression "the rule itself" evidently just means "the rule" as distinguished from some surrounding gloss. And gloss isn't always helpful. Sometimes it muddies the rule, which was performing well on its own (B, E), though it can also bring a wayward rule back into "plain English" (D).

The interpretivist's "rule itself" obviously bears a different burden and comes about in a different way. It expresses the impotence of any rule to determine the particular case. So it refers to an item that is not yet functioning as (what practitioners call) *a rule*, for it is awaiting interpretive assistance in order to make contact with any determine requirements, in order to make a difference. (Similarly, the philosopher's 'fact in itself' is not yet playing the logical role of a fact.) To realize this is bound to be disappointing. It means that our

---

70 *Architecture Domain* "IETF Mandatory Spec Issues List," Internet Draft, March 23, 1998.

71 *Access Currents*, Volume 7, No 2 (March/April 2001) [internet publication concerning Americans with Disabilities Act Accessibility Guidelines (ADAAG)}].

72 *Minnesota v. Pero* 590 N.W.2d 319, Supreme Court of Minnesota, 1999.

73 Federal Trade Commission, "A Business Guide to the Federal Trade Commission's Mail or Telephone Order Merchandise Rule," internet publication, January, 2002.

74 *Melendez v. Illinois Bell Telephone Company*, 79 F.3d 661, 7th Cir., 1996.

sense of familiarity—borne of everyday acquaintance—with "the rule itself" was unwarranted. Without more, talk of inert "rules themselves" introduces nothing more basic, or more easily grasped, than the thesis (of ubiquitous interpretation) it was expected to explain.

8. An often-cited passage of H.L.A Hart's endeavors to break into this tight circle. Hart must have liked the passage, or felt some attachment to it, for it appears on three separate occasions in his work.[75] The original context is his argument— based on a "core" of agreements in judgment needed if anyone is to talk to any- one[76]—for confining "rule-skepticism" to "hard cases" at the periphery. But the passage actually fits only awkwardly into this context. For the contemporary skeptic who speaks of "interpretation" as a condition of the possibility of even "plain cases" (and not merely as a remedy in hard ones)[77] might be remembering something he first heard from Hart:

> [P]articular fact-situations do not await us already marked off from each other, and labeled as instances of the general rule, the application of which is in question; nor can the rule itself step forward to claim its own instances... There will indeed be plain cases... to which general expressions are clearly applicable... but there will also be cases where it is not clear whether they apply or not. Cannons of "interpretation" cannot eliminate, though they can diminish, these uncertainties; for these canons are themselves general rules for the use of language, and make use of general terms which themselves require in- terpretation. They cannot, any more than other rules, provide for their own interpretation. The plain case, where the general terms seem to need no interpretation and where the rec- ognition of instances seems unproblematic... are only the familiar ones... where there is general agreement in judgments as to the applicability of the classifying terms.[78]

Is this an advance? Here the need for interpretation evidently contrasts with a suspect picture of meaning 'taking care of itself,' somehow independently of our activities and responses. So here the interpretivist's "rule itself" evidently contests not the jurist's thought that a rule is sometimes enough, but only some queer version, some special misunderstanding, of this thought. But what misunderstanding? Who is supposed to have thought that the world comes pre-labeled, or that a rule can "step forward to claim its own instances"? And given the evident difficulty of spelling this out—spelling out a properly suspect, as opposed to a practically innocent, sense of "stepping forward"—whence comes Hart's confidence that what is involved is *falsity*, something to be affirma-

---

75 See note 78.

76 See Hart 1994, Chapter 7; cf., PI §242.

77 See, e.g., Fish 1987, 153.

78 Hart 1994, 126. See also Hart 1983 and Hart 1958.

tively denied?[79] (Clearly, we aren't dealing here with the sort of straightforward assertion that might be used to give the Martian visitor his prep: "Now, the world doesn't come with labels on it, mind you; you'll see that as soon as you arrive; fortunately, the language is in place, but you'll have to do all the classifying yourself.") In fact, in a perfectly ordinary sense, it is not false, but *true*, that many bits of the world come with the appropriate labels attached: Simple tasks such as taking aspirin or finding the way home depend on this. (And in an anodyne sense—e. g., "a rule can determine what is to be done"—rules *do* "step forward to claim their own instances." See §11 below.)

Another possibility is that the target picture of 'self-animated' rules isn't intelligible enough—the inferences it supports not wieldy enough—to be considered a true or false account of the use of a rule. It articulates a fantasy. To acknowledge a fantasy here is to recognize that one comes no closer to how things really are by affirming its negation. Fantasy, unlike simple falsehood, persists, even thrives, under negation. Otherwise put, what is suspect in the target picture lies in the structure of a *question* to which it is connected. So reversing the answer ("a rule itself *cannot* determine...") lands one no closer to the truth, because it holds the question fast.[80] Interpretivism, we may say, is a fantastic picture of meaning *under negation*.

One way of seeing that the picture Hart opposes is not false but fantastic is to see that the truth of the picture makes no difference. Suppose someone *has* been thinking that situations come labeled as instances of the rules to be applied? If they were right, would that help secure the rules' application? If the word "rain" always appeared when it was raining, are we to suppose that this would serve to bring words and world together in a way that, say, the criteria for rain (the impressions of wet and cold) do not? One wants to say: If words and world do not already meet in shared judgments concerning "rain," then the appearance of the label will just be one more inert fact about the situation to which our words must be applied; just "in itself," this fact will be impotent to determine what we are to do. Recall again some cases for which the description is correct: Statutes, contracts, deeds, charters, wills, etc., all typically identify themselves as such. The utility of this is obvious. But if it were really true that the rules defining, say, statutory validity could never—save through interpretation—pick out valid statutes, it is hard to see how the presence of an identifying label would make a difference; it would merely add another item to be interpret-

---

**79** Cf., Cornell 1992, 101–2: "[T]he very idea of a rule as a force that pulls us down the track through each new fact situation, determining the outcome of a particular case, is false."
**80** Cf., PI §189: "'But *are* the steps then *not* determined by the algebraic formula?' —The question contains a mistake."

ed. Conversely, if something is, under the rules, a valid statute, the absence of a label must be irrelevant—unless, of course, the rules require one. A general sign of the philosophically fantastic is that it comes to seem important and urgent to deny something whose truth, one finds on closer inspection, couldn't intelligibly make the difference one supposes.

To this may be added the consideration that to say false things about the use of a rule, it must be the right kind of thing—a *rule*—which is under consideration. But someone does not yet have a rule in view if their picture is of an item operating quite independently of us—i.e., of our using it as a guide or a basis of criticism, our following or going against it in particular cases. If a certain pattern of normative judgment is necessary if a rule (as opposed to, say, an inert mark, or a mere regularity of behavior) is to be under consideration,[81] it should have been difficult to find conceptual room for anything to be called "a rule itself," which does not yet make any determinate normative demands. The interpretivist thesis looks like a requirement that a rule be interpreted just to become what it is—a *rule*.

9. The philosophical "rule itself" is evidently an abstraction from what the jurist means by a rule or a "rule itself." It is a rule considered not just apart from any gloss, but somehow apart from our practical concourse with it, our use of it in particular cases. As such, it is normatively inert: It can be applied like *this* or like *that*. Say that it is a rule considered as a mere sign or mark, like ink on a page. Assuming this is intelligible, what philosophical motive is there for treating rules in this strangely abstract way? And once this abstraction is made, is it possible to understand how some further item called "an interpretation" can serve to bring the possibility of a rule's normative power—i.e., the possibility of what jurists know as "a rule" —back into view?

The prospects are dim for manufacturing a jurist's rule out of "a rule itself" plus an "interpretation" of it. (I'll return to the question of the motive for wanting to do so after saying why.)

If interpretation were really ubiquitously needed, it becomes hard to see how there could be anything of the right sort to interpret. Remember that legal interpretation is meaning-preserving; it is not—as with the logician's term "interpre-

---

81 That was at least part of the point of Hart's discussion of the "internal aspect" of rules: "What is necessary [for there to be a rule] is that there should be a critical reflective attitude to certain patterns of behavior as a common standard, and that this should display itself in criticism (including self-criticism), demands for conformity, and in acknowledgments that such criticism and demands are justified, all of which find their characteristic expression in the normative terminology of 'ought', 'must', and 'should', 'right' and 'wrong'" (Hart 1994, 57).

tation"—an *assignment* of meaning to a bare sign. The interpretivist know this; he does not say that judges must invent things from scratch. But how can judges be understood as responsively "interpreting" if the object of their interpretation is not already meaningful, i.e., if it does not in some cases require *this* and not *that?*[82] The interpretivist's "rule itself" makes logically conflicting demands on the object of legal interpretation: something sufficiently meaningless as to leave legal judgment open in any particular case; something sufficiently meaningful to permit such judgment to be a recovery of meaning, and not a mere assignment of it, or a reaction to a Rorschach blot.

This explains why talk of "partial" or "incomplete" determination by a rule is apt to tempt the interpretivist. It is a way of trying to accommodate the required mix of meaningfulness and meaninglessness. Kelsen affords an example. He suggests that we think of every legal rule as only a "frame" for judgment. The rule is meaningful in that some judgments fall outside the frame. But within the frame, various judgments are possible, so an "interpretation," according to Kelsen, is always needed:

> The relationship between a higher and a lower level of the legal order, such... as statute and judicial decision, is a relationship of determining or of binding... This determination can never be complete. The higher norm cannot bind in every direction the act by which it is applied. There must always be more or less room for discretion, so that the higher norm in relation to the lower one can only have the character of a frame to be filled by this act. Even the most detailed command must leave to the individual executing the command some discretion.[83]

> The need for an 'interpretation' results precisely from the fact that the norm to be applied... leaves open several possibilities..."[84]

What is Kelsen getting at? In what sense does even a *not*-so-detailed command— e.g., "Shut the door"—always call for "discretion" or "leave open several possibilities"? After all, someone will satisfy the command if he does just *this*—shuts the door—otherwise not. Kelsen's thought is that different *events* can all count as compliance: The subject might use her left or right hand, complete the action in five or fifteen seconds, etc. In Kelsen's own example, A orders B to arrest C, and B must decide how to proceed.

Despite first impressions, this doesn't support interpretivism, because it doesn't deliver the conceptual hybrid—a rule always in need of interpretation,

---

**82** I'm assuming that to speak of the "meaning" of anything, we must also be able to make use of the notion of actions or judgments which are (or aren't) in accord with that meaning.
**83** Kelsen 1967, 349.
**84** Kelsen 1967, 352.

yet sufficiently meaningful to ground interpretation—that the interpretivist needs. It amounts to remembering that complying with a rule requires an action *type*, one which can be instantiated or tokened—"interpreted," Kelsen confusingly says—in different ways. To see this, let two questions be distinguished: (1) Are further executive decisions needed in complying with a rule? (2) Do those decisions purport to reveal or elucidate the *meaning* of the rule?[85] Applying this to Kelsen's example: (1) Many events would instantiate the type "Arresting C," so executive decisions are needed concerning matters not specified by the command. (2) But "arresting C at 4:00" or "arresting C at 5:00" aren't alternative answers to the question, "What, according to the command, should be done?" So a decision on this matter does not reveal the command's meaning and is therefore not (save in a new technical sense) an "interpretation." Should someone ask whether the command is looking for a particular time of arrest, the answer is not that there can be different "interpretations," but that the command does not make this detail (or innumerable others) relevant. Compare: "Take the five most capable men!" If the sergeant must decide not just the executive details, but also what capacities the command is looking for, then his discretion is an interpretive one.

When Kelsen says "even the most detailed command must leave... some discretion," what he means is undeniable: A command (or a rule) fully determines an action only by determining an action *type*. It may be that a confusion of such normative determination with mechanical determination (of a particular event) lurks in the background here. For the point may also be put like this: A rule determines what is to be done, not by pulling someone who endeavors to comply with it "down the track,"[86] but by delimiting the general shape (type) of performative options. Of course, this doesn't mean that a rule *fails* to "pull us down the track" either.

10. Wittgenstein demonstrates another way of grasping the incoherence of the philosophical "rule itself." He asks how we are to think "an interpretation" placed on the rule could give it the determinacy that, left to itself, it putatively lacks.

Again, what we thought we needed doesn't help.[87] If rules themselves are unable to fix their meaning—if they "cannot step forward"—it seems clear that no further linguistic item is going to help. If that is what an interpretation is sup-

---

85 This distinction might help locate something special about performing-interpretations: here, almost every action is potentially revelatory of the work's meaning.

86 Cornell 1992, 101–2.

87 The next three paragraphs summarize a part of Stone 2004b.

posed to be (*viz.*, a gloss), then interpretations are inert "signs" themselves: Just "in themselves," they don't step forward, but stand in need of interpretation, etc. If interpretation is a necessary condition of a sign meaning anything at all, and interpretations are signs, we face an unhappy regress in which interpretation, rather than animating the sign, merely redoubles the problem of its impotence.[88]

Judges do sometimes gloss the rules. To interpret, in this sense, is to give an explanation where an explanation is needed to remove or avert a doubt about meaning. Given this familiar function of interpretation (§3 above), it is understandable why someone, starting out from an indeterminate "rule itself," might suppose that they could get a functioning rule back into view by making a *general* use of the notion of interpretation. But this is mistaken. One can interpret in this familiar sense only on the condition that interpretation is not generally required. Otherwise, a hopeless regress arises.

Since linguistic items cause trouble, it may be tempting to think of "interpretation" as some mental act of thinking or intending the sign one way rather than another. Yet this seems mysterious.[89] Presumably, whatever is present in one's mind is itself comprised of discrete items; it is not a cognizance of the innumerable situations in which the rule is to be applied.[90] Thus, any items in which "intending a sign a certain way" might be supposed to consist—samples, images, a mental instruction, etc—can always be projected, in future circumstances, in different ways.[91] So we can't really make intelligible to ourselves how a mental item —say, the thought "Shut the door"—can be more determinate, or less in need of interpretation, than a text representing that thought. For we can't really understand what it would be for there to be an item in the mind that had the requisite normative properties of meaning, but that was not, from the get-go, subject to the conditions of representability (or communicability) in signs.

11. In light of these challenges, we can expect to find the interpretivist emphasizing the merely negative aspects of his doctrine, its status as a counter to a suspect picture of a rule as a kind of independent compelling force. In Wittgenstein's image, the rule lays down a rail on which our performances will have to lie if they are to be in accord with it.[92] The interpretivist wants to say: *There is no such rail.* For the reasons canvassed, however, this negative characteriza-

---

**88** See PI §§85, 198, 201.
**89** In Derrida's case, this is also one of the chief critical targets: the idea, allegedly endemic to metaphysical philosophy, of an "inner voice" that is external to "writing." See esp. Derrida 1973.
**90** Cf., PI §§139, 187–8, 197
**91** Cf., PI §§141, 186
**92** See PI §218.

tion of interpretivism can't really be any clearer than the requirement of interpretation it purports to explain.

To sharpen this, consider whether "there is no such rail" unambiguously makes contact with something true, by considering the following two-prong response to it. (1) Of course, grasping a rule doesn't "pull us down the track" in any mechanical sense. Any *actual* mechanism is subject to breakdown. If we are to think of the relation between a rule and its future applications as one of mechanical compulsion, this would have to be a mechanism always functioning *properly*—i. e., a mechanism operating according to a rule![93] Otherwise put, the relation between a rule and its applications is a normative one: The red light means that one *should* stop, not that one *will*. To picture this as something mechanical either mistakes the kind of thing a rule is, or it presupposes a grasp of the very idea one wants to explain. (2) Taken as a figure for a *normative* relation, the picture of a rail, though un-illuminating, seems unobjectionable. It states a truism about the kind of thing a rule is: something affording a standard of correctness for future cases, and to which we can appeal in justifying our performances.[94] The sense of something suspect only arises from a blending of the pictures of normative and mechanical determination.[95]

This response to the interpretivist finds nothing more objectionable in the picture he rejects than an especially colorful way of expressing the grammar of our use of rules.[96] It thereby shows that to understand him we have first to grasp a queer conception of such grammatical commonplaces as "a rule determines what we are to do."[97] This queer conception (the philosophical 'rule itself') and the requirement of interpretation go hand in hand. Returning now to the question of what motivates this treatment of rules, the answer is: the demand for a *philosophical account* of what a rule means.

---

**93** Cf. PI §§193–94.

**94** Similarly, it may be said that the picture Hart sets his face against—that "a rule can itself step forward," etc.—merely characterizes the kind of thing a rule is: viz., something which normatively determines the shape of future options. Consider: "Unlike a mere regularity of behavior, a rule steps forward to claim its own instances: i. e., it sorts those instances into those that are in accord with and those that are not. With a regularity of behavior, in contrast, you've got to start with the instances and induce the shape of the thing from there."

**95** Cf., PI §§191, 195.

**96** See PI §373: "Grammar tells us what kind of object anything is." The thought that the picture to which the interpretivist objects might be understood in this harmless way is suggested by John McDowell (McDowell 2001).

**97** Cf., PI §195: "But of course... [the use itself is present] 'in some sense'! Really the only thing wrong with what you say is the expression 'in a queer way'."

To explain, consider the 'red-light' rule. "Just *by itself*," the interpretivist says, "this didn't determine that you were to do just *this*—stop then and there. A doubt is always possible." Given this, it might seem unexceptional to say that something must have been done to exclude such doubt—an "interpretation." But this should encounter an objection. That a doubt is "always possible" just means that a doubt might arise in *some circumstances*; it doesn't mean that one is presently in doubt, or even that one could make intelligible to oneself what it would be to doubt.[98] In what sense, then, is there always some possibility to be excluded in following a rule, even in the plainest case?

The solution is to see that what drives this description is the wish for a 'philosophical explanation' of a rule's meaning: i.e., one that is not dependent—as our everyday explanations are—on someone's practical uptake under the circumstances. Thus, suppose someone were to ask why the 'red light' rule required one to do *this*—stop there and then. (Suppose she asks seriously: "Why not stop after the light, or stop and then proceed through the light, or...?") In response, we might try various explanations. But in doing so we shall be relying on her ability to take up our words and apply them correctly—i.e., to grasp and follow rules. Should further doubts arise, there can be further explanations, but they will share this feature of dependency on our interlocutor's uptake—on the fact that some doubts do not actually arise. But now the idea might arise of a different kind of explanation of the connection between the red-light rule and its application in a particular case, one that *wasn't* in this way dependent on the contingent patterns of response that are part of the circumstances in which we operate with rules. Such an explanation would seek to remove not just doubts that, under the circumstances, actually arise, but to specify the meaning of the rule (as it were) *absolutely*, in light of *all* the possibilities.[99]

Posing the peculiar question of how 'a rule *itself* determines what one is to do' is really a way of asking for this special sort of explanation. For, as was said, the philosophical "in itself" functions to abstract a rule not just from any glosses, but from the practical circumstances in which rules operate. Hence "in itself" frames a notional point of view from which it seems to make sense to speak of excluded possibilities in every case. By the use of this phrase, a doubt that is always *possible* (i.e., in some circumstances) is represented as already *present*, as if the kind of explanation wanted is one that first considered "all possible doubts."[100] Of course, it is obscure what this means. So the matter might be

---

**98** Cf., PI §§84, 85, 87.
**99** On the idea of such an account, see Diamond 1991, 68–9, which I am following here.
**100** Cf., PI §87.

put just like this: The interpretivist's use of the expression "a rule itself" expresses the same metaphysical demand as the demand for an account of what a rule
means absolutely, in view of "all the possibilities."

Once one asks how a "rule itself" (in the interpretivist's sense) requires one
to do *this*, it might seem compelling to answer: "by virtue of an interpretation
placed on the rule." But these considerations should begin to make clear that
interpretivism shares something crucial in common with the picture of meaning
it sets its face against: Both arise in the service of the demand for a philosophical
—a circumstantially independent—account of what a rule means. In contrast,
from the everyday perspective (where no such demand operates), it is an empirical question, as the jurist knows, whether to follow a rule you need to interpret
it (§7). And from this practical perspective, what is objectionable (if anything is)
in talk of 'a rule *itself* determining its own application' is no less objectionable in
talk of 'ubiquitous interpretation.' Apart from the idea of giving a 'philosophical
account'—one from outside the perspective of our everyday concourse with
rules[101]—there would be no point in speaking (philosophically) of a 'rule *itself*';
and apart from this abstraction, the thought that every case requires an interpretation would appear patently absurd—no less so than the picture of 'labeling' or
'self-animation' to which it is in fact dialectically wedded.

## Conclusion

12. The interpretivist means to object to a bit of philosophy. The trouble is that he
doesn't object to it at the right level of depth. Instead, he ends up replacing one
philosophical account with another.[102] Our story has emphasized the dialectical
dependence of interpretivism on a queer picture of rules (the rule as rail, as stepping forward) it seeks to oppose. The interpretivist finds the requirement of interpretation to be a natural way of rejecting this picture. But his way of rejecting it
inherits and preserves what is suspect about it: the demand for an "absolute"
account of a rule's meaning.

---

**101** "If I see the thought symbol 'from the outside', I become conscious that it could be
interpreted like this or that" (Wittgenstein 1970, §235). Wittgenstein's phrase (in scare quotes)
"from the outside" stands for the fantasy of a special, philosophical point of view on meaning.
In the present context, it finds us thinking that we can retain a grip on the kind of thing a rule is
while prescinding from the practical settings that comprise our concourse—our life—with rules.
**102** A similar moral can be found in David Finkelstein's illuminating "Wittgenstein on Rules
and Platonism" (Finkelstein 2000).

There is another possibility. The present dialectic might end *non-philosophically*[103] by our coming to see "the rule itself" as ill-suited for posing fruitful questions about meaning. The word "interpretation" could then be returned to its everyday use. Given the word's varied career—its institutionalization in theology and law; its employment in literature, performance, history, psychoanalysis, etc.—this isn't without difficulty. For "interpretation" carries with it resonances from these various settings, but we lack a perspicuous view of them. This partly accounts for our sense that interpretivism says something significant but too deep to express.

Still, the interpretivist is counting on our familiarity with the use of "interpretation" in contexts where no philosophical business is at hand.[104] But which features of 'interpretation' are pertinent? That meaning isn't apparent? That there is a gloss? A tokening or iteration? Creativity? The interpretivist will understandably be found to reject these as accounts of his meaning; his aim of speaking philosophically appears to be *frustrated* when it is remembered too clearly how the term 'interpretation' functions in everyday contexts.[105] So he is counting on *both* our familiarity with those contexts *and* our partial forgetfulness of them. Adopting a remark of Wittgenstein's, we might say: It is just the occult character of interpretation that the interpretivist *needs* for his philosophical purposes.[106]

At one point Wittgenstein suggests—against such occultism—that "we ought to restrict the term 'interpretation' to the substitution of one expression of the rule for another."[107] This has puzzled some readers. It remembers one everyday use of the term. But there are of course others—performing-interpretations, interpretations of a painting, etc.—that do not involve linguistic substitution. I take it that Wittgenstein wasn't overlooking this, much less legislating against these other uses.

Remember the context of his restrictive proposal: "There is an inclination to say: every action according to the rule is an interpretation. But we ought to re-

---

**103** Cf., PI §85: "— So I can say, the sign-post does after all leave no room for doubt. Or rather: it sometimes leaves room for doubt and sometimes not. And now this is no longer a philosophical proposition, but an empirical one."

**104** Otherwise a technical term would have served just as well. It is notable that Derrida's "quasi-transcendental" argument concerning the conditions of the possibility of meaning makes use of technical terms like "trace," "arche-writing," "differance," etc., in addition to "interpretation." See Jacques Derrida, "Difference," in: Derrida 1996, 129–60. Such terms conspicuously display the property of being useless outside of philosophy.

**105** Cf., PI §261.

**106** Cf., Wittgenstein 1965, 5.

**107** PI §201.

strict..." What is important here is just the contrast between a philosophical temptation to call on "interpretation" in giving an account of a rule's meaning, and the word's everyday use (to signify a "gloss") in the specific context of 'interpreting a rule.' Clearly, the interpretivist would reject Wittgenstein's restrictive proposal as an account of what he means to say. He is not, after all, someone who mistakenly thinks that in order to apply a rule, one must always attach some linguistic rider to it! So the resulting regress of interpretations doesn't directly refute him. Wittgenstein's recalling this bit of everyday use is rather a challenge, which says roughly: "Here is a familiar sense of interpretation, and clearly interpretation in this sense—*viz.*, a gloss—is not ubiquitous. Since that is not what you mean, what *do* you mean by 'every action according to the rule is an *interpretation*'?"[108]

Nonetheless, there is a more positive point to grasp here. Although bringing "interpretation" back to its everyday use need not mean restricting it to cases of "linguistic substitution," it does mean seeing it as a form of explanation, an endeavor to say or show what an object means when this is not fully apparent. "Linguistic substitution" is perhaps only the most obvious case in which interpretation plays this logical role. But in its obviousness, this case also makes perspicuous other asymmetries between the philosophical and everyday uses of the term. For the philosopher, interpretation is ubiquitous. In everyday settings, it isn't; or is, but only within a limited domain, defined by one's reasons for interpreting (e. g., in cases of literature, performance). In everyday settings, the call for interpretation contrasts with cases of plain meaning. In philosophy, it contrasts with a putatively suspect notion of "plain meaning." To explain this suspect notion, the philosopher speaks of meanings as plain "in themselves."[109] In everyday settings, it is an empirical question whether the meaning of anything is plain "in itself." Pressed further, the philosopher is apt to speak of meanings that are somehow immune to the possibility of doubt or challenge. But interpretation, like any elucidation, is called for in circumstances of actual doubt or uncertainty, not the mere notional possibility of such.

---

108 On this reading, PI §201 keeps faith with Wittgenstein's view that philosophy (as he practices it) advances no theses: PI §128. Indeed, PI §201 can be seen as applying the sort of philosophical procedure that Wittgenstein described in the *Tractatus* as "the only strictly correct one": "to say nothing [philosophical] and then, whenever someone else wanted to say something metaphysical, to demonstrate to him that he had failed to give a meaning to certain signs in his sentences" (Wittgenstein 1961, 6.53). "Bringing words back to their everyday use" is in the service of this procedure. I develop this reading of PI §201 in Stone 2000.
109 See, e. g., Fish 1989, 513.

# Bibliography

Anscombe, G.E.M. (1957), *Intention*, Oxford: Blackwell.

Cavell, Stanley (1979), *The Claim of Reason: Wittgenstein, Skepticism, Morality, and Tragedy*, Oxford: Oxford University Press.

Cornell, Drucilla (1992), *The Philosophy of the Limit*, Second Edition, New York: Routledge.

Davidson, Donald (1984), "Radical Interpretation." In: Donald Davidson, *Inquiries Into Truth and Interpretation*, Oxford: Clarendon Press, 125–39.

De Man, Paul (1979), "Semiology and Rhetoric." In: Paul de Man, *Allegories of Reading: Figural Language In Rousseau, Nietzsche, Rilke, and Proust*, New Haven: Yale University Press, 3–19.

De Man, Paul (1986), "The Resistance to Theory." In: Paul de Man, *The Resistance to Theory*, Minneapolis: University of Minnesota Press, 3–20.

Derrida, Jacques (1992), "Force of Law: The 'Mystical Foundations of Authority.'" In: Drucilla Cornell, Michel Rosenfeld, and David Gray Carlson, *Deconstruction and the Possibility of Justice*, New York: Routledge, 3–67.

Derrida, Jacques (1996), *Speech and Phenomena: And Other Essays on Husserl's Theory of Signs*, David B. Allison (trans.), Evanston, IL: Northwestern University Press.

Diamond, Cora (1991), *The Realistic Spirit: Wittgenstein, Philosophy, and the Mind*, Cambridge, MA: The MIT Press.

Dworkin, Ronald (1986), *Law's Empire*, Cambridge, MA: Harvard University Press.

Dworkin, Ronald (1998), "Comment." In: Antonin Scalia, *A Matter of Interpretation: Federal Courts and the Law*, Princeton: Princeton University Press, 119–26.

Finkelstein, David (2000), "Wittgenstein on Rules and Platonism." In: Alice Crary and Rupert Read (eds.), *The New Wittgenstein*, London: Routledge, 53–73.

Fish, Stanley (1989), *Doing What Comes Naturally: Change, Rhetoric, and the Practice of Theory In Literary and Legal Studies*, Oxford: Clarendon Press.

Gadamer, Hans-Georg (1986), "Composition and Interpretation." In: Hans-Georg Gadamer, *The Relevance of the Beautiful and Other Essays*, Cambridge: Cambridge University Press, 66–73.

Gadamer, Hans-Georg (1994), *Truth and Method*, Joel Weinsheimer and Donald G. Marshall (trans.), New York: Continuum Books.

Grice, Paul (1957), "Meaning." In: *Philosophical Review* 66, 377–88.

Hampshire, Stuart (1966), "Types of Interpretation." In: Sidney Hook (ed.), *Art and Philosophy: A Symposium*, New York: New York University Press, 101–8.

Hart, H.L.A. (1961), *The Concept of Law*, Oxford: Clarendon Press.

Hart, H.L.A. (1983), "Problems In the Philosophy of Law." In: H.L.A. Hart, *Essays In Jurisprudence and Philosophy*, Oxford: Oxford University Press, 106–7.

Hart, H.L.A. (1994), *The Concept of Law*, Second Edition, Oxford: Oxford University Press.

Hart, H.L.A. / Honore, Tony (1985), *Causation In the Law*, Second Edition, Oxford: Clarendon Press.

Heidegger, Martin (1996), *Being and Time*, Joan Stambaugh (trans.), New York: State University of New York.

Hutchinson, Allen (1989), "Democracy and Determinacy." In: *University of Miami Law Review* 43, 541–76.

Juhl, P.D. (1980), *Interpretation: An Essay In the Philosophy of Literary Criticism*, Princeton: Princeton University Press.

Kant, Immanuel (1929), *Critique of Pure Reason*, Norman Kemp Smith (trans.), New York: St. Martin's Press.

Kelsen, Hans (1967), *Pure Theory of Law*, Max Knight (trans.), Berkeley, Los Angeles, and London: University of California Press.

Knapp, Stephen (1993), *Literary Interest: The Limits of Anti-Formalism*, Cambridge, MA: Harvard University Press.

McDowell, John (2001), "Meaning and Intentionality In Wittgenstein's Later Philosophy." In: John McDowell, *Mind, Value, and Reality*, Cambridge, MA: Harvard University Press, 263–78.

Moran, Richard (2004), "Anscombe on 'Practical Knowledge.'" In: John Hyman and Helen Steward (eds.), *Agency and Action*, Cambridge: Cambridge University Press, 43–68.

Moran, Richard / Stone, Martin (2009), "Anscombe on Expression of Intention." In: Constantine Sandis (ed.), *New Essays on the Explanation of Action*, 132–68.

Nehemas, Alexander (1981), "The Postulated Author: Critical Monism as a Regulative Ideal." In: *Critical Inquiry* 8, 133–49.

Nietzsche, Friedrich (1998), *On the Genealogy of Morality*, Maudemarie Clark and Alan J. Swensen (trans.), Indianapolis: Hackett.

Nietzsche, Friedrich (2003), *Writings from the Late Notebooks*, Rudiger Bittner (ed.), Kate Struge (trans.), Cambridge: Cambridge University Press.

Raz, Joseph (2009), *Between Authority and Interpretation: On the Theory of Law and Practical Reason*, Oxford: Oxford University Press.

Ricoeur, Paul (1973), "The Model of the Text: Meaningful Action Considered As a Text." In: *New Literary History* 5, 91–117.

Rorty, Richard (1982), *Consequences of Pragmatism*, Minneapolis: University of Minnesota Press.

Schauer, Frederick (1988), "Formalism." In: *Yale Law Journal* 97, 508–48.

Schauer, Frederick (1993), *Playing By the Rules: A Philosophical Examination of Rule-Based Decision-Making in Law and in Life*, Oxford: Clarendon Press.

Sedivy, Sonia (2004), "Wittgenstein Against Interpretation: 'The Meaning of a Text Does Not Stop Short of Its Facts.'" In: John Gibson and Wolfgang Huemer (eds.), *The Literary Wittgenstein*, London: Routledge, 165–85.

Shelley, Percy Bysshe (1920), *A Philosophical View of Reform*, Oxford: Oxford University Press.

Shelley, Percy Bysshe (2004), "A Defence of Poetry." In: Percy Bysshe Shelley, *A Defence of Poetry and Other Essays*, Whitefish, MT: Kessinger Publishing, 27–45.

Stone, Martin (1995), "Focusing the Law: What Legal Interpretation Is Not." In: Andrei Marmor (ed.), *Law and Interpretation: Essays In Legal Philosophy*, Oxford: Clarendon Press, 31–96.

Stone, Martin (2000), "Wittgenstein On Deconstruction." In: Alice Crary and Rupert Read (eds.), *The New Wittgenstein*, London: Routledge, 83–117.

Stone, Martin (2002), "Formalism." In: Jules Coleman and Scott Shapiro (eds.), *The Oxford Handbook of Jurisprudence and Philosophy of Law*, Oxford: Oxford University Press, 166–205.

Stone, Martin (2004a), "On the Old Saw: Every Reading of a Text Is an Interpretation." In: John Gibson and Wolfgang Huemer (eds.), *The Literary Wittgenstein*, London: Routledge, 186–208.

Stone, Martin (2004b), "Theory, Practice, and Ubiquitous Interpretation: The Basic." In: Gary A. Olson and Lynn Worsham (eds.), *Postmodern Sophistry: Stanley Fish and the Critical Enterprise*, New York: University of New York.

Thompson, Michael (2008), "Naïve Action Theory." In: Michael Thompson, *Life and Action: Elementary Structures of Practice and Practical Thought*, Cambridge, MA: Harvard University Press, 85–148.

Vattimo, Gianni (1997), *Beyond Interpretation: The Meaning of Hermeneutics for Philosophy*, Stanford: Stanford University Press.

Von Wright, G.H. (1971), *Explanation and Understanding*, Cornell: Cornell University Press.

Wittgenstein, Ludwig (1958), *Philosophical Investigations*, G.E.M. Anscombe (trans.), Oxford: Blackwell.

Wittgenstein, Ludwig (1961), *Tractatus Logico-Philosophicus*, D.F. Pears and B.F. McGuiness (trans.), London: Routledge.

Wittgenstein, Ludwig (1965), *The Blue and the Brown Books*, New York: Harper & Row.

Wittgenstein, Ludwig (1970), *Zettel*, G.E.M. Anscombe and G.H. von Wright (eds.), Berkeley, Los Angeles, and London: University of California Press.

Wodehouse, P.G. (1930), "The Ordeal of the Young Tuppy." In: P.G. Wodehouse, *Very Good, Jeeves*, London: W.W. Norton & Company, 234–59.

Jason Bridges
# Rule-Following Skepticism, Properly So Called

Saul Kripke famously argued that there are no facts about what people mean by the words and sentences they utter. His 'skeptical paradox,' as he called it, has generated an enormous secondary literature. Indeed, it's not an exaggeration to say that it gave birth to a new subfield of the philosophy of mind and language. Despite the degree of attention, however, I believe that the real source and character of Kripke's skeptical doubts have never come into clear view. Previous commentary on Kripke has failed to grasp that the doubts fundamentally concern the possibility of a person's *following* a rule. That might seem an absurd charge, given that everyone knows that Kripke conceives the skeptical paradox as a development of Wittgenstein's remarks on rule-following. But the point of the charge is that previous interpretations of the paradox go astray because they miss that its central target is the idea that a person's performance might be *based upon* a rule—that a rule might be *her reason* for proceeding as she does. The skeptical paradox belongs to the philosophy of rational explanation, of explanations that account for what people do or think by citing their reasons for doing or thinking so.

That this feature of the paradox has been overlooked is partly Kripke's fault. His exposition of the skeptical argument intertwines two strands without adequately distinguishing them. The secondary literature has picked up on one of these strands. But the material constituting this strand cannot make sense of crucial steps in the discussion; thus commentators are led to find disappointingly large gaps in the skeptical line of thought. After an analysis of this exegetical state of affairs in the first few sections of this paper, I shall focus on developing the other strand. The exercise will have a number of positive results: it will yield a more satisfying understanding of Kripke's text, it will uncover a skeptical argument of interest and depth, and it will allow for a richer engagement between the skeptical argument and Wittgenstein's own discussions of rule-following.

## 1 The Prescriptive and Evaluative Interpretations of Kripke's Normativity Thesis

Kripke's skeptical argument, on any reading, hinges on the idea that the relationship between the meaning of an expression and the use of that expression is "normative." The standard interpretations of Kripke's talk of the normativity of meaning take their primary cue from the following passage:

> Suppose I do mean addition by '+'. What is the relation of this supposition to the question of how I will respond to the problem '68+57'? The dispositionalist gives a *descriptive* account of this relation: if '+' meant addition, then I will answer '125'. But this is not the proper account of the relation, which is *normative*, not descriptive. The point is *not* that, if I meant addition by '+', I *will* answer '125', but that, if I intend to accord with my past meaning of '+', I *should* answer '125'. Computational error, finiteness of my capacity, and other disturbing factors may lead me not to be disposed to respond as I *should*, but if so, I have not acted in accordance with my intentions. (Kripke 1982, 37)[1]

Some commentators interpret this passage as proposing the following thesis: what a word means has implications for how a speaker of the language ought to use the word. Allan Gibbard, for example, writes:

> The claim I draw from the passage is this: If I mean something by a term, this has implications for what I should do when I use the term, or answer questions couched using the term. The 'should' here is normative: What I mean determines what I *ought* to do. The crux of the slogan that meaning is normative, then, might be another slogan: that *means* implies *ought*. To use... Kripke's example, from statements saying what I mean by the plus sign and other arithmetical terms and constructions, it will follow that I *ought* to answer "125" when asked, "What's 68+57?" Not that I necessarily *will* answer "125", but that is what I ought to answer. (Gibbard 1994, 100)[2]

On Gibbard's reading, then, Kripke's claim is that the meanings of my words determine how I ought to use them. Call the view that the meaning of a word determines how one ought to use it *the prescriptive view of meaning*, and call the claim that this view captures what Kripke intends in speaking of the normativity of meaning the *prescriptive interpretation*. Gibbard applauds the prescriptive view of meaning, and suggests it opens the attractive possibility that a word's having the meaning that it does will prove reducible to facts about how the words ought to be used. Other commentators, such as Paul Horwich (1998, Chapter 8), are less sympathetic, but agree that Kripke must have something along these lines in mind.

But there seems to me very good reasons to reject Gibbard's reading of the passage. *Pace* Gibbard, Kripke does not say that, given what I mean or have meant by "+," I ought to answer "125." What he says, rather, is that if I *intend*

---

1 Henceforth, this text will be cited by page number only.

2 Gibbard actually uses the example of answering the question "What's 5+2?" For ease of exposition I have substituted Kripke's example.

to accord with what I have meant by "+," I ought to answer "125." This distinction is not pedantic: it marks the difference between a hypothetical and categorical imperative, between an "ought" claim whose hold on a person depends on her possession of certain aims, intentions, or desires, and an "ought" claim whose hold on a person is not so dependent. Gibbard ascribes to Kripke the principle, "What I mean determines what I *ought* to do." If Kripke had said or implied that facts about meaning give rise to categorical imperatives, the ascription would be apt. Given that Kripke just asserts a hypothetical imperative, however, the principle fits the text only if understood as shorthand for the following: "Facts about what I mean determine what I ought to do contingent on my possession of particular aims, desires, or intentions." This is hardly a noteworthy thesis, for facts about *anything* can determine what I ought to do contingent on my possession of particular aims, desires, or intentions. If I want clearer vision, I ought to wear corrective lenses. Obviously, the possibility of this kind of remark should not motivate a thesis of the normativity of optics.[3]

If the prescriptive view of meaning is glossed in terms of hypothetical imperatives, it is vacuous; and if it is glossed in terms of categorical imperatives, the prescriptive interpretation has no textual support in the passage under consideration. A charitable reading of Kripke should find the point of his distinction between the normative and descriptive to lie elsewhere.

Such a reading suggests itself when we note that "ought" and "should" are not the only terms in the passage that might reasonably be regarded as normative; "accord" is another. Consider again Kripke's hypothetical imperative: "if I intend to accord with what I have meant by '+', I should answer '125'." Compare the following remark: "If you intend to accord with the rules of the Charleston, at this juncture you should step before you kick." This remark obviously doesn't presuppose that facts about the rules of the Charleston have implications for what you ought to do now irrespective of your particular aims and intentions. What it does seem to imply, however, is that in light of its rules, there is such a thing as a *correct* way (and such a thing as an *incorrect* way) to dance the Charleston. It seems open to read Kripke's hypothetical imperative simply as a way of

---

3 Oddly, many commentators miss the hypothetical character of Kripke's imperatives. The most striking version of this oversight is in Boghossian (2003). Boghossian's quotation of the passage (Boghossian 2003, 31) stops before the final mention of intentions, and, more remarkably, omits the phrase, "if I intend to accord with my past meaning of '+,'" with no ellipsis to indicate the omission. This omission sets the stage for Boghossian to write later in the paper, "Kripke says: 'If I mean addition by '+', then it doesn't follow that I *will* say that '68 57 = 125', but only that I *ought* to say that it does'" (39), and to proceed to criticize the second part of this claim on the ground that whether one ought to give the correct answer will be contingent on one's intentions.

making the analogous point about meaning. The availability of that particular imperative shows that, in light of the meaning of a linguistic expression, there are right and wrong ways to use that expression. The meaning of an expression, like the rules of a dance, provides a standard, or norm, against which performance is determined as correct or incorrect. In this sense, the relationship between meaning and use is normative.

Call the claim that the meaning of an expression determines uses of that expression as correct or incorrect *the evaluative view of meaning*, and call the claim that this view captures what Kripke means in speaking of the normativity of meaning the *evaluative interpretation*. The evaluative interpretation has been endorsed by a few commentators, including Paul Boghossian (1989, but see also Boghossian 2003), John McDowell (2001), and Hannah Ginsborg (2011). In addition to better fitting the text, the evaluative interpretation has a further advantage: unlike the categorical version of the prescriptive view, the evaluative view of meaning seems plausible on its face. At the very least, it can be said to have the support of commonsense, in the sense that the great majority of language speakers would immediately assent to it. Nearly everyone takes it as obvious that words can be used correctly and incorrectly and that the meaning of a word determines which is which.[4]

---

4 Some lexicographers and social commentators appear to set themselves against commonsense here, for they appear to regard the evaluative view of meaning as an expression of elitism. We have long accepted that there is no one "correct way" to dress or otherwise comport oneself; why should we persist in insisting, in the face of the great diversity of dialects, that there is a "correct way" to speak English—say, the way people educated at high-end colleges do? (For citations of this line of reasoning, see Wallace 2001.) But as an objection to the evaluative view, this confuses two dimensions along which linguistic performances might be evaluated for correctness: whether a word is used with its proper meaning, and whether a word is used correctly in light of its meaning—that is, in light of whatever meaning it has on the speaker's lips, be it proper or improper. The meaning it has on your lips may be special to the particular dialect you speak; it may even be special to your idiolect. But if we are genuinely talking about meaning, then it will determine correct and incorrect ways for you to use that word. Two children may decide to communicate in a secret code in which, say, "rain" means snow and "snow" means rain. If one of them on some occasion forgets that that is what they are doing and uses "rain" when intending to speak of rain, then insofar as it is still true to say that in this context the word "rain" on her lips means snow, it is also true to say that on this occasion she is using the word incorrectly in light of that meaning. Now, perhaps one might want to claim that the children's code assigns the 'incorrect' or 'improper' meaning to the word "rain." But that is a different matter. And it is only the latter sort of claim that, at least in some contexts, may merit the charge of elitism.

Some philosophers appear to believe that an item can sort behavior into correct or incorrect only if it has categorical implications for what one ought to do.[5] This would collapse the distinction I have drawn between the evaluative and prescriptive views. But the belief is simply wrong. I might take an hour right now and invent a new dance. If I do so, I will have brought into being a new dimension along which human actions can be judged as correct or incorrect: namely, as performances of that dance. I will have, in that perfectly legitimate sense, introduced a new norm for judging potential human performances correct or incorrect. But the mere fact that the rules of my dance are norms in this sense obviously does not give them any categorical power, not even a *prima facie* power, to dictate what anyone ought to do. We should count ourselves lucky that there is no implication from an item's having the power to sort our performances into correct and incorrect to its having the power to determine, categorically, what we ought to do. As this example shows, the former power can be had very cheaply.

The evaluative interpretation yields an appealingly straightforward explanation of Kripke's dissatisfaction with reductive accounts of meaning. On this interpretation, the gist of Kripke's objection to dispositionalism, for example, would be this: that while one's behaving in a certain way can be inconsistent with the hypothesis that one possesses a certain disposition, there is no sense in saying one's behavior fails to accord with that disposition. Dispositions do not sort behavior into correct and incorrect. But meanings do. Thus, one's meaning something by an expression cannot be identified simply with one's possessing a particular disposition in the use of that expression. Analogous objections can easily be constructed for the other reductive accounts Kripke considers. Whatever the ultimate merits of these objections, they certainly seem to have some *prima facie* force.

# 2 The Evaluative Interpretation and Anti-Reductionism

I do not wish to deny that the evaluative view of meaning is at work in Kripke's discussion of his skeptical paradox. On the contrary, I think it clear that he objects to dispositionalism and the other reductive accounts of meaning at least

---

5 This view appears to be common ground between Gibbard and Boghossian in their debate in Gibbard 2003 and Boghossian 2003. However, I have difficulty finding a consistent interpretation of Boghossian's essay.

partly on the ground that they cannot accommodate the evaluative view. But if we suppose, à la the evaluative interpretation, that the evaluative view exhausts the import of Kripke's appeals to the "normative" relationship between meaning and use, we will be unable to make sense of his dissatisfaction with *anti-reductionism* about meaning. After disposing of the various reductive proposals he considers, Kripke concludes the skeptical argument with a brief consideration of the possibility that states of meaning things by one's words are *"sui generis"* and "primitive," and hence that semantic facts cannot be reduced to facts specifiable in non-semantic terms. Kripke's response is simply to complain that the proposal "leaves the nature of this postulated primitive state... completely mysterious" (51). Why does Kripke think this?

There are two possibilities. The first is that Kripke assumes some version of semantic naturalism—the view that all facts about semantic content must be reducible to facts expressible in non-intentional, non-semantic terms.[6] This view sets a clear research agenda for the philosophy of mind: to explain possession of semantic content and correlative states and properties in non-intentional, non-semantic terms. And it licenses suspicion about the existence of a putative kind of content-involving state if, in light of repeated failed efforts to construct a satisfactory reductive account of what it would be to occupy such a state, the prospects for such an account come to seem dim. If Kripke's discussion proceeded from an assumption of semantic naturalism, then it would be quite clear why, after a wholly unsuccessful series of attempts to produce a reductive account of states of meaning things by words, he should be impatient with the rearguard insistence that we do not after all need such an account to vindicate our belief in the existence of such states.

But the claim that semantic naturalism is a presupposition of Kripke's skeptical argument is extremely dubious. For one thing, Kripke never explicitly registers a commitment to semantic naturalism in his presentation of the skeptical paradox. Indeed, he gives no hint at all that such an assumption plays any role in motivating the skeptical conclusion. Moreover, one might well wonder where the assumption came from. Kripke himself is no friend of semantic naturalism or the constructive philosophical projects it licenses.[7] And surely he is not such a poor interpreter as to suppose that Wittgenstein is committed to semantic

---

6 For an example of this interpretation, see Horwich 1984, 164.

7 That Kripke 1980 served as a foundational text in the development of various 'naturalistic' accounts of reference and content seems to me to show that one of the central lessons of that book was not absorbed.

naturalism either. But if neither Kripke nor Wittgenstein is a semantic naturalist, how did it come about that Kripkenstein is such a knee-jerk one?[8]

We are left with the second possibility. This is that Kripke takes himself to have brought to our attention, in the course of his exposition of the skeptical argument, certain seemingly problematic or paradoxical features of the envisioned states of meaning, features so seemingly problematic, in fact, that we cannot justifiably countenance the existence of anything possessing those features until we have produced a satisfactory philosophical account of what it would be for something to possess them. If Kripke were to believe that he had shown this, then it would be quite understandable why he should feel justified in dismissing the claim that states of meaning are *sui generis* and hence not to be subject to analysis or explanation. When a compelling doubt has been raised about the very intelligibility of a supposed property or state of affairs, it is no defense to style it as *sui generis*. If we simply cannot make sense of the imagined property or state of affairs, the insistence on irreducibility is a smokescreen.

What is the problematic feature of states of meaning that Kripke thinks he has brought to our attention? Evidently it has something to do with normativity. For the claim that meaning is normative is the only positive point about meaning that Kripke makes.[9] Similarly, that an account of states of meaning must provide for the normativity of meaning is the only substantive condition that Kripke explicitly imposes on solutions to his skeptical paradox.[10] And so if Kripke believes he has revealed something paradoxical in the very idea of a state of meaning, he

---

**8** An analogous point applies to Robert Brandom's claim that the skeptical argument presupposes what we might call *normative naturalism,* according to which all normative facts must be reducible to facts specifiable in non-normative terms. In Brandom's words, "Kripke's skeptic implicitly restricts the vocabulary used to specify [past] use to *nonnormative* vocabulary. He thus assumes that normative specifications of proprieties of concept use are in principle intelligible only if they can be reduced without remainder to specifications of nonnormative properties of concept use" (Brandom 2001, 605). But the ascription of normative naturalism to Kripke's skeptic is just as unsatisfying, and for just the same reasons, as is the ascription of semantic naturalism. (People who like bad puns—not me, certainly—will be tempted to call this version of Kripke's skeptical persona Brankenstein, for his argument, if perhaps not quite monstrous, is nonetheless a pitiable creature.)

**9** It is true that Kripke objects to specific accounts of meaning by appealing to further purported facts about meaning, in particular, that the meaning of an expression determines its correct use in an infinite number of possible circumstances and that people are disposed to use their expressions incorrectly some of the time. But Kripke takes these objections to be applications of the basic normativity objection. See 24, 37, 52 fn.

**10** 11. Note that here Kripke states the normativity condition in terms of talk of justification; this is a crucial point to which I shall shortly return.

must take it to be an implication of the idea that states of meaning are normative.

But if there is nothing more behind Kripke's talk of the normativity of meaning than the thesis I labeled the evaluative view, the obvious question is why Kripke should think he has identified an especially problematic feature of meaning. Is the power to sort performances into correct and incorrect really so paradoxical or mysterious? What's the mystery? What's the paradox? Kripke does not say. It is easy to sympathize with Crispin Wright's initial reaction to Kripke's treatment of the anti-reductionist proposal. Wright (1984, 775–7) objects that it is our ordinary concepts of contentful mental states that ascribe normativity and correlative properties to them, and that we need to be given some substantive reason, which Kripke does not provide, for supposing that our ordinary concepts are not in order as they stand. Philosophers who share Wright's sense of the flimsiness of Kripke's case against anti-reductionism include Boghossian (1989) and Donald Davidson (1992).

It would be disappointing if Kripke's celebrated skeptical argument turned out to rest on an unmotivated suspicion of the very idea of a state that sorts behavior into correct and incorrect. But I do not think it does. As we will shortly see, the real culprit here is the going interpretation of the claim that meaning is normative. A central element of Kripke's treatment of normativity, and the real basis for his skepticism, is quite different from anything we have yet considered.

# 3 The Evaluative Interpretation and the Justification Requirement

Early on in his discussion, Kripke announces an essential condition on a satisfactory answer to his skeptical paradox:

> An answer to the sceptic must satisfy two conditions. First, it must give an account of what fact it is (about my mental state) that constitutes my meaning plus, not quus. But further, there is a condition that any putative candidate for such a fact must satisfy. It must, in some sense, show how I am justified in giving the answer '125' to '68+57.' (11)

Here, Kripke says that a satisfactory response to the skeptic must show how it can be the case that a particular use of a linguistic expression (in this case, a response to a question involving that expression) is *justified*. This requirement, which I shall call the *justification requirement*, Kripke presents as a condition that must be satisfied by any putative "account of what fact it is (about my mental state) that constitutes my meaning plus." Given that he states no other requirement on an "account of what fact it is (about my mental state) that constitutes my meaning plus," we can infer that the justificatory role of meaning is the primary topic of the skeptical argument. Elsewhere he indicates that it is this justificatory role that he has in mind when he speaks of meaning as normative. For example, in the paragraph immediately following the passage about the "normative" relationship between use and meaning that was our focus in section 1, Kripke summarizes the thrust of that passage thusly: "Precisely the fact that our answer to the question of which function I meant is *justificatory* of my present response is ignored in the dispositional account and leads to all its difficulties" (37, his emphasis).

According to the evaluative interpretation, Kripke demands of an account of meaning that it provide for the capacity of an expression's meaning to determine uses of that expression as correct or incorrect. Adherents to that interpretation presumably suppose that the justification requirement is just another way of formulating the same demand. And indeed, that "125" is the correct answer to the question "What is 68+57?" can, in certain contexts, be all that one means in saying that this answer is justified. In general, if we are engaging in a kind of activity that essentially involves certain standards of performance—doing addition, dancing the Charleston, using a language—then we might assert that a given response or performance is "justified" as a way of expressing our judgment that the response or performance accords with the relevant standards.

However, a closer look at Kripke's text reveals that the evaluative interpretation cannot in fact account for the particular significance of the skeptic's demands for "justification." Consider the following passages:

> Ordinarily, I suppose that, in computing '68+57' as I do, I do not simply make an unjustified leap in the dark. I follow directions I previously gave myself that uniquely determine that in this new instance I should say '125'. (10)

> The sceptic argues that when I answered '125' to the problem '68+57', my answer was an unjustified leap in the dark. (15)

> How can I justify my present application of such a rule, when a sceptic could easily interpret it so as to yield any of an indefinite number of other results? It seems that my application of it is an unjustified stab in the dark. I apply the rule blindly. (17)

Here the issue raised by the skeptic is said to concern whether, when an ostensibly mathematically competent person computes what is ostensibly an addition problem, her answer is an "unjustified leap/stab in the dark." Now, suppose her answer was correct, and so justified in the sense of talk of what is "justified" mentioned above. Does it follow that her answer was not a stab in the dark? Certainly not: one can take a stab in the dark and happen to hit on the right answer. It seems obvious, however, that in speaking of an "unjustified stab in the dark," Kripke does not mean to point to a contrast between two kinds of stabs in the dark: those that are justified (in virtue of being correct) and those that are not. Rather, Kripke's characterizing the answer as "unjustified" is meant to go hand in hand with his characterizing it as a "stab in the dark": what makes the answer unjustified just *is* its being a stab (or leap) in the dark. And so it would not cease to be unjustified, in the relevant sense, if it happened to be correct.

It follows that the kind of justification provided for by the evaluative interpretation—according to which the meaning of '+' determines answers as "justified" simply in virtue of determining them as correct or incorrect—is not the sort of justification with which the skeptic, as portrayed in these passages, is concerned. Thus the evaluative interpretation is incorrect. Its interpretation of Kripke's talk of normativity cannot after all make sense of the requirement intended by Kripke when he says that answers to the skeptical argument must identify a fact that will "show how I am justified."

# 4 Rule following, Justification and Rational Explanation

So what does Kripke mean when he requires that a candidate for the fact that constitutes his meaning plus by "+" be such as to "show that he is justified in answering '125' to '68+57'"? We can see what he has in mind by registering some simple points about the idea of rule-following.

Before doing so, I should note that from this point forward, I shall be couching my discussion of the skeptical argument largely in terms of rules as opposed to meanings. Kripke himself moves freely between talk of meanings and talk of rules; he evidently regards the use of language as a rule-following activity, with the relevant rules constituted by the meanings of the linguistic expressions. It is because I doubt that Kripke is right about this, and because I nonetheless see Kripke's skeptic as setting forth an important and interesting puzzle about rule-following as such (regardless of whether the use of meaningful expressions counts as a kind of rule-following), that I will key my subsequent exposition to rules rather than meanings.[11] I shall say a bit more about this at the end of this section.

---

11 Proponents of the evaluative interpretation don't run into this difficulty. Meanings and rules

Start with the undeniable point that following a rule is not just a matter of behaving in accord with the rule (cf., Wittgenstein 1965, 13). If I jot a sequence of numbers down on a page, what I write is no doubt in accord with any number of algebraic rules for the development of a series. But it doesn't follow that I am following all of these rules. I've never given a thought to the vast majority of them; indeed, many would require such complex formulae for their expression that I couldn't understand them if I tried. And even if I were aware that what I was writing was in accord with a particular rule—say, with the rule for calculating the Fibonacci sequence—that by itself would not imply that I was following that rule. I may be doing something wholly unrelated to the rule—perhaps I'm recording business expenses, or just listing my favorite integers—and happen to notice the correspondence.

What more is required if my performance is to count as a case of my following the rule for calculating the Fibonacci sequence? At least the beginning of an answer seems obvious: I am following the rule only if the rule is *my reason* for doing what I do. This is to imply, of course, that there is an explanatory connection between the rule and what I do. But not just any explanatory connection: what is at stake when we speak of a person's reason for doing something is not merely a reason in the thin sense in which anything that explains something counts as a reason for it. If last night's heavy wind explains why the tree in my yard fell over, then the wind was the reason the tree fell over. But it was not the *tree's* reason for falling over—the tree had no reasons. By contrast, if I am following the rule for the Fibonacci sequence, then the rule is *my* reason for proceeding as I do—to put it another way, it is the reason *for* or *upon* which I proceed. Rule-following is an exercise of the human capacity of *rationality*, of the capacity to recognize and act (or form attitudes) for reasons.

Let us call an explanation of an action or attitude that cites a person's reasons for that attitude or action a *rational explanation*. One familiar and plausible thought about the content of rational explanations is this: when we say that a person S's reason for A-ing was B, we imply that S took B to be a reason for her to A, and that this fact about S explains her A-ing.[12] This analysans uses

---

are both undeniably normative in the sense identified by the evaluative view: they both sort performances into correct and incorrect. So there is no particular need to distinguish between them for purposes of engaging the text when it is understood in terms of the evaluative interpretation. What is questionable—and matters, on the interpretation of the skeptical argument I will defend—is whether a user of language *follows* meanings, in the way a rule-follower follows a rule.

**12** For elaborations of this thought, see Grice 2005, 40ff; Darwall 1983, 32ff; and Stroud 1979; among many others.

the word "reason" in what philosophers of action call its "normative" sense: a reason in the normative sense (or 'normative reason,' for short) is a consideration that justifies, or at least counts toward justifying, that which it is a reason for.[13] Here nothing especially freighted or demanding is meant by talk of justification; the same point might be made by saying that a normative reason is a consideration that supports, recommends, or counts in favor of S's A-ing.[14] Putting these points together, if I say that Rachel's reason for moving to Toronto was the fact that her mother lives there, then I am saying that Rachel moved to Toronto because she took something to count in favor of her doing so, namely, that her mother lives there. More generally, the view at which we have arrived is that rational explanations explain actions and attitudes in terms of the subject's conception of what supports or counts in favor of them.

Anyone familiar with the voluminous philosophical literature on rational explanation will know that there are a great many controversies about the view of rational explanation just briefly outlined. Does the idea that acting for a reason entails perceiving a normative reason for what one does unrealistically cast people as hyper-vigilant seekers after the good? What role, if any, does this view leave for desires in the rational explanation of actions? Exactly how does a person's taking B to be a reason for A-ing explain her A-ing: do we have here a case of a belief's causing behavior, or is the explanation rather best understood as non-causal, perhaps even as non-psychological? Is the involvement of normativity in a rational explanation limited to the beliefs about normative reasons that such an explanation ascribes to the subject? Or is there a stronger sense in which rational explanations are normative, suggested perhaps by the Davidsonian thought that one can find such an explanation intelligible only to the extent that one shares, or at least finds reasonable, the beliefs about normative reasons ascribed by the explanation to the subject? When, as we say, S's reason for A-ing is B, is her reason best understood as the fact or proposition that B, as her belief that B, or as her belief that the fact that B counts in favor of her A-ing? And so on.

---

**13** B may count toward justifying S's A-ing without flat-out justifying it if, for example, there are stronger reasons against S's A-ing. I will ignore this irrelevant complication in what follows.
**14** Contra Millar 2004, Chapter 2, who argues for restricting talk of "justifying" actions only to special cases. In other cases, he prefers to say not that a reason for an action "justifies" that action, but that it "recommends" it (59), or that it "represent[s] the action as being favoured in some way" (58). Certainly no one would deny that there are distinctions to be drawn among kinds of reasons for actions. But I would argue that nothing Millar says on this score adequately motivates his fastidiousness about the use of "justification."

Fortunately, we don't need get into any of these issues here. The skeptical argument, as we will see, can be understood as a very general challenge to this conception of rational explanation, at least as that conception manifests itself in characterizations of people as following rules. Understanding this challenge will not require taking a stand on any of these matters.

Let's return to the justification requirement: Kripke's demand that our "account of what fact it is (about my mental state) that constitutes my meaning plus... show how I am justified in giving the answer '125' to '68+57'." As we've noted, one might hear this merely as requiring that our account show how Kripke is *correct* in giving the answer '125' to '68+57.' But we've seen that the reading does not square with Kripke's repeated indications that the issue raised by the skeptic is whether Kripke's answer was an "unjustified stab in the dark." Showing that Kripke's answer was correct is one thing; showing that it was not a stab in the dark is another.

What would it take to show that Kripke's answer was not a stab in the dark? To say that his answer was a stab in the dark is to say that it was a guess. And to say that it was a guess is to say that Kripke had no reason for giving that answer as opposed to another. This suggests that the justification requirement is best construed, in application to this particular case, as the demand that our account reveal Kripke's reason for giving the answer '125.' According to the views of rational explanation and rule-following just put on the table, giving Kripke's reason for his answer will involve portraying his answer as explained by his taking the rule for addition to justify that answer. The justification requirement, as I think we ought to construe it, is the demand that our account of what constitutes Kripke's meaning plus by "+" entitle ourselves to this portrayal of Kripke's performance, in which his answer is explained by the justification he takes the rule to provide for it.[15] What will give the requirement bite is a skeptical argument purporting to show that, despite initial appearances, we cannot after all understand how his answer might be explained in this way.

Support for this interpretation of the requirement does not lie merely in the quotations about stabs and leaps in the dark. Once one knows what to look for, it becomes obvious that throughout Kripke's initial "intuitive" presentation of the skeptical paradox, and at several other places in the book (notably, as we will

---

15 In suggesting that, for Kripke, showing that the rule-follower's justification for proceeding as she does amounts to explaining her performance in terms of the justification she takes herself to have for it, I am trading on a familiar and (in this context) harmless ambiguity in the ordinary use of the word "justification," akin to that between "reason" in the sense of a normative reason and "reason" in the sense of a person's reason for doing something. (Compare: "She told me her justification for leaving, but I told her she had no justification.")

later see, his discussion of anti-reductionism), he is articulating a puzzle targeted at the thought that, in giving his answer to the "+" problem, a would-be adder is following a rule and that, in so doing, he is engaging in a rational performance, a performance based upon a reason. Consider, for example, this passage from the second half of the book:

> Almost all of us hesitatingly produce the answer '125' when asked for the sum of 68 and 57, without any thought to the theoretical possibility that a quus-like rule might have been appropriate! And we do so without justification. Of course, if asked why we said '125', most of us will say that we added 8 and 7 to get 15, that we put down 5 and carried 1 and so on. But then, what will we say if asked why we 'carried' as we do? Might our past intention not have been that 'carry' meant *quarry*; where to 'quarry' is...? The entire point of the sceptical argument is that ultimately we reach a level where we act without any reason in terms of which we can justify our action. We act unhesitatingly but *blindly*. (87, ellipsis in original)

The question with which the skeptical argument is concerned is "why we said '125.'" This is an explanatory question; it asks why we performed a particular action. The import of the skeptical argument, as here represented, is that what we are inclined to say in answer to this question does not have the substance with which we credit it. We think we can explain why we answered '125' by portraying ourselves as following a rule, involving adding and carrying and so forth. This explanation is supposed to show our reason for giving that answer—to show that we gave that answer because we took the stated rule to justify our doing so. But as Kripke sees it, the explanation we give in terms of the rule, despite initial appearances, does not succeed. For it prompts a further question about our reasons for proceeding as we do, which can then be pressed in turn, ad infinitum. The upshot of this regress is that we cannot after all explain our answer in terms of our reasons for it. The only option is to conclude that there was no reason for which we acted as we did. "The entire point" of the skeptical argument is that "ultimately we reach a level where we act without any reason in terms of which we can justify our action." We do not act for a reason; we act "blindly."

The next question for us, obviously, is why exactly a regress is supposed to arise here. But before turning to it, I want to briefly connect some of the dots of the discussion to this point.

First, there is the matter of normativity. The passages I've been discussing, which together link normativity to the justification requirement and the justification requirement to the rational character of rule-following, motivate a third interpretation of Kripke's talk of normativity: to say that the relationship between a rule and its application is normative is to say that when a person follows a rule, the rule provides her reason for proceeding as she does. Despite some infelicitous historical connotations of the word "rationalism," I will call the view that the rule is the rule-follower's reason for proceeding as she does the *rationalist view of rules,* and the claim that Kripke's talk of normativity is intended to express this view the *rationalist interpretation* of such talk.[16] The thrust of this section is that the rationalist interpretation is the right one, at least with respect to one significant strand in the exposition of the skeptical argument. And what makes it sensible to associate the rationalist view with talk of normativity is the internal connection, discussed above, between the idea of the reason for which a person acts and the idea of a normative reason.

Second, there is the matter of the irrealist character of the skeptic's conclusion. On the present interpretation, the immediate conclusion of the skeptical argument is that we cannot make sense of the idea that we follow rules. To put it another way, there is no such thing as rule-following. What the skeptic actually concludes, however, is that there is no such thing as rules. It might seem that there is an illicit inferential leap here: that it is possible for there to be rules despite the fact that the idea that we follow them turns out to be untenable. Perhaps being capable of being followed is not an essential property of rules. I will not argue on the skeptic's behalf against this possibility, although pressing this objection to the skeptical argument seems to me likely to be a singularly unrewarding exercise. If one wants to insist on the possibility of unfollowable rules, we may on the skeptic's behalf revise his conclusion to dismiss only rule-following and not rules as such. That result is devastating enough.

Finally, there is the matter of meaning. Throughout the book, Kripke focuses on the example of the '+' problem. In discussing the problem, he shifts seamlessly between talk of rules and talk of meanings. Now, it is certainly an ordinary thought, a thought that any skeptical engagement with our ordinary understanding of our practices is entitled to view as a component of that understanding, that a person who computes an addition problem is following a rule. It is also an ordinary thought, in this sense, that it is in virtue of the meaning of '+' that the rule for addition is the relevant rule for answering the question, "68

---

**16** One might deny that a rule can be a person's reason for doing or thinking something, on the ground that only proposition-like items can be a person's reasons and that a rule is not proposition-like. (For example, one might think that a rule is best modeled not on an assertion, but on a command: "Step, then kick," "Add two to the previous number.") Given this claim, the rationalist view of rules would need to be reformulated thusly: when a person follows a rule, her reason, at each step, for doing what she does is that doing so at that step accords with the rule. It would make no difference for my purposes if the view was reformulated thusly, but I will stick with the simpler formulation in the text. (Thanks to Jon Ellis and Hannah Ginsborg for raising this issue.)

+57?"—in particular, it is in virtue of the fact, as Kripke would put it, that '+' means plus. But it is quite another matter to hold that the meaning of '+' is *itself* a rule, a rule that we follow in responding to problems posed with that expression. A fortiori, it is quite another matter to hold that the meanings of linguistic expressions in general are sensibly construed as rules that we follow in speaking a language. It seems to me that if one wants to claim that our ordinary understanding of linguistic practices is committed to this thesis, then one must do some work to show that that is so. An adequate assessment of this claim would require engagement with an array of difficult matters, and I won't attempt it here.[17] Suffice it to say that, although we have seen the rationalist view of rules to be plausible, we cannot show the analogous *rationalist view of meaning* to be similarly plausible simply by assimilating, without explanation or defense, meanings to rules.

But my interest is in the skeptic's argument against the possibility of rule-following, and the interest of that argument is not diminished even if we reject the assimilation of meanings to rules. If, for example, the skeptic can show that Kripke is not following a rule when he gives his answer to the '+' problem, that would be a remarkable and disturbing result, whatever the precise implications of this result for meaning. Since I want to stay focused on this issue, I will for purposes of argument grant Kripke his view that the use of meaningful expressions is a species of rule-following.

---

**17** The basic question is whether it is right to think that the meanings of linguistic expressions serve as reasons for which we use those expressions as we do. Certainly, the use of language is a rational activity: we generally have reasons for saying the things we do. But it is consistent with this point to suppose that for a fluent speaker of the language, the only descriptions under which her utterances (or responses to utterances) will be intentional (at least in typical cases), and hence the only descriptions under which she will have reasons for those utterances (or responses), are descriptions that cite the utterances' *content*. On this picture, the question of what Kripke's reason was for answering '125' in response to '68+57?', when interpreted strictly, may not have an answer. The answerable question in this vicinity may rather be what Kripke's reason was for answering 125 when asked what 68+57 is. It would certainly be natural to answer *this* question by citing a rule as Kripke's reason, but the rule will not be a rule for the use of a linguistic expression.

# 5 The Skeptical Regress and the Situatedness of Explanation

What, exactly, is the nature of the regress that the skeptic takes to undermine our rational explanation of Kripke's response to the '+' problem? The line of thought articulated in the passage quoted might be construed as follows. We offer an explanation of Kripke's response by citing a rule as his reason for that response. But this explanation only prompts further questions about Kripke's reasons for giving that response. Answers to those questions are met with further such questions. Eventually, we "reach a level" where Kripke's reasons give out, where there's nothing further to be said about his reasons. This result gives the lie to our original explanation. It shows that Kripke did not after all have a reason for his response; rather, he acted "blindly."

If the skeptical argument is to be worth our time, it must contain premises and inferences not made explicit by this characterization. For to think that the argument, thus characterized, is valid would be to make a fairly uninteresting mistake. Granted, in the face of a claim about a person's reasons for doing or thinking something, it's always possible to formulate a further question about the person's reasons. And granted, if we keep pressing such questions, sooner or later we'll get to one we can't answer and about which we may perhaps be inclined to say that it has no answer. But of course it is true of *explanation in general* that one can always respond to an explanation by raising questions about considerations appealed to or presupposed or implied by that explanation. And of course it's true that if we keep pressing such questions, we'll eventually reach a question we can't answer, and indeed such that we don't have a clear idea of what an answer might be. What we need to ask in any such case is this: is the further question well taken? That is, does the adequacy of the original explanation—its capacity to explain that which it is intended to explain—depend upon our being able to provide, or even on there being in principle, an answer to this question? The mere fact that one can *formulate* the question does not suffice to show that it is well taken in this sense. What the possibility of formulation shows at best is only, as is anyway obvious, that every explanation takes something for granted, that it assumes something that it does not itself explain. That a three-year-old keeps asking, "Why?", no matter what his parent says, does not demonstrate that the explanations proffered to him stand in need of additional content. Rather, it demonstrates that the child does not yet have the knowledge or sensibility to appreciate these explanations, situated as they inevitably are against an assumed background of what Wittgenstein calls "agreement in judgments" (1973 §242).[18]

Consider again the scenario discussed in the previous section. I list 0, 1, 1, 2, 3, 5, 8, 13, etc., on a piece of paper. Suppose you ask a third party why I'm doing that and are told that I'm following the rule for the Fibonacci sequence. On the rationalist view of rules, this characterization of my behavior offers a rational explanation of it: it says that at each step, my reason for listing the number I do is the rule for the Fibonacci sequence. This answer may prompt you to ask further questions, for example, why I'm following the rule for the Fibonacci sequence to begin with. (This question may take a particular shape for you, depending on your view of relevant features of the situation. "Why is he following that rule when I explicitly asked him to calculate the Perrin sequence?" "Why is he sitting there calculating sequences while his wife angrily packs her bags in the next room?") I've noted that the mere possibility of pressing such questions does not show that the original explanation is inadequate pending answers to these questions. Perhaps the original explanation *is* inadequate; the point is that we need a better reason for thinking so than the fact that rational explanation, like all other kinds of explanation, has to start somewhere.

But the questions I just imagined you asking seek explanations that are 'upstream,' as we might put it, of the original explanation of my activity; such explanations would provide insight into the larger interests, considerations, or motivations that prompt my rule-following behavior. More pertinent in the present context is the possibility of seeking explanations that are 'downstream' of the original explanation. The rule for producing the Fibonacci sequence may be quasi-formally characterized thusly: to list the $n^{th}$ number in the sequence, list 0 if n=1 and 1 if n=2; otherwise, list the number that is the sum of the $(n-1)^{th}$ and $(n-2)^{th}$ numbers. Obviously, applying this rule for a given n will require as input the previous two numbers on the list. And so if it is said that I am following the rule for the Fibonacci sequence in listing 4,181 at the twentieth step, a fuller statement of the reason for which I am thereby said to list 4,181 is that

---

**18** Of course, there *is* such a thing as a putative explanation taking too much for granted and so failing to adequately explain. Unfortunately, there is no algorithm for determining whether an explanation does say "enough." Explanations aim to yield understanding, or better, to provide people with the opportunity to understand (an opportunity they may fail to take). Whether a given explanation counts as doing its part to achieve this aim is not something we can determine absent an engagement with the discursive context in which it is, or might be, offered. For a classic discussion of the role of context in determining "explanatory relevance," see Van Fraassen, 1980, Ch. 5. (Note that all subsequent references to Wittgenstein, 1973, will be by section number only.)

it is the rule coupled with the fact that (we may assume) the previous two numbers on the list were 1,597 and 2,584. Now, it's possible to imagine someone asking why I took the rule, coupled with that input, to yield that result. Presumably, my reason for taking this to be so was that the sum of 1,597 and 2,584 is 4,181. But what was my reason for believing that the sum of 1,597 and 2,584 is 4,181? (We could imagine a novice in arithmetic wanting an answer to this question.) Probably there is something to be said here concerning my application of the rule for addition. Sooner or later, however, we will reach an arithmetical belief on my part such that even I would be hard-pressed to reconstruct some further reason for which I hold it—beyond that (as I might say) I remember that it's true. In this sense, my reasons will give out. But so far, this shows nothing at all. Everything turns on whether the further questions one might think to ask here—e. g., "What is your reason for taking it that your remembering this putative fact is a reason to believe it to obtain?"—is well taken. If we see the skeptical argument as appealing only to the abstract possibility of responding to rational explanations with further downstream questions about reasons, then we must conclude that it is entirely devoid of force.

# 6 The guidance conception of understanding

We need, then, to find an interpretation of the skeptical argument that rests on more than this. I think the materials for such an interpretation are present in Kripke's text. But the key premise is not made as clear as one might like, either in its motivation or in its role in the skeptical argument.

What is this premise? Kripke repeatedly associates the justification requirement with a further idea. Indeed, he seems almost to run them together. Consider the following passage from the discussion of dispositionalism:

> So it does seem that a dispositional account misconceives the sceptic's problem—to find a past fact that *justifies* my present response. As a candidate for a 'fact' that determines what I mean, it fails to satisfy the basic condition on such a candidate stressed above on p. 11, that it should *tell* me what I ought to do in each instance. (24)

The skeptic challenges us "to find a past fact that *justifies* my present response." As we have seen, what he challenges is the legitimacy of our picture of Kripke as following a rule, and hence of the rule as providing Kripke's reason for his response. Here that challenge is transformed, without comment, into the condition that we find a fact that will "*tell* me what I ought to do in each instance." Language to similar effect pervades Kripke's exposition. Here are a few examples:

> Normally, when we consider a mathematical rule such as addition, we think of ourselves as *guided* in our application of it in each new instance. (17).

> The 'directions'... that determine what I should do in each instance, must somehow be 'contained' in any candidate for the fact as to what I meant. (11)

> The answer to the sceptic's problem, 'What tells me how I am to apply a given rule in a new case?' must come from something outside any images or 'qualitative' mental states... [Even] if there were a special experience of 'meaning' addition by 'plus', analogous to a headache, it would not have the properties that a state of meaning addition by 'plus' ought to have—it would not tell me what to do in new cases. (43)

> Sometimes when I have contemplated the [skeptical paradox], I have had something of an eerie feeling. Even now as I write, I feel confident that there is something in my mind—the meaning I attach to the 'plus' sign—that *instructs* me what I ought to do in all future cases... But when I concentrate on what is now in my mind, what instructions can be found there? How can I be said to be acting on the basis of these instructions when I act in the future?... To say that there is a general rule in my mind that tells me how to add in the future is only to throw the problem back on to other rules that also seem to be given only in terms of finitely many cases. What can there be in my mind that I make use of when I act in the future? It seems the entire idea of meaning vanishes into thin air. (21–2).

If I am to follow a rule, something must "instruct" me how to go on. It must "guide" me. It must provide "directions." It must "tell me how I am to apply [the] rule in new cases." And what is the item that is to guide or instruct me? It is "something in my mind." Elsewhere, Kripke characterizes it as "my mental state" (11). In particular, it is his "state" of "meaning addition by '+'" (51). In a similar vein, it is his "grasp" of the "rule" (7), or his "understanding" (48). Given that the skeptical argument applies to rule-following in general, and given that I do not wish to get sidetracked by the question of whether linguistic meanings are sensibly thought of as rules that we follow, I will tend to favor talk of understanding and grasping rules rather than states of meaning. I will say, then, that what is supposed to guide a rule-follower, for Kripke, is the mental state that constitutes her grasp or understanding of the rule. For Kripke, one species of this state is the state of meaning something by a linguistic expression.

The common kernel expressed by these various locutions is the idea that, when a person follows a rule (at least as we "normally" think of this activity— i.e., in advance of acquaintance with the skeptical argument), there is something in her mind that she consults, something that she refers to, at each step. This item communicates information to her about how to proceed, and she so proceeds. Imagine a person navigating a hedge maze. In her pocket is a guide—perhaps a map, perhaps a set of instructions. At each intersection she takes the guide out of her pocket, consults it, and proceeds on the basis of the information thus gleaned. On the vision of rule-following suggested by Kripke's formulations, rule-following is just like this, with the difference that the rule-follower's guide is in her mind rather than in her pocket. It is in fact the *mental item* that constitutes her grasp, her understanding of the rule.

I shall call this idea *the guidance conception of understanding*, though this label comes with two caveats. First, the word "conception" can have connotations of determinacy and clarity that are out of place here. What I am calling the guidance conception of understanding is not a well thought-out philosophical theory of anything; it is rather a picture our grip upon which is largely intuitive and analogical. Indeed, as we shall see, the main point of the skeptical argument is that we will run into insoluble difficulties when we try to think through the conception more carefully. The second caveat is that we sometimes speak of one item's "guiding" another and mean only that the first item influences the second, with no implication that this influence was mediated by any uptake or comprehension on the part of the item being guided. Thus we speak, for example, of guiding a ship into harbor. But the relation between subject and understanding posited in the guidance conception of understanding is not one in which a person is an uncomprehending instrument of his understanding, as a ship is of its navigator, but rather one in which the subject acquires information about how to proceed, information upon which she then acts. What is at stake is not the guidance of brute causal influence, but what we might call *informed* guidance. Kripke's talk of instruction, direction, showing, and telling all avoid this ambiguity. But I prefer talk of guidance for its greater generality, and so will stick with that term.

Why should we be attracted to the guidance conception, as Kripke implies that we are? Kripke seems to suggest that the phenomenology of rule-following favors the conception: even after being convinced by the skeptical argument, he can't help but "feel confident" that there's something in his mind instructing him how to go on. Now, undoubtedly, there are occasions of rule-following when one will think of oneself as guided or directed by something in one's mind. For example, if you are trying to follow a rule whose application is complex and which you have not fully got the hang of, you may bring to mind instructions, images, and so on that were used as aids in your training. You may then find it natural to say that these images or instructions guide or direct your application, or that they tell you how to proceed. But in other cases, the conception is less obviously apt. For example, if you are following a rule that is second nature to you, or one whose application is exceedingly straightforward (imagine a rule for producing a simple numerical sequence), will you have any sense at all that there is something in your mind that actively instructs or directs you in how to go on? At the very least, the phenomenology is much less clear-cut in such cases.

Is there a motivation for the guidance conception other than the uncompelling appeal to phenomenology? Kripke does not tell us. But I think it's possible to get at least some sense of why the conception has such allure for Kripke by thinking through a natural reaction to remarks by Wittgenstein in the part of the *Philosophical Investigations* that prompt Kripke's own skeptical reflections.

Wittgenstein is prone to a certain kind of characterization of what goes on when a person follows a rule. He speaks, for example, of a rule-follower as doing what comes naturally (§185), as just reacting as he was trained (§198), and as applying the rule as a matter of course (§238). The thrust of these characterizations, and others like them, is that in typical cases, a rule follower is merely responding to the circumstances, without reflection or deliberation, in whatever way he has been trained or habituated. Now, I think it's easy to get the sense that Wittgenstein's characterizations of an ostensible rule-follower are in fact incompatible with viewing him as genuinely following a rule. What the characterizations might seem to conflict with in particular is the very thing I have been harping on here—the rational character of rule-following, the fact that a rule-follower proceeds as she does because she takes the rule to provide a reason for doing so. It might seem that there is a failure of fit between the idea that a person is acting in light of her conception of what the rule gives her reason to do and the idea that, in proceeding as she does, she is just doing what comes naturally to her in light of her training. Wittgenstein himself is happy to encapsulate his vision of what goes on in rule-following with the remark that we "apply the rule *blindly*" (§219). But if our application of the rule is truly "blind," one might want to say, then we are not really following the rule after all. For rule-following is not blind; it is informed by a sense of what, at each step, the rule gives us reason to do.

This worry about Wittgenstein's characterizations of putative instances of rule-following is nicely articulated by Thomas Nagel (1996). Nagel is troubled by these characterizations, which he calls Wittgenstein's "facial descriptions of our practices" (1996, 52). To Nagel, the facial descriptions "suggest that the final and correct conception of what I am doing when I add, for example, is that I am simply producing responses which are natural to me, which I cannot help giving in the circumstances (including the circumstances of my having been taught in a certain way)" (1996, 48). So viewed, the practices "lose their meaning"; they appear as mere "impotent rituals" (1996, 51, 53). And we cannot square this conception of our behavior with how our performances look to us from the "inside," a vantage point from which they are seen as flowing from the thoughts and beliefs that constitute our understanding of what the relevant rules dictate.

Suppose we share Nagel's intuitive sense of the incompatibility of Wittgenstein's "facial descriptions" of behavior with conceiving that behavior as rule-following behavior. Can we fill out this intuition further? What, exactly, is the nature of the incompatibility? A natural first thought here is that acting for a reason is, or involves, a mental process, the presence of which gives the lie to the facial descriptions. But this thought doesn't take us very far: the bare notion of a mental process is too indefinite to do any real work here.[19] We need to specify a particular kind of mental process, one whose incompatibility with the descriptions at issue is evident. Nor can we do much with the most obvious candidate, and cast the process in question as one of thinking, in the sense of active deliberation or reflection. Granted, a person who proceeds on the basis of careful deliberation is not aptly described as, say, applying the rule as a matter of course or as just reacting as she was trained. The problem is that many cases of rule-following (including the kinds of cases upon which Wittgenstein tends to focus) obviously do not involve a process of thinking in the relevant sense. It would seriously over-intellectualize matters to insist that, in following a simple and familiar rule, a competent adult must engage in anything akin to deliberation or reflection.[20]

But even in simple cases, it might appear that we can still conceive the behavior in question as *guided* by the rule-follower's understanding of the rule. Being guided, being instructed or shown or told how to proceed, needn't involve any deliberation or reflection on one's part: if someone or something tells me, "Write down '5' now," I can grasp that instruction, and follow suit, without any intervening deliberation at all. And the proposed mental process meets our other desideratum as well: viewing a person as being guided in her performance comports very poorly with viewing that person as just doing what comes naturally, or just reacting as she was trained. Indeed, to do what comes naturally is precisely *not* to rely on any directions, instructions, or other form of guidance. When you do what comes naturally, you don't consult anyone or anything on what to do; you just do it.

The appeal of the guidance conception for Kripke, I propose, is a function of its apparent capacity to underwrite the intuition articulated by Nagel. It seems to

---

**19** The later Wittgenstein is often read as denying that understanding, and similar phenomena, are mental states or processes. But it seriously misreads his intentions to interpret him as ever flatly giving out such a denial. It's essential in interpreting a remark such as, "Try not to think of understanding as a 'mental process' at all.—For *that* is the expression which confuses you" (§154), to ask to whom he is offering this advice and why.

**20** Compare Wittgenstein 1978, §§VII–60: "One follows the rule *mechanically*. Hence one compares it with a mechanism. 'Mechanical'—that means: without thinking. But *entirely* without thinking? Without *reflecting*."

give flesh to the thought that following a rule, as a species of rational activity, must involve a mental process that is not in play when a creature just reacts to the circumstances in whatever way comes naturally to it.

There is room for further examination of why this thought can so easily get a grip on the philosophical imagination. But before we return to this matter in section 9, I want to consider how incorporating the guidance conception as premise of the skeptical argument enables us to make satisfying sense of the skeptical charge of regress and the rejection of anti-reductionism.

# 7 The Skeptical Regress, Properly Construed

The problem for the guidance conception of understanding flows from an exceedingly simple point: if an item is to successfully tell you something, or direct you or instruct you in some particular way, then you must understand what it tells you, or what it directs or instructs you to do. Recall the map or set of directions in the pocket of the person navigating the hedge maze: that map or set of directions obviously cannot show the person the way through the maze if she does not understand it as showing her anything. And of course the point is perfectly general. To conceive an item as showing or telling a person something, or as instructing or directing her in some way, is to conceive that item as communicating something—which is to say, some content—to her. And successful communication with a person requires two contributions, one from the communicator, and one from the communicatee. The contribution from the former is to express or otherwise make available the relevant content. And the contribution from the latter is to take that content in—to grasp, comprehend, understand it.[21]

But if the point is perfectly general, then it applies in particular to items in the mind that purport to guide or direct one. And so if Kripke's grasp of the rule for calculating "'+' consists in the presence of, as he puts it, "something in my mind... that *instructs* me what I ought to do in all future cases," then we must posit a further state of understanding on the part of Kripke: namely, his understanding of the instruction provided by the item in the mind that constitutes his grasp of the '+' rule. The question we now face is this: how are we to construe the role of this second-order state of understanding in helping to explain Kripke's subsequent performances? More specifically, if we are to conceive of the first-order understanding of the rule on the model of an item that instructs the

---

**21** Obviously, the notion of communication I'm here appealing to is not the notion treated in information theory à la Shannon and Dretske.

rule-follower in how to proceed, are we to conceive the second-order understanding in the same way?

Neither answer is satisfactory. If the answer is no, then we are left with, as Kripke and Wittgenstein would put it, a "level" at which his performance is "blind," and this conflicts with the original motivation for the guidance conception. Let's switch for a moment to the example of my following the rule for producing the Fibonacci sequence. The aim of the guidance conception is to ward off a description of a rule-follower like me as applying a rule "blindly." It seeks to do so by ruling out the possibility that in writing each number that I do, I am simply doing what comes naturally to me, as a result of my training, in those circumstances—such circumstances including, in this case, the numbers I've previously written down. So we posit something in my mind that instructs me what number to write down at each step. If the presence of this item is to be of any use to me, I must understand the instruction it provides. But if my understanding of the instruction does not itself consist of, or involve, an item in my mind that guides me in applying the instruction, then we have not after all ruled out the possibility that I am merely reacting as I was trained to do in the circumstances. All we've done is introduce a further circumstance, namely, the presence of the item in my mind that constitutes my understanding of the rule. Nothing we've said so far blocks the following thought: that in writing each number that I do, I'm simply doing what comes naturally to me given the combined presence of those numbers on the page and that item in my mind. So the original motivation for the guidance conception is left unsatisfied.

On the other hand, if the answer is yes, then we are embarked on a regress. Suppose my understanding of the instruction provided by the item that constitutes my understanding of the Fibonacci rule is itself constituted by an item that instructs me how to proceed. If it is to instruct me, I must understand the instruction it provides. We will need then to posit a third-order state of understanding on my part: an understanding of the instruction provided by the mental item that constitutes my understanding of the instruction provided by the mental item that constitutes my understanding of the Fibonacci rule. If we allow this regress to begin, then, as Kripke's skeptic sees, it cannot be stopped. At each stage of the regress, we come to an item that is supposed to instruct me how to apply the preceding item, but is unable to do so unless a further item has instructed me how to apply it. The result is an endless chain of 'dead' items, each awaiting a breath of 'life' from the next item down the line, and so none receiving any.[22]

---

22 For the life/death imagery, see Wittgenstein 1965).

Arguments of this general thrust, more or less compacted in presentation, occur in several places in *Philosophical Investigations*. To take an occurrence that is less frequently discussed than others, consider the following:

> How is he to know what colour he is to pick out when he hears "red"?—Quite simple: he is to take the colour whose image occurs to him when he hears the word.—But how is he to know which colour it is 'whose image occurs to him'? Is a further criterion needed for that? (§239)

Think of a game in which one of the rules is to identify a sample of red from among an array of color samples when "red" is uttered. Wittgenstein's interlocutor suggests that the participant's grasp of this rule might be partly constituted by an association between that word and an image of a color in his mind. It would be a mistake to take the point of Wittgenstein's response to be that such an association could not possibly be of use in following the rule. Certainly such an insistence would be hard to swallow. Who is Wittgenstein to say what might or might not be of use to a person in following a rule? "Red" is perhaps not a good example, as most of us apply that word as a matter of course. But imagine a native English speaker who's previously acquired little of its extensive vocabulary for speaking of shades (I am such a speaker) and is now being trained, perhaps preparatory to working as a salesperson in a clothing store, in the use of words like "vermilion," "fuchsia," and "cerise." Here it's easy to imagine that his application of those words might be mediated, at least initially, by his calling to mind appropriate images—perhaps memories of samples he's been shown.

There is no reason to take Wittgenstein to deny this possibility. What he points out is simply that a mental image cannot show the person that he is to pick out a certain color unless he understands it as showing him that. If, then, the interlocutor's motivation for positing the image was a worry, however inchoate, to the effect that a person *must* have something in his mind that shows him how to apply the rule if he is to count as genuinely following the rule, we are faced with a dilemma. For what shows him how to apply the image that is to show him how to apply the rule? If we posit a further "criterion," regress threatens. If, on the other hand, we deny that anything shows him how to apply the image, the question presses of whether we have arrived at a picture of what goes on when a person applies a rule that manages to quell the interlocutor's original worry or merely defers it.

Kripke's own account of the skeptical regress also depends upon the guidance conception, as we can see if we attempt first to understand what he says in motivating the regress without appealing to the conception. Consider Kripke's treatment of the regress in the initial "intuitive" exposition of the skeptical paradox. The crucial step occurs after Kripke has noted that his past answers to computational problems expressed using "+" are consistent with "+" standing for a function other than addition, such as 'quaddition,' in which eventuality "68+57" would denote 5. (This possibility is consistent with Kripke's past answers because, by supposition, Kripke has never previously been confronted with the problem "68+57.") Kripke anticipates that the reader will protest that this point on its own does not undermine Kripke's claim that he meant *plus* by "+"in the past. For what fixed Kripke's past meaning is surely not just his finite set of answers to problems couched in terms of "+" or "plus," but the general rule he employed for solving such problems. Kripke's imagined interlocutor suggests that the rule can be explained as follows: "Suppose we wish to add *x* and *y*. Take a huge bunch of marbles. First count out *x* marbles in one heap. Then count out *y* marbles in another. Put the two heaps together and count out the number of marbles in the union thus formed" (15).

Kripke is unimpressed with this protest. His response begins this way:

> Despite the initial plausibility of this objection, the sceptic's response is all too obvious. True if 'count', as I used the word in the past, referred to the act of counting... then 'plus' must have stood for addition. But I applied 'count', like 'plus', to only finitely many cases. Thus the sceptic can question my present interpretation of my past usage of 'count' as he did with 'plus'. In particular, he can claim that by 'count' I formerly meant *quount*... (16)

For all I've said so far, this response is a non-sequitur. The response challenges an assumption about Kripke's past use of the word "count." But Kripke's interlocutor, as I just presented him, said nothing about Kripke's past use of that word. His proposal was limited to Kripke's past use of "+" (and "plus"): he suggested that Kripke had previously understood a certain rule to govern the use of that expression. It is true that in stating this rule, the interlocutor himself used the word "count." But the meanings of the interlocutor's expressions are not now in question. Indeed, it is an explicit ground rule of the skeptical argument that we—those formulating and discussing the paradox—can take for granted that we know what our own words mean: "the sceptic, provisionally, is not questioning my *present* use of the word 'plus'... Not only does he agree with me on this, he conducts the entire debate with me in my language as I *presently* use it" (12).[23]

---

23 The point of couching the skeptical puzzle in this way, as a challenge about past use, is to

What's going on here? The answer is that Kripke understands the interlocutor not only as suggesting a rule that Kripke followed in solving '+' problems, but as offering a particular conception of what his grasp of the rule consisted in. Kripke states the general idea this way: "I learned—and internalized instructions for—a *rule* which determines how addition is to be continued" (15). The parenthetical bit is essential: the point of the interlocutor's suggestion, as Kripke interprets it, is not to restate the basic thought that Kripke is following a rule in responding to the '+' problem, but to identify the item in Kripke's mind that instructs him how to apply the rule. And so when the interlocutor proposes a statement of the rule Kripke previously followed, he is understood as suggesting that Kripke "explicitly gave [himself]" this "set of directions"—that they are "engraved on [his] mind as on a slate" (15). With the interlocutor's proposal thus understood, Kripke's rejoinder is well-taken. If the set of directions Kripke previously gave himself is to be of any use in helping him follow the rule, he must understand it. But in what does his understanding of those directions consist? If it does not consist in any mental item that shows him how to understand—how to apply—the directions, then the interlocutor's proposal does not in the end insulate Kripke from the charge that he follows the rule "blindly." But if we hold that his understanding of the directions does consist in such an item, all the previous difficulties recur.

# 8 Anti-Reductionism and Logical Compulsion

We're at last in a position to return to the matter we left in section 2: Kripke's puzzlingly brusque rejection of the view that mental states and occurrences are irreducible. The rejection becomes explicable when we register two points. First, the treatment of anti-reductionism, like the initial exposition of the skeptical paradox, centers not around the evaluative view of meaning, as commentators have assumed, but around the rationalist view of meaning—the view, recall, that meanings, à la rules, serve as reasons for our using meaningful expressions as we do. Second, and relatedly, Kripke's understanding of rule-following is controlled by his subscription to the guidance conception. Kripke recognizes, as we've seen, that this conception of rule-following yields a regress. But he remains committed to the conditional premise that if there were such a thing as rule-following, it would have to conform to the model of the guidance concep-

---

avoid worries about "whether the discussion is taking place 'both inside and outside language'" (12).

tion. The upshot is that Kripke can make nothing of the appeal to the irreducibility of the mental but an attempt to protect the possibility of rule-following, conceived in terms of the guidance conception, by insisting that any worries about it are improper because states of understanding and meaning are *sui generis* and hence not subject to examination. It is no wonder that Kripke finds this maneuver uncompelling.

But there is in fact a more specific point to be made about Kripke's response to anti-reductionism: in an abbreviated fashion, it recapitulates an important element of Wittgenstein's treatment of rule-following. That element is Wittgenstein's criticism of the idea of "logical compulsion."

When we are in the grip of the guidance conception, it can be tempting to think that mental items are special, in precisely the way that is needed to block the regress. As we noted, there are two contributions to a scene of guidance or instruction: one from the instructor and one from the instructed. The contribution of the former is to provide or make available the instructing content; the contribution of the latter is to understand it. But perhaps the perception that this second contribution is always required stems from modeling the guidance provided by one's understanding too closely on the guidance provided by material things in the outside world. The mental sphere is unique in a great many ways, after all. Suppose in particular that we can make out the following thought: that the mental item you consult when you follow a rule differs from maps, written directions, stop signs, and other physical objects in that its power to communicate information to you is not dependent on your hitting upon the right understanding of what it expresses. We might put the thought this way: the mental item provides for its own understanding. The proper understanding of the direction it provides is built into the item itself. Hence this understanding is not something *you* must contribute to the transaction: it is part of the package with which the item presents you.

Here, it might seem, we have the key for preventing the regress. The regress is set in motion by the fact that the mental item constituting your understanding of a rule, if it is to guide you, must itself be understood. The question arises: what constitutes your understanding of that mental item? The structure then replicates ad infinitum. But if the understanding of what the mental item tells you is somehow built into the item itself, so that the sheer presence of the item in the mind guarantees proper understanding, then the question of what constitutes your understanding of that item has already been answered: it consists in the presence of the original item. And so, it might seem, the regress cannot get started.

Such an item would be one that it is logically impossible for you to understand in any but one way. It is in this context that we can situate Wittgenstein's invocation of "a picture, or something like a picture, that forces its application on us," and the resultant imagined distinction between "psychological" and "logical" compulsion (PI §140). As things stand, you cannot help but understand a stop sign as telling you to stop. Even so, the compulsion at work here is only 'psychological': it is a contingent feature of your psychological makeup. Had you been trained differently, you might now be compelled to understand the stop sign as telling you something else entirely. What we are now envisioning, by contrast, is a compulsion of a different order. In the case of the picture that forces its application upon you, the question of how you are disposed to understand the picture does not so much as arise, for the proper understanding of the picture is, as it were, part of the picture itself. We can no more isolate something about which the question of understanding might arise than we can isolate, say, a triangle from its angles.[24]

It's hard to fill out this idea more fully, because however tempting it may be —and for Wittgenstein, I believe, it belongs among a set of ideas about the nature of mental processes that we can find well-nigh irresistible—it falls apart under scrutiny. There is simply no making sense of the idea of an item, mental or otherwise, that 'logically' forces us to understand it in a particular way. It is perhaps enough just to be fully self-conscious about what it is we are expecting from the envisioned mental items to realize that it cannot be forthcoming. An item cannot tell a person something unless she understands it to tell her that, and there is no getting around the fact that her understanding it this way is something she must bring to the table, not something that the item can itself provide for. No matter what we place before a person, no matter how rich or extensive the materials we display, there can be no guarantee that the person will take those materials to say or otherwise convey what we intend, or indeed to convey anything at all. How could it be otherwise? In the end, the person either understands—or she does not. Of course, the mental item guiding the subject's performance is not conceived as something that we onlookers exhibit to her; it is something she has in her mind. But nothing can circumvent the dependence

---

24 It's important not to run together this idea with the view that contentful mental states have their contents essentially or intrinsically. On that view, insofar as a belief that 68+57=125 can be said to be an "item in the mind" of the person who has it, it is an item identified and individuated by its being a belief with that very content. But the idea we are now considering is that of a mental item *whose conveying or communicating to you a specific content* is an essential property of it. To the extent that we construe mental states as intrinsically contentful entities— and so as not aptly conceived on analogy to signs, images or linguistic expressions—we will be disinclined to construe our relationship to them in terms of communication or guidance to begin with. (This last point warrants elaboration, which I cannot here provide.)

of guidance upon a person's uptake, and so merely stipulating that the guiding materials are mental rather than physical cannot help.

It is true that we have difficulty conceiving how the understanding of some kinds of objects might differ from our own. While the shape of, say, a stop sign may be arbitrary, the ways in which we understand items such as color samples and images seem to us to be based on relationships of similarity and resemblance for which there are no real alternatives. Philosophers are fond of pointing out that everything is similar to everything else in some respect or other, but we may find it hard to take seriously the possibility of creatures who find it natural, say, to use a bit of green paper as a representation of Goodman's grue rather than of green. And that is a perfectly reasonable attitude. Beings whose standards of salience and similarity were such that they understood pictures and samples in ways that differed radically from our own would strike us as extremely, perhaps incomprehensibly, peculiar. We get into trouble, however, if we allow this attitude to generate the sense that the guidance yielded us by color samples, images, or diagrams somehow arises wholly out of the existence of the relevant similarities. Even in these cases, there can be no guidance unless *we* understand the items in such a way as to yield that guidance, and the items themselves cannot force us to do that. Our inability to imagine alternative understandings shows only how strong the 'psychological compulsion' is here (if it pleases us to put it this way); it cannot vindicate the confused idea of 'logical compulsion.'

Let's return to Kripke. Since Kripke takes the guidance conception for granted, he assumes that the anti-reductionist does too. But the anti-reductionist also believes that the skeptical argument can be defused simply by casting our grasp of a rule as a *sui generis* mental state. At the core of the skeptical argument is, of course, the regress. From Kripke's perspective, then, the anti-reductionist is committed to all of the following propositions: that a rule-follower's grasp of a rule consists in an item in his mind that tells him how to proceed, that we needn't worry that this picture generates a regress, and that the reason we needn't worry is that the mental item in question has a *sui generis* character. As we have just seen, Wittgenstein discusses a view that precisely encompasses these three propositions, and that is the view that a rule-follower's grasp of a rule consists in an item in his mind that guides his performances by 'logically compelling' him to understand it in a particular way. Given all this, and given that Kripke understands his work as an elaboration of Wittgenstein's rule-following remarks, it would be unsurprising if Kripke should take the anti-reductionist proposal to be tantamount to the idea that states of meaning and understanding logically compel our understanding of them.

And indeed he does. He presses his charge of mystery-mongering against the anti-reductionist thusly: "Can we conceive of a finite state which *could* not be interpreted in a quus-like way? How could that be? The proposal I am now considering brushes such questions under the rug, since the nature of the supposed 'state' is left mysterious" (52–3). To speak of a state that could not but be interpreted in one way is to speak of an item that logically compels a particular understanding of it. Kripke is right to doubt the possibility of such an item. As soon as we think of our relationship to an item as one of our interpreting or understanding it—as we do when we think of the item as directing, guiding, or instructing us—we cannot avoid the fact that the way in which we understand that item is a contingent fact about us.

To the extent that commentators pick up on Kripke's protest about the idea of a state that could only be interpreted in one way, they fail to grasp its significance. Boghossian's reaction to the protest is a good example. He writes, "[The] objection to the anti-reductionist suggestion is that it is utterly mysterious how there could be a finite state, realized in a finite mind, that nevertheless contains information about the correct applicability of a sign in literally no end of distinct situations. But… this amounts merely to insisting that we find the idea of a contentful state problematic, without adducing any independent reason why we should" (1989, 542). Boghossian here equates the idea of a contentful state with the idea of a "state" that "contains information about the correct applicability of the sign." Perhaps, for Boghossian, talk of "containing information" *is* just a fanciful way of talking about possession of content, in which case his gloss on Kripke's objection overlooks the crucial structuring role played by the guidance conception. On the other hand, if we take Boghossian's talk of "containing information" literally, then the question we should ask is: to whom, or what, is the information "contained" in the "state" to be conveyed? If it is to be conveyed to the rule-follower, in order to guide her application of the rule, then she must grasp that information. To suppose that Kripke has no "independent reason" for finding this proposal problematic is to entirely miss the strand of the skeptical argument that has been the focus of this paper.

# 9 The Appeal to Practice

The skeptical argument occupies, of course, only half of Kripke's book. The second half is given over to the exposition of a "skeptical solution" to the "paradox"—i.e., an account of the significance of our ordinary talk about meaning that is consistent with the conclusion of the skeptical argument, and hence does not presuppose any facts about what we mean by our words. The key ideas seem to be, first, that a satisfactory understanding of the role of semantic talk in our lives can be provided by describing the conditions under which members of our linguistic community are licensed by that community to utter such sentences as, e.g., "Kripke means plus by 'plus'" and "Kripke's answer to '68 plus 57' was incorrect," and second, that we can adequately describe these conditions without supposing that there is any fact of the matter about what Kripke, or anyone else, means by the expressions they use.[25]

In its reliance on the communal setting of our utterances, Kripke takes his skeptical solution to be in the spirit of Wittgenstein's own frequent appeals to customs and practices. But as many commentators have pointed out, it's quite a stretch to read Wittgenstein as endorsing a skeptical solution, in Kripke's sense, to a puzzle about meaning or rule-following. It's true that, in the famous passage in §201, Wittgenstein speaks of a "paradox" about rule-following and that he takes one upshot of reflection on this paradox to be that "'obeying a rule' is a practice" (§202). But Wittgenstein's attitude to the putative paradox is manifestly not that the perception of a paradox is correct and that we must learn to live with the consequences, but rather that the perception is predicated on a "misunderstanding" (§201). Wittgenstein evidently believes that thinking of rule-following in terms of customs and practices can help us to dissolve the perception of paradox, not to make peace with it.

Given the argument for the skeptical conclusion as I have interpreted it here, how can the appeal to customs and practices work to counter it? The argument turns on the soundness of the intuition that there is an incompatibility between conceiving a person as just reacting to the circumstances in the way she was trained and conceiving her as following a rule, with its attendant implication that the rule is her reason for going on as she does. It is this intuition that prompts the guidance conception. And it is precisely this intuition, I believe, that Wittgenstein, in reminding us of the possibility of conceiving our rule-following behavior in terms of customs and practices, means to undercut.

Wittgenstein's basic point is encapsulated in the following remark: "What, in a complicated surrounding, we call 'following a rule' we should certainly not call that if it stood in isolation" (Wittgenstein 1978, §§VI–34). Abstracted from the complicated surroundings in which it takes place, your doing what comes naturally in response to my order, "Add two," is not readily conceived of as your following a rule. But seen in the context of these surroundings, which is how we see it in everyday life, no such difficulty arises. With that context in view, we can simply take in stride that you react to my order in the way that comes naturally to you in light of your training. Registering that fact will have no tendency, in and of itself, to undermine our sense of the rational char-

---

**25** Both of these ideas seem to me quite wrong, but that is not my concern here.

acter of what you do. Your doing what comes naturally, in these circumstances, given these surroundings, is something we all recognize as a case of following a rule, hence of rational activity.

For Wittgenstein, the relevant "complicated surroundings" encompass a great deal. They include no less than the "whole hurly-burly" of human activity, in all its variegation, richness, and complexity:

> How could human behavior be described? Surely only by sketching the actions of a variety of humans, as they are all mixed up together. What determines our judgment, our concepts and reactions, is not what one man is doing now, an individual action, but the whole hurly-burly of human actions, the background against which we see any action. (Wittgenstein 19701970, §567)

In discussing rule-following and related phenomena, Wittgenstein is especially prone to characterize this background of human activity in terms of practices, customs, institutions, and uses. There is no indication that he invests this talk with any special or technical meaning. Indeed, it would be counterproductive for him to do so, for he wants it to be an uncontroversial claim that each of us participates in numerous customs, practices, and institutions. As ordinarily used, these terms speak of common activities—of things people typically or regularly do. And they often suggest an element of conventionality: walking is not, as such, naturally described as a custom, but walking on the right side of a sidewalk or hallway is (at least in the United States). The conventional element of customs and practices is in turn often characterizable in terms of rules.

We find a relatively straightforward illustration of what Wittgenstein aims to accomplish with his appeal to customs and practices in the following much-discussed passage:

> "But how can a rule show me what I have to do at *this* point? Whatever I do is, on some interpretation, in accord with the rule."—That is not what we ought to say, but rather: any interpretation still hangs in the air along with what it interprets, and cannot give it any support. Interpretations by themselves do not determine meaning.
>
> "Then can whatever I do be brought into accord with the rule?"—Let me ask this: what has the expression of a rule—say a sign-post—got to do with my actions? What sort of connection is there here?—Well, perhaps this one: I have been trained to react to this sign in a particular way, and now I do so react to it.
>
> "But that is only to give a causal connection; to tell how it has come about that we now go by the sign-post; not what this going-by-the-sign really consists in." On the contrary; I have further indicated that a person goes by a sign-post only in so far as there exists a regular use of sign-posts, a custom. (§198)[26]

---

26 Following the practice of McDowell (1998), I have put quotes around the first sentence of the

The first paragraph raises the regress problem for the guidance conception, and extracts the following moral: we must reject the idea that the relationship between the expression of a rule and what I do in response to it is mediated by a mental item (an "interpretation") guiding my performance ("showing me what I have to do"). In the wake of this rejection, Wittgenstein proposes an alternative account of the relationship: I was trained to react in a certain way when confronted with the expression of a rule, and that is how I now react. But the interlocutor is baffled by this suggestion. The point of the guidance conception is to underwrite the thought that what is going on here is precisely a case of *going by* a sign—which is to say, a case of *following* a rule—rather than a brute, non-rational reaction. The contrasting picture of the relationship between expression and action drawn by Wittgenstein, which I am portrayed as just reacting as I was trained, seems to fail on this score. But Wittgenstein takes this response to miss his point. When we train a child to react in a certain way to, say, a walk sign, we introduce the child to a going practice in the use of those signs. This is a practice of *going by* or *following* the sign: of walking when the sign says "walk'" and of refraining from walking when it says "don't walk." To recognize that a person has been initiated into our practice in the use of walk signs is thereby to recognize that what that person does now when confronted by such a sign counts as a case of her going by the sign, and so of her following a rule, and so of her acting for a reason. In citing our training, Wittgenstein seeks to remind us that we have been initiated into such practices, practices of following rules.

As this example illustrates, practices and customs are especially useful for Wittgenstein's purposes because they have two salient features: (1) once a person has been successfully trained into a given practice, it will often come naturally to her to do whatever conforms to the practice on the appropriate occasions—it will simply be a matter of her reacting as she was trained; and (2) many practices are rule-following practices, practices of following or going by particular rules, signs, and the like. These are features of practices that everyone takes for granted. But taken at face value, they entail that it is a mistake to think that doing what comes naturally and following a rule cannot comport. For most adults, participation in the practice of walking when the sign says "walk" and waiting when it says "don't walk" does not require any deliberation, reflection, or guidance; one just reacts in the pertinent situation as one was trained. But those who participate in this practice are following a particular rule; it just *is* a practice of fol-

---

final paragraph to indicate the interlocutor's voice. My treatment of this passage is strongly influenced by McDowell's on a more substantive level as well.

lowing rules. We might put Wittgenstein's suggested therapy this way: if you find yourself doubting that any given tract of behavior can satisfy both the description "following a rule" and the description "doing what comes naturally," then remind yourself that the behavior may well satisfy a third description, namely, that by which we characterize some specific rule-following practice.

I suggested that the characteristic of rule-following that makes these descriptions seem incompatible is that it is a species of rational activity, in which the rule-follower's performance is explained, at each step, by the justification she takes the rule to provide. In §198 and similar passages, Wittgenstein points us toward the recognition that this perception of incompatibility is not justified by our ordinary thought and discourse, by the ways in which think and talk about relevant phenomena in everyday life. For on the one hand, we do ordinarily conceive rule-following, even of simple rules, as a form of rational activity. That is to say, on appropriate occasions we cite traffic rules, arithmetical rules, and so on, as people's reasons for doing what they do. At the same time, we are perfectly aware that competent participants in familiar rule-following practices are often just doing what comes naturally to them in the circumstances. Indeed, we generally take the effortless, natural, non-deliberative character of a rule-follower's responses as reflective of her *mastery* of the rules. (It is precisely this effortless, non-deliberative quality that we aim to inculcate in those we train in the relevant rule-following practices.) And so the idea that rule-following involves a special mental process—a mental process that, if it is not strictly speaking deliberation or reflection, is nonetheless like deliberation or reflection in virtue of rendering inappropriate Wittgenstein's 'facial descriptions' of the activity —certainly does not come from observation of a divide between the behavior we ordinarily classify as done for a reason and the behavior we ordinarily classify as a natural reaction to the situation (or as a product of habituation, as done as a matter of course, etc.). There is no such divide.

How effective is the appeal to practice, so construed, as a response to the skeptical line of thought? It seems to me that the point Wittgenstein is making is a good one. The idea that rule-following must involve a special mental process, one whose presence removes rule-following behavior from the realm of natural reactions, may be an idea we find attractive during philosophical reflection. It is perhaps in the context of such reflection that one is most likely to "feel confident," with Kripke, that there must be something in our mind that instructs us how to proceed when we follow a rule. But this idea finds no support from observation of the cases in which, in ordinary life, we think of people as participating in given rule-following practices. In particular, that a given person is evidently just doing what comes naturally to her in the circumstances is no bar to our ordinarily thinking of her as, say, obeying a walk sign, producing a simple arithmetical sequence, and so on.

At the same time, it seems to me that the appeal, if it is to be effective, must go hand-in-hand with a diagnosis of why the idea of the special mental process should be so tempting in the context of philosophical reflection. If the intuition articulated by Nagel is in tension with the judgments and reactions we have when, as in everyday life, we see a person's actions against the background of the "whole hurly-burly of human actions," then why are philosophers as insightful as Kripke and Nagel so gripped by that intuition? Presumably there is a fairly deep-seated mindset at work here. Until we know what that mindset is well enough to take the measure of it, no reminder about ordinary practices and customs is likely to block its influence.

This is a topic on which Wittgenstein could say much more than he does. He does make some diagnostic moves in *Philosophical Investigations* and elsewhere. For example, there is the discussion in the *Blue Book* of the philosopher's "preoccupation with the method of science," understood as "the method of reducing the explanation of natural phenomena to the smallest possible number of primitive natural laws" (1965, 18). This preoccupation has "made the philosopher dismiss as irrelevant the concrete cases, which alone could have helped him to understand the usage of the general term" (1965, 19–20). We might, in the present case, see this preoccupation as leading the philosopher to posit an underlying mental mechanism that unifies and explains the varied rule-following practices that we observe and participate in every day, whereas for Wittgenstein it is our familiarity with the "concrete cases"—going by a sign, calculating, performing a dance, and so on—that constitutes our understanding of what it is to follow a rule.

But a diagnosis at this high a level of generality is, I think, not fully satisfying. For it seems to me a natural suspicion that it is specifically the rational character of rule-following—its location in the "space of reasons," as Sellars and McDowell say—that gives the philosopher trouble. It is plausible to suspect, in other words, that the intuition is at bottom an instance of the familiar difficulty of reconciling two conceptions of ourselves: as rational beings, on the one hand, and as natural beings on the other. Wittgenstein's hypothesis of a favoritism for the general over the concrete does not really make anything of this.

It would be good to follow out the suspicion just mentioned, but I will not do so here. This paper is already long enough.

# 10 Conclusion

Let's recap. Kripke's talk of the normative relationship between meaning and use may be partially explicable as an expression of the evaluative view of meaning—the view according to which uses of linguistic expressions can either accord or fail to accord with their meanings. But that interpretation of his normativity-talk cannot explain his attitude toward anti-reductionism. Moreover, Kripke ties the normativity-talk to the justification requirement he imposes upon accounts of meanings, and that requirement, given that it is articulated as the demand to show that Kripke's responses to '+' problems are not mere stabs in the dark, cannot be understood in terms of the evaluative view. It flows rather from three premises. The first is the rationalist view of rules: to characterize a person as following a rule is to offer a rational explanation of her performance, with the rule serving as her reason for proceeding as she does. The second is the idea that rational explanations of what people do explain their performances in terms of their own conception of what justifies their proceeding as they do. The third is the view that language-use involves following rules laid down by the meanings of expressions.

Now, Kripke assumes that viewing rule-following as a species of rational activity (i. e., as performances susceptible to rational explanation) will require taking on board the guidance conception, according to which a rule-follower's grasp of a rule involves a mental item that guides her applications of the rule. This assumption can be understood as arising from our intuitive sense of the incompatibility of conceiving a rule-follower as acting on the basis of the justification she takes the rule to provide and conceiving her, à la Wittgenstein, as just doing what comes naturally to her in the circumstances, given her training and background. But the guidance conception generates a dilemma. If we do not reapply the guidance conception at the level of the person's understanding of the guidance provided by the mental item constituting her understanding of the rule, then the conception turns out just to temporarily defer a description of the putative rule-follower as doing what comes naturally to her in the circumstances. Hence it does not after all provide an account of rule-following that validates the aforementioned intuition of incompatibility. If, on the other hand, we do reapply the conception at this level, the dilemma simply reappears at the next level up. The pull of the conception can be so strong that we may be led to a vision of occupants of the mental realm as regress-proof, in virtue of their 'logically compelling' our understanding of the guidance they provide. But this vision proves unintelligible. The skeptic concludes that rule-following, and the application of linguistic meanings in particular, is impossible.

Is the argument for this conclusion sound? Suppose we accept, as I've suggested we should, the premise that rule-following is a form of rational activity, coupled with the view of rational explanation that casts such explanations as appealing to the subject's own conception of what justifies her performances. Suppose we accept, as I've been doing for purposes of exposition, that Kripke is right to assimilate the use of meaningful expressions to the following of rules. And suppose we accept, as I've argued we must, that the guidance conception generates the dilemma just summarized and that the idea of 'logical compulsion,' being a confusion, cannot help resolve the dilemma.

One issue then remains outstanding. Is the intuition that I have portrayed as the motivation for the guidance conception sound? Are, as Nagel worries, Wittgenstein's "facial descriptions" of putative rule-following behavior incompatible with conceiving the person as genuinely following a rule? Wittgenstein's appeal to the customs and practices that surround everyday episodes of rule-following, that and inform our ordinary understanding of those episodes, aims to challenge this intuition. That appeal would benefit from supplementation with a diagnosis of why the intuition, in the context of philosophical reflection, can seem so compelling. Wittgenstein offers something along these lines, but there is room for a good deal more.

# Bibliography

Boghossian, Paul (1989), "The Rule-Following Considerations." In: *Mind* 98, 507–549.

Boghossian, Paul (2003), "The Normativity of Content." In: *Philosophical Issues* 13, 31–45.

Brandom, Robert (2001), "Modality, Normativity, and Intentionality." In: *Philosophy and Phenomenological Research* 63, 587–609.

Darwall, Stephen (1983), *Impartial Reason*, Ithaca: Cornell University Press.

Davidson, Donald (1992), "The Second Person." In: *Midwest Studies in Philosophy* 17, 255–67.

Gibbard, Allan (1994), "Meaning and Normativity." In: *Philosophical Issues* 5, 95–115.

Gibbard, Allan (2003), "Thoughts and Norms." In: *Philosophical Issues* 13, 83–98.

Ginsborg, Hannah (2011), "Primitive Normativity and Skepticism about Rules." In: *The Journal of Philosophy*, pp. 227–254.

Grice, Paul (2005), *Aspects of Reason*, Oxford: Oxford University Press.

Horwich, Paul (1984), "Critical Notice on *Wittgenstein on Rules and Private Language*." In: *Philosophy of Science* 51, 163–71.

Horwich, Paul (1998), *Meaning*, Oxford: Clarendon Press.

Kripke, Saul (1980), *Naming and Necessity*, Cambridge: Harvard University Press.

Kripke, Saul (1982), *Wittgenstein on Rules and Private Language*, Cambridge: Harvard University Press.

McDowell, John (2001), "Meaning and Intentionality In Wittgenstein's Later Philosophy." In: John McDowell, *Mind, Value, and Reality*, Cambridge, MA: Harvard University Press, 263–78.

Millar, Alan (2004), *Understanding People*, Oxford: Oxford University Press.

Nagel, Thomas (1996), *The Last Word*, Oxford: Oxford University Press.

Stroud, Barry (1979), "Inference, Belief and Understanding." In: *Mind* 88, 179–96.

Van Fraassen, Bas (1980), *The Scientific Image*, Oxford: Oxford University Press.

Wallace, David Foster (2001), "Tense Present: Democracy, English and the Wars over Usage." In: *Harper's Magazine*, 39–58.

Wittgenstein, Ludwig (1966), *The Blue and Brown Books*, New York: Harper & Row.

Wittgenstein, Ludwig (1970), *Zettel*, G.E.M. Anscombe and G.H. von Wright (eds.), Berkeley, Los Angeles, and London: University of California Press.

Wittgenstein, Ludwig (1978), *Remarks on the Foundations of Mathematics*, Revised Edition, Cambridge, MA: The MIT Press.

Wittgenstein, Ludwig (1973), *Philosophical Investigations*, Third Edition, New York: Prentice Hall.

Wright, Crispin (1984), "Kripke's Account of the Argument Against Private Language." In: *Journal of Philosophy* 81, 759–78.

**Part III:   After Cavell**

Stephen Mulhall
# Inner Constancy, Outer Variation: Stanley Cavell on Grammar, Criteria, and Rules

1. In the book on Stanley Cavell's work that I published seven years ago,[1] my account of his understanding of Wittgenstein's notion of a criterion implied that he thought of criteria as rules of grammar and of grammatical investigations as designed to recall us to the rules governing our uses of words. In this respect, my account of Cavell conformed to a very common pattern in the writings of many contemporary commentators on Wittgenstein's later philosophy—Baker and Hacker preeminent amongst them. But it was quickly made clear to me that, for some of those familiar with, and influenced by, Cavell's teaching and writings, this aspect of my account of his work was deeply problematic. Not only did it fail to register the very striking fact that Cavell himself typically avoids any such invocation of the concept of a rule when discussing and deploying the Wittgensteinian concepts of grammar and of criteria; it also failed to recognize that this avoidance was not accidental but motivated—motivated by the conviction that such invocations fundamentally distort Wittgenstein's vision of language and hence of philosophical method. On this alternative reading of Cavell's reading of Wittgenstein, the idea that language is a framework or structure of grammatical rules is not part of the perspective that the *Philosophical Investigations* aims to cultivate; it is what it most fundamentally aims to subvert.

This objection to my book thus raised three important and closely related questions. What is Cavell's conception of the grammar of words? What is Wittgenstein's conception of the grammar of words? And what is the right conception of the grammar of words? Since the participants at the conference in Amsterdam whose proceedings are collected in this volume included a number of people who shared this concern (or at least an interest in this concern) about my book, and since Steven Affeldt (who had first, and most forcefully, raised these issues in print)[2] had been invited to reply to my contribution to those proceedings, it seemed fitting that I should take my own invitation to participate as an opportunity to return to those issues in some detail.

---

1 Mulhall 1994.
2 Affeldt 1998.

The topic of linguistic normativity is, after all, directly related to the conference's stated themes; for one way of characterizing this debate about how best to interpret Cavell and Wittgenstein on grammar is as a debate about skepticism. Unlike many Wittgenstein commentators, Cavell sees humanly serious expressions of skepticism as using words in a not-wholly-unnatural way, and as having some account to give of that less-than-full-naturalness. Hence he sees skepticism not as a (more or less duplicitous) refusal of the transparent grammatical conditions of intelligible speech, but as responsive to certain aspects of ordinary language use that must not, from a genuinely Wittgensteinian perspective, be denied—in particular, the capacity of words to undergo projection into unforeseen contexts. On this view, the common Wittgensteinian presentation of grammatical reminders as demonstrations of the inexpressibility or emptiness of skepticism amounts to a repression of something internal to the ordinariness of ordinary language-use; and insofar as talk of rules of grammar is implicated in such repressive strategies, it must itself be understood as a further expression of the very skepticism it claims to set itself against.

However, the intellectual substance of a good conference amounts to far more than can be represented by the sum total of the papers delivered there; and this was a particularly good conference. The discussions that I was able to have with Steven Affeldt both before, and in the immediate context of, our joint session seemed, I think I can say for both of us, to advance our understanding of the nature of our disagreement so significantly that we wanted the published versions of our contributions to reflect this deepening and clarification. Hence, this paper is not a transcription of my address to the conference,[3] but rather a further reflection upon the issues it raised, and—I would like to think—a better reflection of the enhanced understanding of those issues with which I left Amsterdam, for which I must thank the conference organizers, the participants, and in particular Steven Affeldt.

2. Looking back at the exegetical strategy of my book, with its apparent obliviousness to what now seems an utterly pivotal issue, I can think of three reasons why I might simply have taken it for granted that Cavell's highly distinctive account of Wittgenstein's notions of grammar and criteria might nevertheless be given expression without essential distortion in terms of the familiar Wittgensteinian rhetoric of a rule. The first two of these reasons relate to the apparent im-

---

**3** That text can be found in full in Mulhall 2003, to which some of Steven Affeldt's discussion will refer.

port of certain passages of Cavell's work; the third relates to the import of the work of those happy to employ that rhetoric.

Cavell himself regularly refers to the opening essay of his first book, *Must We Mean What We Say?*,[4] as the earliest of his writings that he continues to use (hence, presumably, to find philosophically productive); hence, my account of his work oriented itself from the beginning in relation to that essay (whose title is that of the book as a whole). And it is striking in the present context to see that, in this defense of the cogency of Austin's philosophical method of recalling what we say and when we say it, a defense that turns upon the view that saying something is one kind of doing (so that when we talk about talking we are talking about a species of action), Cavell's invocations of linguistic normativity are frequently couched in terms of rules.

> When we say how an action is done (how to act) what we say may report or describe the way we *in fact* do it... but it may also lay out a way of doing or saying something which is to be *followed*. Whether remarks... 'about' ordinary language, and equally about ordinary actions... are statements or rules depends upon how they are taken: if they are taken to state facts and are supposed to be believed, they are statements; if they are taken as guides and supposed to be followed, they are rules... Statements which describe a language (or a game or an institution) are rules (are binding) if you want to speak that language (play that game, accept that institution); or rather, *when* you are speaking that language, playing that game, etc... (Cavell 1976, 15–16, 22)

Here, the question of what is normative for any particular moment of speech is presented as a matter of what the rules governing that act require. Cavell goes on to declare that "[r]ules tell you what to do when you do the thing at all" (Cavell 1976, 28) and that Austin's reminders of what we say when might be said to formulate "the rules [as opposed to] the principles of grammar" (Cavell 1976, 32). Against this background, with Cavell seemingly happy to describe the philosopher who proceeds from ordinary language as establishing (that is, confirming or proving) the existence of norms (cf., Cavell 1976, 32), and to describe those norms as rules, it is not hard to see why I was happy to characterize his later talk of the Wittgensteinian practice of grammatical investigations, of recalling criteria, as a matter of reminding us of rules of grammar.

There are, of course, other passages or portions of Cavell's work in which he appears to express a resolute hostility to such formulations. For example, in his Carus lecture on Kripke's reading of the rule-following remarks in the *Philosophical Investigations*, he declares that "I... do not share the sense that Wittgenstein attaches salvational importance to rules... Indeed, I take Wittgenstein to say fair-

---

4 Cavell 1976.

ly explicitly that rules cannot play the fundamental role Kripke takes him to cast them in" (Cavell 1990, 67). Such declarations are, however, ambiguous as they stand; for they might be taken to express not a settled hostility to any explication of the notion of criteria in terms of rules, but rather a rejection of a particular philosopher's explication of it. My sense that the latter reading of such passages was the more plausible was reinforced by the specific form of the criticisms Cavell offered of Kripke's reading of Wittgenstein.[5]

To take just one example: when Kripke defines what it is right to do in following a rule of a given community in terms of the matching of one's inclinations to go on in a certain way, Cavell takes this to embody a conception of the community that is the reverse of inviting.

> [W]hat could my inclination, or profound faith, ever have to do with justifying him here (or licensing him, or judging his action to be correct)? Suppose that driving you to work I say 'I'm inclined to run this red light; if you reply 'My inclination agrees with yours', have you licensed me to run the light? You may be encouraging license. If when the light turns green I say 'I have faith in going now', and you reply 'My faith agrees with yours', have you made sense of me and I of you?... If the situation is as Kripke says Wittgenstein says, why ever say more than: 'I agree with you. That is my inclination too'? Paraphrasing a wonder of Wittgenstein's: What gives us so much as the idea that human beings, things, can be right?... If the matching of inclinations is all Wittgenstein's teaching leaves us with, then I feel like asking: What kind of solution is that to a sceptical problem? Then I can express my perplexity this way: This solution seems to me more sceptical than the problem it is designed to solve. (Cavell 1990, 74–5)

Kripke's talk of inclinations, confident or otherwise, induces a loss of the very idea of rightness or justification, say normativity, that he presents himself as wishing to defend from the skeptic. Hence, there is a clear sense in which the conception of rules he proffers as a solution to his skeptical paradox is itself an expression of skepticism. But Cavell's way of reaching this conclusion depends so critically upon the precise implications of every key term in Kripke's commentary that it neither offers, nor seems designed to offer, a reason for believing that the same charge must apply to any commentator who gives any conception of a rule a central place in their account of Wittgenstein's philosophical designs.

My sense that these specific criticisms of Kripke left the general idea of equating criteria or grammar with rules untouched was confirmed by Cavell's way of introducing his disagreement with Kripke:

---

**5** I provide a much more extensive and detailed justification of this judgment in Mulhall 1994.

In taking rules as fundamental to Wittgenstein's development of scepticism about meaning, Kripke subordinates the role of criteria in the *Investigations*, hence appears from my side of things to underrate drastically, or to beg the question of, the issue of the ordinary, a structure of which is the structure of our criteria and their grammatical relations. In my seeing criteria as forming Wittgenstein's understanding of the possibility of scepticism, I take this to show rules to be subordinate; but since Kripke's interpretation of rules seems, in turn to undercut the fundamentality of the appeal to the ordinary, my appeal to criteria must appear to beg the question from his side of things. (Cavell 1990, 65–6)

This way of putting the dispute precisely occludes the possibility that the familiar idea of rules of grammar holds open—that criteria are no more subordinate to rules than rules are to criteria, but that criteria are rather a species of rule, that their articulation displays an aspect of the manner in which our uses of words are rule-governed. The key idea here is not subordination (of one concept to another, as in a codification or calculus), but clarification (of one concept by another, as in a recounting of grammar)—an option that is passed over by Cavell's assumption throughout this passage that rules and criteria are to be contrasted or opposed. To think that rules are fundamental to Wittgenstein's vision of language does not entail thinking that criteria, and hence the ordinary, are subordinate to rules; but then Cavell's critique of Kripke will not generalize.

3. In effect, then, the thought (familiar in the Wittgenstein literature) that criteria might be regarded as rules of grammar can easily appear to be at least consistent with what Cavell says in many parts of his work and, in some places, to be no more than a summary of what he does say. And this sense that nothing essential to Cavell's way of reading Wittgenstein and of understanding language use is lost or distorted if it is reformulated in such terms (even if Cavell himself—perhaps rightly—saw no necessity to employ them) was reinforced by my sense of what this familiar thought (at least in the contexts in which I became acquainted with it) was intended to encapsulate. In the influential work of Baker and Hacker, for example, the notion of rules of grammar is developed and presented in essential opposition to certain philosophical assumptions to which it is clear that Wittgenstein, and Cavell himself, are also opposed.[6]

In developing this notion, whether as an interpretation of the *Philosophical Investigations*[7] or as an instrument in more polemical disputes, Baker and Hacker are primarily concerned to distinguish the concept of following a rule from

---

6 My primary sources for the following summary of their position are two central essays in Backer/Hacker 1985, 34–64, 154–181.
7 Wittgenstein 1998 (hereafter: PI).

that of acting in accord with a rule and from that of a behavioral regularity. On their account, a phenomenon does not count as an instance of rule-following simply because it is regular: the orbit of the moon may be law-like, but it is not generated by the moon's following a rule; and a repeated gesture in a tribe's rain-dance may accord with a particular rule even though the dancers are not actually following that rule (they may be following a different rule which results in the same sequence of gestures, or indeed no rule at all). For a regularity in behavior to count as rule-following, it must not only be in accord with what the rule requires; it must be done *because* that is what the rule requires. This is not a causal link: the point here is that the rule constitutes the agent's reason for acting as she did. If an agent is following a given rule, then she must be able to explain what she is doing by reference to it, teach others how to follow it, justify her actions by reference to it, and/or acknowledge that her actions can be evaluated as right or wrong by reference to it. In short, talk of human behavior as rule-following behavior brings it into the realm of normativity; the rule functions as a standard of correctness, a means by which the relevant action can be guided and evaluated, a norm that constitutes the action as the specific (rule-following) action it is.

By linking the Wittgensteinian idea of grammar with this idea of a rule, Baker and Hacker mean to equip themselves with a weapon against philosophical accounts of language-use and word-meaning that invoke an idea of rule-following but sever the link between rules and what they call the background normative activities of teaching, explaining, defining, justifying, and evaluating—the context within which human behavior can count as an instance of a rule-governed activity. This allows them to question the coherence of Chomskyan notions of depth grammar, which appear to presuppose that a speaker's behavior can be governed by (as opposed to being in accord with) rules that they are incapable either or articulating or of understanding when articulated by others. It also allows them to reject dispositional or more generally causal accounts of meaning, which attempt to reduce the notion of our grasp of a word's meaning to the presence or absence of a tendency to deploy and respond to a given word in specific, regular ways.

If we were to substitute the word 'inclination' for 'tendency' in the previous sentence, it would be clear just how far Baker and Hacker's notion of a rule of grammar differs from that of Kripke's Wittgenstein and how, hence, it is not only untouched by Cavell's criticisms of Kripke but deeply in tune with them. But Baker and Hacker are also careful to distinguish their conception of a rule of grammar from certain other conceptions with which it might otherwise be confused and to which Cavell also takes exception. For example, whilst their conception of such rules certainly includes dictionary definitions, it extends far beyond them: it includes concrete samples, charts, blueprints, signposts, lists of examples—indeed any of the indefinitely many ways in which speakers can explain and justify their uses of words to others. They also stress that a linguistic activity can be rule-governed even when no explicit rule-formulation is used by an agent to guide her activity (she may simply cite the rule when challenged or asked to explain herself) and sometimes even when no rule-formulations are involved in acquiring or displaying a mastery of the activity (she might simply point out the mistakes of others, display chagrin at her own slips, and so on). Moreover, such explanations as are employed in the activity are not and could not be designed to remove all possible misunderstandings or to cover all possible cases of a word's applications; they are in order if they do their job—if they actually overcome the specific misunderstanding that is causing trouble, or allow a pupil to go on successfully with a particular word. And of course, circumstances may demand that we judge how best to extend or adapt existing norms to cope with new contexts. The focus throughout is thus not on a canonical form of explanation, but upon the use to which certain objects or forms of words are put in any given context; the basic idea is that something counts as a rule of grammar if it is used in the relevant way, if the activity in which it is employed is normative.

This emphasis on the variety and context-specificity of grammatical rules is Baker and Hacker's way of acknowledging the various demystifications to which Wittgenstein subjects the idea of an explanation of meaning in the opening eighty or so sections of the *Investigations*, in the course of his discussion of ostensive definitions, family resemblance, and other topics. One might think of Wittgenstein's overall strategy as one of emphasizing that his own talk of language-games (despite its many concrete examples of such games in which tables, charts, and samples are explicitly deployed for explanatory purposes) is meant to suggest the systematic normativity of our practices of employing words without implying that each such mode of linguistic activity is explicitly or implicitly governed by a book of rules, an articulated, codified system of precise norms. On the contrary, Wittgenstein makes it clear in §81 that such a conception of linguistic normativity—the idea that "if anyone utters a sentence and *means* or *understands* it he is operating a calculus according to definite rules"—is his central target. Of course, despite this, some commentators give accounts of Wittgenstein's own position that project exactly such a view upon it; Cavell's early essay "On the Availability of Wittgenstein's Philosophy"[8] identifies such a projection in David Pole's account of Wittgenstein's idea of grammar and subjects it to withering criticism. Since, however, Baker and Hacker are careful to

---

**8** In: Cavell 1976.

incorporate into their own conception of grammatical rules the various ways in which Wittgenstein distinguishes his account of language-games from a calculus conception of language, there is—at least on the face of it—no reason to think that their position differs from Cavell's in this respect.

4. Taken together, then, there seems to be good reason to think that a conception of grammar such as that of Baker and Hacker, and the conception worked out in Cavell's writings, might be essentially complementary despite their striking differences in rhetorical register. Since Cavell is not always unhappy to talk of rules of grammar himself, since his explicit criticisms of philosophers who do employ such talk focus on confusions that are not obviously displayed by all who so express themselves, and since at least one highly influential pair of commentators who talk of grammatical rules thereby appear to develop a position whose main emphases are congenial to Cavell's own conception of grammar and uncongenial to conceptions to which he too is hostile, why might one still wish to resist the idea that an account of Cavell's vision of language might make use of the notion of grammatical rules without essential loss or distortion?

Of course, matters are not to be settled so simply or quickly. To begin with, we should recall that the essay in which Cavell seems happiest to employ the terminology of rules ("Must We Mean What We Say?") is explicitly devoted to an explication of Austin's rather than Wittgenstein's philosophical method; it was in fact written before Cavell had engaged in any systematic reading of Wittgenstein at all. When (as in the succeeding essay, "The Availability of Wittgenstein's Philosophy") he does turn to the *Investigations*, he appears far more hostile to such terminology and its implications: "That everyday language does not, in fact or in essence, depend upon such a structure and conception of rules, and yet that the absence of such a structure in no way impairs its functioning, is what the picture of language drawn in [Wittgenstein's] later philosophy is about" (Cavell 1976, 48). It might therefore be argued that Cavell's essay on Pole marks the point at which his conception of the correct philosophical method attains its Wittgensteinian maturity by sloughing off an Austinian rule-based conception of criteria. Any such argument must, however, depend upon the sharp distinction that Cavell comes to draw between Austin's and Wittgenstein's conception of criteria and grammar, to the latter's benefit; but the argumentative basis for this contrast appears only in *The Claim of Reason*,[9] a text with which we have not yet engaged.

---

9 Cavell 1979.

Second, even if we accept that the ways in which commentators such as Baker and Hacker employ the concept of a rule is not obviously vulnerable to some of Cavell's essentially *ad hominem* critiques of other commentators, it may well be that there are other, more general reasons that Cavell's work provides for feeling suspicious of certain implications that talk of 'rules' brings into play. Once again, those who are most sensitive to this concern tend to point to the central arguments of *The Claim of Reason* as grounding their suspicion.

And finally, of course, we should recognize the very general possibility that a philosopher might find herself betrayed by the distinction between programme and practice in this domain. For of course, Wittgenstein's conception of grammar determines not only his vision of language but his vision of philosophical method; insofar as he understands philosophy to be a process of grammatical investigation, of recalling criteria, then the grammatical articulations of language are not just one topic of his philosophical explorations, but rather constitute the medium of any and every such enterprise. In short, his view of what grammar is essentially conditions his sense of what philosophy is, of what it can and cannot do, of how it can and must be practiced. Hence, any philosopher who claims allegiance to Wittgenstein's conception of the subject as a matter of grammatical investigation must ensure that the substance and implications of her conception of grammar inform the way she conducts her business as a philosopher more generally. With respect to our specific concerns, then, even if we acknowledge that Baker and Hacker's account of Wittgenstein's conception of grammar and criteria in terms of rules does not essentially misrepresent the Wittgensteinian texts, we can still ask whether the form of their philosophical practice as a whole is true even to their own account of this aspect of the substance of those texts.

5. In turning now to the highly detailed and elaborate account of criteria with which *The Claim of Reason* opens, I cannot here reproduce the rather more detailed discussion of it that I offered in the paper I originally gave at the Amsterdam conference. If I were to summarize its general import, I would venture the formulation that, whilst nothing that Cavell says in outlining and putting to use his highly distinctive understanding of Wittgenstein's notion of a criterion *requires* the use of the concept of a rule of grammar (and Cavell himself does not use it), the most salient aspects of his account can be restated in such terms without distortion, and certain turns of his argument seem in fact to embody assumptions that would be highly congenial to commentators who prefer to employ such terms.

One example of this latter phenomenon must suffice to illustrate my point. It concerns an apparent paradox in Wittgenstein's conception of criteria as Cavell has presented it:

> Criteria were to be the bases (features, marks, specifications) on the basis of which certain judgements could be made...; agreement over criteria was to make possible agreement about judgements. But in Wittgenstein it looks as if our ability to establish criteria depended upon a prior agreement in judgements. (Cavell 1979, 30)

Cavell proceeds to dissolve the air of paradox here by reminding us that our agreement in criteria is not meant to explain our agreement in judgment nor to provide a further foundation of agreement when we find ourselves disagreeing in judgment; for the two kinds of agreement are interwoven. To agree in the criteria for a given word just is to agree in how we apply the word in the context of specific judgments; and if we find that we disagree in a specific judgment employing that word, we thereby show that, to that extent, we disagree in our criteria.

> [This idea of mutual attunement] is meant to question whether a philosophical explanation is needed, or wanted, for the fact of agreement in the language human beings use together, an explanation, say, in terms of meanings or conventions or basic terms or propositions which are to provide the foundations of our agreements. For nothing is deeper than the fact, or the extent, of agreement itself. (Cavell 1979, 32)

Cavell is here identifying a version of the deep philosophical desire for foundations—in this case, a desire to found or ground our agreements in the ways we use words on something independent that might provide a guarantee of their continuance or at least a secure basis from which to identify and criticize disagreements. And even those Wittgensteinians whose general accounts of language-mastery do not explicitly present agreement in criteria as providing a foundation for agreement in specific applications of words may nevertheless find that their philosophical practice betrays them—if, for example, they assume that a philosopher's divergent application of a word can simply and definitively be corrected by reminding her of its 'agreed' criteria. For Cavell, Wittgenstein's insight entails that, when our attunements in application become dissonant, we have no independent source of authority or guidance to appeal to in determining how to respond to that dissonance. Citing criteria cannot constitute an objective resolution to a genuine disharmony in judgments (say, in response to a skeptic's anxieties); for if our agreement in criteria runs no further or deeper than our agreements in judgments, then citing criteria can never authoritatively demonstrate the deviance of one party to the disagreement. It can at best amount to an invitation to reconsider that disagreement and what is truly at stake in it, to ask ourselves whether we wish to take a stand upon it and what stand we wish to take.

I think it is undeniable that there are moments in Baker and Hacker's work when their philosophical practice subverts their own official account of its grammatical basis in just this way.[10] And any such mismatch between theory and practice is surely to be regretted in the work of any Wittgensteinian philosopher. But it must surely be acknowledged that, at such moments, what their practice subverts is their own official account; in other words, such failures in practice do not invalidate their theoretical stance, as if that stance entailed such forms of practice, but are rather identifiable as such by reference to it. One might say, then, that their official account is honored rather than discredited by such breaches in its practical observance. Hence, even if they can be criticized in this way, such criticism does not invalidate their reliance upon the concept of a rule to elucidate Wittgenstein's notion of grammar and of criteria. One might perhaps argue that the very idea of a rule—insofar as it brings with it visions of rulebooks, or codified systems of independently established norms governing a practice—can encourage us to fall into the forms of philosophizing under criticism here; but nothing in the specific inflection of that concept as it is elucidated in Baker and Hacker's work (an inflection which repeatedly averts itself from the model of a calculus or rulebook) in fact offers any such encouragement.

Moreover, Cavell's way of developing from a Wittgensteinian perspective this rather Kierkegaardian (even Heideggerian) concern that the content of one's philosophizing be acknowledged in its form is rather striking in this context. For he makes it clear that the argument just summarized for the non-foundational status of criteria amounts to a gloss upon Wittgenstein's famous remark that "If language is to be a means of communication there must be agreement not only in definitions but also (queer as this may sound) in judgements" (PI, §242). But the ideas about agreement in language, definition, and judgment which are crystallized in that remark are developed in the extended discussion of rule-following that precedes it in the *Investigations*. In other words, Cavell's argument applies conclusions that Wittgenstein develops from his consideration of the concept of a rule to his notion of criteria, and thus appears to presuppose that criteria can be regarded as a species of rule in just the way that commentators such as Baker and Hacker themselves argue.

---

**10** Ed Witherspoon identifies one such moment in the essays on which I have been basing my account of Baker and Hacker's position, in Witherspoon 2000.

6. I have already identified one understandable, but in my view mistaken, reason for thinking that any invocation of rules in elucidating Wittgenstein's notion of grammar will distort his key insights—the belief that the concept of a rule necessarily carries with it the idea that we might invoke the impersonal authority of a rulebook to settle philosophical disagreements over the legitimacy of going on in a certain way with a given word. A further, related anxiety, also having to do with the ways we project words into new contexts, is plainly under consideration in another, highly significant part of *The Claim of Reason:* Cavell's "Excursus on Wittgenstein's Vision of Language." His primary example is the word 'feed': we learn to 'feed the cat' and to 'feed the lions,' and then, when someone talks of feeding the meter or feeding our pride, we understand them; we accept this projection of the word. Cavell's view is that tolerating such projections is of the essence of words. We could, of course, have used other words than 'feed' for this new context, either by projecting another established word or inventing a new one. If, however, we talked of 'putting' money in the meter as we do of putting a dial on the meter, we would lose a way of making certain discriminations (between putting a flow of material into a machine and putting a part made of new material on a machine); we would begin to deprive ourselves of certain of our concepts (could we dispense with talk of feeding our pride and still retain our concept of emotions as capable of growth?); and we would in effect be extending the legitimate range of our alternative word in just the manner we were trying to avoid. If instead we invented a new word, we would lose a way of registering connections between contexts, open up questions about the legitimate projections of this new word, and at the limit deprive all words of meaning (since no word employed in only one context would be a word).

At the same time, however, our projections of our words are also deeply controlled. We can, for example, feed a lion, but not by placing a bushel of carrots in its cage; and its failure to eat them would not count as a refusal to do so. Such projections of 'feed' and 'refusal' fail because their connection with other words in their normal contexts do not transfer to the new one; one can only refuse something that one might also accept, hence something that one can be offered or invited to accept. And what might count as an offer and an acceptance in the context of a meal is both different from and related to what counts as an offer and acceptance in the context of mating or being guided. These limits are neither arbitrary nor optional; they show how (what Cavell elsewhere calls) a word's grammatical schematism determines the respects in which a new context for a word must invite or allow its projection.

In short:

> [A]ny form of life and every concept integral to it has an indefinite number of instances and directions of projection; and this variation is not arbitrary. *Both* the 'outer' variance and the 'inner' constancy are necessary if a concept is to accomplish its tasks—of meaning, understanding, communicating, etc., and in general, guiding us through the world, and relating thought and action and feeling to the world. (Cavell 1979, 185)

There is a certain tension in this key passage between its surface rhetoric and the underlying tendency of its argument, a tension that is centered on Cavell's talk of 'outer' variance and 'inner' constancy. For that contrast between outer and inner suggests, on the face of it, that the constancy of a concept is more internal or integral to its capacity to accomplish its tasks than is its variance. And yet the evident thrust of the passage is to claim that *both* the inner and the outer aspects of the concept are necessary to it. To be sure, Cavell registers a certain sense of discomfort with his own contrast by putting both of its terms within scare quotes; but its apparent implications are not simply in need of softening or qualification to be rendered consistent with his fundamental claim—as if they might mislead but can otherwise make a positive contribution to his argument. Insofar as they are taken seriously, they appear to run entirely counter to it.

Suppose, however, we concentrate for a moment on the general thrust of the account of concepts that this passage encapsulates, and focus on the claim that a concept needs both outer variance and inner constancy—that, as Cavell puts it, he is "trying to bring out, and keep in balance, two fundamental facts about human forms of life, and about the concepts formed in those forms" (Cavell 1979, 185). Those suspicious of the baggage that talk of grammatical rules may bring with it into this debate will naturally find themselves placing emphasis on the fact of outer variance, and will ask whether it is really possible to imagine that any rule-formulation might capture or ground it. Might there be a rule governing the route of projection that our word 'feed' displays, not to mention the further steps or leaps we might find ourselves taking with it in the future? But those less suspicious of the idea of a rule will equally naturally find themselves struck by the balancing fact of inner constancy, and ask whether it is really possible to capture it—as it is manifest, say, in our responsibility to show how a concept's new context can tolerate the applications of the concepts to which its criteria relate it—without adverting to some idea of a systematic web of norms or standards. Surely some such invocation must be made if the fact of outer variance is not to eclipse its inner twin?

As Cavell's own talk of attempting to keep two facts in balance itself suggests, it may seem that the solution to our problem here is to accept the need for an account of grammar and criteria that accommodates both fundamental facts. Perhaps, then, we should imagine the web of norms, standards or rules as setting a certain kind of limit on the degree of variance that a concept's projections can be permitted: the rules give constancy, and individual or collective imagination, natural reactions, and so on engender variance, with the life of the concept being formed from the interaction of these two aspects of human forms of life. We might then consider that the debate with which this paper concerns itself is predicated upon allowing one of Cavell's pair of fundamental facts to eclipse the other. Each position, taken on its own, is inadequate, unbalanced; but the two taken together would provide a complete and balanced picture of the grammatical essence of concepts.

Unfortunately, this picture of compromise and ultimate complementarity would entirely miss the real point of Cavell's vision of Wittgenstein's vision of language. We might begin to see this if we return for a moment to his apparently misleading inner/outer contrast, and try regarding the 'scare quotes' he assigns to them as quotation marks; for that pair of terms is employed in some of Wittgenstein's most famous remarks about the relationship between the human mind and the human body—as when he declares that "an 'inner process' stands in need of outward criteria" (PI §580), or that "the human body is the best picture of the human soul" (PI II, §iv). In these contexts, Wittgenstein's point is not to give the inner priority over the outer, or indeed to reverse that order of priority; his concern is to suggest that the inner and the outer are not two independent realms or dimensions at all, but are rather internally related, the significance or import of each inseparable from that of the other.

If we transpose that suggestion to the context of Cavell's discussion of the grammatical essence of concepts, it would appear to follow that his characterization of constancy and variance as two fundamental facts is rather more misleading than his characterization of them as inner and outer. For this transposition would suggest that we should stop thinking of a concept's essence as determined by a conjunction or dovetailing of two separable components or elements (its constancy and its variance); we should rather think of its projectibility as having an indefinitely variable kind of constancy, or an essentially non-arbitrary kind of variation. In other words, Cavell's two fundamental facts are in fact two aspects of a single or singular fact; hence they do not need to be kept in balance, because to downgrade or entirely to overlook one is to distort the other.

What accounts for that single fact, in all its singularity, is identified in a vital early part of Cavell's specification of his (and Wittgenstein's) notion of a criterion.

[Wittgensteinian] criteria do not relate a name to an object, but, we might say, various concepts to the concept of that object. Here the test of your possession of a concept... would be your ability to use the concept in conjunction with other concepts, your knowledge of which concepts are relevant to the one in question and which are not; your knowledge of how various relevant concepts, used in conjunction with the concepts of different kinds of objects, require different kinds of contexts for their competent employment. (Cavell 1979, 73)

For example, knowing what a toothache is is in part a matter of knowing what counts as having a toothache, what counts as alleviating a toothache, and so on. In other words, what Cavell calls the grammatical schematism of a word is its power to combine with other words—"the word's potency to assume just those valences, and a sense that in each case there will be a point of application of the word, and that the point will be the same from context to context, or that the point will shift in a recognizable pattern or direction" (Cavell 1979, 77–8). Hence, when the acceptability or naturalness of a new projection of a given word is in question, our final judgment will turn upon the speaker's capacity to show that and how the new context into which he has projected it either invites or can be seen to allow that projection by inviting or allowing (at least some modified form of) the projection of those other words to which its criteria relate it and which are accommodated in familiar contexts of the word's use.

Many of Cavell's examples of projections of words in his "Excursus" are utterly obvious to us; they show the untroubled reach of our mutual attunements. We accept that placing a bushel of carrots in a lion's cage does not count as 'feeding' him because (amongst other things) we can see nothing that could count as his accepting or refusing to eat it; but we also accept talk of feeding the meter and feeding our pride despite the fact that much of the word's familiar valences either will not carry over or must be modified in order to do so. We understand someone who says that the meter has refused her coins, or that her pride refuses to feed on such gross flattery; the valences of 'refusal' in these contexts differ not only from one another but from their more familiar contexts (in the lion's cage or the fast-food restaurant), but the point of their modified retention—the point of the word's application—is clear. In other cases, however, the acceptability or unacceptability of the projection is less clear; it isn't obvious how and why we should accommodate ourselves to it, because it isn't clear how the word's valences might be carried over into its new context. Can we point out Manhattan—could anything count as pointing out Manhattan—to a child who does not yet grasp the concept of maps? Perhaps not, if we're walking with her on 58th Street; but what if we are looking out of a window as our plane banks on its approach to La Guardia airport? Is a plank stood on end about the height and width of a human being, tipped and braced back slightly from the vertical, into which are fitted at right angles two pegs to go under the armpits and a saddle peg in the middle—is such a thing a chair? Well, would we be inclined to count the tribesman comfortably arranged on its pegs as sitting on it?

Different kinds and instances of questionable projection will elicit different forms of justification and criticism and will reach different kinds of individual and communal resolution. It will not be clear or specifiable in advance exactly what will or might be said to justify or to criticize a disputed projection—that will depend on the disputants' knowledge of the new context for the word, their capacity to give explicit articulation to their implicit grasp of the word's criteria, the depth and range of their imaginations, their willingness to accommodate change in exchange for insight, their sense of a given concept's grammatical center of gravity, and so on. But to know how to speak is to know what kinds of consideration are and are not pertinent to the justification and criticism of a given word's projections; we might see good reason to dispute the suggestion that what the tribesman is doing with his plank is sitting on it, but we thereby acknowledge that determining whether anything might count as sitting on the plank contributes to determining whether that plank counts as a chair. Without that shared grasp of what we might call canons of relevance, there would be nothing of the systematic normativity in language-use to which Wittgenstein and Cavell are so sensitive, and without which grammatical investigations could have no claim on our attention.

7. The phrase 'canons of relevance' is one I derive from another stretch of *The Claim of Reason* (its third part), in which Cavell disputes broadly emotivist understandings of moral discourse. There he castigates philosophers such as Stevenson, who claims that any kind of statement that any speaker considers likely to alter attitudes may be adduced for or against an ethical judgment. Cavell, by contrast, argues that morality's claim to rationality depends upon its being constituted by a shared commitment to certain modes of argument—although ones that (unlike those of the sciences) do not necessarily lead to agreement on conclusions. For example, if someone makes a promise, she commits herself to performing a certain action; hence, if she fails to perform it, she must (if she is to maintain credibility as a moral agent) explain why the circumstances in which she found herself justified this failure to honor her commitment, why she did not give advance warning of this to the promisee, and so on. Her interlocutor might dispute the precise weight she attached to the factors that led to her decision and might offer reasons for his disagreement—reasons that will themselves invoke considerations that must relevantly counter her excuse; and the promisor might dispute the weight her interlocutor attaches to them; and so on. The rationality of their enterprise is determined by their shared acknowledgement of the canons and procedures that control or limit what might competently be of-

fered as a relevant ground for defense and criticism; but the relevance of these grounds can be acknowledged by both without them both assigning the same weight to any given ground.

> What is enough to counter my claim to be right or justified in taking a certain action is up to me, up to me to determine. I don't *care* that he is an enemy of the state; it's too bad that he took what I said as a promise... I can *refuse to accept* a "ground for doubt" without impugning it as false, and without supplying a new basis, and yet not be dismissed as irrational or morally incompetent. What I *cannot* do, and yet maintain my position as morally competent, is to deny the *relevance* of your doubts ("What difference does it make that I promised, that he's an enemy of the state..."), fail to see that they require a determination by me. (Cavell 1979, 267)

Hence Cavell's objection to the Rawlsian idea that what counts as an adequate basis for a moral judgment is determined by the practice or institution of morality or justice or promising (an objection that he motivates in part through a long discussion of the role of rules in games). The response that a given moral agent makes to a specific moral issue—to accept a ground for doubt another offers her, to contest it, or simply to deny its significance—reveals not what the practice impersonally determines the right conclusion to be, but rather what she personally regards as justified, what she is prepared to be answerable for; it reveals the moral position for which she is taking responsibility, and hence it reveals *her.* And it is then open to others to determine their stance towards that position, to determine whether they can agree with it, or disagree with it whilst respecting it (and hence her), or discover that she and they are not in the same moral universe. In short, the criteria of relevance shared by those competent in the practice of moral argument open a space in which the right to acknowledge and determine for oneself the relative importance of multiple and competing cares and commitments can coexist with the achievement of a community of mutual understanding and respect. Cavell sees in this human mode of criterially governed interaction a way in which the search for community can be prosecuted without the sacrifice of individuality.

8. I trust that the basic pattern of Cavell's conception, both here and in the apparently more general case of projecting words, is clear. Once seen, its recurrence (with variations) throughout his work becomes striking; and it might help to clarify matters further if I briefly examine the inflection of it that structures his study of cinematic comedies of remarriage, *Pursuits of Happiness.*[11]

---

11 Cavell 1981.

The analytical spine of the book is a highly distinctive notion of genre, which he defines not by a list of essential features that must be manifest in any film that will count as an instance of the genre (as a type of object might be defined by the set of properties that any instance of the type must possess), but rather by the fact that its members share the inheritance of certain conditions, procedures and subjects and goals of composition, and that each member represents a study of those conditions. What distinguishes each member from its fellows is that it bears the common responsibility of its inheritance differently; it may, for example, introduce new features to the genre, but in so doing it must show how it can be understood either as compensating for any hitherto-standard feature that it lacks, and/or as contributing to a deeper characterization of the genre as a whole. Thus, any genre must be understood as essentially open to change, sometimes very radical change, and no single feature of it can be held to be immune to removal as long as the member in which that removal is effected can be shown to provide a compensation for it. On the other hand, no such alteration in the inheritance can properly be effected without the provision of compensation; and if a film provides no compensation for an absence it effects, if what it provides in its stead cannot be seen as a further interpretation of the genre's inheritance, then it can be said to have negated that feature—and in so doing, it generates or places itself within an adjacent genre, a different inheritance.

Once again, then, we see an inflection of the familiar pattern. Anyone wishing to make a film that is a member of a given genre (call her the director) must acknowledge her inheritance, which means neither denying its central features nor simply reiterating them, but rather studying them—seeking to deepen her own and our understanding of the multiple, interrelated, and multidimensional terms of that inheritance by subjecting them to forms of compensatory alteration that can be understood to draw out hitherto-implicit ranges of their significance. We might think of this as the director's capacity to project the genre into a new context, one which we can come to accept as an unpredictable but retrospectively justifiable step in its development. A successful contribution to the genre thus amounts to a non-arbitrary variation in the genre's inheritance, and each such contribution reveals the genre's indefinitely variable constancy.

9. The relevance of this excursus on film to the matter of Cavell's Wittgensteinian vision of language is, I hope, clear. Since the criteria of any given concept locate it in a system or web of concepts that informs and is informed by human forms of life (call it the word's inheritance), its grammatical schematism possesses a flexible inflexibility, an intolerant tolerance. Its projections into new contexts must either show that its usual valences are carried over into it, or that they can be modified in acceptable ways, or that (and how) the context's inability

to tolerate the projection of certain concepts to which the given concept is normally related can itself be tolerated. This is the concept's essential inflexibility, that which allows us to say that what has been projected into the new context is the same old concept. But there are no formulae that determine in advance how broad a field of the concept's related concepts must carry over, or what degree of modification of any given conceptual relation might be acceptable, or whether (and, if so, when and why) something about a given projection might compensate for the absence of a given conceptual relation; such judgments will be context-specific and dependent upon the reach of the speaker's understanding and imagination. This is the concept's essential flexibility, its capacity to elicit new reaches of significance from itself, from those who use it, and from the contexts it proves capable of inhabiting.

This means that Wittgensteinian criteria must be so characterized as to bring out the play in their systematicity, the way in which their interrelatedness establishes structure without occluding individual judgment. This is not a matter of making room in one's account for something other than normativity (say, freedom or individual judgment); it is a matter of showing that and how the kind of normativity they exemplify enables or rather constitutes such freedom of judgment—the openness of our words (and hence ourselves) to an essentially unpredictable (even if retrospectively explicable) future. It is precisely because the grammatical schematism of a word locates it in a horizon of interrelated words embedded in human forms of life that our projections of those words are at once deeply controlled and creative, displaying the kind of imaginative reach that only an acknowledgement of constraint makes possible.

Once we have seen this, however, it seems to me that the question of whether this vision of the normativity of language should be given expression in terms of rules becomes essentially semantic. On the one hand, we should recognize that invocations of rule-governed activity—so often exemplified by games such as chess or baseball—might mislead us into thinking that disagreements (particularly deeply charged philosophical disagreements) over the legitimacy of a certain projection of a word can be settled by reference to the impersonal authority of a rulebook containing determinations for every possible eventuality. Some aspects of Rawls's account of moral and political discourse seem to imply such a misconception (both of games and of language-games); and so do some aspects of Baker and Hacker's philosophical practice (for example, their occasional tendency to regard their philosophical interlocutors as if they were deviant pupils). On the other hand, we should also recognize that attempting to motivate or reinforce the rejection of that misconception by rejecting talk of rules altogether might be equally (if oppositely) misleading. For what is needed in place of that misconception is an account of word-use that makes room for a speaker's need to take responsibility for determining whether and how she accepts a given word's projections, whilst acknowledging that such responsibilities can only be exercised within a horizon of linguistic normativity of almost unimaginable range and systematicity.

The conception of rule-following, and hence of grammatical rules, that informs Baker and Hacker's official account of grammar and criteria plainly has a place for the main considerations that generate this vision of linguistic normativity in Wittgenstein's texts—for example, his emphasis upon the interweaving of definitions and applications, of rule-following activities with the general normative background of teaching, explaining, justifying, and criticizing; and of ways of using words with forms of human life and patterns of natural reaction and response—even if they lack Cavell's awareness of their importance and their vulnerability to methodological repression. If that is so, then nothing of substance will hang on whether we follow such commentators in thinking of those normative articulations as rules or talk instead of norms, or standards, or canons. What matters is that we properly acknowledge their distinctive normative character, both in what we say about them and in what we say as philosophers (that is, as recounters of grammar) about anything.

# Bibliography

Affeldt, Steven (1998), "The Ground of Mutuality: Criteria, Judgment and Intelligibility in Stephen Mulhall and Stanley Cavell." In: *European Journal of Philosophy* 6, 1–31.

Baker, G.P. / Hacker, P.M.S. (1985), *Wittgenstein: Rules, Grammar and Necessity*, Oxford: Blackwell.

Cavell, Stanley (1976), *Must We Mean What We Say?*, Cambridge: Cambridge University Press.

Cavell, Stanley (1979), *The Claim of Reason: Wittgenstein, Skepticism, Morality, and Tragedy*, Oxford: Oxford University Press.

Cavell, Stanley (1981), *Pursuits of Happiness: The Hollywood Comedy of Remarriage*, Cambridge, MA: Harvard University Press.

Cavell, Stanley (1990), *Conditions Handsome and Unhandsome: The Constitution of Emersonian Perfectionism*, Chicago: University of Chicago Press.

Mulhall, Stephen (1994), *Stanley Cavell: Philosophy's Recounting of the Ordinary*, Oxford: Oxford University Press.

Mulhall, Stephen (2003), "Stanley Cavell's Vision of the Normativity of Language: Grammar, Criteria, and Rules." In: Richard Eldrige (ed.), *Stanley Cavell*, Cambridge: Cambridge University Press, 79–106.

Witherspoon, Edward (2000), "Conceptions of Nonsense in Carnap and Wittgenstein." In: Alice Crary and Rupert Read (eds.), *The New Wittgenstein*, London: Routledge, 315–347.

Wittgenstein, Ludwig (1998), *Philosophical Investigations*, G.E.M. Anscombe (trans.), Oxford: Blackwell.

Steven G. Affeldt
# The Normativity of the Natural

> Underlying the tyranny of convention
> is the tyranny of nature.[1]

## §1

In "The Ground of Mutuality,"[2] I argued that by characterizing language as a framework of rules and construing operating within such a framework as the condition for intelligible speech, Stephen Mulhall's *Stanley Cavell*[3] had departed significantly from Cavell's work and had failed to capture the central thrust of his presentation of, and inheritance of, Wittgenstein's vision of language. One way of specifying this thought is to say that Mulhall's text failed to capture the way in which—and the depth at which—for Cavell, Wittgenstein's vision of language is formed in response to the continuous threat of skepticism, understood as the "human drive to transcend itself, make itself inhuman, which should not end until, as in Nietzsche, the human is over,"[4] and consequently that it failed to capture what I might call Cavell's and Wittgenstein's sense of the individual burden of intelligibility. What I mean, briefly, is this: The nature of Mulhall's focus on rules meant that his account did not seem to have captured the manner in which, or the depth at which, Cavell and Wittgenstein bind intelligibility to maintaining connection with human desires, interests, purposes, forms of life, natural reactions, and the like; nor had it adequately captured the possibilities of and drives toward the emptiness that comes of repudiating this connection—a drive that I understand Cavell to register in speaking of a wish to "empty out my contribution to words, so that language itself, as if beyond me, exclusively takes over the responsibility for meaning"[5]; and so, consequently, it had not adequately captured Cavell's and Wittgenstein's understanding of the ground of, but also the fragility of, mutual intelligibility—the importance of our revealing

---

1 Cavell 1979, 125. Further references to *The Claim of Reason* will be included in the text as CR followed by page numbers.
2 Affeldt 1998.
3 Mulhall 1994.
4 Cavell 1989, 56–57.
5 Cavell 1989, 57.

and our being able to discover in others, from moment to moment, the human desires, interests, purposes, and the like that inform speech and action.[6]

The two papers of Mulhall's under consideration here—"Stanley Cavell's Vision of the Normativity of Language: Grammar, Criteria, and Rules" and "Inner Constancy, Outer Variation: Stanley Cavell on Grammar, Criteria, and Rules"—mark a significant development in thought about these matters.[7] In particular, they not only develop sustained and provocative interpretations of central moments in Cavell's work, but they also clarify the conception of rules that Mulhall wishes to employ, illuminate why he feels free to employ such a conception, and more importantly, illuminate why he finds it necessary to employ such a conception in order to capture Wittgenstein's and Cavell's vision of language.[8] These papers—together with a couple of extensive and fruitful conversations with him—have provided me with a much greater appreciation of the subtlety of Mulhall's views, and I know that several of the arguments advanced in "The Ground of Mutuality" would require, at least, reformulation in light of them.

However, I continue to have concerns, concerns about some of the interpretive claims that Mulhall advances regarding Cavell and Wittgenstein and about the vision of language, the normativity of language-use, and the possibility and fragility of intelligibility that he presents. In the pages to follow, I will endeavor to articulate some of these concerns.

Before beginning to do so, two final introductory words are in order. First, the papers under consideration are primarily devoted to considering specific mo-

---

**6** I have elsewhere tried to capture the thought sketched here by saying that, for Wittgenstein, mutual intelligibility depends (a) upon our individually revealing the position within the circuit of human desires, interests, purposes, forms of life, natural reactions, and the like from which we speak or act, and (b) upon others being able to discover, and their being interested in discovering, that position. See Affeldt 1999.

**7** Mulhall 2003, Mulhall 2014 (in this volume).

**8** It should be noted that Mulhall's explicit strategy in Mulhall 2003 is to argue that Cavell's view of grammar and criteria is *compatible* with the claim that they are rules rather than to argue that they *must* be rules, and that in Mulhall 2014 he remarks that "whilst nothing that Cavell says in outlining and putting to use his highly distinctive understanding of Wittgenstein's notion of criterion *requires* the use of the concept of a rule of grammar (and Cavell himself does not use it), the most salient aspects of his account can be restated in such terms without distortion, and certain turns of his argument seem in fact to embody assumptions that would be highly congenial to commentators who prefer to employ such terms" (2014, 299). (So then, one wonders, what makes Cavell's account "highly distinctive"?) But the thrust of his argument in both papers, although more directly in Mulhall 2014, suggests that some notion of rules—whether called by that term or not—is necessary for understanding Wittgenstein's (and Cavell's) vision of language and accounting for the normativity of language-use. I will note several specific moments in support of this claim toward the close of §2 below.

ments in Cavell's work. The arguments and interpretations that Mulhall develops in doing so are often powerful and they all deserve, and would repay, detailed examination. However, while I will exam Mulhall's treatment of a couple of moments in Cavell's work explicitly and will touch on others, the focus of my attention lies elsewhere. In particular, it lies in exploring a number of more general thoughts underlying and informing his discussion. For these thoughts, it seems to me, not only lie at the heart of his orientation toward Wittgenstein and Cavell (and at the heart of my concerns about that orientation), but they also motivate his efforts to show that Cavell's view of criteria and grammar is compatible with regarding them as species of rules and that Cavell's specific criticisms of rule-based conceptions of language do not generalize. Second, while this essay bears only a minimal relation to the remarks I offered at the conference the proceedings of which are collected in the present volume, I have tried to preserve the spirit of those remarks. By this I mean that I have tried to preserve the tone and the structure of remarks offered in response to a paper—sometimes making quite specific points or raising specific questions, sometimes moving at a more general level, but always with the aim not of settling any issues but of provoking further thought about them.

## §2

There are three closely related Wittgensteinian (and Cavellian) thoughts that are central to much of Mulhall's discussion. I will begin by sketching them.

First, our uses of language and our agreement in language are, as Cavell expresses it, "pervasively, almost unimaginably, systematic" (CR, 29) and these uses and this agreement have an equally pervasive normative character. That is, we for the most part agree in what we call things and in when, where, and how we use our words. This is to say that we agree in what ranges of additional concepts must normally be applicable in order for a given concept to be applicable; in the implications of the use of a given concept or of a given remark; in what is, or may be, a relevant, illuminating, amusing, intelligible, etc., response to a given remark; in what sort of challenges or questions must be accepted as pertinent in response to a remark; in the kinds of ways in which such challenges or questions must be met; and in a host of similar matters. Competent speakers of a language know such things, even if they have not and perhaps could not have explicitly formulated them for themselves. And if you are to be judged a competent speaker of the language, then you must acknowledge that the competent employment of a given concept requires the applicability of certain other concepts (or be able to show why, in this instance, it does not); you must acknowledge certain challenges to the use of a concept as relevant (or be able to show why, in this instance, you do not), must meet such challenges in a range of acceptable ways (or be able to show why, in this instance, you do not), and so on. Of course, such matters are importantly open-ended—there is, for example, no fixed range of further concepts that must be applicable in order for a given concept to be applicable—but they are also deeply controlled. We might say that the ways in which such matters are open-ended are not themselves open-ended.

Second, speaking a language is fundamentally different from merely acting from a disposition to produce and respond to certain words in certain situations. This is not to deny that there may be, say, causal mechanisms of some kind at work in speaking and understanding language, but only to say that speaking and understanding language are not to be understood in terms of these causal mechanisms.[9] This thought is part of what I understand Mulhall to be invoking in speaking of Baker and Hacker's account of language as meant to "allow them to reject dispositional or more generally causal accounts of meaning, which attempt to reduce the notion of our grasp of a word's meaning to the presence or absence of a disposition to deploy and respond to a given word in specific, regular ways" (Mulhall 2014, 296). Further, this difference between speaking and understanding language and the disposition to produce and respond to words is not to be accounted for in terms of any accompanying and animating mental act—which is to say that speaking and understanding language are not to be understood as behavior from a disposition to produce and respond to words *plus* a mental act of meaning or grasping meaning.

And third, there are specific, open-ended—but non-arbitrarily open-ended—conditions on/for everything that we are able to do. There are specific conditions on/for saying something, doing something, thinking something, experiencing something, understanding something, and so on. That is, Wittgenstein is concerned to remind us that not just anything that one does or says in any circumstances whatever will count as, will be, doing, saying, meaning, understanding,

---

9 Wittgenstein speaks directly to this issue in Wittgenstein 1968 §493 (henceforth: PI).

We say: "The cock calls the hens by crowing"—but doesn't a comparison with our language lie at the bottom of this? Isn't the aspect quite altered if we imagine the crowing to set the hens in motion by some kind of physical causation?

But if it were shewn how the words "Come to me" act on the person addressed, so that finally, given certain conditions, the muscles of his legs are innervated, and so on—should we feel that that sentence lost the character of a *sentence*?

I take it that we do not, and that the idea of a person being "addressed" cannot be captured in terms of a causal mechanism.

experiencing something in particular—for example, expecting Mr. N.N., asking the name of a thing, paying a bill, declining an invitation, meaning a building by 'bank,' and so on. And he is further concerned to remind us that what makes what we do or say doing or saying anything in particular is not an independent, animating mental act *accompanying* our words or actions—for, to go no further, there are conditions on/for "mental acts" as well. Here Wittgenstein may be understood as writing in response to a twofold sense. First, he is writing in response to a sense that the very possibility of our doing anything has become mysterious—that it has become mysterious how it is so much as possible for us to think something, mean something, expect something, understand something, perform some action, and so on. When we reflect philosophically upon our words and actions they can seem dead, impotent to mean or accomplish anything. And second, he is writing in response to a sense that the ways in which we try to redeem the possibility of our doing anything—predominantly by positing a mental act lying behind and animating what we regard as the in-themselves dead sounds and movements we make, a mental act that transforms those sounds and movements into meaning, understanding, expecting, and so on—only make the possibility of our doing anything all the more mysterious.[10] Accordingly, when the possibility of some phenomenon becomes mysterious to us, Wittgenstein undertakes to remove this sense of mysteriousness by reminding us of the ordinary circumstances in which this phenomenon is said to occur, of the criteria for this phenomenon, and in this way to direct our attention to the ordinary conditions for our counting someone as having experienced, done, or said something in particular and to the role that the surrounding circumstances play in our counting it as such. So, for example, if the possibility of someone pointing to the color of an object begins to seem mysterious to us, the pointing gesture of the hand impotent to *mean* the color as opposed to the object itself, or its shape, or whatever, and we are inclined to imagine that the power of the pointing hand to mean the color must lie not in the hand (in the gesture) but in some mental act of meaning the color (as though through a radiating mental beam of some sort), then Wittgenstein will undertake to remind us of ordinary

---

**10** Here is one juncture at which the temptation to read Wittgenstein as some form of behaviorist, a temptation he registers in allowing an interlocutory voice to ask whether he isn't "really a behaviorist in disguise" (PI §307), emerges. Happily, this temptation is now less frequently acceded to than it once was. For what Wittgenstein undertakes to show is that the temptation toward behaviorism and the temptation toward animating mental acts both begin from the same mistake—regarding our words and actions as, in themselves, dead. The behaviorist accepts this "fact" while what we might call the mentalist seeks to breathe life into our words and actions.

circumstances in which, and ordinary ways in which, one may point to the color of an object—say, by pointing to another object of the same color—and the sense of mysteriousness and of the need for a special mental act of meaning is dispelled.[11]

Mulhall and I do not differ in regarding these three thoughts, at least on a certain understanding of them, as central to Wittgenstein and Cavell. We differ primarily, but not exclusively, in our understanding of the relation of these thoughts to a conception of rules. For Mulhall, making sense of each of these thoughts requires some conception of rules. That he regards a conception of rules as essential to making sense of our agreement in language and its normativity is made clear by the number of times in which he moves without argument from the claim that normativity is at issue to the claim that *therefore* rules must be at issue. (See, for example, Mulhall 2003, 85 – 87, 93, 98)[12] He explicitly argues that the idea of language-use as a rule-following activity is essential to accounting for what it is to speak a language—indeed, there is a suggestion that he regards rule-following as *the* essential determinant of what it is to speak (Mulhall 2014). In the same vein he claims that Wittgenstein's discussion of rule-following "appears designed to give [his] own account of linguistic meaning" (Mulhall 2003, 105), suggesting again that a conception of rules is essential to Wittgenstein's understanding of meaningful speech. And, finally, throughout both articles, he argues that the criteria for and the grammatical conditions on saying something, doing something, meaning something, experiencing something, and so on are rules.[13]

Given, then, that Mulhall regards a conception of rules as essential to making sense of central Wittgensteinian and Cavellian thoughts, and given that Cavell's work on Wittgenstein does not explicitly assign any central place to a conception of rules, Mulhall must maintain that Cavell is implicitly relying upon a conception of rules. Accordingly, he must argue, first, that Cavell's explicit criti-

---

**11** This example derives from Cavell's consideration of *Philosophical Investigations* §33 in CR, 74 – 5.

**12** Here Mulhall seems to be in at least prima facie disagreement with Cavell. For following his remark that our uses of language are "pervasively, almost unimaginably, systematic," Cavell adds that no "current idea of 'convention'" could explain this intimacy of agreement that is revealed in eliciting criteria. He remarks that "there would have to be, we could say, too many conventions in play, one for each shade of each word in each context" (CR, 31). Mulhall's reliance upon an idea of rules of language suggests that he thinks otherwise.

**13** In Mulhall 2003, he seems somewhat more guarded—and is certainly more elusive. For while he does speak of grammar and criteria as rules and as constituting a web of rules, he also frequently speaks of them as a species of rules, as akin to rules, and as illuminatingly glossed in terms of rules.

cisms of readings of Wittgenstein that make a conception of rules central do not carry weight against a more nuanced conception of rules and, second, that Cavell's own interpretation of Wittgenstein may be expressed in terms of rules without distortion.

I approach these matters otherwise. Rather than taking the fact that Cavell shares with Wittgenstein the three thoughts I have noted to imply that he must be implicitly relying upon a conception of rules, I take the fact of his criticisms of rule-based conceptions of language and the absence of any explicit place for rules in his own work on Wittgenstein to mean that for Cavell, and for Wittgenstein as he understands him, making sense of these thoughts does not require any central place for a conception of rules. Indeed, I take Wittgenstein and Cavell to argue that to appeal to a conception of rules in making sense of these thoughts is to fundamentally distort not only these thoughts themselves, but the nature of human language and our life with and in language. It is a distortion rooted in *comparing* language to logic or to games and calculi with fixed rules. This is what I take Wittgenstein to be suggesting in saying that if "you say that our languages only *approximate* to such calculi you are standing on the very brink of a misunderstanding" and what I take Cavell to be suggesting in claiming that Wittgenstein's "new, and central, concept of 'grammar' is developed in opposition to" a view of language based around a conception of rules.[14] It is not *equating* ordinary language and a calculus with fixed rules that is distorting; it is the comparison itself that misdirects and distorts our thinking. To adapt a remark of Wittgenstein's, the comparison of language to a calculus represents a "misunderstanding of the logic of language" (PI §93)— not a misunderstanding of the logic of some aspect of our language, but a misunderstanding of the logic of the concept 'language.'[15] Accordingly, as I understand it, the distortion will not be avoided or rectified, as Mulhall holds, through offering a more nuanced account of rules.

I can put the issue here as follows. In giving a central place to the three thoughts that I have noted, Mulhall is accurately registering deep and important affinities between Wittgenstein and the logicism of Frege and the positivism of early Carnap. In particular, he is accurately registering their shared antipathy to psychologism and their shared embrace of forms of the context principle. However, in regarding a conception of rules as essential to making sense of these three ideas, Mulhall leaves Wittgenstein too close to logicism and positi-

---

**14** PI §81; Cavell 1976, 48.
**15** Here I am following Rush Rhees, and in particular his discussions of the logic of language in "Wittgenstein's Builders" and "The Philosophy of Wittgenstein," both of which are reprinted in Rhees 1970.

vism. On Mulhall's view, Wittgenstein's general orientation to these issues remains within the same horizon as that of Frege and Carnap, while the specific conception of rules is (importantly) altered. In contrast, I understand Wittgenstein to have sought to effect a deeper and more radical overcoming of logicism and positivism, an overcoming that effectively displaces any central role for even a quite nuanced conception of rules. Toward the close of these pages, I will say something about how I understand the nature of this overcoming of logicism and positivism and about the horizon of thought about language, and about our life with and in language, that it opens.

# §3

I want now to consider in some detail a couple of Mulhall's more general claims noted above, in particular his claims that Wittgenstein's discussion of rule-following appears designed to give his own account of linguistic meaning and that Wittgenstein seems to understand language-use as fundamentally a rule-governed activity. Although these claims are given more sustained treatment in Mulhall 2013 than in Mulhall 2003, it must be said that it is not part of Mulhall's direct purpose in either paper to argue for them extensively. Nevertheless, it is important that they be considered, for as I noted in §1, these claims lie at the heart of Mulhall's orientation toward both Wittgenstein and Cavell and they motivate his examination of specific moments in Cavell's work.

As with most of the thoughts Mulhall advances in these papers, these two central claims are intimately bound together. However, I will somewhat artificially separate them, and begin with the claim that Wittgenstein's discussion of rule-following gives his own account of linguistic meaning.

This claim seems to have two aspects. First, the meaning of a word is, or is constituted through, what Mulhall sees as the grammatical and criterial rules linking its employment to the employment of other words so that to know the meaning of a word is to know or to grasp, even if not explicitly, the grammatical and criterial rules governing its use. Second, to speak, as opposed to behaving from a disposition to produce and respond to certain words in certain situations, consists in rule-following. (Clearly, this second aspect is closely connected to the idea that language-use is fundamentally a rule-following activity and it will be considered more fully in connection with that idea.)

This claim is, self-evidently, enormous and for that reason alone it would be folly to imagine that it can be addressed at all thoroughly in a brief compass. Accordingly, I will restrict myself to a few specific and a few more general remarks.

First, in both articles, the thought that Wittgenstein's discussion of rule-following provides a substantive account of linguistic meaning is pervasive and represents, for Mulhall, a deep point of continuity between Wittgenstein and other philosophers—a point to which I will return. Here, however, I want to look briefly at the context in which the claim emerges directly in Mulhall 2003. It emerges at the close of an extended consideration of Cavell's criticism of Kripke's assimilation of the words of ordinary language to mathematical functions—an assimilation represented in Kripke's claim that mathematical examples bring out "most smoothly" problems that "apply throughout language" and in his construction of the concept "tabair" on the model of his construction of the mathematical function "quus."[16] Cavell's criticism of this assimilation appears to cast doubt upon the relevance, or at least the *direct* relevance, of Wittgenstein's discussion of mathematical rule-following in illuminating ordinary language. That is, it appears to suggest that his discussion of mathematical rule-following cannot offer any general illumination concerning what Mulhall understands to be linguistic rule-following—following the rules governing the words of ordinary language. In this connection, Mulhall remarks that

> ... of course, the main reason most Wittgenstein commentators have assumed that the example of addition casts light on the nature of linguistic rules and hence upon grammar is that the text of the *Philosophical Investigations* appears to share that assumption. It takes a mathematical example as normative for the whole of its discussion of rule-following, and that discussion appears designed to give Wittgenstein's own account of linguistic meaning. (Mulhall 2003, 104-5)

What is happening here, it seems to me, is this. Mulhall recognizes and wishes to acknowledge the force of Cavell's criticism of Kripke. Therefore, he seeks a way of accommodating that criticism, and since he shares the assumption that the discussion of rule-following gives Wittgenstein's own account of linguistic meaning, his strategy of accommodation is to deny that Wittgenstein takes the mathematical as normative for his discussion of rule-following (and, therefore, for the nature of linguistic rules in general). He suggests that Wittgenstein, through using a mathematical example in his considerations of rule-following, is acting out a fantasy of linguistic rules for therapeutic purposes (Mulhall 2003, 105). However, I find this strategy interpretively implausible. It seems interpretively more plausible to allow that Wittgenstein does, as the surface of his texts suggests, take the mathematical as normative for his discussion of rule-following. He takes a mathematical rule, and in particular a mathematical rule as simple as '+2,' as norma-

---

16 Kripke 1982, 19. Cavell's criticism of this assimilation occurs in Cavell 1990, 87 ff.

tive for his discussion of rule-following because it provides a best case for investigating the idea of rule-following and so for bringing to light our confusions about the normative power of rules and the fantasies concerning the nature of rules that we construct in order to account for that power as we confusedly imagine it. However, if this suggestion is accepted, then accommodating Cavell's arguments against Kripke's assimilation of mathematics and ordinary language will mean allowing that Wittgenstein's discussion of rule-following is not intended as normative for, or representative of, language in general—even though, as is true enough, the discussion issues in some general conclusions about language. This is to say that it is not intended to give his own account of the nature of linguistic meaning. If we allow this, we may be prepared to reconsider Cavell's early claims about "Wittgenstein's 'purpose' in investigating the concept of a rule," namely, that this investigation "allows him to formulate one source of a distorted conception of language—one to which, in philosophizing, we are particularly susceptible, and which helps to secure distortion in philosophical theorizing," and that "[h]e wishes to indicate how inessential the 'appeal to rules' is as an explanation of language."[17]

Second, it must be acknowledged, however, that there are moments in Cavell (and in Wittgenstein) that can appear to support Mulhall's claim that the meaning of a word is (or is given by) its grammatical relations and that to know the meaning of a word is to know these grammatical relations. However, whether these moments in fact support the claim remains, for me, doubtful. I'll sketch three reasons why.

Consider first Cavell's elaboration of the idea of the grammatical schematism of a word—an idea that plays a key role in Mulhall's discussions (I shall return, in §4, to Mulhall's use of the idea). Cavell says the following:

> To think of a word as embodying a concept is to think of the word as having a grammatical schematism of the sort I have sketched for "chair" and "pointing to"; the schematism marks out the set of criteria on the basis of which the word is applied in all the grammatical contexts into which it fits and will be found to fit (in investigating which we are investigating part of its grammar). The concept is this schematism—a sense of the word's potency to assume just those valences, and a sense that in each case there will be a point of application of the word, and that the point will be the same from context to context, or that the point will shift in a recognizable pattern or direction. In this sense a concept is the meaning of a word. (CR, 77–8)

These remarks can certainly seem to support Mulhall's view. However, Cavell follows these remarks by saying: "So it is empty to explain the meaning of a word

---

**17** Cavell 1976, 51–2.

by appealing to its concept [i.e. to its grammatical schematism]. If anything, its concept is explained, unwrinkled before us, by going through the meanings of, what we mean in using, the word" (CR, 78). Why is it empty to explain the meaning of a word by appealing to its concept? I can imagine several possible reasons for this claim, but will mention only the one that I regard as most weighty. It is empty to explain the meaning of a word by appealing to its grammatical schematism because to be able to recognize the point of application of a word as the same from context to context or as shifting in recognizable patterns depends upon your already being within the life of the meaning of the word. That is, the notions of sameness and of recognizable patterns of shift in the employment of a word depend upon your appreciating the meaning of the word, upon your being an initiate of the forms of life expressed in and through the use of that word. Accordingly, unless you are already within the life of the meaning of the word, there is for you no grammatical schematism of the word. Which is to say that what it is to know the meaning of a word cannot (only) be, and is not explained by, knowing the grammatical schematism of the word.[18]

Consider further, in this same connection, an essential feature of the grammatical schematism of "chair" as Cavell sketches it; namely, the use of the demonstrative in "It is part of the grammar of the word 'chair' that *this* is what we call 'to sit on a chair'" (CR, 71). Cavell remarks that the function of the demonstrative is to "[register] that we are to recollect those very general facts of nature or culture which we all, all who can talk and act together, do (must) in fact be using as criteria; facts which we only need to recollect, for we cannot fail to know them in the sense of never having acquired them" (CR, 73). This invocation of very general facts of nature or culture points to the background of our biological and social forms of life within which we use our words, which informs those uses, and apart from which they would not have the relations, connections, and significances they have. These very general facts of nature or culture include, for example, that our bodies are of a certain stature and configuration; that the extent of our reach is less than the extent of our step and far less than the extent of our (normal) vision; that objects are more or less enduring, offer resistance to our touch, and do not (generally) move or change shape on their own; that there is day and night; that we orient ourselves more by sight than by smell; that we are capable of many tones of voice and that we regard these tones as significant; that

---

**18** In sketching this thought, I am indebted to some ideas developed in Minar 2010. In the context of explaining why there is liable to be a certain dogmatism in our sense that the child in PI §§185 ff. is missing something "already there" in the meaning of the rule "+2," Minar suggests that this is "because the patterns and connections already there in the practice cannot be apprehended prior to one's beginning to gain a mastery of it" (Minar 2010, 199).

we can make facial expressions; that we laugh; that we eat together but do not (generally) bathe together; and untold other facts of the same sort.[19] But these background facts of nature or culture, these facts characterizing our forms of life, will not and cannot be captured in a grammatical rule governing the use of a word—a point to which I will return in discussing one part of Mulhall's discussion of Cavell's criticism of Kripke on rules. And this suggests, at a minimum, that grasping grammatical rules cannot be all that is involved in knowing the meaning of a word and how much is left out in saying that in learning words we are learning rules governing their use.

To mention just one final thought in this connection: Cavell consistently emphasizes that for Wittgenstein criteria are recalled or grammatical investigations are undertaken "when we 'don't know our way about,' when we are lost with respect to our words and to the world they anticipate. Then we start finding ourselves by finding out and declaring the criteria upon which we are in agreement" (CR, 34). The recounting of criteria and the conducting of grammatical investigations, for Wittgenstein (as Cavell understands him), occur in response to specific moments of confusion or disorientation.[20] But then this suggests that it would be a mistake to think that in conducting these recuperative exercises we are uncovering what it is to know the meaning of a word, or what we know in knowing the meaning of a word, or a structure of grammar or of grammatical rules that we are always basing ourselves upon in speaking meaningfully. These exercises, as Cavell says, are "academic" or "reconstructed" (CR, 79). But further, (1) the structure of the recounting of criteria and grammatical investigation will be determined by the specific nature of the confusion or disorientation to which it responds, (2) it can involve matters that do not seem to be any part of the ordinary meaning of the word (in the *Blue Book*, for example, Wittgenstein suggests that to recover our sense of the meaning of talk of sensations it will help to accustom ourselves to the idea of having pain in another person's body or in an inanimate object), and

---

**19** In emphasizing the importance of these kinds of very general facts of nature, Wittgenstein joins—and perhaps even goes beyond—Nietzsche in working to recall the philosophical significance of the fact of human embodiment. Cavell distinguishes between a biological and a social sense of forms of life, and emphasizes the importance to Wittgenstein of the biological sense, in his "Declining Decline: Wittgenstein as a Philosopher of Culture" in Cavell 1989.

**20** A form of this idea occurs in Cavell's work as early as "Must We Mean What We Say?" In that essay, he writes:

> When should we ask ourselves when we should (and should not) say "The x is F" in order to find out what an F(x) is?... The answer suggested is: When you have to. When you have more facts than you know what to make of, or when you do not know what new facts would show. When, that is, you need a clear view of what you already know. When you need to do philosophy. (Cavell 1976, 21)

(3) we can "invent fictitious natural history for our purposes" (PI, p. 230). As I understand them, then, these recuperative exercises do not reveal the always-present ground of our intelligibility and linguistic competence but provide us with methods for finding our way back to these, however they are grounded—a matter on which these procedures are silent.[21]

Here, as at the end of the first specific point sketched above, we touch once again upon a much larger issue. The issue is nothing less than whether, or in what sense, Wittgenstein intends to provide a substantive account of linguistic meaning—in his discussion of rule-following or elsewhere. It was primarily for this reason that I said it would be folly to imagine that Mulhall's claim that Wittgenstein's discussion of rule-following gives his own account of linguistic meaning could be discussed at all thoroughly in this context. However, something must be said about this issue, for it is one of the deepest points of difference in how Mulhall and I approach Wittgenstein (and Cavell).

As I noted above, Mulhall regards what he sees as Wittgenstein's attempt to provide an account of linguistic meaning as bespeaking his affinity with the philosophical tradition in the West since Plato. In the introductory section of Mulhall 2003, after sketching some of the interpretive issues surrounding how to understand Cavell's and Wittgenstein's notions of grammar and criteria, he says the following:

> It is worth emphasizing that the issues at stake here are not of significance only to those who have an already-established interest in Wittgenstein's vision of language. For when Wittgenstein talks of our capacity to grasp or to recall the criteria or grammar of words, he is concerned with what philosophers in the analytic tradition would refer to as our mastery of a certain fragment of a natural language; and they would equate that ability aptly to apply words with mastery of the corresponding concepts. So understood, clarifying the nature of our linguistic abilities will cast light on what it is to master concepts, and hence illuminate a question that has been central to philosophical reflection since Plato. Moreover, since analytic philosophers have tended to assume that our mastery of words is a mastery of rules which govern their use, arguing instead about how best to understand the nature of those rules... to question whether Wittgenstein would think of criteria as rules at all amounts to suggesting that Wittgenstein's work—rather than conforming in this fundamental respect to analytic assumptions—in fact aims to place them in question. (Mulhall 2003, 80–1)

This passage makes explicit what is clear enough from the tenor of both of the Mulhall papers under discussion—namely, that Mulhall regards Wittgenstein's work as "conforming in this fundamental respect to analytic assumptions."

---

**21** I discuss the issues touched on in this paragraph much more fully in Affeldt 1998.

But at this point the conformity to analytic assumptions of interest to me is not simply the narrow issue of whether our mastery of concepts is to be understood as a grasp of rules that govern their use. What is of concern to me is the more pervasive issue of Wittgenstein's approach to traditional philosophical questions—questions such as, for example, "What is it to master concepts?" I believe it is fair to say that Mulhall regards Wittgenstein as sharing the approach to such questions that is characteristic of the philosophical tradition since Plato. The questions are accepted as having a clear sense. It is accepted, that is, that we have a clear idea of what we are asking and why we are asking the questions and the task of philosophy is to provide responses to these questions. The task of philosophy, that is, is to provide philosophical accounts addressing philosophical questions. On this view, Wittgenstein's difference from other philosophers will rest primarily upon the nature of the accounts that he offers.[22]

But it is just here that many readers of Wittgenstein, myself among them, have sought to locate his decisive difference from the previous history of philosophy in the West—to identify why it was that he understood his work as introducing a "kink" or rupture in the history of philosophy.[23] These readers take remarks of Wittgenstein's such as "[a] philosophical problem has the form: 'I don't know my way about'" (PI §123) to mean, at least, that in philosophy we are not confronted with clear problems. Rather, we confront "one or another piece of plain nonsense" (PI §119). Or, better, what we confront is one or another piece of "disguised nonsense"—disguised, in this instance, in the form of apparently clear and pressing questions (PI §464). Accordingly, these readers of Wittgenstein do not understand him to be accepting traditional philosophical questions as

---

22 In "The Availability of Wittgenstein's Later Philosophy," Cavell allows that the investigation of the grammar of an assertion "will doubtless be reminiscent of procedures which have long been part of the familiar texture of analytic philosophy." He goes on, however, to remark that "[a] profitable way, I think, to approach the thought of the later Wittgenstein is to see how his questions about grammar differ from these... more familiar questions." One of the differences he specifies is worth noting here. He remarks:

> It is true that an explanation of the grammar of an assertion can be asked for by asking "How would you verify that?" But first, where that is what the question asks for, it is not to be assumed that the question itself makes good sense; in particular it is not sensible unless there is some doubt about how that assertion is conceived to be verified, and it therefore leads to no theory of meaning at all. (Cavell 1976, 55–6)

It is a question for me how broadly we are to conceive the scope of that final clause.

23 One place in which this sense of rupture emerges is in the following *Blue Book* remark: "If, e. g., we call our investigations 'philosophy,' this title, on the one hand, seems appropriate, on the other hand it certainly has misled people. (One might say that the subject we are dealing with is one of the heirs of the subject which used to be called 'philosophy')" (Wittgenstein 1965, 28).

well-posed and attempting to provide alternative answers. They see his descriptions, his "looking into the workings of our language" (PI §109), as intended to enable us to pass from disguised nonsense to "something that is patent nonsense" (PI §464). More specifically, they understand this descriptive work as in each case (1) directed toward enabling us to recognize as illusory our sense of a philosophical problem, to recognize this sense of a problem as in fact a muddle, and (2) *locally* directed toward the particular muddle that we are in and so as incapable of being pressed into service as part of a general philosophical account of some phenomenon.[24] In this sense, they take his claim that "[w]e must do away with all *explanation*, and description alone must take its place" (PI §109) very seriously. When Wittgenstein remarks that "[t]he philosopher's treatment of a question is like the treatment of an illness" (PI §255), I take it that part of what he means to convey is that one wants to understand the etiology and the symptoms of the question. But he also means that one wants to heal it, to remove it.[25]

---

**24** In the *Blue Book*, Wittgenstein says this: "Our problem, in other words, was not a scientific one; but a muddle felt as a problem" (Wittgenstein 1965, 6).

**25** It is true that, in PI §109 and elsewhere, Wittgenstein speaks of problems being solved. But "lösen" might also, and better, have been translated "dissolved." The strategy for reading Wittgenstein that I have been sketching is quite widespread. Indeed, at this level of generality it might almost deserve to be called an (emerging) orthodoxy. It is, in different forms, represented in Cavell's *The Claim of Reason*, in Goldfarb 1986, in much of the work on Wittgenstein by David Cerbone, James Conant, Alice Crary, Cora Diamond, David Finkelstein, and Martin Stone—representative instances of work by each of whom can be found in Crary/Read 2000—and in the work of many others. So far as I know, however, one of the first to explicitly and consistently adopt and argue for this strategy for reading Wittgenstein was O.K. Bouwsma in his extraordinary review of the *Blue Book*. Toward the close of that review, he makes the following remarks, which I indulge in the pleasure of quoting in full:

> When Protagoras was consulted about what would happen to the young Hippocrates if he associated with Protagoras, Protagoras answered: "Young man, if you associate with me, on the very first day you will return home a better man than you came, and better on the second day than on the first and better every day than you were on the day before." And now if we were to ask concerning some young Hippocrates from Harvard or Yale what would happen to him if he reads this book [the *Blue Book*], we should certainly not with the courage of Protagoras' convictions say anything like what Protagoras said. Let us try a few answers. "Young man, if you read this book as you read most books nothing whatsoever will happen to you and it won't take long. On the very first day you will return home a no-better man than you came, on the second day the same, and so on." Or: "Young man, if you read this book diligently, digging as you are used to digging in the books you read, coming up with a shining truth here and a nice bristling idea there, the chances are that you will have got it all wrong. You will go home full of indigestibles, and oh, the pity of it! a worse man than you came, not much worse, but let us say, four or five misunderstandings worse."

In making these remarks, I do not mean to deny that one can come to understand much through studying Wittgenstein's treatments of muddles disguised as meaningful (and pressing) philosophical questions. His work is not, as he sometimes seems to worry, nothing but destruction. For, to go no further, these muddles and our persistent drive toward them reveal aspects of our human nature (as currently constituted).[26] Nor do I mean to deny that Wittgenstein's work helps us to understand much about human language and speaking human language. One of the things that Wittgenstein tells us, and which his work is directed toward helping us to recognize and accept, is that "commanding, questioning, recounting, chatting, are as much a part of our natural history as walking, eating, drinking, playing" (PI §25). He wants to show us that and how our uses of language are part of our natural history, how, we might say, the fact that we use language as we do characterizes the kind of creatures that we are. It marks an ontological determination of the human being. And this is to allow, indeed to urge, that his work shows us much about what Cavell has called the life form of us talkers.[27] But then it is also to say that an "account" of human language or of linguistic meaning will be nothing less than an "account" of what it is to be human. And it is also to suggest that the felt need for a philosophical account of linguistic meaning, of a problem calling for a philosophical solution, arises out of our having refused to accept, or repudiated, our human forms of life.[28]

Let me turn now to the second central claim of Mulhall's I have identified: his claim that Wittgenstein understands language-use as fundamentally a species of rule-governed activity.

---

Or: "Young man, if you read this book with your mind wide open, and take time to stew in it or to let it stew in you; if with a little bit of luck, it should cling to you like a bramble and it should hurt and sting and all the while the agitations keep you alert, then inkling by inkling, glimpse by glimpse, chink by chink, on the very first day ten years later, you will return home a different man than you came. (Bouwsma 1965, 199–200)

I am grateful to Kelly Jolley for sending me back to this essay.

**26** This positive moment of Wittgenstein's therapeutic work is something that I regard as essential and something that I find to be insufficiently considered in some work exemplifying a therapeutic approach to Wittgenstein. I undertake to elaborate some limitations of a certain conception of the therapeutic approach to Wittgenstein in Affeldt 2010.

**27** Cf., Cavell 1989, 47–48.

**28** Here I am adapting the following thought of Cavell's:

In Wittgenstein the gap between mind and world is closed, or the distortion between them straightened, in the appreciation and acceptance of particular human forms of life, human "convention". This implies that the *sense* of a gap originates in an attempt, or wish, to escape (to remain a "stranger" to, "alienated" from) those shared forms of life, to give up responsibility for their maintenance. (CR, 109)

Given the importance of this claim for Mulhall, it is, in one sense, surprising how little direct argument he offers in support of it.[29] However, in another sense

---

29 One of his few direct supports for this claim is the following: "Wittgenstein's comparison of moments of speech to moves in a game implies that language [use] is a rule governed activity" (Mulhall 2003, 83). I want to offer a few remarks about this claim.

First, it is not clear to me what Mulhall has in mind in speaking of Wittgenstein's comparison of moments of speech to moves in a game. The only instance that I am able to locate in *Philosophical Investigations* where Wittgenstein directly makes such a comparison occurs in §81, where he speaks of a tendency in philosophy to "*compare* the use of words with games and calculi with fixed rules." Of course it is true that in PI §§83–4 Wittgenstein develops and explores an "analogy between language and games." However, in these passages he is clearly warning against this comparison and the focus that it produces on rules and following rules. Where the comparison is mentioned directly in §81, he says that we "cannot say that someone who is using language *must* be playing such a game," and then goes on to caution us against the danger that I mentioned in §2, of saying that our language only *approximates* to such games or calculi. In §81, Wittgenstein speaks of "fixed rules," and in §83 he speaks of "definite rules," so these passages taken alone might suggest that his cautions and criticisms are directed only against thinking of the use and meaning of words as requiring such an idea of rules. However, this is not the case in §84, where he remarks that "the application of a word is not everywhere bounded by rules." Nor is this the case in §80, where Wittgenstein presents us with a chair that seems alternately to appear and disappear and asks whether we are to "say that we do not really attach any meaning to [the word 'chair'] because we are not equipped with rules for every possible application of it." To which question the intended answer seems to be "no" and the point of the question seems to be to encourage us to think about why we might be tempted to think otherwise.

Second, it might be that what Mulhall has in mind in speaking of Wittgenstein comparing moments of speech to moves in a game is his use of the idea of language-games. This suggestion is given some support in Mulhall 2003, where he speaks of "Wittgenstein's investigation of the ways in which games (and hence language games?) are rule governed" (Mulhall 2003, 96). But Mulhall's question mark here indicates reservations, and for good reason. For not only are language-games not to be thought of on strict analogy with games (for reasons that I will mention immediately below), it would be flatly question-begging were Mulhall to be understood as appealing to the idea of language-games as the basis of this comparison and asserting that they are typically rule-governed. For what is at issue is exactly whether language-games are or must be rule-governed. Further, when Wittgenstein explains why he introduces the idea of language-games and what he means it to highlight, he does not speak of rules. Rather, what he says, memorably, is that "the term 'language-*game*' is meant to bring into prominence the fact that the *speaking* of language is part of an activity, or of a form of life" (PI §23). While I will return to this idea later in this essay, I will gloss it for now by saying that speaking is fundamentally a way of relating ourselves to (actual or imagined) others, occupying specific positions (characterized by their beliefs, expectations, knowledge, histories, desires, and the like), in specific circumstances, for specific purposes.

Finally, for reasons that are closely connected to these considerations about speaking as part of a form of life, it seems to me unhelpful and misleading to compare moments of speech to moves in a game. For as Cavell argues in Part Three of *The Claim of Reason*, games—at least most games —are delightfully free of the various complexities, burdens, and responsibilities of trying to

it is not surprising. For the real bases of his conviction in the claim lie not in specific remarks or arguments of Wittgenstein's, but elsewhere. In particular, they lie (1) in the thought that *the* way to distinguish what it is to speak and mean (as opposed, for example, to behaving from a mere disposition to produce and react to words) is to see speaking as a species of rule-following (for it is just this, for Mulhall, that allows speaking to be open to normative assessment in a way that behavior from dispositions is not), and (2) in the fact of our systematic agreement in language and the highly normative character of this agreement. While these two thoughts work together, each lending force to the other, I will discuss them separately.

Since I shall say more about the first of these ideas below, here I will just say the following.

First, as I have noted above, I share Mulhall's thought that part of what characterizes speaking is that it is open to normative assessment. But Mulhall regards the possibility of normative assessment as requiring rules and rule-following and as *the* determinant of what it is to speak. And these thoughts I do not share. Although the comparison of speaking and playing games may be used in ways that are importantly misleading, here it may be helpful to consider games. Part of what is involved in playing games is following rules, and these rules allow for normative assessment of some of our moves or plays as being (or failing to be) in accord with the rules. But much of our play, while open to normative assessment, is not so in virtue of rules. It may be assessed as strategically shortsighted ("He should have tried to bunt the runner to second base"), as sloppy ("She isn't giving enough attention to her defensive position"), as mean-spirited ("They had the game well in hand and could have/should have played substitutes for the last several minutes. There was no need to humiliate

---

speak intelligibly and pertinently. What frees them from such complexities is at least in large part the fact that (1) at any point in the game. the rules dictate a fixed range of moves or plays that are open to you at that point—dictate a fixed range of ways of going on intelligibly—and (2) when a move or play has been made, you and other competent players of the game know what move or play has been made—what exactly has been done—and how the making of that move or play alters the circumstances in which the next move or play may be made. But none of this is true of moments of speech. In speaking there is no corresponding idea of a definite range of moves that are open to you at a given point, no set of ways of speaking pertinently and therefore intelligibly, and even when we know the language used. it may not be clear what exactly a person has said—what move, if you like, was made—or how to go on from it. Indeed, one of our tasks in understanding and speaking together is to come to understand just this. (Rhees too, for these and other kinds of reasons, powerfully challenged the assimilation of speaking and making moves in a game. See his "Wittgenstein's Builders" in Rhees 1970.)

the opponents"), as selfish ("He is hogging the ball"), etc. Further, following rules does not constitute the essence of what it is to *play* a game. "Playing a game," Cavell notes, "is 'a part of our [that is, we humans'] natural history' ([PI] §25), and until one is an initiate of this human form of activity, the human gesture of 'citing a rule' can mean nothing."[30] Indeed, one might justly be said not to be *playing* a game even when one is following—and not merely acting in accord with—the rules. Think of those occasions on which we say, for example, that a person's heart is not in the game, that he is not trying (to win), and the like. What we mean here is that while he is going through the motions of the game, he isn't *playing*.

But more important than these thoughts is the idea, in line with my remarks above concerning Wittgenstein's approach to philosophical questions, that in wishing to provide an account of what in general distinguishes speaking (from, for example, mere dispositions to produce and respond to words), Mulhall is allowing that we face a clear question to which we might provide a meaningful response. More specifically, he appears to be acceding to a skeptical surmise that (what we call) speaking may be mere behavior, merely producing and responding to words. He appears to be acceding to this surmise in allowing it as coherent, allowing that we have a clear idea of what we are imagining in (trying to) imagine this possibility and in attempting to meet it. But I think it is not clear that a coherent idea is expressed in this surmise. And it seems to me that Wittgenstein's approach to this issue is to try to show us just that and, in so doing, to free us from our muddle in imagining that we face a question to which we might meaningfully respond the further muddles in which we involve ourselves in our attempts to respond to this imagined question. For when we fail to recognize an apparent question as nonsense and seek to respond to it, we can produce only further nonsense. (This might stand as an encapsulation of Wittgenstein's view of philosophy, of how it begets its griefs, and of how, in philosophy, we lead ourselves deeper and deeper into darkness.)[31]

---

30 Cavell 1976, 49.

31 Here too I recommend Edward Minar's "The Philosophical Significance of Meaning-Blindness." He remarks:

> A philosophy that tries to ferret out the underlying ground of our capacity to mean *begins*, Wittgenstein suspects, with a posture of meaning-blindness. Philosophy starts with a picture of our capacity for responding to the world by putting it to words as somehow lifeless and mechanical, and then adds whatever elements (if any) are necessary to breathe life, or to secrete meaning, into the proceedings (Minar 2010, 192).

However, Minar goes on to argue that Wittgenstein's interest in the idea of meaning-blindness is not to use the idea to provide a general account of what we have that the meaning-blind lack, but to show us that, the further we try to think through the idea of meaning-blindness, the more

In turning now to the second of what I have suggested are the real bases of Mulhall's claim that language-use is fundamentally rule-governed activity—the fact of our systematic agreement in language and the highly normative character of this agreement—my awareness of the danger of failing to register the subtlety of Mulhall's view is heightened. I will return to this danger below. However, chancing this danger for the moment, his thought here seems to be the following. If we agree systematically in our uses of words, there must be a rule that we are following, even if it is not explicitly formulated and grasped, which accounts for that agreement. The fact of agreement itself attests to the presence of the rule and to our following the rule. And, equally, if we are able to normatively evaluate one another, there must be a rule, even if it is not explicitly formulated and grasped, with reference to which we are able to do so. The fact of normative evaluation itself attests to the presence of the rule and to our following the rule. In short, his thought seems to be that there must be something beyond our individual uses of language themselves—our presenting ourselves in speech at the moment—that undergirds those uses, that makes them the specific uses of language that they are, and that constitutes the standard of correctness against which they may be assessed.[32] Mulhall remarks:

---

we lose our grip on the idea and so lose our conviction that we are confronted with a general question about our capacity to mean that stands in need of a general answer. Minar remarks:

> The more we read their familiarity and liveliness out of the picture, the less apparent it is what the possibilities we are trying to imagine really amount to, and the less clear it is whether we should say that they [the meaning-blind] really speak language. We do not know how to arbitrate these matters. We are tempted, Wittgenstein thinks, to account for whatever is lacking in these people by positing *something* in us which they must be missing—the senses or ideas or experiences, the whatevers, that inform our livelier and more thoughtful relation to the words we use—our questions have taken on a certain unreality.
>
> We should be wary, that is, of drawing conclusions about the nature of language that go beyond describing how what the meaning-blind do with words differs from our sayings and doings (Minar 2010, 198)

**32** In a sense, I do not disagree with the thought that there must be something beyond our uses of language themselves—although not something that undergirds them and that constitutes their standard of correctness. I mean our being initiates of forms of life held in language, our sharing natural reactions, and the like. Here, I am thinking of the justly famous passage from Cavell's "The Availability of Wittgenstein's Later Philosophy" in which he says the following:

> We learn and teach words in certain contexts, and then we are expected, and expect others, to be able to project them into further contexts. Nothing insures that this projection will take place (in particular, not the grasping of universals nor the grasping of books of rules), just as nothing insures that we will make, and understand, the same projections. That on the whole we do is a matter of our sharing routes of interest and feeling, modes of res-

For a regularity in behavior to count as rule-following, it must not only be in accord with what the rule requires; it must have been done *because* that is what the rule required. This is not a causal link; the point here is that the rule constitutes the agents reason for acting as she did. If an agent is following a given rule, then she must be able to explain what she is doing by reference to it, teach others how to follow it, justify her actions by reference to it, and/or acknowledge that her actions can be evaluated as right or wrong by reference to it. In short, talk of human behavior as rule-following behavior brings it into the realm of normativity; the rule functions as a standard of correctness, a means by which the relevant action can be guided and evaluated, a norm which constitutes the action as the specific (rule-following) action it is. (Mulhall 2014, 296)

These are strong claims. According to them, whenever we perform any specific action—which is to say, whenever we do anything that counts as an action—there is a rule that we are *following*, being guided by, in performing that action, and indeed, the rule is our *reason* for acting as we do. A rule that guides our activity and is our reason for acting as we do is insinuated beneath the surface description of everything that we do. For it is just the rule that constitutes the action as the action that it is, and apart from the rule our action could not be normatively evaluated.

What I mean in saying that a rule is being insinuated beneath the surface description of what we do is just that these claims do not match the surface description of our proceedings—how we would ordinarily think of them. For most of what we do we do not ordinarily conceive of ourselves as following a rule and, of course, the rule that we are said to be following—and that we must be following, according to Mulhall—will not in most instances, be the reason that we *give*

---

ponse, senses of humor and of significance and of fulfillment, of what is outrageous, of what is similar to what else, what a rebuke, what forgiveness, of when an utterance is an assertion, when an appeal, when an explanation—all the whirl of organism Wittgenstein calls "forms of life." Human speech and activity, sanity and community, rest upon nothing more, but nothing less, than this. It is a vision as simple as it is difficult, and as difficult as it is (and because it is) terrifying. (Cavell 1976, 52)

But even here the sense in which this 'something beyond our uses of language' undergirds or explains them is complex. For while Cavell's talk of human speech and activity as resting upon the whirl of organism that Wittgenstein calls forms of life may encourage a foundationalist reading of this passage, this is, I think, mistaken. It is not as though we, for the most part, make and understand the same projections of words *because* we share senses of humor, significance, and the like. Our sharing senses of humor and significance, for example, is the same fact as our making and understanding the same projections. Accordingly, shared forms of life are not the foundation for our agreement in language. They are the same fact differently described, and the description of our shared forms of life shows us what is involved in our sharing and agreeing in language.

for our action. Walking along a beach on a late autumn afternoon, I come out with, "It does the soul good!" Suppose you ask me: "Why did you say [what is your reason for saying] that?" I reply: "Oh, I was just thinking how nice it is to be able to see an expanse of horizon, to see the curvature of the earth. For me, it puts things into perspective and calms me." You say: "No, I didn't mean that. I meant, why did you say what you said just as you did?" "What do you mean 'as I did'? Do you mean why did I say that it does the *soul* good?" "No. I mean…" And here it becomes difficult to realistically imagine your asking the question that we need to get you to ask. But let's just suppose that you come out with: "I mean, what rule were you following in saying what you did?" I am likely not to understand what you are asking. And supposing that I sufficiently quell my growing impatience at the fact that a moment of calm for me is being ruined, I am likely to say, impatiently: "I wasn't following *any* rule. I was just talking. Are you suggesting that I have some kind of script that I am following—that a genuine expression of feeling was *inauthentic?*" (The idea raised here—that to suggest, in the ordinary sense, that I am following rules in all that I do will seem to charge me with a kind of inauthenticity—strikes me as important and again suggests that some non-ordinary idea of following rules and of reasons for acting is being insinuated.) But whatever I say, it is extremely unlikely that I will give as my reason for acting as I did a rule that I was following or even that I will understand what you are seeking in asking for the rule that I am following.

I believe that this is significant. In the ordinary sense of the idea of "reasons for acting as we do," our reasons are generally not purported rules governing what it is to perform some action; rather, they are reasons for performing the action. And, in the ordinary sense, when we want to know why someone did something as he did, we have in mind some specific puzzlement about how he did it. Which is to suggest, again, that there is something philosophically suspect in the thought that there is some general question to be addressed about why we perform any of the actions that we perform as we perform them. Or if we try to answer the general question, the answer will be: We perform actions as we do because that is how, or a way to, perform them—and knowing *that* is knowing both less and more than any rule. But I will return to this.

Mulhall's push to insinuate a rule that is being followed beneath the surface description of our practices emerges quite clearly in some of his remarks on *Investigations* §83. Mulhall quotes the following from §83:

> We can easily imagine people amusing themselves in a field by playing with a ball so as to start various existing games, but playing many without finishing them and in between throwing the ball aimlessly into the air, chasing one another with the ball and bombarding

one another for a joke and so on. And now someone says: The whole time they are playing a ball-game and following definite rules at every throw.

And is there not also the case where we play and—make up the rules as we go along? And there is even one where we alter them—as we go along.

In response to this quotation, Mulhall remarks:

> We are plainly meant to baulk at saying what Wittgenstein's imagined observer says; but is that because invoking the idea of rules to understand any aspect of these people's play is unhelpful, or because the observer invokes the specific idea of definite rules governing every move in a seamless sequence of games? To think of these people as variously following, altering and making up rules as they go along seems rather less forced; and the aimlessness which may resist such a thought in this context is certainly not a salient feature of the examples of flexibly inflexible projections of words that are central to Cavell's discussion. (Mulhall 2003, 96-7)

Mulhall is driven to suggest that these people are variously following, altering, and making up rules as they go along because this play is characterized by agreement and is open to normative assessment, and he regards these as requiring the following of rules. But is this less forced? Isn't it simply acceding to a metaphysical demand for a rule informing and making possible the agreement and the normativity of this play?

It should be noted that Wittgenstein introduces the thought of making up or altering rules as you go along with the words: "And is there not also the case..." This suggests that he is not glossing the example of play just sketched, but is inviting us to imagine a further, different example. (One might imagine the vote counting for the 2000 U.S. presidential election in Florida.) But beyond that textual point, what seems less forced is to say that all of the play that Wittgenstein describes is characterized by agreement and is open to normative assessment, but only some of it involves rules and rule-following—namely, those periods of play in which these people are playing games with rules. It is all characterized by agreement and is open to normative assessment because not just anything that people take it into their heads—or hands or feet—to do with a ball in a field will count as, will be, "amusing themselves in a field by playing with a ball." But I do not see that we must appeal to rules and rule-following in order to say this.

Take throwing the ball aimlessly into the air—which Mulhall seems to regard as not a rule-following activity and so not open to normative assessment. Under the circumstances that Wittgenstein's example invites us to imagine, this activity is fine: it can certainly count as part of 'amusing ourselves in a field with a ball.' But if one of us keeps throwing the ball into the air for too long—and how long is too long will depend upon many things—then this will no longer count as amusing ourselves in a field with a ball. (Unless, as we might learn or imagine, the person is introducing a new game, the point of which is to throw the ball into the air over your own head and to see how many consecutive catches can be made. So in this case, it wasn't aimless after all. But then we need to imagine that the players as children, or as people who are for some other reason not especially adept at catching a ball thrown over their own heads—perhaps they have had a couple of bottles of wine with a picnic lunch, or perhaps they are perfectly adept but it is dark, or there is dense fog, or the ball is greased, or very small, or very large. For otherwise, catching a ball thrown over your head will be too easy, and each will be able to do it for too long for this to count as amusing ourselves together with a ball in a field. And if the players are children, they will have to be of a certain age. For otherwise those not throwing the ball are likely to become bored or impatient; they have to be old enough to throw and catch the ball enough times to make it interesting, and also old enough to enjoy the drama and competition involved in others doing so. I regard what I have just sketched as conditions on/for amusing ourselves together in a field with a ball by throwing it over your own head. But they do not seem to me to be rules.) It also seems to me that, under normal circumstances, it will not count as 'amusing ourselves in a field with a ball,' and so will be inappropriate in these circumstances, for one of us to deflate the ball, if it is inflatable, or to smash it to bits if can be smashed to bits, or to throw the ball at someone or to bombard the same person repeatedly, or—even if the ball belongs to her—to take it from another without explanation, and so on. So all of this play is characterized by agreement and is open to normative assessment. But is that because, perhaps without explicitly formulating or grasping them, we have (made up) rules that we are following? Must it be?

I have so far suggested two problems with this specific instance of insinuating a rule that is being followed beneath the surface description of our practices: that doing so seems forced and that it wrongly casts the aimless beyond the purview of agreement and normativity. However, there are further problems with this general move. I will mention three that are closely related.

First, Wittgenstein repeatedly emphasizes that, as he puts it in PI §75, my knowledge, my possession of a concept (here, for example, the concept 'game') is completely expressed in the explanations that I could give. That is, my possession of the concept 'game' is completely expressed in "my describing various kinds of games; showing how all sorts of other games can be constructed on the analogy of these; saying that I should scarcely count this or this among games; and so on." And he further emphasizes, as for example in PI §§69, 71, 208, and 210, that in teaching others concepts by giving them these sorts of examples and explanations, we do not teach them less than we know ourselves.

Since our own possession of concepts is completely expressed in such examples and explanations, in giving others these examples and explanations we are not gesturing toward some further knowledge that we possess but are unable to formulate and that the other must somehow divine. However, insinuating a rule that we must be following beneath the surface description of our activity invites the idea that we do—must—possess more than these examples and explanations, and it also invites the idea that in learning concepts through the examples and explanations provided by others we must make a leap from what they offer to the rule that they are unable to offer.

Second, the purported rule informing and justifying our uses of words will, in actual cases of explaining or justifying our uses of words, be idle. It will do no explanatory or justificatory work and so the idea of such a rule will be, in that sense, empty. Here I am thinking again of Wittgenstein's remarks about our uses of the word 'game' in PI §66 and surrounding sections. I take Wittgenstein to be working in these sections to show that, while we can formulate a rule to describe our uses of the word 'game,' this rule will be exclusively retrospective and summary and so will have no prescriptive force in informing or justifying further uses of the word. But more importantly, I take him also to be working to show that since the rule-formulation is wholly parasitic on what we say about games in particular instances it adds nothing and does no explanatory or justificatory work. What explains or justifies our uses of the word 'game' in particular instances is not the rule but the particular considerations that we are able to offer in these individual cases.[33]

Third, as I understand him, Wittgenstein is not attempting to provide us with a conception of a standard of correctness that guides our uses of words, that makes them the specific uses they are, and in terms of which they can be evaluated. He is, rather, trying to bring us to see that we have no clear conception of the problem for which a standard of correctness is the solution. Or, better, that there is no such problem and when we imagine otherwise, we are under an illusion. We are under an illusion produced by neglecting the ordinary circumstances of speech or by attempting to reflect on our uses of language from an (imagined) perspective beyond any actual context of speech.

This strategy is pervasive throughout PI §§80–8. It is evident in Wittgenstein's countering, in §80, of the idea that we do not really attach any meaning to the word 'chair' unless we are not equipped with rules for every possible application of the word and in his discussion in §83 of people amusing themselves with a ball in a field. It also seems to me clearly in evidence in §82 where he dis-

---

**33** The points developed here are indebted to Goldfarb 1997.

cusses the idea of the rule by which a person proceeds in speaking and in his concluding: "Or, to ask a better question: What meaning is the expression 'the rule by which he proceeds' supposed to have left here?" And it is in evidence in §84, in Wittgenstein's question: "But what does a game look like that is everywhere bounded by rules? whose rules never let a doubt creep in, but stop up all the cracks where it might?" For the point of this question, contrary to a common reading of the passage, is not to provoke us to discover that we cannot imagine such a game. After all, in an ordinary frame of mind we might say that most of the games that we play are exactly such games. We do not, in an ordinary frame of mind, feel that our games are missing some needed rules, or face doubt about how to play them in accordance with the rules. The point is rather to show us that if we think that we cannot imagine such a game, that our ordinary games are not such games, we have fallen prey to the illusion of thinking that there is some coherent idea of a need that the ordinary rules of our games do not meet. We have fallen prey, that is, to the illusion of a need that a standard of correctness will satisfy.

But here I want to make a point, drawing on some ideas Wittgenstein develops in §87, about Mulhall's idea of a standard of correctness.

About the idea of a standard of correctness—of the rules that govern our uses of words, that constitute them as the specific uses they are, and in terms of which they may be normatively assessed—that he is employing and that he takes from Baker and Hacker, Mulhall says the following:

> For example, whilst their conception of such rules certainly includes dictionary definitions, it extends far beyond them: it includes concrete samples, charts, blue-prints, signposts, lists of examples—indeed any of the indefinitely many ways in which speakers can explain and justify their uses of words to others. They also stress that a linguistic activity can be rule-governed even when no explicit rule-formulation is used by an agent to guide her activity (she may simply cite the rule when challenged or asked to explain herself), and sometimes even when no rule-formulations are involved in acquiring or displaying mastery of the activity (she might simply point out the mistakes of others, display chagrin at her own slips, and so on). Moreover, such explanations as are employed in the activity are not and could not be designed to remove all possible misunderstandings or to cover all possible cases of a word's applications; they are in order if they do their job—if they actually overcome the specific misunderstanding that is causing trouble, or allow a pupil to go on successfully with a particular word. (Mulhall 2014, 296–97)

The idea of a standard of correctness here is meant to be philosophically weak and non-tendentious. There is no particular form that this standard of correctness must possess since it may be of the indefinitely many ways in which speakers explain and justify their uses of words; it need not involve an explicit rule-formulation; and it is not meant to cover all possible uses or misunderstandings of words. But this philosophically weak conception of a standard of correctness preserves the thought that there is a job for, and that there are things that serve as, explanations or justifications of words (or actions) apart from the specific situations in which they are employed as explanations or justifications in response to specific confusions, doubts, questions, and so on. For unless it preserves this thought, Mulhall's talk, throughout both the paper under consideration, of our speech and action being governed by rules, guided by rules, of our grasping (even if not explicitly) rules, and so on will lose its point.

However, the idea that there are things that function as explanations or justifications apart from specific contexts of confusions, doubts, questions, and so on is a central target of Wittgenstein's critique in §87 (and elsewhere). That is, the problem with the felt need for a standard of correctness is not that we imagine that it must cover all possible cases. The problem is that we imagine that something can count as a standard of how to go on in the absence of an actual need for some explanation of how to go on. Something is an explanation when and only when it "serves to remove or to avert a misunderstanding"—a misunderstanding that I can foresee as natural in the situation (PI §87). "You must play the suit led if you have it" only counts as an explanation of the rule if you are confused about the rule—otherwise, it might be taken as an impatient way of saying that you ought to pay attention to the game or as a warning not to try to cheat. Handing you a paint sample only counts as an explanation or justification of my, say, calling this color 'puce' if there is some question or doubt about it.

Challenging the idea that there are things that function as explanations or justifications apart from specific confusions and the like must be a central target of Wittgenstein's. For the idea that there just *are* things that function as explanations is the twin of the idea that there just *are* questions about what we do and say, that there just *are* things that need to be explained or justified—that there are just *are* "gap[s] in the foundations" (PI §87). But if we allow that it will seem, and rightly, "that secure understanding is only possible if we first doubt everything that *can* be doubted, and then remove all these doubts" (PI §87). And here we are pushed toward a full-blown standard of correctness—something that must remove all possible misunderstandings and cover all possible cases of a word's applications.[34]

This is a point at which to return to the danger of failing to register the subtlety of Mulhall's view. In particular, my speaking of insinuating a rule beneath the surface description of our activity and my distinguishing between rules

---

34 I will just note that Mulhall *seems*, although it is difficult to be certain, to accept the coherence of the idea of "all possible misunderstandings."

(standards of correctness) that are always governing or guiding our speech and action and examples and explanations given in particular instances may seem unfair to Mulhall's conception of rules. For Mulhall is quite explicit that neither he nor Baker and Hacker wish to conceive of the rules that they see as central to an account of language as beyond or beneath our activities. They are immanent in, or—perhaps better—they are forms of those activities themselves. So, for example, beyond the remarks that I have already quoted about what, for him and for Baker and Hacker, counts as a rule, Mulhall is also clear that the "focus throughout is thus not on a canonical form of explanation, but upon the use to which certain objects or forms of words are put in any given context; the basic idea is that something counts as a rule of grammar if it is used in the relevant way, if the activity in which it is employed is normative" (Mulhall 2014, 297). And he emphasizes that what Baker and Hacker "call the background normative activities of teaching, explaining, defining, justifying, and evaluating" constitute "the context within which human behavior can count as an instance of rule-governed activity" (Mulhall 2014, 296).

These points must be acknowledged in considering Mulhall's conception of rules and the centrality of rules to his account of language and linguistic meaning. I have tried, I hope successfully, to honor their force and import in raising the questions and challenges that I have raised. But here I will say the following. Whatever other concerns and questions I have about Mulhall's view as I understand it, and however successful my attempts to give force to those concerns and questions, it seems to me that there is a deep and unresolved tension running throughout Mulhall's discussion of rules and rule-following. The tension is this. On the one hand, he wants the ideas of rules and rule-following to do heavy philosophical labor: to provide an account of linguistic meaning, to provide an account of our agreement in language and its normative character, to explain how and why our actions are the specific actions they are, and so on. And if we want rules and rule-following to do this heavy philosophical labor, then we seem to need a fairly robust conception of rules and rule-following. We must have a conception of rules as governing and guiding what we say and do, as constituting the standard of correctness for what we say and do, and we must conceive of ourselves as following rules, even if not explicitly formulated or grasped, in everything that we do and say. (As I have argued above, I do not read Wittgenstein as wishing for rules, or anything else, to do this kind of heavy philosophical labor.) However, on the other hand, Mulhall is also leery of any philosophically freighted conception of rules and rule-following and he wants his own conception to be as weak and non-tendentious as possible. Indeed, I think it is fair to say that Mulhall wishes us to understand his talk of rules and of rule-following as nothing more than a re-description of various aspects of our speech and conduct. To talk of rules and a "web of rules" is, according to this idea, simply to talk of the manifold ways in which we are able to explain, justify, correct, and clarify what we say and do and of the fact that there are conditions we recognize on/for doing and saying what we do and say. To talk of our following rules and of our speech and activity being governed or guided by rules is simply to re-describe the fact that, in manifold ways, we correct ourselves and others, acknowledge this correction, and that, again, we recognize conditions on/for what we say and do. It is, I think, in large part because Mulhall wishes us to understand his talk of rules and rule-following as nothing more than a re-description of aspects of our normative life with language that he suggests that "the question of whether this vision of the normativity of language should be given expression in terms of rules becomes essentially semantic" (Mulhall 2014, 309).

But I do not think that we can take this weak understanding of Mulhall's talk of rules fully seriously. The conception of rules that Mulhall presents cannot be taken as weakly as he wishes. For, in the first instance, if we (try to) take Mulhall's talk of rules and rule-following in a very weak sense, as nothing more than a re-description of aspects of our normative life with language, then, as I have suggested, it will not do the heavy philosophical labor that he means it to do.

There is, however, a much more important problem that remains irrespective of whether Mulhall's weak understanding of his conception of rules can do the work he wants it to do, and a problem that, I believe, accounts for a certain *essential* unclarity and elusiveness in Mulhall's conception of rules, rule-following, and the place of rules and rule-following in our speech (and action). As I have noted, Mulhall suggests that it is an essentially semantic matter whether we characterize the normativity of our uses of language in terms of rules. But this is importantly mistaken. Talk of rules and rule-following cannot be merely a re-description of aspects of our normative life with language. For in suggesting that this matter is essentially semantic, Mulhall is unfaithful to his own appreciation of the fact that there are ordinary conditions on/for the meaningful use of our words. What I mean is this. We know what it means, in the ordinary sense, to follow a rule, to be guided by a rule, for our actions to be governed by a rule, for a rule to be the reason we speak or act as we do, and the like. The ideas of a rule, of following a rule, of being guided by a rule, of a rule governing an activity, and so on have (a range of) ordinary and clear senses. But these ordinary senses, the ordinary conditions on/for the meaningful use of these words, do not license the claim that all of our meaningful uses of language and all of our activities involve rule-following, that all of our uses of language are governed by rules, or guided by rules, and so on. For, to go no further, in the ordinary sense we distinguish between actions that involve rule-following and that are governed or guided by rules and those that do not or are not, and in the ordinary sense we distinguish between instances in which a rule is, and those in which it is *not*, our reason for doing what we do (as we do). In claiming that we are always following rules, guided by rules, governed by rules, and the like, the ideas of rule, of following a rule, of being guided by a rule, of being governed by a rule, and so on are philosophically stretched out of shape. And when we recognize that the ordinary senses of these ideas—the ordinary conditions on/for their meaningful employment—do not fit the extended employment that Mulhall wishes to make of them, we discover that we, quite literally, do not know what the claims involving these extended employments *mean*. They have (Mulhall's efforts notwithstanding) been given no clear meaning, and the sense that we understood, more or less, what they meant was an illusion produced by imagining that the ordinary sense of the ideas of a rule, rule-following, and so on could be transferred unproblematically to these extended employments.[35]

# §4

I noted at the close of §1 that all of Mulhall's arguments and interpretive claims concerning specific moments of Cavell's work deserved sustained attention that I would not be able to give them. I do, however, want to consider a couple of these arguments and claims. I focus on those I do not because I regard them as, in general, more interesting or important than the others, but because considering them will allow me to bring out some thoughts that are of more general relevance for me in thinking about differences between Mulhall and myself regarding how we understand our uses of language, the normativity of our uses of language, and the possibility and fragility of our intelligibility in language. In particular, I want to consider one central aspect of Mulhall's discussion of Cavell's treatment of Kripke and his discussion of projecting a word as developed in Mulhall 2014.

Early in Cavell's consideration of Kripke's interpretation of Wittgenstein, he says the following:

---

35 I suspect that Mulhall will want to say that, while his uses of the concepts of rule, following, governing, guiding, and the like may not match our ordinary uses of them in all respects, he is projecting these concepts into a new context. In that case, my suggestion here is that the projections do not work. They are not, as Cavell says projections must be, natural (CR, 190). I will also note that the thoughts sketched in this paragraph strike me as *one way* into thinking about why Cavell may have moved away from the talk of rules that is present in "Must We Mean What We Say?"

In taking rules as fundamental to Wittgenstein's development of skepticism about meaning, Kripke subordinates the role of criteria in the *Investigations*, hence appears from my side of things to underrate drastically, or to beg the question of, the issue of the ordinary, a structure of which is the structure of our criteria and their grammatical relations. In my seeing criteria as forming Wittgenstein's understanding of the possibility of skepticism, or say his response to the threat of skepticism, I take this to show rules to be subordinate; but since Kripke's interpretation of rules seems, in turn, to undercut the fundamentality of the appeal to the ordinary, my appeal to criteria must appear to beg the question from his side of things. These positions repeat the sides of what I will call the argument of the ordinary, something I will take as fundamental to the *Investigations*. It is an argument I seek a way out of, as I suppose the *Investigations* does in seeking to renounce philosophical theses.[36]

Mulhall quotes from this passage and offers the following comments:

Cavell's formulation will certainly appear question-begging to anyone attracted to the traditional idea that criteria are akin to rules. For he puts the point against Kripke in such a way as to occlude the possibility that that traditional idea holds open: that criteria are no more subordinate to rules than rules are to criteria, but that criteria are rather a species of rule—that their articulation displays an aspect of the normativity of our language use. The key idea here is not subordination (of one concept to another, as in a codification or calculus) but clarification (of one concept by another, as in a recounting of grammar)—an option foreclosed by Cavell's assumption throughout this passage that rules and criteria are to be contrasted or opposed. To think that rules are fundamental to Wittgenstein's vision of language (hence meaning, and hence scepticism) does not entail thinking that criteria, and hence the ordinary, are subordinate to rules. Such may be Kripke's way of attaching salvational significance to rules; but then Cavell's critique of Kripke will not generalize. (Mulhall 2003, 98-9; cf., Mulhall 2014, for a parallel set of remarks)

It is undeniable that Kripke's understanding of Wittgenstein's conceptions of meaning and of rules is not Mulhall's. But it is not clear that the force of Cavell's critique of Kripke can be so quickly or easily turned aside. That is, Kripke attributes to Wittgenstein views of meaning and of rules that are utterly detached from our ordinary criteria, or rather, are such that criteria *could not* be relevant to them. In Kripke's account, criteria become invisible. But is the force of Cavell's critique of this view met by reminding us that rules have a grammar? Is that what Cavell is doing?

Mulhall suggests that it is and that it does. In Mulhall 2003, he quotes the following from Cavell:

---

**36** Cavell 1990, 65–6.

How do I know that what I called Wittgenstein's "tone" is what I say it is? My claim is based, for example, on taking Wittgenstein's remark at §199, "This is of course a note of the grammar of the expression 'to obey a rule',"—in response to a question whether obeying a rule could be something only one man can do and only once in his life—to apply to his entire discussion of rules, for example, to questions of what counts as obedience, following, interpretation, regularity, doing the same, ordering, custom, technique, example, practice, explaining, understanding, guessing, intuition, possibility, intention... no one of which is less or more fundamental than the concept of a rule, and each of which is to be investigated grammatically (hence by way of eliciting criteria).[37]

Mulhall comments on this passage as follows:

Cavell... reminds us that Wittgenstein's rule-following considerations (say, from 143–243 and beyond) form part of a grammatical investigation into the concept of a rule, hence involve the eliciting of criteria. Given his previous assumption that rules and criteria are utterly distinct, with its companion assumption that one must be subordinate to the other, his intended conclusion would appear to be that, since Wittgenstein explores the concept of a rule by eliciting our criteria for the use of the term, then criteria must be more fundamental than (let's say superordinate to) rules in Wittgenstein's philosophical method.

However, pointing out that the concept of a rule has a grammar, and hence that Wittgenstein's discussion of it proceeds by way of eliciting criteria, simply fails to engage with the traditional suggestion that a criterion can be illuminatingly compared with—perhaps seen as an inflection of the concept of—a rule, and hence that neither is more fundamental than the other. (Mulhall 2003, 100)

It is important to note that what Mulhall speaks of as Cavell's "assumption that rules and criteria are utterly distinct" is not *Cavell's*. It is Kripke, not Cavell, who presents a view of language-use and its normativity according to which rules and criteria are utterly distinct—that is, according to which the focus on rules renders criteria invisible or irrelevant. Furthermore, this is not simply an *assumption* of Kripke's. In order to explain why, I need to say that—as I understand it—in the passage upon which Mulhall is commenting, Cavell is not simply reminding us that the concept of rule has a grammar.[38] If that were what the passage is

---

37 Cavell 1990, 68.
38 Cavell has offered this reminder in "The Availability of Wittgenstein's Later Philosophy," when he remarks:

"Following a rule" is an activity we learn against the background of, and in the course of, learning innumerable other activities—for example, obeying orders, taking and giving directions, repeating what is done or said, and so forth. The concept of a rule does not exhaust the concepts of correctness or justification ("right" and "wrong") *and indeed the former concept would have no meaning unless these latter concepts already had.* (Cavell 1976, 49; my emphasis).

doing, then what Cavell calls the argument of the ordinary would be very quickly and easily resolved. But the argument of the ordinary cannot be so quickly and easily resolved. For it is an argument between fundamentally divergent orientations toward language, one of which, as I have said, makes criteria and grammar invisible and the appeal to them irrelevant. Cavell's interest is in our temptation toward this view of language—which is to say, his interest is in what he calls our disappointment with criteria and our wish to be free of responsibility for them. It is because the argument of the ordinary has this kind of shape and depth that Cavell speaks of it as "fundamental to the *Investigations*."

The passage of Cavell's under consideration is, rather, reminding us of the range of concepts that figure in the normativity of our uses of language (as well as in our understanding of that normativity), and cautioning against regarding the concept of a rule as more or less central than any of these other concepts to this normativity (and this understanding). The reason for entering this caution, I suggest, is that to focus narrowly on the concept of a rule—to try to make the concept of a rule *the central concept* in capturing the normativity of our language-use or in seeking to understand that normativity—will drive one to "evade Wittgenstein's preoccupation with the ordinary (hence with 'our criteria,' which articulate the ordinary)" or will bespeak such an evasion.[39] My thought, in other words, is that Cavell is suggesting that, if we privilege the concept of rule in an account of language, we are either involved in, or will end up, evading or drastically underrating the issue of the ordinary and our criteria. We need not begin with Kripke's view, and we may not end by embracing his specific view. But if we try to make rules central, we are either involved in or will end up underrating, or miscasting, the role of criteria—and hence the nature of the normativity of our language-use. If this suggestion is correct, then Cavell's treatment of Kripke will generalize—albeit not through the straightforward application of any specific conclusion regarding Kripke's view per se. That is, although Cavell explores the details of Kripke's view his interest is not simply (or, indeed, primarily) in Kripke or the details of his view. He takes Kripke as offering *one formulation* of one of the positions in the argument of the ordinary; and it is that position and that argument that is the center of his interest.

In order to develop the suggestion that privileging the notion of rules bespeaks or begets an evasion of the issue of the ordinary, I want to look at Cavell's consideration of Kripke's concept of a "tabair"—the concept of something that is a table when not at the base of the Eiffel Tower but is, when there, a chair. Briefly, what Cavell says about this concept is that it severs the connection between

---

**39** Cavell 1990, 68.

our concepts—what we call, count as, things—and our interests, our natural reactions, our biological and social forms of life, facts about the world in which we live, act, speak, and so on. For it is quite mysterious why what we count as something should depend upon its being or not being at the base of the Eiffel Tower. In severing this connection, it gives us no way of understanding the fact that there are reasons, reasons of which we can bethink ourselves, why we count things as we do and, more importantly, obscures the fact that there are such reasons. It reduces our uses of words to the expression of mere inclinations—as though our calling things what we do and as we do were mere inclination. And since our criteria for counting something as we do—the criteria we can articulate in response to specific need—express these reasons, the role of criteria has been underrated, miscast, or as I have suggested, made invisible. In going on to sketch some of our ordinary criteria for "table" Cavell is reminding us of the fact that, and of the ways in which, our concepts and our lives are interwoven.[40] This, I think, is at least a good part of what he means in saying that "ordinary concepts have histories."[41]

What I want from these remarks, at this juncture, is simply this: To possess a concept, to be able to go on with a concept, is to appreciate how its significant employment is bound up with our interests, desires, purposes, biological and social forms of life, facts about our social and natural world, and the like. Or, in order to avoid the erroneous impression that concepts stand alone and that we come to possess them one by one, it is more accurate to say that to possess concepts, to be able to go on with them, is to appreciate the weave of connections both among our concepts and between our concepts and our interests, desires, purposes, forms of life, natural reactions, facts about our world, and so on. In coming into possession of concepts—learning to speak significantly—we are coming to appreciate this weave of connections. It is in this sense that coming into possession of concepts is becoming an initiate of forms of life. And in the matter of becoming initiates of forms of life light dawns gradually over the whole.

Even though Mulhall speaks of our learning language as learning rules, he clearly means to be sensitive to these kinds of considerations for he insists that

---

**40** Cavell 1990, 93–4. This is, then, the same sort of procedure he had employed more extensively in considering Wittgenstein's example of people who sell piles of wood according to the area covered, irrespective of the height of the pile. Making sense of these people, of *what* they are doing, depends upon coming to understand how their concepts of "more," "less," "bigger," "smaller," "selling," and so on are woven together with their lives and interests. This example is developed in CR, 115–7.
**41** Cavell 1990, 94.

the rules of which he speaks are not to be understood as separate from our natural reactions, forms of life, and the like. To offer only one instance of this insistence, in "Inner Constancy" he remarks:

> The conception of rule-following, and hence of grammatical rules, that informs Baker and Hacker's official account of grammar and criteria plainly has a place for the main considerations that generate this vision of linguistic normativity in Wittgenstein's text—for example, his emphasis upon the interweaving of definitions and applications, of rule-following activities with the general normative background practices of teaching, explaining, justifying, and criticizing, and of ways of using words with forms of human life and patterns of natural reactions and responses. (Mulhall 2014, 310)

Nevertheless, I continue to believe that Mulhall's emphasis upon rules—upon our learning rules in learning language, upon our following rules in using words, upon rules as governing our uses of words, and the like—is not, and cannot be, fully responsive to these matters. I will mention three closely connected reasons for this belief.

First, to repeat a concern I raised in "The Ground of Mutuality" and that I believe remains relevant, on Mulhall's view our interests, desires, purposes, natural reactions, biological and social forms of life, and so on, represent the bases upon which rules of grammar have meaning. However, it is the rules that govern, guide, represent the standards of correctness, and constitute the conditions on/ for the intelligible use of specific words and the performance of specific actions. Mulhall does insist that these rules cannot be understood as inflexible or impersonal, and that citing them cannot constitute the objective resolution of a disagreement about how one may go on in speaking and acting. However, my concern is that the rules are still coming apart from our interests, desires, purposes, and so on. These are coming apart in that the locus of normativity is the rules rather than our interests, desires, purposes, etc., themselves. One sign and consequence of this separation, to which I will return is this: given Mulhall's insistence that rules are not inflexible, impersonal, and do not constitute an objective resolution of a disagreement, when disagreements arise, his view leaves him very little to say about how they might be understood and addressed.

Second, my reasons for this belief begin from the thought that the ways in which our concepts, and so our intelligible speech and action, are interwoven with one another and with our interests, desires, purposes, biological and social forms of life, facts about our world, and so on are essentially inexhaustible and so importantly unchartable. I do not mean here, although it is of course true and important, that the weave of connections between and among these are essentially inexhaustible because they are open to change. Rather, I mean that at any point in time they are essentially inexhaustible and so importantly unchartable. Our concepts as well as our interests, desires, purposes, forms of life, and so on are radically holistic. This is part of the point, perhaps even the principle point, of Cavell's speaking of our coming into the possession of concepts as becoming initiates of forms of life and it is the point of my remarking that in this matter light dawns gradually over the whole. While one is obviously learning much in coming into the possession of concepts—although "learning" here, as Cavell reminds us, should not be understood narrowly or academically—what one is learning is not capturable as an enormous number of facts. What one is learning, or coming to appreciate, is what it is to be one of us. Better put, one is *becoming* one of us.

This is not to deny that when we are confronted with empirical confusion or philosophical disorientation (in the face of some phenomenon, action, or remark) we can bethink ourselves of some of these connections—can chart them to that extent—and so can help ourselves to understand (perhaps to resolve) the confusion or to understand (perhaps to overcome) the disorientation. However, the connections of which we might bethink ourselves are not *the* connections that constitute the meaning of the concept, but those we regard as relevant to the specific confusion or problem we are facing in the specific situation.[42] These connections of which we bethink ourselves do not, then, provide us with a general account of the meaning of our concepts or of why we use them when and as we do. They present us with enough to address our specific concerns, but on the basis of an inexhaustible background of further connections that we appreciate in being initiates of our forms of life. What I am suggesting is that the idea of a weave of connections, both among our concepts and between our concepts and our interests, desires, purposes, forms of life, natural reactions, and so on, is to be taken seriously. We can, for particular purposes, trace a particular pattern in this weave. This pattern will be what Mulhall, as I understand him, means by a rule of grammar. But then it is not enough to say, as Mulhall in effect does, that this pattern is only the pattern that it is against the background

---

42 This is also a point that I made in Affeldt 1998, 13, and from which, among other considerations, I concluded that it is a mistake to regard us as *having* criteria. What I meant was that we have criteria only in the sense that we can bethink ourselves of relevant criteria as need arises, and that it is a mistake to regard us as always, somehow, possessing criteria on the basis of which we make ordinary, unproblematic judgments. This was one thought, among others, to which Mulhall took strong exception in his response to that essay (see: Mulhall 1998). He did so, in large part, because it seemed to him to eliminate the possibility of normativity in judgments. That is, it seemed to him that to deny that we have criteria on the basis of which we make judgments implies that there is nothing controlling or regulating our judgments. I hope that the thoughts that I am in the process of developing here help to explain why I do not think there is this implication.

of the fabric as a whole—that these rules only have meaning against the background of our interests, desires, purposes, forms of life, natural reactions, and so on. For the point of emphasizing the inexhaustibility of the connections among our concepts and between them and our interests, desires, and the like, is to suggest that, in the face of this inexhaustible weave of connections, it is both arbitrary and distorting of our life with and in language to call any particular pattern that we trace for particular purposes the meaning of our concepts or that which informs and guides their significant employment. In doing so, we evade or underrate the issue of the ordinary. Which is to say that Cavell's idea of our becoming initiates of forms of life does not *supplement* the idea of rules or show that talk of rules is not *sufficient*. The idea of our becoming initiates of forms of life *displaces* the appeal to rules.

A third reason for believing that Mulhall's view cannot be fully responsive to the centrality of our interests, desires, forms of life, and so on, is this: If we take seriously what I have just been suggesting about our coming into possession of concepts being a matter of coming to appreciate the weave of connections between concepts and interests, desires, purposes, forms of life, natural reactions, and so on, then we will give up the idea that any idea of a rule specifies what is involved in—what are the conditions on/for—intelligibly doing or saying anything in particular. For what these considerations suggest is that what is required for intelligibly doing or saying anything is that what you do or say be understandable as a *natural* way of doing or saying what you mean to do or say in terms of interests, desires, purposes, forms of life, natural reactions, and so on. These interest, desires, and the like, need not be *ours*—although appreciating the intelligibility of what you do, understanding *what* you do, will likely be easier to the extent that they are. What is required in order to intelligibly do or say something is that what you do or say be understandable as natural in terms of (what we come to recognize) as *your* interests, desires, and the like.[43] Of course there may well be some things that we cannot (at least at the moment) understand as naturally connected to interests, desires, purposes, and so on in this way—perhaps because we do not understand the interests, desires, and purposes, or perhaps because we (think we) do but cannot understand how what you have done (what we take you to have done) is naturally connected to them. But the problem with appealing to rules to specify the conditions on/for intelligibly doing or saying something in particular is not simply that the ways in which these connections can be established and maintained in a manner that may be appreciated as natural are radically open in a way that no rule could capture.

---

43 Here again Cavell's discussion of Wittgenstein's imagined wood-sellers is relevant.

The problem with appealing to the idea of rules here is, more fundamentally, that this appeal miscasts the nature of the conditions on/for intelligibly speaking and acting. As I have noted, Mulhall's conception of rules is not Kripke's and does not make criteria invisible. However, in casting rules in the role of the conditions on/for intelligibly speaking and acting, he is, it seems to me, miscasting the role of our interests, desires, purposes, forms of life, natural reactions and the like, and so miscasting the role of criteria. For on his view establishing a natural connection with interests, desires, forms of life, and the like is not the condition on/for speaking or acting intelligibly. They are, rather, the background for the rules that function as these conditions. So, again, in appealing to rules here we are evading or underrating the issue of the ordinary.

I will now turn to Mulhall's consideration of Cavell's discussion of projecting words—using words learned in one context and with one sense in other contexts and with related but differing senses. These considerations constitutes the bulk of the second half of Mulhall 2013, and they represent a rich and important discussion of this clearly central idea. What I find most interesting and illuminating is Mulhall's consideration of Cavell's apparent contrast between what he calls the "inner" constancy and the "outer" variance of our uses of words. I will not attempt to recapitulate here the various aspects of Mulhall's discussion, but will simply note the following. He suggests that there is a certain tension in this apparent contrast. For, he remarks,

> that contrast between outer and inner suggests on the face of it that the constancy of a concept is more internal or integral to its capacity to accomplish its task than its variance. And yet the evident thrust of the passage [in which Cavell draws this apparent contrast] is to claim that *both* the inner and the outer aspects of the concept are necessary to it. (Mulhall 2014, 303)

He then suggests that those readers of Wittgenstein and Cavell who are sympathetic to assigning a central place to rules will likely focus on the "inner" constancy of a words use, while those suspicious of assigning a central place to rules will focus on its "outer" variance. However, he argues, both of these moves would be fundamentally mistaken in treating the "inner" constancy and the "outer" variation as separate aspects of a word's use. For, taking a cue from Cavell's placing "inner" and "outer" in quotation marks, Mulhall suggests that he is perhaps alluding to "some of Wittgenstein's most famous remarks about the relationship between the human mind and human body" (Mulhall 2014, 304) in which the concepts of the inner and outer figure. He then concludes this portion of his considerations with a passage that I will quote at length.

In these contexts, Wittgenstein's point is not to give the inner priority over the outer, or indeed to reverse that order of priority; his concern is to suggest that the inner and the outer are not two independent realms or dimensions at all, but rather internally related to one another—the significance or import of each inseparable from that of the other. If we transpose that suggestion to the context of Cavell's discussion of the grammatical essence of concepts, it would appear to follow that his characterization of constancy and variance as two fundamental facts is rather more misleading than his characterization of them as inner and outer. For this transposition would suggest that we should stop thinking of a concept's essence as determined by a conjunction or dovetailing of two separable components or elements (its inner constancy and its variance); we should rather think of its projectibility as having an indefinitely variable kind of constancy, or an essentially non-arbitrary kind of variation. In other words, Cavell's two fundamental facts are in fact two aspects of a single or singular fact; hence they do not need to be kept in balance, because to downgrade or entirely to overlook one is to distort the other. (Mulhall 2014, 304)[44]

---

[44] As I have said, I find Mulhall's discussion here rich and important, and especially his raising the question what Cavell might mean in speaking of the inner and the outer. In that same spirit, I would like to offer a speculation of my own. In his "Excursus on Wittgenstein's Vision of Language," from which are taken the passages upon which Mulhall is commenting, Cavell speaks of the stability and tolerance of the use of words and also of the "inner" constancy and "outer" variation of uses of words. My suggestion is that he is not here differently designating the same (apparent) distinction, but is identifying two different aspects of our life with words. The notions of stability and tolerance are meant to capture what Mulhall speaks of as the singular fact that our uses of words have an indefinitely variable kind of constancy or an essentially non-arbitrary kind of variation. But then, on this suggestion, the idea of "outer" variation is meant to cover both the stability and tolerance of our uses of words. That is, it is meant to capture the fact that the same word is used in different context and in different ways. And the notion of "inner" constancy is meant to capture the idea of a continuity—not an identity —of meaning or sense across these different uses. It speaks to what we recognize in recognizing a continuity within the alteration of sense across—to use Cavell's example—"feed the kitty," "feed the meter," "feed his pride," and so on. We might speak of what we recognize here as the inner life of a word: our sense that its meaning continues, while shifting, throughout its various uses.

This can, however, be only a suggestion. The text of the "Excursus" does not mark this proposed distinction between stability and tolerance, on the one hand, and "inner" constancy and "outer" variation on the other clearly enough for me to be certain that the terms are being used as I am suggesting. In the passage from CR, 185, on which Mulhall focuses, both sets of terms are used in a manner that can be followed in terms of my suggestion, but does not require it. In making the suggestion, I am prompted, in part, by Cavell's reflections on the meaning of "inner" and "outer" at CR, 98–9. There, he says, among other things, the following:

> "Inner" means, in part, something like inaccessible, hidden (like a room). But it also means *pervasive*, like atmosphere, or the action of the heart. What I have in mind is carried in phrases like "inner beauty," "inner conviction," "inner strength," "inner calm". This suggests that the more deeply a characteristic pervades a soul, the more obvious it is. (CR, 99)

What I want chiefly to focus on is Mulhall's account of, or his explanation of, what he calls the singular fact of the indefinitely variable constancy of our uses of words. He says the following:

> What accounts for that single fact, in all its singularity, is identified in a vital early part of Cavell's specification of his (and Wittgenstein's) notion of a criterion.
>
> [Wittgenstein's] criteria do not relate a name to an object, but, we might say, various concepts to the concept of that object. Here the test of your possession of a concept... would be your ability to use the concept in conjunction with other concepts, your knowledge of which concepts are relevant to the one in question and which are not; your knowledge of how various relevant concepts, used in conjunction with the concepts of different objects, require different kinds of contexts for their competent employment." (CR, 73)
>
> For example, knowing what a toothache is is in part a matter of knowing what counts as having a toothache, what counts as alleviating a toothache, and so on. In other words, what Cavell calls the grammatical schematism of a word is its power to combine with other words—"the word's potency to assume just those valences, and a sense that in each case there will be a point of application of the word, and that the point will be the same from context to context, or that the point will shift in a recognizable pattern or direction (CR, 77–78)." (Mulhall 2014, 304–05)[45]

In short, for Mulhall, what accounts for the indefinitely variable constancy of our uses of words is the schematism of a word. He remarks that "these limits [on a word's projection] are neither arbitrary nor optional; they show how (what Cavell elsewhere calls) a word's grammatical schematism determines the respects in which a new context for a word must invite or allow its projection" (Mulhall 2014, 302). And in the same vein he argues that "it is precisely because the grammatical schematism of a word locates it in a horizon of interrelated words em-

---

In one sense, this suggestion does not effect the core of Mulhall's argument. If found plausible, it would simply mean that the singular fact of which he speaks pertains to stability and tolerance rather than to "inner" constancy and "outer" variation. It *might*, however, raise questions about whether Mulhall's account of that singular fact is sufficient to account for the sense of "inner" constancy that I am proposing, that is, whether it is sufficient to account for our appreciation of the inner life of a word. For our appreciation of the inner life of a word—its continuous but altering meaning across different uses—seems to be a matter of our appreciating its continuing, but varying, weave of connections with our interests, desires, purposes, forms of life, natural reactions, and so on, which is a matter of our being what Cavell refers to as initiates of forms of life held in language. And, as I have argued, Mulhall's view does not seem to me to properly maintain these connections.

**45** It is worth noting that what Cavell speaks of as "the test" of your possession of a concept is treated by Mulhall as an account of what it is to possess a concept. But, of course, what tests your possession of a concept need not be an account of that possession. And as I argued above, I do not regard Cavell's talk of the schematism of a word as giving an account of the meaning of the word, or what it is to know the meaning of the word—to possess the concept.

bedded in human forms of life that our projections of those words are at once deeply controlled and creative, displaying the kind of imaginative reach that only an acknowledgment of constraint makes possible" (Mulhall 2014, 309). Accordingly, he says that:

> when the acceptability or naturalness of a new projection of a given word is in question, *our final judgment* will turn upon the speaker's capacity to show that and how the new context into which he has projected it either invites or can be seen to allow that projection by inviting or allowing (at least some modified form of) the projection of those other words to which its criteria relate it, and which are accommodated in familiar contexts of the word's use. (Mulhall 2014, 305; my emphasis)

But I do not see that the notion of the schematism of a word can do, or is intended by Cavell to do, the kind of work that Mulhall wishes. For Mulhall, the schematism of a word is regulative; it constitutes one form of what he means by a rule governing the use of the word. It controls our projections of words by determining the ways in which a new context must invite or allow that projection. And it is because the schematism of a word controls our projections of words in this way that it can function as an explanation of, as well as a limitation on, the indefinitely variable constancy of our uses of words. However, the schematism of words is not, as I understand it, regulative but reflective. It *reflects* (aspects of) what we regard as intelligible projections of words—(aspects of) the range of contexts in which we accept words as used intelligibly, (aspects of) the range of connections with other words involved in uses we accept as intelligible, and so on. Accordingly, the schematism of a word does not provide an answer to the question of what controls our projections; it shows us (aspects of) the ways in which those projections are controlled. It shows us, that is, what requires explanation.

More specifically, the schematism of a word reflects (aspects of) what we accept as natural ways of speaking and acting given our interests, desires, purposes, forms of life, natural reactions, and so on. Accordingly, what controls our projections of words—what explains at one and the same time both the stability and tolerance of our uses of words—is what we regard as (or what can be seen as) *natural*.[46] So I am agreeing with Mulhall that both aspects of our uses of

---

46 Cavell concludes his "Excursus on Wittgenstein's Vision of Language" with the following: The phenomenon I am calling "projecting a word" is the fact of language which, I take it, is sometimes responded to by saying that "All language is metaphorical." Perhaps one could say: the possibility of metaphor is the same as the possibility of language generally, but what is essential to the projection of a word is that it proceeds, or can be made to proceed,

words are to be explained by the same idea, but disagreeing with his account of what that idea is as well as with his (apparent) suggestion that the stability of our uses cannot be captured "without adverting to some idea of a systematic web of norms or standards" (Mulhall 2014, 303).

Of course, if, as I am urging, the schematism of a word reflects (aspects of) what we accept as natural ways of employing it, then what we regard as natural projections of a word will, for the most part at least, display those features of projections Mulhall emphasizes. That is, it will be the case that natural projections of a word into new contexts will be projections in which the new contexts can be seen to invite or to allow at least some modified form of the projection of other words with which the given word is naturally connected. But the point is not only, as I argued above, that the projection must be understandable as natural in terms of *your* interests, desires, purposes, and so on, so that the schematism of a word (what *we* regard as the schematism of a word) cannot be employed as the basis for a final judgment regarding the acceptability or intelligibility of a projection. Nor is the point only, as I also argued above, that the naturalness of a use of a word is bound up with the entire weave of connections among our concepts and between them and our interests, desires, and the like, and so is not determined or controlled by any *discrete* features of its use. The point is, more generally, that the locus of the normative control of our uses of words must be properly located in interests, desires, purposes, forms of life, natural reactions, and so on. It must be properly located, that is, in what we regard as, or can come to understand as, natural.

The idea that the locus of normativity is to be lodged in an idea of the natural takes me to a final set of thoughts about Mulhall's papers that I would like to sketch. These thoughts center on how Mulhall's appeals to rules and to the schematism of a word shape the possibilities of (philosophical) criticism—the options open to us in the face of ways of going on with words (or actions) that we regard as in one way or another unclear or problematic. Different moments of Mulhall's discussion appear to be at odds with one another on this point and two at least apparently quite different postures are presented neither of which is satisfactory.

Some aspects of Mulhall's discussion suggest that he imagines, and that in at least one sense his view commits him to imagining, a quite robust response to what he calls divergent application of words. In saying that he *does* imagine

---

*naturally*; what is essential to a functioning metaphor is that its "transfer" is *unnatural*—it breaks up the established, normal directions of projection. (CR, 189–90)

such a response, I am thinking of his speaking of the schematism of a word as providing us with the basis for a final judgment regarding the acceptability or naturalness of a new projection of that word—a remark in which he seems to be drawing quite close to an idea that he criticizes, the idea of assuming that a person's "divergent application of a word can simply and definitively be corrected by reminding her of its 'agreed' criteria" (Mulhall 2014, 300).

What I have in mind in saying that in at least one sense his view *commits* him to a robust response requires more extensive development.

In defending his conception of rules derived from Baker and Hacker, it is important to Mulhall to argue that nothing in that conception of rules implies or licenses what he acknowledges to be unfortunate moments in their criticisms of other philosophers—moments in which, as I noted above, "they assume that a philosopher's divergent application of a word can simply and definitively be corrected by reminding her of its 'agreed' criteria." He argues that in these moments Baker and Hacker's "philosophical practice subverts their own official account of its grammatical basis" and that since these unfortunate moments are "identifiable as such by reference to [their theoretical stance]... their official account is honored rather than discredited by such breaches in its practical observance" (Mulhall 2014, 301). He goes on to remark:

> One might perhaps argue that the very idea of a rule—insofar as it brings with it visions of rulebooks, or codified systems of independently established norms governing a practice—can encourage us to fall into the forms of philosophizing under criticism here; but nothing in the specific inflection of that concepts as it is elucidated in Baker and Hacker's work (an inflection that repeatedly averts itself from the model of a calculus or rulebook) in fact offers any such encouragement. (Mulhall 2014, 301)

In short, Mulhall wants to establish that Baker and Hacker's philosophically unfortunate moments of criticism are failings of practice that have no relation to their theory of rules of grammar.

But it is not clear to me that this separation of theory and practice can be maintained. I suspect that this conception of rules does imply and license, if not quite the sorts of philosophical practice that one sometimes finds in Baker and Hacker, an equally troubling posture toward a person's "divergent application of a word." My reasons for this suspicion are not based on the thought that any idea of rules will invite thoughts of rulebooks or codified systems of independently established norms. They are based, rather, on the role that rules play for Mulhall in determining what someone has done or said. Let me try to explain.

I suggested above that, as I understand Wittgenstein and Cavell to argue, the conditions on/for a person speaking or acting intelligibly is that what he says or does be understandable as natural in terms of his interests, desires, purposes, forms of life, natural reactions, and so on. However, determining *what* a person has done or said is a matter of understanding or imagining how it is (can be seen as) a natural expression of comprehensible human interests, desires, and the like. Until and unless we can understand or imagine this, we do not know *what* the person has done or said. And so, consequently, we don't know how to assess it as intelligible, legitimate, permissible, divergent, etc., or not. (I knock twice on my garage door before entering. What am I doing? A bird nests in my garage, and if I simply enter it often startles me in flying out. A newspaper headline reads: "British Left Waffles On Fauklands." You don't know how to make sense of this headline apart from determining what the writer was trying to convey.) That is, we cannot take *what* is said or done as given simply by the words used or the actions performed and then assess it as meeting or failing to meet our criteria for doing or saying that thing. Another way to put this thought is to say that we don't know *what* someone has said until we know what they (might have) meant—and we may misunderstand what a person has said or done because we wrongly imagine, or take for granted that we know, the interests, desires, etc., being expressed.

But if rules are cast in the role of the conditions on/for doing or saying something in particular, then these rules represent our only way of determining what someone has done or said. And this amounts to taking *what* is said or done as given—given by the rules. What a person has said or done is determined by the rules governing words or actions, and then this saying or acting is assessed as legitimate, acceptable, divergent, and so on in terms of these rules.[47] Mulhall's insistence that the rules of interest to him should not be regarded as fixed, impersonal, or as constituting an objective resolution of a dispute about how to go on does mean that the fact of divergence in *how* you have done what you are taken to have done will not license its simply be dismissed as illegitimate. Your divergent application of a word cannot simply and definitively be corrected by reminding you of its agreed criteria—the rules governing its application. However, the problem that remains is that the idea that your application of a word *is divergent* is taken for granted—that is, it is taken as given *what* you are trying to

---

[47] It may seem that the problem that I am suggesting here depends upon my neglecting the fact that rules function within a context. So the problem would be eliminated if one were to add that rules are context-dependent and determine what a person has said or done in some context. However, as I argue in Affeldt 1998 (18–9), such appeals to context are not helpful. For knowing what the context is itself depends upon understanding what is (or what may be found to be) intelligibly done or said "within" it.

say. And it must be taken as given, because, as noted, our rules are our only way of determining what you are saying or doing.[48]

There seems to be, then, on the one hand a certain essential dismissiveness, or perhaps chauvinism, built into a view that assigns to rules the role that Mulhall gives them. To the extent that we are able to understand what a person is saying or doing, our understanding will be given by our approaching it in terms of our rules for doing or saying something in particular.

On the other hand, however, the role that Mulhall's view assigns to rules in determining what is said or done, when conjoined with other aspects of his discussion, seems to leave him not in an overly robust critical posture, but rather in an overly weak posture, a posture in which we have essentially nothing to say in the face of ways of going on that we find unclear or problematic.

Here I have two related but distinct thoughts in mind.

First, as I have noted, Mulhall insists that the rules he sees as essential to an account of our agreement in language and the normativity of that agreement are

---

**48** I have more or less suggested that one place in which this move of taking *what* is said or done as given occurs in Mulhall's remark about a philosopher's "divergent application of a word." But another place that I have in mind, and that led to my saying at the close of the previous paragraph that we don't know what someone has said until we know what they meant, occurs in Mulhall's reply to "The Ground of Mutuality." Toward the close of his paper, Mulhall says the following:

> My present way of putting what Affeldt wants to say more generally would be that nothing compels me to speak, to apply particular words to a specific action, event, object, or person; but once I do... I open myself to certain ranges of questions and responses whose legitimacy I cannot deny, and I restrict myself to certain ranges of possible elaborations of my original judgment in responding to those questions... In short, we can say whatever we want to say; but we cannot mean whatever we want to mean by what we say. (Mulhall 1998, 43)

I will note that I do not think that we can say whatever we want to say—even though, but for limitations of vocabulary, we can utter whatever words we like. We cannot say whatever we want because there are some things that, given our position and our situation, we cannot *mean*. But I point to these remarks of Mulhall's because the separation that he effects between saying and meaning represents a clear instance in which what is said is taken as given. In my view, however, while we can say what words a person has used, there is no way of specifying what a person has said apart from what she means.

The structure of concern that I am raising about Mulhall's view here follows what I understand to be the structure of the disagreement between Cavell and Barry Stroud with respect to Wittgenstein's example of the wood-sellers. In Stroud's consideration of this example (in Stroud 1968), he takes it as given *what* these people are doing, although unclear *how* exactly they are doing it. And I take Cavell to be arguing that we cannot know *what* they are doing apart from knowing (or imagining) *how* they are doing it, and that Stroud's mistake is precisely to regard it as clear, as given, *what* they are doing.

not to be regarded as rigidly fixed, impersonal, or as constituting an objective resolution to a disagreement about how to go on. He remarks, for example:

> Citing criteria cannot constitute an objective resolution to a genuine disharmony in judgments (say in response to a skeptic's anxieties); for if our agreement in criteria runs no further or deeper than our agreements in judgment, then citing criteria can never authoritatively demonstrate the deviance of one party to the disagreement. It can at best amount to an invitation to reconsider that disagreement and what is truly at stake in it, to ask ourselves whether we wish to take a stand upon it and what stand we wish to take. (Mulhall 2014, 300 – 01)

Mulhall means these remarks to acknowledge what Cavell calls the power and powerlessness of appeals to criteria and what, in earlier work, he speaks of as the irrelevance of a direct appeal to "what we say" in philosophical criticism.[49] But given the structure of Mulhall's view, this acknowledgment is critically eviscerating. For by simultaneously locating the conditions on/for saying something in rules governing the use of words and repudiating the impersonal authority of those rules, Mulhall's view leaves us with no resources for understanding the position of the other in a genuine disharmony of judgments. If we abandon the impersonal authority of rules to determine what the other is saying or doing, the view leaves us no resources for trying to approach what the other is saying or doing. He will be simply mysterious. Further, and consequently, our consideration of the disagreement and of what is at stake in it can be undertaken only from our own position.

I don't, of course, mean to suggest that my argument that the conditions on/for doing or saying something are bound up with what is or can be seen as natural in terms of interests, desires, and so on eliminates the difficulty of understanding others in such a situation. However, it does provide us with a path into understanding the other and his position in the disagreement. For we may undertake to imagine the interests, desires, purposes, natural reactions, and so on that might lead the other to speak as he does.

Second, a similar problem emerges directly in connection with Mulhall's discussion of the schematism of a word. After having developed his conception of how the schematism of a word controls its projections, its indefinitely variable constancy, Mulhall says the following:

> But there are no formulae that determine in advance how broad a field of the concept's related concepts must carry over, or what degree of modification of any given conceptual re-

---

**49** Cf., "The Availability of Wittgenstein's Later Philosophy" (in Cavell 1976) and *The Claim of Reason* (Cavell 1979).

lation might be acceptable, or whether (and if so when and why) something about a given projection might compensate for the absence of a given conceptual relation; such judgments will be context-specific, and dependent upon the reach of the speaker's understanding and imagination. (Mulhall 2014, 309)

Mulhall is acknowledging that the schematism of a word cannot rigidly and inflexibly restrict and control its competent projections. However, having located the normative control of our uses of words in the schematism of a word, this acknowledgment, again, leaves him with essentially nothing to say about the specific ways in which—and the specific reasons why—our projections of words are controlled. The structure of his view means that he can only be left with a rather diffuse appeal to the speaker's understanding and imagination. If, however, we locate the normative control of our uses of words in the idea of what is, or can be seen as, natural in terms of interests, desires, purposes, forms of life, natural reactions, and so on, then we can acknowledge that there are no formulae that determine in advance how one may intelligibly go on with a word, and yet preserve our ability to be quite specific about the open-ended constraints on uses of words, about why those constraints are as they are, are alterable as they are, and about exactly how a particular use of words falls afoul of these open-ended constraints. Here again, we preserve the ability to undertake to understand the other, but we also preserve our ability to engage in the sort of highly specific interrogation and criticism of uses of words that is characteristic of Wittgenstein's later work.

# §5

Mulhall is understandably impressed by a point of (at least apparent) discontinuity between "Must We Mean What We Say?" and Cavell's later work on Wittgenstein: the fact that, in the early essay, Cavell seems happy to speak of the normativity of our speech and action and of the conditions on/for doing or saying something in terms of rules and that in his later work he does not. I am equally, but oppositely, impressed by a point of deep continuity between Cavell's early and later reflections on these issues: his emphasis throughout on the ideas of the normal and natural. In "Must We Mean What We Say?" he remarks that "[w]hen the philosophers asks, 'What should we say here?', what is meant is 'What would be the normal thing to say here?', or perhaps, 'What is the most natural thing to say here?'"[50] And while the control of the normal and natural

---

**50** Cavell 1976, 20.

in what we do and say (and in what we say of what others do and say) is most directly explored in Chapter Five of *The Claim of Reason*, "Natural and Conventional," I think it is fair to say that the ideas of the normal and natural are fundamental to all of Cavell's writing about Wittgenstein.[51] The centrality of these ideas marks Cavell's appreciation of Wittgenstein's efforts to remind us of "the fact that the *speaking* of language is part of an activity, or of a form of life" (PI §23) or, as Cavell puts it at one point, his efforts "to put the human animal back into language" (CR, 207). He wants to remind us, we might say, of the fact that, and of the importance of the fact that, language is spoken by embodied, desiring creatures. And the need to be reminded expresses our forgetfulness of, or our repudiation of, our human animality (within philosophy and without); it expresses, as I quoted Cavell remarking at the outset of this essay, our skepticism understood as our subjection to "the human drive to transcend itself, make itself inhuman."

---

**51** While I cannot explore the issue in detail here, I will note that this point of continuity may place in question whether Cavell's talk of rules in "Must We Mean What We Say?" can have quite the shape or force that Mulhall suggests. For while I don't find the essay perfectly clear on this point, the emphasis on what is normal or most natural at least suggests that the force of such remarks as "Rules tell you what to do when you do the thing at all" (Cavell 1976, 28) is that these rules articulate *a way* of doing the thing that is normal or natural. That is, there may well be other ways of doing the thing. But in any case, what is required to have done the thing at all—what determines whether you can be said to have done the thing at all—is not that you do it as the rules dictate, but that what you do be comprehensible as a normal or natural way of doing the thing in question, normal or natural, that is, given your circumstances, interests, tastes, and so on. (At least this may be the force of such remarks *when they are applied to ordinary speech and to performing ordinary actions.* There are, of course, some kinds of actions, e. g., some moves in some games, and some kinds of speech, e. g., some kinds of perfomative utterances, that must be done in a quite particular manner in order to count as having been done at all. But this is not the case for most of what we do and say. Indeed, I suspect that Cavell's focus on rules in this early essay is at least in part a result of his being somewhat too heavily under the spell of thinking about games and so subject to a temptation to construe speaking and acting too closely upon the model of making moves in a game.) This is also a point at which to consider the relevance of Cavell's claim that what are sometimes called "misuses" of language "break our understanding" (Cavell 1976, 21) (as opposed to violating rules?) as well as the following remarks.

> Since saying something is never *merely* saying something, but is also saying something with a certain tune and at a proper cue and while executing the appropriate business, the sounded utterance is only a salience of what is going on when we talk (or the unsounded when we think); so a statement of "what we say" will give us only a feature of what we need to remember. But native speaker will normally know the rest; learning it was part of learning the language (Cavell 1976, 32–3).

While I have focused in the preceding pages on the idea of the natural, the ideas of the normal and the natural as they figure in the work of Cavell (and as his work enables us to see them figuring in the work of Wittgenstein) are closely connected. For the idea of the normal, as Cavell suggests, is an idea of what normal people do. He remarks: "It isn't that people normally (on the whole, statistically) don't sing [for example] that way; but that *normal people don't*, people don't" (CR, 88). And this idea of what normal people do is made out in terms of what it is natural for people—for us—to do. I have attempted to articulate some of the ways in which emphasizing the importance of this idea of the natural effects a shift in our orientation to our uses of language and to the issue of the normativity of those uses.

Notwithstanding their important differences, the logicism of Frege and the positivism of Carnap may be understood as enacting a removal of the human animal from language. We might say that, in correctly repudiating psychologism, their reflections on language incorrectly turned away from the ordinary conditions of our human life with and in language as such, away from the fundamental importance of our interests, desires, purposes, forms of life, natural reactions, and so on. In so doing, these views turned away from exactly the same ordinary conditions of human meaning as had the psychologism that they contested, and so preserved just the problem of the possibility of meaning that psychologism had created by turning against these ordinary conditions. But where psychologism sought to solve the problem that it had created by locating meaning in occurrent psychological acts, logicism and positivism sought to solve the same problem that their manner of turning against psychologism had preserved by appealing to a framework of rules: the meaning of a sign being determined by its location within this framework and by the rules governing its possible combinations with other signs. In terms of this obviously quite schematic account, the originality of Wittgenstein's work may be seen to lie in its recognition of, and in its overcoming of, the shared problem at the root of psychologism, logicism, and positivism. Which is to say that the originality of his work lies in its returning us to the ordinary conditions of human meaning and so *dissolving* the problem that occurrent psychological acts as well as frameworks of rules were meant to solve.

Mulhall clearly does not (as psychologism, logicism and positivism had) simply ignore or repudiate the ordinary conditions of human meaning; the significance of our human embodiment, our interests, desires, purposes, forms of life, natural reactions, and so on. However, as I have tried to argue, his view does seem both to bespeak and to effect an attenuated relation to these matters. It bespeaks an attenuated relation to these matters in that it preserves the idea of a problem about meaning that requires solution and seeks the solution to the problem in a framework of rules that govern and determine the meaning of our speech and action. These rules are, to be sure, understood differently from how they are understood in logicism or positivism, but the requirement for rules of some sort remains. And this focus on rules, as I have argued, then effects an attenuation of our relation to these matters by miscasting the place and role of the ordinary—of our interests, desires, purposes, forms of life, natural reactions, and so on, and of what is natural in terms of these. Which is to say, as I said at the outset, that for all of its specific differences from them, Mulhall's view remains within the same horizon of thinking about language as does logicism and positivism. And that is to suggest that, as I understand it, his view remains within the horizon of the skepticism against which Wittgenstein's work is recurrently directed.[52]

# Bibliography

Affeldt, Steven (1998), "The Ground of Mutuality: Criteria, Judgment and Intelligibility in Stephen Mulhall and Stanley Cavell." In: *European Journal of Philosophy* 6, 1–31.

Affeldt, Steven G. (1999), "Captivating Pictures and Liberating Language: Freedom as the Achievement of Speech in Wittgenstein's *Philosophical Investigations.*" In: *Philosophical Topics* 27, 255–85.

Affeldt, Steven G. (2010), "On the Difficulty of Seeing Aspects and the 'Therapeutic' Reading of Wittgenstein." In: William Day and Victor J. Krebs (eds.), *Seeing Wittgenstein Anew*, Cambridge: Cambridge University Press, 268–290.

Bouwsma, O.K. (1965), "The Blue Book." In: O.K. Bouwsma, *Philosophical Essays*, Lincoln: NE: University of Nebraska Press, 175–202.

Cavell, Stanley (1976), *Must We Mean What We Say?*, Cambridge: Cambridge University Press.

Cavell, Stanley (1979), *The Claim of Reason: Wittgenstein, Skepticism, Morality, and Tragedy*, Oxford: Oxford University Press.

Cavell, Stanley (1989), *This New Yet Unapprochable America*, Albuquerque, NM: Living Batch Press.

Cavell, Stanley (1990), *Conditions Handsome and Unhandsome: The Constitution of Emersonian Perfectionism*, Chicago: University of Chicago Press.

Crary, Alice M. / Read, Rupert J. (eds.) (2000), *The New Wittgenstein*, London: Routledge.

Goldfarb, Warren (1983), "I Want You to Bring Me a Slab: Remarks on the Opening Sections of the *Philosophical Investigations.*" In: *Synthese* 56, 265–82.

---

**52** Versions of this paper were presented at a conference on "Skepticism and Interpretation" at the University of Amsterdam as well as for the Wittgenstein Workshop at the University of Chicago. I would like to thank the participants at these occasions for their questions, comments, and suggestions, and I would like especially to thank Stephen Mulhall for the provocation to further thinking that his papers have provided.

Goldfarb, Warren (1997), "Wittgenstein on Fixity of Meaning." In: William W. Tait (ed.), *Early Analytic Philosophy: Frege, Russel, Wittgenstein*, Chicago and La Salle, IL: Open Court Press.

Kripke, Saul A. (1982), *Wittgenstein on Rules and Private Language*, Cambridge, MA: Harvard University Press.

Minar, Edward (2010), "The Philosophical Significance of Meaning Blindness." In: William Day and Victor J. Krebs (eds.), *Seeing Wittgenstein Anew*, Cambridge: Cambridge University Press, 183–203.

Mulhall, Stephen (1994), *Stanley Cavell: Philosophy's Recounting of the Ordinary*, Oxford: Oxford University Press.

Mulhall, Steven (1998), "The Givenness of Grammar: A Reply to Steven Affeldt." In: *European Journal of Philosophy* 6, 32–44.

Mulhall, Stephen (2003), "Stanley Cavell's Vision of the Normativity of Language: Grammar, Criteria, and Rules." In: Richard Eldrige (ed.), *Stanley Cavell*, Cambridge: Cambridge University Press, 79–106.

Mulhall, Stephen (2014), "Inner Constancy and Outer Variation: Stanley Cavell on Grammar, Criteria and Rules." In: James Conant and Andrea Kern (eds.), *Varieties of Skepticism: Essays After Kant, Wittgenstein, and Cavell*, Berlin and New York: Walter de Gruyter.

Rhees, Rush (1970), *Discussions of Wittgenstein*, London: Routledge & Kegan Paul.

Stroud, Barry (1968), "Wittgenstein and Logical Necessity." In: George Pitcher (ed.), *Wittgenstein: The* Philosophical Investigations, New York: Doubleday Press, 477–96.

Wittgenstein, Ludwig (1965), *The Blue and the Brown Books*, New York: Harper & Row.

Wittgenstein, Ludwig (1968), *Philosophical Investigations*, G.E.M. Anscombe (trans.), London: Macmillan.

Christoph Menke
# Tragedy and Skepticism: On *Hamlet*

## I

In ancient Pyrrhonian and modern epistemological skepticism, it has been claimed that philosophy's "pure" form of enquiry calls into question our convictions and certainties.[1] Even prior to this, however, uncertainty was described as an effect of tragedy. For Plato and Nietzsche, respectively, it is uncertainty that constitutes the dangerous truth and blindness of tragedy: tragedy replaces trust and confidence with doubt and uncertainty. Moreover, Aristotle (against Plato) and Nietzsche (against Schopenhauer) tried to show—in very different ways—that tragedy "purifies" us of the uncertainty that it itself produces. Whatever the final effect of tragedy may be, its last *word* is the expression of an attitude of uncertainty. In *Oedipus Rex*, the chorus's closing words read as follows:

> Citizens of Thebes. / Here is Oedipus, who solved the riddle / And was most famous. / Who of you, gazing at him, was not envious? / Behold him now, wrecked by the stormiest seas. / Know then, we should call no man happy / Till he has passed that frontier where all pain ceases. (v. 1524–30)[2]

And earlier:

> O human generations, I consider / Life but a shadow. Where is the man / Ever attained more than the semblance / Of happiness but it quickly vanished? (v. 1186–92)

According to Sophocles's chorus, the contemplation of tragic fate teaches us uncertainty. In *Oedipus Rex*, this uncertainty is related to happiness—to the success of a whole life. Before it is too late, we cannot know what, in our delusion, we believe we know: that a life is really happy. Nothing that has happened in this life—and certainly nothing that we can do about it—can ensure its happiness. In its song about the monstrosity of humanity, the *Antigone* chorus relates this insight to the "skillfulness" and "arts" of mankind, from agriculture to the arts of war and rhetoric: "Ingenious beyond dreams, his diverse skills / Lead sometimes towards good, sometimes bad, ends" (v. 365–7). The first thing that

---

1 See Williams 2005, Chapter 2; Williams 1996, Chapter 5. For a profound discussion of epistemic skepticism, see Kern 2006.
2 Sophocles 1994.

can be said about tragedy, then, is that, by concentrating on the reaction and interpretation of the chorus, it represents not only a tragic fate, but also the effect of this representation on the spectator. This effect is one of doubt and uncertainty—a doubt and uncertainty concerning the happiness of our lives and the success of our actions.

At the same time, this effect tells us something about the relationship between tragedy and skepticism. Skepticism is a position that fundamentally doubts the possibility of secure, well-founded judgment. In this sense, the chorus of Sophoclean tragedy draws a skeptical conclusion from its contemplation of tragic fates. Rather than articulating a general skepticism, the chorus's doubt and uncertainty concerns only a particular class of judgments: those in which we express our convictions about the actions that will fulfill our intentions.[3] These judgments, the possibility of which the Sophoclean chorus doubts, are not only special, but also fundamental. They are judgments that express our practical knowledge. Practical knowledge refers to our actions and, consequently, to the abilities that we must possess if our intentions are to succeed. Practical knowledge gives us the capacity to steer our actions. As a whole, it allows us to lead a conscious, self-determined life. To the extent that it doubts the success of judgments of practical knowledge, the Sophoclean chorus's skepticism thus expresses doubt about this ability to effectively steer our actions and lead a self-determined life. The skepticism of tragedy concerns our practical reason; it is practical skepticism.

It is this preoccupation with practical reason that distinguishes the skepticism of tragedy from the skepticism of modern epistemology—which is concerned with 'theoretical' reason and knowledge. The doubt that overcomes both chorus and spectator when confronted by a tragic fate does not affect our ability to acquire reliable empirical knowledge. Practical skepticism necessarily follows from epistemic skepticism, but it is not necessarily grounded on it. Practical skepticism necessarily follows from epistemic skepticism because, without reliable empirical knowledge of facts, no dependable practical knowledge about correct modes of behavior can be acquired. But practical skepticism is not necessarily *grounded* on epistemic skepticism, because practical knowledge—knowledge about how to act—cannot be reduced to empirical knowledge. It is precisely this irreducibility with which tragedy is concerned: with the experience that we lack the practical knowledge—or the particular forms of practical

---

**3** It is not, therefore, a "radical skepticism" in Michael Williams's sense: "The most interesting sceptical arguments imply *radical* scepticism, the thesis that we never have the slightest justification for believing one thing rather another." See Williams 2001, Chapter 5.

knowledge—that would enable our actions to succeed. Action can only succeed when we know how the various basic orientations of human life meaningfully relate to one another (*Antigone*); when we know to what extent we can meaningfully explore our origins and control our lives (*Oedipus*); or when we know how to combine authenticity with shrewdness (*Philoctetes*). In the tragic irony of an action that turns against its author, tragedy shows what happens when we lack such practical knowledge. At the same time, tragedy renders our lack of this knowledge probable—not in principle, but performatively, in the situation of action. This lack is not the consequence of the unreliability and incompleteness of our empirical knowledge (which the tragedies of Sophocles also show). *Antigone, Oedipus Rex*, and *Philoctetes* make it likely that practical reason can provide no reliable guidance for the problems of action—a guidance that the most reliable and complete system of empirical knowledge also could not provide.

Classical tragedies are tragedies of action: they show the failure of our practical capabilities, of our skills, arts, and virtues. Even when, as in *Oedipus Rex*, the search for factual knowledge stands in the center, it is dealt with as a mode of behavior that raises practical and not cognitive problems. Teiresias, for instance, warns Oedipus against continuing with the search through which he attempts to prove himself a good ruler. Teiresias's argument is that it is better—in an ethical, political, or religious sense—not to know certain things (or at least not to search after them).[4] In contrast, many modern tragedies appear to be tragedies of knowledge: they show the failure of our epistemic capabilities—of our capacity to know. For Hamlet, unlike Oedipus, the question is not whether, in order to want our actions to succeed, we should attempt to know everything that we can know. Rather, it is whether, in order to want our actions to succeed, we *can* know everything that we need to know. For Hamlet, being able to know is not a practical question. Rather, being able to act is a theoretical one—a question of being able to know. According to Hamlet's conviction, we cannot know what is most essential and important; therefore, we cannot act—our actions and lives cannot succeed. Why do we vacillate, inwardly torn, between two possibilities: either bearing the accidents of history and the capriciousness of our oppressor, or acting to evade these things by committing suicide? Because knowledge fails us—knowledge concerning what awaits us after death. If what came after death were not an "undiscover'd country, from whose bourn / No traveller returns" (III,

---

4 For a reading of Oedipus as a discussion of the desire to know. see Knox 1998 and, for a more acute reading, Goux 1993.

I, 79–80);[5] if it were a country of which we had certain tidings, then it would also be possible for us to decide whether we should further endure our fate or withdraw from it. Only secure knowledge—Hamlet's lament seems to presuppose—results in correct action; knowledge allows action to succeed. However, we do not and cannot possess this knowledge. As a consequence, we cannot act, and our actions and lives cannot succeed.

From Hamlet's perspective—or, more cautiously, from the perspective of Hamlet's reflection—the problems of practical knowledge are reduced to those of the limitedness and unreliability of our empirical knowledge. On this view, the practical skepticism of tragedy would be nothing more than an expression, in reflective thought, of epistemic skepticism. I want to show, however, that this applies only to the character of Hamlet and not to *The Tragedy of Hamlet*, Shakespeare's play. Furthermore, Hamlet's conviction that our practical problems can be reduced to empirical ones mirrors a positioning of knowledge at the center of action and life.[6] Rather than concurring in this positioning, *Hamlet* reflects upon it as (partly) responsible for the descent into misfortune. *Hamlet* shows the tragic consequences of an attitude that places knowledge at the center. Most importantly, it also shows the reason for this attitude. *Hamlet* writes a genealogy of Hamlet's outlook—one that makes the intention to act dependent upon knowledge and that despairs of action because it doubts the possibility of knowledge. *Hamlet* shows that it is difficult, indeed impossible, for Hamlet not to have the attitude that reduces practical to empirical skepticism. This means, however, that *Hamlet*, like classical tragedy, gives rise to the effect of practical skepticism. For the impossibility of avoiding the reduction to epistemic problems proves itself to be a practical problem: a problem of action. *Hamlet* shows that epistemic skepticism is not our real problem; but also that we cannot avoid it, because it is the consequence of a practical problem for which we have no convincing ("rational") solution.[7]

---

**5** In the following, I quote from the Arden edition of *Hamlet* (Shakespeare 1982).

**6** When, in the following, I talk of "knowledge" without further qualification, I am always dealing—as a result of the central position it is given in the play—with empirical or theoretical knowledge: concerning facts or, more precisely, their connections and causes.

**7** This formulation indicates the indebtedness of my reading to Stanley Cavell, in particular to his great Lear essay ("The Avoidance of Love," in: Cavell 1976, 267–353). In the following section —section 2—I dispense with the need to point out this connection in detail and at every point. In section 3, it should become clear how my reading departs from Cavell's model.

# II

In the first three acts of the play, Hamlet shifts between two poles: the lack of and the hope for knowledge. The ghost, who introduces himself to Hamlet as his father's spirit (I,v,9), has unequivocally called for revenge. With the urgent demand "Remember me" (I,v,91), he disappears before the dawn, the light of which he shuns. Hamlet, however, does nothing—other than bewail the fact that, of all people, the lot has fallen to him to set right a time that is out of joint.[8] Hamlet reacts to this momentarily inexplicable inhibition of action, of which he once again accuses himself ("Why, what an ass am I!" [II,ii,578]), with a program for the acquisition of epistemic certainty. Hamlet wants to find out for himself whether the ghost spoke the truth when it accused his uncle and mother of murder. From the beginning, the ghost's form understandably appeared "questionable" (I,iv,43) to him. How can we know whether it is "a spirit of health or goblin damn'd," whether it brings with it "airs from heaven or blasts from hell," whether it harbors "intents wicked or charitable" (I,iv,40 ff.)? The only way Hamlet can dissolve this questioning is by acquiring certainty about the ghost's accusations against his uncle and mother:

> The spirit that I have seen / May be a devil, and the devil hath power / T'assume a pleasing shape, yea, and perhaps, / Out of my weakness and my melancholy, / As he is very potent with such spirits. / Abuses me to damn me. I'll have grounds / More relative than this. (II, ii,594–600)[9]

However reasonable or self-evident this idea appears at first, the arrangement that Hamlet devises in order to put it into effect—the famous "mousetrap" in which he wants to catch Claudius—is hardly promising. Exactly observed, it resembles the paradox of the Cretan. Let us look once more at Hamlet's reaction to the ghost's speech. In a curious scene—one that shows the play's irony with regard to its hero—the first thing that Hamlet does after hearing this speech is make a note about the given possibility (at least in Denmark!) of hypocrisy, as though there were a danger that he could forget the conclusion he has drawn from the ghost's words:

---

8 "The time is out of joint. O cursed spite, / That ever I was born to set it right" (I,v,196–7).
9 "More relative" means here, according to Jenkins' commentary, "more directly relating to (connected with) the circumstances; perhaps also... relatable (able to be told) to the public" (Shakespeare 1982, 273).

> O most pernicious woman! / O villain, villain, smiling damned villain! / My tables. Meet it is
> I set it down / That one may smile, and smile, and be a villain— / At least I am sure it may
> be so in Denmark. (*Writes*). (I,v,105–9)

The first conclusion Hamlet draws from the ghost's speech is the suspicion of
hypocrisy; for if the ghost is right, Hamlet's uncle and mother are criminals con-
cealing themselves behind gestures of respectability, mourning, and care. In a
next step, however, the second conclusion that Hamlet comes to is that, if his
uncle and mother can be hypocrites, then this can just as well—indeed, all the
more—be true of the ghost; the deceitful spirit of hell could speak through it.
There is a contradiction between these two consequences that the "mousetrap"
should resolve: by producing, at least once, a situation in which it is impossible
for a criminal to dissimulate. In this respect, the "mousetrap" resembles a scientific experiment: it is an artificial arrangement that should cut through everything artificial, apparent, and secondary in order to reveal things as they really
are. More precisely, the experiment by means of which Hamlet wants to find the
truth resembles a lie detector. It should give rise to a situation of involuntary expression in which the suspected hypocrite loses control over her remarks and no
longer says what she wants to say, but says how things are.

In Hamlet's opinion, this succeeds in the theater:

> Hum—I have heard / That guilty creatures sitting at a play / Have, by the very cunning of the
> scene, / Been struck so to the soul that presently / They have proclaim'd their malefactions.
> / For murder, though it have no tongue, will speak / With most miraculous organ. (II,
> ii,584–90)

In order for this to work—in order that the trap be able to snap shut—there would
indeed have to be a "miraculous" occurrence. In fact, Claudius certainly reacts to
the play that is acted out before him at the intended point (III,ii,254 ff.): Claudius
stands up ("The King rises," says Ophelia), asks for a lamp ("Give me some
light"). and exits (*"Exeunt all"*). But how are we to know what this reaction
*means?* In order to know what Claudius's standing up implies, we must first of
all know—although we do not know—which kind of play he has actually seen.
Has he seen what Hamlet sees: that a king is poisoned in his sleep and that
the murderer—according to Hamlet's explanation of further events—wins the
love of his victim's wife? Or has he seen that a nephew—as Hamlet says, "This
is one Lucianus, nephew to the King" (III,ii,239)—poisons his uncle in order to
win his wife? Has he seen, therefore, a play that reenacts his murder of Hamlet's
father, or one that anticipates his own murder at the hands of Hamlet? As long as
we do not know this, and consequently do not know what significance Claudius's behavior has, then we certainly cannot know whether Hamlet's assump-

tion—which he has drawn only from hearsay ("I have heard...")—is correct, that is, whether, at certain points, a theater audience reacts wholly involuntarily. If we do not know—that is, *cannot* know—whether Claudius's reaction is conscious or unconscious, then we cannot know whether, instead of dissimulating, he is for once unwillingly—and therefore sincerely—revealing his true feelings. That is, we cannot know here whether expression and what is expressed correspond to each other (independently of the first problem: that we cannot know in what the expressed content consists). Hamlet's confidence in the "mousetrap" resembles the attempt to resolve the paradox of the Cretan by asking the Cretan, once again, whether he now really thinks that all Cretans lie. In order to find out whether the ghost is speaking the truth, Hamlet wants to use the "mousetrap" to cross-examine those who—assuming that the ghost is speaking the truth—do not speak it themselves. This is the paradoxical (and as much despairing as comical) attempt to want to make a decision about the existence of sincerity at the same time as this existence is presupposed.

Hamlet's search for certainty cannot, therefore, result in success. There is no experimental method by means of which sincerity can be securely ascertained. In order to be ascertained, sincerity must—at least selectively—be presupposed. If the "mousetrap" is to determine whether Claudius is sincere in mourning his brother, Hamlet must presuppose, that is, he must trust, that Claudius is sincere when he reacts to the reenacted crime by jumping up and walking out. As long as presupposition and trust are understood as knowledge, however, they will give rise to the alternately skeptical and comical paradox that confronts a triumphant Hamlet after the apparent success of the "mousetrap."[10] This paradox only resolves itself, indeed, could only be resolved, if the presupposition of or trust in sincerity—without which we cannot even test for the existence of sincerity—were

---

10 Hamlet himself is convinced that the "mousetrap" has answered his doubt concerning the ghost's words and appearance. His conclusion runs as follows: "O good Horatio, I'll take the ghost's word for a thousand pound" (III,ii,280–1). It is not only unclear, however, how much weight Hamlet in fact gives to the ghost's words, but also, in the ensuing dialogue with Horatio, why he does so. To Hamlet's question, "Didst perceive?", Horatio laconically replies, "Very well, my lord." To Hamlet's enquiry, "Upon the talk of poisoning?" (which, incidentally, does not occur in the play, but can only refer to Hamlet's commentary on it; cf. III,ii,255 ff.), Horatio replies evasively: "I did very well note him" (III,ii,281 ff.). Earlier, when Hamlet infers his qualification to be a theater director from the putative success of the "mousetrap" ("Would no this, sir... get me a fellowship in a cry of players?"), Horatio shows himself as at best half convinced of Hamlet's success in the theater: "Half a share" (III,ii,273). Below, I will propose a reading of the second part of the play (the part after the "mousetrap") that is based on Hamlet's sharing Horatio's view. Hamlet also believes, I will argue, that the success of the "mousetrap" is just as uncertain as are the words of the ghost—the certainty of which it was intended to establish.

of a different form or order from the knowledge that we want to attain. Doubt about our ability to know has to become doubt about our desire to know: doubt about whether secure knowledge is the right objective when we are concerned with our relationships with others and their sincerity. This reflection, however, lies outside Hamlet's realm of possibility.

Why, though, is it impossible for Hamlet to recognize the difference between the presupposition and knowledge of sincerity? Why can there be no alternative for Hamlet to knowledge about sincerity or insincerity? One answer would be to see this as Hamlet's "flaw"—a flaw that gives rise to the tragic descent into misfortune. However, Hamlet's incapability of admitting to himself the paradox of his search for knowledge has a deeper and more solid ground, one that is first brought into play by Hamlet's search for knowledge itself. I have already mentioned that Hamlet undertakes his search for secure knowledge—for "grounds more relative than this," that is, than the the ghost's speech—in order to solve a *practical* problem; knowledge should help him to act. However, Hamlet's practical problem is not that he does not know *what* he should do, but that he does not do it even though he knows it. It is this inhibition of action that should be overcome by the acquisition of certainty.

This hope appears absurd. Hamlet's attempt to acquire certain knowledge does not appear condemned to failure only because it employs unsuitable methods, but because it is itself the wrong means—it cannot result in the expected practical success. Hamlet's undertaking of the search for certainty appears to be founded on a simple category mistake: the confusion of practical or, more precisely, motivational problems with epistemic problems of secure knowledge. Things are not, however, so simple, as is shown in the scene in which Hamlet first formulates his project for the acquisition of knowledge. With the formulation of this intention—"The play's the thing / Wherein I'll catch the conscience of the King" (II,ii,600 – 1)—the play's second act closes. Hamlet's plan for the acquisition of knowledge is to be fulfilled in the same place in which it is made: the theater. In making this plan, however, Hamlet is not centrally concerned with the spectator. In the "mousetrap," the King is experimentally placed in the position of a theater spectator and, on his part, is observed by Hamlet who, at the same time, is the director of this theatrical arrangement. Before the "mousetrap," in contrast, Hamlet's interest in the theater was directed towards the actor. For it is the player—"Of all people, the player!" we might say—who Hamlet takes to exemplify the capacity for decision and action that he himself lacks. While Hamlet remains passive, "peak / Like John-a-dreams, unpregnant of my cause" (II,ii,562 – 3), even though he possesses "the motive and the cue for passion" (555), the player acts precisely when he is not affected: he weeps for Hecuba.

Let us briefly remember the situation that gives rise to Hamlet's surprising modeling of the capacity for action upon the player. The band of players has arrived in Elsinore, and Hamlet remembers the earlier recitation of a speech that he particularly liked. Initially, this speech, which one of the players then recites again at Hamlet's request, is the account of an event: Aeneas tells Dido how, during the invasion of Troy, Pyrrhus killed Priam. As things develop, however, the account turns from the event itself to Hecuba's despairing reaction to Priam's —her husband's—murder. The aim of this account is to describe the feelings that must overcome every spectator—even the gods—when Hecuba, herself an observer, is observed: "The instant burst of clamour that she made, / Unless things mortal move them not at all, / Would have made milch the burning eyes of heaven / and passion in the gods" (II,ii,511–4). At this point, when the player recites Aeneas's account of the weeping of the gods in the face of Hecuba's reaction to Priam's death, the player himself begins to weep. It is the player's weeping that Hamlet interprets as the sign of a capacity for action—the absence of which he bitterly reproaches himself for:

> O what a rogue and peasant slave am I! / Is it not monstrous that this player here, / But in a fiction, in a dream of passion, / Could force his soul so to his own conceit / That from her working all his visage wann'd, / Tears in his eyes, distraction in his aspect, / A broken voice, and his whole function suiting / With forms to his conceit? And all for nothing! / For Hecuba! / What's Hecuba to him, or he to her, / That he should weep for her? What would he do / Had he the motive and the cue for passion / That I have? (II,ii,544–56)

Hamlet thus interprets the player's weeping not as an involuntary reaction (of the kind that he later relies on in setting the mousetrap), but as a conscious act. For Hamlet, what conduct requires and consists in is clear: action or conduct arises out of power, more precisely, out of the power to "force" the "soul," by means of "conceits", into movement ("working") so that it expresses itself in corresponding external and bodily events or forms. The (good)[11] player has at his disposal the power to give outer expression to the inner. It is precisely this power—as becomes clear when he is compared with the player—that Hamlet lacks.

It seems all the more incomprehensible, then, that Hamlet's observation of the player leads him to plan the acquisition of secure knowledge about the other's sincerity. How could knowledge, even the most certain knowledge, give rise

---

**11** On the classical sources of this conception of the actor and of the ability to make oneself weep as the sign of a good actor, see Harold Jenkins's notes to the Arden edition (Shakespeare 1982, 481 ff.).

to this power to act? More than anyone, the player shows that these two things have nothing to do with each other. The player's action consists in his reaction to the scene that he has himself recited and represented. Every such reaction contains an interpretation not only of the situation but also, at the same time, of the relation to it of she who reacts—of the significance of the events for her. In the case of the player, it is precisely this implicit interpretation that is without real content; he acts "in a fiction, in a dream of passion." For the player who possesses the capacity for action, the question of knowledge does not occur.

Again, however, it is not a simple (category) mistake that compels Hamlet—following his confrontation with the player's capacity for action—to resort to the idea that knowledge is the precondition of his own action. With regard to the question concerning the condition for and possibility of action, the player is a deeply ambiguous case. Anybody who, like Hamlet, takes play-acting as the paradigm of the capacity for action must, at the same time, fundamentally question the *meaning* of action. In *Hamlet*, this holds true generally, far beyond this particular scene. Whenever Hamlet is confronted by a character exemplifying the capacity to act, he tends to doubt the meaning and possibility of action. The power of resolution of young Fortinbras, for example—by means of which he attacks Poland and for which Hamlet admires him—stands in complete disproportion to the objective for which it is (apparently) employed. Just as the player weeps for Hecuba, the Norwegians and Poles fight literally "for nothing"—"a little patch of ground / That hath in it no profit but the name" (IV,iv,18–9). In *Hamlet*, "examples" (IV,iv,46) of action always furnish at least as good a reason for inaction.

In the example of Fortinbras, this is the result of what Hamlet sees as the emptiness of the objective of action[12]—of the disproportion between end and means, gains and sacrifices. To speak of "disproportion" here points to the fact that the capacity for action presupposes more than the capacity that Hamlet admires in the player—the capacity to translate one's own ideas into bodily expressions by means of a self-generated movement of the soul. To be able to act, we must be able to recognize (and most of all, to expect) a meaningful connection between ends, means, results, and consequences. (I shall return to this point below.) The example of the player is not, however, so ambiguous because this internal connection of the elements of action is missing. It is so ambiguous because it leads us to doubt whether another connection is ensured—one that constitutes the external context of response (*Antwortzusammenhang*) of action,

---

**12** Fortinbras's attack on Poland is the real—and, in contrast to Hamlet's, successful—'mousetrap" in this play. In it, Norway catches the throne of Denmark.

without which action is meaningless. Any action stands in a context of response with the actions of others and derives its meaning from this context. However, when play-acting is taken as the paradigm of action—when we have to assume or fear that everyone who acts play-acts—then we no longer know whether the other's action is sincere or insincere; we no longer know what motivates the other's actions; and, finally, we no longer know how our own actions—which always respond to the actions of others—should be oriented. Action becomes impossible because response has become impossible. Every action is certainly the outer bodily expression of something inner, of an idea and a successive movement of the soul. Hamlet realizes this in his confrontation with the player. At the same time, the example of the player reminds Hamlet of what he took note of following the appearance of the ghost: that all action can be hypocrisy. The fact that every action is the bodily expression of an idea implies nothing about its real content: it can be true or imaginary, sincere or feigned. The ability to act is a question of strength (to "*force* his soul to his own conceit"); he who lives "in a fiction, in a dream of passion" also has it at his disposal. In order to be able to weep for Hecuba, we must be able to imagine her pain to such a degree that our souls are compelled to work and express themselves bodily. This is not to say, however, that Hecuba actually means anything to anybody— the player weeps "for nothing." This is the ambiguity of the example of the player: because it describes the player's weeping as an action, it shows that the person who is capable of action can force herself to weep. It thus increases the suspicion that this person forces herself to do everything, that all action can be compelled by an idea that means nothing to the agent. This idea can always be something wholly other than what the agent expresses in her actions.

Hamlet calls this experience "monstrous." It is alarming because it shows that the capacity for action is intertwined with the permanent possibility of insincerity or unreality; to be able to act is to be able to deceive. If this is true of all others, however, then how should we ourselves act? Our actions are only meaningful when we know what other actions they are responding to— when we know the motives that they express or that lie behind them. In order for us to act meaningfully, it is not necessary that the other's action always be sincere. We must be able to know, however, whether it is sincere. The player who is capable of action also reminds Hamlet that he does not possess this knowledge. Therefore, it is completely reasonable, and at the same time absurd, that the experience with the player leads Hamlet to formulate the "mousetrap": an experimental device by means of which certainty about the other's sincerity is to be obtained. It is completely reasonable because, in order to be able to act meaningfully, we must know whether the other to whom we respond is sincere or not. It is absurd because, if the possibility of play-acting always exists, then it also exists in the experimental situation of the "mousetrap." The experience with the player both renders necessary the search for secure knowledge about the other's sincerity and compels its failure.

The reconstruction of the genesis of Hamlet's search for certainty shows that it is not grounded on a mere mistake, but instead on an experience: the experience that Hamlet has during his confrontation with the player. This confrontation affects Hamlet so deeply, however, only because it helps him to formulate a suspicion that he has harbored from the beginning—and which he finds confirmed by the assertions of the ghost. This is the suspicion of living in a world of mere appearance. All outer expressions of grief, clothing, facial expressions, ways of speaking, "together with all forms, moods, shapes of grief," can be mere appearance (as Hamlet, right at the beginning, explains to his mother when she, with good reason, finds his behavior "particular"): "These indeed seem, / For they are actions that a man might play" (I,ii,83 – 4). And Ophelia, who allows herself to be used as a spy by her father and King, is described by Hamlet as follows: "I have heard of your paintings well enough. God hath given you one face and you make yourselves another. You jig and amble, and you lisp, you nickname God's creatures, and make your wantonness your ignorance" III,i,144 – 8). This explains why, for Hamlet, the confrontation with the player has such far-reaching implications, and why he responds to it by formulating a project to obtain certainty about the other's sincerity. The encounter with the player makes explicit for Hamlet something that, according to his own experience, is generally valid of the other's behavior: that we cannot know whether the motives and interpretations expressed by a person's behavior are true. For Hamlet, the player's behavior becomes the paradigm of all behavior. In its structure, Hamlet's experience is theatrical.

This brings out a characteristic of Hamlet's experience that at first seems opposed to the picture of action that he derives from the player. This characteristic determines Hamlet's experience (and execution) of action in the second part of the play, that is, in the scenes that come after the "mousetrap's" failed attempt to attain knowledge about the true intentions and opinions of the other. Hamlet's formative experience here is no longer one of the mere playfulness of action; rather, it is an experience of the fact that action can be at the mercy of an unalterable fate. In the "mousetrap," the play within the play, the King had already spoken of this before his murder:

Our wills and fates do so contrary run / That our devices still are overthrown: / Our thoughts are ours, their ends none of our own. (III,ii,206 – 8)

Hamlet picks up on this motif again in his apology to Laertes, when he claims that the ill consequences of his actions where without evil intention:

> Sir, in this audience, / Let my disclaiming from a purpos'd evil / Free me so far in your most generous thoughts / That I have shot my arrow o'er the house / And hurt my brother. (V,ii,236–40)

The question of course arises here whether he who shoots arrows over houses (or runs through curtains with his sword)—without having made sure who or what stands on the other side—carries responsibility for his actions. This question fails to materialize, however, not only because Laertes—the person to whom this apology is offered—has in general little inclination or talent for enquiry; but also because Hamlet's point here is much more far-reaching than the claim that one should only ascribe responsibility to someone for the intended consequences of their actions. Hamlet claims that it was not he himself who did Laertes wrong:

> Was't Hamlet wrong'd Laertes? Never Hamlet. / If Hamlet from himself be ta'en away, / And when he's not himself does wrong Laertes, / Then Hamlet does it not, Hamlet denies it. (V,ii,229–32)

To the further question, who was it then, if not Hamlet ("Who does it then?")—a question that Hamlet puts to himself—Hamlet replies (speaking of himself in the third person): "His madness" (233). "Madness" here describes a condition of transportedness (*Entrücktheit*): a condition in which the agent is separated ("ta'en away") from himself. (Earlier, Claudius had said of the insane Ophelia that she is "divided from herself and her fair judgement" [IV,v,85].) This explains why we can only ascribe madness—to the other or to ourselves—externally or retrospectively. "Madness" is the condition in which somebody does something that she does not intend—indeed, something that runs contrary to her intentions. It is a condition of hostility to oneself: "His madness is poor Hamlet's enemy" (235).

With this turn, it becomes clear that "insane" self-transportedness is based on an entirely normal model. In his apology to Laertes, Hamlet complains that he has found himself in the situation of a dramatic character—for such characters belong not to themselves but to their fate (which in Hamlet is characterized both in ancient terms as *fate* and in Christian terms as *providence*). Hostility to oneself is the fundamental characteristic of the characters in classical drama. The figure of this hostility is termed "dramatic irony." According to Aristotle, the expression "drama" stems from the imitation of "those who act" (*drontes*, from *dran*).[13] Because it imitates particular agents and actions, drama is the imitation of *an* action—a ("plausible") story or fable (*mythos*). By means of the "synthesis" of individual actions, drama represents a total action. This synthesis, however, and the total action that it implies, exceeds the individual actions. The individual actions are split into what they are for themselves and what they are in the totality of action. In drama, we always experience individual actions in two different ways: in terms of the on-the-spot significance they have for the agent and in terms of their contribution to the total action. For structural reasons, because of the form of representation, dramatic action is ambiguous: it intends and means (*meint*) one thing and causes and signifies (*bedeutet*) something else. This ambiguity is dramatic irony. Dramatic irony distinguishes two levels of meaning that belong to two different perspectives: that of the individual dramatic character and that of the dramatic fate that encompasses her. By distinguishing these two perspectives, dramatic irony also combines them with each other. Because of this, the dramatic—in contrast to the epic—experience of fate is the experience that all action contributes to the production of a context that exceeds the agent and, indeed, can turn against her.[14]

If Hamlet's experience of the other's action in the first part of the play can be termed "theatrical," his experience of his own action in the second part can be termed "dramatic." A distinction (and a recombination of what has been distinguished) lies at the center of both experiences. In Hamlet's theatrical experience of others, it is a distinction between role and player, play and reality; in Hamlet's dramatic experience of himself, it is a distinction between individual and total action, intention and fate. In the theater, we experience that the two things

---

**13** Aristotle 1987, 1448a.

**14** In the same way that Hamlet talks of "fate" as well as "providence," the figure of dramatic irony is neutral with regard to the strict philosophical-historical (*geschichtsphilosophisch*) opposition according to which Benjamin understands the difference between ancient tragedy and the experience of fate in modern tragedy (*Trauerspiel*). Benjamin understands the moment of tragic irony when speech is derailed and becomes indiscreet as the sudden change from the one meaning of action to its opposite at the hands of a polytheistic and mythic "world-order" (Benjamin 1998, 100 ff). Similarly, see also Vernant 1990, 113 ff. In comparison, fate in the sense of the *Trauerspiel* has its basis, according to Benjamin, not in the multiplicity of meanings, but in the abandonment to the meaning*less* nature of "the profane world of things" (which "has no place" in ancient drama) (Benjamin 1998, 133). Hamlet's own experience of fate no doubt corresponds to this second model; it is the experience that "once human life has sunk into the merely creaturely, even the life of apparently dead objects secures power over it" (Benjamin 1998, 132). However else it might be interpreted, the chain of circumstances that drama (as dramatic irony) presents has primarily neither a mythic nor material, but rather a textual character. It *appears* to us—according to Empson 1965, 38 ff.)—as the web of linguistic references that make up the dramatic text.

are not the same, that behind the role there is a player and above our intentions, a fate. Both distinctions, the theatrical and the dramatic, give rise, in the figure of irony, to a recombination of what has been distinguished: the (theatrical) irony of the player over against his role, which, according to his whims, he puts on or takes off like a mask; the (dramatic) irony of fate, over against the agent's intentions, which themselves give rise to what turns against them.

This double irony defines the structure of (our) theater as apparatus and drama. Hamlet, however, transposes this irony to action in his everyday reality. He derives two different and conflicting[15] models from the theater, according to which he interprets action in general: the other's action as theatrical, one's own as dramatic. Interpreting the other's action as theatrical gives rise to the suspicion of a universal hypocrisy; interpreting one's own action as dramatic gives rise to the no less disquieting suspicion of an uncontrollable determinism. Both models can also be combined with one another: we can dissimulate a dramatic-deterministic self-interpretation (there is a suspicion of this in Hamlet's apology to Laertes) or be determined to a theatrical-hypocritical mode of behavior (there is a suspicion of this in the scheming of Rosencrantz and Guildenstern). Both, however, render action impossible—the interpretation of action according to the model of theater makes action impossible. For both experiences, the theatrical and the dramatic, are experiences of disintegration: the disintegration of each of the two contexts in the existence of which we have to be able to trust in action. If the theatrical interpretation of action is correct, then the external and social context of response in which all action is situated dissolves. Because then it is true of all behavior that it can be an action "that a man might play" (I,ii,84). If all action can be merely played, then we can no longer know what our own actions respond to. If, on the other hand, the dramatic interpretation of action is correct, then the internal and structural context of meaning that constitutes all action is dissolved. For then it is true of all action that, from the perspective of the agent, no comprehensible and predictable context holds sway between intentions and consequences; instead, the context of action is determined from outside. If all action can be fatefully over-determined, then we no longer know what our actions involve us in.

In the first part of the play, Hamlet's theatrical experience of others gives rise to an interminable doubt and hesitation. In the second part, the dramatic experience of himself leads Hamlet to vacillate between a resigned belief in fate ("The

---

15 This becomes clear inasmuch as they provide two distinct views of the same thing: the dramatic role. From one perspective, the role appears as played by the actor, and from the other, as determined by a (self-produced) fate.

readiness is all. Since no man, of aught he leaves, knows aught, what is't to leave betimes? Let be" [V,ii,220]) and an unconscious action that no longer cares about its relationship to reality.[16] The murder of Polonius, hidden behind the curtain, is only the first of a series of actions for which Hamlet does not consider himself responsible, precisely because—as he protests to Laertes—it was not he himself who carried them out. Whereas, in the first part of the play, Hamlet does not act because of an experience of theatrical irony, in the second part, he does not act because of an experience of dramatic irony—assuming, that is, that action presupposes decision and carries with it responsibility.

# III

Hamlet's experience of the world is characterized by the threat of irony: by the irony of the player who can play everything out for us, and by the irony of a fate that can turn against our actions. In a world of irony, nothing is to be taken literally; everything can always mean something else. There are a number of possible reactions to such an experience: search for certainty, sheer decisionism, and lastly, melancholy. What, however, is the status of the experience of irony itself? In a short paragraph on *Hamlet*, with which the first part of *The Origin of German Tragic Drama* concludes, Walter Benjamin has described Hamlet's fundamental experience as follows: "The secret of his person is contained within the playful, but for that reason fairly circumscribed, passage through all the stages in this complex of intentions, just as the secret of his fate is contained in an action which, according to this, his way of looking at things, is perfectly homogeneous. For the *Trauerspiel* Hamlet alone is a spectator by the grace of God; but he cannot find satisfaction in what he sees enacted, only in his own fate."[17] Hamlet's gaze refers to his fate, and his fate corresponds to his gaze— his gaze is his fate. This gaze is that of the spectator. Everything leads back to the fact that Hamlet is a spectator both of himself and of the other. A process that, according to Nietzsche, began with Euripides—the bringing of the spectator

---

16 In the first part of the play, then, the theatrical experience of others is central; in the second part, the dramatic experience of himself. This explains why, in this second part, doubt about the other's sincerity no longer plays a role. Where Hamlet interprets himself as a dramatic character, he no longer sees himself as a responsible actor. It is from the perspective of the actor, however— and from this perspective alone—that the question of the other's sincerity acquires its significance.

17 Benjamin 1998, 157–8.

onto the stage[18]—applies in its full consequences to *Hamlet*. Hamlet is the hero as spectator, the spectator who has become a hero (and who, because of this, can no longer be a hero, that is, can no longer act).

It does not suffice, however, simply to describe Hamlet as a spectator, for we can be spectators in quite different ways. Hamlet is a spectator in a special sense. This sense is characterized by the fact that Hamlet is a spectator of theater—his spectatorship is theatrical. However, we can also be spectators of theater in quite different ways. Hamlet is not only a spectator, but also a spectator of theater, in a special sense. During the performance of the "mousetrap," which Hamlet interrupts with explanations and commentaries, Ophelia sees him as playing the role of the classical chorus ("You are as good as a chorus, my lord" [III,ii,240]), which, as Jenkins remarks, "explains or 'interprets' the action of a play" (Shakespeare 1982, 302). This description, however, is only half correct, for Hamlet does not behave here as a spectator who—like the chorus of classical tragedy—is gripped and moved by the events unfolding before him. Hamlet's commentary is directed much more towards the background of events. Because it determines the immediate events from the perspective of the whole of the play, this background exceeds and interrupts the dramatic present. In the other scene that shows Hamlet in the theater, during the recitation of Aeneas's speech to Dido, the situation is the same. Hamlet's attention is again directed not only toward the present dramatic events being played out or summoned up before him, but also toward the player who produces them. In both scenes in which Hamlet is a spectator in the theater, his spectatorship dissolves, or rather exceeds, the presentness of the characters. As a spectator of theater, Hamlet is never fully absorbed either by the presentness of a dramatic character or by what happens to it.[19] In the theater, indeed, because of it—because of what constitutes it as a medium and apparatus—Hamlet is conscious both of the means by which the presentness of dramatic characters is produced, that is, of the player and his skills, and of that which is produced by these characters, that is, of fate and its turns. (He is also conscious of the effect of both the player and fate on the audience.) Hamlet's spectatorship in the theater is characterized by its interruption of the absorption in the presentness of dramatic events and characters in adhering to the rebukes of an irony that dissolves the dramatic present.

As we have seen, it is precisely this ironic fragmentation of the present that also characterizes Hamlet's experience of action. Hamlet's experience of action

---

**18** Nietzsche 1999, 57.

**19** Dramatic absorption, the opposite of theatrical reflection, is Michael Fried's concept, which Cavell makes the basis for his interpretation of Shakespeare; cf., Fried 1980. See the critical discussion in Rebentisch 2003, esp. Part 1.

is constituted in the same way as is his experience of theater. Both experiences are characterized by a theatrical attitude of spectatorship. This interrelation between Hamlet's experience of action and his experience of theater is significant both structurally and functionally. In *structural* terms, the connection between Hamlet's theatrical experience and the ironic fragmentation of the present allows a more exact characterization of his experience of action. This experience can be grasped by means of the concept of reflection; and, so understood, it enters into a systematic interrelation with epistemic skepticism. The interrelation between Hamlet's experience of action and his experience of theater is *functionally* significant because his experience of theater has to be understood as the model for his experience of action. This raises the question of the justifiability as well as the necessity of Hamlet's theatrical spectatorship. To the extent that this is a question of attitude—that is, to the extent that spectatorship, as an attitude, is itself a mode of action—the question of tragedy and its practical skepticism is raised at the same time.

Firstly, however, what does it mean to describe Hamlet's theatrical attitude of spectatorship as an attitude of "reflection"? The reason for this characterization is the ironic dissolution of presentness that determines not only Hamlet's experience of theater, but also his attitude of spectatorship in general. In this experience, everything appears as relative to something else. Agents and characters are not taken in their immediate presentness; they are observed as making up one side of a distinction. Theatrical spectatorship operates, however, with a particular form of distinction; and it is this particular form that first characterizes it as reflective. Without (some) distinctions, nothing whatsoever can be experienced. In perception, for example, these are distinctions the two sides or terms of which lie on one level (for instance, the distinction between different colors, degrees of brightness, or forms). Reflection, on the other hand, is concerned with asymmetric distinctions: between something that is present to us and something that lies behind or underlies it. Reflection exceeds presentness by retreating behind it. It asks for the ground of presentness and, in this respect, renders it a mere effect of something else. Hamlet's reflective spectatorship operates—first in the theater and then in reality—with the distinction between appearance and ground. Reflection is the dissolution of presentness in the recollection of its ground—the dissolution of every presentness in (mere) appearance.[20]

---

20 In this respect, the attitude of reflective spectatorship is "modern" and stands in contrast to the ancient model of "theoretical" spectatorship. The Greek concept of theory "derives from the pre-philosophical concept of *theoros*, the envoy to the holy games." "Theory" hence refers to a form of spectatorship, the sense of which is "the celebrating of the god on viewing the divine": "While some at this festival pursue their own pleasure and others use the opportunity to offer

If it is accurate to see in Hamlet's doubly ironic experience of action forms—perhaps even basic forms—of an attitude of reflective spectatorship of the world, then also the consequences to which this experience leads Hamlet can be understood as consequences of reflective spectatorship. These consequences consist in a dissolution of the contexts of meaning and response without which action is impossible; and this dissolution, this rendering-impossible of action, can now be understood as a consequence of the attitude of reflective spectatorship. For reflection cannot give rise to any certainty. More precisely, reflection cannot replace a dissolved present certainty with a second-order certainty—concerning the "ground" or "essence" of appearances—that would make action possible. This is true of both aspects of Hamlet's doubly ironic experience of action. In the context of this discussion, however, the first aspect is of greater significance.[21] The theatrical experience of action dissolves the presentness of the character into the irony of the player. This is its reflective operation: it sees manifest actions and motives only as appearances and relates them to hidden intentions and deeds. Because of this, the reflective experience of action brings into play the search for knowledge—knowledge of the other's true intentions. At the same time, however, as the example of the "mousetrap" has shown, this search can come to no conclusion as long as it is conditioned by such a reflective experience of action. Knowledge of the other's hidden intentions is only possible if we do not regard all expressions of intention in action as mere appearance. Hamlet's reflective experience of action renders his search for certainty both necessary and, at the same time—if it is conceived as total—unfulfillable. It leads to a fundamental doubt about our capacity to know (the intentions of) the other. The attitude of reflective spectatorship is the ground of epistemic skepticism, and epistemic skepticism is the consequence of the attitude of reflective spectatorship.

The first part of this diagnosis formulates the *genealogy* of epistemic skepticism that *Hamlet* presents. *Hamlet* shows the conditions under which epistemic skepticism must arise: precisely when, in the reflective attitude of spectatorship,

---

their wares for sale, the philosopher is he who grasps the meaning of the festival of theory" (Ritter 1977, 16). In keeping with this model, Gadamer also describes spectatorship in the theater as a "being-there" (*Dabeisein*) that attests to presentness: "The being of the spectator is determined by his 'being there present' [*Dabeisein*]. Being present does not simply mean to participate... Thus watching something is a genuine mode of participating. Here we can recall the concept of sacral communion that lies behind the original Greek concept of *theoria*. *Theoros* means someone who takes part in a delegation to a festival" (Gadamer 1994).

**21** An action-dissolving effect follows also from the second aspect—the experience of dramatic irony. Although this experience can certainly give rise to certainty, it is both retrospective and contemplative. It cannot be effective in or from the performative perspective.

the presentness of action begins to dissolve into mere appearance. In order to be able to act in this situation, we need secure knowledge. But it is precisely in this situation that we can no longer attain secure knowledge. The second part of the claim formulates the problematization of reflection that *Hamlet* carries out. *Hamlet* shows the consequences that the attitude of reflective spectatorship of the world (of action) has: this attitude falls prey—as Walter Benjamin has said about the "allegorical intention"—to "the dizziness of its bottomless depths."[22] Because of this, no certainty can be attained in the reflective attitude: "if contemplation is not so much patiently devoted to truth, as unconditionally and compulsively, in direct meditation, bent on absolute knowledge, then it is eluded by things, in the simplicity of their essence."[23]

*Hamlet* carries out a problematization of reflection by showing that the attitude of reflective spectatorship leads to epistemic skepticism. Conversely, the skeptical doubt about our capacity to know (the motives and sincerity of) the other is a consequence of the attitude of reflective spectatorship: in this attitude, epistemic skepticism is unavoidable. How do things stand, however, with the attitude of reflective spectatorship itself? In Benjamin's investigation, its ground—and, therefore, its necessity—remains undetermined. In contrast, Stanley Cavell—not with reference to *Hamlet*, but rather to *King Lear*—has placed the question of the theatricality of spectatorship in the center. Moreover, he sees it as constituting the "flaw" that sets the tragedy going: the tragedy occurs because the hero behaves toward others (and, in *Hamlet*, also toward himself) as a spectator or, more precisely, as a theatrical spectator. The attitude of theatrical spectatorship in the face of the presentness of dramatic events becomes the decisive element with regard to the events themselves. In modern tragedy, the dramatic characters are no longer only the object of a theatrical spectatorship that reflects upon them in their relation to their external conditions (fate and player); in relation to one another, they are themselves theatrical and reflective spectators. The spectator is not external to tragedy, that is, to this modern tragedy; she is "implicated" in it. It is this entry of the spectator into the tragedy that first gives rise to the tragedy itself.[24]

---

22 Benjamin 1998, 232. In this problematization of reflection, *Hamlet* embodies the "idea" of the *Trauerspiel*, as constructed by Benjamin in opposition to an ahistorical concept of the tragic. *Trauerspiel* is a reflection on reflection—a staging of the aporias to which a reflective attitude to the world leads.

23 Benjamin 1998, 229.

24 Cavell 1976, 313. Cavell formulates here the direct counter-thesis to the widely disseminated view that the theatrical self-reflection of tragedy dissolves (the representation of) the tragic. I

Although Cavell goes beyond Benjamin in making this decisive insight, he does not pursue its consequences—ones that can be drawn from *Hamlet*—in his discussion of *King Lear*. This is true in two different respects. The first concerns Cavell's concept of theatricality. Cavell certainly traces the characters' "loss of presentness" back to the fact that they take up the attitude of spectatorship with regard to one another. He also connects the attitude of spectatorship within the play to the one that is taken up toward it; it is because of this that he terms it "theatrical." At the same time, however, he does not describe this attitude in its specific theatrical constitution. Cavell's discussion of theatricality is related exclusively to the loss or dissolution of presentness. It does not, however, characterize this loss or dissolution theatrically (or aesthetically), but epistemologically, because such spectatorship follows modern philosophy in conceiving of knowledge as the representation and ascertainment of an object by a subject who confronts it.[25] In his reading of *King Lear*, Cavell understands theatrical spectatorship as objectifying what confronts it (and as rendering the spectator a "subject"). In theatrical spectatorship, however, as it is represented in *Hamlet*, presentness is not dissolved by the objectification of what confronts the spectator, but by the irony of (aesthetic) reflection. If Cavell's insight—that the hero's attitude of reflection within the play has to be understood as the internal mirroring of the perspective of its audience—is taken seriously, then this attitude of reflection and spectatorship cannot only be characterized by its negative effect, that is, by its dissolution of presentness. It is much more important to ascertain how this effect is produced: not by the modern idea of epistemic certainty, but by the ("ironic") consciousness of what produced the present events (the player's play) and of what these events themselves produce (the embroilments of fate).

This suggests a second difference between my reading of *Hamlet* and Cavell's understanding of theatrical spectatorship in *King Lear*. This difference concerns not the structure but the genesis—and thus the necessity and legitimacy—of theatrical spectatorship. If the attitude of spectatorship is described according to the epistemological model of the objectification of what confronts the subject, then it remains unclear whether and why the theatrical attitude of spectatorship *must* appear in tragedy. If the attitude of spectatorship is described according to the theatrical model of a doubly ironic reflection, however, then this question can be answered in a way continuous with Cavell's thesis that modern tragedy

---

have described (and criticized) this view as the "romantic" paradigm of the theory of tragedy; see Menke 2009, Part 2.

**25** Cavell 1976, 322ff. See also "Knowing and Acknowledging," in: Cavell 1976, 238–66. On this point, Cavell's reading again coincides with Benjamin's: both are diagnoses of the modern will to knowledge and its consequences. Cf., Haverkamp 2001, esp. Part 1.

"implicates" the viewer. The attitude of spectatorship has to arise in tragedy whenever, and because, tragedy itself becomes self-reflective. It is precisely this that occurs in, and indeed constitutes, the step from classical to modern tragedy. Modern tragedy emerges out of classical tragedy by absorbing and representing within itself that which is constitutive of classical tragedy yet remains external to it. The doubly ironic reflection in Hamlet's spectatorship, which, according to Benjamin, makes up his fate, is not an attitude that is assumed voluntarily (nor is it transposed from modern epistemology); it is already the basic characteristic of the spectator of classical tragedy. In classical tragedy, however, this spectator—who dissolves the dramatic present by referring to the whole of the play and to what lies behind the masks—is not herself represented. The spectator constitutes classical tragedy as theater, but is not represented in it. In modern tragedy, on the other hand, the spectator is represented. This explains the theatrical spectatorship of its heroes: they have learned this attitude in the theater.

This does not yet explain, however, why Hamlet does not restrict this theatrical spectatorship to the world of theater, but instead relates it to the world of action. Is this not an unjustified and, indeed, arbitrary move—one that is as wrong as it is avoidable?[26] Nietzsche describes Hamlet as standing on the boundary between theater and reality. Hamlet's situation is characterized by the fact that, after he has experienced the irony of theater, "everyday reality re-enters consciousness,"[27] and he interprets this reality according to the model of theater; the scene with the player (II,ii) makes this explicit. It is this process of interpretation—on the model of theater—that first gives rise to Hamlet's doubly ironic experience of action and, thus, to his doubt about the possibility of both knowing the other's intentions and being responsible for his own actions. However, neither these fateful consequences nor this grounding on the model of theater let Hamlet's theatrical attitude of spectatorship appear as if it had an alternative (that is, an alternative for Hamlet, in the play). For Hamlet, that is, there is no alternative to the attitude of reflection that constitutes his theatrical spectatorship. This, I want to claim finally, is the essential tragic experience in *Hamlet*: the attitude of reflection, even given an awareness of its skeptical consequences

---

26 On the question of necessity and freedom in modern tragedy, see Cavell 1976, 317 ff., 340 ff.
27 Nietzsche 1999, 40 (translation modified). This recourse to Nietzsche's interpretation presupposes that if it is at all possible to understand the "ecstasy of the Dionysiac state, in which the usual barriers and limits of existence are destroyed," from which Nietzsche sees Hamlet return to the consciousness of everyday reality, it is only as a theatrical experience. Such a way of reading the Dionysian, which I cannot develop here, follows the thread of the "original phenomenon of drama" (43) more than that of intoxication.

and its theatrical ground, is unavoidable. The effect of the tragedy of Hamlet, like that of classical tragedy, is one of practical doubt or skepticism.

This claim—that the attitude of reflective spectatorship, despite its problematic, is unavoidable, that there is no alternative to it in *Hamlet*—must be qualified. There is an alternative, even in this play, but it is no more appealing than the attitude of reflection is. It consists in the attitude of unreflective and immediate action. In the conflict between Hamlet and Laertes, these two attitudes are set against one another. Hamlet and Laertes are doubles (*Doppelgänger*). Their "causes" resemble one another, as Hamlet realizes: "For by the image of my cause I see / The portraiture of his" (V,ii,77–8). Their behavior, however, could not be more different: as soon as Laertes is convinced who has killed his father and driven Ophelia mad, he decides on revenge, resolves a plan, and undertakes steps to execute it. Whereas Hamlet, in his reflection, sees appearances and asks after their hidden essence, things and people become apparent to Laertes in their present form. Hamlet and Laertes are doubles in the sense of a mirror image: an exact inversion of the same outlines. It is precisely because of this that the conflict that unfolds between them is undecidable; in it, they must both come to an end. Hamlet destroys or loses everything that is important to him—in the end, even the throne of Denmark, one of the objects, of course, of his dispute with his uncle and his mother. Laertes, however, fares no better. Where Hamlet doubts, Laertes trusts. But where Laertes trusts—in the support of the scheming Claudius, for example—he would have done better to doubt. This is the problem that is posed by the mirror-image confrontation between Hamlet and Laertes: one reflects, the other trusts, and both actions end in the same disaster. The problem that this pair of doubles presents is that we do not and *cannot* know whether we should trust the presentness of people and things or reflectively doubt their appearance.

This knowledge—the possibility of which stands in question here—is not empirical or theoretical knowledge that, in its unattainability, leads to epistemic skepticism. Rather, it is practical knowledge: knowledge about the practical correctness of attitudes and modes of behavior. For the question of whether we should believe in the present form of people or things, or doubt and reflect upon it as appearance, cannot be answered by our ascertainment of their constitution. Rather, we can only ascertain this if we have already taken up an attitude of trust or belief with regard to things and people—if we have already decided the question in the spirit of Laertes. Conversely, the decision of this question in the spirit of Hamlet makes it impossible for us to securely ascertain the constitution of people and things: reflective doubt about their presentness is endless. Epistemic doubt about the possibility of knowing the other and her motives is—as we experience in *Hamlet*—a consequence of the attitude of reflective spectatorship (which, for its part, has its ground in the theater). With regard to the attitude of reflective spectatorship itself, however—one that leads to epistemic skepticism—the play leaves us with a practical doubt: doubt about our capacity of knowing how to rationally decide between reflective spectatorship and practical belief and trust.

Although according to Benjamin, the *Trauerspiel* of Hamlet is far removed from ancient tragedy, it ultimately leads back to the practical skepticism of classical tragedy. Classical tragedy is a tragedy of action, modern tragedy (or *Trauerspiel*) a tragedy of reflection; classical tragedy is the tragedy of the acting hero, modern tragedy that of the reflective spectator. But to be a reflective spectator—as Hamlet is when, on the threshold of theater, "everyday reality re-enters consciousness"—is also to behave in a certain way. We experience the consequences of a particular mode of behavior practically. Moreover, it is a practical question—a question of practical reason—whether, in the face of these consequences, we should behave in one way or another. Hamlet confronts this question—the practical question concerning the place that we should allocate to the attitude of reflection (and spectatorship) in wanting our actions and lives to succeed—in its unanswerability. If the tragedy of Hamlet shows that epistemic skepticism is one of the consequences of the attitude of reflective spectatorship, then *practical* skepticism is the attitude to which it itself gives rise.

# Bibliography

Aristotle (1987), *Poetics*, Stephen Halliwell (trans.), London: Duckworth.

Benjamin, Walter (1998), *The Origin of German Tragic Drama*, John Osbourne (trans.), London: Verso.

Cavell, Stanley (1976), *Must We Mean What We Say?*, Cambridge: Cambridge University Press.

Empson, William (1965), *Seven Types of Ambiguity*, Harmondsworth: Penguin Books.

Fried, Michael (1980), *Theatricality and Absorption: Painting and Beholder in the Age of Diderot*, Chicago: Chicago University Press.

Gadamer, Hans-Georg (1994), *Truth and Method*, Joel Weinsheimer and Donald G. Marshall (trans.), New York: Continuum Books.

Goux, Jean-Joseph (1993), *Oedipus, Philosopher*, Stanford: Stanford University Press.

Haverkamp, Anselm (2001), *Hamlet: Hypothek der Macht*, Berlin: Kadmos.

Kern, Andrea (2006), *Quellen des Wissens. Zum Begriff vernünftiger Erkenntnisfähigkeiten*, Frankfurt am Main: Suhrkamp.

Knox, Bernard (1998), *Oedipus at Thebes: Sophocles' Tragic Hero and His Time*, New Edition, New Haven: Yale University Press.

Menke, Christoph (2009), *Tragic Play: Irony and Theater from Sophocles to Beckett*, New York: Columbia University Press.

Nietzsche, Friedrich (1999), *The Birth of Tragedy*, Ronald Spiers (trans.), Cambridge: Cambridge Ubniversity Press.

Rebentisch, Juliane (2003), *Ästhetik der Installation*, Frankfurt: Suhrkamp.

Ritter, Joachim (1977), "Die Lehre von Ursprung und Sinn der Theorie bei Aristoteles." In: *Metaphysik und Politik*, Frankfurt: Suhrkamp, 9–33.

Shakespeare, William (1982), *Hamlet*, Harold Jenkins (ed.), Walton-on-Thames: Nelson & Sons.

Sophocles (1994), *Oedipus Tyrannus*, Hugh-Lloyd Jones (trans.), Cambridge, MA: Harvard University Press.

Vernant, Jean-Pierre (1990), "Ambiguity and Reversal: On the Enigmatic Structure of *Oedipus Rex.*" In: Jean-Pierre Vernant and Pierre Vidal-Naquet, *Tragedy and Myth in Ancient Greece*, New York: Zone Books, 113–40.

Williams, Bernard (2005), *Descartes: The Project of Pure Enquiry*, London: Routledge.

Williams, Michael (1996), *Unnatural Doubts: Epistemological Realism and the Basis of Scepticism*, Princeton: Princeton University Press.

Williams, Michael (2001), *Problems of Knowledge: A Critical Introduction to Epistemology*, Oxford: Oxford University Press.

Arata Hamawaki
# Cavell, Skepticism, and the Idea of Philosophical Criticism

## 1 Introduction: The Idea of Philosophical Criticism

A striking feature of Stanley Cavell's treatment of the philosophical problem of skepticism is its intense and sustained focus on the nature of the problem itself, on describing the problem correctly and comprehensively, and on arriving at the terms in which it could be satisfactorily resolved. For Cavell, philosophical problems, such as the problem of skepticism about the external world or about other minds, are themselves peculiar—peculiar as intellectual problems—and require, if any genuine headway is to be made on them, an understanding of just what it is that makes the problem a *philosophical* one. This is for him part and parcel of the special difficulty that a philosophical problem presents. Many intellectual problems are hard nuts to crack. With philosophical problems, it turns out to be a trap to take the problem at face value and simply to try to come up with the solution to it. Rather, one must see why there is going to be something unsatisfying about dealing with the problem in such a straightforward way, and that is something that one can do only by coming to understand the peculiar nature of the problem itself, to understand what distinguishes the problem as a philosophical one.[1] Thus, for Cavell, any satisfying engagement with a philosophical problem such as the one posed by skepticism must shed light on the nature of philosophical problems as such: on their source, on the prospects of a satisfactory resolution of them, and on how they differ from intellectual problems in other fields, however intractable they may be. There is for him no way to separate the task of arriving at a conception of philosophy, and with it a conception of the methods that philosophy must hew to and the "data" that it can appeal to, and the enterprise of dealing with and potentially resolving the problem itself. If this is right, it might go some way towards characterizing the challenge

---

[1] Cavell writes, "If I deny a distinction, it is the still fashionable distinction between philosophy and meta-philosophy, the philosophy of philosophy. The remarks I make *about* philosophy (for example, about certain of its differences from other subjects) are, where accurate and useful, nothing more or less than philosophical remarks, on a par with remarks I make about acknowledgment or about mistakes or about metaphor. I would regard this fact—that philosophy is one of its own normal topics—as in turn defining for the subject, for what I wish philosophy to do" (Cavell 1976, xviii).

one faces in trying to understanding Cavell. One must do at least two things, and do them more or less simultaneously: one must seek both to absorb his special conception of philosophy and to understand the way that conception structures and guides his dealings with something that has the shape of a familiar philosophical problem, such as skepticism about the external world or skepticism about other minds. One must conduct these tasks more or less simultaneously, since it becomes quickly evident to any reader of Cavell that one can fully understand his conception of philosophy only by seeing how it both arises from and in turn guides his dealings with the philosophical problem at hand.

Cavell's intense focus on the nature of the problem or conflict that skepticism poses is reminiscent of Kant's approach to problems in metaphysics. For Kant, the worst thing that one can do is to try to simply answer a metaphysical question, for metaphysics itself exists in a state of unavoidable conflict. In answering a metaphysical question, one simply stakes oneself to one side of the conflict and so ignores that the opposing position is equally defensible. Thus, the straightforward way with metaphysical questions simply reinforces the conflict between forces of the mind that lies at the heart of metaphysics, a conflict rooted in reason itself. For Kant, metaphysics is a kind of seemingly endless repetition of Groundhog Day. The only way forward is to inquire into and to articulate the nature of the conflict itself; to find its source in principles of the human mind; and to seek, if possible, a way of satisfying, in a more satisfactory, less conflicted way, the ineluctable need to which metaphysics is a response. It is this turn to the nature and roots of philosophical conflict that gives rise to Kant's particular conception of philosophy as "critical," and I think that it is useful to see Cavell's conception of philosophy as a descendant of Kant's "Critical Philosophy."[2] Indeed, I think that it is Cavell's affinity to Kant here that marks the sharpest and deepest break between his approach to skepticism and others on offer in contemporary philosophy.

In order to diagnose and resolve the conflict within reason, Kant believed that both sides in metaphysical disputes must be seen as laboring under what he called "transcendental illusion."[3] The sort of thing that a transcendental illusion is, Kant tells us, is to be understood by seeing how it is distinguished, on the one hand, from what he calls "empirical illusion" and, on the other, from what

---

2 Cavell acknowledges that the situation of "modernity" described here has its roots in Kant: "This new significance in philosophical repudiation itself has a history. Its most obvious precursor is Hegel, but it begins, I believe, in Kant. For it is in Kant that one finds an explicit recognition that the terms in which the past is criticized are specific to one's own position, and require justification from within that position" (Cavell 1976, xix).

3 See Kant 1998, A293/B349–A298/B355.

he calls "logical illusion." An empirical illusion—such as the sun's looking larger when it is appears closer to the horizon—tends to persist even after it is pointed out; it concerns the appearance of an empirical fact and has its roots in the constitution of our empirical psychology. A logical illusion—such as the fallacy of affirming the consequent—concerns a logical matter and so can be corrected a priori, but vanishes once it is pointed out. Unlike an empirical illusion, transcendental illusion has its source and corrective in reason itself, but unlike a logical illusion, a transcendental illusion tends to persist even after its nature as an illusion is discovered. Kant argued that though the opposed positions on a metaphysical question present themselves as contradictories—so that it looks as though each side could simply defend its own position by refuting its competitor—that is a transcendental illusion: they are, he argues, contraries.[4] The transcendental illusion is that one or the other of the opposed positions must be right. For example, the world as a whole is either finite or infinite in extension, infinitely divisible or made up of indivisible atoms, and so on. Kant points out that both sides in the disputes suppose that there is such an object as the world as a whole—a totality over and above the objects that make up the world—and that this object possesses determinate properties such as size. This is the source of the illusion. And once this illusion is exposed, the way is open toward resolving the conflict of reason through an acceptance of transcendental idealism.

What interests me here are not the specific details of Kant's doctrine of transcendental illusion, or of his claim that it is only through an acceptance of transcendental idealism that it is possible to avoid being taken in by the illusion.[5] Rather, my aim in describing those features of Kant's philosophy is to tease out how he conceived of the intellectual situation that calls for what he called "criticism" and how he conceived of the enterprise of "criticism" itself, in particular, how "criticism" differs from what might be described as "straightforward" philosophical argumentation offered in defense of, or in opposition to, one or another philosophical position.[6]

As Kant understood it, "criticism" isn't simply the application of critical reflection to a philosophical position. In that sense of "criticism," philosophy is obviously "critical" from the start, since it generally involves critical reflection on one's position, the offering of a justification for it, a refutation of opposing

---

4 See Kant 1998, A502/B530–A507/B535.
5 I take up the issue of the relation between Kantian critique and Kantian idealism at the end of the paper, by raising the question of whether Cavell's methodology is linked with idealism.
6 For an illuminating discussion of Kant's conception of philosophy as criticism and Hegel's own critical reception of this conception of philosophy, see Bristow 2007.

positions, and so on. Rather, criticism in Kant's special sense is a response to a particular intellectual predicament, and the response itself is an enterprise that involves more than what might be called "the activity of defense and refutation." First, criticism requires unraveling an illusion rather than simply uncovering an error of reasoning or a false premise in an argument. And unraveling an illusion requires entering into the point of view of a position and understanding the source of the hold that the position has on the mind. One must enter into the illusion in order to lead someone out of it, that is, in order to lead someone out of being taken in by it. One must in that sense work on an illusion "from the inside." This requires, among other things, allowing the illusion the greatest freedom to express itself.[7] Second, criticism begins at a point at which reason already seems to have had its say, a point, you might say, of the apparent exhaustion of reason. Further argumentation seems at this juncture either to be the spinning of idle wheels, or to serve simply to further entrench the opposing positions and so give fuel to a skeptic who uses the standoff as the basis for attacking reason itself. This condition leads to skepticism about reason itself, followed on its heels by a kind of weariness or boredom, which ushers in the height of decadence that Kant called "indifferentism": "the mother of chaos and night." Third, criticism is essentially self-criticism. It is an exercise in self-knowledge. Resolution requires self-recognition on the part of the one under the sway of the illusion. One can't simply be argued out of an illusion as one can be argued out of a mistaken belief. Rather, while others can have a hand in leading you out of an illusion, an illusion is ultimately something that one must find one's own way out of. A defense of an argument can be successful even if no one as a matter of fact thinks so. But philosophical criticism is nothing if it does not issue in *actual agreement.* Fourth, since the illusion is transcendental, it cannot be explained away as an empirical quirk of our psychology—as can the illusion of the sun looking larger when it is seen on the horizon—but must have its seeds planted deep in our rational nature. This means that transcendental illusion itself has a "logic"; it is a playing-out of forces of reason itself.[8] Transcendental illusion is a non-pathological and permanent condition. This suggests that while illusion can lead to falsehood, it must also express a significant truth: if nothing else, a truth about reason itself. Finally, criticism is ushered onto the scene by a crisis in reason itself, one that is characterized by reason seeming to be in the position of opposing itself, to be split in two. Thus, what is at

---

7 The idea that philosophy deals with illusion, and that illusion in philosophy has a specific nature, is something that has been impressed upon me by conversations with Kelly Jolley.
8 Thanks to Bill Bristow for stressing this point to me.

stake in criticism is reason itself, and so what stands in need of defense, and criticism, is not one or another philosophical position (for Kant it's too late in the day for that), but the very faculty of reason itself.

I think that Cavell conceives of his philosophical project in such terms. For Cavell also, skepticism represents not just a standoff between philosophical positions, but a crisis in reason itself. And also for him, the time has passed in which it makes sense to go on defending or criticizing the opposing sides of a philosophical problem such as skepticism.[9] And so I believe that Cavell's conception of philosophical criticism shares with Kant's all five of the abovementioned features: it involves dealing with illusion rather than simply with mistakes; it begins at a point of apparent rational exhaustion or impasse; it is an exercise in self-knowledge; it deals with intellectual forces that are deeply rooted in our rational nature; and it constitutes a critique and defense of reason itself, a defense of reason based on a delimitation of what it can and cannot accomplish. However, it is not easy to see how Cavell arrives at a conception of philosophical criticism that is characterized by these features or how these features play a role in Cavell's specific engagement with the skeptic about the external world or about other minds. My aim in this paper is to elaborate on Cavell's inheritance of the idea of Kantian critique, with the aim of articulating just where he follows Kant's model and where he is compelled to depart from it, and why. By doing so, I hope to illuminate both the nature of Cavell's unique engagement with skepticism and the special conception of philosophy that arises from and informs this engagement.[10]

## 2 Austin's Challenge

As I have said, philosophical criticism itself is not simply critical reflection on one or another philosophical view. Rather, as Kant understood it, philosophy becomes critical when reason seems to be in conflict with itself. With this in mind, we might ask what it is that motivates the turn to criticism for Cavell: what is the conflict that necessitates criticism? What is the nature of this conflict? And in

---

**9** Of course, just as Kant's diagnosis of the situation with regard to metaphysical problems didn't deter many from continuing with the old metaphysical debates, so after Cavell's diagnosis of the situation with regard to skepticism, philosophers have continued, and no doubt will continue, to attempt refutations of skepticism.

**10** Sanford Shieh also explores this connection in his attempt to explain what Cavell calls "the truth of skepticism." My view of Cavell's conception of philosophy is, I think, in agreement with his, although I stress different aspects of that conception. See Shieh 2006.

what sense does the conflict embody a conflict within reason itself, so that the conflict calls for "critique" in something like the Kantian sense? The reader of Cavell is made quickly aware that these are the central questions that drive the long and dense story he tells in the first 240 or so pages of *The Claim of Reason*. But it is not immediately obvious that there should be such complexity in understanding the nature of the conflict. As it is normally understood, the conflict is conceived of as one in which skepticism is pitted against what might be called "common sense." The skeptic claims that we don't, or can't, know anything about the world around us, or about other minds. This seems to offend against common sense, and it seems to do so because it contradicts a "position," or a "belief," held by common sense or by the so-called "plain" person. I stress here that a difference in belief seems to be the locus of the conflict because it will soon emerge that that is *not* what Cavell sees as the locus of the conflict at all. But I will begin by taking the appearances at face value and suppose for now that this is the conflict that Cavell takes to be posed by skepticism, letting us revise our view about the nature of the conflict in due course. How readily does the conflict admit of resolution, and what is its source? These are two questions that Kant taught us to ask with respect to philosophical conflicts in general.

Let me start with the first question (the second will occupy me for approximately the rest of the paper).[11] Cavell notes that it is a central feature of the skeptic's argument that it seems to rely on very little that might be characterized as a specific philosophical position or view, a position or view that seems to require independent defense. Instead, the skeptic's argument seems to follow a pattern that is common to similar inquiries we all conduct in the course of everyday life and so seems to draw only on our familiarity with such inquiries. The rootedness of the skeptic's manner of proceeding in ordinary epistemic inquiries is largely responsible for what Cavell, and others, have observed to be a striking and powerful fact about skepticism: its naturalness.

J. L. Austin memorably laid out the structure of an ordinary epistemic inquiry.[12] If someone claims that there is a goldfinch in the garden, then he opens himself up—at least in certain circumstances—to the question how he knows this. And we can imagine him answering: "By its red head." In certain circumstances, his offering such a basis for his claim could be challenged by saying: "But goldcrests also have red heads." Once such a challenge is entered, it is

---

**11** My focus throughout in this paper will be on Cavell's treatment of Cartesian skepticism about the external world. Due to space considerations, I will leave to one side his fascinating discussion of skepticism about other minds.

**12** See Austin 1961.

not, of course, open for the person to go on with the knowledge-claim as before. He must find some way of neutralizing the challenge or else give up the claim. He could say any of an indefinite number of things—again, depending on the circumstances—that might achieve that. He might say, for example, "Yes, but goldcrests are no longer found in these parts," or "Yes, but the goldcrest's heads are a kind of pinkish red, whereas the goldfinch's heads are a wine red," and so on.

And Cavell rightly observes that the skeptic's inquiry seems to follow a parallel pattern.[13] We all know how this goes. The skeptic supposes that he knows, say, that there is a tomato before him or that he is dressed in his nightclothes, seated before a fire. How does he know this? "By means of his senses," he says. Given the entering of that basis, it looks as though it constitutes a legitimate challenge to say: "But it's possible that I am/you are dreaming." And as with the goldfinch case, it doesn't seem open at this point for one to respond: "So what? I know nonetheless." No, it looks as though one needs first to remove the challenge in order to preserve one's entitlement to the claim. But as we all know, this turns out to be, perhaps surprisingly, a tall—even maybe an impossible—order to fill. For one thing, there doesn't seem to be the possibility in the skeptic's case of making a response that parallels the response that goldcrests are no longer found in these parts. The possibility that one is dreaming isn't one that is dependent on circumstances, at least not on circumstances that can vary across contexts in which one makes claims to know. That possibility, or its relevance, seems to be underwritten not by the environment in which we find ourselves, but by nothing more than a simple fact about human nature itself, the fact that we dream.[14] Obviously, it would not be open for one to say, "But people don't dream much around these parts." You might say that the possibility that one is dreaming follows one wherever one goes, whereas other possibilities—such as the possibility that a given bird is a goldcrest, or even the possibility that one is a brain in a vat—don't seem to do so.

The other common way of rebutting a challenge to one's basis for a knowledge-claim is to appeal to something specific about the basis, as we saw with the response that the goldcrest's head is a kind of wine-red. This type of approach also doesn't seem to be a promising way of dealing with the skeptic's challenge.

---

**13** See Cavell 1979, 132–4 (hereafter: CR).

**14** Indeed, this is precisely how Descartes prefaces his introduction of the challenge. He reminds himself, "A brilliant piece of reasoning! As if I were not a man who sleeps at night, and regularly has all the same experiences while asleep as madmen do when they are awake" (Descartes 1984, 77). Compare this to a statement such as, "But I must remember that I am on Alpha Centauri, and that here on Alpha Centauri there are brains in vats enjoying lifelike experiences," to which it can be replied, "But here on earth, there aren't."

For we can't, it seems, point to any feature of our sensory experience that would decisively distinguish it from a dream experience—something along the lines of the particular shade of the goldcrest's red head—since it seems to be possible for any given dream to be qualitatively indistinguishable from waking experience. A bird that has all the qualities of a goldcrest would be a goldcrest, but an experience that has all the qualities of a waking experience is not necessarily a waking experience. Again, the possibility that what appears to be a waking experience is in fact a dream seems to be contained in the nature of sensory experience itself; it doesn't seem to depend on what is the case in the world. Having a certain kind of red head implies, given what else is true about the world, that a bird with that kind of red head is a goldfinch—or so we can coherently suppose. But there seems to be no comparable basis in the case of our classifying an experience as a waking experience. We think that if x is the basis for our knowledge that an object belongs to a certain kind, then there must be something about the basis that implies that the object belongs to that kind. But the qualities we can predicate of our sensory experience don't seem to be able to function as such a basis, since they do not decisively determine whether it is to be classified as a waking, and so veridical, experience, or as a dream experience. I think that this discovery is, as Descartes describes it, "bewildering" or "dizzying."[15] Now imagine that you are in such a situation with respect to the basis for your claim that what you see is a goldfinch. And imagine that you see that your basis doesn't decisively determine that what you see is a goldfinch and not a goldcrest. Isn't it obvious that you would have to retract your claim to know that the bird is a goldfinch?[16] So by parity of reasoning, we must retract our claim to know that there is a tomato there or that we are seated before the fire. There is, as Cavell puts it, "a sense of discovery" in this conclusion, just as there would be a comparable sense of discovery if we learned that our basis for claiming that the bird is a goldfinch were found to be an inadequate basis for the claim.[17] And it is precisely here that the conflict with common sense emerges. Such considerations display, if not the irresolvability of the conflict, at least a kind of surface intractability of the sort that can seem to mark the problem as a philosophical one.

A common way of resolving the conflict is to challenge the correctness of the skeptic's view of what our concept of knowing actually requires for someone to

---

15 Descartes 1984, 77.

16 Of course, you might still have fairly good reasons for continuing to believe that what you see is a goldfinch. But you wouldn't, I think, be justified in persisting in your claim that you know—or so it seems to me.

17 See CR, 129.

count as knowing. In particular, the skeptic is charged with wrongly supposing that knowing requires ruling out every conceivable possibility that is incompatible with one's having knowledge in the particular circumstance, such as the possibility that one is dreaming. In taking it that ruling out such possibilities is a condition of knowledge, the skeptic, it seems, must be assuming what is now widely known as "the epistemic closure principle" and, as an instance of it, the principle that in order to know that p, one must know that one is not dreaming that p.[18] However, all that is required—so the argument runs—for one to possess knowledge is to rule out those possibilities that are *relevant* to the case at hand, which normally do not include remote possibilities such as those the skeptic traffics in. It is possible to find the basis for such a criticism in Austin's "Other Minds," a paper that is pivotal to Cavell's treatment of skepticism. However, it is important to see that Cavell does not view the significance of that paper in that way, that is, as lying in its offering an alternative analysis of our concept of knowledge, one that would reveal the skeptic to be mistaken about what knowing in general requires. Rather, for Cavell, the observations that Austin makes about what in ordinary life would count as a reasonable challenge to a knowledge-claim cannot fail to be already known by the skeptic and so cannot form the basis of what Cavell calls a "direct criticism" of the skeptic.

Austin observed that a legitimate doubt is raised only if it involves specifying a concrete way in which one might be mistaken and a special reason for considering that way of being mistaken as a possibility in the particular circumstances. Thus, when I say that I know that's a goldfinch on yonder tree, I need to possess enough to show that it isn't some other species of bird found around these parts. I don't need to rule out every competing description of the bird, such as its being a stuffed bird. The question, "How do you know it's a goldfinch—maybe it's stuffed?" may become relevant in special circumstances. As Cavell writes, "If we watch a blackbird fly into a tree and sit on a wet branch thirteen ways, no one (including the philosopher) is going to raise, or accept the question 'But is it real?', without some special reason. But if I say 'Don't forget that Mr. Stevens (the next door neighbor) is not only an inventor but an expert taxidermist', that might make us accept the question about the reality of our blackbird on the fourteenth look."[19] And when the question, "Stuffed?" becomes relevant because we live next door to the amazing Mr. Stevens, then there are more or less recognized procedures for answering the question. And finally, no way of answering such

---

**18** More recently, Fred Dretske and Robert Nozick have pressed this line. See Dretske 1999 and Nozick 1991. Since then, the literature on this topic has grown to cottage-industry proportions. For a qualified or partial defense of the skeptic against this strategy, see Stroud 1984, 39–82.
**19** CR, 56–7

questions is protection against every conceivable type of failure. As Austin memorably wrote, "'Being sure it's real' is no more proof against miracles or outrages of nature than anything else is or, *sub specie humanitatis*, can be. If we have made sure it's a goldfinch, and a real goldfinch, and then in the future it does something outrageous (explodes, quotes Mrs. Woolf, or what not), we don't say we were wrong to say that it was a goldfinch, we don't know what to say. Words literally fail us."[20]

But the ease with which we accept the above observations might itself be the source of misgivings. And indeed it is for Cavell. He helpfully directs us to attend to the terms of criticism that a philosopher employs as a clue to understanding what the philosopher is up to.[21] What are the terms of criticism that are implicit in Austin's characterizations of the skeptic? The terms 'being mistaken,' 'unjustified,' do not seem to go far enough, do not seem to be apt terms for describing the nature of the philosopher's failure. Rather, terms such as 'outrageous,' 'ridiculous,' and 'absurd' seem more fitting. For Austin, the philosopher doesn't simply make a mistake in reasoning, or assume a false premise; rather, she evinces a laughable incompetence in distinguishing what is and is not a legitimate challenge to a claim to know. But it is hard to take Austin's characterizations of the skeptic as even close to decisive. After all, they seem to implicate us as well—didn't we go along with the philosopher, at least up to the point where he drew his conclusion? He didn't seem outrageous or incompetent. He seemed to be serious and worth taking seriously.[22] So how, if Austin is right, could we not have seen his maneuvers for what they were? Further, we must expect the skeptic himself to nod in agreement with everything that Austin says about the ordinary requirements for making a challenge to a claim to know that is worth taking seriously. The skeptic knows how to engage in this kind of back-and-forth as well as anyone. Are we to suppose that the skeptic just forgot how to do so? What could explain such a temporary loss of good sense? As Cavell puts it, all that

---

20 Austin 1961, 88.

21 "And the specific terms of criticism in which one philosophy formulates its opposition to another philosophy or to everyday beliefs is as definitive of that philosophy as any of the theses it may produce" (Cavell 1976, 238).

22 Cavell writes, "I take this to mean that any really formidable criticism of the traditional philosopher must show that his investigation does not, in the way he depends upon it to, *fully* follow an ordinary investigation of a claim to knowledge. It seems to me undeniable that it *apparently* does (to deny that would mean, for me, denying that large groups of competent persons had ever been convinced by it)" (CR, 165).

Austin is doing is recounting norms that anyone who so much as knows how to speak must already know, including the skeptic himself.[23]

We have, then, the following triad of propositions: (1) the skeptic, or as Cavell often calls him, "the traditional philosopher," fails to observe the standards that govern the raising of epistemic challenges in ordinary life; (2) Someone who fails to observe such standards in ordinary life is epistemically incompetent; (3) The skeptic, or the traditional philosopher, is not epistemically incompetent. It is difficult to hold all three propositions together. Cavell takes Austin to reject the third, but he finds such a rejection implausible. He writes,

> So if we can make the ordinariness, the naturalness of traditional investigations explicit in terms of our untutored understanding of ordinary language, then if there is some lack of reasonableness in the investigations, it must turn out to be subtle enough, or something enough, and the way of avoiding its recognition explained convincingly enough, that we can fully imagine a master of language, under the pressure of philosophical meditation, to have failed to see his mastery failing him.[24]

The predicament here resembles the one that Kant believed characterized the state of metaphysics. For Kant, both thesis and antithesis on a metaphysical question seem to have equally compelling backing in reason. Given that acknowledgement, it would be futile to continue the argumentation in a straightforward way: each position is already as entrenched as it could be in reason. And reason is not decisive. Continuing the argument at this point would be nothing less than indulging in a species of madness. How then to move forward? Kant takes it that what is called for is not the taking of sides, but the undertaking of criticism, which means finding new terms on which the two sides can come to agreement with each other. Criticism is the method of enabling reason to arrive at a kind of "agreement with itself." For Cavell, the conflict between Austin and the philosopher presents itself in a similarly acute and vexing way. It seems that both must be right, and yet it is hard to see how both could be right. And so merely defending one side against the other seems futile, perhaps even somewhat crazy. The way forward calls for a kind of retracing of steps, a search for

---

23 Cavell writes, "While it was explicit in my procedures throughout Part One that I understood traditional epistemologists to require 'reasonableness,' of some kind, in their investigations, it remained implicit that the reasonableness of the philosopher's considerations was a function of their being just those ordinary and everyday considerations that any person who can talk and can know anything at all will recognize as relevant to the claim ('belief') under scrutiny" (CR, 131). The strength of the ordinary-language philosopher's position has one and the same source as that of the traditional philosopher.
24 CR, 132

a touchstone of agreement—in short, for "criticism" in the Kantian sense. It is this that Austin does not, for all his acuity, seem to attempt, or even see the need for. Thus, for Cavell, Austin forms only the necessary starting point of an adequate treatment of skepticism. He supplies us with important data that need to be accounted for in any such treatment. But his is the first, not the last, word.

# 3 "Specific" and "Generic"

What explains the skeptic's apparent departure from the norms that Austin observes to be operative in our ordinary epistemic inquiries? Cavell tries to explain the skeptic's bracketing of Austinian considerations as beside the point by appealing to a distinction between "specific" and "generic" objects. He suggests that if we see the skeptic as concerned with knowledge of a "generic," rather than of a "specific," object, we will see why he is intellectually forced to suppose that remote skeptical possibilities, such as the dreaming possibility, form the basis of a legitimate epistemic challenge.

In setting up his problem, the skeptic typically draws from a small store of stock examples—tomatoes, tables, chairs, apples, trees in the Quad, and so on. This might be taken by a casual observer to manifest a striking impoverishment of imagination. Mightn't we be better served by considering more concrete, more typical, examples of the sort we encounter in real life, ones teeming with the rich and vivid detail of reality, than to be offered the string of the usual, tired, artificial examples? Cavell argues, however, that the unremarkableness—the obviousness—of the philosopher's examples is forced on the philosopher by the nature of his quest.[25] The philosopher is concerned to assess our knowledge as a whole, to evaluate whether we are ever in a position to know anything about the world at all. In order to pursue this question, he needs to put before us a representative case of knowing, a case which is such that failure to know in that particular case has global implications for our ability to know in *any* case. What is at stake in whether I know that there is a tomato before me is whether I can know anything at all about the world. In ordinary life, we do not understand epistemic challenges as addressed to such a global matter, to whether we are ever in a position to know anything at all about the world. For example, if I am challenged on my claim that the bird on the tree is a goldfinch, then what is typically at issue are such things as whether I have the relevant expertise to make such a judgment

---

25 I am indebted to Kelly Jolley for stressing this point to me.

reliably or whether I am in a position to do so in the particular circumstances. Such cases concern what Cavell calls "specific objects." Knowledge of a "specific object" is a matter of correctly identifying an object as belonging to a certain kind, such as 'goldfinch,' 'prairie dog,' or 'heirloom tomato.' Where "specific" objects are in question, failures to know do not threaten our ability to know *überhaupt*. Cavell argues that the philosopher needs to put before us what he calls a "generic object." Generic objects resist being inserted into the kind of exchange Austin is describing, an exchange in which what is at issue is the correct identification of the object, an exchange that has as part of its background the possibility of actually informing someone of something, of telling someone something significant. The idea is that if it is obvious how an object is to be classified then if a genuine epistemic question were to arise with respect to it, it would have to be a question concerning the thing's existence. Generic objects are "generic" in the sense that they are a kind of stand-in for any object at all. You might say that to have a generic object before one is to take the object as exemplifying not a particular kind, but rather "objecthood" or "materiality" as such. If a question arises with regard to a generic object, there can be no question of differences in the distribution of authority. For one to have gotten hold of a question about a generic object, one must already take oneself to be in the best position one could be in for knowing it; and furthermore, one must take one's position to be one that anyone is already in. If a tomato will not do, because it is for you something strange and exotic, then pick another object, one that could count for you as "generic." The idea is that everyone can find an object that would figure "generically," as one that could stand for the world as such. Only by raising a question about an object so understood can conclusions that are arrived at with respect to the particular case have implications for the assessment of our knowledge as a whole.

These considerations bear on Austin's requirement of special reasons, the requirement that the backing of a special reason is needed to raise a competent challenge to knowledge. If an example admits of a challenge to know that is backed by a special reason, then the example would have to be viewed as one in which our position as knowers is not representative. And if the case is not representative, then failure to know in that case will fail to carry implications for our knowledge as a whole. Thus, an accurate understanding of the philosopher's enterprise *mandates* or *forces* a waiving of the special-reasons requirement even if Austin is right that ordinarily the special-reasons requirement is in force. It isn't that the skeptic fails to realize, or has temporarily forgotten, that that requirement is usually in force; it's that the nature of his inquiry leads him deliberately to focus on an example in which questions of authority, and so the requirement of special reasons, have no place. As Cavell writes,

> But suppose that traditional epistemologists have had no choice in this matter, that their obsession is dictated by, and reveals, the nature of the question they are obsessed by... There is something common among all their objects: they are ones specifically about which there just is no problem of recognition or identification or description; ones about which the only "problem", should it arise, would be not to say what they are but to say whether we can know that they exist, are real, are actually there. I am going, for heuristic purposes, to call such things "generic objects" and contrast them with such things as Austin takes for his examples, which I will call "specific objects".[26]

Cavell thus argues that we can say this much in defense of the skeptic or "the traditional epistemologist": if a problem about knowing the generic object has presented itself, then it is not unreasonable to ask how we know the object, without having a special reason for raising the question in the particular circumstances.[27] In particular, the possibility that one is now dreaming—remote as that possibility is—would constitute a fully legitimate challenge to a question regarding a generic object. And this is because what has come to be called "the principle of epistemic closure" would hold with respect to knowledge of a generic object. Knowledge of a generic object would require not just that the possibilities that are incompatible with my knowing do not in fact obtain, but would require also my *knowing* that those possibilities do not obtain. And as anyone who has studied the problem of skepticism can attest, granting the skeptic the closure principle seems tantamount to granting him all he wants and needs.

If Cavell is right, he has made a beginning toward reconciling what it seemed impossible to reconcile. He has begun to give an explanation of how the triad of propositions I mentioned earlier could all be true. He has begun to find a way of reconciling the evident absurdity of the skeptic's line of inquiry with its evident reasonableness, its obvious unnaturalness with its patent naturalness, and to do so without appealing to the *ad hoc* maneuver of appealing to different senses of "know." The skeptic's line of inquiry is unnatural if the skeptic is taken to be dealing with a specific object, but it is natural if the skeptic is taken to be dealing with a generic object. And this would also explain why the

---

26 CR, 52

27 I think that this point is important in part because if Cavell is right here, this has wide ramifications for much of contemporary epistemology. I take it that the same intuitions that fuel our sense that Austin is right about the range of possibilities that are in play in the investigation of an ordinary claim to know are the very same intuitions that are drawn on by externalists and by counterfactual tracking analysts of the concept of knowledge. But then it would seem to follow that such treatments of the skeptic would be committed to accusing the skeptic of having failed to notice the very requirements that are in play in ordinary life, the very ones that he himself seems adept at enforcing when he is not doing philosophy.

skeptic's conclusion is unstable. In ordinary life, our claims to know always concern a specific, not a generic, object, and so questions about generic objects fail to get a grip on—fail to have direct implications for—our inquiries concerning specific objects. Our claims to know specific objects do not in that sense seem to presuppose our knowledge of generic objects.

What reflection on Austin's criticism of the traditional philosopher shows is that the relation between philosophy and ordinary life is not as straightforward as it initially seems. Initially, it seems that there is a straightforward conflict between what the philosopher asserts and something that is implicitly believed in ordinary life. But what is emerging is that what the philosopher is putting into question, what he means by a statement such as "There's a tomato there—that is something that I know," and the question, "But do I really know it?" are simply not accessible in the context of ordinary life at all. The contexts of ordinary life simply prevent us from hearing those words in the way that the skeptic needs to mean them. This is why the philosopher must, if he is so much as to get his project off the ground, suspend the grounds that govern the raising and answering of questions in everyday life, for his question—a question concerning a generic object—must already be understood as one that simply could not arise in everyday life. The point here is not just that the philosopher's inquiry is not circumscribed by ordinary life, that the philosopher has no particular practical interest in inquiring into what he does. That is true enough, but it is a commonplace. Rather, the point is that the very norms that characterize inquiries in ordinary life must be placed in suspension if the statements that the philosopher makes are to be understood in the sense in which the philosopher means them.[28] And so I think that if Cavell is right then from the philosopher's standpoint, it is bound to seem that his particular examples, and the way he intends those examples to be taken, are simply not available to Austin, given that Austin is devoted to the careful description of how we proceed in ordinary life. Thus, the philosopher is bound to feel that he hasn't been responded to at all, simply because he has not been understood. Here, the stricture that Cavell holds to be fundamental to the method of proceeding from ordinary language—namely, the stricture of understanding the one who is being criticized "from the inside"—is not observed by Austin, and this lack constitutes a serious shortcoming in Austin's attempt to engage with the skeptic.[29]

---

**28** See Clarke 1972, 754–9.

**29** Yet it might be said that this failing on Austin's part is also part of his achievement. He has displayed the relation between ordinary life and philosophy by in a sense being tone-deaf, perhaps deliberately so, to how the philosopher seeks to mean the words he uses. In doing so, he has placed the onus on the philosopher to make himself intelligible, to explain how he means

But can Cavell's distinction between "specific" and "generic" objects do the work that it is supposed to do? Can that distinction constitute the basis for a partial defense of the skeptic against Austin's criticism? It might seem that the answer has to be, "No."

To review, with a generic object, questions regarding identification or classification do not arise: the only question it would make sense to raise about a generic object is whether the object exists. Expertise cannot be at issue with a generic object: once you get to a question of existence, concepts have already done all the work they can do, as Kant argued in claiming that existence is not a predicate. But the notion of a generic object doesn't stand for a particular kind, such as 'kohlrabi' or 'manatee.' Any kind of object can in some circumstance count as a specific object. No kind of object—say, a tomato—is *simply* a generic object. Rather, the distinction between generic and specific must be formulated in, broadly speaking, epistemological terms. The distinction marks something like the attitude we take toward objects, how we think about the object. As it happens, some kinds of objects are easy to think of generically, others are not. This may lead one to press the question of what it is to think of an object generically, particularly given that the mere fact that we are raising a question of existence about an object doesn't entail that we are thinking of the object generically. What is it to understand something in such a way that the *only* question that could arise with regard to it is one of its existence? As I have mentioned, what Cavell seems to be after is the thought that a generic object is a kind of stand-in for objects in general, representative of materiality as such. This is why the only question that could arise with respect to a generic object is one of existence. And this is to say that there is nothing about the object in particular that is relevant to assessing our knowledge of it.

It seems to follow from this that a question that arises with respect to a generic object would have to be a question that is understood as one that could be asked at any time, at any place, and with regard to any object at all. The fact that it is being asked just at this moment and of this object must be irrelevant to our understanding of the question. There couldn't, in effect, be any point to asking the question at any particular time. And so it doesn't seem that a question of this sort could ever arise in ordinary life. For Austin, the questions we raise in ordinary life are constrained by considerations of relevance, in particular relevance as to whether a particular person knows in a particular concrete situation. The particularity of both the subject who claims or assumes knowledge, and the sit-

---

the words he is compelled to use. Nevertheless, in not seeking a ground for mutual intelligibility, he seems to leave us with a rupture between our philosophical and ordinary selves.

uation in which the knowledge is claimed or assumed, governs what questions it is appropriate—or even intelligible—to raise, and what responses to the question would count as appropriate or intelligible. And so the raising of a question that could be raised in any situation whatsoever, and by anybody, of anybody, no matter their position or level of expertise, would seem to have no place in ordinary life. If challenges to know in ordinary life are governed by these particularities, then the philosopher's question would seem to be one that could have no relevance. There could be no answer to the question of why it is being asked "just now."

But this is just to say that we have a generic object before us—or more precisely, are conceiving of an object as a "generic" one—just in case a question can be raised about it without that question being based on a special reason, a reason that would be rooted in the particularities of the situation. But if that's the case, using the specific/generic distinction in a partial defense of the skeptic seems to beg the question against Austin, for it looks as though the distinction amounts to this: specific objects are ones with regard to which one can only raise a challenge on the basis of a special reason; not so in the case of generic objects. But then why couldn't Austin say that the concept of a generic object has no extension: there is nothing that counts as a generic object so understood? Doubt makes sense only when there is a special reason for doubt, and since in such cases there is by definition no special reason for doubt, the concept of doubt lacks an application to such cases.[30]

Although Cavell does not explicitly consider this objection, I think that he has the resources to answer it and that this answer reveals something important about how he conceives of philosophical criticism. Austin presents his observations about ordinary language as constituting what Cavell calls "a direct criticism" of the skeptic. A "direct criticism" would show that the skeptic has made a mistake, for example, that he has distorted the meaning of words or has spoken emptily or unintelligibly. But according to Cavell, to suppose that there can be a direct criticism of the skeptic along these lines is to fail to understand a limitation that is intrinsic to claims that are "based on ordinary language."[31] This limitation follows from the fact that, unlike a perception-based claim, claims concerning ordinary language, those concerning "what we

---

30 Thanks to James Shelley, who pressed this objection in conversation.
31 This point is missed by many commentators on Cavell. They tend to see Cavell as seeking a "direct criticism" in the manner of Austin, that is, as criticizing the skeptic as making a mistake about "the conditions of being intelligible." See, for example, Williams 1996, 151–2; McGinn 1989, 85–6. I have found James Conant to be very helpful here; see Conant 2005.

would say when," rely on making, in a certain sense, *oneself* the "basis" for the claim. Cavell writes,

> Understanding from inside a view you are undertaking to criticize is sound enough practice whatever the issue. But in the philosophy which proceeds from ordinary language, understanding from the inside is methodologically fundamental. Because the way you must rely upon yourself as a source of what is said when, demands that you grant full title to others as sources of that data—not out of politeness, but because the nature of the claim you make for yourself is repudiated without that acknowledgement: it is a claim that no one knows better than you whether and when a thing is said, and if this is not to be taken as a claim to expertise (a way of taking it which repudiates it) then it must be understood to mean that you know no better than others what you claim to know. With respect to the data of philosophy our positions are the same.[32]

The skeptic must be acknowledged to be equally authoritative with regard to the claims of the ordinary-language philosopher. This means for Cavell that agreement in our judgments about these matters simply follows from our being able to speak to each other—if such agreement actually exists. They are matters with regard to which if anyone knows them, everyone does—their nature is such as to preclude the possibility of expertise. This is why the skeptic must be granted "full title" to his own claim of intelligibility. So if the skeptic is less than fully intelligible, this is not something that can be chalked up to an ordinary mistake, such as faulty reasoning or a perceptual error. The skeptic must be under a kind of illusion of intelligibility, and that particular "plight of mind" would itself require an explanation. It couldn't simply be a brute fact that the skeptic is not fully intelligible. Thus, "understanding from the inside" cannot be for the ordinary-language philosopher simply a matter of "diagnosis," as that is usually understood, namely, as an activity that is supplemental to the primary, basically impersonal activity of criticizing the view at hand. For the ordinary-language philosopher, philosophical criticism is ineluctably criticism not just of a disembodied "view," but of a human being, or at least of an imagined human being. The stakes here are different from the usual philosophical ones, for they are best figured not in terms of the possibility that one is in error, but in terms of the possibility of a loss of mind or self.[33]

---

32 Cavell 1976, 239.

33 However, if the methods of the ordinary-language philosopher put the human self back into philosophy, as Cavell claims, they can also seem to threaten the line that separates philosophy from psychology. Cavell writes, "We know of the efforts of such philosophers as Frege and Husserl to undo the 'psychologizing' of logic (like Kant's undoing Hume's psychologizing of knowledge): now, the shortest way I might describe such a book as the *Philosophical Investigations* is to say that it attempts to undo the psychologizing of psychology, to show the

The idea that what is at issue is a matter of self-knowledge may be helpful in describing what is involved in adjudicating the conflict between Austin and the skeptic. Critics of the so-called "Cartesian" view that we are infallible with regard to the content of our mental states, and that our own mental states are transparent to us, have been fond of pointing out both that we can be mistaken with regard to our beliefs about our own mental states and that we can be in mental states of which we are not conscious. But recently some philosophers have attempted to mount a qualified defense of the traditional Cartesian view. [34] While admitting that Descartes's critics are surely right on the issues of incorrigibility and transparency, these philosophers argue that there remains, nonetheless, an important sense in which we possess a special authority with regard to the contents of our own mental states. In particular, what is ruled out in the case of our beliefs about our own mental states is the possibility of a kind of brute error or ignorance. For example, I couldn't simply fail to know that I believe that the airplane has taken off, as I can simply be wrong with respect to a perception-based claim, such as the claim that there is a bird in the garden. There must be a certain sort of explanation, such as that, due to my fear of flying, I repressed that knowledge, or something along those lines.[35] Where such an explanation is in the offing, the connection in me of what I actually believe with my evaluative judgments about what I should believe is severed. I won't know what I do believe simply by virtue of knowing what I should believe. I will have a "third-person" rather than a "first-person" relation to my belief. Although I can stand in a "third-person" relation to some isolated beliefs, I can't in general stand in such a relation to my own beliefs, for if I did, "my beliefs" would not be fully "mine." To be minded in the way that a rational being is minded requires having a "first-person" relation to one's beliefs.

For Cavell, we are similarly authoritative about the matter of what is ordinarily said and what is to be understood by what is said. We must, insofar as we can speak at all, be in a position to speak *for* others, to articulate the conditions under which a particular use of words is intelligible. In this sense, you yourself are the "basis" of the claims that are made by the ordinary-language philoso-

---

necessity controlling our application of psychological and behavioral categories; even, one could say, show the necessities in human action and passion themselves. And at the same time it seems to turn all of philosophy into psychology—matters of what we call things, how we treat them, what their role is in our lives" (Cavell 1976, 91).

**34** The view about self-knowledge sketched here draws on Moran 2001.

**35** Cavell makes the similar point that I can't simply fail to know that someone is in pain where certain "criteria" of being in pain, such as writhing, are present. There has to be some explanation, such as: the person was feigning, or rehearsing for a part in a play, etc.

pher. You could say that this characterizes the "form" of such claims. Claims such as the ones Austin makes aren't empirical generalizations that would issue in predictions about how we in fact use words. If others disagree with, or diverge from, what is stated in such claims—as the skeptic appears to—that does not falsify the claim, as it would if the claim were to be understood as a prediction.[36] For Cavell, what follows from disagreement in such cases is a narrowing of one's scope of authority—one discovers that one doesn't "speak for" the person with whom one finds oneself in "disagreement." The discovery of such a gap between oneself and others has a "transcendental" flavor, for it is not disagreement with regard to a matter of fact, something with respect to which we can treat one side as holding a mistaken belief. Rather, it is a "disagreement" that would compromise our ability to agree or disagree about specific matters of fact. The failure here would be something like a failure of reason. The scope of one's authority is contingent on the existence of actual agreement. However, the claims of the ordinary-language philosopher don't merely report the existence of such agreement, as an empirical generalization would. Such claims are in a sense unfalsifiable—they measure the limits of one's authority to speak for others, measure the limits of "my world" or "our world." But despite the contingency of one's authority on such a matter, the authority doesn't rest on the "evidence" of actual agreement—as a prediction would—but simply on one's capacity to speak to others.

Just as there is no guarantee that we are always right about the claims that we make about our own minds, so there is no guarantee that we always speak for others when we give voice to "criteria." But as with our authority to say how it is with our own minds, we can't simply lose our authority to give voice to criteria. To lose that authority would be tantamount to losing one's mind altogether. (For Cavell, rationality, you could say, depends on our being able to speak for one another, to speak representatively.)[37] If the skeptic must be granted "full title" to his own claim of intelligibility, then where he is less than fully intelligible, a certain kind of explanation is called for. It couldn't, as it were, be a brute fact that the skeptic is mistaken. To treat the skeptic thus would be tantamount to impugning one's *own* title to "speak for others" on the matter of intelligibility. Cavell writes, "Here what we do not know comprises not our ignorance but our alienation."[38] And so the problem would be to discover with regard to the skeptic "the specific

---

36 Cavell writes, "In such appeals such a philosopher is voicing (reminding us of) statements of initiation; telling himself or herself, and us, how in fact we (must) go about things, not predicting this or that performance" (CR, 179).

37 See Cavell 1976, 67.

38 Cavell 1976, 69.

plight of mind and circumstance within which a human being gives voice to his condition."[39]

# 4 The Skeptic's Plight of Mind

Cavell connects the skeptic's plight, or our plight with respect to the skeptic, with one that we necessarily face insofar as we are speakers of a language at all. This plight is expressed by what Cavell calls "Wittgenstein's vision of language." Cavell thinks that the skeptic's particular use of the words "I know that there is a tomato there," uttered when the tomato is in clear view and nothing seems to be amiss, has a kind of surface ambivalence with respect to intelligibility: the skeptic's use is not clearly intelligible, but also not clearly unintelligible either. For example, the questions, "How much?" and "All of it?" have a clear sense with respect to certain statements while having no sense with respect to others. Those questions have a clear sense when they are addressed to the claims, "I polished the table" or "I played the Brahms concerto." They are manifestly without sense when they concern the statements, "I entered the room" or "I hit the target." But there is a third category of statements with respect to which the sense of those questions is neither "perfectly clear" nor "perfectly unclear." Here Cavell mentions "I played the violin" and "I scratched the table." While it might initially seem that those questions lack sense when raised with respect to those statements, it is possible on reflection to imagine ways in which they could have a sense. For example, as Cavell points out, it may make sense for someone to ask how much of the violin you played if he wanted to know "whether you tested it by playing chromatic scales on the fingerboard." And it may make sense to ask "How much?" with respect to scratching the table if there was a concern to determine whether an undercoat of paint had been used to cover the entire surface. If a question falls into this third category, then the sense of the question must be made out—it doesn't, so to speak, wear its sense on its sleeve. Cavell writes, "But about expressions which have some sense—as it were, a sense that needs *completion*—we feel that there is a *right* context for its use, and that 'figuring out' its application is a matter of hitting upon *that* context."[40]

Cases of this sort Cavell calls "projecting a concept into a new context." When one projects a concept into a new context, one is obligated to explain

---

**39** Cavell 1976, 240.
**40** CR, 196.

how the particular context "invites" the projection. When the application of a concept has clear sense, we implicitly imagine a certain limited range of contexts in which it has application. That we all more or less imagine the same range of limited contexts is, I take it, a condition of our being able to speak to each other at all. But not all meaningful applications of a concept are like that. Cavell contends that it is essential to language that it tolerate a certain degree of "freedom" with regard to the projection of concepts. And there are no rules that determine in advance how much freedom in "projection" language tolerates. He writes,

> If I ask "Have you eaten all of the apple?" and you answer flatly "Yes", then what will your response be if I walk over to look and say, "But you haven't eaten it all; you've left the core, and the stem and the seed to waste"? You *may* tolerate that. Perhaps that is my form of life with apples; I "eat apples" that way and that is not so bizarre but that you may be willing to accept my version of "eating all the apple" and fit yours to it, conceding, "I ate all of it except the core". But this tolerance has its limits. If on another occasion someone objects, "But you haven't smoked all of the cigarette, you have left the whole filter to waste", then even if he normally drags on the filter until the ash gives out, and then chews and swallows the rest, we are not likely to accede to his version of "smoking the whole cigarette" and effect a reconciliation between his and our version of that activity, saying, "Well, I smoked it all except the filter": his way of "smoking" is *too* bizarre. You can't talk to everyone about everything.[41]

Someone who has such a bizarre notion of smoking is not altogether someone with whom we do not share a world at all. But other disagreements in projection can seem to place another beyond the reach of communication: the differences in "form of life" would be too thoroughgoing or systematic. This is basically a matter of degree. In both cases, what is shown is that it is essential to language that we have freedom to project concepts into new contexts, but it is equally essential that there are limits to such freedom. And there is no saying in advance which projections are "tolerable" and which not. We can speak to each other only because we agree—generally—in our judgments about the contexts that invite new projections and those that don't. This is Cavell's way of understanding Wittgenstein's well-known claim that language presupposes agreement in "form of life." Somehow, when we acquire language we manage to acquire the ability to project concepts into new contexts and are initiated into the "forms of life" the limits of which are measured by our judgments about which projections are "tolerable" and which not.[42]

---

**41** CR, 196.
**42** "But though language—what we call language—is tolerant, allows projection, not just any projection will be acceptable, i.e., will communicate. Language is equally, definitively, intolerant

Donald Davidson pointed out that the possibility of agreement or disagreement with respect to particular beliefs requires a background of shared beliefs.[43] This is the idea behind what Davidson calls the "principle of charity" in the interpretation of others. And it is the main reason why Davidson questions the coherence of the idea of an alternative conceptual scheme. A radically exotic conceptual scheme would render tenuous our grip on the exotic "other" as having any beliefs at all. If we are to understand others as holding beliefs then we can't avoid viewing them as holding beliefs that are largely in line with our own. And that would seem to be tantamount to others necessarily being "of the same world" as us. But the judgmental affinity that Cavell has in mind is not a matter of overlap in *beliefs*, nor of agreement in *definitions*. What he has in mind goes back to his idea that it is essential to language that terms in it are both "tolerant"—that is, allow for projection into new contexts—and "intolerant," since not every projection is acceptable. What determines our judgments as to which projections are tolerable (intelligible) and which not (unintelligible) is not itself something that is readily explainable. Cavell writes,

> On a given occasion one may fail to recognize a given object as a shoe—perhaps all we see is a twist of leather thong, or several blocks of wood. But what kind of failure is this? It may help to say: What we fail to see here is not *that* the object is a shoe (that would be the case where, say, we failed to notice what it was the hostess shoved under the sofa, or where we had been distracted from our inventory of the objects in a painting and later seem to remember a cat's being where you say a shoe lies on its side), but rather we fail to see *how* the object in question would be a shoe (how it would be donned, and worn, and for what kind of activities or occasions).[44]

What we might fail to see is not something that could be corrected by our gaining a better understanding of what the word "shoe" means—by redefining the word "shoe"—and the failure isn't a matter of having incorrect beliefs. We might encounter a similar failure before certain objects that make a claim to be viewed as a work of art: we may be at a loss to understand how *this*—e.g., a "readymade" by Duchamp—is a work of art at all (never mind whether it is a good or a bad one). We may similarly be at a loss as to how continuing a series "1000, 1004, 1008..." is going on "in the same way" when the series began with "2, 4, 6, 8... " To share a world—one that includes art, shoes, and claims of knowledge—requires a shared attunement in judgments, an attunement that

---

—as love is tolerant and intolerant of differences, as materials or organisms are of stress, as communities are of deviation, as arts or sciences are of variation" (CR, 182).
**43** See the essays in Davidson 1984.
**44** CR, 183.

cannot be characterized either in terms of an agreement in beliefs or an agreement in definitions or meaning (as that has traditionally been understood). Yet it is such "agreement" that enables our thoughts to have a bearing on the world.

It is agreement of this kind that is registered by what Cavell, following Wittgenstein, calls "criteria": criteria are expressed in essentially singular judgments, such as "This is what we call 'going on in the same way'"; "This is what we call 'following a rule'"; "This is what we call 'being in pain'"; "This is what we call 'a claim to know.'" Unlike the sort of criteria that determine membership in a kind, such as the criteria for being a goldfinch—what Cavell calls "Austinian criteria"— one cannot simply be told what Wittgensteinian criteria are. To lack Austinian criteria is to lack a specific piece of information, such as that goldfinches have certain external markings, and so deficiencies in Austinian criteria are tantamount to a failure of expertise. Wittgensteinian criteria concern that with regard to which no one can be any more authoritative than anyone else. One cannot, then, "be told" what Wittgensteinian criteria are, and you can't be told because you can't exactly be ignorant of them.[45] Rather, you can find yourself out of "attunement," which compromises your ability to be told something (to learn something) and to tell something (to teach something). You could say that Wittgensteinian criteria condition the possibility of teaching and learning Austinian criteria, and in that sense serve as conditions of the possibility of knowledge. Where we diverge in criteria, you and I fail to "share the same world."[46]

These are, as I understand it, the central features of what Cavell calls "the vision of language" that underlies the method of proceeding from ordinary language. What a consideration of Austin has shown for Cavell is that the philosopher's "projection" of questions such as "Do you see all of the object>", or "How do you know?" in the particular contexts in which the philosopher must imagine those questions being asked falls into the third category of "projections" described above. Such projections don't have a clear sense, but neither do they manifestly lack sense. The skeptic, if he is to counter Austin's observations, is obligated, then, to give an explanation that shows how *his* context invites the projection of these concepts, these questions. [47]

---

45 The similarity here with aesthetic judgment is striking, for it seems that the authority to make an aesthetic judgment is similarly not transferrable through testimony. For example, to be in a position to say that an object is beautiful requires that one be in a position to see exactly how it is beautiful—to see that and how for oneself.

46 It is hard here not to think of criteria as a new version of what Kant called "the categories."

47 In this respect, the skeptic's projection is similar to those that populate Wittgenstein's *Philosophical Investigations*. There, one makes odd projections of a concept intelligible by

But there is, Cavell argues, an in-principle obstacle to the skeptic's ever making good on showing his particular projection of concepts to be fully intelligible, on imagining his context so that it invites just the words he needs. In order for the skeptic to raise a question about a generic object, it must be possible for a string of words such as, "There is a tomato there," or "I am seated before the fire," to be used to enter a claim in his context, one that the skeptic could then turn on and ask, "But do I really know that there is a tomato there?" or "Do I really know that I am seated before the fire?" Cavell contends that while those words can indeed be used to enter a claim in *some* contexts, they cannot be used to enter a claim in the context the skeptic needs to imagine.

Cavell claims that the skeptic must, like all of us, observe the following constraints on intelligibility. You need the words "There is a tomato there" or "I am seated before the fire" to express a thought, and it can only do so if there is something that *you* mean by those words. But *you* can mean something by those words only if you use them in a linguistic activity, such as that of making a claim or an assertion. And you can count as using those words in such an activity only if there is a point to the activity. But, of course, any point will be dependent on the particular circumstances in which the word is used. Thus, acknowledging that there is such a condition on the intelligible use of words would defeat the skeptic's aim of interrogating a representative case.

Cavell, of course, does not deny that the words "There is a tomato there" can be used to make a claim. One point of using those words to make a claim might be to inform someone of something. Perhaps the person you are speaking to doesn't know that cherry tomatoes are tomatoes, or perhaps the person you are informing comes from a land that has no tomatoes. Or perhaps there are some wax tomatoes mixed together in a basket with some real tomatoes, and you mean to single out the ones in the basket that are the real tomatoes. Or perhaps you are looking from a distance at what you've been told is a tomato patch, and at first you aren't sure that it is the much ballyhooed tomato patch you've heard about over in Loachapoka until you spy what looks like a tomato hanging from a branch. In such contexts, there would be a discernible point to saying "There is a tomato there." But in each of those contexts, the availability of a point to the utterance compromises the representativeness of the situation, the generic-ness of the generic object. The point marks the situation as a special one, or at least as a particular one, and so seems not to allow the objects in

---

imagining a form of life against which a strange use of the concept would make sense. If Wittgenstein is right, such cases illustrate the extent to which our understanding of a concept is conditioned by our form of life. But that, of course, is not an option in dealing with the oddness of the skeptic's projections.

such situations to serve as stand-ins for any object at all (for externality as such).[48] Thus, he writes,

> The "dilemma" the traditional investigation of knowledge is involved in may now be formulated this way: "It must be the investigation of a concrete claim if its procedure is to be coherent; it cannot be the investigation of a concrete claim if its conclusion is to be general. Without that coherence it would not have the obviousness it has seemed to have; without that generality its conclusion would not be skeptical.[49]

The point isn't that there is something that the skeptic is trying to say, but hasn't found the occasion to mean it. The skeptic doesn't fail to mean by his words what he wants to mean; rather, he hasn't given any clear sense to what he wants to mean.[50]

To review, I have been stressing the differences between Austin and Cavell. Austin argues that the skeptic's use of his concepts have become unmoored from the ordinary criteria that govern their use. In that sense, the skeptic is speaking unintelligibly, has failed to introduce a genuine reason for doubt that we are obligated to countenance and answer. And so for Austin, it is enough to remind the skeptic what our ordinary criteria are to set him aright. But for Cavell, the skeptic cannot simply have failed to perceive what the ordinary criteria are—there must be something about his "plight of mind" that explains this lapse. And indeed, as we have seen, the skeptic is motivated by the nature of his investigation to use

---

48 It might be objected that there may be a point to using the words "There is a tomato there" even when doing so wouldn't be informative. Imagine that you have been summoned to the stage during a magic act, and you are brought before a table on which there sits, ever so innocently, a tomato. The magician asks you what's on the table. When you say, "There is a tomato there," you wouldn't take yourself to be informing anyone of anything. But there would still be a point to your *saying* that; your saying it would be intelligible. But, again, your utterance would have a point only because there is something particular about the case that prompts it. It is a case in which a magician is about to show everyone how wrong you are. And that marks the case as non-representative. I can also imagine the following objection (I thank Eric Marcus for suggesting it). Granted, the fact that there is a tomato there may be too obvious, or too unnoteworthy, to be worth remarking, but surely you *believe* that there is a tomato there, as shown by the fact that you may do things that could only be explained by appealing to your having the belief that there is a tomato there. For example, you may reach for the salt. Why do you reach for the salt? Because you believe that there's a tomato there. But again, I don't think that such an example will do for the skeptic. For what's relevant about that case is that it's a *tomato* that's there, not, say, an ice cream cone or a Chihuahua—things that you presumably wouldn't be interested in sprinkling with salt. And so, again, the object fails to be representative, representative, as Cavell puts it, of "materiality" itself. See CR, 53.
49 CR, 220.
50 See Conant 2005.

concepts detached from their ordinary criteria. [51] The true nature of the conflict between the skeptic and the ordinary person comes out only when we press on the skeptic the request to make his use of his concepts intelligible, to show how his context invites his use of the concepts. And it is here that it emerges that the skeptic must—once again, because of the nature of his project—refuse any such request. Thus, what marks the difference between the skeptic and the ordinary person isn't that the skeptic simply diverges from the ordinary criteria that govern the use of his concepts, but rather that the skeptic must refuse any criteria for his use of his concepts. The skeptic's project itself is one that requires a refusal to make himself intelligible.[52]

Of course, that is not how the skeptic would see his predicament. For him, the need to make himself intelligible has not been fully made out, for he operates under the conviction that he is *already* intelligible. This conviction is of a piece with the idea that there is something that he has gotten a hold of independently of his ability to make intelligible the projection of a concept into new contexts. That confidence would, it seems, have to be underwritten by the idea that there is something called grasping a concept independently of our ability to project the concept in particular contexts. It's not that the skeptic has simply fallen out of intelligibility; it is that he is, for Cavell, in the grip of a certain fantasy or illusion of intelligibility.[53]

Here we've reached, I think, the crux of Cavell's analysis of the skeptic. But what is the source of this fantasy? I find that Cavell doesn't go into this question directly, but it can be teased out from a number of things he does say. I believe that, for him, the fantasy has its roots in a certain conception of the objectivity of thought and meaning, in what might be called "the traditional conception of the logical," a conception that is motivated by the desire to secure the possibility of

---

**51** This way of putting the difference treats Austinian criteria and Wittgensteinian criteria as amounting to the same thing. They don't. Austinian criteria are criteria on the basis of which a particular kind of thing, say, a bird, belongs to a certain kind, such as a 'gold-finch'. If one fails to know the Austinian criteria, one is simply ignorant of certain facts. Wittgensteinian criteria are closer to what might be called a category. If one lacks the criteria for X, then one is unable to discourse about X: one is unable to make any judgments about X. Having criteria for X is necessary for being in a position to learn anything about X. This is an important distinction for Cavell, and so worth noting, but for my purposes here, I see no harm in ignoring it.
**52** Here I agree with Affeldt 1998
**53** There is an affinity here with Wittgenstein's famous parable of the private linguist. A private language would involve withdrawing oneself from meaning in the sense that there is no room in a private language of *making* oneself intelligible: in a private language, questions of intelligibility could not arise, and that, for Cavell, disqualifies it as the exercise of a linguistic capacity.

the communicability and objectivity of our thoughts.[54] The idea is that, unless the content of what we are thinking is determined by factors that are independent of the particular subject who is thinking them—and of the particular circumstances in which the subject is placed—then what determines what a particular thought commits the subject to would be a psychological matter. And this would make complete hash of logic.[55] There would be no way to identify the strictly logical content of a thought and to distinguish the strictly logical content from all the psychological contributions that particular subjects make to any act of thinking. Thus, it is essential that we be able to view an act of thinking from a purely logical point of view, a standpoint from which we prescind from all that is contributed by the subject's psychology. This includes, in particular, what the subject might take to be the point of making a particular utterance—for example, whether the point of making the utterance is to inform the hearer, to remind her, to issue a command, and so on. These are particular uses to which language can be put, and from the standpoint of logical analysis, they are basically psychological, subjective matters, as opposed to the meaning itself, which must be objective.

Cavell's idea that meaning or sense is governed by criteria can seem to threaten the traditional view of the objectivity of meaning, since criteria are, in some sense, supposed to bottom out in "agreement in judgment."[56] Cavell writes, "Our ability to communicate with him depends upon his 'natural understanding', his 'natural reaction', to our directions and our gestures. It depends upon our mutual attunement in judgments."[57] To imagine different criteria involves imagining a different "form of life," where imagining a different form of life would entail imagining different natural facts about us and our environ-

---

54 This is a rather familiar idea, stressed by, among others, Frege. Here is a representative instance of the idea from the unduly neglected Oxford philosopher C. R. Morris: "*Prima facie* at least there is a task and a procedure for logic quite distinct from those of psychology; namely, to throw light on the nature and limits of proof, and thereby of knowledge strictly so-called, by determining the meaning and implications, not of particular persons, but of statements" (Morris 1933). I thank Kelly Jolley for reference to this book.

55 It is this worry that Wittgenstein is expressing when he writes, "If language is to be a means of communication there must be agreement not only in definitions but also (queer as this may sound) in judgments. This seems to abolish logic, but does not do so" (Wittgenstein 1998, §242).

56 "There is no logical explanation of the fact that we (in general, on the whole) will agree that a conclusion has been drawn, a rule applied, an instance to be a member of a class, one line to be a repetition of another (even though it is written lower down, or in another hand or color); but the fact is, those who understand (i.e., can talk logic together) do agree" (CR, 118–9).

57 CR, 115.

ment or different cultural facts about the ways we do things.[58] For Cavell there are, as we have seen, certain activities within which our utterances have a point, such as the activity of informing, reminding, and so on, only because there is widespread agreement in judgment on the criteria that determine when an act is an act of informing, reminding, and so on. And given that language-use always has a point, then, to that extent, it could be said that in order for anything to count as a use of language, it must be governed by criteria, and given that criteria have the parochiality described above, it follows that what counts as a use of language seems itself to be infected by the parochial.[59]

Of course, the simple fact that what counts as a use of language is infected with the parochial in that sense does not of itself pose a threat to the skeptic. That is, Cavell's argument cannot just be that the skeptic seeks to transcend the parochial yet still count as engaging in a use of language. That would no doubt be incoherent—at least if Cavell is right that he can only count as using language in terms of the criteria that determine when an act is a linguistic act, and that criteria are by their nature parochial. For such a criticism would leave the skeptic an easy out. He could reply that, while what counts as informing, reminding, and so on may be subject to Cavellian criteria, *what* is said when one informs, reminds, and so on is not. And this is all that the skeptic would need if he is to raise the question he seeks to raise. In fact, the whole point of the traditional conception of the logical was to distinguish the objective from the subjective aspects of thought, and from the beginning, those who held this conception viewed the point of expressing a thought in an utterance as belonging to the subjective side and so as needing to be abstracted from in any strictly logical analysis of thought. Adherents of the traditional conception of the logical did not think of the notion of the logical so understood as anything more than an abstraction, albeit a necessary one.

---

**58** For example, Wittgenstein's much-discussed wood-sellers have the bizarre practice of "measuring" wood not as we do, but by the amount of ground-surface a pile of wood covers. While on the surface nonsensical, their practice might be something we can, nonetheless, make sense of if we could but fill in the details of the form of life within which their practices of "measuring wood" takes place. Cavell resists the view that such agreement in judgment can be usefully modeled on the idea of convention. The key idea behind a conventionalist account of our criteria—that the criteria are somehow optional, that we could have adopted different criteria or arrived at different agreements—belies their nature. One cannot readily imagine our operating with different criteria as one can our operating with different traffic rules or different rules of etiquette. Our criteria possess in that sense a kind of necessity.

**59** I borrow the word "parochial" from Charles Travis, who uses it to describe a potential threat to the objectivity of thought and meaning that seems to accompany the "occasion sensitivity" of meaning and thought-content. See Travis 2006.

Proponents of the traditional conception would have recognized that many enabling conditions would have to be met for there to be anything that possesses the logical properties that thought does. For example, in order for someone to have a thought, certain physical processes would have to take place in the brain and nervous system. And for a thought to be expressed in language, certain other physical occurrences would have to take place, such as the making of certain sounds, or marks on paper, blackboard, or what have you, and further, someone would have to produce those physical processes as part of an activity that would count as informing, reminding, joking, etc., and they would have to do so in a context in which such an activity would have a point. Any genuine use of language would require the meeting of such minimal, and indeterminate, enabling conditions. But for the proponents of the traditional conception, these enabling conditions are not relevant to determining the *content* of the thought itself, the purely logical features of the thought. And it is just such a conception of thought, a conception according to which thought must possess a purely logical content, to which the skeptic helps himself. For him, there must be something wholly impersonal and objective that determines the content of a thought such as "I know that there's a tomato there" and so determines what it would be for a thought that would be expressed using those words to be true, independently of such things as the point with which those words are used. The latter is merely subjective, part of what a speaker means, belonging to the pragmatic implications of the utterance, not to its semantic content. On this traditional conception of meaning, there must be a *something* that you mean by using certain words that can be pried apart from what *you* mean in using those words. As long as such a distinction can be made, then the conflict between the skeptic's need to fulfill the conditions on making an intelligible assertion and the requirement that what he asserts be understood to bear on a representative case would seem to imply only that he cannot meet the conditions under which he could intelligibly count as asserting what he seeks to assert. But then he would fail only in *asserting* the statement he needs: the meaning of the statement would remain intact. This still preserves the idea that there is a thought that he could assert.[60] It is this conception of meaning, I think, that Cavell views as characterizing the skeptic's "plight of mind."

Cavell's larger point is that it's this particular philosophical construction of meaning that is responsible for the other philosophical constructions that the

---

60 I think that something like this traditional conception of the logical is what is assumed by Barry Stroud in his reply to Cavell in an APA symposium on *The Claim of Reason*. See Stroud 1980.

skeptic needs, the construction of "the senses" as the basis of our knowledge as a whole and of the "world" as that which would be known by "the senses" so understood and so on. He writes,

> I also suggested that the philosopher's notions of "the senses", and "the feeling itself", were inventions of a similar sort, ideas of what things *must* be like in order to match what he must mean, has the illusion of meaning. The philosopher's idea of "the senses" or "(sense) experience" is made to order with his ideas of "the whole object", and "the thing itself": his idea of "the feeling itself" is made to order with his idea of "behavior"; and the latter members are themselves inventions. It is as though the philosopher, having begun in wonder, a modern wonder I characterized as a feeling of being sealed off from the world, within an eternal round of experience, removed from the daily round of action, from the forms of life which contain the criteria in terms of which our concepts are employed, in which, that is, they are *of* a world—or, as Wittgenstein would put it, a position in which one *must* speak "outside language games"—it is as though the philosopher, on that position, is left only with his eyes, or generally, the ability to sense.[61]

That there is a single basis that could settle the question whether someone knows, say, that there is a tomato there would depend on whether the skeptic has gotten hold of a claim that can function in a representative way. Otherwise, what the basis of a knowledge-claim is would be determined in part by the point of the claim. There wouldn't be a single basis that could be singled out as the basis of all of our knowledge claims considered as a whole. There would just be the individual bases that we appeal to in particular circumstances, but none of these would serve to back a representative claim to know.[62] Accordingly, the notion of the world as the object of our purportedly representative knowledge-claim would also go by the boards. If we can't so much as get such a claim or thought in view then the idea of a world that would answer to the request for a basis would lack all possible application. We wouldn't be able to put ourselves in the position of being able so much as to formulate the necessary conception of a world.[63] We would simply have nowhere to stand from which to

---

61 CR, 223–4.

62 Cavell says, "If the mechanic tells me that my automobile will start now, his reason is not going to be—unless he is chiding my absent-mindedness—that now the ignition is turned on (though it is true that if it weren't turned on, the car wouldn't start); nor will his reason be—unless he is abusively telling me that I wouldn't understand anyway—that now the wires won't turn into string (though if the car were "wired" with string then no doubt the car wouldn't start)" (CR, 217).

63 I take it that one large issue at stake here is the possibility of the very question often posed in epistemology, namely, the question of what knowledge requires. If Cavell is right, then that question is not a fully intelligible one. He isn't simply saying, as contextualists have recently argued, that what knowing requires depends on the particular context. According to contex-

bring the "world" before us, and so the "world" so understood cannot withdraw from us either. Such a notion of the world begins to sound like Kant's conception of the world as "thing-in-itself."

I think that Cavell's most interesting claim here is that all of this stands or falls together. It is only if the skeptic has managed to get a hold of a thought, as it were, "purely," apart from its expression in particular contexts in which the expression would have a particular point, that he would have managed to bring into view our knowledge as a whole, and with it the idea of our senses as such as a basis, and likewise the corresponding idea of the world. Whether the skeptic has managed to make intelligible his inquiry into our knowledge as a whole rests, then, on whether the conception of objectivity he uses to deflect the ordinary-language-based criticism is left standing.[64]

If Cavell is right then the only questions that can arise with regard to our knowledge are ones that are restricted in their scope, questions that cannot have the sort of generality the skeptic is aiming for. But if that is so then this seems to contain implications for how we must think of what our senses offer up to us. It can be admitted that we cannot be certain in any particular case—even an optimal one—that our senses afford us facts about the world and not just the appearance of such facts. By itself, such an admission amounts to nothing more than an acknowledgement of our fallibility, and that is not equivalent to skepticism, which depends on the further idea that there is gulf between the world and what our senses in general afford us. But if Cavell is right, it would seem, so to speak, to be built into the structure of the questions that we can meaningfully raise that it must be supposed, unless we have reason to think otherwise, that what our senses afford us in general are facts about the world and not mere appearances of such facts. You might say that our sensory experience carries with it the default assumption of trustworthiness, even though it may not in each case be possible to establish its trustworthiness. Such a default assumption would prevent any global conclusion to be drawn from the failure of one's senses to afford facts about the world in any *particular* situation. The unavaila-

---

tualism, the operative standard that determines whether someone knows varies across contexts. But for a contextualist, what standard it is that is relevant in a particular context is not itself something that is determined by context, but rather is absolute. It is an understanding that anyone who grasps the concept of knowledge must possess. In this sense, the contextualist is engaged in the traditional approach to epistemological questions: he is asking what knowing requires. And this supposes that our having the concept of 'knowing' is one thing, and our use of the concept in particular situations is another. These are obviously large issues. I do not claim to have put myself in a position to adjudicate them.

**64** The affinity between Cavell and Thompson Clarke here is worth noting. See Clarke 1972.

bility of an inquiry that puts our senses as a whole on trial all at once, that seeks to establish the trustworthiness of our senses *tout court*, is equivalent to the existence of a default assumption of trustworthiness. Only if such an inquiry were intelligible would it make sense to suppose, as the skeptic does, that sensory experience is not trustworthy unless it can be shown to be trustworthy.

I have been stressing that Cavell is best read as inheriting Kant's notion of philosophy as "critique" and as following a dialectic that is in its broad shape Kantian. I think that the final step that I have described in Cavell's engagement with the skeptic bears an interesting affinity with Kant's move against dogmatic metaphysics.[65] Rationalist metaphysicians suppose that it is possible to gain substantive knowledge about the world through concepts alone, that is, without any appeal to the intuitions to which the concepts are related. As I mentioned earlier, Kant argued that the supposition that it is possible to gain knowledge in that way leads to unavoidable contradictions in trying to answer speculative metaphysical questions. He argued further that the only way to avoid such contradictions is to suppose that our concepts can have meaningful application only to what could possibly be given to us through our faculty of sensible intuition, in particular, to what conforms to the spatial and temporal forms of our sensibility. His claim here wasn't simply that what we can know is in fact restricted to what could be given to us through our faculty of sensibility. Rather, his claim was that it is only insofar as concepts have a relation to intuition that they can be used (in combination with other concepts, or to use Kant's term, in "synthesis") to formulate a judgment on the world at all. Without a relation to intuition, concepts could be used to describe what are at best logical possibilities: they could not be used to describe a content that the world could in principle answer, a content that would be "answerable to the world." In Kant's terms, no combination of concepts would offer up the possibility of knowledge, or what he calls "experience." There would be no ground for the synthesis of concepts that is a condition of the possibility of knowledge or experience. Thus, for Kant, if by "world" is meant something to which our representations are answerable, then the impossibility of knowledge through concepts alone does not represent a restriction on

---

**65** It is interesting that the parallel is with Kant's move against dogmatism rather than his move against the Cartesian skeptic. This doesn't, however, represent a breakdown in the comparison, for on Kant's view it is dogmatism that contains the roots of the more troubling, and challenging, form of skepticism: skepticism with regard to reason itself. I have been arguing that, for Cavell, the conflict between the Cartesian skeptic and the ordinary-language philosopher, like Austin, embodies a similar sort of skeptical crisis, a skeptical crisis within reason itself. Kant simply didn't view the threat posed by Cartesian skepticism in such terms—for him, it is enough simply to show how the Cartesian skeptic goes wrong.

our knowledge of the world. The "world" so understood is constituted by the conditions of the possibility of our knowing the world. This does not mean for Kant that it is impossible for us to *think* a world that is not subject to those conditions. However, such a "world" would not be something that we could coherently have in our sights as a possible object of knowledge. Such a representation of the world is not one that would be of any use for us *as knowers* of the world. Insofar as it possesses some significance, it would have to be figured in terms of a different orientation toward the world than that which we have as knowers: for example, our orientation as practical agents.[66] For Kant the possibility of a "*revelation* of how things are" must take place within the constraints built into our faculty of sensibility.

Similarly, for Cavell, the possibility of a "revelation of how things are"[67] must take place within an imaginable language-game. He writes, "And where Kant speaks of 'transcendental illusion'—the illusion that we know what transcends the conditions of possible knowledge—Wittgenstein speaks of the illusions produced by our employing words in the absence of the (any) language game which provides their comprehensible employment."[68] It is only in an imaginable language-game that a claim can be entered, a basis produced, and the basis assessed. All such activity, which is essential to expressing a thought at all—and so to having one—itself rests on certain natural affinities that speakers of a language must share if they are to engage in this sort of activity at all, call it "epistemic activity." Such is the background that is necessary for our concept of knowledge to gain a foothold, for there to be a revelation of how things are. And here Cavell seems to follow Kant in asking not "How can we know what there is?", but rather "What makes our knowledge *of* a world of objects at all?"[69] In other words, such a background serves as the condition, you could say, of "having a world,"[70] one to know or even think about. Thus, the philosopher's attempt to prescind from those conditions in asking the question he wants to ask about the validity of our knowledge as a whole fails to so much as pose a meaningful question.[71] His conclusion that our senses are an inadequate basis

---

66 Kant leaves room for "practical postulates" regarding the world. These are beliefs about the world considered as noumenon that we are justified in holding, not because we possess evidence that points to their truth, but because they serve a need of practical reason.

67 See CR, 224.

68 Cavell 1976, 65.

69 See CR, 225.

70 I take this phrase from Kelly Jolley, who used it in conversation.

71 Again, this isn't because the words or their combination would somehow be lacking in meaning, but because *one* could not mean anything by them: "[W]hat happens to the philo-

for knowledge is, according to Cavell, not false, but rather neither true nor false.[72]

We can distinguish between two senses in which the world might be pictured as withdrawing from us. If you think that our sensory experience fails to give us knowledge of the world, since what it gives us in the way of evidence for our beliefs about the world is compatible with the possibility that we are dreaming—as the skeptic argues—then it looks as though the world withdraws from what we can establish on the basis of our sensory experience. It looks as though our sensory experience falls short of the world, that the world lies out of the reach of our sensory experience or of any evidence that our sensory experience can provide. This, of course, is the withdrawing of the world that is at issue in Cartesian skepticism. But there is another way in which the world can threaten to withdraw from us. It can threaten to withdraw from us as something we can think about at all, as something that could in principle answer to our thoughts.[73]

For Kant, metaphysicians lose the world because they seek to transcend the forms of sensibility in terms of which it is possible for us to have a world at all. In Kant's case, the fantasy is one of knowing the world through pure reason alone. But for Cavell, both the skeptic and those who try to refute the skeptic (those who fall under Cavell's rubric "traditional epistemologist") lose the world because both seek to leave behind the criteria in terms of which it is possible for us to have a world at all.[74]

---

sopher's concepts is that they are deprived of their ordinary criteria of employment (which does not mean that his words are deprived of meaning—one could say that such words have nothing *but* their meanings) and, collecting no new ones, leave his concepts without relation to the world (which does not mean that what he says is false), or in terms I used earlier, remove them from their position among our system of concepts" (CR, 226).

72 "What I wish to convey is not that the conclusion that sense-experience is inadequate as a basis for knowledge as a whole (or that we can never really know the experience of another person) is *false*, and in *that* sense not a discovery; but rather that it is neither false nor true, that it is not what we should call a 'discovery'" (CR, 223).

73 These two ways of losing the world correspond to the distinction that Jim Conant has drawn between Cartesian skepticism and Kantian skepticism. See Conant 2004 (a shorter version of which is reprinted in this volume).

74 Something similar to the philosopher's falling back on the senses takes place in the philosopher's falling back on a notion of behavior to help secure his connection to other minds. It's not, of course, that behavior doesn't play an essential role in the connection. But those who, like Norman Malcolm, argue that there are certain criteria of pain, like wincing and groaning, which logically imply the existence of pain, view criteria as a superior form of evidence. For Cavell, to mobilize criteria in this way is itself an expression of skepticism. Criteria don't constitute a

Another way to put the point is to say that the skeptic seeks to find a basis for knowing in something that essentially has nothing to do with him, nothing to do with anything that he can assume responsibility for. This is connected with the philosopher's need to have a generic object as the subject of his inquest, a need that is tied to the skeptic's "craving for generality," his quest to answer a question about whether our senses are ever reliable sources of our knowledge.[75] For Cavell, this craving for generality expresses a wish to exempt oneself, one's own involvement in making sense, from the demand to make oneself intelligible. For him, whether one is intelligible at any point rests simply on an authority to speak for others. But since the scope of such authority, as we have seen, depends on sharing a sensibility with others, a sensibility that is expressed by one's voicing of criteria, this involves risking the possibility that one may very well fail to speak for others. (Remember that such claims are not based on evidence or argument.) The skeptic is driven to avoid that risk altogether and so to relinquish that authority. But in doing so, the skeptic removes himself from the conditions under which it is possible to speak to one another, to share a world, to have a world to know. (This is tantamount to abandoning one's role in offering oneself as the basis of one's claim of making sense.) He writes, "It is as though we try to get the world to provide answers in a way which is independent of our responsibility for claiming something to be so (to get God to tell us what we must do in a way which is independent of our responsibility for choice.)"[76] The search for a Cartesian guarantee rests on the prior assumption of what one might call a Kantian guarantee, the guarantee that there is something—say, our transcendental subjectivity—that insures that the world does not withdraw from us in the Kantian sense. (It is perhaps in this sense that Cavell might well regard Kant as being himself a skeptic.)

I end by briefly raising a possible worry. Kant, of course, was a kind of idealist, and so one may wonder whether the parallel I have been sketching with Kant indicates an idealist strain in Cavell's thought. If criteria constitute conditions on human knowledge much as the forms of sensibility do for Kant, then wouldn't criteria, like the forms of sensibility, constitute specifically human constraints on our knowledge?

---

superior form of evidence; rather they constitute the possibility of talking about—discoursing about, judging—pain.

**75** Granted, the senses are a condition of knowing, but Cavell points out that it doesn't follow from the fact that something is a condition of knowing that in order to know we must know that the condition obtains. Here, Cavell anticipates the by now quite familiar externalist analyses of knowledge and evidence.

**76** CR, 216.

But here I think there is an important point of difference between Cavell and Kant. Kant thought that if you look at the conditions under which our concepts could be applied to objects, those conditions must include reference to specifically human conditions of sensibility. But Kant was able to make this claim only because specifically human constraints do not for him condition any use of concepts at all, which would make all thought specifically human in nature. If that were not so, he would have been deprived of a standpoint from which he could so much as claim that there are specifically human conditions on the application of concepts. Kant was able to preserve a standpoint from which he could think this thought only because he held that thought as such was not specifically human. The very fact that he could think the thought that there are specifically human conditions on the application of concepts entails that thought as such is not specifically human. And Kant was able to preserve such a "transcendent" standpoint, one which is assumed by his doctrine of transcendental idealism, because he distinguished between thinking (the conditions of thought as such) and applying a concept to an object (the conditions of knowledge) in an act that could at least in principle make a claim on the world, and so count as knowledge.

Now, it may seem that Cavell's criteria constitute a similar restriction on our relation to the world. It may seem that they constitute the specifically human conditions on knowing, or on the concept of knowing, that mediates our relation to the world. And so Cavell would seem to be in a situation like Kant's. But as I have said, there is an important difference. For Cavell, it is not possible to formulate a *thought* that is independent of the criteria—the idea that it is possible to do so is for him an illusion. Thus, we do not have a standpoint from which we could make sense of criteria as merely parochial or as a constraint on what we can and cannot think. And so the idea of the parochial as a constraint, and the associated idea of judgment—one that Kant himself was working with—is revealed to be an illusion. Cavell thus sees the conflict between the skeptic and the ordinary-language philosopher as a conflict between that tendency of the mind to think of the conditions on human knowing as constraints on it and the view that there is no standpoint from which they can be viewed as constraints.

It is relevant here to remind ourselves of the nature of criteria. As we've seen, criteria are for Cavell available to us only insofar as we have the capacity to use language. We are each authoritative about the criteria of pain or the criteria for making a knowledge-claim. These are not matters about which anyone can be in a better position than others, which is to say that each of us must, insofar as we can speak to each other, be in a position to speak for others, to speak with, in Kant's phrase, "a universal voice." There are, no doubt, empirical conditions of this possibility, but the criteria themselves cannot simply be the registering of these empirical conditions. The judgments in which we give voice to the criteria cannot simply be about some specific community of speakers, predictions about how speakers in the community will in fact comport themselves. They are expressions of our rationality, and as such they cannot be viewed as merely contingent constraints on us, such as the forms of sensibility are for Kant. The fact that there is no guarantee that others will agree in the judgments through which we give voice to criteria does not constitute a restriction on the criteria themselves, for our entitlement to give voice to criteria does not rest on the evidence of *de facto* agreement with others. Although our ability to speak for others is conditioned by empirical facts, it is not based on empirical facts. Like Kant, Cavell, under the pressure of responding to the skeptic, proposes nothing less than a new way of conceiving of our rationality.[77]

# Bibliography

Affeldt, Steven (1998), "The Ground of Mutuality: Criteria, Judgment and Intelligibility in Stephen Mulhall and Stanley Cavell." In: *European Journal of Philosophy* 6, 1–31.

Austin, J.L. (1961), "Other Minds." In: J.L. Austin, *Philosophical Papers*, Oxford: Oxford University Press, 76–116.

Bristow, William F. (2007), *Hegel and the Transformation of Kantian Critique*, Oxford: Oxford University Press.

Cavell, Stanley (1976), *Must We Mean What We Say?*, Cambridge: Cambridge University Press.

Cavell, Stanley (1979), *The Claim of Reason: Wittgenstein, Skepticism, Morality, and Tragedy*, Oxford: Oxford University Press.

Clarke, Thompson (1972), "The Legacy of Skepticism." In: *Journal of Philosophy* 69, 754–69.

Conant, James (2004), "Varieties of Scepticism." In: Denis McManus (ed.), *Wittgenstein and Scepticism*. New York: Routledge, 97–136.

Conant, James (2005), "Stanley Cavell's Wittgenstein." In: *Harvard Review of Philosophy* 13, 50–65.

---

**77** This paper grew out of a seminar I gave with my colleague Kelly Jolley on Cavell's *The Claim of Reason* at Auburn University in the Fall Term of 2008. I thank Kelly for countless stimulating and illuminating conversations on the topics addressed in the paper. I would also like to single out among the students of that course Benjamin Pierce, whose Senior Thesis on Cavell has been helpful for me in thinking through these topics. Conversations I have had (over the course of many years) with Steven Affeldt, William Bristow, James Conant, Eli Friedlander, Richard Moran, and Sanford Shieh have played a large role in my understanding of Cavell's work. I thank them for these. A version of this paper was presented at the Wittgenstein Workshop at the University of Chicago in April of 2010. I thank the audience on that occasion for their thoughtful feedback. Also, I thank Dafi Agam-Segal, Silver Bronzo, Keren Gorodeisky, Tom Lockhart, Eric Marcus, and James Shelley for conversations that I know had a significant influence on the paper. Finally, my thanks go out to Stanley Cavell, my teacher.

Davidson, Donald (1984), *Inquiries Into Truth and Interpretation*, Oxford: Clarendon Press.

Descartes, Réne (1984), *Meditations on First Philosophy*. In: Réne Descartes, *The Philosophical Writings of Descartes, Volume II*, John Cottingham, Robert Stoothoff, and Dugald Murdoch (trans.), Cambridge: Cambridge University Press.

Dretske, Fred (1999), "Epistemic Operators." In: Keith De Rose and Ted A. Warfield (eds.), *Skepticism: A Contemporary Reader*, Oxford: Oxford University Press, 131–44.

Kant, Immanuel (1998), *Critique of Pure Reason*, Paul Guyer and Allen Wood (trans.), Cambridge: Cambridge University Press.

McGinn, Marie (1989), *Sense and Certainty: A Dissolution of Scepticism*, New York: Blackwell.

Moran, Richard (2001), *Authority and Estrangement: An Essay on Self-Knowledge*, Princeton: Princeton University Press.

Morris, C. R. (1933), *Idealistic Logic: A Study of Its Aim, Method and Achievement*, London: Macmillan.

Nozick, Robert (1991), *Philosophical Explanations*, Cambridge: Harvard University Press.

Shieh, Sanford (2006), "The Truth of Skepticism." In Alice Crary and Sanford Shieh (eds.), *Reading Cavell*, London: Routledge, 131–166.

Stroud, Barry (1980), "Reasonable Claims." In: *Journal of Philosophy* 77, 731–44.

Stroud, Barry (1984), *The Significance of Philosophical Scepticism*, Oxford: Oxford University Press.

Travis, Charles (2006), *Thought's Footing*, Oxford: Oxford University Press.

Williams, Michael (1996), *Unnatural Doubts: Epistemological Realism and the Basis of Scepticism*, Princeton: Princeton University Press.

Wittgenstein, Ludwig (1998), *Philosophical Investigations*, G.E.M. Anscombe (trans.), Oxford: Blackwell.

Simon Glendinning
# Cavell and Other Animals

## Cavell's Criteria

In *The Claim of Reason*, Stanley Cavell proposes a deceptively simple typographical shift of emphasis in the formulation of "Wittgensteinian criteria." Such criteria, Cavell suggests, should not be thought of as criteria for something's *being* so, but for something's being *so*.[1] Simple as it seems, Cavell's shift of emphasis leads to a completely novel reading of what Wittgenstein was hoping to achieve with that term, particularly in relation to the threat of skepticism concerning other minds. The standard reading is that Wittgenstein's work on criteria allows one to affirm that the presence of one ("outer") event or state is a non-empirical basis or ground (perhaps "in certain circumstances") for *certainty* concerning the presence of another ("inner") event or state. On this broadly epistemological interpretation, Wittgenstein's appeal to criteria offers a distinctive response to the threat of skepticism that many regard as conclusive: criteria are logically adequate ways of telling, from the outward behavior of something, how things really *are* in the interiority of its inner life. Wittgenstein's appeal to criteria is thus understood as belonging to a novel refutation of skepticism, allowing a confident affirmation, from a reflective or philosophical standpoint, that we can know or be certain of the existence or presence of other minds through or via the behavior of other bodies.[2]

The promise held out by this reading is obviously attractive. However, Cavell's shift of emphasis suggests that it radically misconceives the trajectory of Wittgenstein's discussion. Indeed, for Cavell, it effaces an acknowledgement in Wittgenstein's thinking of something like "the truth of skepticism" (Cavell 1979, 7). In this section, I will outline a central strand in Cavell's reading of Wittgenstein's appeal to criteria.[3] The outline will not, however, give itself over in every respect to the words that articulate Cavell's revision of the standard reading. Not only will I want to raise an objection to his interpretation of the "publicness" of language; there is

---

1 Cavell 1979, 45.
2 On this interpretation, Wittgenstein thus successfully discharges us from at least one dimension of the Kantian complaint regarding 'the scandal of philosophy.'
3 Some of the early phase of this presentation draws on material from the final chapter of Glendinning 1998. However, since writing that book, my thinking about human animality has been profoundly reshaped by my further reading of Jacques Derrida and Cora Diamond. My ongoing debts to them on this subject are evident throughout this essay.

also something that I will want to bracket out or neutralize in it altogether, a neutralization that should prepare for certain questions, directed here at Cavell, that seem to me too quickly and too conveniently settled not only in his work but by traditional philosophy generally. These questions concern the way in which animal life is typically framed in the work and conceptuality of philosophical reflection as we have inherited it. What I want to neutralize in what follows will be an (already fundamentally traditional) identification by Cavell, very near the outset of his reading of Wittgenstein, on a (or *the*) singular difference between human beings and animals, an identification all the more effective and determining for its appearing so innocent.

Presenting Cavell's discussion under these constraints still allows me to begin more or less where he does, with a rejection of the attempt to divine in Wittgenstein's text a special or technical conception of criteria. Cavell is impressed instead that "the bulk of Wittgenstein's rhetoric in manipulating the term... is just the rhetoric of the ordinary word" (Cavell 1979, 7). Thus for example, in Wittgenstein's cases, criteria are the sort of thing:

(1) Which we fix (Wittgenstein 1958, §322).
(2) Which are used, accepted, or adopted (Wittgenstein 1958, §§182, 141, 160).
(3) Of which we can apply different ones in different circumstances (Wittgenstein 1958, §164).
(4) Of which there can be usual ones (Wittgenstein 1958, §185).
(5) Of which we can introduce completely new ones (Wittgenstein 1958, p. 222).[4]
(6) Which can be much more complicated than might appear at first sight (Wittgenstein 1958, §182).
(7) To which someone can have his or her attention drawn (Wittgenstein 1958, p. 181).

Cavell then undertakes an exploration of this 'rhetoric' in order to prepare for a return to Wittgenstein's use of the term. And what Cavell finds in this preliminary exploration is that criteria are typically "specifications... on the basis of which to judge (assess, settle) whether something has a particular status or value" (Cavell

---

4 Cavell does not mention this example, perhaps because he wants to protect the naturalness of Wittgensteinian criteria from contamination by the idea of 'convenience' that he finds as one aspect of convention (Cavell 1979, 110). Cavell rightly regards Wittgensteinian criteria as profoundly misunderstood when construed as 'mere conventions.' See esp. the discussion of "the conventionality of human nature," (Cavell 1979, 111). Similar arguments can be found in Merleau-Ponty. The emphasis on structures of repetition that I will trace in Wittgenstein's remarks on criteria will support this effort to avoid the radical separation of the natural and the conventional.

1979, 9). That is, criteria provide the regulations by means of which something is assigned a certain status (rather than another or none) or is granted a particular title (rather than another or none).

Holding this understanding in view, Cavell goes on to acknowledge that, once we grant that the rhetoric of Wittgensteinian criteria is more or less ordinary, it should remain surprising that the kind of thing with respect to which Wittgenstein talks of criteria are not the kind of thing that we would ordinarily think of as requiring criteria at all. That is, it is not the way he uses the term that is odd, but rather in respect of *what* he claims them. The kinds of thing for which Wittgenstein suggests there are criteria include the following:

(a) 'Fitting,' 'being able to,' 'understanding' (Wittgenstein 1958, §§182, 146).
(b) Mastery of the series of natural numbers (Wittgenstein 1958, §185).
(c) Demonstrating a capacity (Wittgenstein 1958, p. 181).
(d) 'Inner states' (Wittgenstein 1958, p. 181; §§580, 572).
(e) The truth of a confession (Wittgenstein 1958, p. 222).
(f) Saying someone is seeing a drawing three-dimensionally (Wittgenstein 1958, p. 203).
(g) Someone's being of such-and-such an opinion (Wittgenstein 1958, §573).
(h) The identity of pains, etc. (Wittgenstein 1958, §§253, 288, 322).
(i) The sameness of two images (Wittgenstein 1958, §377).
(j) Personal 'identity' (Wittgenstein 1958, §404).
(k) Looking at something but not seeing it (Wittgenstein 1958, p. 211).
(l) The way a formula is meant (Wittgenstein 1958, §§190, 692).
(m) Reading (Wittgenstein 1958, §§159, 160, 165).

P.M.S. Hacker states: "We fix criteria by laying down grammatical rules" (Hacker 1986, 310). This formulation brings the concept of criteria into (grammatical) relation with the concept of grammar, but I am not at all sure I know what it means. It looks (grammatically) as if we are dealing with a case as straightforward as this: "We settle the result by drawing out numbered tickets." But it is precisely the oddness of Wittgenstein's cases that makes it hard to imagine what Hacker's formulation is saying. One might reproduce it more suggestively (though certainly less smoothly) so as to let it remark this difficulty by saying: "We" "fix" "criteria" by "laying down" "grammatical" "rules." The rhetoric of each of these may, in Wittgenstein's use of them, be ordinary, but with respect to the list (a)–(m) that only serves to highlight the strangeness of his claim.[5]

---

5 When and why did we *fix* them? And did *we* (all, collectively) fix them? Did I have a hand in this?

Thus, while one can readily understand why, say, judges in a diving competition need to agree on a system or set of regulations for adjudicating the excellence of a dive, it is none so clear that we have, let alone need, anything like that in the kinds of cases Wittgenstein considers. Indeed, what is clear is that if there *are* criteria in play in these kinds of cases, then they are *not* laid down anywhere in the form of systematic regulations or definite rules. So if Wittgensteinian criteria remain, nevertheless, (grammatically) instruments of regulation of judgments, then in these cases, it will be misleading to conceive them as an externalized tool, as layed down in a consultable guide. One might rather say that, in these cases, *we are ourselves functioning as the instrument of regulation.*

For Cavell, then, what we imagine or recall in response to being asked, "What in particular cases do we regard as criteria for...?" is not a hitherto unnoticed system or set of 'decisive criteria' for judgment (Cavell 1979, 13). We cannot conceptually clarify the criteria Wittgenstein is concerned with in terms of definite rules or codified conventions. Thus, while a philosopher may try to produce a systematic formalization of them, the result is bound to be disappointing: "The systems that occur to him are inadequate, and he suddenly finds himself in a wilderness instead of the well laid out garden that he knew so well. Rules occur to him, no doubt, but the reality shows nothing but exceptions" (Wittgenstein 1980, §557).

Cavell's reading of the fix of criteria for inner states of others aims fully to respect this informal form. Acknowledging one's possession of them is not a matter of laying out one's knowledge of specifications that are recognized to be satisfied or unsatisfied in particular cases. Rather, what is at issue is more like seeing a rough textural patterning *woven right into* a fabric's fabric. In the case of an investigation of criteria for "inner states," for example, what we need to recall are the kinds of occasion on which we respond to living thing in ways that incorporate the use of particular psychological concept-words, concepts of "inner states," cases in which we repeat—or, as Cavell puts it, where we '"retain"—them (Cavell 1979, 45).

How should we bethink such occasions for ourselves? On the standard reading, Wittgensteinian criteria are usually conceived as behavioral conditions of some type. And in a sense, Cavell does not dispute this. However, for Cavell what is in question here is never simply the presence of some typical condition that *then* elicits some typical response. On the contrary, the behavioral condition in question is not something that can be established to obtain independently of one's response.[6]

---

Did you? Are they actually *laid down* somewhere? If criteria really are used in the cases he considers, why do I seem to be ignorant of this fact?
**6** This formulation derives from McDowell, but the Cavellian root is duly acknowledged (see McDowell 1982, 462).

That is, the identification or recognition of such a behavioral condition—the recognition of certain behavior as, say, 'a wince' and thus as *an expression of pain*—is already a response. The presence of criteria, one might say, cannot be reduced to the presence of a kind of behavior that is perceptually available to just anyone you please.[7] To perceive the satisfaction or non-satisfaction of criteria requires that the behavior of a living thing must, as Cavell comes to put it, be "read" (Cavell 1979, 356).

Cavell thus identifies the following crucial feature of Wittgenstein's appeal to criteria: namely, that they implicate their users in the *"what"* of "what is recalled." As Wittgenstein puts it, "my relation to the appearance here is part of my concept" (Wittgenstein 1981, §543; cf., Cavell 1979, 93). On this account, in each case, what is recognized (for example, "a wince" or "a wink") is not something that can be established to obtain independently of its recognition, or its reading. A consequence of this interpretation is a sense of disappointment with criteria. For Cavell, the correct answer to the question, "When is behavior a (satisfied) criterion of *p?*" is simply "When it is identified as a behavioral *expression of p*." For example, "the criteria of pain are satisfied by the presence of (what we take as, fix, accept, adopt, etc., as) pain-behaviour" (Cavell 1979, 44). On the standard reading of Wittgenstein, this is no help at all, for there the satisfaction of criteria was expected to give us logically adequate (if, for some, defeasible) grounds for certainty for the *truth* of statements such as, "He *is* in pain." For Cavell, however, the basic error of the standard reading lies precisely in its effort to conceive cases of, say, pain-behavior *without* pain (pretense, etc.) as cases that should be (if, for some, defeasibly) excluded by the satisfaction of criteria. Against such an approach, Cavell stresses that what can be called (out) or recalled in such "problem" cases are still, for example, cases of feigning *pain*, acting as if in *pain*, simulating *pain*-behavior, pretending to be in *pain*, etc. That is, what is at issue are still cases in which there is a response (again) to certain behavior as an expression of *pain* (and not some other thing). In all such cases, the criteria for pain are satisfied. For this just means that these are all cases in which we respond (again) with, among other things, this concept-word. In the fabric of our lives with this word, *this* is also where we (do) repeat it, *this* is also where we (do) retain it.

On this view, and *pace* the standard reading of Wittgenstein, the satisfaction of criteria is not a way of telling *how* things are, but rather our basic way of telling *what* things are. Here we arrive at the fundamental shift of emphasis proposed by Cavell's reading of Wittgensteinian criteria: "Criteria are," he suggests, "'criteria

---

7 This formulation is from J.L. Austin's essay "Other Minds," but it fits well with what Cavell has to say about 'reading the other.'

for something's being so', not in the sense that they tell of a thing's existence, but of something like its identity, not of its *being* so but of its being *so*. Criteria do not determine the certainty of statements, but the application of the concepts employed in statements" (Cavell 1979, 45). For Cavell, then, the concept of (the satisfaction of) criteria does not provide any sort of theoretical or technical account of the behavioral grounds for our claims to know the inner states of others, but belongs to an account that is encouraging us to recall our involvement or (what Cavell calls) our 'intervention' in the counting of the behavior of a living thing as *expression*. However, if that is, as it were, all they can achieve, as Cavell insists it is, then not only is no refutation of skepticism in the offing, but we can also see why skepticism itself will remain as a "natural possibility" or "standing threat" wherever there are judgments controlled by criteria (Cavell 1979, 47), a threat that will show itself whenever there is "a wish for the connection between my claims of knowledge and the objects upon which the claims are to fall to occur without my intervention, apart from my agreements" (Cavell 1979, 351–2). As Wittgenstein puts it:

> The following is true: I can't give criteria which put the presence of the sensation beyond doubt; that is to say *there are no such criteria*—But what sort of fact is that? A psychological one, concerning sensations? Will one want to say that it resides in the nature of sensation, or the expression of sensation? I might say, it is a peculiarity of our language-game—But even if that is true, it passes over a main point: In certain cases I am in some uncertainty whether someone else is in pain or not, I am not secure in my sympathy with him—and no expression on his part can remove this uncertainty. (Wittgenstein 1980, §137; emphasis mine)

For Cavell, then, a decisive characteristic of the standard reading is that it wants criteria to do *more* than they can. However, in closing this sketch of one strand of Cavell's interpretation and reevaluation of Wittgensteinian criteria, I want to suggest that, for his part, Cavell seems to want them to do rather *less* than they can.

Consider, first, that if we accept (as I think we should) that Cavell is right to say that the recognition of criteria is internal to the identification of a stretch of behavior as an *expression*, then it surely becomes both striking and significant to recall Wittgenstein's observation that *in one's own case*—in the case, for example, of the expression of one's own sensations—"what I do is not, of course, to identify my sensation by criteria: but to *repeat an expression*" (Wittgenstein 1958, §290; emphasis mine; cf., §377). Cavell does not, as far as I know, make use of or have anything to say on this point. But in hand with what he does say, it would follow that the criterial individuation or identification of sensations, and hence the identity of our various *concepts* of sensation in general, is bound up with a logic of repetition that is irreducibly related to others. Indeed, it is this logic that explains both why the language of the inner is necessarily and through-and-through "not one intelligible to me alone" (Wittgenstein 1958, §261) and why the identified "what" of inner states and processes fundamentally "stands in need" of outward criteria—and hence stands in need of a response from the other:[8] "Do I say in my own case that I am saying something to myself, because I am behaving in such-and-such a way? —- I do *not* say it from observation of my behavior. *But it only makes sense because I do behave in this way*" (Wittgenstein 1958, §357; emphasis mine).

The profoundly anti-Cartesian consequence of this logic is, I think, unavoidable: namely, that I have no (identifying) relation to myself that does not pass through a relation to *another repetition* or the repetition of another—the retaining response of another. This is a dimension of Wittgenstein's confrontation with the problem of other minds that is not in view at all on the standard reading. But nor, as we shall see, is it something that is clearly or consistently articulated by Cavell.[9] According to the skeptic, unlike the situation in one's own case, the real presence of the other's inner life seems vulnerable to doubt. The standard reading of Wittgenstein simply claims that the notion of criteria can help us to dispel this doubt. The great strength of Cavell's reevaluation lies in its emphasis on the fact that there are no behavioral criteria that do not *already* implicate singular responses of repetition (or retention) of psychological concepts. For this reason alone, it is illegitimate to appeal to criteria to refute skepticism. As a refutation of skepticism, recourse to criteria will always beg the question: with their identification, we will have already been caught responding to the other *as such*. Indeed, it is precisely characteristic of what is recalled that it could not be described without invoking (repeating, retaining) the very concepts of life that the skeptic would like to suspend. In short, a "we" will have already been put into play. On the other hand, however, in its elision of the distinctive difference between repetitions in the first and third person, Cavell's discussion makes the use of criteria seem more vulnerable to a threat of skepticism than I find in Wittgenstein. Of course, Cavell does not endorse the skeptical assumption that, if the sincerity or authenticity of an expression is unpresentable, this is because it relates to a subject whose inner goings-on (for example, whose sensations) are in a fundamental sense "hidden" from me. On his reading, however, the scene is simply recast in terms of the fate of individuals who can meet the minds of others only if they naturally find themselves "willing to judge" in the way others do, and thus share criteria with them (Cavell 1979, 35). This achievement of mutual publicness is, as we shall see further in the next section, something

---

8 This is the basic significance of (and explains the diacritics in) *Philosophical Investigations* §580.
9 What I mean is that Cavell does not pursue this line of thought directly; his emphasis is not on it. But things are complicated. See, for example, Cavell's suggestion that "being human is the power to grant being human" (Cavell 1979, 397). On the other hand, I am not so confident that we should think of this as a distinction (a power) reserved for human beings alone.

that Cavell regards as essentially "fragile" (Cavell 1979, 36). In the possibility of for-going the conditions of human community, skepticism becomes "a natural possibil-ity" (Cavell 1979, 36).

With the non-criterial repetition of psychological expressions in view, however, Cavell's way of resituating the threat of skepticism looks like an individualistic mis-construal of what is, in fact, a structural feature of the language-game itself. The crucial point here is that the "game" is essentially (and at both ends, as it were) bound up with *repetition* (retention), so that what we recall when we recall criteria always carries us beyond the "one man once" singularity of an isolated occasion of behavior. However, since the "not once" of repeatability belongs (grammatically) to the regulation of judgments afforded by criteria as such,[10] then so too does the pos-sibility of (in various ways) *mimicking* them. And if anything, it is this *structural pos-sibility* that I would want to call "the truth of skepticism" (Wittgenstein calls it a "constitutional uncertainty" [Wittgenstein 1980, §141]). But then this power of rep-etition in general—what Cavell might call, still rather individualistically perhaps, the insinuation in every scene of 'my intervention'—is precisely what renders non-doubting (saying with certainty, for example, that "Sophie is concerned") pos-sible too. As I say, I will come back to Cavell's problematic interpretation of public-ness. For it is, as I hope to show, indissociable from that aspect of his account of criteria that I have tried to hold in reserve altogether up to this point. It is to this that I turn in the next section.

# A Natural Tongue

Let me begin now to bring in what I have tried to bracket out in presenting Cav-ell's reading of Wittgensteinian criteria. Cavell presents his reading as aiming faithfully to elaborate Wittgenstein's well-known hostility to the tendency in phi-losophy to focus on words and sentences in isolation from their actual use. Sug-gestively, Cavell characterises this tendency as tantamount to "reject[ing] the human" (Cavell 1979, 207, 222). He then styles the corrective task as the effort "to put the human animal back into language" (Cavell 1979, 207).

This opening of Wittgenstein's philosophy onto the question of human ani-mality is, I think, both profoundly important and helpful. However, for all the attempts made by Cavell to recover the unity of body (or 'flesh') and language, of tool and thought prior to philosophy's disarticulation of and emphasis on the originality of the one and the other, he still does not, I will suggest, every-

---

10 Wittgenstein 1958, §199.

where sustain his critique of the abstraction of the human from animality. Indeed, as we shall see, he will even have recourse to the concepts that have habitually served to affirm a fundamental difference between human beings and animals. So, ultimately, I wonder or worry whether Cavell is right to see his retrieval of the human animal as so foreign to traditional philosophy. It is at least not foreign to that tradition's insistence that it offers (or, indeed, is itself) the best picture of this animal's distinction. True, in this tradition, this has typically led to the near eclipse of, or even denial of, human animality, and Cavell has undoubtedly made great strides to restore it. Nevertheless, and even if Cavell is right to see this threatened eclipse as the result of looking at words and sentences in isolation, it seems to me that his mode of retrieval of the human animal remains, in its most decisive movements, at one with that tradition's distinctive focus on the human in isolation, its tendency to picture the human in terms of its unique distinctiveness, as isolated in its distinction, as if what characterizes the human most deeply is what distinguishes it most radically from other animals. My claim, then, is that in retrieving the human animal, Cavell retains a rather traditional estimation of the idea of the difference between human beings and animals. And my worry is that this leads to a rather traditional distortion or inflation of human "finitude" and perhaps especially of what, taking a certain Cavell as my guide here as well, I have called the power of repetition.

In "The Availability of Wittgenstein's Later Philosophy," Cavell famously says that Wittgenstein "'wishes an acknowledgement of human limitation which does not leave us chafed by our own skins" (Cavell 1976, 61). I think that is right, but I will suggest that Cavell's neglect (at certain points) of the skins of animals brings relief at a price: namely, of conceiving us as at home in our own skins in a way that occludes our participation in and distinctive kinship to our most "other" others, i.e., to animals.

But wait! Is there really a neglect of animal life in Cavell? Since there is so much insistence on human animality in his work, non-human animals could hardly avoid being caught up in its embrace. Yet their entry is surprisingly rare, and at times that entry is rather brusquely curtailed. Cavell gives to the skeptic about other minds the dogmatic gesture of "omitting [animals] for convenience" (Cavell 1979, 420), but the inconvenience of letting them in is not something that I find Cavell dwells on or amends.

And so, inconveniently enough, I want simply to ask: What, then, if this other, this finite creature, was an animal?[11] What if, what Cavell calls in "What

---

11 I want this to resonate with something Cavell says towards the end of his essay "What is the Scandal of Skepticism?" Shortly after having unforgettably declared that "I am the scandal," he

is the Scandal of Scepticism?", the "variation of examples" called for in the inquiry into the other did not just happen normally to exclude animals, but that animals, in their absence from the examples actually considered, are the finite figure that this discourse both needs and needs to protect itself from? So I ask this (ask to imagine a further variation of the examples called on in the inquiry into others) not in order to have a supplementary addition to our inquiry, a factual complication or limiting case of the other, but in order to take us to the point where we can comfortably accept (without chafing) that the finite other might (also) be an animal.

In order to see how Cavell keeps animals out of the frame in his counter-traditional affirmation of human animality, I want very briefly to look at what, in Cavell's foray into the theme of Wittgensteinian criteria, first manifests the movement of thought that I have tried to neutralize in my initial presentation. In the first chapter of *The Claim of Reason*, entitled "Criteria and Judgment," and already combating the traditional tendency to separate human capacities from the life of an animal, Cavell's discussion is framed not with the idea of judgments as, say, the proper work of the mind, but rather, as the distinctive mark, of "a creature that has speech" (Cavell 1979, 15). But now, and from now on, having pre-delimited the object of his investigation as in this way distinguished from other living 'creatures,' this moment of combat with (a certain intellectualist strain in) our tradition is also one of fundamental alliance with it. The accusation against the tradition (that it 'rejects the human') could not be radical, since it still moves within its basic conceptuality (the insistence on the radical distinction of the human). And thenceforth, his discussion of criteria is framed 'always' within a human horizon: criteria, Cavell will insist, are "always 'ours'" (Cavell 1979, 18), and the group here is explicitly identified as "the human group."

Emphasizing Cavell's constant emphasis on the idea of *'our* criteria' may seem unfair, since Cavell also wants to invoke, and again appeals to Wittgenstein to invoke, the idea that there might (even) be human beings who do not share them. To illustrate this, he cites a remark from Part II of the *Philosophical Inves-*

---

writes of a (perhaps) non-theological mode of overcoming such scandal though an "investment of a certain kind in a particular finite other" in which you "suffer the other's separation, perhaps by allowing that the other knows who you are, perhaps by forgiving them for not knowing." Here again (and in fact throughout nearly every line of this extraordinary essay, which was the major inspiration for my own here), I want to haunt Cavell's words (and further deflect them from a certain religious source) with the question: What if this finite other were also an animal? In doing so, I am also haunting Cavell with his own words, his own acknowledgement that "animals are also our others" (Cavell 1979, 412).

*tigations* in which Wittgenstein notes that "one human being can be a complete enigma to another" (Wittgenstein 1958, p. 223). However, Cavell's invitation to consider such cases as moments of disagreement over criteria (a suggestion to which I shall return) is not part of a retreat from his general conception of criteria as 'ours,' but rather forms part of the more adventurous claim that the appeal to criteria is always also a search for a 'human community' (something that, in particular cases, might turn out to be unfounded or forgone). Within a paragraph, Cavell couples this search to the search for reason, surely serving to announce that the life of this 'creature with speech' supposedly recovered by Cavell remains in close contact to traditional philosophy and its classical anthropology of the *zoon logon echon* (the animal with the capacity for '*logos*'). Indeed, we should remember that the Aristotelian anthropology also sought, like Cavell's, to distinguish humanity from natural animality *naturally*—a natural distinction in the sense that, as Cavell puts it, it flows from the "naturalness of a natural tongue" for human beings (Cavell 1979, 122). This is (as Cavell more or less concedes) a naturalism that never radically disallows an invocation of the supernatural, and is strictly opposed to any sort of scientific naturalism.

There is no doubt that human beings 'keep discovering themselves' in opposition to or in their difference to animals.[12] Cavell will confirm this, and indefatigably repeat it. He will also find Wittgenstein saying this too. However, what I find problematic at the heart of Cavell's more or less classical humanism here is something he actually shares with the scientific naturalist opponent he principally wants to shun: namely, the same fundamental *cognitivism* with regard to the idea of the difference between human beings and animals. The humanist asserts the reality of the difference, the naturalist (a continuist by tradition) denies it—but both regard their position as deriving from a perception of how things really are.

Now, in the context of a discussion of the idea of a radical separation of man and beast, one might be a little surprised to find that *The Claim of Reason* makes nothing of *Philosophical Investigations* §25, a remark in which Wittgenstein explicitly addresses the idea of human beings as (naturally) language-users. But perhaps the reason for this omission is due to the fact that this passage does not exactly speak for Cavell. It runs as follows:

> It is sometimes said that animals do not talk because they lack the mental capacity. And this means: 'they do not think, and that is why they do not talk.' But—they simply do not talk. Or to put it better: they do not use language—if we except the most primitive

---

12 See Cavell 1979, 495. Cavell is here suggesting that human beings "keep discovering themselves in opposition to nature," but the contrast with animals is naturally fitting too.

forms of language. —Commanding, questioning, recounting, chatting, are as much a part of our natural history as walking, eating, drinking, playing. (Wittgenstein 1958, §25)

The rather insistent voice that simply declares 'they simply do not talk' resonates with Cavell's formulations about the speaking creature. But Wittgenstein does not stop there, and moreover, in my view, the supplementary conditional attached to the formulation affirmed as 'better' should be particularly stressed. The remark suggests not only that it is not best to think of animals as 'simply non-talkers' (hence not best to conceive ourselves as uniquely the creature that has speech) and not best to privilege one way of using language among others (speech), but also that *if* we want to mark the (undeniable) originality of human language with the (radical) character of 'uniqueness,' then we can do so only by dogmatically excluding from our considerations the primitive forms of language that are *in fact* exhibited in the lives of other animals. And what could possibly motivate that (no doubt convenient) exclusion—except perhaps an antecedent desire to discover the human in its distinction from animals and thus see what is natural to humanity as situating it at least in part (but this part is not one part among others) as set radically apart from the rest of nature? So *Investigations* §25, while it no doubt emphasises how natural using a language is for human beings—*for that creature that tends to identify itself first by insisting that "they (animals) do not talk"*—it does nothing to underwrite the idea that this creature's use of language (original as it is) can be appealed to in order to delimit a uniquely human mode of community. The irony here is, to borrow a phrase of Jacques Derrida's, that human language, original as it may be, does not allow us to 'cut' once and for all, where we would in general *like* to cut.[13] Indeed, contrary to what we would like to do here, we can and should remain open-minded, for the discussion *at this level* concerns factual differences between different living things, *differences* between human beings and animals, not the (historically momentous) *imaginative elaboration* within humanity of the idea of the *difference* between human beings and animals.[14] Of

---

13 Derrida 1992, 116–7.

14 The analysis here appeals to a thought-provoking distinction articulated by Cora Diamond in her essay "Eating Meat and Eating People": "The difference between human beings and animals is not to be discovered by studies of Washoe or the activities of dolphins. It is not that sort of study or ethology or evolutionary theory that is going to tell us the difference between us and animals: the difference is, I have suggested, a central concept for human life and is more an object of contemplation than observation (though that might be misunderstood; I am not suggesting it is a matter of intuition). One source of confusion here is that we fail to distinguish between 'the difference between animals and people' and 'the differences between animals and

course, in this context—in the context of an investigation that challenges the standard cognitivist way in which philosophy (and not just philosophy) has typically interpreted the idea of that difference (as if it were one among the natural, factual differences)—the facts here are not just any facts, for they allow us to see a decisive articulation of traditional philosophical thinking in a certain *a priori* anthropology.[15] And if Cavell is right, as I think he is, to see Wittgenstein's work as a response to a rejection of the human and as an attempt to "to put the human animal back into language," then one cannot fail to see it as a hunting-down and a being-on-the-scent-of what that philosophy and that anthropology, to say what it says, dogmatically passes over.

Coming back to criteria, it is now worth noting that the paradigmatic Cavellian emphasis on the idea of criteria as always ours is not something that Wittgenstein seems especially keen to invite. What *is* typical in Wittgenstein is the way he invites his reader (i. e., in each case, *you*) to acknowledge, in the examples he looks at, that there really are (what one might fairly call) "criteria" that you accept and that you are, in some way, already familiar with. What Wittgenstein is doing here, I think, is reminding his reader that what he or she ordinarily does and says (his or her own practice in the use of language) is other than he or she is inclined to suppose 'when doing philosophy,' when, that is, he or she becomes self-consciously reflective. Of course, this is not something Cavell would deny at all. But I take it as significant that his (Cavell's) primary and favored way of designating this conflict is in terms of a philosopher's "disagreement" not with his or her own practice, but "with the words of ordinary human beings" (Cavell 1979, 34). Thus, for Cavell, the appeal to criteria is made when philosophy comes to the point where our mutual "attunement... is threatened or lost" (Cave;; 1979, 34). For Wittgenstein, by contrast, the *emphasis* is on the fact that philosophical problems arise when someone is reflectively out of tune with what he or she himself or herself prereflectively says and does—an *internal conflict* with what, in a certain way, he or she already knows.[16] Now, that will *be* to be

---

people'; the same sort of confusion occurs in discussions of the relationship of men and women. In both cases people appeal to scientific evidence to show that 'the difference' is not as deep as we think; but all that such evidence can show, or show directly, is that the differences are less sharp than we think. In the case of the difference between animals and people, it is clear that we form the idea of this difference, create the concept of the difference, knowing perfectly well the overwhelmingly obvious similarities" (Diamond 1991, 324).

**15** I explore the cognitivism of traditional philosophical anthropology at greater length in the final chapter of Glendinning 2007.

**16** "What is it that is repulsive in the idea that we study the use of a word, point to mistakes in the description of the use and so on? First and foremost one asks oneself: How could *that* be so important to us? It depends on whether what one calls a 'wrong description' is a description that

out of tune with others, but not at all because these others ('ordinary human beings') are blessedly free of those tendencies that threaten our original attunement, but as one might put it, because they will be out of tune with, for example, what one learned to *do* when one learned, say, English.[17] To put it bluntly (and no doubt far too quickly), it seems to me that what occurs here (in acquiring one's 'natural tongue') is, in each case, the development and prodigious expansion of natural dispositions to or powers of repetition that afford the disciplined inhabitation of the maturing human being into behavioral repertoires and regimes ('language-games') that can belong to (be repeated by) others and which are made to do (function) without (every) me. As I have indicated, however, it is significant that, for Cavell, *that* structure of publicness is not something regarded as *built into* the functioning of (among other things) 'speech,' but rather is something *built on* 'fragile' acts of human speech; moments in which individuals reach out for a 'we' of human community (Cavell 1979, 36).

I do not wish to deny that there is a distinctively existential moment in every act of 'going on in the same way'.[18] Moreover, the emphasis that I want to give here to a structural publicness to every use of language (or indeed of 'marks' or 'gestures' in general) does not in the least imply that I am abandoning the possibility for another to speak my part or that I am challenging the possibility of another appealing to criteria that are also mine. But I do want to explore how Cavell's way of situating the emphasis on criteria (as always "ours") threatens to produce an illegitimate delimitation of the very entity it aims to isolate: the human animal.

My central concern here is that the Cavellian emphasis invites an all-too-traditional tendency to regard it as methodologically appropriate—indeed, as a merely methodological matter—to 'omit for convenience' attention to the lives of animals, a tendency that, I think, closes us off to opportunities to get clear about dimensions of our lives that, while not (naturally enough) simply exclusive

---

does not accord with established usage—or one which does not accord with the practice of the person giving the description. *Only* in the second case does a philosophical conflict arise" (Wittgenstein 1980, §548; final emphasis mine). It would be surprising if Cavell showed no awareness of the idea of internal conflict—and he *does* when he suggests that "the one philosophizing" is "out of agreement" with "his own words when he is not philosophizing" (Cavell 1979, 34). But my worries are in many respects about emphasis, and so, for me, it is significant that Cavell makes this point only in parenthesis, and does so without the emphatic 'only' that I am emphasizing in Wittgenstein's remark.

**17** I develop this account of philosophical problems, and Wittgenstein's understanding of them, in Glendinning 2004.

**18** See Glendinning 1998, 101

to human beings, are nevertheless basic to the life of the finite creature that we are.

Wittgenstein's regular and frequent consideration of patterns of animal life as offering more perspicuous illustrations of far more complex patterns of human life is an obvious and crucially important case in methodological point. But I also have a more abstract and more generally anthropological case (or indeed 'result') of such investigations in mind here. Cavell broaches the theme I want to focus on with the example of those humans who are said to have "a distinctive lack of hold on their world and their condition," namely, psychotics. Cavell says this: "Part of the difficulty in treating psychotics is the inability one has in appreciating *their* world, and hence in honoring them as persons; the other part of the difficulty comes in facing how close our world is... to theirs" (Cavell 1979, 90). Quite so. And what I want to suggest and develop in what follows is the thought that the human encounter with animals has an uncannily similar structure. And as such, it provides, I will suggest, a basic lesson concerning human finitude in general.

## Uncanny Kindness

Animals are a wonderfully natural kind of phenomenological puzzle.[19] There they are, in the world, familiar enough. In herds, or flocks, or swarms, or shoals, or packs, or on their own. On farms, in forests, in the air, in the rivers and seas, in the wild, and also, whether invited or not, in our spaces—in our gardens, our homes, our cities, as pets or pests. And yet, however familiar they are, they are never *simply* 'part of the furniture' nor *simply* 'part of the family.' The animal—that is the name for what (clearly) never *quite* fits in, or for what, to use Cavell's word, can never be *fully* accommodated.

Philosophy has never stopped trying to fit the animal in. Their entry disrupts the philosophical home, gnawing at the contours of our concepts and categories. So they are forced in. The animal—that is also the name for what cannot survive well in the texts of traditional philosophy, the name for the one whose appearance always risks disappearance, risks being made to fit in. Can we make room for animals? Let them in and they might run amok, ruin the demonstration. Take them to the tribunal and they'll make a monstrous show, an unruly display.

---

**19** The first phase of this section draws on and reworks material from an earlier (and from where I now stand, somewhat unsuccessful) attempt at a philosophical study of animal life in Glendinning 2000.

Bloody nuisance. For convenience's sake, let's squeeze them in next to the rocks and plants. There. Gone. That's better.

I'm about to let one in too. But this one should be no trouble, because it is already dead. My mother's now-no-longer-living dog, called Sophie. Sophie was not an easy dog to have around, and I would be mad to think I had her under control now, now she is dead. That is what I like best about Sophie, even now that she has gone. I'll never catch her. Neighbors, and the neighbor in me, would complain to my mother. "Can't you get her under control?" Of course, we all thought we could master her, or at least have a go. No chance. And for just that reason, Sophie will help me out again here, help me by not helping out at all, by remaining, to the end and well beyond her death, delinquent, unruly. Here is her entrance:

> There is (what I definitely want to call) a game I used to play with my mother's dog Sophie, in which we would run around a small pond [in my mother's former garden in London]. My aim was to catch her; hers to avoid being caught... Sophie has a lot of Collie in her and I never caught her. But one day while we *(we)* were playing this game I slipped as I tried to change direction too quickly on damp grass. Almost immediately Sophie ran straight up to me. I was unhurt, but she licked my face anyway. I do not see why this cannot be counted as a case of 'mutual intelligibility.' The dog could see my distress and I could see her sympathy. (Glendinning 1998, 142)

Now, as I have described it, this scene does nothing to support a fundamental or radical division between human beings and other animals. Whatever our differences, Sophie and I are not in fact separated by a clean divide or an uncrossable abyss. There is, for reasons I will specify later, what I want to call an uncanny mutuality to the game we engaged in. I was not playing with Sophie; we were both playing. And when I fell, she saw my distress and I saw her sympathy.

There are clearly many ways one might want to go on with this presentation, and I want to stress that I am not advocating that, in Cavell's words, we can do justice to this situation only if we 'naturalize' the human in the manner of the biological sciences. Cavell calls this the "attempt... to understand this being in relation to (non-human) nature, an attempt sometimes described as locating the human being's place in nature" (Cavell 1979, 465). He rightly sees this attempt as "slated to disappointment" (Cavell 1979, 465). However, as I have indicated, he explains this failure only in terms of what looks like a classic philosophical recoil: namely, in terms of finding that, as it were willy-nilly, "human beings keep discovering themselves in opposition to nature" (Cavell 1979, 465). This oscillation between scientific naturalism and its classical humanist recoil is not further explored by Cavell. And the reason for this is not hard to see: namely, that the recoil position is the milieu and not the object of his thinking. In saying this, I do not want to deny that what one might risk calling 'Cavell's humanism' is original and distinctive. But it is, I want to suggest, no less stubborn and insistent for all that.

But, again, wait! Why should Sophie prove a problem for Cavell? For unlike either scientific naturalists or classical humanists, there is no reason why he should dismiss Sophie's apparent sympathy (and, in fact, particularly not her daft name) as mere psychological candy floss belonging to a pre-scientific 'folk psychology,' or would want to attempt to explain (away) her behavior in terms of organic events capable of a fully and exhaustively natural, causal explanation, an explanation in terms of laws of the kind found in the natural sciences.

Thus, even while I am penning Cavell in with a humanist recoil from scientific naturalism, I accept that there is nothing in his work that suggests his conception of our criteria disallows their application beyond the human case, nothing that suggests they do not hold for the non-human. Indeed, it is part of his view that to respond to anything as a living thing is precisely *not* to withhold them (Cavell 1979, 83). Nevertheless, it is equally true that this is not something he spends much time on. I think that omission is unfortunate, and I want briefly to explain why.

We might begin here by considering the thought that the Wittgensteinian aphorism that features so heavily in Cavell's thinking (the idea that 'the human body is the best picture of the human soul') is a variant of a more general formulation where Wittgenstein, in the context of a scene of someone observing a dog, suggests that "if you see the behaviour of a living thing you see its soul" (Wittgenstein 1958, §357). Now, one of the things I like about the more general formulation is that the kind of generality it aims for precisely resists the philosophical tendency (not one to be found in Cavell, I think) to appeal to the idea of something-in-general called "the animal." That is, Wittgenstein's formulation is, as before, open-minded. There is no simple category of "the animal" here that is bluntly opposed to "the human." To cite what I think is Cavell's only use of the Wittgensteinian aphorism in a non-human case, we might talk about seeing the distinctive "soul of a frog" (Cavell 1979, 396), and no doubt, that will be something to be contrasted with, say, the soul of a dog. Now, the first crucial consequence of this approach is that it also removes the tendency to see either *some* or *all* of human behavior (the standard humanist concession and scientific-naturalist insistence respectively) as something that might be simply shared in common with or simply matching the behavior of animals. These ways of fitting animals in are, to my mind, unsatisfactory. Why should we assume *a priori* that *any* animal trait or structural organization should be, just like that, 'the same' as or 'simply matching' a human one? Indeed, isn't it precisely when animals are *most* like humans that we find them most *uncanny?*[20] Here we have behaviors and responses that are not *simply* and *not quite* matching human ones. They are uncanny because the animal's behavior *so closely* resembles something human and yet *remains* the behavior of a cat or ape or, indeed, Sophie the dog.

What we need here is not another way of making animals fit in, but a way of acknowledging that *what we perceive* in these cases is something that we *cannot* quite fit in, that we can never completely or securely capture: we need to acknowledge a certain lack of hold on our world, and hence acknowledge too our lack of hold on our finite condition.[21]

## Wittgenstein's Lion

I take it as significant that Wittgenstein reaches for and finds astonishing words for the human encounter with animals. Here is the reference to the enigmatic other that Cavell cites in his discussion of agreement and disagreement in criteria, now cited with a little more of its immediate context, a context that also confirms that Wittgenstein is on the scent of what underlies philosophy's tendency to reject the human:

> If I were to talk to myself out loud in a language not understood by those present my thought would be hidden from them...

---

**20** My sense of Sophie's aliveness to my state of mind had seemed to me to justify breaking with the habitual tendency to confine the scope of "mutual intelligibility" to the forms of intercourse that can go on between humans. However, there were reservations in my descriptions even then. With respect to her response to me, I did not say "her whole manner and demeanour was concernful" but that it was so "in the dog way" (Glendinning 1998, 142). And I did not say that "both Sophie and I were satisfied" that our modes of responsiveness to the other in this case had been warranted and appropriate, but that "both Sophie and I were (in an uncanny, non-matching way) 'satisfied' about these things" (Glendinning 1998, 142). My sense of the peculiarity of our kinship—what I want now to call (following Coetzee 1999) the perception of *our uncanny 'kindness'*—is something that I have always wanted to keep in view. As should be clear, I no more wish to regard other animals as 'basically the same' as human beings (reductive or scientific naturalism) than I want to regard them as 'essentially distinct' from us (classical humanism). What we need, it seems to me, are discourses that do not wind up bringing our aliveness to the uncanny kindness of the other animal to a premature end. (For example, by denying animals a proper relation to death.)

**21** As Rilke puts it: "and the noticing beasts are well aware that we are not very securely at home in the interpreted world" (Rilke 1975, 25; translation modified). And if we are properly to avoid the oscillation between humanism and scientific naturalism, we should leave open (as Rilke rather typically does not) that the human can see that this also holds for animals too. In their own ways, many animals are 'the same too,' uncannily.

> If I see someone writhing in pain with evident cause I do not think: all the same, his feelings are hidden from me.
>
> We also say of some people that they are transparent to us. It is, however, important as regards this observation that one human being can be a complete enigma to another. We learn this when we come into a strange country with entirely strange traditions; and what is more, even given a mastery of the country's language. We *do not* understand the people. (And not because of not knowing what they are saying to themselves.) We cannot find our feet with them.
>
> 'I cannot know what is going on in him' is above all a picture. It is the convincing expression of a conviction. It does not give the reasons for the conviction. They are not readily accessible.
>
> If a lion could talk, we *could not* understand him. (Wittgenstein 1958, 223, emphasis mine)

As I have noted, Cavell interprets the idea of the encounter with the enigmatic other as illustrating the possibility that there may be disagreement in criteria within the human 'group.' But the fact that Wittgenstein includes 'mastery of the country's language' in his description of this scene seems to render problematic that reading of his remark. For in this case, we can assume that the technique of any given word's use, and so also, one might suppose, the criteria for something's being *so,* will not, in fact, be disputed. So what differs between them, then, is not, I would suggest, something in the order of criteria.

Putting that to one side, however, and as the immediately surrounding paragraphs serve to indicate, the central theme of Wittgenstein's remarks is more obviously about why, in philosophy, we can become convinced that, with respect to any and every other, "I cannot know what is going on in him." And it seems to me that the remarks about encounters with the enigmatic other and with the impenetrable lion are invitations to bethink oneself of cases where we might really want to say something like this. For example, in both cases we might hedge from predicting, on the basis of observing their behavior, what they are going to do. Or again, when they do what they do, one might hedge from explaining why they might have done it. But of course, Wittgenstein's examples are not illustrative equivalents; there is clearly a step beyond the enigmatic when he introduces the lion. Indeed, here the philosopher's form of words looks particularly apt. So, yes, Wittgenstein is suggesting that the philosopher rejects the human. That is, the philosopher finds himself or herself as interpreting other human beings as if they were, ultimately, always something of a lion. (A thought that, in fact, one might not want always to reject.)

But that is not the end of the matter. For the aptness of these words in this case is itself telling of the human. We could put the point like this: within the world as we find it there is a spectrum of cases of encounters with other human beings that ranges from the 'completely transparent' to the 'completely enigmatic,' and (the suggestion seems to be) the typical human encounter with animals cannot be placed on that spectrum.[22] Thus, it would be misleading to say that, for the human, the life of an animal, say the life of a lion, is an 'enigma' to us. Indeed, if there is something distinctive here, as I think there is, it does not always preclude a willingness on our part (or, uncannily, on the part of many animals) to repeat (retain), and often enough to repeat pretty much without hesitation, certain psychological concepts (or behaviors and displays that are uncannily related to the function of these concepts) with respect to, and so attribute a 'subject' character to, the other animal. There is not, as it were, an uncrossable abyss here (indeed one might say that many animals are—uncannily like human beings—deeply marked by the disposition to re-mark), but there are what one might call 'structural breaks' between the lives of different animals that render such scenes of repetition remarkable. It is only because 'the spirit of the lion' (to use the words of the early Wittgenstein) is manifest *as such*, as *another* spirit,[23] that Wittgenstein could be alive to the thought that 'if a lion could talk we could not understand it.'

---

**22** In "Other Minds," J.L. Austin gives a list of those he finds it "hard to divine... what it must feel like to be," which includes royalty, fakirs, bushmen, Wykehamists [pupils and former pupils of Winchester School], and simple eccentrics. He goes on to contrast this list with a cat and a cockroach, cases in which, he claims, "we don't know (can't even guess or imagine) really, what it would feel like to be" one. There is something very strange and unhelpful in this talk "what it feels like to be something." I wouldn't know what to say (or where to begin) if someone asked me what it felt like to be me, although I can imagine someone having something to say when being asked, for example, what it felt like to be a bushman *for a week*. Comparison and contrast is essential in every area of language. Moreover, I think that I do have some uncanny (uncannine!) affinity with cats (domestic or not), and one that is, in its own way, *less* problematic than any encounter I might have with, say, bushmen or Wykehamists. The step beyond the completely enigmatic other-human to the animal-other is not, as I have tried to indicate, a step towards an *even more* enigmatic other. I think Austin's willingness to use the philosophically familiar phrasing of "what it feels like to be something" in this context is reflected in his (maddening) concession to tradition, in the same footnote, that there really *is* a sense in which we don't *ever* know what "accompanies" the behavior of another (Austin 1979, 104–5 fn. 1). This acknowledgment of, as it were, the truth in skepticism seems to amount simply to the claim that skepticism is, in some deep sense, *true*, or at least that other humans are, ultimately, always *something* of a cat or a cockroach. Again, this latter thought is not something I would want, always and everywhere, to reject. (As it were, from Kafka to DNA.) Here, no doubt, it is just terrible. Cavell's formulation, cited above (footnote 9), seems to me a better point of departure for thinking about human seperateness. (Equally good, I think, is Levinas in *Totality and Infinity* [Levinas 1979].)

**23** This acknowledgement of the radical alterity of the other animal is something the early Wittgenstein could not achieve. On the contrary, it belongs to the early Wittgenstein's conception of "the spirit" of the animal that it is essentially "my spirit" and so not *another* spirit at all. (See Wittgenstein 1961, 85; see also Glendinning 1998, 71–2.)

***

When our usual forms of expression seem limited in their power to come to terms with the world as we find it, we can find ourselves without a path or passage (*poros*) available and are left without knowing a way to go (*aporos*). Like many readers of Wittgenstein today, I have learned from Cavell that Wittgenstein's writing is itself a form of responsiveness to this kind of *aporia* of inhabitation. But Cavell's own response to the difficulty—his response to the situation that arises "when we are lost with respect to our words and the world they anticipate" (Cavell 1979, 34)—seems to me to misrepresent our (naturally) always limited hold on the world and our condition, to misrepresent the limited hold that, in the actual practice of language (in finding, *in der Tat*, passages into a future that we cannot completely anticipate) we *endure* everyday, indeed as the everyday itself.[24] For Cavell, "an acknowledgement of human limitation which does not leave us chafed by our own skins" is achieved by "finding ourselves" by way of "finding out and declaring" our criteria, "our attunement with words" (Cavell 1979, 34). In my view, the philosophical quest of coming to terms with human finitude requires a somewhat different emphasis (and, really, throughout this essay what has been at issue at each turn are matters of *emphasis*). When "finding ourselves" requires finding our way back to "the words of ordinary human beings" (Cavell 1979, 34), the task is not to write texts that resist what threatens to wrest us from community with other human beings. The task is to write texts that resist elaborating the difference of 'an ordinary life with words' in terms that conceal its uncanny kindness to the lives of animals.

# Bibliography

Austin, J.L. (1979), "Other Minds." In: J.L. Austin, *Philosophical Papers*, Oxford: Oxford University Press.

Cavell, Stanley (1976), *Must We Mean What We Say?*, Cambridge: Cambridge University Press.

Cavell, Stanley (1979), *The Claim of Reason: Wittgenstein, Skepticism, Morality, and Tragedy*, Oxford: Oxford University Press.

Coetzee, J.M. (1999), *The Lives of Animals*, Princeton: Princeton University Press.

Derrida, Jacques (1976), *Of Grammatology*, G. Spivak (trans.), Baltimore: John Hopkins University Press.

Derrida, Jacques (1992), "'Eating Well' or the Calculation of the Subject." In: E. Cadava, et. al. (eds.), *Who Comes After the Subject?*, New York: Routledge.

---

**24** I develop the idea that philosophical investigations aim to enable us reflectively to endure what (in deed) we endure in (as) the everyday in Glendinning 2004.

Diamond, Cora (1991), "Eating Meat and Eating People." In: Cora Diamond, *Realism and the Realistic Spirit: Wittgenstein, Philosophy, and the Mind*, Cambridge, MA: The MIT Press, 319–34.

Glendinning, Simon (1998), *On Being With Others: Heidegger-Derrida-Wittgenstein*, London: Routledge.

Glendinning, Simon (2000), "From Animal Life to City Life." In: *Angelaki* 5, 19–30.

Glendinning, Simon (2003), "A Different Difference: Humans and Animals." In: *The Philosophers' Magazine* 23, 35–7.

Glendinning, Simon (2004), "Philosophy as Nomadism." In: *What Philosophy Is*, H. Carel and D. Gamez (eds.), London: Continuum, 155–67.

Glendinning, Simon (2007), *In the Name of Phenomenology*, Abingdon: Routledge.

Hacker P.M.S. (1986), *Insight and Illusion*, Revised Edition, Oxford: Clarendon Press.

Levinas, Emmanuel (1979), *Totality and Infinity: An Essay on Exteriority*, Dordrecht: Kluwer.

McDowell, John (1982), "Criteria, Defeasibility, and Knowledge." In: *Proceedings of the British Academy* 68, 455–79.

Rilke, R.M. (1975), *Duino Elegies*, J.B. Leishman and S. Spender (trans.), London: The Hogarth Press.

Wittgenstein, Ludwig (1958), *Philosophical Investigations*, G.E.M. Anscombe (trans.), Oxford: Blackwell.

Wittgenstein, Ludwig (1961), *Notebooks: 1914–1916*, G.E.M. Anscombe (trans.), Oxford: Blackwell.

Wittgenstein, Ludwig (1980), *Remarks on the Philosophy of Psychology, Vol. I*, G.E.M. Anscombe (trans.), Oxford: Blackwell.

Wittgenstein, Ludwig (1981), *Zettel*, G.E.M. Anscombe (trans.), Oxford: Blackwell.

# Contributors

**Steven Affeldt** is Assistant Professor of Philosophy and Director of the McDevitt Center for Creativity and Innovation at Le Moyne College, NY. He does research in the fields of moral, political, and social philosophy as well as aesthetics. He has published papers on Rousseau, Wittgenstein, and Stanley Cavell.

**Jason Bridges** is Associate Professor in the Philosophy Department at the University of Chicago. He focuses his research on the philosophy of mind, the philosophy of language, and the philosophy of action. His current work is on epistemic and semantic contextualism as well as on rational explanation and the normativity of rationality. In 2011, he co-edited *The Possibility of Philosophical Understanding: Reflections on the Thought of Barry Stroud,* to which he contributed the article "Dispositions and Rational Explanation."

**James Conant** is Chester D. Tripp Professor of Humanities, Professor of Philosophy, and Professor in the College at the University of Chicago. His research interests lie in the philosophy of mind, the philosophy of language, epistemology, and aesthetics. He has published numerous articles on topics in these areas, as well as on thinkers such as Kant, Nietzsche, Kierkegaard, Frege, Carnap, Wittgenstein, Putnam, Cavell, Rorty, and McDowell. He has edited, among many others books, *Hilary Putnam: Pragmatism and Realism* (2002) and *Analytic Kantianism* (2006).

**Cora Diamond** is Professor Emeritus at the University of Virginia. Her research is primarily focused on the philosophy of language, as well as on analytical, moral, and political philosophy. In addition to her writings on ethics and animal rights, she is best known for spearheading a new interpretive approach to the philosophy of Ludwig Wittgenstein. She is the author of *The Realistic Spirit: Wittgenstein, Philosophy, and the Mind* (1991) as well as numerous articles.

**Paul Franks** is Professor of Jewish Philosophy and Professor of Philosophy at Yale University. His main research areas are Kant, German idealism, post-Kantian approaches within analytic and Continental philosophy, transcendental arguments, metaphysics and epistemology, mind and meaning, and Jewish philosophy. He has published numerous articles and is the author of *All or Nothing: Systematicity, Transcendental Arguments, and Skepticism in German Idealism* (2005).

**Simon Glendinning** is Reader in European Philosophy and Director of the Forum for European Philosophy in the European Institute at the London School of Economics. He specializes in philosophy of Europe, phenomenology and deconstruction, and is also interested in Wittgenstein and ordinary-language philosophy. He has written numerous articles and books, including *On Being with Others: Heidegger–Derrida–Wittgenstein* (1998) and *In the Name of Phenomenology* (2007).

**Arata Hamawaki** is Assistant Professor at Auburn University in Alabama. He works on Kant, nineteenth-century German philosophy, Early Modern philosophy, Wittgenstein, and on Kantian and Hegelian themes in contemporary philosophy of mind, philosophy of action, aesthetics, ethics, and moral psychology.

**Andrea Kern** is Professor of Philosophy at the Universität Leipzig. Her research interests lie in the areas of epistemology, the philosophy of perception, skepticism, the philosophy of action, and aesthetics. She has published numerous articles on these topics, as well as two monographs: *Schöne Lust. Eine Theorie der ästhetischen Erfahrung nach Kant* (2000) and *Quellen des Wissens. Zum Begriff vernünftiger Erkenntnisfähigkeiten* (2006).

**Christoph Menke** is Professor of Philosophy at the Goethe-Universität in Frankfurt on the Main. His research focuses on political theory, theories of law, theories of subjectivity, ethics, and aesthetics. In addition to numerous articles, he has published monographs such as *Kraft. Ein Grundbegriff ästhetischer Anthropologie* (2008) and *Die Gegenwart der Tragödie* (2009). He is the co-author of *Philosophie der Menschenrechte* (2007, with Arnd Pollmann) and has co-edited books including *Philosophie der Dekonstruktion* (2002, with Andrea Kern).

**Stephen Mulhall** is Professor of Philosophy at the University of Oxford. He is especially interested in Wittgenstein, post-Kantian philosophy, post-analytic philosophy, ethics, philosophy of religion, philosophy and literature, and philosophy and film. His publications include *Heidegger and Being and Time* (2005), *Wittgenstein's Private Language* (2006), *The Conversation of Humanity and The Wounded Animal: J.M.Coetzee and the Difficulty of Reality in Literature and Philosophy* (2009).

**Hilary Putnam** is John Cogan University Professor Emeritus in the Department of Philosophy at Havard University. His extensive work focuses on problems in metaphysics and epistemology, the philosophy of science, the philosophy of language, and the philosophy of mind. He has also written on the relations between scientific and non-scientific knowledge and on American pragmatism. His more recent publications include *Ethics Without Ontology* (2004) and *Jewish Philosophy as a Guide to Life: Rosenzweig, Buber, Levinas, Wittgenstein* (2008).

**Sebastian Rödl** is Professor of Philosophy at the Universität Leipzig. His research, by integrating aspects of epistemology, philosophy of mind, philosophy of language, and philosophy of action, examines the nature of human thinking and acting. He is the author of *Self-Consciousness* (2007) and *Categories of the Temporal: An inquiry into the Forms of the Finite Understanding* (2011), as well as numerous articles on subjects including normativity, practical knowledge, and reason.

**Martin Stone** is Professor of Law at the Benjamin N. Cardozo School of Law of Yeshiva University and Adjunct Professor of Philosophy at the New School University Graduate Faculty. He is a specialist in the philosophy of law, but has also written on Wittgenstein, formalism, and interpretation.

**Albrecht Wellmer** is Professor Emeritus at the Freie Universität Berlin. His work concentrates on the philosophy of language, hermeneutics, aesthetics, and moral and social philosophy. He has written extensively on pragmatism, truth and meaning, Critical Theory, Modernity and Postmodernity, as well as on philosophy and music. His recent publications include *Sprachphilosophie* (2004), *Wie Worte Sinn machen* (2007), and *Versuch über Musik und Sprache* (2009).

**Michael Williams** is the Krieger-Eisenhower Professor and Chair of the Department of Philosophy at the Johns Hopkins University. His research focuses on epistemology, the philosophy of language, and the history of modern philosophy. He is the author of *Groundless Belief: An Essay on the Possibility of Epistemology* (1977), *Unnatural Doubts: Epistemological Realism and the Basis of Scepticism* (1992), *Problems of Knowledge: A Critical Introduction to Epistemology* (2001), and numerous articles.

# Index of Persons

Made in the USA
Middletown, DE
10 January 2017